Using Stata

For *Principles of Econometrics, Fourth Edition*

Using Stata

For *Principles of Econometrics, Fourth Edition*

LEE C. ADKINS
Oklahoma State University

R. CARTER HILL
Louisiana State University

JOHN WILEY & SONS, INC
New York / Chichester / Weinheim / Brisbane / Singapore / Toronto

Lee Adkins dedicates this work to his lovely and loving wife, Kathy

Carter Hill dedicates this work to Stan Johnson and George Judge

---

This book was set by the authors.

To order books or for customer service call 1-800-CALL-WILEY (225-5945)

ISBN-13   978-1-118-03208-4

10 9 8 7 6 5 4 3 2 1

PREFACE

This book is a supplement to *Principles of Econometrics, 4th Edition* by R. Carter Hill, William E. Griffiths and Guay C. Lim (Wiley, 2011), hereinafter *POE4*. This book is not a substitute for the textbook, nor is it a stand alone computer manual. It is a companion to the textbook, showing how to perform the examples in the textbook using Stata Release 11. This book will be useful to students taking econometrics, as well as their instructors, and others who wish to use Stata for econometric analysis.

Stata is a very powerful program that is used in a wide variety of academic disciplines. The website is **http://www.stata.com**. There you will find a great deal of documentation. One great and visual resource is at UCLA: **http://www.ats.ucla.edu/stat/stata/**. We highly recommend this website.

In addition to this computer manual for Stata, there are similar manuals and support for the software packages EViews, Excel, Gretl and Shazam. In addition, all the data for *POE4* in various formats, including Stata, are available at **http://www.wiley.com/college/hill**.

Individual Stata data files, errata for this manual and the textbook can be found at **http://www.principlesofeconometrics.com/**.

The chapters in this book parallel the chapters in *POE4*. Thus, if you seek help for the examples in Chapter 11 of the textbook, check Chapter 11 in this book. However within a Chapter the sections numbers in *POE4* do not necessarily correspond to the Stata manual sections. Data files and other resources for *POE4* can be found at **http://www.stata.com/texts/s4poe4**.

We welcome comments on this book, and suggestions for improvement. We would like to acknowledge the help of the Stata Corporation, and in particular Bill Rising, for answering many of our questions and improving our prose and code.

Lee C. Adkins
Department of Economics
Oklahoma State University
Stillwater, OK 74078
lee.adkins@okstate.edu

R. Carter Hill
Economics Department
Louisiana State University
Baton Rouge, LA 70803
eohill@lsu.edu

BRIEF CONTENTS

CONTENTS

CHAPTER 1

Introducing Stata

1.1 STARTING STATA

Stata can be started several ways. First, there may be shortcut on the desktop that you can double-click. For the Stata/SE Release 11 it will look like

Earlier versions of Stata have a similar looking Icon, but of course with a different number. Alternatively, using the Windows menu, click the **Start > All Programs > Stata 11**.

A second way is to simply locate a Stata data file, with ***.dta** extension, and double-click.

1.2 THE OPENING DISPLAY

Once Stata is started a display will appear that contains windows titled

> **Command**—this is where Stata commands are typed
> **Results**—output from commands, and error messages, appear here
> **Review**—a listing of commands recently executed
> **Variables**—names of variables in data and labels (if created)

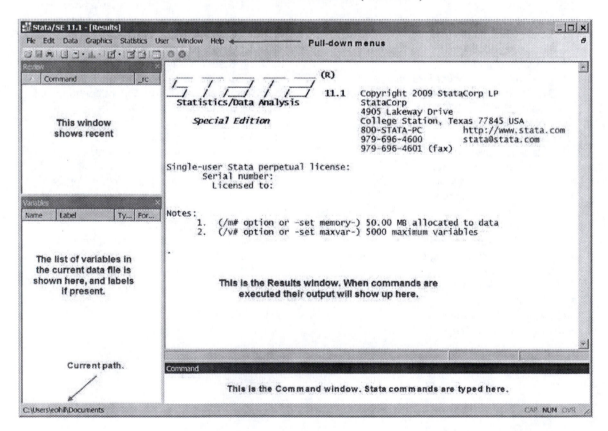

Across the top are Stata **pull-down menus**. We will explore the use of many of these. In the lower left-hand corner is the **current path** to a working directory where Stata saves graphs, data files, etc. We will change this in a moment.

1.3 EXITING STATA

To end a Stata session click on **File**

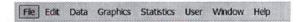

and the **Exit** on the pull-down menu

We will denote sequential clicking commands like this as **File > Exit**. Alternatively, simply type

```
exit
```

in the **Command** window and press **Enter**.

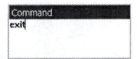

1.4 STATA DATA FILES FOR *PRINCIPLES OF ECONOMETRICS*

Stata data files have the extension ***.dta**. These files should not be opened with any program but Stata. If you locate a ***.dta** file using double-click it will also start Stata.

For *Principles of Econo metrics, 4th Edition* all of the data used in the book has been converted into Stata data files for your use. These files, in a format compatible with Stata Version 9 and later can be found at

1. The John Wiley & Sons website for the book: http://www.wiley.com/college/hill. You can download the entire collection of Stata data files to your computer or a "memory stick" with adequate storage.
2. Book data and other resources are available at the authors' website http://www.principlesofeconometrics.com.
3. Individual data files, and other book materials, can found at the Stata web site http://www.stata.com/texts/s4poe4/.

1.4.1 A working directory

You should copy the data into a convenient directory. How to accomplish this will depend on your computer system. In this Windows-based book we will use the subdirectory **c:\data\poe4stata** for all our data and result files. We are doing this for our convenience and if you are in a laboratory setting this is a bad choice. If you are working in a computer laboratory, you may want to have a storage device such as a "flash" or "travel" drive. These are large enough to hold the Stata data files and definition files. Make a subdirectory on the device. Calling it **X:\DATA** or **X:\POE4**, where **X:** is the path to your device, would be convenient.

To change the working directory use the pull-down menu **File > Change Working Directory**. In the resulting dialog box navigate to your preferred location and click **OK**. to this location type

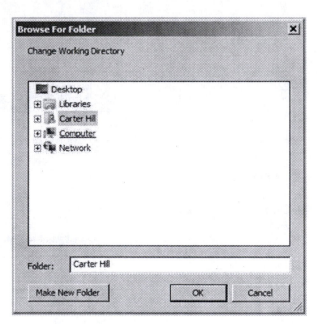

Stata will show the implied command

```
cd "C:\data\poe4stata"
```

This can be entered into the **Command** window and press **Enter**.

The result of this command is

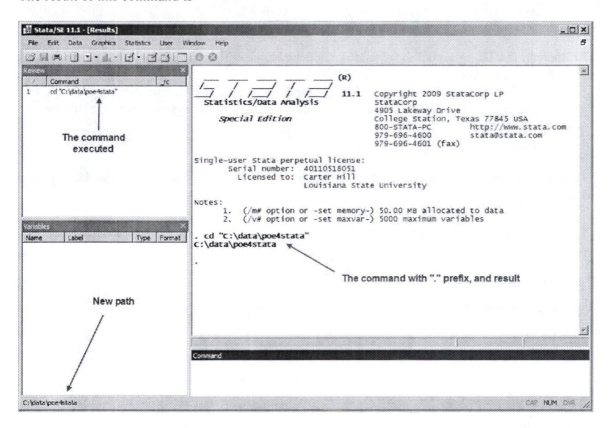

Note that in the **Results** window the command is echoed, and it appears in the **Review** window as well. The new path is indicated at the bottom left of the screen.

1.5 OPENING STATA DATA FILES

There are several ways to open, or load, Stata data files. We will explain a couple of them.

1.5.1 The use command

With Stata started, <u>change your working directory</u> to the where you have stored the Stata data files. In the **Command** window type **use cps4_small** and press **Enter**.

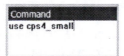

If you have a data file already open, and have changed it in some way, Stata will reply with an error message.

```
. use cps4_small
no; data in memory would be lost
r(4);
```

If you click on r(4); you will be able to read the error message in a **Viewer box**. Sometimes this is helpful. To close the Viewer box click the **X**.

This feature will prevent you from losing changes to a data file you may wish to save. If this happens, you can either save the previous data file [more on this below], or enter the command

    `clear`

The **clear** command will erase what is in Stata's memory. If you want to open the data file and clear memory, enter

    `use cps4_small, clear`

1.5.2 Using the toolbar

To open a Stata data file using the tool bar click the **Open (use)** icon on the Stata toolbar.

Open (use)

Locate the file you wish to open, select it, and click **Open**. In the Review window the implied Stata command is shown.

    `use "C:\data\poe4stata\cps4_small.dta", clear`

In Stata opening a data file is achieved with the **use** command. The path of the data file is shown in quotes. The quotes are necessary if the path name has spaces included. The option **clear** indicates that any existing data is cleared from memory.

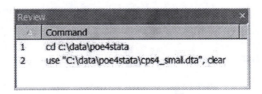

1.5.3 Using files on the internet

Stata offers a nice option if you are connected to the internet. Files can be loaded from a web site. The Stata data files are stored at **http://www.stata.com/texts/s4poe4/**. For example, to load *cps4_small.dta*, after saving previous data and/or clearing memory, enter in the **Command** window

    `use http://www.stata.com/texts/s4poe4/cps4_small, clear`

Once the data are loaded onto your machine, you can save it using **File > Save as** and filling in the resulting dialog box.

1.5.4 Locating book files on the internet

If you would like to browse the book data sets, use your internet browser to visit http://www.stata.com/texts/s4poe4 or http://www.principlesofeconometrics.com where you will find individual data files listed, along with other book materials. **Double click** on the Stata data file you wish to use and Stata will start and load the data file. Of course you must do this from a machine with Stata on it, and there may be a warning box to deal with.

1.6 THE VARIABLES WINDOW

In the **Variables** window the data file variables are listed. Also shown are variable **Labels**, if they are present, along with the **Type** of variable and its **Format**. We will only display the variable **Name** and **Label** in future screen shots.

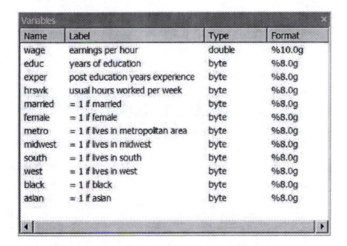

Labels are useful and can be easily added, changed or deleted.

1.6.1 Using the data editor for a single label

On the Stata pull-down menu select the **Data Editor** icon.

In the resulting spread sheet view, right-click in the column defined by the variable and select **Variable Properties**.

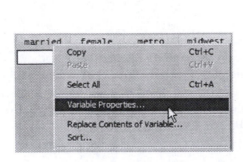

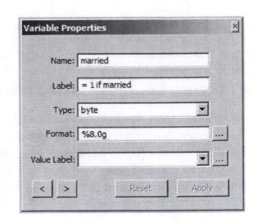

Enter the modified variable **Label** and select **Apply**.

1.6.2 Using the data utility for a single label

On the Stata pull-down menu select **Data** > **Data utilities** > **Label utilities** > **Label Variable** .
That is,

Then

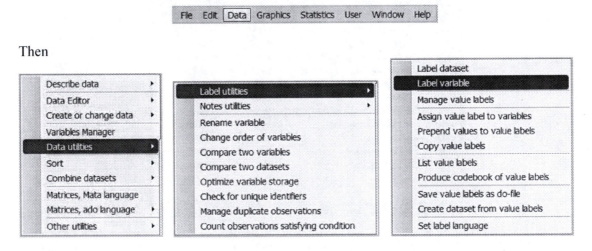

In the resulting dialog box, you can alter the existing label by choosing **Attach** a label to a variable, choosing the variable from the **Variable**: pull-down list and typing in the **New** variable label. Click **OK**.

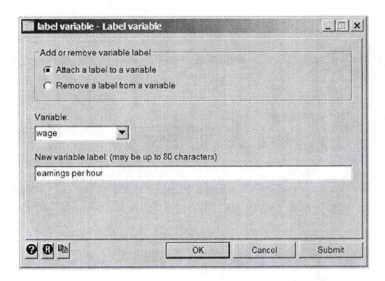

Instead of the dialog box approach, enter the **Command**

```
label variable wage "earnings per hour"
```

This will create the label, and it will write over an already existing label for wage. In the dialog box you can also choose to **Remove** a label.

1.6.3 Using Variables Manager

A one-stop place to manage your variables is the **Variables Manager**. On the Stata pull-down menu click the icon

For extended help on the many features of **Variables Manager** enter the command **help varmanage**. In the resulting Viewer there is a link to the full documentation.

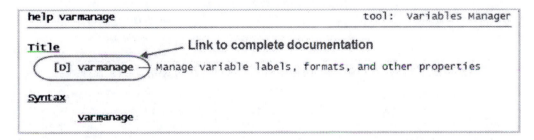

There we also see syntax of the command **varmanage**. The underlined portion represents the minimal command required to open the **Variables Manager**. Near the bottom of the Viewer you will find a link to the *Getting Started with Stata* discussion of the **Variables Manager**. This is perhaps the best place, other than this manual, to "get started."

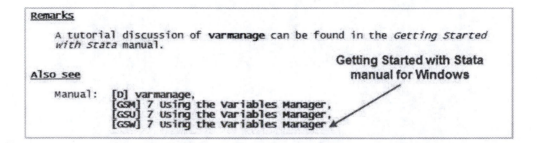

Remarks

A tutorial discussion of **varmanage** can be found in the *Getting Started with Stata* manual.

Getting Started with Stata manual for Windows

Also see

Manual: [D] varmanage,
[GSM] 7 Using the Variables Manager,
[GSU] 7 Using the Variables Manager,
[GSW] 7 Using the Variables Manager

Within the **Variables Manager** click a variable to open the **Variable Properties**. Here you can change the variable label, add notes, and manage both individual variables and groups of variables.

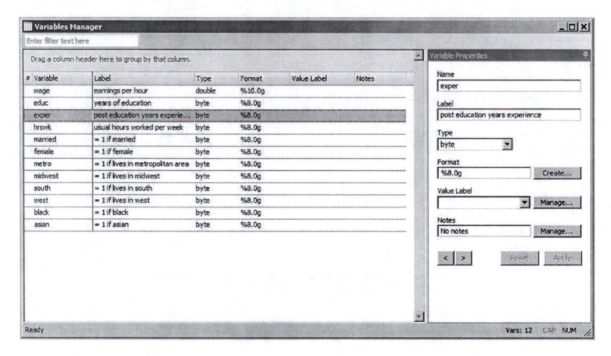

Right-click the high-lighted variable to find more options

The **Variables Manager** has become even more functional in Version 11 as it may be left open while working.

1.7 DESCRIBING DATA AND OBTAINING SUMMARY STATISTICS

There are a few things you should do each time a data file is opened. First, enter the **Command**

      `describe`

This produces a summary of the dataset in memory, including a listing of the variables, information about them, and their labels. A portion of the results is

```
. describe

Contains data from cps4_small.dta
  obs:         1,000
  vars:           12
  size:       23,000 (99.9% of memory free)
```

variable name	storage type	display format	value label	variable label
wage	double	%10.0g		earnings per hour
educ	byte	%8.0g		years of education
exper	byte	%8.0g		post education years experience
hrswk	byte	%8.0g		usual hours worked per week
married	byte	%8.0g		= 1 if married
female	byte	%8.0g		= 1 if female

Next, enter the **Command**

      `summarize`

In the **Results** window we find the **summary statistics**. A portion is

```
. summarize
```

Variable	Obs	Mean	Std. Dev.	Min	Max
wage	1000	20.61566	12.83472	1.97	76.39
educ	1000	13.799	2.711079	0	21
exper	1000	26.508	12.85446	2	65
hrswk	1000	39.952	10.3353	0	90
married	1000	.581	.4936423	0	1
female	1000	.514	.5000541	0	1

Should you forget a Stata command the pull-down menus virtually assure that with enough clicking you can obtain the desired result. To illustrate, click on Statistics on the Stata menu list

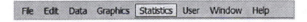

You will find a long list of possible statistical analyses, some of which we will use. For now select **Summaries, tables, and tests. S** elect **Summary and descriptive s tatistics,** and then **Summary statistics,** as shown below.

Recall that we will abbreviate such as path of commands as

Statistics > Summaries, tables, and tests > Summary and descriptive
statistics > Summary statistics

A **dialog box** will open that shows many options. For the basic summary statistics table no options are required. Select **OK**. Stata automatically will provide the summary statistics for all the variables in the data set. You can select individual variables by typing their names in the **Variables** box. The **Standard display** will produce the number of observations, the arithmetic mean, the standard deviation, the minimum and maximum of the data values.

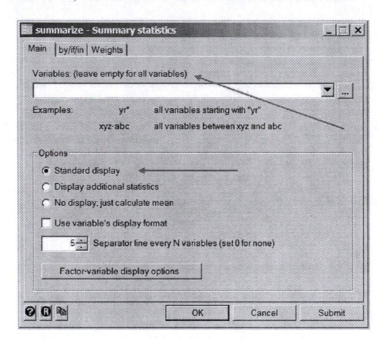

1.8 THE STATA HELP SYSTEM

The Stata help system is one if its most powerful features. Click on **Help** on the Stata menu, then **Contents**.

Each of the blue words is linked to further screens. You should explore these to get a feel for what is available.

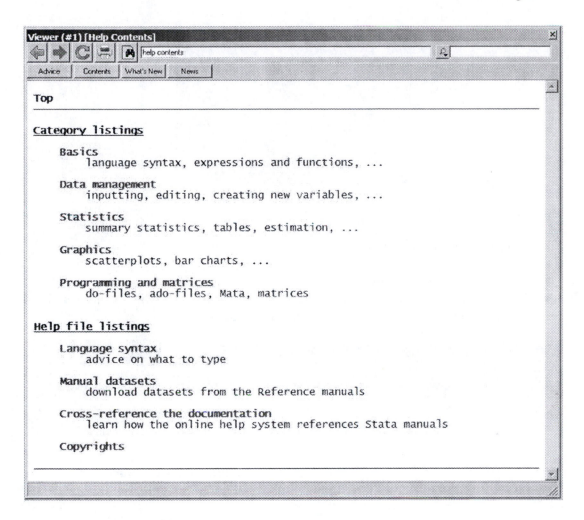

1.8.1 Using keyword search

Now click on **Help > Search**

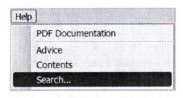

In the Dialog box that opens there are several search options. To search all the Stata documentation and Frequently Asked Questions (FAQs) simply type in phrase describing what you want to find. It does not have to be a specific Stata command. For example, let's search for **Summary Statistics**.

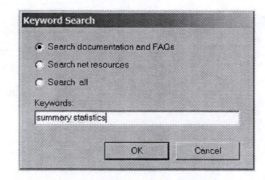

The **Command** line entry is

```
search summary statistics
```

Up comes a list of topics that might be of interest. Once again blue terms are links. Click on **Summarize**. The resulting **Viewer** box shows the command syntax, which can be used when typing commands in the **Command** window, and many options.

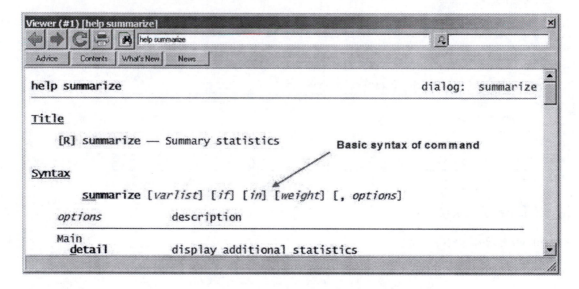

> **Tip:** Note under the syntax that <u>su</u> is underlined. It is the minimum abbreviation. This means that the command **summarize** can be abbreviated as **su** or, say, **summ**.

A broader keyword search uses the **findit** command. For example, enter the command

```
findit mixed models
```

For more on these search options use **help search**.

1.8.2 Using command search

If you know the name of the Stata command you want help with, click **Help > Stata Command**

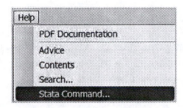

In the resulting dialog box type in the name of the command and click OK.

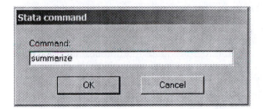

Alternatively, on the command line type

```
help summarize
```

and press **Enter**.

1.8.3 Opening a dialog box

If you know the name of the command you want, but do not recall details and options, a dialog box can be opened from the Command window. For example, if you wish to summarize the data using the dialog box, enter **db summarize**

Or, enter **help summarize**, and click on the blue link to the dialog box.

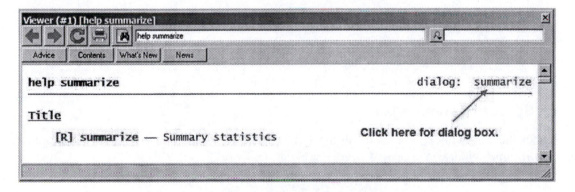

1.8.4 Complete documentation in Stata manuals

Stata has a complete set of reference manuals consisting of thousands of pages and about two feet of shelf space. Stata 11 installation comes with these manuals as PDF files. One way to access them is through the Viewer window from help.

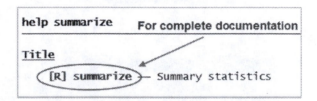

The **[R]** denotes Reference Manual, and the blue `summarize` is a link to the stored PDF documentation for the command **summarize**. Manual documentation is more complete than that in the Viewer from **help summarize** and usually has several examples.

1.9 STATA COMMAND SYNTAX

Stata commands have a common syntax. The name of the command, such as **summarize** is first.

        command [varlist] [if] [in] [weight] [, options]

The terms in brackets [ ] are various optional command components that could be used.

- **[varlist]** is the list of variables for which the command is used.
- **[if]** is a condition imposed on the command.
- **[in]** specifies range of observations for the command.
- **[weight]** when some sample observations are to be weighted differently than others.
- **[, options]** command options go here.

For more on these options use a **Keyword Search** for **Command syntax**, then click **Language**.

> **Remark:** An important fact to keep in mind when using Stata is that its commands are case sensitive. This means that lower case and capital letters have different meanings. That is, Stata considers **x** to be different from **X**.

1.9.1 Syntax of summarize

Consider the following examples using the syntax features. In each case type the command into the **Command** window and press **Enter**. For example,

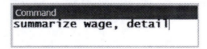

summarize wage, detail computes detailed summary statistics for the variable wage. The percentiles of wage from smallest to largest are shown, along with additional summary statistics (e.g., skewness and kurtosis) that you will learn about. Note that Stata echoes the command you have issued with a preceding period (.).

```
. summarize wage, detail
```

```
                        earnings per hour

              Percentiles      Smallest
 1%              5.53            1.97
 5%              7.495           2.3
10%              8.255           2.5          Obs              1000
25%             11.25            2.52         Sum of Wgt.      1000

50%             17.3                          Mean          20.61566
                                Largest       Std. Dev.     12.83472
75%             25.63           72.13
90%             37.55           72.13         Variance      164.7302
95%             47.375          72.13         Skewness      1.583909
99%             70.44           76.39         Kurtosis      5.921362
```

summarize wage if female==1 computes the simple summary statistics for the females in the sample. The variable **female** is 1 for females and 0 for males. In the "**if qualifier**" equality is indicated by "==".

summarize if exper >= 10 computes simple summary statistics for those in the sample whose experience (**exper**) is greater than or equal to 10 years, or missing.

summarize in 1/50 computes summary statistics for observations 1 through 50.

summarize wage in 1/50, detail computes detailed summary statistics for the variable wage in the first 50 observations.

> If you notice at bottom left of the Results window —**more**—: when the Results window is full it pauses and you must click —**more**— in order for more results to appear, or press the space bar.

1.9.2 Learning syntax using the review window

At this point you are wondering "How am I supposed to know all this?" Luckily you do not have to know it all now, and learning comes with repeated use of Stata. One great tool is the combination of pull-down menus and the **Review** window. Suppose we want detailed summary statistics for female wages in the first 500 observations. While you may be able to guess from previous examples how to do this, let's use the point and click approach. Select

Statistics > Summaries, tables, and tests > Summary and descriptive statistics > Summary statistics

In the resulting dialog box we will specify which variables we want to include, and select the option providing more detailed statistics. Then click on the **by/if/in** tab at the top.

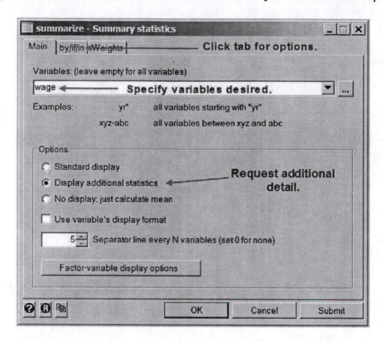

In the new dialog box you can enter the if condition in a box. Click the box next to **Use a range of observations**. Use the selection boxes to choose observations 1 to 500. Then click **OK**.

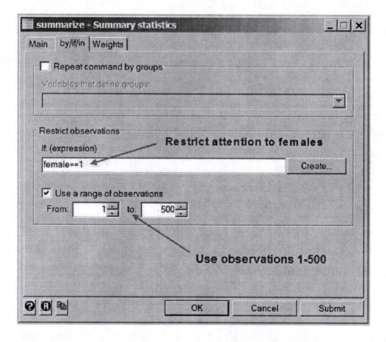

Stata echoes the command, and produces detailed summary statistics for the women in the first 500 observations

```
. summarize wage if female == 1 in 1/500, detail
```

                                earnings per hour

	Percentiles	Smallest		
1%	6.25	1.97		
5%	7.25	5.2		
10%	8	6.25	Obs	269
25%	10	6.35	Sum of Wgt.	269
50%	15.25		Mean	18.98892
		Largest	Std. Dev.	12.35847
75%	24.05	61.11		
90%	38.23	72.13	Variance	152.7318
95%	43.25	72.13	Skewness	1.78174
99%	72.13	72.13	Kurtosis	6.640641

Now look at the **Review** window

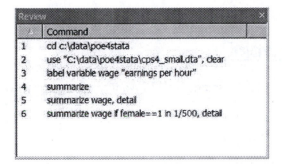

In the **Review** window is the list of commands we have typed. You will also find the list of commands generated using the dialogs. Line 6 is the command you would enter into the **Command** window to achieve the results of all that pointing and clicking. After experimenting for just a few minutes you will learn the syntax for the command `summarize`.

Suppose you want to change the last command to include observations 1 to 750. You can enter the command

```
summarize wage if female == 1 in 1/750, detail
```

into the **Command** window, but Stata offers us a much easier option. In the **Review** window, simply click on the command in line 6.

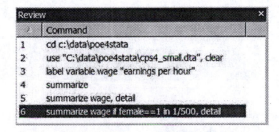

Instantly, this command appears in the **Command** window

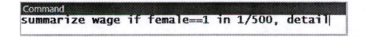

Edit this command, changing 500 to 750, then press **Enter**

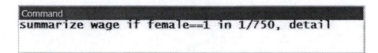

To edit a previously used command, click on that command in the **Review** window. The past command will zip to the Command window, where it can be edited and executed. Not only do you obtain new results, but the modified command now appears as the last item in the **Review** window.

> **Stata Tip**: Many commands will be too long to fit into the **Review** window. In the **Command** window use **Page Up** and **Page Down** to navigate through previous commands.

1.10 SAVING YOUR WORK

When you carry out a long Stata session you will want to save your work.

1.10.1 Copying and pasting

One option, though certainly not recommended as a general procedure, is to highlight the output the **Results** window, then **right-click**.

```
. summarize wage if female==1 in 1/500, detail

                        earnings per hour

         Percentiles      Smalles┌──────────────────────────────┐
  1%         6.25            1.  │ Copy Text         Ctrl+C     │
  5%         7.25            5.  │ Copy Table                   │
 10%            8            6.2 │ Copy Table as HTML           │
 25%           10            6.3 │ Copy as Picture          269 │
                                 │                          269 │
 50%        15.25                │ Select All        Ctrl+A     │
                                 │                              │
                        Larges   │ Preferences...      18.98892 │
 75%        24.05           61.1 │ Font...             12.35847 │
 90%        38.23           72.13│ Print...                     │
 95%        43.25           72.13└─ Variance         152.7318 ──┘
 99%        72.13           72.13   Skewness          1.78174
                                    Kurtosis          6.640641
```

This gives you options to copy (Ctrl+C) the output as text, and then paste it into a document using the shortcut (Ctrl+V) or by clicking the paste icon.

If you paste into a word processing document you may find that the nicely arranged Stata results become a ragged, hard to read, mess. Part of the results might look like

```
. summarize

    Variable |    Obs      Mean   Std. Dev.     Min      Max
-------------+--------------------------------------------------
        wage |   1000   10.21302   6.246641    2.03    60.19
        educ |   1000    13.285    2.468171      1       18
        exper |  1000     18.78    11.31882      0       52
      female |   1000      .494    .5002142      0        1
       black |   1000      .088    .2834367      0        1
```

This is due to the word processor changing the font. While you may be using Times New Roman font for standard text, use Courier New for Stata output. You may have to reduce the font size to 8 or 9 to make it fit. A partial output is

```
. summarize

    Variable |       Obs        Mean    Std. Dev.       Min        Max
-------------+--------------------------------------------------------
        wage |      1000    10.21302     6.246641      2.03      60.19
        educ |      1000      13.285     2.468171         1         18
       exper |      1000       18.78     11.31882         0         52
      female |      1000        .494     .5002142         0          1
       black |      1000        .088     .2834367         0          1
```

Copying the highlighted material as a **Picture** places your selection into a graphic that makes for nice looking output that can be pasted into a document. As a graphic, though, it cannot be edited using a word processor. See the output from the **describe** command on page 11 of this manual.

1.10.2 Using a log file

Stata offers a better alternative. In addition to having results in the **Results** window in Stata, it is a very good idea to have all results written (echoed) to an output file, which Stata calls a **log file**. Enter the Stata command

```
help log
```

Log files come in two types: a **text** format, or a **smcl** format.

1.10.2a Log files with text format

The **text** format is a simple ASCII file. The advantage of text format is that the contents can be copied and pasted into, or opened with, a word processing software, or with a utility like Notepad. The text format also has the virtue of being usable on computers without Stata installed. To open a Stata log in text format, enter the command

```
log using chap01, replace text
```

In the Results window we find the echoed command and the full name of the file, **chap01.log** with path **c:\data\poe4stata**.

```
. log using chap01, replace text
```

```
      name:  <unnamed>
       log:  c:\data\poe4stata\chap01.log
  log type:  text
 opened on:   8 Dec 2010, 08:18:45
```

If you wish to name the output file something including spaces, then quotes must be used, as

```
log using "chapter 1 output", replace text
```

The option **replace** will result in previous versions of the log file being written over, and the option **text** indicates that the log file is to be in ASCII or text format. After the log file is opened, all output written to the **Results** window will be echoed to the log file. To close the output file enter the command

```
log close
```

After closing the log file navigate to it and open it with Notepad or a word processor.

1.10.2b Log files with smcl format

The **smcl** format is a Stata Markup and Control Language format. This type of file cannot usefully be opened with a word or text file processor because like HTML code there is a great deal of coding that is incomprehensible to the uninitiated. However, like output in the **Results** window, portions of it can be highlighted and then copied using a right-click as a picture, then pasted into a word processing document. It will have the appearance of the output in the **Results** window, nicely formatted and spaced. It can be copied and pasted text or a table as well. To begin a log file in **smcl** format, enter the command

```
log using chap01, replace
```

Since **smcl** format is the Stata default, it is not necessary to indicate the format type. In the Results window we see

```
. log using ch01, replace
(note: file c:\data\poe4stata\ch01.smcl not found)
```

```
      name:  <unnamed>
       log:  c:\data\poe4stata\ch01.smcl
  log type:  smcl
 opened on:   8 Dec 2010, 08:21:44
```

To close the log file, enter **log close**.

Stata is used to view a **smcl** log file. On the Stata menu choose **File > View**

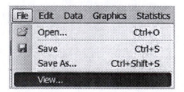

In the resulting dialog box enter the log file pathname, or use **Browse** to locate it, and then enter **OK**.

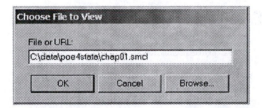

The log file **chap01.smcl** opens in a new Viewer window. To print the **smcl** log file click the printer icon.

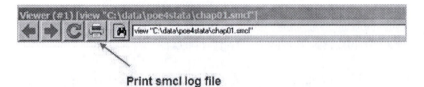

Print smcl log file

A dialog box opens that allows you to enter header information, then select **OK**.

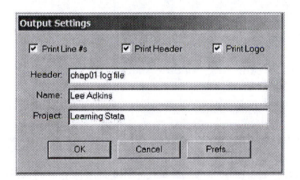

Advantages of the **smcl** formatted log file include the ability to view the formatted output, and to easily print it. A disadvantage of *.smcl files is that they cannot be easily viewed without having Stata open. They are like *.html files in that while they are text files, they also include lots and lots of formatting commands. This means that if you want to work on the output on a machine without Stata you are out of luck. Stata allows you the best of both worlds. You can translate the Stata *.smcl log files into simple text files.

On the Stata toolbar select **File > Log > Translate**.

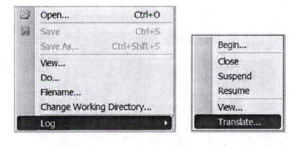

Fill in the resulting dialog box. If the Output File named already exists, you will be queried if you want to replace it or not. Select **Translate**.

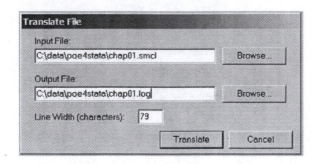

Alternatively, enter the command

        translate chap01.smcl chap01.log, replace

So that the file type will be recognized as a text file, you might instead use

        translate chap01.smcl chap01.txt, replace

1.10.2c Log files summary

To open a log file using the **Command** window, enter

        log using chap01

This will open **chap01.smcl** in the current directory. Variations of this command are:

log using chap01, replace will open the log file and replace one by the same name if it exists.

log using chap01, append will open an existing log file and add new results at the end.

log close closes a log file that is open.

To translate the *.smcl to a text file, in the current directory, enter

        translate chap01.smcl chap01.txt

If the text file already exists, and you wish to write over it, use

        translate chap01.smcl chap01.txt, replace

To print directly from the Command window, enter

        print chap01.smcl

Using the pull-down menu approach, click on the **Log Begin/Close/Suspend/Resume** icon on the Stata toolbar.

1.11 USING THE DATA BROWSER

It is a good idea to examine the data to see the magnitudes of the variables and how they appear in the data file. On the Stata toolbar are a number of icons. Sliding the mouse pointer over each icon reveals its use. Click on **Data Browser**

The browser allows you to scroll through the data, but not to edit any of the entries. This is a good feature that ensures you do not accidentally change a data value. Use the slide bar at the bottom (shown on next page) and the one on the right to view the entire data array. Alter the size of the spreadsheet by dragging the "window size" corner. In Stata 11 the **Data Editor** or **Data Browser** can be open while working without doing any harm.

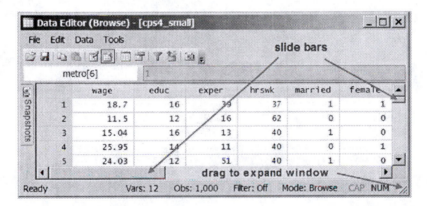

1.12 USING STATA GRAPHICS

Stata does very nice graphics of high quality many tools for enhancing the figures. We encourage the use of dialog boxes when learning graphics, combined with careful reading of the Graphics Manual (**help graph**), to learn the scope of graphics features. We will illustrate a Histogram and a Scatter Plot. Later in this manual we will illustrate various options to the basic graphs.

1.12.1 Histograms

Select **Graphics > Histogram** on the Stata menu.

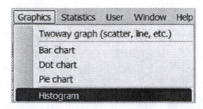

In the resulting dialog box there are many options. For a simple histogram all you need to is select is the variable from the pull-down list. For illustration, we have entered a title and axis labels by clicking the Titles, Y axis and X axis tabs and filling in a boxes. Choose Percent to have histogram bin heights reflect percent of sample contained in the bin. Select **OK**.

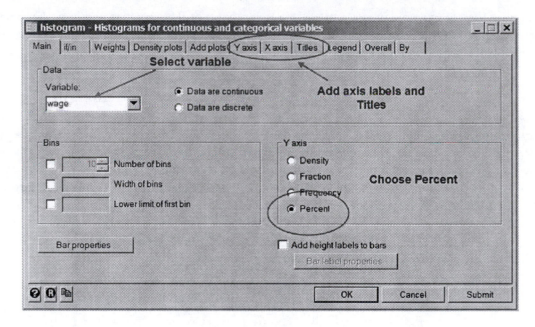

The resulting figure is

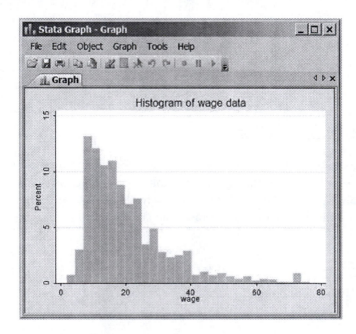

On the graph toolbar you have several options.

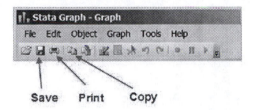

Click on the **Save** graph icon. The resulting dialog box shows that the graphics file will be saved into your working director, which for this book is **c:\data\poe4stata**. Attach a file name and choose the type of graphics file from the drop-down list. The default type ***.gph** is a Stata graphics format, which is convenient if you will do further editing in Stata. Other available formats, such as ***.png** files are widely used for images, like screen shots. If the graphs are to be included in document Microsoft Word use the ***.emf** format (Enhanced Metafile), or on a Mac use ***.pdf**.

The corresponding Stata command is

```
graph save Graph "C:\data\poe4stata\histogram of wages.gph", replace
```

Quotes are required because the file name includes spaces. The **replace** option indicates that it is okay to replace a file with the same existing file name. This command can be shortened to

```
graph save chap01hist, replace
```

The file will be saved, in our case, as **C:\data\poe4stata\chap01hist.gph**.

The saving process can be done in one step using

```
histogram wage, percent title(Histogram of wage data)
        saving(chap01hist,replace)
```

The advantage of the two-step process is that you can edit the figure before saving. The one-step process ensures that you won't forget.

Having saved the file, in your word processor you can insert the image as a figure into a document. Alternatively, if you choose the **Copy** graph icon the figure will be copied to the clipboard, and then the figure can be pasted (Ctrl+V) into an open document. The figure below was saved in ***.emf** format and inserted as a picture.

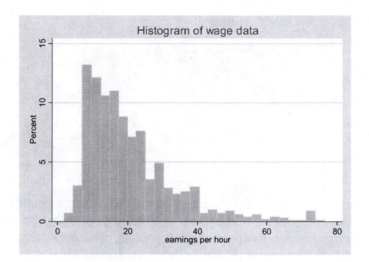

Note that our pointing and clicking could have been replaced by the command

```
histogram wage, percent ytitle(Percent) xtitle(wage) title(Histogram
        of wage data) saving(chap01hist, replace)
```

> **Remark: Long lines**—The command above is rather long. Stata has no trouble with long commands, but in our document and in do-files we will sometimes make the long command fit onto two, or more, lines using a "line-join indicator", *///*. That is, the command in the do-file could be
>
> ```
> histogram wage, percent ytitle(Percent) xtitle(wage) ///
> title(Histogram of wage data) saving(chap01hist, replace)
> ```

1.12.2 Scatter diagrams

A scatter diagram is a **Two-way Graph**. From the graphics menu select this option

In the dialog box, click **Create**.

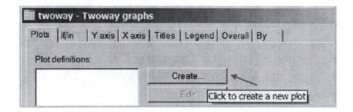

A dialog box opens.

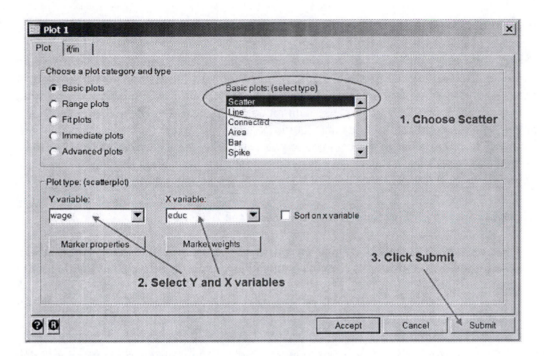

Choose the **Y variable** (vertical axis) and **X variable** (horizontal axis). Select the **Scatter plot**, and click **Submit**. The resulting graph can be saved to a file, or copied and pasted into a document, as with the histogram. The result shows "dots" for each data pair (educ, wage), and by casual inspection we see that more education is associated with higher wages. Aren't you glad? The Stata command used to create this scatter plot is (with saving option added)

```
twoway (scatter wage educ), saving(wage_educ, replace)
```

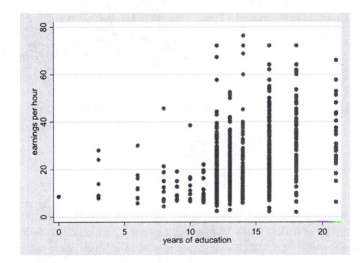

1.13 USING STATA DO-FILES

While it is possible to point and click your way to success such an approach requires a new pointing and clicking odyssey each time you do a new problem. In our view it is more convenient is to use Stata's Do-files as a method for executing commands. These are files containing lists of commands that will be executed as a batch.

Do-files are very convenient after having pointed and clicked enough so that the commands you want to execute appear in the Review window. If you have been carrying along on the computer with the examples we have been doing, then your Review window is a clutter of commands right now. Let's take those commands to a new **Do-file** called chap01.do. The extension ***.do** is recognized by Stata and should be used.

One way to retain a list of the commands you enter is to use a **command log file**, which is a simple text file containing a record of what you type during your Stata session. Since it contains only what you type it is a subset of the full log file. Open a command log file using

```
cmdlog using filename [, append replace]
```

where *filename* can be specified without an extension—Stata will add **.txt**. These ASCII files then can be turned into do-files. To close a command log, temporarily suspend logging, or resume logging use

```
cmdlog {close|on|off}
```

Alternatively, **Right-click** in the **Review** window, and on the pull-down menu click **Select All**. After all commands are selected right-click again and choose **Send to Do-file Editor**.

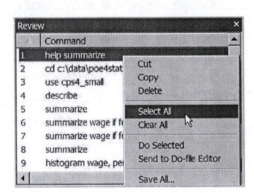 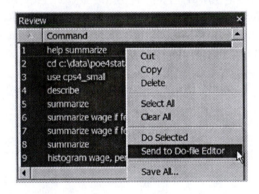

The **Do-file Editor** is opened. To save this file click on **File > Save**, or the **Save** icon,

and enter the file name **ch01.do**. The Stata Do-file editor is a simple text editor that allows you to edit the command list to include only those commands to keep. In the file below we have eliminated some commands, done some rearranging, and added some new commands. It also presumes that the log file is new, that you have saved and cleared any previous work, and that the working directory has been specified. Recall that comment lines are preceded with "*****" and comments can be added in lines using "**//**". Long lines can be split using "**///**".

* file ch01.do is a comment identifying the file when you open it

version 11.1 specifies the version used. This is quite useful because when Stata is installed, it includes previous versions. If you have a Do-file used with a previous version and wish to recreate the output, then you can specify instead version 10.1, or whatever.

capture log close is protection against the error of trying to open a new log file while another is open.

set more off prevents Stata from pausing when the Review window is full.
log close should be included at the end.

When using Do-files, which are collections of commands run together, or in "batch mode," the **replace** option is used to write over old saved results and graphs with new ones.

```
Do-file Editor - ch01                                                    _ |□| x|
File  Edit  Tools  View

  ch01 | Untitled.do |

 1    * file ch01.do
 2    cd c:\data\poe4stata
 3
 4    * setup
 5    version 11.1              // specify version used
 6    capture log close        // closes any unclosed logs
 7    set more off             // does not pause when review window is full
 8
 9    * open log file
10    log using chap01, replace text      // use log file with text format
11
12    * open data and examine
13    use cps4_small, clear               // clear memory before opening data
14    describe
15    summarize
16
17    * summarize options
18    summarize wage if female==1 in 1/500, detail
19    summarize wage if female==1 in 1/750, detail
20
21    * histogram--save graph and replace previous versions
22    histogram wage, percent ytitle(Percent) xtitle(wage) title(Histogram of wage data)
23    graph save Graph "C:\data\poe4stata\histogram of wages.gph", replace
24
25    * scatter diagram
26    twoway (scatter wage educ)
27    graph save Graph "C:\data\poe4stata\wage vs education scatter.gph", replace
28
29    log close              // close the log file

Ready                                                 Line: 1, Col: 14  CAP  NUM  OVR
```

The remainder of the Do-file is from the list of commands we have explored.
To execute this series of commands click the **Do icon** on the Do-file Editor toolbar.

The results appear in the **Result** window and will be written to the specified log file.

The Do-file editor has some useful features. Several Do-files can be open at once, and the Do-file editor can be used to open and edit any text file. By highlighting several commands in the Do-file and selecting Do Selected Lines parts of the Do-file can be executed one after the other. Of course the data file *cps4_small.dta* must be open prior to attempting to execute the selected lines.

```
Do-file Editor - ch01                                                    _ □ ×
File  Edit  Tools  View
┌────────────────────────────────────────────────────────────────────────────┐
│ ch01  Untitled.do                          Execute Selection (do)        ▾ × │
│  2      cd c:\data\poe4stata                                               ▲ │
│  3                                                                           │
│  4    * setup                                                               │
│  5    version 11.1             // specify version used                      │
│  6    capture log close        // closes any unclosed logs                  │
│  7    set more off             // does not pause when review window is full │
│  8                                                                           │
│  9    * open log file                                                       │
│ 10    log using chap01, replace text    // use log file with text format    │
│ 11                                                                          │
│ 12    * open data and examine                                               │
│ 13    use cps4_small, clear            // clear memory before opening data  │
│ 14    describe                                                              │
│ 15    summarize                                                            ▼ │
└────────────────────────────────────────────────────────────────────────────┘
```

> **Stata Tip:** If the Do-file tab shows an asterisk (*) that means changes have been made to the file and the changes have not yet been saved. Be sure to Save the Do-file!
>
> ```
> Do-file Editor - ch01*
> File  Edit  Tools  View
> □ ☞ 🖫 🖼 | 🖊 | 🖎 🖻 🖺
> ch01*  Untitled.do
> ```

At the end of each chapter in this book we will present a Do-file summarizing the chapter.

1.14 CREATING AND MANAGING VARIABLES

Stata offers a wide variety of functions that can be used to create new variables, and commands that let you alter the variables you have created. In this section we examine some of these capabilities.

1.14.1 Creating (generating) new variables

To create a new variable use the generate command in Stata. Let's start with the pull-down menu. Click on **Data > Create or change variables > Create new variable** on the Stata menu.

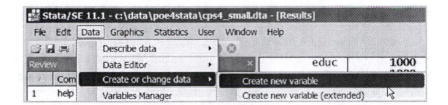

A dialog box will open.

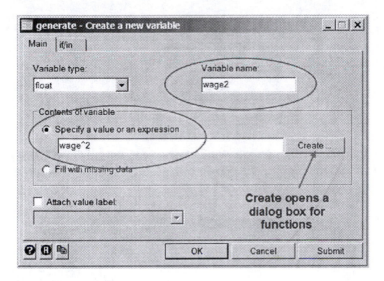

Alternatively, in the Command window, enter **db generate** to open the dialog box. In the dialog box you must fill in

New variable name: choose something logical, informative and not too long.

Contents of new variable: this is a formula (no equal sign required) that is a mathematical expression. In the example above **wage2** is a new variable that will be the square of wage. The operator "**∧**" is the symbol Stata uses for "raise to a power, so **wage∧2** is the square of wage, **wage∧3** would be wage cubed, and so on.

Variable type: the default is float, which stands for **floating point**. This relates to the way in which the variable will be stored internally. Enter the command **help data type** if you are curious.

Click **OK**. In the **Results** window (and **Review** window) we see that the command implied by the menu process is

```
generate wage2 = wage∧2
```

The command can also be shortened to

```
gen wage2 = wage∧2
```

1.14.2 Using the expression builder

Suppose in the process of creating a new variable you forget the exact name of the function. This happens all the time. To illustrate let us create a new variable **lwage** which will be the natural logarithm of *WAGE*. Go through the steps in Section 1.14.1 until to you reach the **generate** dialog box. Type in the name of the new variable, and then click Create, opening Expression builder.

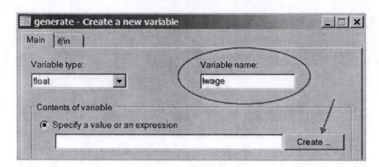

In the **Expression builder** dialog box you can locate a function by choosing a category, scrolling down the function list while keeping an eye on the definitions at the bottom until you locate the function you need.

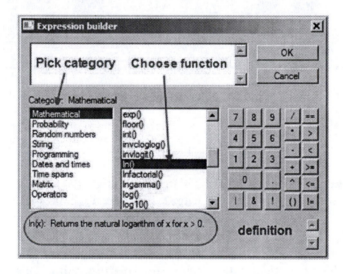

Double-click on the function **ln()**, and it will appear the Expression builder window

Now fill in the name of the variable **wage** in place of "**x**" and click **OK**.

In the generate dialog box you will now find the correct expression for the natural logarithm of wage in the Contents of new variable space. Click OK.

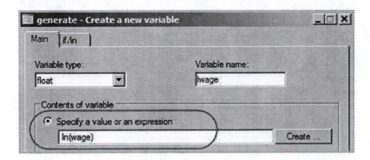

The command will be executed, creating the new variable **lwage** which shows up in the **Variables** window. Stata echoes the command to the **Results** window

```
generate lwage = ln(wage)
```

and to the **Review** window. The simple direct command is

```
gen lwage = ln(wage)
```

1.14.3 Dropping and keeping variables and observations

Enter the command **help drop**. There you will find commands and variations for dropping variables, or observations.

Drop variables: use **drop varlist**, where **varlist** is a list of variables. For example, **drop wage2 lwage** will drop these two variables.

Instead of deleting variables using **drop**, you may wish to only **keep** certain variables or observations.

Keep variables: use **keep varlist**, where **varlist** is a list of variables. For example, **keep wage2 lwage** will drop all variables except these two.

Should you forget this, from the Stata menu choose **Data > Variables Manager**

The **Variables Manager** window will open where you can change various aspects of the data. To **drop** or **keep** variables, highlight several and then **right-click**.

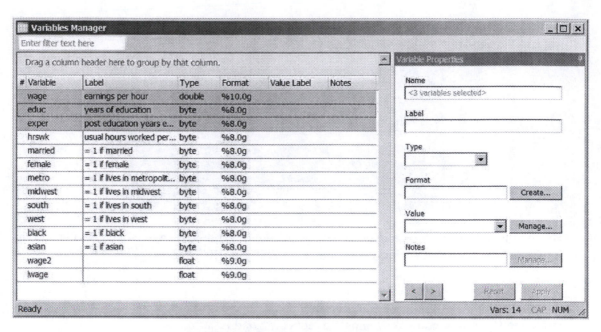

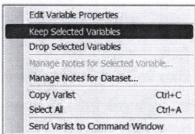

If you wish to drop or keep certain observations use the pull-down menu **Data > Create or change data > Keep or drop observations**.

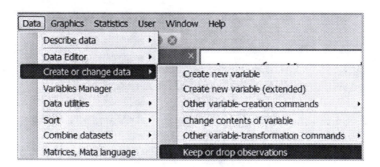

To drop all observations for which the variable wage is greater than 5.50, enter into the dialog box

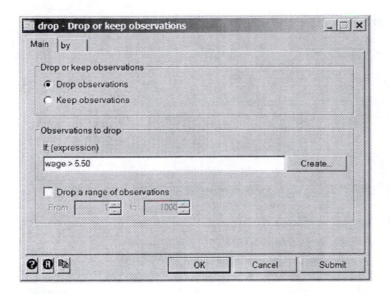

Or, in the **Command** window:

Drop observations: use **drop if exp**, where *exp* is a Stata expression. For example, **drop if wage > 5.50** will drop all observations for which **wage** is greater than 5.50, or missing.

> **Tip:** The command **drop if _n > 100** will drop all observations in data rows 100 and above, keeping only the first 100 observations. The variable **_n** is the observation number in Stata, which is an automatic variable that is always present.

Drop a range of observations: use **drop in 1/50** to drop the first 50 observations.

Keep observations: use **keep if exp**, where **exp** is a Stata expression. For example, **keep if wage <= 5.50** will drop all observations for which **wage** is greater than 5.50.

In passing we note that there are many other data utilities, such as for renaming variables. See the pull-down list

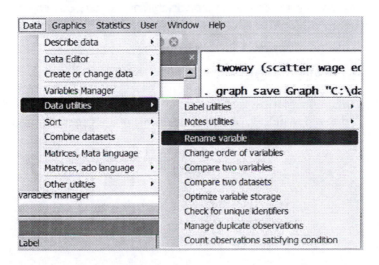

1.14.4 Using arithmetic operators

The Arithemetic operators are:

+ addition
- subtraction (or create negative of value, or negation)
* multiplication
/ division
^ raise to a power

To illustrate these operators consider the following generate statements:

```
generate wage1 = wage+1 (addition)
generate negwage = -wage (negative or negation)
generate blackeduc = black*educ (multiplication)
generate blackeduc_south = black*educ*south (multiplication)
generate blackeduc_west = blackeduc*west (multiplication with created variable)
generate wage_yr = wage/educ (division)
generate blackeduc_midwest = (black*educ)*midwest (multiplication)
```

The last line shows the use of parentheses. Like regular algebra parentheses control the order of operations, with expressions in parentheses being performed first.

Several of these constructions were for demonstration purposes only. We'll drop them using

```
drop blackeduc_west blackeduc_midwest wage1 negwage wage_yr
```

> **Stata shortcut:** With a list of variables to type it is easier to type the command name, here drop, and then click on the names of the variables in the Variables window. When selected they appear in the Command window. Another way to quickly enter a variable name is to take advantage of Stata's **variable name completion feature**. Simply type the first few letters of the variable name in the Command window and press the **Tab** key. Stata will automatically type the rest of the variable name for you. If more than one variable name matches the letters you have typed, Stata will complete as much as it can and beep at you to let you know that you have typed a non-unique variable abbreviation. See Chapter 10 in *Getting Started with Stata* for other such shortcuts.

1.14.5 Using Stata math functions

Stata has a long list of mathematical and statistical functions that are easy to use. Type **help functions** in the Command window. We will be using math functions and density functions extensively.

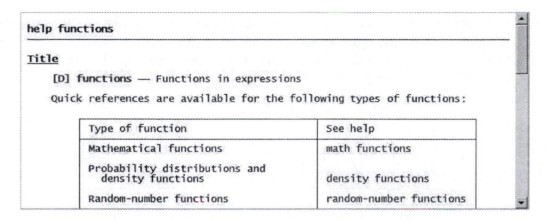

Click on **math functions**. Scrolling down the list you will see many functions that are new to you. A few examples of the ones we will be using are:

> **generate lwage = ln(wage)** (natural logarithm)
> **generate elwage = exp(lwage)** (exponential function is antilog of natural log)
> **generate rootexper = sqrt(exper)** (square root)

Note that the exponential function is e^x. Use the Stata **browser** to compare the values of **wage** and **elwage**. These are identical because the exponential function is the antilog of the natural logarithm. The variable **lwage** is the logarithm of **wage**, and **elwage** is the antilog of **lwage**. The function **ln(wage)** is the natural logarithm and so is **log(wage)**. In *Principles of Econometrics* the notation **ln(x)** is used to denote the natural logarithm.

1.15 USING STATA DENSITY FUNCTIONS

Enter **help functions** in the **Command** window. Click on **density functions**. There are many probability distributions available in Stata, such as the binomial, chi-square, *F*, normal and *t*. Stata provides several classes of functions for describing each probability distribution. We will discuss **cumulative distribution functions**, or *cdf*s, and a type of inverse function that permits calculation of distribution critical values. This section is for completeness and is meant to serve as a reference for when the distributions are encountered.

1.15.1 Cumulative distribution functions

If X is a random variable, and x is some particular value, we might like to compute the probability that X is less than or equal to x. If $F(x)$ denotes the cumulative distribution function of X, then the desired probability is

$$P(X \leq x) = F(x)$$

The *cdf*s for key distributions are:

normal(z) returns the cumulative standard normal distribution for a given z. If X has a normal distribution with mean μ and variance σ^2 then $Z = (X - \mu)/\sigma$ is a standardized normal random variable, with mean 0 and variance 1. All normal probabilities are calculated in terms of the standard normal distribution. That is,

$$P(X \leq x) = P\big(Z \leq (x - \mu)/\sigma\big) = F(z) = \Phi(z)$$

where $\Phi(z)$ is the common symbol used for the standard normal *cdf*, rather than F. To use the function we must calculate $z = (x - \mu)/\sigma$.

For the chi-squared distribution we have two functions. One computes the usual *cdf* value and the other computes its complement. If the *cdf* value gives $P(X \leq x)$ then complement function gives $1 - P(X \leq x)$

chi2(n,x) for a given value $x > 0$, returns the cumulative chi-squared distribution with n degrees of freedom.

chi2tail(n,x) for a given value $x > 0$ returns the reverse cumulative (upper-tail) chi-squared distribution with n degrees of freedom. **chi2tail(n,x) = 1 - chi2(n,x)**

For the F distribution we have two functions. One computes the usual cdf value and the other computes its complement. Recall that Stata is case sensitive, and the use of upper case **F** below is required.

F(n1,n2,f) for a value $f > 0$ returns the cumulative F distribution with $n1$ numerator and $n2$ denominator degrees of freedom.

Ftail(n1,n2,f) for a value $f > 0$ returns the reverse cumulative (upper-tail) F distribution with $n1$ numerator and $n2$ denominator degrees of freedom. **Ftail(n1,n2,f) = 1 - F(n1,n2,f)**

For the t distribution we have only the "tail" probability function.

ttail(n,t) for a given t value, returns the reverse cumulative (upper-tail) Student's t distribution with n degrees of freedom; it returns the probability $T > t$

1.15.2 Inverse cumulative distribution functions

Cumulative Distribution Functions tell us the probability that a random variable X takes a value "less than or equal to" a specific value x. The opposite question is "What is the value of x such that p probability is to its left?" In this case we are given the probability $p = P(X \leq x)$ and we wish to determine the value of x. These are actually percentiles of the distribution. Stata also provides the "tail probability" version that gives the value x such that the probability $p = P(X > x)$. The statistical Tables 2-5 in *Principles of Econometrics* report selected percentile values p, which can be computed using these functions.

invnormal(p) for a given $0 < p < 1$ returns the inverse cumulative standard normal distribution: if **normal(z) = p,** then **invnormal(p) = z.**

invchi2(n,p) for a given $0 < p < 1$ and degrees of freedom *n*, returns the inverse of **chi2()**: if **chi2(n,x) = p,** then **invchi2(n,p) = x.**

invchi2tail(n,p) for a given $0 < p < 1$ and degrees of freedom *n*, returns the inverse of **chi2tail():** if **chi2tail(n,x) = p,** then **invchi2tail(n,p) = x.**

invF(n1,n2,p) for a given $0 < p < 1$, numerator degrees of freedom *n1*, and denominator degrees of freedom *n2*, returns the inverse cumulative *F* distribution: if **F(n1,n2,f) = p,** then **invF(n1,n2,p) = f.**

invFtail(n1,n2,p) for a given $0 < p < 1$, numerator degrees of freedom *n1*, and denominator degrees of freedom *n2*, returns the inverse reverse cumulative (upper-tail,) *F* distribution: if **Ftail(n1,n2,f) = p,** then **invFtail(n1,n2,p) = f.**

invttail(n,p) for a given $0 < p < 1$ and degrees of freedom *n*, returns the inverse reverse cumulative (upper-tail) Student's *t* distribution: if **ttail(n,t) = p,** then **invttail(n,p) = t.**

1.16 USING AND DISPLAYING SCALARS

When computing a probability or a percentile value we usually want a single value, rather than 1000 values. Stata allows these single values or scalars [**help scalar**] to be computed and displayed [**help display**].

1.16.1 Example of standard normal cdf

To illustrate, lets compute the probability that a standard normal random variable *Z* takes a values less than or equal to 1.27. This is computed using the *cdf* normal. Enter the following commands into the **Command** window.

scalar phi = normal(1.27) computes a scalar variable that is the desired probability.

display phi reports the value of the computed probability on the next line.
          .89795768

display "Prob (Z <= 1.27) = " phi illustrates inserting text into display.
          Prob (Z <= 1.27) = .89795768

di "Prob (Z <= 1.27) = " phi shows that display can be abbreviated **di.**
          Prob (Z <= 1.27) = .89795768

We do not have to first create **phi** at all. We can simply display the value by including the function to be evaluated in the display statement.

```
di "Prob (Z <= 1.27) = " normal(1.27)
Prob (Z <= 1.27) = .89795768
```

1.16.2 Example of t-distribution tail-cdf

Compute the probability that a *t*-random variable with $n = 20$ degrees of freedom takes a value greater than 1.27.

```
scalar p = ttail(20,1.27)
```

```
di "Prob (t(20) > 1.27) = " p
Prob (t(20) > 1.27) = .1093311
```

or

```
di "Prob (t(20) > 1.27) = " ttail(20,1.27)
Prob (t(20) > 1.27) = .1093311
```

1.16.3 Example computing percentile of the standard normal

Compute the value of the standard normal distribution *z* such that $p = 0.90$ of the probability falls to its left, so that $P(Z < z) = 0.90$. In this case *z* is the 90th percentile of the standard normal distribution.

```
scalar z = invnormal(.90)
di "90th percentile value of standard normal is " z
90th percentile value of standard normal is 1.2815516
```

1.16.4 Example computing percentile of the t-distribution

Compute the value *t* of the *t*-distribution with $n = 20$ degrees of freedom such that $p = 0.90$ of the probability falls to its left, so that $P(t(20) < t) = 0.90$. In this case *t* is the 90th percentile of the *t* distribution with 20 degrees of freedom. This problem is complicated by the fact that Stata provides only the "tail" function for the *t*-distribution, so the 90th percentile value is found by locating the point such that $p = 0.10$ of the probability lies in the upper-tail of the distribution, that is $P(t(20) > t) = 0.10$.

```
scalar t = invttail(20,.10)
di "90th percentile value of t(20) distribution is " t
90th percentile value of t(20) distribution is 1.3253407
```

You will note that the 90th percentile of the *t*(20) distribution is larger than the 90th percentile of the standard normal distribution. This is as it should be, as the *t*-distribution is "wider" than the standard normal. As noted earlier the **invttail** function can go into the display statement

```
di "90th percentile value of t(20) distribution is " invttail(20,.10)
```

```
90th percentile value of t(20) distribution is 1.3253407
```

1.17 A SCALAR DIALOG BOX

We will be using scalar functions frequently, yet there is no pull-down menu access to them. However there is a trick that can be used. Enter

help scalar

The help Viewer opens. Click on **define**.

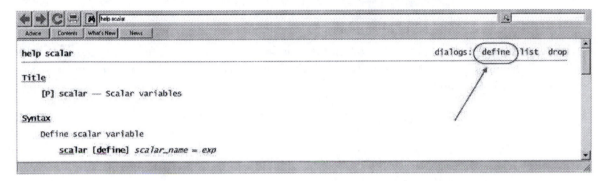

Alternatively enter **db scalardefine** in the Command window. A dialog box opens in which you can enter the scalar name and a function expression. For example let us find a percentile from the *t*-distribution with 20 degrees of freedom. For the 95th percentile we will find the value, say **t95**, of *t* such that $P(t(20) > t) = 0.05$ using **invttail(20,.05)**. In the dialog box we would enter the following, and click **OK**.

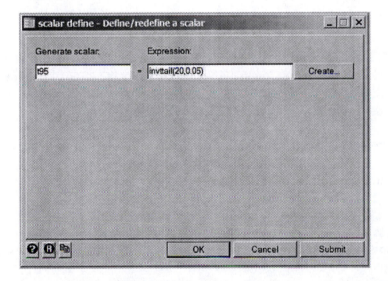

However the important advantage of this dialog box is if you forget the name of the function you seek. Click on **Create** in the **scalar define** dialog box, which opens an **Expression builder** dialog box.

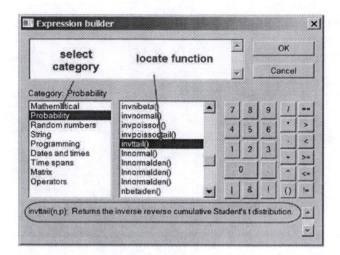

Choose a category of functions, scroll down the function list, using the definition appearing at the bottom of the dialog box. Now **double-click** on `invttail()`. The function then goes to the **Expression builder** window

Fill in the values for *n* and *p* that you desire, here *n* = 20 (degrees of freedom) and *p* = 0.05 (upper tail probability), then click **OK**.

In the scalar define dialog box `invttail(20,.05)` appears, leaving you only the task of naming the scalar and clicking **OK**. In the Command window appears the implied command

```
scalar define t95 = invttail(20,0.05)
```

Here `define` is optional and can be omitted if desired. The results can be displayed using

```
di "95th percentile of t(20) is " t95
95th percentile of t(20) is 1.7247182
```

While the process of using **Create** and the **Expression builder** looks tedious, it is sometimes quicker than looking up the required function using the Help menu, unless of course you remember the name of the function, which we often do not.

Close the log file. You may wish to translate it into a text file.

```
log close
```

If you use the **smcl** format of log file (`log using chap01, replace`) at this point you may wish to translate it to a text file

```
translate chap01.smcl chap01.txt
```

1.18 USING FACTOR VARIABLES

In Stata Version 11 a new feature has been added for use with **categorical variables** and discrete, binary or **indicator variables**. A categorical variable is one that identifies a group. Individuals might be categorized into groups according to where they live (North, South, Midwest, etc.) or their profession (White collar, Blue collar, etc.) or race/ethnicity (White, Black, Asian, Native American, etc.). Variables such as a woman's number of children, or a household's number of computers, is a count variable (a nonnegative integer) which can also be thought of as categorizing individuals. A special case of a categorical variable is an **indicator variable**, which has only two categories: male or female, for example. Another name for indicator variable is a **dummy variable**. The term "dummy" is meant to convey the idea that we are using a numerical value, such as 0 or 1, to represent a qualitative characteristic such as gender.

Stata treats categorical variables as **factor variables**. They are designated in operations with an "**i.**" prefix, such as **i.female** or **i.black**. To designate a variable as continuous use the prefix "**c.**", as in **c.wage**. Variables such as years of education or experience can be treated as either. This designation can be used in statistical analyses by using these prefixes. See **help factor variables**. For example,

```
summarize i.female
```

```
. summarize i.female
```

Variable	Obs	Mean	Std. Dev.	Min	Max
1.female	1000	.514	.5000541	0	1

The results are shown for the females (if **female = 1**) in the sample. The base category in this case is males (if **female = 0**), which is not shown. To show the base level use

```
summarize i.female, allbaselevels
```

```
. summarize i.female, allbaselevels
```

Variable	Obs	Mean	Std. Dev.	Min	Max
female					
0	1000	(base)			
1	1000	.514	.5000541	0	1

To define female = 1 (males) to be the base group use

```
summarize ib1.female
```

```
. summarize ib1.female
```

Variable	Obs	Mean	Std. Dev.	Min	Max
0.female	1000	.486	.5000541	0	1

To show summary statistics for all levels (no base group is omitted) use

```
summarize ibn.female
```

```
. summarize ibn.female
```

Variable	Obs	Mean	Std. Dev.	Min	Max
female					
0	1000	.486	.5000541	0	1
1	1000	.514	.5000541	0	1

Factor variables and continuous variables can be interacted with each using the operator "#"

```
summarize c.wage#i.female i.female#i.married
```

```
. summarize c.wage#i.female i.female#i.married
```

Variable	Obs	Mean	Std. Dev.	Min	Max
female#					
c.wage					
0	1000	10.76123	14.19308	0	72.13
1	1000	9.85443	13.25106	0	76.39
female#					
married					
0 1	1000	.296	.4567194	0	1
1 0	1000	.229	.4203995	0	1
1 1	1000	.285	.4516403	0	1

The interaction of the continuous variable wage and the indicator variable female reveals that the average wage of males is $10.76 and the average value of females is $9.85. The interaction of the two indicator variables **female** and **married** shows that in this sample of 1000 29.6% of males are married, 22.9% of females are not married, and 28.5% of females are married. The remaining category, unmarried males, makes up the remainder.

A "fully interacted" set of variables can be created using the operator "##". The notation A##B is interpreted by Stata as A and B and A#B. For example, and showing all groups,

```
summarize ibn.female##(c.wage ibn.married)
```

```
. summarize ibn.female##(c.wage ibn.married)
```

Variable	Obs	Mean	Std. Dev.	Min	Max
female					
0	1000	.486	.5000541	0	1
1	1000	.514	.5000541	0	1
wage	1000	20.61566	12.83472	1.97	76.39
married					
0	1000	.419	.4936423	0	1
1	1000	.581	.4936423	0	1
female# c.wage					
0	1000	10.76123	14.19308	0	72.13
1	1000	9.85443	13.25106	0	76.39
female# married					
0 0	1000	.19	.3924972	0	1
0 1	1000	.296	.4567194	0	1
1 0	1000	.229	.4203995	0	1
1 1	1000	.285	.4516403	0	1

1.18.1 Creating indicator variables using a logical operator

To create an indicator variable we use the generate command with a condition to be satisfied. If the condition is true, then the variable is assigned the value 1 and if it is not true the variable is assigned the value 0. For example, if we wish to create an indicator variable for a person who has an education level of between 9 and 12 years, use

```
generate hs = (9 <= educ)&(educ <=12)
```

The *cps4_small* data does not include any missing values. If the dataset contains missing values you may wish to make sure that they are propagated properly by adding the **if qualifier** shown below

```
generate hs = (9 <= educ)&(educ <=12) if !missing(educ)
```

If the variable **educ** takes a value greater than or equal to 9, or less than or equal to 12, then the variable **hs** is assigned the value 1, and otherwise **hs** = 0.

The "&" represents an operator. It is the logical equivalent of "and." For other operators, and the order of precedence, enter **help operators**.

```
help operators

Title

     Operators in expressions (found in [U] 13 Functions and expressions)

Syntax

                                                     Relational
               Arithmetic          Logical      (numeric and string)

          +    addition          &   and          >    greater than
          -    subtraction       |   or           <    less than
          *    multiplication    !   not          >=   > or equal
          /    division          ~   not          <=   < or equal
          ^    power                              ==   equal
          -    negation                           !=   not equal
          +    string concatenation               ~=   not equal

     A double equal sign (==) is used for equality testing.

     The order of evaluation (from first to last) of all operators is ! (or ~), ^, - (negation), /, *, -
     (subtraction), +, != (or ~=), >, <, <=, >=, ==, &, and |.
```

1.18.2 Creating indicator variables using tabulate

To create a separate indicator variable for each level of a categorical variable, the **tabulate** command is convenient. For example, suppose we wanted a separate 0-1 variable for each possible year of education.

```
tabulate educ, gen(ed)
```

This command counts the number of observations in each education level

```
. tabulate educ, gen(ed)
```

years of education	Freq.	Percent	Cum.
0	1	0.10	0.10
3	6	0.60	0.70
6	8	0.80	1.50
8	11	1.10	2.60
9	8	0.80	3.40
10	11	1.10	4.50
11	16	1.60	6.10
12	328	32.80	38.90
13	171	17.10	56.00
14	109	10.90	66.90
16	217	21.70	88.60
18	88	8.80	97.40
21	26	2.60	100.00
Total	1,000	100.00	

The option **gen(ed)** generates a series of 13 indicator variables, **ed1-ed13**, for each possible value of the variable **educ**. We see the listing of these variables in the **Variables** window.

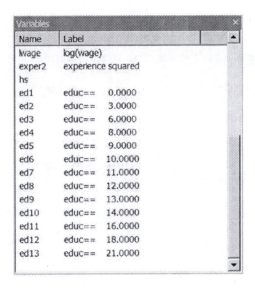

KEY TERMS[1]

arithmetic operators

categorical variable

cd

cdf

clear

command syntax

command window

cumulative distribution function

current path

data browser

data utilities

definition files

density functions

describe

dialog box, **db**

display

do selected

do-file

do-file editor

drop

exit

expression builder

factor variables

generate

help

help *command*

histogram

if

in

indicator variable

inverse cdf

keep

keywork search

label

log close

log file

log using

logical operators

math functions

operators

options

results window

review window

scalar

scalar dialog box

scatter diagram

search

search command

smcl format

standard normal distribution

summarize

summarize *variable*

summarize, detail

syntax

text format

translate

two-way graph

use

use *"data file"*, **clear**

variable manager

variables window

varmanage

working directory

---

[1] Stata terms in **bold** font

CHAPTER 1 DO-FILE [CHAP01.DO]

The following code includes most of the commands used in the chapter.

```
* file chap01.do for Using Stata for Principles of Econometrics, 4e

cd c:\data\poe4stata

* Stata do-file
* copyright C 2011 by Lee C. Adkins and R. Carter Hill
* used for "Using Stata for Principles of Econometrics, 4e"
* by Lee C. Adkins and R. Carter Hill (2011)
* John Wiley and Sons, Inc.

* setup
version 11.1
capture log close // this is a comment too
set more off

* open log file
log using chap01, replace text

* open data
use cps4_small, clear
describe

* assign or modify label
label variable wage "earnings per hour"

*----------------------------------------------------------------
* this is a comment
*
/* this type of comment "/*  */" can contain other comments  */
*
* these commands presume you have changed to the working
* directory. To change to a working directory enter
*
*        cd c:\data\poe4
*
* use the clear option if previous work in memory can be erased
*----------------------------------------------------------------

/*
 With few exceptions, the basic language syntax is

        [prefix :] command [varlist] [=exp] [if] [in] [weight]
                        [using filename] [, options]


    see                 language element        description
    ----------------------------------------------------------------
    help prefix         prefix :                prefix command
    help command        command                 Stata command
    help varlist        varlist                 variable list
    help exp            =exp                    expression
    help if             if                      if exp qualifier
    help in             in                      in range qualifier
    help weight         weight                  weight
    help using          using filename          using filename modifier
    help options        options                 options
    ----------------------------------------------------------------
*/
```

```
* summarize and variations
summarize
summarize wage, detail
summarize if exper >= 10
summarize in 1/50
summarize wage in 1/50, detail
summarize wage if female == 1 in 1/500, detail


*------------------------------------------------------------
* path to dialog box via pull-down menu
*
* Statistics > Summaries, tables, and tests > Summary and descriptive
*         statistics > Summary statistics
*
* or enter: db summarize
*
* or enter: help summarize
*------------------------------------------------------------

* illustrating help commands
help viewer
search mixed model
findit mixed model

* histogram menu: Graphics > Histogram
help histogram
db histogram
histogram wage, percent title(Histogram of wage data)
more


*--------------------------------------------------------
* the above command -more- causes execution of
* the Do-file to pause so that the histogram can
* be inspected before the next command is carried out
* Press the space bar to continue
*--------------------------------------------------------

* saving graphs
graph save Graph "C:\data\poe4stata\histogram of wages.gph", replace

* alternative saving option
graph save chap01hist, replace

* one-part construction
histogram wage, percent title(Histogram of wage data)
        saving(chap01hist,replace)
more

* enhanced figure with long lines indicator "///"
histogram wage, percent ytitle(Percent) xtitle(wage) title(Histogram of wage data) ///
        saving(chap01hist, replace)

* scatter diagram

twoway (scatter wage educ), saving(wage_educ, replace)
more

* creating new variables
generate lwage = ln(wage)
label variable lwage "ln(wage)"
generate exper2 = exper^2
label variable exper2 "experience squared"
```

```
*--------------------------------------------------------
* Note: to drop variables use command: drop lwage exper2
*--------------------------------------------------------

* Computing normal probabilities
help functions
help normal
scalar phi = normal(1.27)
di phi
display phi
display "Prob (Z <= 1.27) = " phi
di "Prob (Z <= 1.27) = " phi
di "Prob (Z <= 1.27) = " normal(1.27)

* Computing percentile values
scalar z = invnormal(.90)
di "90th percentile value of standard normal is " z

* factor variables
help factor variables
summarize i.female
summarize i.female, allbaselevels     // identify base level
summarize ib1.female                  // change base level, omitted group, to female=1
summarize ibn.female   // show summarize statistics for all levels (no omitted group)

* interacting factor variables
summarize c.wage#i.female i.female#i.married

* fully interacted or full factorial
summarize ibn.female##(c.wage ibn.married)

* create indicator variables
generate hs = (9 <= educ)&(educ <=12)
label variable hs "=1 if 9<=educ<=12"
tabulate educ, gen(ed)

log close
```

CHAPTER **2**

The Simple Linear Regression Model

2.1 THE FOOD EXPENDITURE DATA

An example that recurs in the first few chapters of Principles of Econometrics, 4th edition (abbreviated as POE4) is an economic model of the relationship between weekly household food expenditure and weekly household income. First, start Stata and change the working directory. How this is done depends on your computer hardware and operating system.

In this Windows-based book we use the working directory c:\data\poe4stata, and to change the working directory type

```
cd c:\data\poe4stata
```

on the command line and press Enter. Or follow the path **File > Change Working Directory** on the Stata pull-down menu.

2.1.1 Starting a new problem

If you are beginning a new problem you must start by closing any log file that is open and clearing any data from memory. To **Begin or Close** a Stata log file click on the toolbar icon.

If you have a log file open, a dialog box will appear giving you some options. Before beginning a new log file you must close the old one. Or, in the Command window enter

    log close

To clear Stata's memory enter

    clear

2.1.2 Starting a log file

To Begin or Close a Stata log file click on the toolbar icon, or enter the command

    log using chap02, replace text

This will open the log file in a text format in the current directory. The option replace will cause any previous version of **chap02.log** to be written over, and erased.

> **Remark**: Users should open a log file for each chapter, or part of a chapter. We will remind you to Begin and Close log files in the early chapters, but will not thereafter. Make it a habit to use log files.

2.1.3 Opening a Stata data file

The data for the food expenditure example is in the Stata data file *food.dta* and the definition file is *food.def*. To open the Stata data file click on **Open (use)** on the toolbar

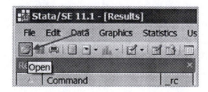

Locate *food.dta*, select it, and click **Open**. In the Command window, to open the data file in the current directory, enter

```
use food
```

If you wish to clear Stata's memory at the same time the new data file is opened, enter

```
use food, clear
```

The clear option clears any previously opened data set from memory. However, it is safer to carry out data file "housekeeping" prior to opening a new data file.

To load the data from the Stata internet site, enter

```
use http://www.stata.com/texts/s4poe4/food
```

In the **Variables** window two variables are listed, **food_exp** and **income**, along with their labels. Other information about the variable Type and Format may also appear. We have chosen to cover up those columns.

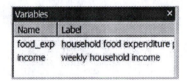

2.1.4 Browsing and listing the data

At the start of each new problem, it is prudent to examine the data. Enter into the command line

```
describe
```

For more on these options enter **help describe** in the **Command** window. None are required for a simple summary, so click **OK**.

```
. describe

Contains data from food.dta
  obs:            40
  vars:            2
  size:          800 (99.9% of memory free)

              storage  display    value
variable name   type   format     label      variable label

food_exp        double %10.0g                household food expenditure per week
income          double %10.0g                weekly household income
```

The output is general information about the data file *food.dta*.

One good motto for studying econometrics is the X-files mantra "Trust No One!" So we will check our data. Use the **Data Browser**.

The spreadsheet view opens that allows you to see the data values

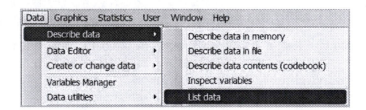

Close the Data Browser by clicking the "**x**"

If you wish to "print" or list some of the data lines, on the pull-down menu click **Data > Describe data > List data**

In the dialog box that opens simply click **OK** to list all the data to the **Results** window. The Stata command is `list`. The syntax of the list command is

```
list [varlist] [if] [in] [, options]
```

To list the values of specific variables, enter the variable names. The range of values to be listed can be modified using the logical "if" or "in" to denote specific lines. For example

```
list in 1/5
list food_exp in 1/5
list food_exp if income <= 10
```

The **Results** window shows

```
. list in 1/5
```

	food_exp	income
1.	115.22	3.69
2.	135.98	4.39
3.	119.34	4.75
4.	114.96	6.03
5.	187.05	12.47

```
. list food_exp in 1/5
```

	food_exp
1.	115.22
2.	135.98
3.	119.34
4.	114.96
5.	187.05

```
. list  food_exp if income <= 10
```

	food_exp
1.	115.22
2.	135.98
3.	119.34
4.	114.96

If the Results window fills, you may find —more— at the bottom. This indicates a pause. Either click —more— or press the space bar. The Stata command **set more off** will turn off the pause feature.

2.2 COMPUTING SUMMARY STATISTICS

Now, check to determine if the data have the same summary statistic values as reported in the definition file. Using the pull-down menu, click on

> **Statistics > Summaries, tables, and tests > Summary and descriptive statistics > Summary statistics**

In the resulting dialog box simply click **OK** for summary statistics on all the variables in the data set. You can also enter into the command line **db summarize** or **db su** to open the dialog box. The **Command** window equivalent is to enter

```
summarize
```

The syntax of the **summarize** command is

```
summarize [varlist] [if] [in] [weight] [, options]
```

A key option allows us to obtain more detailed summary statistics. The Stata command is

```
summarize food_exp, detail
```

. summarize

Variable	Obs	Mean	Std. Dev.	Min	Max
food_exp	40	283.5735	112.6752	109.71	587.66
income	40	19.60475	6.847773	3.69	33.4

```
.
. * summarize food expenditure with detail
. summarize food_exp, detail
```

household food expenditure per week

	Percentiles	Smallest		
1%	109.71	109.71		
5%	115.09	114.96		
10%	127.66	115.22	Obs	40
25%	199.245	119.34	Sum of Wgt.	40
50%	264.48		Mean	283.5735
		Largest	Std. Dev.	112.6752
75%	367.46	447.76		
90%	443.025	460.36	Variance	12695.7
95%	471.455	482.55	Skewness	.4920827
99%	587.66	587.66	Kurtosis	2.851522

In the **Results** window the Percentiles of the data are shown, as are the **Smallest** and **Largest** observations, the number of observations (**Obs**) and **Sum of Wgt** that you can ignore. Stata will report many things you do not understand. The trick is to be able to identify what you do know. For example, the results include

Mean	283.5735
Std. Dev.	112.6752
Variance	12695.7

These are summary statistics for the variable **food_exp**.

- Mean is the sample mean, $\bar{y} = \sum y_i / N$
- Std. Dev. is the sample standard deviation, which is the square root of the Variance
- Variance is the sample variance, $\text{var}(y) = \sum(y_i - \bar{y})^2 / N - 1$.

The values of **Skewness** and **Kurtosis** will be discussed later.

2.3 CREATING A SCATTER DIAGRAM

In the simple regression model it is important to plot the data values in a **Scatter Diagram**. On the Stata pull-down menu choose **Graphics > Twoway graph (scatter, line, etc.)**. For the details enter `help twoway`.

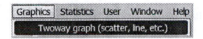

In the dialog box click **Create**

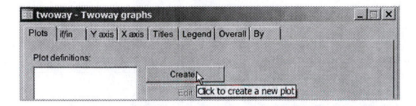

In the resulting dialog box choose **Basic plots, Scatter** then choose the Y variable (vertical axis) and the X variable (horizontal axis) using the pull-down arrows.

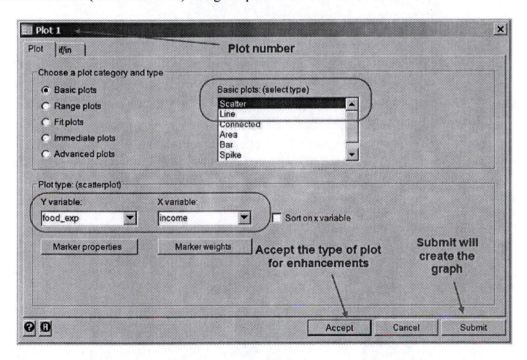

If you click **Submit** the scatter diagram will be created. The Stata command is

```
twoway (scatter food_exp income)
```

If you select **Accept** Plot 1 will appear in the Plot definitions window and the graph will be created when you click OK.

To save the graph to disk to the default directory with the Stata graph extension ***.gph** use

```
graph save food1, replace
```

Graphing and saving to disk can be accomplished in one-step using the **saving** option

```
twoway (scatter food_exp income), saving(food1, replace)
```

Instead of saving to disk, you can save to memory using the **name** option. This may be handy if you are in a lab environment

```
twoway (scatter food_exp income), name(food1, replace)
```

2.3.1 Enhancing the plot

To enhance the plot, in the Plot 1 dialog box, click **Accept**. In the Graphics dialog box this creates a Plot definition, or profile, called **Plot 1**.

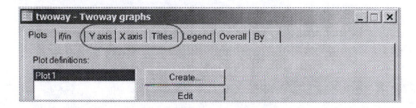

Click the tab Y axis. In the resulting dialog box select

There are several options, but let us specify the range of the vertical axis.

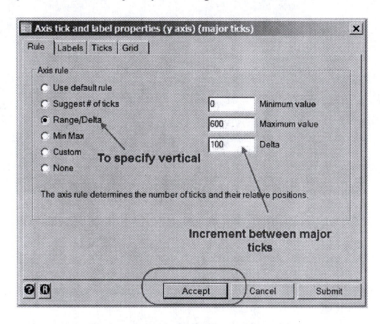

Click the **Range/Delta** option. From the data summary statistics we know the minimum and maximum values of **food_exp**. So that we can view the entire range of data select Minimum value 0 and Maximum value 600. **Delta** is the units of measure for the axis—the space between tick marks. Set this value to 100. Click **Accept**.

Repeat this process for the X axis, using as Maximum value 35 and a Delta of 5. Click **Accept**

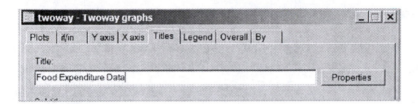

To add a title click the **Titles** tab in the **Twoway Graph Dialog Box**.

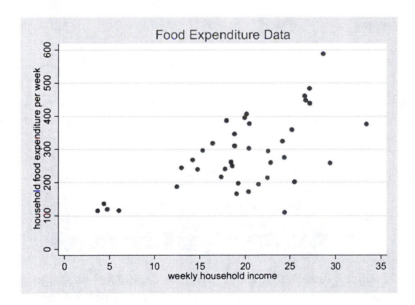

Click **OK** to create the graph and close the window. This produces a nice plot with Y-axis and X-axis labeled with the Variable labels in the data set.

The Stata command used to create this figure is

```
twoway (scatter food_exp income), ///  /* basic plot control        */
       ylabel(0(100)600)          ///  /* Y axis 0-600 & ticks at 100 */
       xlabel(0(5)35)             ///  /* X axis 0-35 & ticks each 5  */
       title(Food Expenditure Data)    /* graph title               */
```

In this command the "///" continues the command onto the next line. This is useful when commands are long, or when comments are inserted after specific parts of a command as we have done here. The comment form "/* .... */" is useful because it can be inserted anywhere and the content is ignored by Stata. For discussion of alternative comment commands enter **help comments**.

twoway (scatter food_exp income), is the same command used to produce the simple scatter. The comma is important, and indicates options that will be applied.

ylabel(0(100)600) specifies the range of the Y axis, 0 to 600, and space between the major ticks, 100.

xlabel(0(5)35) specifies the range, 0 to 35, and increment for the X axis, 5.

title(Food Expenditure Data) specifies the primary title.

Once again you can add the **saving** option to the **twoway** command, or use the option **name** to save to memory, or use a **graph save** command. We use **graph save** commands in the do-file for this chapter.

2.4 REGRESSION

The simple linear regression model is

$$y = \beta_1 + \beta_2 x + e$$

Given data on the dependent variable, y (**food_exp**), and the independent variable, x (**income**), we can use Stata to estimate the unknown parameters. Regression analysis uses the pull-down menu from

Statistics > Linear models and related > Linear regression

In the **Regress - Linear regression** dialog box select the dependent variable to be **food_exp**. This is the left-hand side variable in the regression model. Select (or enter) **income** as the independent (right-hand side) variable. Stata will automatically include an intercept term in the estimation. Click **OK**.

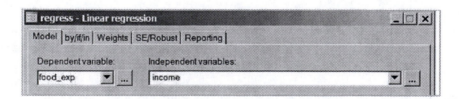

Alternatively the command line syntax is

```
regress depvar [indepvars] [if] [in] [weight] [, options]
```

See **help regress**. This shows that the dependent variable **depvar** is listed first and then the independent variable or variables (for a multiple regression), **indepvars**. You can use **if** or **in** to limit the sample, assign weights to the observations or use options, if desired. We discuss these options more in future chapters.

For the food expenditure the simple regression command is

```
regress food_exp income
```

which can be shortened to

```
reg food_exp income
```

In the **Results** window the Stata command for the regression is given, and a display of regression results. We will explore all of these items, but for now focus on the first two columns labeled **food_exp** and **Coef.**

The first column gives the variable names. Remember that computer software will not know that you call the estimates "b1" and "b2" and will instead list these with variable names. Stata lists the slope coefficient first, **income**. The y-intercept is labeled **_cons**, short for "constant" or "constant term," which is another common name for the y-intercept.

```
. regress food_exp income
```

Source	SS	df	MS		
Model	190626.984	1	190626.984	Number of obs =	40
Residual	304505.176	38	8013.2941	F(1, 38) =	23.79
				Prob > F =	0.0000
				R-squared =	0.3850
				Adj R-squared =	0.3688
Total	495132.16	39	12695.6964	Root MSE =	89.517

food_exp	Coef.	Std. Err.	t	P>|t|	[95% Conf. Interval]	
income	10.20964	2.093264	4.88	0.000	5.972052	14.44723
_cons	83.416	43.41016	1.92	0.062	-4.463279	171.2953

2.4.1 Fitted values and residuals

The fitted, or predicted, values $\hat{y}$ are obtained using what are called "postestimation" commands. They are called "postestimation" options because they follow the estimation of the regression model. After **help regress** the link to the postestimation options is in the upper right-hand corner.

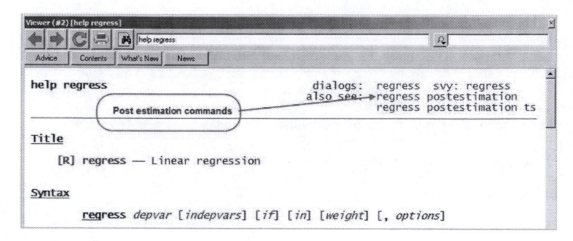

The path on the Stata menu bar is

Statistics > Postestimation > Predictions, residuals, etc.

Click **Statistics** then

In the resulting dialog box there are several alternatives. To obtain the fitted values, click on Linear prediction and enter a name for the fitted values, say **yhat**. Click OK.

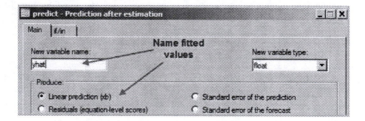

To obtain the least squares residuals,

$$\hat{e}_i = y_i - \hat{y}_i = y_i - b_1 - b_2 x_i$$

open the dialog box again, click on **Residuals** and enter a name for the residuals, say **ehat**. Click OK.

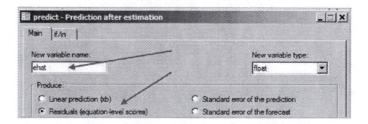

These commands have created two new variables, **yhat** and **ehat**, which appear in the **Variables** window.

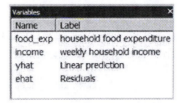

Examine these values by selecting the **Data Browser**, or use the command

> `Browse`

The Stata commands that compute the fitted values and least squares residuals are obtained using the fundamental postestimation command `predict`. Close the browser and in the **Command** window type

> `help predict`

The basic syntax for predict is

> `predict [type] newvar [if] [in] [, single_options]`

What is required is the name of the variable, **newvar**, and an option. To obtain fitted values use the option **xb** which is short for "x times b".

> `predict yhat, xb`

Obtaining predictions are actually the default for this command, so we could have used

> `predict yhat`

To obtain residuals use the option **residuals**. For the food expenditure model these are

> `predict ehat, residuals`

The option **residuals** can be shortened to the minimum of **r**, or a bit longer like **res** or **resid**.

2.4.2 Computing an elasticity

Given the parameter estimates, and the summary statistics for the variables, we can easily compute other quantities, like the elasticity of food expenditure with respect to income, evaluated at the means

$$\hat{\varepsilon} = b_2 \cdot \frac{\bar{x}}{\bar{y}} = 10.21 \times \frac{19.60}{283.57} = 0.71$$

One of Stata's post-estimation commands allows computing this elasticity automatically. Select **Statistics > Postestimation > Marginal effects**.

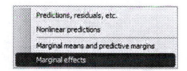

In the resulting dialog box select the radio button for **Elasticities** and the **Variable**. In our simple regression model there is only one variable to select, **income**. To evaluate the elasticity at the sample means select the **At** tab, and click the radio button for **All covariates at their means in the sample.**

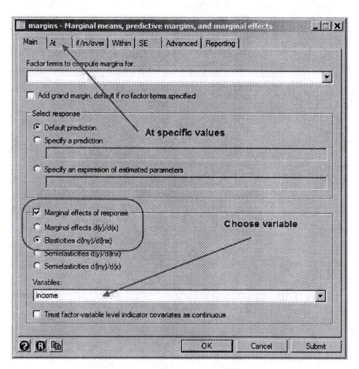

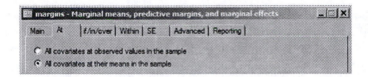

In the Results window we find the **Conditional marginal effects**

```
. margins, eyex(income) atmeans
```

```
Conditional marginal effects                    Number of obs   =        40
Model VCE     : OLS

Expression    : Linear prediction, predict()
ey/ex w.r.t. : income
at            : income       =    19.60475 (mean)
```

	ey/ex	Delta-method Std. Err.	z	P>|z|	[95% Conf. Interval]
income	.7058399	.1489436	4.74	0.000	.4139159 .9977639

The **Margins** dialog box is very powerful and will do calculations you may not understand at the moment. We present it to make a couple of points. In Economic analysis the change in one variable resulting from the change in another, holding all else constant, is called a **marginal effect**. In the linear regression model this is the interpretation of the slope parameter and in the simple linear regression model is the derivative dy/dx. Stata will compute this value in more complex models and we will return to this feature later.

For the linear (straight-line) regression model the elasticity is

$$\varepsilon = \frac{\text{percentage change in } y}{\text{percentage change in } x} = \frac{\Delta y / y}{\Delta x / x} = \frac{\Delta y}{\Delta x} \cdot \frac{x}{y}$$

Replace the Δ by the "d" to put it in the form of a derivative.

$$\varepsilon = \frac{dy / y}{dx / x} = \frac{dy}{dx} \cdot \frac{x}{y} = \beta_2 \frac{x}{y}$$

In calculus $d\ln(y) = dy/y$ and $d\ln(x) = dx/x$, thus an economical way to write the elasticity for a straight line regression model is

$$\varepsilon = \frac{d \ln(y)}{d \ln(x)} = \frac{dy / y}{dx / x}$$

The Stata post-estimation command for this elasticity following a regression is

```
margins, eyex( income ) atmeans
```

Note only does Stata report the elasticity, but computes a standard error for this quantity and a confidence interval as well[1]. It shows the value of income at which this quantity is calculated, which is the sample mean. Most commonly the elasticity is calculated at the "point of the means" $(\bar{x}, \bar{y}) = (19.60, 283.57)$ because it is a representative point on the regression line.

> **Remark**: Computer software is dangerous to the learning process. You must not rely on pointing and clicking to obtain an answer without understanding what calculation is occurring, and how the quantity is interpreted. Neat computing tricks are not a substitute for really learning the material.

Rather than computing the elasticity at one specific point we can alternatively find the elasticity at each value of y and x and then average this quantity across all observations. This is called an **Average marginal effect**, in this case average elasticity. That is, compute

$$AME = \bar{\varepsilon} = \frac{1}{N} \sum_{i=1}^{N} b_2 \frac{x_i}{y_i}$$

Stata will compute

$$\widehat{AME} = \frac{1}{N} \sum_{i=1}^{N} b_2 \frac{x_i}{\hat{y}_i} = \frac{1}{N} \sum_{i=1}^{N} b_2 \left(\frac{x_i}{b_1 + b_2 x_i} \right)$$

The Stata margins command for this quantity omits the previously used "**atmeans**" option

        margins, eyex(income)

The results are[2] now **Average marginal effects**, rather than Conditional marginal effects as above.

```
. margins, eyex( income )

Average marginal effects                      Number of obs    =         40
Model VCE      : OLS

Expression     : Linear prediction, predict()
ey/ex w.r.t.   : income
```

	ey/ex	Delta-method Std. Err.	z	P>|z|	[95% Conf. Interval]	
income	.6796126	.1466535	4.63	0.000	.3921769	.9670482

We can verify this calculation. After a regression Stata saves the estimated coefficients in its memory, though not indefinitely. Regression coefficients are designated **_b[varname]**. After the food expenditure regression, the estimated slope is stored as **_b[income]**. The elasticity calculation, evaluated for each observation in the sample, is then

---

[1] The calculation of the standard error is discussed in an appendix to this chapter.
[2] More details of this calculation are given in an appendix to this chapter.

```
generate elas = _b[income]*income/yhat
```

The average elasticity is

```
summarize elas
```

We have then in the Results window

```
. generate elas = _b[income]*income/yhat

. summarize elas
```

Variable	Obs	Mean	Std. Dev.	Min	Max
elas	40	.6796126	.1168024	.3111216	.8034579

In these results the **Std. Dev.** reported is the sample standard deviation. The margins command produces something called a **Delta-method Std. Err.** These are not the same. The Delta method is introduced in Chapter 5 of *POE4*.

2.4.3 Plotting the fitted regression line

To plot the fitted regression line use the pull-down menu **Graphics > Twoway graph (scatter, line, etc.).** If you are continuing this session and have done the scatter plot in Section 2.3 then **Plot 1**, the scatter diagram, already exists. We will create a new plot for the linear prediction. Click **Create**. In the Plot 2 dialog box, choose **Fit plots** and **Linear prediction** with Y variable and X variable as **food_exp** and **income**.

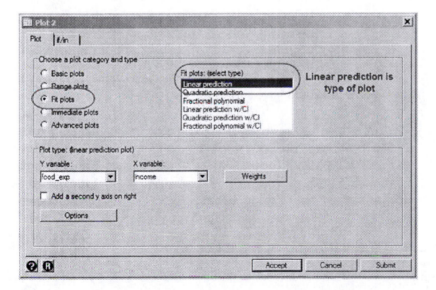

Click on **Accept**. Change the title by clicking on **Titles**, enter a new title. Return to Plots tab. Clicking **Submit** will create the graph and leave the window open.

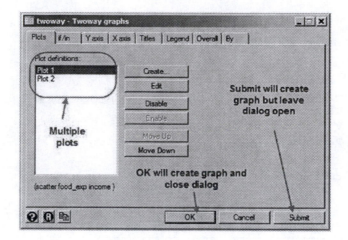

When several Plot definitions are present and active in memory, Stata will overlay one graph on top of another. The figure produced is

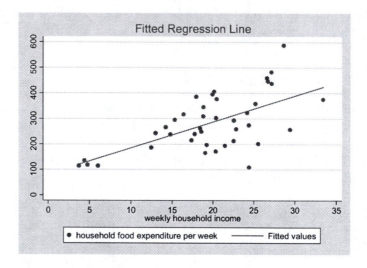

Into the Command window we could have entered

```
twoway (scatter food_exp income)        ///    /* basic plot control */
       (lfit food_exp income),          ///    /* add linear fit */
       ylabel(0(100)600)                ///    /* label Y axis */
       xlabel(0(5)35)                   ///    /* label X axis */
       title(Fitted Regression Line)           /* graph title */
```

2.4.4 Estimating the variance of the error term

Besides the regression coefficients another important parameter is the variance of the error term,

$$\text{var}(e_i) = \sigma^2 = E[e_i - E(e_i)]^2 = E(e_i^2)$$

This parameter is estimated as

$$\hat{\sigma}^2 = \frac{\sum \hat{e}_i^2}{N-2}$$

where $\hat{e}_i = y_i - \hat{y}_i = y_i - b_1 - b_2 x_i$ are the least squares residuals. The "2" in the denominator is the number of regression parameters, here β_1 and β_2. In the Stata regression output this quantity is given in the Analysis of Variance table.

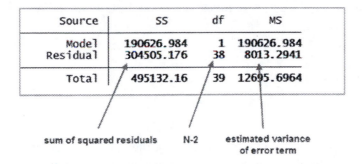

Focus on the row **Residual**. The column labeled **SS** contains Sums of Squares. The value 304505.176 is the sum of squared least squares residuals

$$SSE = \sum_{i=1}^{N} \hat{e}_i^2 = \text{SS Residual}$$

The column labeled **df** is the (residual) degrees of freedom, which in this case is $N - 2 = 38$. The model degrees of freedom is 1, which is the number of parameters other than the intercept, here β_2. The column header **MS** stands for Mean Square. The mean of the squared residuals is the estimated error variance

$$\hat{\sigma}^2 = \frac{\sum \hat{e}_i^2}{N-2} = \text{MS Residual} = 8013.2941$$

The other components of the table will be explained later.

2.4.5 Viewing estimated variances and covariance

After a regression is estimated there are many regression related statistics calculated but not reported by Stata. The estimated variances and covariance of the least squares estimators for the food expenditure model are

$$\widehat{\text{var}}(b_1) = \hat{\sigma}^2 \left[\frac{\sum x_i^2}{N \sum (x_i - \bar{x})^2} \right] = 1884.4423$$

$$\widehat{\text{var}(b_2)} = \frac{\hat{\sigma}^2}{\sum(x_i - \bar{x})^2} = 4.3817522$$

$$\widehat{\text{cov}(b_1, b_2)} = \hat{\sigma}^2 \left[\frac{-\bar{x}}{\sum(x_i - \bar{x})^2} \right] = -85.903157$$

These can be viewed using the **estat** command. Enter on the command line

```
help estat
```

To obtain the estimated variances and covariance enter

```
estat vce
```

The result is a table with the estimated variances of the regression coefficients reported on the diagonal and the estimated covariance between the regression coefficients on the "off-diagonal." Stata's arrangement has the variance of b_2 being in the upper left corner.

$$\text{Stata covariance matrix} = \begin{bmatrix} \widehat{\text{var}(b_2)} & \widehat{\text{cov}(b_1, b_2)} \\ \widehat{\text{cov}(b_1, b_2)} & \widehat{\text{var}(b_1)} \end{bmatrix}$$

```
. estat vce

Covariance matrix of coefficients of regress model
```

e(V)	income	_cons
income	4.3817522	
_cons	-85.903157	1884.4423

The square roots estimated variances are the standard errors of the estimated coefficients.

$$se(b_1) = \sqrt{\widehat{\text{var}(b_1)}} = 43.41016$$

$$se(b_2) = \sqrt{\widehat{\text{var}(b_2)}} = 2.093264$$

These are automatically produced by Stata when a regression is performed and are labeled **Std. Err.**

food_exp	Coef.	Std. Err.	t	P>|t|	[95% Conf. Interval]	
income	10.20964	2.093264	4.88	0.000	5.972052	14.44723
_cons	83.416	43.41016	1.92	0.062	-4.463279	171.2953

2.5 Using Stata to obtain predicted values

The predicted value of weekly food expenditure for a household with $2000 income per week, based on the estimated food expenditure model is

$$\hat{y}_i = 83.42 + 10.21x_i = 83.42 + 10.21(20) = 287.61$$

We will trick Stata into doing the work for us by adding an incomplete observation to the data file. On the Stata toolbar click the **Data Editor** icon

This will open a spreadsheet view, like the **Data Browser**, with the difference being that in the **Data Editor** view we can change the data file. Scroll down to the 40th and last observation, highlight the cell for income in row 41. Type the value **20** in the "formula bar" window and press **Enter**.

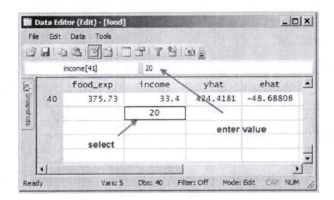

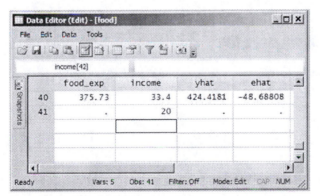

The **Data Editor** will now show that income has the value 20 for observation 41, but the other values have a period "." showing. In Stata a period means that a numeric data value is missing, which in this case is what we want. Close the **Data Editor** by clicking the **x**. The equivalent Stata commands are

```
edit
```

```
set obs 41
replace income = 20 in 41
```

The command **set** is a utility that controls many system parameters, including the number of observations. The command **replace** is a Data utility, that can be found using the menu path **Data > Create or change data > Change contents of variable**. The syntax of **replace** is

```
replace oldvar = exp [if] [in] [, nopromote]
```

We have replaced the value of **income** in line 41 with the value 20. You can view more about these commands using **help set** and **help replace**.

Obtain the predicted or fitted values, which we will now call **yhat0** because the variable **yhat** already exists. We can omit the **xb** option as it is the default with **predict**.

```
predict yhat0
```

The predict command will compute predicted, or fitted, values for all values of **income**, including income = 20 in observation 41. List the data for **income** and **yhat0** in observation 41.

```
list income yhat0 in 41
```

In the **Results** window we see

```
. list income yhat0 in 41
```

	income	yhat0
41.	20	287.6089

The value of **yhat0** is the predicted weekly food expenditure for a household with income $2000 per week.

2.5.1 Saving the Stata data file

To save the Stata data file, since it has been changed by adding several variables, click **File > Save as**

Save the data file under a new name such as **chap02.dta**. The Stata command is

```
save chap02.dta
```

As the final step you will **Close** the log file.

```
log close
```

2.6 ESTIMATING NONLINEAR RELATIONSHIPS

The linear regression model can be used to estimate nonlinear, curvilinear, relationships. This is not a contradiction because **linear regression** refers to a model in which the parameters do not enter in a nonlinear fashion. The regression $y = \beta_1 + \beta_2 x + e$ is linear. The variables y and x can be transformations of other variables. The regression $y = \exp(\beta_1 + \beta_2 x) + e$ is **not** a linear regression because the parameters are involved in a nonlinear way, as an exponent.

Two popular variable transformations are using polynomial terms and logarithmic terms. In this section we examine quadratic and log-linear models

2.6.1 A quadratic model

Using real estate data we will estimate the quadratic model $y = \beta_1 + \beta_2 x^2 + e$. Begin a new log file, and open data *br.dta*.

```
log using chap02_quad, replace text
use br, clear
describe
summarize
```

The descriptions and summary statistics are, in part,

variable name	storage type	display format	value label	variable label
price	float	%9.0g		sale price, dollars
sqft	float	%9.0g		total square feet

. summarize

Variable	Obs	Mean	Std. Dev.	Min	Max
price	1080	154863.2	122912.8	22000	1580000
sqft	1080	2325.938	1008.098	662	7897

The most straightforward way to proceed is to create a new variable **sqft2** that is the square of the variable **sqft**.

```
generate sqft2=sqft^2
```

Regress house price on the square of house size and obtain fitted values, **priceq**.

```
regress price sqft2
predict priceq, xb
```

```
. regress price sqft2
```

Source	SS	df	MS
Model	1.1286e+13	1	1.1286e+13
Residual	5.0150e+12	1078	4.6522e+09
Total	1.6301e+13	1079	1.5108e+10

Number of obs =	1080
F(1, 1078) =	2425.98
Prob > F =	0.0000
R-squared =	0.6923
Adj R-squared =	0.6921
Root MSE =	68207

price	Coef.	Std. Err.	t	P>|t|	[95% Conf. Interval]	
sqft2	.0154213	.0003131	49.25	0.000	.014807	.0160356
_cons	55776.56	2890.441	19.30	0.000	50105.04	61448.09

To plot the fitted line we will introduce some new options in a **twoway graph**. First, we plot the raw data. The second plot is the fitted line using **twoway** plot type **line**. See `help twoway` for other plot types. The option **sort** must be added so that the fitted line is smooth and continuous instead of the jagged result obtained by plotting the observations sequentially, with houses of varying sizes following one another. To make the fitted line a bit thicker than the default, add `lwidth(medthick)`.

```
twoway (scatter price sqft)        /// /* basic plot */
       (line priceq sqft,          /// /* 2nd plot: line is continuous */
        sort lwidth(medthick))         /* sort & change line thickness */
graph save br_quad, replace
```

The resulting plot shows the curvilinear shape of the fitted quadratic function. The slope is not constant, and larger houses have larger increase in price per additional size. The function is increasing at an increasing rate. Slope and elasticity calculations must be altered from the "straight line" or linear relationship functional form we considered earlier.

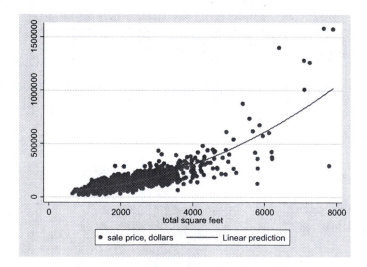

The slope of the fitted quadratic regression function $\hat{y} = b_1 + b_2 x^2$ is $dy/dx = 2b_2 x$. To compute the slope at different values of $x = $ **sqft** we can use a simple `display` (see `help display`), which can be abbreviated as `di`. As earlier in this chapter we will access the regression coefficient using `_b[sqft2]`. Calculating the slope at **sqft** = 2000, 4000 and 6000 we have

```
        di "slope at 2000 = " 2*_b[sqft2]*2000
        di "slope at 4000 = " 2*_b[sqft2]*4000
        di "slope at 6000 = " 2*_b[sqft2]*6000
```

```
. * slope and elasticity calculations
. di "slope at 2000 = " 2*_b[sqft2]*2000
slope at 2000 = 61.685207

. di "slope at 4000 = " 2*_b[sqft2]*4000
slope at 4000 = 123.37041

. di "slope at 6000 = " 2*_b[sqft2]*6000
slope at 6000 = 185.05562
```

Using the same approach we can see the predicted values from the estimated regression

```
        di "predicted price at 2000 = " _b[_cons]+_b[sqft2]*2000^2
        di "predicted price at 4000 = " _b[_cons]+_b[sqft2]*4000^2
        di "predicted price at 6000 = " _b[_cons]+_b[sqft2]*6000^2
```

```
. di "predicted price at 2000 = " _b[_cons]+_b[sqft2]*2000^2
predicted price at 2000 = 117461.77

. di "predicted price at 4000 = " _b[_cons]+_b[sqft2]*4000^2
predicted price at 4000 = 302517.39

. di "predicted price at 6000 = " _b[_cons]+_b[sqft2]*6000^2
predicted price at 6000 = 610943.42
```

An elasticity for the fitted function is $\hat{\varepsilon} = \left(d\hat{y}/dx\right)\times\left(x/\hat{y}\right)=2b_2 x^2/\hat{y}$. Using the estimated coefficients to form this value we have

```
        di "elasticity at 2000 = " 2*_b[sqft2]*2000^2/(_b[_cons]+_b[sqft2]*2000^2)
        di "elasticity at 4000 = " 2*_b[sqft2]*4000^2/(_b[_cons]+_b[sqft2]*4000^2)
        di "elasticity at 6000 = " 2*_b[sqft2]*6000^2/(_b[_cons]+_b[sqft2]*6000^2)
```

```
. di "elasticity at 2000 = " 2*_b[sqft2]*2000^2/(_b[_cons]+_b[sqft2]*2000^2)
elasticity at 2000 = 1.0503027

. di "elasticity at 4000 = " 2*_b[sqft2]*4000^2/(_b[_cons]+_b[sqft2]*4000^2)
elasticity at 4000 = 1.6312505

. di "elasticity at 6000 = " 2*_b[sqft2]*6000^2/(_b[_cons]+_b[sqft2]*6000^2)
elasticity at 6000 = 1.8174084
```

A more stylish and efficient approach is to use factor variables. If we use $x^2 = x\times x$, with the continuous variable x = **sqft** denoted in factor variable notation **c.sqft**, we can estimate the quadratic function directly without creating a new variable.

```
        regress price c.sqft#c.sqft
```

```
. regress price c.sqft#c.sqft
```

Source	SS	df	MS
Model	1.1286e+13	1	1.1286e+13
Residual	5.0150e+12	1078	4.6522e+09
Total	1.6301e+13	1079	1.5108e+10

```
Number of obs =     1080
F(  1,  1078) = 2425.98
Prob > F      =  0.0000
R-squared     =  0.6923
Adj R-squared =  0.6921
Root MSE      =   68207
```

price	Coef.	Std. Err.	t	P>|t|	[95% Conf. Interval]	
c.sqft#c.sqft	.0154213	.0003131	49.25	0.000	.014807	.0160356
_cons	55776.57	2890.441	19.30	0.000	50105.04	61448.09

The predictions from this specification are the same as from the previous estimation, as you can confirm by **browsing** the data.

> **predict price2**

The great advantage of using the factor notation is that Stata will correctly compute slopes and elasticities using the **margins** command. First, the slopes use margins with **dydx(*)**, the * denoting a request for slopes for all model variables, which in this case is just **sqft**. Conveniently we can specify the slope to computed at several values with the **at** option.

> **margins, dydx(*) at(sqft=(2000 4000 6000))**

```
. margins, dydx(*) at(sqft=(2000 4000 6000))

Conditional marginal effects                    Number of obs    =      1080
Model VCE    : OLS

Expression   : Linear prediction, predict()
dy/dx w.r.t. : sqft

1._at        : sqft            =        2000

2._at        : sqft            =        4000

3._at        : sqft            =        6000
```

	dy/dx	Delta-method Std. Err.	z	P>|z|	[95% Conf. Interval]	
sqft _at						
1	61.68521	1.252385	49.25	0.000	59.23058	64.13983
2	123.3704	2.504769	49.25	0.000	118.4612	128.2797
3	185.0556	3.757154	49.25	0.000	177.6917	192.4195

Not only are slopes computed correctly, but we are provided a standard error and interval estimate as well. Elasticities use the **eyex(*)** option.

> **margins, eyex(*) at(sqft=(2000 4000 6000))**

```
. margins, eyex(*) at(sqft=(2000 4000 6000))
```

```
Conditional marginal effects                    Number of obs   =        1080
Model VCE      : OLS

Expression     : Linear prediction, predict()
ey/ex w.r.t.   : sqft

1._at          : sqft              =           2000

2._at          : sqft              =           4000

3._at          : sqft              =           6000
```

		Delta-method				
	ey/ex	Std. Err.	z	P>|z|	[95% Conf. Interval]	
sqft						
_at						
1	1.050303	.0336868	31.18	0.000	.9842778	1.116328
2	1.631251	.0203148	80.30	0.000	1.591434	1.671067
3	1.817408	.0112071	162.17	0.000	1.795443	1.839374

The slopes and elasticities computed above are **Conditional** because they are computed at specific values. To compute the **Average** marginal effects or average elasticities use the margins command without the **at** option.

margins, eyex(*)

```
. margins, eyex(*)
```

```
Average marginal effects                        Number of obs   =        1080
Model VCE      : OLS

Expression     : Linear prediction, predict()
ey/ex w.r.t.   : sqft
```

		Delta-method				
	ey/ex	Std. Err.	z	P>|z|	[95% Conf. Interval]	
sqft	1.102401	.0292176	37.73	0.000	1.045135	1.159666

To verify that these **Average marginal effects** are what we expect, we can compute them directly by accessing the save regression coefficients. It can be difficult at first to know how to refer to individual coefficients. This can be resolved by replaying the regression with the option **coeflegend**.

regress, coeflegend

This returns to ANOVA table and the coefficient legend.

price	Coef.	Legend
c.sqft# c.sqft	.0154213	_b[c.sqft#c.sqft]
_cons	55776.57	_b[_cons]

For the factor model specification the **_b[varname]** is **_b[c.sqft#c.sqft]**.

```
generate elas2 = 2*_b[c.sqft#c.sqft]*(sqft^2)/price2
summarize elas2
```

. generate elas2 = 2*_b[c.sqft#c.sqft]*(sqft^2)/price2

. summarize elas2

Variable	Obs	Mean	Std. Dev.	Min	Max
elas2	1080	1.102401	.3528353	.2161448	1.890364

Note that the average elasticity is indeed what **margins** has computed, but once again **summarize** computes a sample standard deviation and **margins** computes a Delta-method standard error. Now close the log file.

```
log close
```

2.6.2 A log-linear model

Using the same data we will estimate a log-linear model $\ln(y) = \beta_1 + \beta_2 x + e$. The fitted line will be

$$\widehat{\ln(y)} = b_1 + b_2 x$$

To obtain the fitted value of y the most natural thing to do is compute the antilog as

$$\hat{y} = \exp\left(\widehat{\ln(y)}\right) = \exp(b_1 + b_2 x)$$

The slope of the fitted log-linear curve is $d\hat{y}/dx = b_2\hat{y}$ and the elasticity is $\hat{\varepsilon} = (d\hat{y}/dx) \times (x/\hat{y}) = b_2 x$. Open a new log, and use *br.dta*. Detailed summary statistics for the variable **price**, and its histogram, show it to have a skewed distribution, with a long tail to the right.

```
log using chap02_llin, replace text
use br, clear
summarize price, detail
```

```
. summarize price, detail
```

                         sale price, dollars

	Percentiles	Smallest		
1%	31000	22000		
5%	59897.5	22000		
10%	74450	22654	Obs	1080
25%	99000	23000	Sum of Wgt.	1080
50%	130000		Mean	154863.2
		Largest	Std. Dev.	122912.8
75%	170325	1280000		
90%	244200	1400000	Variance	1.51e+10
95%	315000	1575000	Skewness	6.291909
99%	610000	1580000	Kurtosis	60.94976

Note that the sample mean is quite a bit greater than the median (50th percentile) because of some extremely large values about $1.5 million. The Skewness coefficient is positive rather than the zero we expect for symmetric distributions like the normal.

```
histogram price, percent
graph save price, replace
```

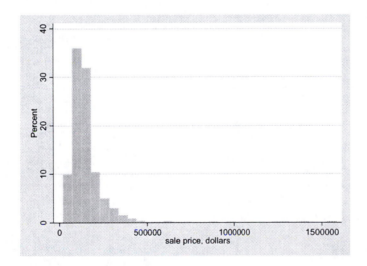

Now generate the logarithm of price and plot its histogram.

```
generate lprice = ln(price)
histogram lprice, percent
graph save lprice, replace
```

As shown below it is more symmetrical, if not bell shaped like the normal.

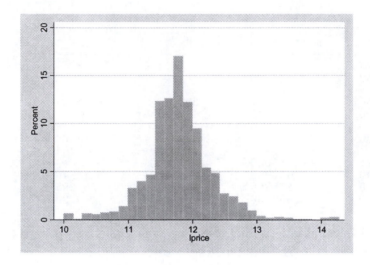

The log-linear regression model is

```
reg lprice sqft
```

```
. reg lprice sqft
```

Source	SS	df	MS
Model	185.472091	1	185.472091
Residual	111.400275	1078	.103339773
Total	296.872366	1079	.275136577

Number of obs = 1080
F(1, 1078) = 1794.78
Prob > F = 0.0000
R-squared = 0.6248
Adj R-squared = 0.6244
Root MSE = .32147

lprice	Coef.	Std. Err.	t	P>|t|	[95% Conf. Interval]
sqft	.0004113	9.71e-06	42.36	0.000	.0003922 .0004303
_cons	10.8386	.0246075	440.46	0.000	10.79031 10.88688

The predicted values are obtained using

```
predict lpricef, xb
generate pricef = exp(lpricef)
```

The variable pricef is the predicted (or forecast) price. Plot the fitted curve

```
reg lprice sqft
predict lpricef, xb
generate pricef = exp(lpricef)

twoway (scatter price sqft) ///
        (line pricef sqft, sort lwidth(medthick))
graph save br_loglin, replace
```

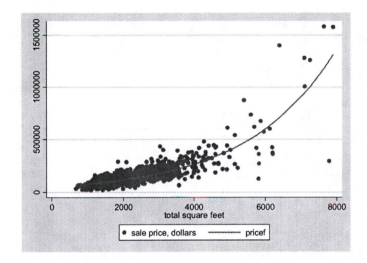

Because the fitted curve is not a linear relationship, the slope and elasticities must be calculated at specific points. It is worth noting here that margins will not do the calculations here, because Stata does not recognized the logarithmically transformed dependent variable. So we must calculate the slope and elasticity in the straightforward manner. Note that the slopes are calculated assuming specific house prices, rather than at predicted prices for a give house size.

```
di "slope at 100000 = " _b[sqft]*100000
di "slope at 500000 = " _b[sqft]*500000
di "elasticity at 2000 = " _b[sqft]*2000
di "elasticity at 4000 = " _b[sqft]*4000
```

```
. di "slope at 100000 = " _b[sqft]*100000
slope at 100000 = 41.126885

. di "slope at 500000 = " _b[sqft]*500000
slope at 500000 = 205.63442

. di "elasticity at 2000 = " _b[sqft]*2000
elasticity at 2000 = .82253769

. di "elasticity at 4000 = " _b[sqft]*4000
elasticity at 4000 = 1.6450754
```

We can also compute average marginal effects at each fitted house price in the sample.

```
generate me = _b[sqft]*pricef
summarize me
```

```
. generate me = _b[sqft]*pricef

. summarize me
```

Variable	Obs	Mean	Std. Dev.	Min	Max
me	1080	61.00072	42.91725	27.51118	539.2198

Similarly the average elasticity is

```
        generate elas = _b[sqft]*sqft
        summarize elas
```

. generate elas = _b[sqft]*sqft

. summarize elas

Variable	Obs	Mean	Std. Dev.	Min	Max
elas	1080	.9565858	.4145993	.27226	3.24779

Close this log file

```
        log close
```

2.7 REGRESSION USING INDICATOR VARIABLES

Indicator variables are usually binary 0-1 variables. These can be used in regression to indicate qualitative factors, such as location in a real estate model. Open a new log and the data *utown.dta*. The **describe** and **summarize** the data.

```
        log using chap02_indicator, replace text
        use utown, clear
        describe
        summarize
```

The description shows that the variable **utown** is 1 if a house is close to a university, and implicitly 0 otherwise.

variable name	storage type	display format	value label	variable label
price	double	%10.0g		house price, in $1000
sqft	double	%10.0g		square feet of living area, in 100s
age	byte	%8.0g		house age, in years
utown	byte	%8.0g		=1 if close to university
pool	byte	%8.0g		=1 if house has pool
fplace	byte	%8.0g		=1 if house has fireplace

The summary statistics show that of the 1000 observations, about 52% are in the university neighborhood.

```
. summarize
```

Variable	Obs	Mean	Std. Dev.	Min	Max
price	1000	247.6557	42.19273	134.316	345.197
sqft	1000	25.20965	2.91848	20.03	30
age	1000	9.392	9.426728	0	60
utown	1000	.519	.4998889	0	1
pool	1000	.204	.4031706	0	1
fplace	1000	.518	.4999259	0	1

Creating histograms for the house prices in a single graph with common axis values will allow us to compare them easily. First create and save two separate histograms using bins that are $12000 [**width(12)**] wide and beginning at $130000 [**start(130)**] which is below the sample minimum. Using $12000 wide bins was based trial and error. The **xlabel** statement indicates that ticks are to begin at 130 with 24 between ticks up to 350. The **histogram** commands use the logical operator, for example **if utown == 0**, to select the two subsets of data defined by the variable **utown**.

```
histogram price if utown==0, width(12) start(130) percent  ///
        xtitle(House prices ($1000) in Golden Oaks)        ///
        xlabel(130(24)350) legend(off)
graph save utown_0, replace

histogram price if utown==1, width(12) start(130) percent  ///
        xtitle(House prices ($1000) in University Town)     ///
        xlabl(130(24)350) legend(off)
graph save utown_1, replace
```

The saved graphs are combined into one using the **graph combine** command. To stack them one atop the other we choose them to go into a single column [**col(1)**]. Using **help graph combine** reveals that "…iscale(1) means that text and markers should appear the same size that they were originally." The graph names are put in quotes to identify them as *.gph files.

```
graph combine "utown_0" "utown_1", col(1) iscale(1)
graph save combined, replace
```

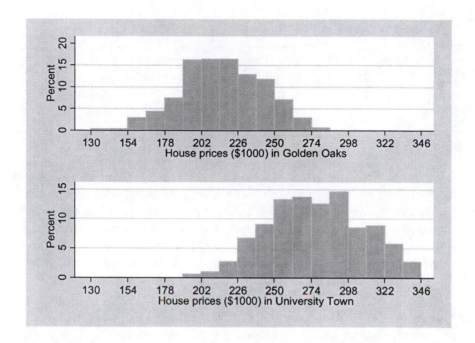

The graphs show that prices in the university neighborhood are centered at a higher value than the houses in the other neighborhood.

Rather than create two graphs and combine them, we can use a very important feature in Stata, the **by** command, which will repeat a Stata command over subsets of data. When using **by** it is important to use labels. In the two statements that follow we first create a label definition called **utownlabel**, specifying 0 for Golden Oaks and 1 for University town. In the second statement we apply the label to the variable *UTOWN*.

```
label define utownlabel 0 "Golden Oaks" 1 "University Town"
label value utown utownlabel
```

The histogram uses the by option, specifying that the data subsets are defined by *UTOWN*.

```
histogram price, by(utown, cols(1))            ///
        start(130) percent                     ///
        xtitle(House prices ($1000))           ///
        xlabel(130(24)350) legend(off)
graph save combined2, replace
```

The resulting graph has as a single scale for price, and a footnote indicating the use of the **by** option.

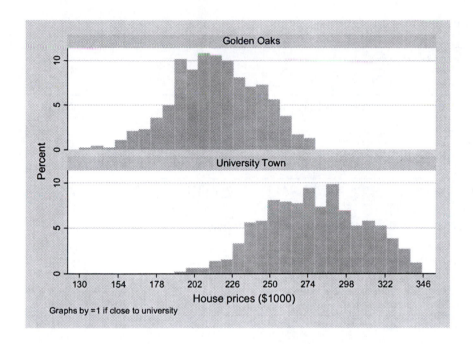

Graphs by =1 if close to university

This is revealed further by examining the summary statistics for prices in the separate neighborhoods.

```
summarize price if utown==0
summarize price if utown==1
```

. summarize price if utown==0

Variable	Obs	Mean	Std. Dev.	Min	Max
price	481	215.7325	26.73736	134.316	276.977

. summarize price if utown==1

Variable	Obs	Mean	Std. Dev.	Min	Max
price	519	277.2416	30.78208	191.57	345.197

Again it is easier and more efficient to use a **by** option. When using the **by** command the data must be sorted according to the values of the variable defining the subsets of observations. The sorting can be done within the command, as follows.

```
by utown, sort: summarize price
```

```
. by utown, sort: summarize price
```

```
-> utown = Golden Oaks
```

Variable	Obs	Mean	Std. Dev.	Min	Max
price	481	215.7325	26.73736	134.316	276.977

```
-> utown = University Town
```

Variable	Obs	Mean	Std. Dev.	Min	Max
price	519	277.2416	30.78208	191.57	345.197

A more terse command that is equivalent to the above is

bysort utown: summarize price

```
. bysort utown: summarize price
```

```
-> utown = Golden Oaks
```

Variable	Obs	Mean	Std. Dev.	Min	Max
price	481	215.7325	26.73736	134.316	276.977

```
-> utown = University Town
```

Variable	Obs	Mean	Std. Dev.	Min	Max
price	519	277.2416	30.78208	191.57	345.197

A regression with the indicator variable as explanatory variable has the same syntax as usual, though we could have used i.**utown**.

regress price utown

```
. regress price utown
```

Source	SS	df	MS			
Model	944476.744	1	944476.744			
Residual	833969.397	998	835.640678			
Total	1778446.14	999	1780.22637			

```
Number of obs =    1000
F(  1,   998) = 1130.24
Prob > F      =  0.0000
R-squared     =  0.5311
Adj R-squared =  0.5306
Root MSE      = 28.907
```

price	Coef.	Std. Err.	t	P>|t|	[95% Conf. Interval]	
utown	61.50911	1.829589	33.62	0.000	57.91882	65.09939
_cons	215.7325	1.318066	163.67	0.000	213.146	218.319

Note that the estimated constant term is the average price when **utown = 0**, and the coefficient of **utown** is the difference between the sample means.

You may have done a test of whether two population means are equal in a statistics course. Stata includes the command **ttest** for this approach.

```
      ttest price, by(utown)
```

. ttest price, by(utown)

Two-sample t test with equal variances

Group	Obs	Mean	Std. Err.	Std. Dev.	[95% Conf. Interval]	
Golden O	481	215.7325	1.219119	26.73736	213.337	218.128
Universi	519	277.2416	1.351183	30.78208	274.5871	279.8961
combined	1000	247.6557	1.334251	42.19273	245.0375	250.274
diff		-61.50911	1.829589		-65.09939	-57.91882

```
    diff = mean(Golden O) - mean(Universi)                           t = -33.6191
Ho: diff = 0                                          degrees of freedom =      998

      Ha: diff < 0                  Ha: diff != 0                  Ha: diff > 0
   Pr(T < t) = 0.0000        Pr(|T| > |t|) = 0.0000          Pr(T > t) = 1.0000
```

log close

APPENDIX 2A AVERAGE MARGINAL EFFECTS

The calculation of marginal effects in Stata has been much improved in recent versions, but understanding the calculation does require some effort. We consider a couple of cases.

2A.1 Elasticity in a linear relationship

For the linear relationship $y = \beta_1 + \beta_2 x + e$, elasticity is defined as

$$\varepsilon = \frac{dy/y}{dx/x} = \frac{dy}{dx} \cdot \frac{x}{y} = \beta_2 \frac{x}{y}$$

To obtain a representation point on the curve Stata takes a given $x = x_0$ and computes the corresponding fitted value $\hat{y}_0 = b_1 + b_2 x_0$. Then the estimated elasticity is

$$\hat{\varepsilon}_0 = b_2 \frac{x_0}{\hat{y}_0} = b_2 \frac{x_0}{b_1 + b_2 x_0}$$

This is a complicated nonlinear function of the least squares estimates which is easy enough to calculate, but we econometricians want a standard error of any estimate we obtain. Simple variance rules like $\text{var}(b_1 + b_2 x_0) = \text{var}(b_1) + x_0^2 \text{var}(b_2) + 2x_0 \text{cov}(b_1, b_2)$ do not apply. Instead the standard error of the estimated elasticity must use the Delta-method, which is explained in Chapter 5. For now we will simply note that there is a Stata command, **nlcom**, that will calculate nonlinear functions of estimates and compute a correct standard error.

To illustrate, open the food data and **summarize income**. After Stata estimation commands certain things are saved. After **summarize** we can see the saved items using the command **return list**.

```
log using chap02_ame, replace text
use food, clear
summarize income
return list
```

```
. return list

scalars:
                  r(N) =  40
              r(sum_w) =  40
               r(mean) =  19.60475
                r(Var) =  46.89198967948718
                 r(sd) =  6.847772607168492
                r(min) =  3.69
                r(max) =  33.4
                r(sum) =  784.1899999999999
```

The saved items have "returned" values, such as the mean, denoted by **r(mean)**. These can be saved as scalars and used in subsequent expressions.

```
scalar xbar = r(mean)
```

To evaluate the elasticity "at the means" we can use margins, as shown in the chapter. The regression output is suppressed since we have seen it before

```
quietly regress food_exp income
margins, eyex(*) atmeans
```

```
. margins, eyex(*) atmeans

Conditional marginal effects                    Number of obs   =        40
Model VCE     : OLS

Expression    : Linear prediction, predict()
ey/ex w.r.t.  : income
at            : income         =    19.60475 (mean)
```

	ey/ex	Delta-method Std. Err.	z	P>|z|	[95% Conf. Interval]	
income	.7058399	.1489436	4.74	0.000	.4139159	.9977639

The elasticity can be computed directly by using **nlcom** to compute the nonlinear function of the parameter values. The values match. The **Std. Err.** computed by **nlcom** uses the Delta-method.

```
nlcom _b[income]*xbar/(_b[_cons]+_b[income]*xbar)
```

```
. nlcom _b[income]*xbar/(_b[_cons]+_b[income]*xbar)

    _nl_1:  _b[income]*xbar/(_b[_cons]+_b[income]*xbar)
```

food_exp	Coef.	Std. Err.	t	P>|t|	[95% Conf. Interval]	
_nl_1	.7058399	.1489436	4.74	0.000	.4043194	1.00736

The test statistics and interval estimates will be discussed in Chapter 3. The interval estimates [95% Conf. Interval] differ because the **margins** command uses percentiles from the Standard normal distribution (note that the test statistic is called "*z*") while **nlcom** uses percentiles from the *t*-distribution (note that the test statistic is called "*t*").

```
log close
```

2A.2 Elasticity in a quadratic relationship

Using factor notation for quadratic models allows Stata to correctly compute slopes and elasticities. An elasticity for the fitted quadratic model function is $\hat{\varepsilon}_0 = 2b_2 x_0^2 / \left(b_1 + b_2 x_0^2 \right)$. Using the logic from the previous section calculate the elasticity for a 2000 square foot home.

```
log using chap02_quad_ame, replace text
use br, clear
quietly regress price c.sqft#c.sqft
margins, eyex(*) at(sqft=2000)
```

```
. margins, eyex(*) at(sqft=2000)

Conditional marginal effects                    Number of obs   =        1080
Model VCE    : OLS

Expression   : Linear prediction, predict()
ey/ex w.r.t. : sqft
at           : sqft            =        2000
```

	ey/ex	Delta-method Std. Err.	z	P>|z|	[95% Conf. Interval]	
sqft	1.050303	.0336868	31.18	0.000	.9842778	1.116328

The analogous **nlcom** command and output, which echos the command, are

```
nlcom 2*_b[c.sqft#c.sqft]*(2000^2)/
        (_b[_cons]+_b[c.sqft#c.sqft]*(2000^2))
```

```
. nlcom 2*_b[c.sqft#c.sqft]*(2000^2)/(_b[_cons]+_b[c.sqft#c.sqft]*(2000^2))

      _nl_1:  2*_b[c.sqft#c.sqft]*(2000^2)/(_b[_cons]+_b[c.sqft#c.sqft]*(2000^2
> ))
```

price	Coef.	Std. Err.	t	P>|t|	[95% Conf. Interval]	
_nl_1	1.050303	.0336868	31.18	0.000	.9842035	1.116402

```
      log close
```

2A.3 Slope in a log-linear model

Using the same data we will estimate a log-linear model $\ln(y) = \beta_1 + \beta_2 x + e$. The fitted line will be

$$\widehat{\ln(y)} = b_1 + b_2 x$$

To obtain the fitted value of y the most natural thing to do is compute the antilog as

$$\hat{y} = \exp\left(\widehat{\ln(y)}\right) = \exp(b_1 + b_2 x)$$

The slope of the fitted log-linear curve is $d\hat{y}/dx = b_2 \hat{y} = b_2 \times \exp(b_1 + b_2 x)$. In Section 2.6.2 we simply chose a value of y at which to evaluate the slope. In keeping with the spirit of the margins calculations, we can instead evaluate the slope at a given value of x, say **sqft** = 2000, using the **nlcom** command.

```
      log using chap02_1lin_me, replace text
      use br, clear
      gen lprice = log(price)
      quietly regress lprice sqft
      nlcom _b[sqft]*exp(_b[_cons]+_b[sqft]*2000)
      log close
```

```
. nlcom _b[sqft]*exp(_b[_cons]+_b[sqft]*2000)

      _nl_1:  _b[sqft]*exp(_b[_cons]+_b[sqft]*2000)
```

lprice	Coef.	Std. Err.	t	P>|t|	[95% Conf. Interval]	
_nl_1	47.6971	1.080834	44.13	0.000	45.57632	49.81788

APPENDIX 2B A SIMULATION EXPERIMENT

In Appendix 2G of *Principles of Econometrics*, 4th edition, a simulation experiment[3] is described. We generate artificial data and then try out our statistical techniques on the data we have created. In the experiment we use a sample size of 40 with

$$E\left(y_i \mid x_i = 10\right) = 100 + 10x_i = 100 + 10 \times 10 = 200, \quad i = 1, \ldots, 20$$

$$E\left(y_i \mid x_i = 20\right) = 100 + 10x_i = 100 + 10 \times 20 = 300, \quad i = 21, \ldots, 40$$

The random error is assumed to have a normal distribution $N\left(0, 2500 = 50^2\right)$. We generate such data, and save it as a representative Monte Carlo sample

```
clear all
log using chap02_app2G, replace text
```

First we create some **global** "macros" that contain constants for the experiment.

```
global numobs 40        // sample size
global beta1 100        // intercept parameter
global beta2 10         // slope parameter
global sigma 50         // error standard deviation
```

A Monte Carlo experiment uses random numbers. See Appendix B4 in *Principles of Econometrics*, 4th edition. Also enter the Stata command **help random numbers**. Random numbers are created iteratively, and require a starting point. If none is provided Stata picks one. Therefore, so that we can all get the same results, we set the system parameter **seed**.

```
set seed 1234567
```

Normal random numbers with mean zero and standard deviation $\sigma = 50$ are created using **rnormal(0,$sigma)**, with the **$** sign indicating that a global variable is to be used. The data generation process for x and y is

```
set obs $numobs
generate x = 10
replace x = 20 if _n > $numobs/2
generate y = $beta1 + $beta2*x + rnormal(0,$sigma)
```

We can estimate a regression with this data to see how close the estimates are to the true values.

```
regress y x
di "rmse " e(rmse)
estat vce
```

---

[3] For more on simulation using Stata, see A. Colin Cameron and Pravin K. Trivedi (2010) "Microeconometrics Using Stata, Revised Edition," Stata Press.

```
. regress y x
```

Source	SS	df	MS
Model	76256.9134	1	76256.9134
Residual	82705.2254	38	2176.4533
Total	158962.139	39	4075.95227

Number of obs =	40
F(1, 38) =	35.04
Prob > F =	0.0000
R-squared =	0.4797
Adj R-squared =	0.4660
Root MSE =	46.652

y	Coef.	Std. Err.	t	P>|t|	[95% Conf. Interval]	
x	8.73252	1.475281	5.92	0.000	5.745971	11.71907
_cons	127.2055	23.32624	5.45	0.000	79.98398	174.427

```
. di "rmse " e(rmse)
rmse 46.652474

. estat vce
```

Covariance matrix of coefficients of regress model

e(V)	x	_cons
x	2.1764533	
_cons	-32.646799	544.11332

The data we have generated can be saved for further study

```
save mc1, replace
```

The result of one regression does not reveal the repeated sampling properties of the least squares estimator. We must carry out this process many times. Using Stata's **simulate** command we can do this. The simulate command will repeat the same sequence of steps, written as a **program**, and collect the results from each repetition. A program is a self-contained series of commands. For example, the following program, called **chap02sim**, creates the artificial data, estimates the regression and returns the results. Because it returns results it is called an **rclass** program. Note that we reset the **seed** value, and close the program with **end**.

```
program chap02sim, rclass
      version 11.1
      drop _all
      set obs $numobs
      generate x = 10
      replace x = 20 if _n > $numobs/2
      generate ey = $beta1 + $beta2*x
      generate e = rnormal(0, $sigma)
      generate y = ey + e
      regress y x
      return scalar b2 =_b[x]                 /           / saves slope
      return scalar b1 =_b[_cons]                         // saves intercept
      return scalar sig2 = (e(rmse))^2                    // saves sigma^2
end
```

The simulate command names variables **b1r**, **b2r** and **sig2r** that contain the returned program values; **reps(1000)** indicates that we will execute this program 1000 times, **nodots** and **nolegend** suppress some output, the **seed(1234567)** is specified, and the program name is specified at the end by **:chap02sim**.

```
simulate b1r = r(b1) b2r=r(b2) sig2r=r(sig2) , ///
         reps(1000) nodots nolegend seed(1234567): chap02sim
```

It takes Stata only a few seconds to complete the simulation. We then summarize the results.

```
di " Simulation parameters"
di " beta1 = " $beta1
di " beta2 = " $beta2
di " N = " $numobs
di " sigma^2 = " $sigma^2
summarize, detail
```

To illustrate, the summary statistics for **b2r=r(b2)** show that the average value of the 1000 estimates is very near the true value of 10, and that the sample variance 2.31 of these estimates is close to the true $\text{var}(b_2) = 2.50$.

```
. di " Simulation parameters"
 Simulation parameters

. di " beta1 = " $beta1
 beta1 = 100

. di " beta2 = " $beta2
 beta2 = 10

. di " N = " $numobs
 N = 40

. di " sigma^2 = " $sigma^2
 sigma^2 = 2500
```

r(b2)

	Percentiles	Smallest		
1%	6.403119	5.009561		
5%	7.381377	5.379227		
10%	7.95141	5.506445	Obs	1000
25%	8.966896	5.726702	Sum of Wgt.	1000
50%	9.988169		Mean	9.997464
		Largest	Std. Dev.	1.558116
75%	11.06335	14.48513		
90%	11.98034	14.83626	Variance	2.427726
95%	12.56822	14.84318	Skewness	-.0553848
99%	13.52443	14.93775	Kurtosis	2.97382

A histogram for these estimates, with a normal distribution superimposed [See POE4, Appendix C.10 or use **help kdensity**]. The resulting figure shows the histogram of the estimates to closely follow the shape of the normal density, which is as it should be.

```
histogram b2r, percent normal
```

```
graph save b2r, replace
log close
```

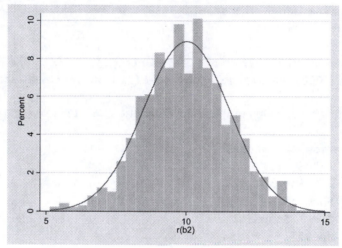

KEY TERMS

atmeans
by
bysort
cd
clear
data browser
data editor
delta method
di
display
dydx
elasticity
estat
estat vce
eyex
factor variable
gen
generate
global
graph
graph combine
graph save
graph save
histogram
label define
label value
lfit

list
list in
log
log close
log-linear model
lwidth
marginal effects
margins
mean
model, linear
model, log-linear
model, quadratic
msymbol
name
nlcom
postestimation
predict
program
quadratic model
random number
range/delta
reg
regress
replace
residuals
return list
return scalar

rnormal
save
saving
scalar
scatter
seed, random number
set more off
set obs
set seed
simulate
standard deviation
standard error
std. dev.
std. err.
summarize, detail
title
ttest
twoway
twoway lfit
twoway line
twoway scatter
use
variance
xb
xlabel
ylabel

CHAPTER 2 DO-FILE [CHAP02.DO]

At the end of each chapter we will provide a list of the commands used, as they would appear in a Do-file. Lines beginning with * are comments. It is a good idea to comment your computer code so that at some later point it will make sense.

```
* file chap02.do for Using Stata for Principles of Econometrics, 4e

cd c:\data\poe4stata

* Stata Do-file
* copyright C 2011 by Lee C. Adkins and R. Carter Hill
* used for "Using Stata for Principles of Econometrics, 4e"
* by Lee C. Adkins and R. Carter Hill (2011)
* John Wiley and Sons, Inc.

* setup
version 11.1
capture log close
set more off

* open food data
log using chap02_food, replace text
use food, clear

* examine data
describe

* browse
list
list in 1/5
list food_exp in 1/5
list food_exp if income < 10

* compute summary statistics
summarize

* summarize food expenditure with detail
summarize food_exp, detail

* simple plot data
twoway (scatter food_exp income)
graph save food1, replace          // open for editing with: graph use food1

* save graph using saving
twoway (scatter food_exp income), saving(food1, replace)

* store the graph in memory only
twoway (scatter food_exp income), name(food1, replace)

* enhanced plot /* with comments */
twoway (scatter food_exp income),     ///  /* basic plot control */
     ylabel(0(100)600)                ///  /* Y axis 0 to 600 with ticks each 100 */
          xlabel(0(5)35)              ///  /* X axis 0 to 35 with ticks each 5 */
               title(Food Expenditure Data)   /* graph title */
graph save food2, replace

* compute least squares regression
regress food_exp income

* calculate fitted values & residuals
```

```
predict yhat, xb
predict ehat, residuals

* compute elasticity at means
margins, eyex(income) atmeans

* compute average of elasticities at each data point
margins, eyex(income)
generate elas = _b[income]*income/yhat
summarize elas

* plot fitted values and data scatter
twoway (scatter food_exp income)      ///      /* basic plot control */
       (lfit food_exp income),        ///      /* add linear fit */
       ylabel(0(100)600)              ///      /* label Y axis */
       xlabel(0(5)35)                 ///      /* label X axis */
       title(Fitted Regression Line) /* graph title */
graph save food3, replace

* examine variances and covariances
estat vce

* add observation to data file
edit
set obs 41
replace income=20 in 41

* obtain prediction
predict yhat0
list income yhat0 in 41
log close

* to save changes to food data
* save chap02.dta, replace

* Chapter 2.8.2 Using a Quadratic Model

* new log file
log using chap02_quad, replace text

* open br data and examine
use br, clear
describe
summarize

* create new variable
generate sqft2=sqft^2

* regression
regress price sqft2
predict priceq, xb

* plot fitted line
twoway (scatter price sqft)           ///                /* basic plot */
       (line priceq sqft,             ///                /* 2nd plot: line is continuous */
           sort lwidth(medthick))                        /* sort & change line thickness */
graph save br_quad, replace

* slope and elasticity calculations
di "slope at 2000 = " 2*_b[sqft2]*2000
di "slope at 4000 = " 2*_b[sqft2]*4000
di "slope at 6000 = " 2*_b[sqft2]*6000
di "predicted price at 2000 = " _b[_cons]+_b[sqft2]*2000^2
```

```
di "predicted price at 4000 = " _b[_cons]+_b[sqft2]*4000^2
di "predicted price at 6000 = " _b[_cons]+_b[sqft2]*6000^2
di "elasticity at 2000 = " 2*_b[sqft2]*2000^2/(_b[_cons]+_b[sqft2]*2000^2)
di "elasticity at 4000 = " 2*_b[sqft2]*4000^2/(_b[_cons]+_b[sqft2]*4000^2)
di "elasticity at 6000 = " 2*_b[sqft2]*6000^2/(_b[_cons]+_b[sqft2]*6000^2)

* using factor variables
regress price c.sqft#c.sqft
predict price2
margins, dydx(*) at(sqft=(2000 4000 6000))
margins, eyex(*) at(sqft=(2000 4000 6000))
margins, eyex(*)
regress, coeflegend
generate elas2 = 2*_b[c.sqft#c.sqft]*(sqft^2)/price2
summarize elas2

log close

* Chapter 2.8.4 Using a Log-linear Model

log using chap02_llin, replace text
use br, clear

* distribution of prices
summarize price, detail
histogram price, percent
graph save price, replace

* distribution of log(price)
generate lprice = ln(price)
histogram lprice, percent
graph save lprice, replace

* log-linear regression
reg lprice sqft
predict lpricef, xb

* price prediction using anti-log
generate pricef = exp(lpricef)
twoway (scatter price sqft) ///
       (line pricef sqft, sort lwidth(medthick))
graph save br_loglin, replace

* slope and elasticity calculations
di "slope at 100000 = " _b[sqft]*100000
di "slope at 500000 = " _b[sqft]*500000
di "elasticity at 2000 = " _b[sqft]*2000
di "elasticity at 4000 = " _b[sqft]*4000

* average marginal effects
generate me = _b[sqft]*pricef
summarize me

generate elas = _b[sqft]*sqft
summarize elas

log close

* Section 2.9 Regression with Indicator Variables

* open new log
log using chap02_indicator, replace text
```

```
* open utown data and examine
use utown, clear
describe
summarize

* histograms of utown data by neighborhood
histogram price if utown==0, width(12) start(130) percent    ///
        xtitle(House prices ($1000) in Golden Oaks)          ///
                xlabel(130(24)350) legend(off)
graph save utown_0, replace

histogram price if utown==1, width(12) start(130) percent    ///
        xtitle(House prices ($1000) in University Town)      ///
                xlabel(130(24)350) legend(off)
graph save utown_1, replace

graph combine "utown_0" "utown_1", col(1) iscale(1)
graph save combined, replace

* using by option
label define utownlabel 0 "Golden Oaks" 1 "University Town"
label value utown utownlabel
histogram price, by(utown, cols(1))               ///
        start(130) percent                        ///
        xtitle(House prices ($1000))              ///
        xlabel(130(24)350) legend(off)
graph save combined2, replace

* summary stats
summarize price if utown==0
summarize price if utown==1

* summary stats using by
by utown, sort: summarize price

* summary stats using bysort
bysort utown: summarize price

* regression
regress price utown

* test of two means
ttest price, by(utown)
log close

* Appendix 2A on calculation of Average marginal effects

* food expenditure example
log using chap02_food_me, replace text
use food, clear
summarize income
return list
scalar xbar = r(mean)
quietly regress food_exp income
margins, eyex(*) atmeans
nlcom _b[income]*xbar/(_b[_cons]+_b[income]*xbar)
log close

* quadratic house price example
log using chap02_quad_me, replace text
use br, clear
quietly regress price c.sqft#c.sqft
margins, eyex(*) at(sqft=2000)
```

```
nlcom 2*_b[c.sqft#c.sqft]*(2000^2)/(_b[_cons]+_b[c.sqft#c.sqft]*(2000^2))
log close

* slope in log-linear model
log using chap02_llin_me, replace text
use br, clear
gen lprice = log(price)
quietly regress lprice sqft
nlcom _b[sqft]*exp(_b[_cons]+_b[sqft]*2000)
log close

* Appendix 2B

*clear memory and start new log
clear all
log using chap02_app2G, replace text

* define some global macros
global numobs 40                    // sample size
global beta1 100                    // intercept parameter
global beta2 10                     // slope parameter
global sigma 50                     // error standard deviation

* random number seed
set seed 1234567

* create artificial data using y = beta1+beta2*x+e
set obs $numobs
generate x = 10
replace x = 20 if _n > $numobs/2
generate y = $beta1 + $beta2*x + rnormal(0,$sigma)

* regression with artifical data
regress y x
di "rmse " e(rmse)
estat vce

* data file mc1.data created using following command
save mc1, replace

* program to generate data and estimate regression
program chap02sim, rclass
    version 11.1
    drop _all
    set obs $numobs
    generate x = 10
        replace x = 20 if _n > $numobs/2
    generate ey = $beta1 + $beta2*x
        generate e = rnormal(0, $sigma)
        generate y = ey + e
        regress y x
    return scalar b2 =_b[x]                // saves slope
        return scalar b1 =_b[_cons]        // saves intercept
        return scalar sig2 = (e(rmse))^2   // saves sigma^2
end

* simulate command
simulate b1r = r(b1) b2r=r(b2) sig2r=r(sig2) , ///
        reps(1000) nodots nolegend seed(1234567): chap02sim

* display experiment parameters
di " Simulation parameters"
di " beta1 = " $beta1
```

```
di " beta2 = " $beta2
di " N = " $numobs
di " sigma^2 = " $sigma^2

* summarize experiment results
summarize, detail

* histogram sampling distribution of LS estimates
histogram b2r, percent normal
graph save b2r, replace
log close
```

CHAPTER **3**

Interval Estimation and Hypothesis Testing

CHAPTER OUTLINE

3.1 INTERVAL ESTIMATES

Interval estimates are also known as confidence intervals. When Stata carries out a regression analysis part of its standard output is a 95% interval estimate for each of the coefficients. Begin a new Stata session and change to your working directory. Open a log file and estimate the food expenditure model, as demonstrated in Section 2.4 of the previous chapter.

```
log using chap03, replace text
use food, clear
reg food_exp income
```

The regression output includes [`95% Conf. Interval`] which are the lower and upper bounds of the interval estimates for the corresponding coefficients.

food_exp	Coef.	Std. Err.	t	P>|t|	[95% Conf. Interval]	
income	10.20964	2.093264	4.88	0.000	5.972052	14.44723
_cons	83.416	43.41016	1.92	0.062	-4.463279	171.2953

The interval estimates are computed as **Coef. ± t-critical*Std. Err.** The values of the coefficients are given, as are the standard errors. The remaining ingredient is the *t*-critical value. This can be found in Table 2 of *Principles of Econometrics*, or using Stata, as we now show.

3.1.1 Critical values from the t-distribution

We can use Stata to compute critical values of many probability distributions, which is very handy in many contexts. Critical values are created as scalars in Stata and carry the general prefix **inv**, indicating that they are "inverse" functions. To recall the command for a particular scalar value enter

```
help scalar
```

Click on **define** in the Viewer box if you wish to use a dialog box. Using the **Expression builder** (see Section 1.12.8 in this manual) box locate **invttail()**, double click, and fill in the degrees of freedom $N - 2 = 38$ and the amount of the probability in the upper tail of the *t*-distribution required for a 95% interval estimate: 2.5% of the probability in the upper tail defines the 97.5 percentile of the *t*-distribution. Click OK.

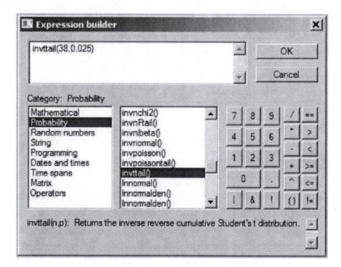

In the scalar define box we now have

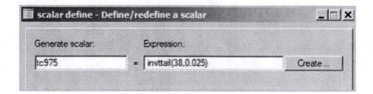

Click on **Submit** at the bottom of this box. In the **Results** window (and in the **Review** window) the Stata command is shown to be

```
scalar define tc975 = invttail(38,0.025)
```

The optional define is not required, so the command can be simplified to

```
scalar tc975 = invttail(38,0.025)
```

To view the value of this scalar we must display it

```
di "t critical value 97.5 percentile = "  tc975
```

which produces

```
. di "t critical value 97.5 percentile = "  tc975
t critical value 97.5 percentile = 2.0243942
```

Other examples of t-critical values are:

```
di "t(30) 95th percentile = " invttail(30,0.05)
```

```
. di "t(30) 95th percentile = " invttail(30,0.05)
t(30) 95th percentile = 1.6972609
```

```
di "t(20) 5th percentile  = " invttail(20,0.95)
```

```
. di "t(20) 5th percentile  = " invttail(20,0.95)
t(20) 5th percentile  = -1.7247182
```

```
di "t(30) 2.5th percentile  = " invttail(30,0.975)
```

```
. di "t(30) 2.5th percentile  = " invttail(30,0.975)
t(30) 2.5th percentile  = -2.0422725
```

3.1.2 Creating an interval estimate

Using the regression results and the t-critical value we have just calculated a 95% interval estimate can be computed using a calculator. You can also use results saved in Stata's memory to obtain an interval estimate. As noted previously, when a regression is estimated certain results are saved and are accessible for further use. The estimated coefficients and standard errors are saved as **_b[varname]** and **_se[varname]**, respectively. After the food expenditure equation estimation the estimated slope coefficient is known as **_b[income]** and the estimated intercept is **_b[_cons]**. Their standard errors are **_se[income]** and **_se[_cons]**. For more information on these, enter **help _variables** in the **Command** window. The 95% interval estimates are $b_k \pm t_c \mathrm{se}(b_k)$. The upper bound and lower bound of the interval estimates for the slope are

```
scalar ub2 = _b[income] + tc975*_se[income]
scalar lb2 = _b[income] - tc975*_se[income]
```

These can be displayed using

```
        di "beta 2 95% interval estimate is " lb2 " , " ub2
```

producing

```
. di "beta 2 95% interval estimate is " lb2 " , " ub2
beta 2 95% interval estimate is 5.9720525 , 14.447233
```

3.2 HYPOTHESIS TESTS

The t-statistics used for hypothesis tests about the parameters can be computed using a calculator from the regression output and a t-critical value from a statistical table. However in this section we will compute the test statistic values, critical values and p-values using Stata. As an example we will continue with the food expenditure regression model.

3.2.1 Right-tail test of significance

To test the null hypothesis $H_0 : \beta_2 = 0$ against the alternative hypothesis $H_1 : \beta_2 > 0$. We can construct and display the t-statistic value and critical value using

```
        scalar tstat0 = _b[income]/_se[income]
        di "t statistic for Ho: beta2=0 = " tstat0
        di "t(38) 95th percentile = " invttail(38,0.05)
```

```
. scalar tstat0 = _b[income]/_se[income]

. di "t statistic for Ho: beta2=0 = " tstat0
t statistic for Ho: beta2=0 = 4.8773806

. di "t(38) 95th percentile = " invttail(38,0.05)
t(38) 95th percentile = 1.6859545
```

Note that the critical value comes from the right tail of the t-distribution and we use the `invttail` command to find the critical value. The t-statistic values for the null hypothesis that the coefficients are zero are automatically produced by Stata when a regression model is estimated in the column labeled "t".

food_exp	Coef.	Std. Err.	t	P>|t|	[95% Conf. Interval]	
income	10.20964	2.093264	4.88	0.000	5.972052	14.44723
_cons	83.416	43.41016	1.92	0.062	-4.463279	171.2953

t-statistic for testing hypotheses that
the parameters are zero

Sometimes we will want to test more complicated hypotheses about coefficients, and these can be implemented using the post-estimation command `lincom`. From the Stata pull-down menu select **Statistics > Postestimation > Linear combinations of estimates.**

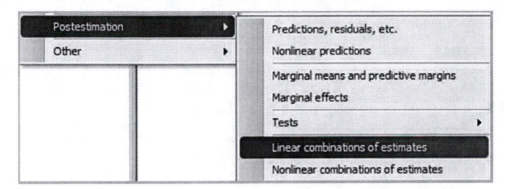

Type the expression that you want to estimate in the dialog box. It can be any linear expression, called a linear combination, involving the two coefficients b_1 and b_2, such as $5b_2 - 3b_1 = 1$. Of course Stata does not make reference to b_2 and b_1 directly but rather through `_b[income]` and `_b[_cons]`. In the case of the command `lincom` we can simply refer to the variable names, such as `5*income - 3*_cons-1`. The command will compute the value of the expression and its standard error, and produce a *t*-statistic and an interval estimate.

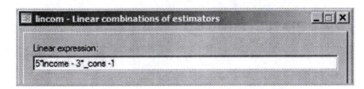

```
. lincom 5*income - 3*_cons -1

 ( 1)   5*income - 3*_cons = 1
```

food_exp	Coef.	Std. Err.	t	P>|t|	[95% Conf. Interval]	
(1)	-200.1998	140.1664	-1.43	0.161	-483.9518	83.55225

As another example, simply enter

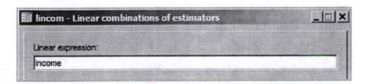

Click **OK**. In the **Result** window we find that the implied Stata command and the same result presented in the regression output.

```
. lincom income

 ( 1)   income = 0
```

food_exp	Coef.	Std. Err.	t	P>|t|	[95% Conf. Interval]
(1)	10.20964	2.093264	4.88	0.000	5.972052 14.44723

3.2.2 Right-tail test of an economic hypothesis

To test $H_0 : \beta_2 \leq 5.5$ against the alternative hypothesis $H_1 : \beta_2 > 5.5$ we can again do the basic calculations of the test statistic and 0.01 right-tail critical value

```
scalar tstat1 = (_b[income]-5.5)/_se[income]
```

Note that we have used parentheses to control the order of operation.

```
di "t-statistic for Ho: beta2 = 5.5 is " tstat1
di "t(38) 99th percentile = " invttail(38,0.01)
```

This produces the results

```
. di "t-statistic for Ho: beta2 = 5.5 is " tstat1
t-statistic for Ho: beta2 = 5.5 is 2.2499045

. di "t(38) 99th percentile = " invttail(38,0.01)
t(38) 99th percentile = 2.4285676
```

Using **lincom** enter

```
lincom income-5.5
```

The result shows that the value of $b_2 - 5.5$ is computed [**Coef.**] and the t-statistic [**t**]calculated, along with a 95% interval estimate of this value.

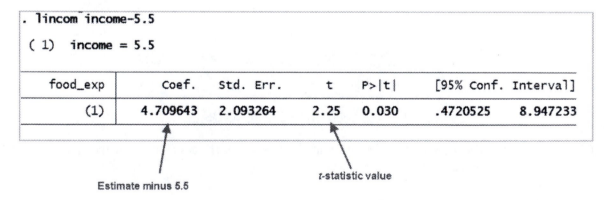

3.2.3 Left-tail test of an economic hypothesis

To illustrate a left tail test, let the null hypothesis be $H_0 : \beta_2 \geq 15$ with alternative hypothesis $H_1 : \beta_2 < 15$. The command sequence is

```
scalar tstat2 = (_b[income]-15)/_se[income]
di "t-statistic for Ho: beta2 = 15 is " tstat2
```

We again use **invttail** to compute the 0.05 critical value. Since the rejection region is in the left tail, this time we require 95% of the probability in the right tail.

```
di "t(38) 5th percentile = " invttail(38,0.95)
```

Producing

```
. di "t-statistic for Ho: beta2 = 15 is " tstat2
t-statistic for Ho: beta2 = 15 is -2.2884634

. di "t(38) 5th percentile = " invttail(38,0.95)
t(38) 5th percentile = -1.6859545
```

To use **lincom** enter

```
lincom income-15
```

```
. lincom income-15

 ( 1)   income = 15
```

food_exp	Coef.	Std. Err.	t	P>|t|	[95% Conf. Interval]
(1)	-4.790357	2.093264	-2.29	0.028	-9.027948 -.5527666

3.2.4 Two-tail test of an economic hypothesis

A two-tail test has the same mechanics as a one tail-test except for the calculation of the critical values. For a test at the 0.05 level of significance the critical values must be the 2.5 and 97.5 percentiles of the *t*-distribution. To test $H_0 : \beta_2 = 7.5$ against alternative hypothesis $H_1 : \beta_2 \neq 7.5$ use the following commands

```
scalar tstat3 = (_b[income]-7.5)/_se[income]
di "t-statistic for Ho: beta2 = 7.5 is " tstat3
di "t(38) 97.5th percentile = " invttail(38,0.025)
di "t(38) 2.5th percentile = " invttail(38,0.975)
```

The results are

```
. di "t-statistic for Ho: beta2 = 7.5 is " tstat3
t-statistic for Ho: beta2 = 7.5 is 1.2944586

. di "t(38) 97.5th percentile = " invttail(38,0.025)
t(38) 97.5th percentile = 2.0243942

. di "t(38) 2.5th percentile = " invttail(38,0.975)
t(38) 2.5th percentile = -2.0243942
```

Because the Stata command **invttail** works with the upper tail of the t-distribution, calculating the critical values for the lower tail can be confusing. At all times let your brain continue to function. The t-distribution is symmetric and the percentiles 90, 95, 97.5 and 99 are positive values, and percentiles 1, 2.5, 5 and 10 are negative.

To use **lincom** enter

```
lincom income-7.5
```

```
. lincom income-7.5

 ( 1)   income = 7.5
```

food_exp	Coef.	Std. Err.	t	P>|t|	[95% Conf. Interval]	
(1)	2.709643	2.093264	1.29	0.203	-1.527948	6.947233

3.3 p-VALUES

The ability to compute p-values easily is a powerful feature of Stata. Recall that

- if $H_1 : \beta_k > c$, p = probability to the right of t
- if $H_1 : \beta_k < c$, p = probability to the left of t
- if $H_1 : \beta_k \neq c$, p = sum of probabilities to the right of $|t|$ and to the left of $-|t|$

> **The p-value rule for testing hypotheses**: Reject the null hypothesis when the p-value is less than, or equal to, the level of significance α. That is, if $p \leq \alpha$ then reject H_0. If $p > \alpha$ then do not reject H_0.

Critical values for the t-distribution can be looked up in tables, or computed using the function **invttail**. However p-values must be calculated using the computer. Stata uses the function **ttail**. The syntax of the command and its definition are obtained by entering **help ttail** in the Command window.

```
ttail(n,t) "returns the reverse cumulative (upper-tail) Student's t
distribution; it returns the probability T > t."
```

where **n** is the number of degrees of freedom and **t** is the value of the t-statistic. Once again the **ttail** function returns an upper-tail probability value.

3.3.1 *p*-value of a right-tail test

In Section 3.2.2 above we tested $H_0 : \beta_2 \le 5.5$ against the alternative hypothesis $H_1 : \beta_2 > 5.5$. We calculated the *t*-statistic value using

```
scalar tstat1 = (_b[income]-5.5)/_se[income]
```

To compute and display the *p*-value use

```
di "p value right tail test ho:beta2 = 5.5 is " ttail(38,tstat1)
```

With result

```
. di "p-value for right-tail test ho:beta2 = 5.5 is " ttail(38,tstat1)
p-value for right-tail test ho:beta2 = 5.5 is .01516329
```

Recall that if you forget the syntax, you can find the scalar define dialog box by entering the command **help scalar**. In the resulting Viewer click **define**. Click **Create** and then in the **Expression builder** dialog box select **Probability functions** and scroll down to something that looks right. The definitions of the functions show up at the bottom of the box which is a great help. Then double-click the name of the function, and in the Expression builder box enter the degrees of freedom **n** and the *t*-statistic value **t** and click **OK**.

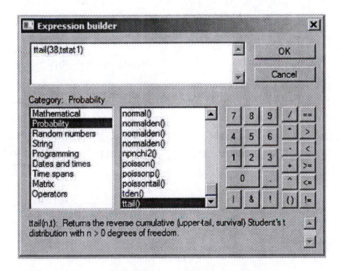

In the resulting box enter a name for the expression and click OK.

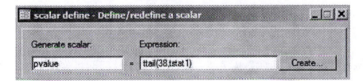

3.3.2 *p*-value of a left-tail test

To illustrate a left-tail test *p*-value use the example in Section 3.2.3 above. Let the null hypothesis be $H_0 : \beta_2 \geq 15$ with alternative hypothesis $H_1 : \beta_2 < 15$. We computed

```
scalar tstat2 = (_b[income]-15)/_se[income]
```

The *p*-value for a left tail test, is in the left, or lower, tail of the *t*-distribution. Enter the command

```
di "p value left tail test ho:beta2 = 15 is " 1-ttail(38,tstat2)
```

We have to use **1 − ttail(38,tstat2)** because we want to compute the area to the left of **tstat2** while **ttail(38,tstat2)** calculates the area to the right of **tstat2**. The result is

```
. di "p-value for left-tail test ho:beta2 = 15 is " 1-ttail(38,tstat2)
p-value for left-tail test ho:beta2 = 15 is .01388071
```

3.3.3 *p*-value for a a two-tail test

In Section 3.2.4 above we tested $H_0 : \beta_2 = 7.5$ against alternative hypothesis $H_1 : \beta_2 \neq 7.5$. The t-statistic was calculated using

```
scalar tstat3 = (_b[income]-7.5)/_se[income]
```

The *p*-value for a two-tail test is the sum of the areas to right of $|t|$ and the left of $-|t|$. Use

```
scalar phalf = ttail(38,abs(tstat3))
```

This command computes ½ the *p*-value, the portion in the upper tail of the *t*-distribution to the right of the absolute value (the function **abs**) of the *t*-statistic. Multiply this value by 2 and display

```
scalar p3 = 2*phalf
di "p value for two tail test ho:beta2 = 7.5 is " p3
```

The result is

```
. di "p-value for two-tail test ho:beta2 = 7.5 is " p3
p-value for two-tail test ho:beta2 = 7.5 is .20331828
```

Of course separate calculations are not required. The calculation is

```
di "p value for ho:beta2 = 7.5 is " 2*ttail(38,abs(tstat3))
```

```
. di "p-value for ho:beta2 = 7.5 is " 2*ttail(38,abs(tstat3))
p-value for ho:beta2 = 7.5 is .20331828
```

3.3.4 *p*-values in Stata output

When a regression is estimated, and when the post-estimation command `lincom` is used, a *p*-value is reported. For example, the regression output is:

food_exp	Coef.	Std. Err.	t	P>|t|	[95% Conf. Interval]
income	10.20964	2.093264	4.88	0.000	5.972052	14.44723
_cons	83.416	43.41016	1.92	0.062	-4.463279	171.2953

p-value for a two-tail test that the
coefficient is zero

The column labeled $P > |t|$ is the two-tail *p*-value for the null hypothesis that the coefficient is zero. The symbol itself is taken to the mean the probability **P** greater than the absolute value of the *t*-statistic value $|t|$. This translates into two statements really, the probability greater than the positive value of *t* and the value less than the negative value of *t*. If a one-tail test of significance is desired, the *p*-value is ½ the *p*-value of the two-tail test as long as the estimate satisfies the alternative hypothesis, since it occurs in only one-tail of the distribution.

When `lincom` is used the same elements are present

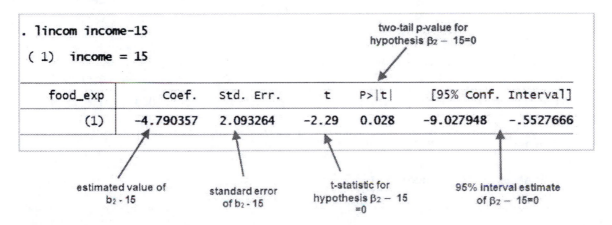

```
. lincom income-15

( 1)   income = 15
```

two-tail p-value for
hypothesis β₂ – 15=0

food_exp	Coef.	Std. Err.	t	P>|t|	[95% Conf. Interval]
(1)	-4.790357	2.093264	-2.29	0.028	-9.027948	-.5527666

estimated value of
b₂ - 15

standard error
of b₂ - 15

t-statistic for
hypothesis β₂ – 15
=0

95% interval estimate
of β₂ – 15=0

3.3.5 Testing and estimating linear combinations of parameters

A more general linear hypothesis involves both parameters and may be stated as

$$H_0 : c_1\beta_1 + c_2\beta_2 = c_0$$

where c_0, c_1 and c_2 are specified constants. The test of this hypothesis uses the *t*-statistic

$$t = \frac{(c_1 b_1 + c_2 b_2) - c_0}{se(c_1 b_1 + c_2 b_2)}$$

The rejection regions for the one- and two-tail alternatives (i)-(iii) are the same as those described in Section 3.3, and conclusions are interpreted the same way as well. The standard error in the denominator of the t-statistic is the square root of

$$\text{var}\left[c_1 b_1 + c_2 b_2\right] = c_1^2 \widehat{\text{var}(b_1)} + c_2^2 \widehat{\text{var}(b_2)} + 2c_1 c_2 \widehat{\text{cov}(b_1, b_2)}$$

To compute this value manually use the estimated covariance matrix of the least squares estimates, obtained post-estimation using **estat vce**.

. estat vce

Covariance matrix of coefficients of regress model

e(V)	income	_cons
income	4.3817522	
_cons	-85.903157	1884.4423

Using **lincom** we can estimate a linear combination such as $c_1 \beta_1 + c_2 \beta_2$, and test the more general form of linear hypothesis. For example, if $c_1 = 1$, and $c_2 = 20$, then

    lincom _cons + income*20

. lincom _cons + income*20

 (1)   20*income + _cons = 0

food_exp	Coef.	Std. Err.	t	P>|t|	[95% Conf. Interval]
(1)	287.6089	14.17804	20.29	0.000	258.9069	316.3108

To test the null hypothesis that this linear combination equals 250, use

    lincom _cons + income*20 - 250

. lincom _cons + income*20 - 250

 (1)   20*income + _cons = 250

food_exp	Coef.	Std. Err.	t	P>|t|	[95% Conf. Interval]
(1)	37.60886	14.17804	2.65	0.012	8.906915	66.31081

APPENDIX 3A GRAPHICAL TOOLS

To illustrate graphically one-tail and two-tail rejection regions and p-values we first generate the t-distribution values, and then "shade" the appropriate tail areas. For example, the two-tail rejection region for a *t*-distribution with 38 degrees of freedom is *t*-values greater than 2.024 or less than −2.024.

First, clear memory. The density function values $f(t)$ are obtained using the Stata function `tden(n,t)` where n is the degrees of freedom and t is a value. The **graph twoway function** (`help twoway function`) will generate a line plot for a specified function. The command syntax is

```
twoway function [[y]=] f(x) [if] [in] [, options]
```

Within the twoway function we can obtain as shaded area using the **recast** option, which specifies a new plot type—an **area** instead of a line plot.

```
twoway (function y=tden(38,x), range(-5 -2.024) ///
                color(ltblue) recast(area)) ///
       (function y=tden(38,x), range(2.024 5)   ///
                color(ltblue) recast(area)) ///
       (function y=tden(38,x), range(-5 5)),    ///
       legend(off) plotregion(margin(zero))      ///
       ytitle("f(t)") xtitle("t")     ///
       text(0 -2.024 "-2.024", place(s))         ///
       text(0 2.024 "2.024", place(s))           ///
       title("Two-tail rejection region" "t(38), alpha=0.05")
```

The option **plotregion** (`help region options`) eliminates graph margins. The **text** option allows placement of text into a graph at given coordinates (help graph text) in relative position given by **place**, here south (**s**).

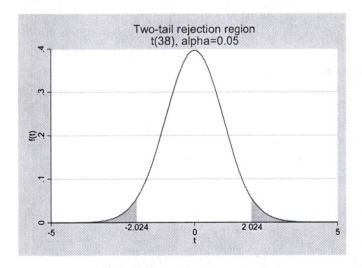

Similarly, for a right-tail rejection region use

```
twoway (function y=tden(38,x), range(1.686 5) ///
                color(ltblue) recast(area)) ///
       (function y=tden(38,x), range(-5 5)), ///
       legend(off) plotregion(margin(zero)) ///
       ytitle("f(t)") xtitle("t") ///
```

```
text(0 1.686 "1.686", place(s)) ///
title("Right-tail rejection region" "t(38), alpha=0.05")
```

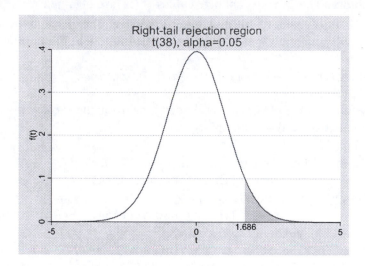

APPENDIX 3B MONTE CARLO SIMULATION

Using the same experimental design as in the Chapter 2 simulation, we now explore the repeated sampling properties of hypothesis tests and interval estimators. A test at the 5% level of significance should result in rejecting a true null hypothesis 5% of the time. A 95% interval estimator should cover, or contain, the true parameter value 95% of the time. We can verify these properties using a Monte Carlo simulation.

```
clear all
log using app3c, replace text
global numobs 40
global beta1 100
global beta2 10
global sigma 50

set seed 1234567

set obs $numobs
gen x = 10
replace x = 20 if _n > $numobs/2
gen y = $beta1 + $beta2*x + rnormal(0,$sigma)

quietly regress y x
```

Test the true null hypothesis that the slope parameter is 10 by constructing the *t*-statistic from saved results.

```
scalar tstat = (_b[x]-$beta2)/_se[x]
```

```
di "ttest of ho b2 = 10 " tstat
```

The program that will be repeated in the simulation process now returns both the *t*-statistic value and also the upper and lower bounds of a 95% interval estimate.

```
program chap03sim, rclass
        version 11.1
        drop _all
        set obs $numobs
        gen x = 10
        replace x = 20 if _n > $numobs/2
        gen ey = $beta1 + $beta2*x
        gen e = rnormal(0, $sigma)
        gen y = ey + e
        regress y x
        scalar tc975 = invttail($numobs-2,0.025)
        * calculating 95% interval estimate
        return scalar b2 = _b[x]
        return scalar se2 = _se[x]
        return scalar ub = _b[x] + tc975*_se[x]
        return scalar lb = _b[x] - tc975*_se[x]

        * calculating t-statistic
        return scalar tstat = (_b[x] - $beta2)/_se[x]
end
```

In a Monte Carlo experiment concerning rejection probabilities or interval estimation success, the number of Monte Carlo experimental samples is quite important. Here we choose to use 10,000 samples for the following reason. A 95% confidence interval estimator should contain the true parameter value 95% of the time in repeated samples. The M repeated samples in a Monte Carlo experiment are independent experimental trials in which we expect a "success," an interval containing the true parameter value, with probability of success $P = 0.95$. The number of successes follows a **binomial** distribution. The **proportion** of successes $\hat{P}$ in M trials is a random variable with expectation P and variance $P(1-P)/M$. If the number of Monte Carlo samples M is large, the probability is 0.95 that the proportion of Monte Carlo successes is $P \pm 1.96\sqrt{P(1-P)/M}$. Similarly, for a test with probability of rejection $\alpha = 0.05$, the probability is 0.95 that the percent of rejections will fall within $\alpha \pm 1.96\sqrt{\alpha(1-\alpha)/M}$.

These bounds for 10,000 and 1000 samples are given by

```
di "lower bound with 10000 replications " 0.05 -
        1.96*sqrt(0.05*0.95/10000)
di "upper bound with 10000 replications " 0.05 +
        1.96*sqrt(0.05*0.95/10000)
di "lower bound with 1000 replications " 0.05 -
        1.96*sqrt(0.05*0.95/1000)
di "upper bound with 1000 replications " 0.05 +
        1.96*sqrt(0.05*0.95/1000)
```

```
. di "lower bound with 10000 replications " 0.05 - 1.96*sqrt(0.05*0.95/10000)
lower bound with 10000 replications .04572828

. di "upper bound with 10000 replications " 0.05 + 1.96*sqrt(0.05*0.95/10000)
upper bound with 10000 replications .05427172

. di "lower bound with 1000 replications " 0.05 - 1.96*sqrt(0.05*0.95/1000)
lower bound with 1000 replications .03649163

. di "upper bound with 1000 replications " 0.05 + 1.96*sqrt(0.05*0.95/1000)
upper bound with 1000 replications .06350837
```

With 10,000 Monte Carlo samples the probability is 0.95 that the observed percent of rejections will fall within the interval 0.0457 and 0.0543. With only 1000 samples the interval is 0.0365 to 0.0635.

The **simulate** command generates new variables **b2r**, **se2r** as in Chapter 2. In addition we add **ubr**, **lbr** and **tstatr** for the upper and lower interval estimate bounds and the t-statistic for the true null hypothesis that $\beta_2 = 10$.

```
simulate b2r = r(b2) se2r = r(se2) ubr = r(ub) lbr=r(lb) ///
        tstatr=r(tstat) , reps(10000) nodots nolegend ///
        seed(1234567): chap03sim
```

To count the number of successful interval estimations we count how many times the interval estimate contains the true parameter value 10.

```
gen cover = (lbr < $beta2) & ($beta2<ubr)
```

The hypothesis test should reject the true null hypothesis 5% of the time. Here we demonstrate using a right-tail alternative. We can examine and summarize these values.

```
gen reject = (tstatr > invttail($nobs,0.05))
list b2r se2r tstatr reject lbr ubr cover in 101/120, table
```

	b2r	se2r	tstatr	reject	lbr	ubr	cover
101.	8.318099	1.502351	-1.119513	0	5.276749	11.35945	1
102.	10.95639	1.548826	.6174955	0	7.82096	14.09183	1
103.	13.36436	1.70848	1.96921	1	9.905719	16.82299	1
104.	9.740551	1.876146	-.1382883	0	5.942492	13.53861	1
105.	12.34023	1.627542	1.437893	0	9.045445	15.63502	1

```
summarize cover reject
```

```
. summarize cover reject
```

Variable	Obs	Mean	Std. Dev.	Min	Max
cover	10000	.9518	.2141993	0	1
reject	10000	.0473	.2122904	0	1

```
log close
```

We see that the interval estimates contain the true parameter value 95.18 % of the time, and the hypothesis test rejects 4.73 % of the time, which is within the bounds of sampling error we calculated.

KEY TERMS

_b[_cons]	interval estimate	**scalar**
_b[varname]	**invttail**	set obs
_se[_cons]	left-tail test	simulate
_se[varname]	**lincom**	**tden**
confidence interval	linear combinations of estimates	**ttail**
coverage probability	postestimation	two-tail test
define	p-value	**twoway**
estat vce	**recast(area)**	
expression builder	right-tail test	

CHAPTER 3 DO-FILE [CHAP03.DO]

```
* file chap03.do for Using Stata for Principles of Econometrics, 4e

cd c:\data\poe4stata

* Stata Do-file
* copyright C 2011 by Lee C. Adkins and R. Carter Hill
* used for "Using Stata for Principles of Econometrics, 4e"
* by Lee C. Adkins and R. Carter Hill (2011)
* John Wiley and Sons, Inc.

* setup
version 11.1
capture log close
set more off

* open log
log using chap03, replace text

* open food
use food, clear

* estimate regression
reg food_exp income

* compute t-critical value
scalar tc975 = invttail(38,.025)
di "t critical value 97.5 percentile = "  tc975

* calculating 95% interval estimate
scalar ub2 = _b[income] + tc975*_se[income]
scalar lb2 = _b[income] - tc975*_se[income]
di "beta 2 95% interval estimate is " lb2 " , " ub2

* examples of computing t-critical values
di "t(30) 95th percentile = " invttail(30,0.05)
```

```
di "t(20) 95th percentile = " invttail(20,0.05)
di "t(20) 5th percentile  = " invttail(20,0.95)
di "t(30) 97.5th percentile = " invttail(30,0.025)
di "t(30) 2.5th percentile  = " invttail(30,0.975)

* right-tail test ho:beta2 = 0
scalar tstat0 = _b[income]/_se[income]
di "t statistic for Ho: beta2=0 = " tstat0
di "t(38) 95th percentile = " invttail(38,0.05)

* using lincom
lincom income

* right-tail test ho:beta2 = 5.5
scalar tstat1 = (_b[income]-5.5)/_se[income]
di "t-statistic for Ho: beta2 = 5.5 is " tstat1
di "t(38) 99th percentile = " invttail(38,0.01)

* using lincom for calculation
lincom income-5.5

* left-tail test ho:beta2 = 15
scalar tstat2 = (_b[income]-15)/_se[income]
di "t-statistic for Ho: beta2 = 15 is " tstat2
di "t(38) 5th percentile = " invttail(38,0.95)
lincom income-15

* two-tail test ho:beta2 = 7.5
scalar tstat3 = (_b[income]-7.5)/_se[income]
di "t-statistic for Ho: beta2 = 7.5 is " tstat3
di "t(38) 97.5th percentile = " invttail(38,0.025)
di "t(38) 2.5th percentile = " invttail(38,0.975)
lincom income-7.5

* two-tail test ho:beta1 = 0
lincom _cons

* p-value for right-tail test
scalar tstat1 = (_b[income]-5.5)/_se[income]
di "p-value for right-tail test ho:beta2 = 5.5 is " ttail(38,tstat1)

* p-value for left-tail test
scalar tstat2 = (_b[income]-15)/_se[income]
di "p-value for left-tail test ho:beta2 = 15 is " 1-ttail(38,tstat2)

* p-value for a two-tail test
scalar tstat3 = (_b[income]-7.5)/_se[income]
scalar phalf = ttail(38,abs(tstat3))
scalar p3 = 2*phalf
di "p-value for two-tail test ho:beta2 = 7.5 is " p3
di "p-value for ho:beta2 = 7.5 is " 2*ttail(38,abs(tstat3))

* linear combinations of parameters
* estimating a linear combination
estat vce
lincom _cons + income*20

* testing a linear combination
lincom _cons + income*20 - 250

log close

* Appendix 3A Graphing rejection regions
```

```
clear

* specify critcal values as globals
global t025=invttail(38,0.975)
global t975=invttail(38,0.025)

* draw the shaded areas, then draw the overall curve
twoway (function y=tden(38,x), range(-5 $t025)        ///
                   color(ltblue) recast(area))        ///
        (function y=tden(38,x), range($t975 5)        ///
                        color(ltblue) recast(area))   ///
        (function y=tden(38,x), range(-5 5)),         ///
        legend(off) plotregion(margin(zero))          ///
                    ytitle("f(t)") xtitle("t")        ///
           text(0 -2.024 "-2.024", place(s))          ///
           text(0 2.024 "2.024", place(s))            ///
           title("Two-tail rejection region" "t(38), alpha=0.05")

* one-tail rejection region
twoway (function y=tden(38,x), range(1.686 5)         ///
                   color(ltblue) recast(area))        ///
        (function y=tden(38,x), range(-5 5)),         ///
        legend(off) plotregion(margin(zero))          ///
                     ytitle("f(t)") xtitle("t")       ///
           text(0 1.686 "1.686", place(s))            ///
           title("Right-tail rejection region" "t(38), alpha=0.05")

* Appendix 3C

* set up
clear all

* open log
log using app3c, replace text

* define global variables
global numobs 40
global beta1 100
global beta2 10
global sigma 50

* set random number seed
set seed 1234567

* generate sample of data
set obs $numobs
gen x = 10
replace x = 20 if _n > $numobs/2
gen y = $beta1 + $beta2*x + rnormal(0,$sigma)

* regression
quietly regress y x

* test h0: beta2 = 10
scalar tstat = (_b[x]-$beta2)/_se[x]
di "ttest of ho b2 = 10 " tstat

* program to generate data and to examine
*        performance of interval estimator and
*        hypothesis test
program chap03sim, rclass
    version 11.1
```

```
    drop _all
    set obs $numobs
    gen x = 10
        replace x = 20 if _n > $numobs/2
    gen ey = $beta1 + $beta2*x
        gen e = rnormal(0, $sigma)
        gen y = ey + e
        regress y x
        scalar tc975 = invttail($numobs-2,0.025)

        * calculating 95% interval estimate
        return scalar b2 = _b[x]
        return scalar se2 = _se[x]
        return scalar ub = _b[x] + tc975*_se[x]
    return scalar lb = _b[x] - tc975*_se[x]

        * calculating t-statistic
    return scalar tstat = (_b[x] - $beta2)/_se[x]
end

* display 95% interval for test size with different number
*       of monte carlo samples

di "lower bound with 10000 replications is " 0.05 - 1.96*sqrt(0.05*0.95/10000)
di "upper bound with 10000 replications is " 0.05 + 1.96*sqrt(0.05*0.95/10000)
di "lower bound with 1000 replications is " 0.05 - 1.96*sqrt(0.05*0.95/1000)
di "upper bound with 1000 replications is " 0.05 + 1.96*sqrt(0.05*0.95/1000)

* simulate command
simulate b2r = r(b2) se2r = r(se2) ubr = r(ub) lbr=r(lb)      ///
        tstatr=r(tstat) , reps(10000) nodots nolegend          ///
        seed(1234567): chap03sim

* display experiment parameters
di " Simulation parameters"
di " beta1 = " $beta1
di " beta2 = " $beta2
di " N = " $numobs
di " sigma^2 = " $sigma^2

* count intervals covering true beta2 = 10
gen cover = (lbr < $beta2) & ($beta2 < ubr)

* count rejections of true h0: beta2 = 10
gen reject = (tstatr > invttail($numobs-2,0.05))

* examine some values
list b2r se2r tstatr reject lbr ubr cover in 101/120, table

* summarize coverage and rejection
summarize cover reject

log close
```

CHAPTER **4**

Prediction, Goodness-of-Fit and Modeling Issues

CHAPTER OUTLINE

4.1 LEAST SQUARES PREDICTION

We have touched on prediction in Chapter 2. Now we include the standard error of the forecast as a measurement of the precision of the prediction, or forecast, and a prediction interval. Change to your working directory, begin a log file for the chapter, and open the food expenditure data.

```
version 11.1
capture log close
set more off

log using chap04_food, replace text
```

123

```
use food, clear
```

Let us obtain the predicted value of household food expenditure for a household with income of $2000 per week.

4.1.1 Editing the data

We will edit the data, entering income = 20 in observation 41. The steps are explained in Section 2.5 of this manual.

```
edit
set obs 41
replace income = 20 in 41
```

4.1.2 Estimate the regression and obtain postestimation results

Now estimate the food expenditure regression, suppressing the output since we have seen it.

```
quietly regress food_exp income
```

Using the post-estimation **predict** command, obtain the fitted values (**yhat**), the least squares residuals (**ehat**). These we have seen before in Section 2.4.1.

```
predict yhat
predict ehat, residuals
```

A new option that we will add is **stdf** which will compute the standard error of the forecast. Let the new observation for which we wish a forecast be defined by

$$y_0 = \beta_1 + \beta_2 x_0 + e_0$$

where e_0 is a random error. We assume that $E(y_0) = \beta_1 + \beta_2 x_0$ and $E(e_0) = 0$. We also assume that e_0 has the same variance as the regression errors, $\text{var}(e_0) = \sigma^2$, and e_0 is uncorrelated with the random errors that are part of the sample data, so that $\text{cov}(e_0, e_i) = 0$ $i = 1, 2, \ldots, N$. The least squares predictor of y_0 comes from the fitted regression line

$$\hat{y}_0 = b_1 + b_2 x_0$$

That is, the predicted value $\hat{y}_0$ is given by the point on the least squares fitted line where $x = x_0$. To evaluate how well this predictor performs we define the forecast error, which is analogous to the least squares residual,

$$f = y_0 - \hat{y}_0 = (\beta_1 + \beta_2 x_0 + e_0) - (b_1 + b_2 x_0)$$

The estimated variance of this forecast error is

$$\widehat{\text{var}(f)} = \hat{\sigma}^2 \left[1 + \frac{1}{N} + \frac{(x_0 - \bar{x})^2}{\sum(x_i - \bar{x})^2} \right]$$

The square root of this estimated variance is the standard error of the forecast

$$\text{se}(f) = \sqrt{\widehat{\text{var}(f)}}$$

This is the quantity calculated using the command

```
predict sef, stdf
```

Browsing the data, we find

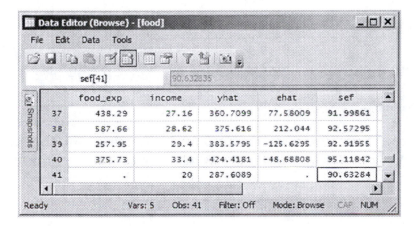

The predicted value **yhat** and the standard error of the forecast **sef** have values. The dependent variable **food_exp** and the least squares residual **ehat** have missing values for observation 41.

4.1.3 Creating the prediction interval

Defining the critical value t_c to be the $100(1-\alpha/2)$-percentile from the t-distribution, we can obtain a $100(1-\alpha)\%$ prediction interval as

$$\hat{y}_0 \pm t_c \text{se}(f)$$

We create the t-critical value using **invttail(n,p)**.

```
scalar tc = invttail(38,.025)
di "t critical value 97.5 percentile = "  tc
```

```
. di "t critical value 97.5 percentile = "  tc
t critical value 97.5 percentile = 2.0243942
```

The value created is 2.0243942. Now, we use this value, along with **yhat** and **sef** to generate new variables that are the lower and upper bound of the prediction interval. The generate command can be shortened to **gen**.

```
gen lb = yhat - tc*sef
gen ub = yhat + tc*sef
```

We can view the values of these variables in observation 41 using **list**. We will list the variables income, lb, yhat and ub in observation 41.

```
list income lb yhat ub in 41
```

```
. list income lb yhat ub in 41
```

	income	lb	yhat	ub
41.	20	104.1323	287.6089	471.0854

Because we will use observation 41 no longer, let us drop it from the data file

```
drop in 41
```

The command **drop** has several functions. It can be used to delete particular observations from the data file, as we have done above, and it can be used to drop variables. Enter **help drop** to see the syntax.

4.2 MEASURING GOODNESS-OF-FIT

The goodness of fit measure R^2 is motivated by the sum of squares decomposition

$$\sum(y_i - \overline{y})^2 = \sum(\hat{y}_i - \overline{y})^2 + \sum\hat{e}_i^2$$

These "sums of squares" are:

- $\sum(y_i - \overline{y})^2$ = total sum of squares = SST: a measure of total variation in y about the sample mean.
- $\sum(\hat{y}_i - \overline{y})^2$ = sum of squares due to the regression = SSR: that part of total variation in y, about the sample mean, that is explained by, or due to, the regression. Also known as the "explained sum of squares."
- $\sum\hat{e}_i^2$ = sum of squares due to error = SSE: that part of total variation in y about its mean that is not explained by the regression. Also known as the unexplained sum of squares, the sum of squared residuals, or the sum of squared errors.

Using these abbreviations the sum of squares decomposition becomes

$$SST = SSR + SSE$$

Then the goodness of fit measure R^2 is

$$R^2 = \frac{SSR}{SST} = 1 - \frac{SSE}{SST}$$

When a regression is estimated, all of these quantities appear in the **Analysis of Variance Table** just above the regression coefficients. In the table **source (Model, Residual, Total)** refers to the same breakdown as the sums of squares decomposition. The column labeled **SS** refers to sums of squares. The column **df** is for degrees of freedom. The Model "degrees of freedom" is 1 because the model contains one explanatory variable. The Residual degrees of freedom is $N - 2$, which is the number of observations minus the number of model parameters, including the intercept. The column **MS** is for **Mean Square**. This column contains the ratio of the **SS** column divided by the **df** column. Thus the **Residual MS** is our estimated error variance.

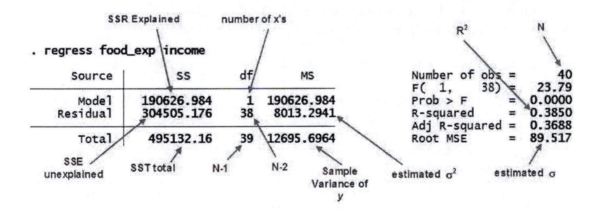

4.2.1 Correlations and R^2

It is also noted in *POE* that in the simple regression model R^2 is the squared simple correlation between the y and x variables. Also, in general, R^2 is the squared correlation between y and its fitted value, $\hat{y}$. From the Stata pull-down menu choose

> **Statistics > Summaries, tables, and tests > Summary and descriptive statistics > Pairwise correlations**

In the **Pairwise correlations** dialog box fill in the names of the variables using the pull-down list. Click **OK**. The Stata command is

```
pwcorr food_exp income yhat
```

The Results window shows the correlations.

```
. pwcorr food_exp income yhat
```

	food_exp	income	yhat
food_exp	1.0000		
income	0.6205	1.0000	
yhat	0.6205	1.0000	1.0000

Then squaring the correlation between **food_exp** and **income** gives $r_{xy}^2 = .62^2 = .385 = R^2$.

4.3 THE EFFECTS OF SCALING AND TRANSFORMING THE DATA

Data in a regression model can be scaled without any real loss of meaning. The scaling of variables should result in reasonable units of measurement, with no extremely large numbers or extremely small numbers. Scaled and transformed variables are easily created using the **generate** command.

For the food expenditure data the variable income is measured in units of $100, so **income** = 20 means that the household has a monthly income of $2000. To change the income variable to dollars and estimate the resulting regression, enter into the Command window

```
gen inc_dollar = income*100
```

Estimate the food expenditure regression with this new income variable. Note that we have shortened the **regress** command to **reg**.

```
reg food_exp income
```

food_exp	Coef.	Std. Err.	t	P>|t|	[95% Conf. Interval]	
income	10.20964	2.093264	4.88	0.000	5.972052	14.44723
_cons	83.416	43.41016	1.92	0.062	-4.463279	171.2953

```
reg food_exp inc_dollar
```

food_exp	Coef.	Std. Err.	t	P>|t|	[95% Conf. Interval]	
inc_dollar	.1020964	.0209326	4.88	0.000	.0597205	.1444723
_cons	83.416	43.41016	1.92	0.062	-4.463279	171.2953

In the regression results note the change in the size of the coefficient of income and its standard error, and thus the confidence interval.

```
log close
```

4.3.1 The linear-log functional form

The linear regression model can represent relationships between variables that are nonlinear using simple transformations of variables. For the food expenditure example the linear-log model is

$$FOOD\_EXP = \beta_1 + \beta_2 \ln(INCOME) + e$$

To estimate this model we will create a new variable that is the log of income, and then apply least squares regression.

```
log using chap04_linlog, replace text
use food, clear
gen lincome = ln(income)
reg food_exp lincome
```

```
. reg food_exp lincome
```

Source	SS	df	MS		
Model	176519.828	1	176519.828		
Residual	318612.333	38	8384.53507		
Total	495132.16	39	12695.6964		

Number of obs =	40
F(1, 38) =	21.05
Prob > F =	0.0000
R-squared =	0.3565
Adj R-squared =	0.3396
Root MSE =	91.567

food_exp	Coef.	Std. Err.	t	P>|t|	[95% Conf. Interval]	
lincome	132.1659	28.80461	4.59	0.000	73.85397	190.4777
_cons	-97.18645	84.23744	-1.15	0.256	-267.7162	73.34333

Use the post-estimation command **predict** to obtain fitted values and residuals from the log-linear model regression that we use in Section 4.3.2.

```
predict lyhat
predict lehat, resid
```

For the linear-log model the slope is $\beta_2/INCOME$. How can we use Stata to compute this? First we must select a value for income. The sample mean is a good choice when no other specific value is of interest. Calculate the summary statistics for income.

```
summarize income
```

Stata saves a number of calculated results. You can see these by entering the command

```
return list
```

```
. summarize income
```

Variable	Obs	Mean	Std. Dev.	Min	Max
income	40	19.60475	6.847773	3.69	33.4

```
. return list

scalars:
              r(N) =  40
          r(sum_w) =  40
           r(mean) =  19.60475
            r(Var) =  46.89198967948718
             r(sd) =  6.847772607168492
            r(min) =  3.69
            r(max) =  33.4
            r(sum) =  784.1899999999999
```

We see that a number of scalars are returned, including the mean. Save it as a scalar.

> **scalar xbar = r(mean)**

Now use **lincom** to calculate the slope formula

> **lincom lincome/xbar**

```
. lincom lincome/xbar

 ( 1)   .051008*lincome = 0
```

food_exp	Coef.	Std. Err.	t	P>|t|	[95% Conf. Interval]	
(1)	6.741522	1.469267	4.59	0.000	3.767147	9.715897

At the mean level of income an increase of \$100 weekly household income is estimated to increase food expenditure by \$6.74. The slope of the estimated linear-log function can be computed at other values as well.

> **lincom lincome/10**
> **lincom lincome/20**
> **lincom lincome/30**

```
. lincom lincome/10

 ( 1)   .1*lincome = 0
```

food_exp	Coef.	Std. Err.	t	P>|t|	[95% Conf. Interval]	
(1)	13.21659	2.880461	4.59	0.000	7.385397	19.04777

```
. lincom lincome/20
```

```
( 1)   .05*lincome = 0
```

food_exp	Coef.	Std. Err.	t	P>|t|	[95% Conf. Interval]	
(1)	6.608293	1.440231	4.59	0.000	3.692698	9.523887

```
. lincom lincome/30
```

```
( 1)   .0333333*lincome = 0
```

food_exp	Coef.	Std. Err.	t	P>|t|	[95% Conf. Interval]	
(1)	4.405528	.9601537	4.59	0.000	2.461799	6.349258

4.3.2 Plotting the fitted linear-log model

Using the fitted values and residuals computed in the previous section, we overlay two plots using the **twoway** graphs, the first being a scatter diagram and the second a line plot. The figures will overlay nicely because the data are sorted on *INCOME*.

```
twoway (scatter food_exp income, sort) ///
       (line lyhat income, sort lwidth(medthick)), ///
       xtitle(Income) ytitle(Food Expenditure) ylabel(0(100)600) ///
       title(Linear Log Model)
graph save linlog, replace
```

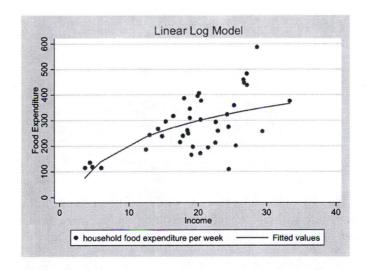

This relationship is not a straight-line. Near the center of the data the fitted line is not very steep. The slope, 6.74, is smaller from the simple linear regression. To see this more clearly let us overlay three plots. Estimate the linear relationship, using the **quietly** option to suppress output, and obtain predicted values and residuals.

```
quietly reg food_exp income
```

```
predict yhat
predict ehat, resid
```

Add the fitted line with another new option, **lpattern(dash)**.

```
twoway (scatter food_exp income, sort) ///
        (line lyhat income, sort lwidth(medthick)) ///
        (line yhat income, sort lpattern(dash) lwidth(medthick)), ///
        xtitle(Income) ytitle(Food Expenditure) ylabel(0(100)600) ///
        title(Linear Log Model)
graph save linlog2, replace
```

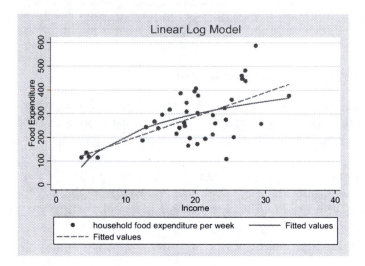

4.3.3 Editing graphs

Using the **Graph Editor** aspects of the graph can be altered interactively.

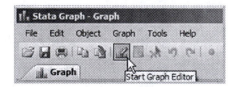

On the right-side is a list of graph elements with "+" denoting elements that open to more detailed list. Clicking elements shows highlighted fields with which they are associated. To change the label "Fitted Values" for the linear-log model select **label[2]**.

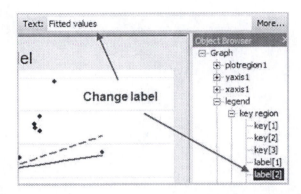

Selecting **label[2]** reveals along the top editing options for color of label, size and text. Simply type in the text you desire and press **Enter**.

Select **plotregion**, and **plot3**. As **plot3** is selected the linear-fitted line shows crosses to indicate it has been selected. To change the line pattern from dash to another, select from the pull-down menu.

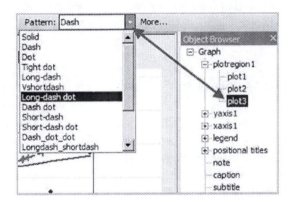

Select **Apply** to have the changes made. Then **Save** your changes and **Stop** the plot editor

save   stop plot
editor

Our graph is now

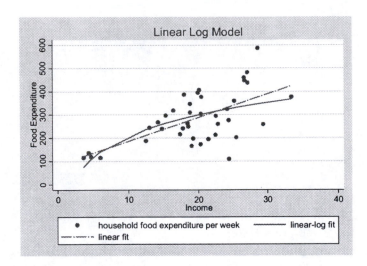

Virtually every aspect of your graph can be controlled in the Graph Editor. The edits you have made can be recorded using the **graph recorder** and re-played on other graphs. Enter **help graph recorder** for more on this feature.

4.4 ANALYZING THE RESIDUALS

One of the key elements in determining if the selected functional form is adequate is analyzing the model residuals. In Section 4.1.2 above we computed the least squares residuals for the linear model. They should be in the dataset in memory. If not, re-estimate the linear food expenditure model and calculate the residuals, which we call **ehat**. If you have an extended session you must remember to save the variables you will need for later use. This requires a little planning ahead, or simply to recalculate.

As a first step, construct a histogram of the least squares residuals. We always hope that the result is reasonably bell-shaped, reminding us of a normal distribution.

```
histogram ehat, percent title(Linear Model Residuals)
graph save olsehat_hist, replace
```

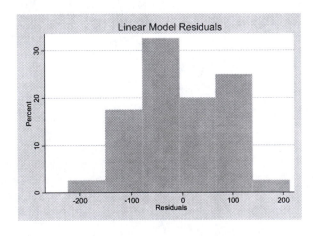

Secondly, we can summarize the residuals in detail

summarize ehat, detail

. summarize ehat, detail

```
                          Residuals

         Percentiles      Smallest
 1%      -223.0255       -223.0255
 5%      -133.9407       -142.2519
10%      -115.6628       -125.6295      Obs                40
25%      -52.94326       -119.058       Sum of Wgt.        40

50%      -6.324473                      Mean          4.77e-08
                          Largest       Std. Dev.      88.3619
75%       68.72928        117.4039
90%      112.8848         120.0951      Variance      7807.825
95%      121.0697         122.0443      Skewness     -.0973187
99%      212.044          212.044       Kurtosis      2.989034
```

4.4.1 The Jarque-Bera test

The detailed analysis includes the **Skewness** and **Kurtosis** coefficients that are ingredients of the **Jarque-Bera test for normality**. Define the sample moments for a variable Y as

$$\tilde{\mu}_2 = \sum \left(Y_i - \bar{Y}\right)^2 \Big/ N = \tilde{\sigma}^2$$

$$\tilde{\mu}_3 = \sum \left(Y_i - \bar{Y}\right)^3 \Big/ N$$

$$\tilde{\mu}_4 = \sum \left(Y_i - \bar{Y}\right)^4 \Big/ N$$

Note that in these calculations we divide by N. Using these sample estimates of the central moments we can obtain estimates of the **skewness coefficient (S)** and **kurtosis coefficient (K)** as

$$\widehat{skewness} = S = \frac{\tilde{\mu}_3}{\tilde{\sigma}^3}$$

$$\widehat{kurtosis} = K = \frac{\tilde{\mu}_4}{\tilde{\sigma}^4}$$

As noted earlier when summarize is used, a number of items are saved. Enter

return list

Some of the returned items are

```
. return list

scalars:
                    r(N)  =  40
                r(sum_w)  =  40
                 r(mean)  =  4.76837158203e-08
                  r(Var)  =  7807.824984910715
                   r(sd)  =  88.36189781184373
             r(skewness)  =  -.0973187365457582
             r(kurtosis)  =  2.989033831200444
```

Using the returned values of N, **skewness** and **kurtosis** we can use Stata (or a calculator) to compute the Jarque-Bera statistic

$$JB = \frac{N}{6}\left(S^2 + \frac{(K-3)^2}{4} \right)$$

The commands to create the statistic and display it are:

```
scalar jb = (r(N)/6)*( (r(skewness)^2) + ((r(kurtosis)-3)^2)/4 )
di "Jarque-Bera Statistic = " jb
```

The result is

```
. di "Jarque-Bera Statistic = " jb
Jarque-Bera Statistic = .06334
```

4.4.2 Chi-square distribution critical values

The critical value for this distribution comes from a chi-square distribution with 2 degrees of freedom. Critical values are computed using **inv** type functions. To locate the correct function type **help scalar**, then click define as we have done several times before. Another fast alternative is to enter

```
db scalar
```

The "db" stands for "dialog box." The Stata command is

```
scalar chic = invchi2tail(2,.05)
di "Chi-square(2) 95th percentile = " chic
```

The resulting value is

```
. scalar chic = invchi2tail(2,.05)

. di "Chi-square(2) 95th percentile = " chic
Chi-square(2) 95th percentile = 5.9914645
```

The value of the Jarque-Bera statistic 0.06334 is far below the test critical value 5.99, so we fail to reject the hypothesis that the regression errors are normally distributed.

4.4.3 Chi-square distribution *p*-values

Instead of obtaining the chi-square critical value, we could perform the test by obtaining the *p*-value for the Jarque-Bera test statistic value. To locate the correct function type **db scalar**. The Stata command is

```
scalar pvalue = chi2tail(2,jb)
di "Jarque-Bera p-value = " pvalue
```

The resulting *p*-value is

```
. scalar pvalue = chi2tail(2,jb)

. di "Jarque-Bera p-value = " pvalue
Jarque-Bera p-value = .96882624
```

Because the *p*-value 0.9688 is greater than the probability of Type I error, $\alpha = 0.05$, we fail to reject normality, as previously note.

```
log close
```

4.5 POLYNOMIAL MODELS

As an example of a polynomial model we consider wheat yield over time in some shires of Western Australia. The data file is *wa_wheat.dta*. Open this file and clear Stata's memory. Obtain descriptions of the variables and summary statistics.

```
log using chap04_wheat, replace text
use wa_wheat, clear
describe
summarize
```

Variable	Obs	Mean	Std. Dev.	Min	Max
northampton	48	1.168654	.4250324	.3024	2.3161
chapman	48	1.072385	.3328069	.4167	2.0244
mullewa	48	.9840625	.3352854	.3965	1.7992
greenough	48	1.15306	.3653873	.4369	2.2353
time	48	24.5	14	1	48

The summary statistics are show that there are $T = 48$ observations on 4 different shires. So that our terminology will parallel *Principles of Econometrics, 4e,* create a new variable called *YIELD* for the production in Greenough shire.

```
gen yield = greenough
label variable yield "wheat yield greenough shire"
```

Create a scatter plot showing the relationship between *YIELD* and *TIME*.

```
twoway (scatter yield time, sort) , ///
        xtitle(Time) ylabel(0(.5)2.5) ytitle(Yield) ///
        title(Wheat Yield)
graph save wawheat, replace
```

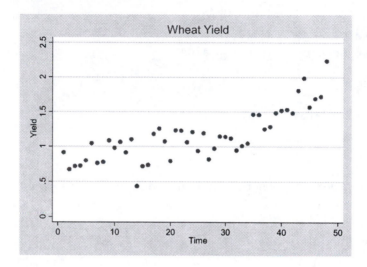

4.5.1 Estimating and checking the linear relationship

The rate of increase in wheat yield increases, especially towards the end of the period. A linear relationship between *YIELD* and *TIME* will not be suitable because it will not capture the changing slope. To demonstrate, estimate the linear regression between *YIELD* and *TIME* and compute both the fitted value and least squares residual.

```
reg yield time
predict yhat
predict ehat, residuals
```

The estimation results are

```
. reg yield time
```

Source	SS	df	MS
Model	4.07486005	1	4.07486005
Residual	2.20000947	46	.047826293
Total	6.27486952	47	.133507862

Number of obs =	48
F(1, 46) =	85.20
Prob > F =	0.0000
R-squared =	0.6494
Adj R-squared =	0.6418
Root MSE =	.21869

yield	Coef.	Std. Err.	t	P>|t|	[95% Conf. Interval]
time	.0210319	.0022785	9.23	0.000	.0164455 .0256184
_cons	.6377778	.0641305	9.94	0.000	.5086898 .7668658

The fitted least squares line and the data scatter are obtained with

```
twoway (scatter yield time, sort) ///
       (line yhat time, sort lwidth(medthick)) , ///
       xtitle(Time) ytitle(Yield) ylabel(0(.5)2.5) ///
       title(Wheat Yield Fitted Linear Model)
graph save wheat_fit, replace
```

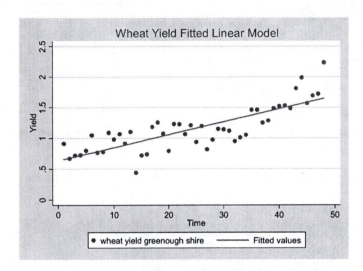

> **Remark**: Variables with long labels may result in text below graph being illegible. Edit the Graph using the Graph editor and enter a new label.

With practice you will be able to spot the cluster of positive residuals at the beginning and end of the time period, and the cluster of negative residuals in the middle. To see this more easily we can plot the residuals against time. A simple plot can be obtained using

```
twoway (scatter ehat time, sort) , ///
       xtitle(Time) ytitle(Residuals) yline(0) ///
       title(Wheat Linear Model Residuals)
graph save wheat_ehat, replace
```

The option `yline(0)` creates the horizontal reference line at zero.

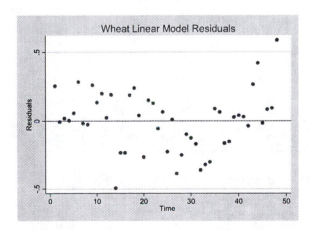

Alternatively, Stata has some built in post-estimation residual diagnostic plots. On the Stata menu bar select the following:

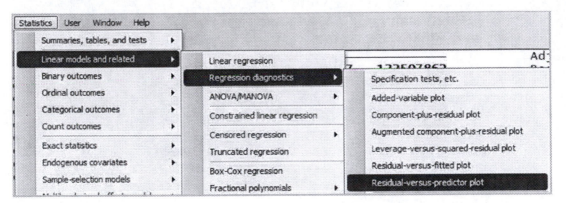

Using **help regress postestimation** we find links to dialogs and descriptions of available plots.

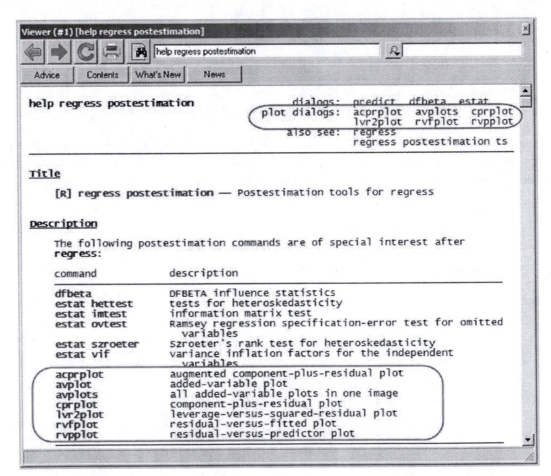

One example is, using the **recast(bar)** option to obtain a bar graph rather than a scatter diagram,

```
rvpplot time, recast(bar) yline(0)
```

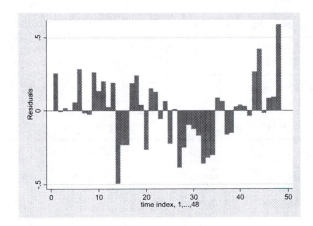

This plot clearly shows the cluster of positive residuals at the two ends of the time period and the large cluster of negative residuals in the center. Patterns in the residuals are not desirable and may indicate a need to find a better functional form.

4.5.2 Estimating and checking a cubic equation

Generate the variable **time0 = time/100**. This scaling will prevent the cubic variable being very large, and make the estimated coefficient comparably larger. Estimate the cubic equation using factor variable notation, and obtain fitted values and residuals, naming them **yhat3** and **ehat3** because **yhat** and **ehat** exist from the previous regression.

```
generate time0=time/100
list yield time0 in 1/5
```

	yield	time0
1.	.9141	.01
2.	.6721	.02
3.	.7191	.03
4.	.7258	.04
5.	.7998	.05

```
summarize time0
```

Variable	Obs	Mean	Std. Dev.	Min	Max
time0	48	.245	.14	.01	.48

```
reg yield c.time0#c.time0#c.time0
```

```
. reg yield c.time0#c.time0#c.time0
```

Source	SS	df	MS
Model	4.71126527	1	4.71126527
Residual	1.56360425	46	.033991397
Total	6.27486952	47	.133507862

```
Number of obs =      48
F( 1,    46) =  138.60
Prob > F      =  0.0000
R-squared     =  0.7508
Adj R-squared =  0.7454
Root MSE      =  .18437
```

yield	Coef.	Std. Err.	t	P>|t|	[95% Conf. Interval]	
c.time0# c.time0# c.time0	9.681516	.8223546	11.77	0.000	8.026202	11.33683
_cons	.8741166	.0356307	24.53	0.000	.8023958	.9458374

Compute the least squares residuals and predicted values.

```
predict yhat3
predict ehat3, residuals
```

The advantage of the factor notation is that **margins** will correctly compute the slope for us.

```
margins, dydx(*) at(time=(0.15 0.30 0.45))
```

		dy/dx	Delta-method Std. Err.	z	P>|z|	[95% Conf. Interval]	
time0	_at						
	1	.6535024	.0555089	11.77	0.000	.5447069	.7622979
	2	2.61401	.2220357	11.77	0.000	2.178827	3.049192
	3	5.881521	.4995804	11.77	0.000	4.902361	6.86068

A plot of the data and fitted line shows that the curvature of the cubic function fits the data better at the beginning and end of the period.

```
twoway (scatter yield time, sort) ///
       (line yhat3 time, sort lwidth(medthick)) , ///
       xtitle(Time) ytitle(Yield) ylabel(0(.5)2.5) ///
       title(Wheat Yield Fitted Cubic Model)
graph save wheat_cubic_fit, replace
```

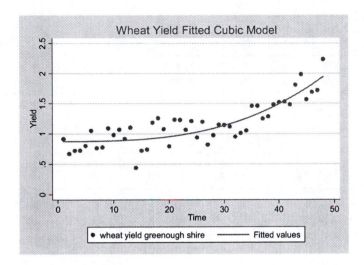

Using the residual diagnostic plot we find that the runs of positive and negative residuals are reduced.

```
twoway (scatter ehat3 time, sort) , ///
        xtitle(Time) ytitle(Residuals) yline(0) ///
        title("Residuals Wheat" "Cubic Specification")
graph save wheat_cube_ehat, replace
```

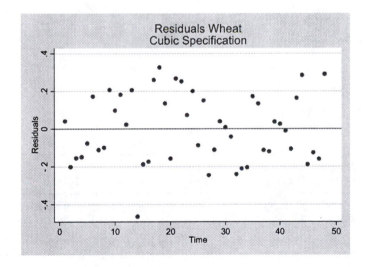

4.5.3 Estimating a log-linear yield growth model

As alternative to the cubic model of the previous section, a log-linear growth model can be used.

```
gen lyield = ln(yield)
reg lyield time
```

```
. reg lyield time
```

Source	SS	df	MS
Model	2.93313558	1	2.93313558
Residual	1.82466561	46	.039666644
Total	4.75780119	47	.101229813

Number of obs =	48
F(1, 46) =	73.94
Prob > F =	0.0000
R-squared =	0.6165
Adj R-squared =	0.6082
Root MSE =	.19916

lyield	Coef.	Std. Err.	t	P>|t|	[95% Conf. Interval]
time	.0178439	.0020751	8.60	0.000	.0136669 .0220208
_cons	-.3433665	.0584042	-5.88	0.000	-.460928 -.2258049

We estimate an annual growth rate of 1.78%. More will be said about the log-linear functional form in the following section.

```
log close
```

4.6 ESTIMATING A LOG-LINEAR WAGE EQUATION

Begin a new log, open the data file *cps4_small.dta*, and obtain variable descriptions and examine the summary statistics. Tabulate the values of *EDUC*.

```
log using chap04_lwage, replace text
use cps4_small, clear
describe
summarize
tabulate educ
```

The variables we will use are

variable name	storage type	display format	value label	variable label
wage	double	%10.0g		earnings per hour
educ	byte	%8.0g		years of education

Plot a scatter diagram of wage versus years of education, using small symbols with the msize(small) option.

```
twoway (scatter wage educ, msize(small)) , ///
       xtitle(Education) ytitle(Wage) ///
       title(Wage-Education Scatter)
graph save wage_educ, replace
```

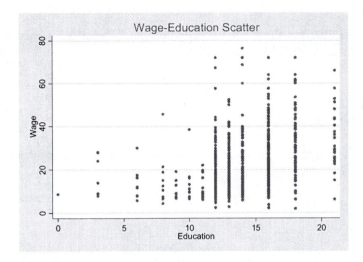

Using these data we will study the relationship between wages and years of education. The plot of wage against education shows the tendency for some wages at higher levels of education to be skewed. This is typical of wage, salary and income data.

4.6.1 The log-linear model

This is a log-linear model, which means the dependent variable is transformed.

```
gen lwage = ln(wage)
```

Now plot the scatter of **ln(wage)** against education. The transformed data are noticeably less skewed.

```
twoway (scatter lwage educ, msize(small)), ///
      xtitle(Education) ytitle(ln(Wage)) ///
      title(ln(Wage)-Education Scatter)
graph save lwage_educ, replace
```

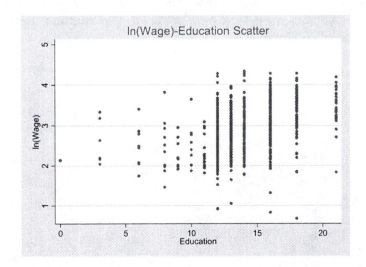

In this example we will predict the wage of a person with 12 years of education. So edit the data file by adding in observation 1001 the value $EDUC = 12$.

```
edit
set obs 1001
replace educ=12 in 1001
```

Estimate the log-linear regression, and compute the fitted values, the least squares residuals and the standard error of the forecast.

```
reg lwage educ
```

. reg lwage educ

Source	SS	df	MS
Model	60.015841	1	60.015841
Residual	276.76489	998	.27731953
Total	336.780731	999	.337117849

```
Number of obs =     1000
F( 1,    998) =   216.41
Prob > F      =   0.0000
R-squared     =   0.1782
Adj R-squared =   0.1774
Root MSE      =   .52661
```

lwage	Coef.	Std. Err.	t	P>|t|	[95% Conf. Interval]	
educ	.0904082	.0061456	14.71	0.000	.0783484	.1024681
_cons	1.609444	.0864229	18.62	0.000	1.439853	1.779036

Compute fitted values, residuals and the standard error of the forecast for future use.

```
predict lwagehat
predict ehat, residuals
predict sef, stdf
```

Based on the regression results we estimate that each additional year of education leads to approximately 9% higher wages.

Below we will use the estimated variance of the error term in a calculation, so while regression results are in Stata's memory, we will obtain it. Use **ereturn list** to view the list of items saved by Stata after a regression.

```
ereturn list
```

. ereturn list

scalars:
```
      e(N) =  1000
   e(df_m) =  1
   e(df_r) =  998
      e(F) =  216.4140443756974
     e(r2) =  .1782044973688944
   e(rmse) =  .5266113647668089
    e(mss) =  60.01584096379838
    e(rss) =  276.764890442558
```

Among the scalars returned are the degrees of freedom (**df_r**) and the sum of squared residuals (**ssr**). Compute a scalar that is the estimated variance of the error term.

```
scalar sig2 = e(rss)/e(df_r)
di "sigma-hat squared = " sig2
```

```
. di "sigma-hat squared = " sig2
sigma-hat squared = .27731953
```

Now, using the same commands as earlier construct a histogram, and calculate the Jarque-Bera test for normality.

```
histogram ehat, percent title(log(Wage) Model Residuals)
graph save lwage_ehat, replace
```

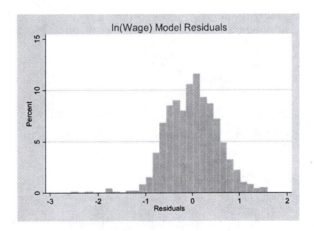

```
summarize ehat, detail
scalar jb = (r(N)/6)*( (r(skewness)^2) + ((r(kurtosis)-3)^2)/4 )
```

```
di "Jarque-Bera Statistic = " jb
scalar chic = invchi2tail(2,.05)
di "Chi-square(2) 95th percentile = " chic
scalar pvalue = chi2tail(2,jb)
di "Jarque-Bera p-value = " pvalue
```

```
. di "Jarque-Bera Statistic = " jb
Jarque-Bera Statistic = 27.528329
```

```
. scalar chic = invchi2tail(2,.05)
```

```
. di "Chi-square(2) 95th percentile = " chic
Chi-square(2) 95th percentile = 5.9914645
```

```
. scalar pvalue = chi2tail(2,jb)
```

```
. di "Jarque-Bera p-value = " pvalue
Jarque-Bera p-value = 1.053e-06
```

The normality of the residuals is rejected. The plot of the residuals is obtained using

```
rvpplot educ, yline(0)
```

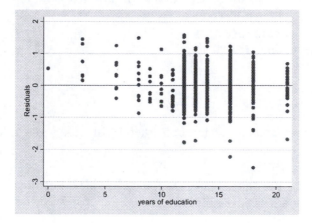

The residuals show both a downward trend and increasing variation as education increases.

4.6.2 Calculating wage predictions

The predicted value from the log-linear model is $\widehat{\ln(y)} = b_1 + b_2 x$. To obtain a prediction of the dependent variable y we take the antilog, obtaining the "natural predictor"

$$\hat{y}_n = \exp\left(\widehat{\ln(y)}\right) = \exp(b_1 + b_2 x)$$

The Stata function **exp()** is the exponential function. To create the antilog of the predicted ln(wage) use

```
gen yhatn = exp(lwagehat)
```

In larges samples a better predictor is the "corrected" predictor

$$\hat{y}_c = \widehat{E(y)} = \exp\left(b_1 + b_2 x + \hat{\sigma}^2/2\right) = \hat{y}_n e^{\hat{\sigma}^2/2}$$

Recall that we calculated the estimated error variance $\hat{\sigma}^2$ calling it **sig2**. Using this scalar, the corrected predictor can be generated using

```
di "correction factor = " exp(sig2/2)
```

```
. di "correction factor = " exp(sig2/2)
correction factor = 1.1487332
```

```
gen yhatc = yhatn*exp(sig2/2)
```

The correction factor is 1.1487, and thus the "corrected" predictions are larger than the "natural" ones. This will always be so because the correction factor $e^a > 1$ for any value $a > 0$, and the estimated variance $\hat{\sigma}^2$ is always greater than zero.

4.6.3 Constructing wage plots

It would be good to see a graph comparing the two predictors.

```
twoway (scatter wage educ, sort msize(small)) ///
       (line yhatn educ, sort ///
    1      width(medthick) lpattern(dash)) ///
       (line yhatc educ, sort lwidth(medthick) lpattern(solid))
graph save lwage_predict, replace
```

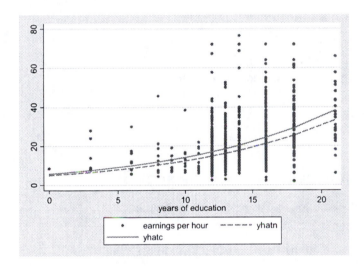

The plot shows that **yhatc** is always greater than **yhatn**. To view the natural and corrected predictions we will list the observation 1001.

```
list educ yhatn yhatc in 1001
```

	educ	yhatn	yhatc
1001.	12	14.7958	16.99643

Are these values reasonable? We can do a rough check by calculating the summary statistics for wage for those with 12 years of education in our sample.

```
summarize wage if educ==12 in 1/1000
```

. summarize wage if educ==12 in 1/1000

Variable	Obs	Mean	Std. Dev.	Min	Max
wage	328	15.99329	8.843706	2.5	72.13

We see that the predictions are in line with the actual mean of wages for individuals with 12 years of education.

4.6.4 Generalized R^2

The generalized R^2 measure is the square of the correlation between the "best" predictor **yhatc** and the variable **wage**. In this case **yhatc** and **yhatn** differ only by a multiplicative constant, so their correlation with **wage** is the same. To compute the correlations use

```
correlate wage yhatn yhatc
di "r2g = " r(rho)^2
```

```
. correlate wage yhatn yhatc
(obs=1000)

             |     wage     yhatn     yhatc
-------------+---------------------------------
        wage |   1.0000
       yhatn |   0.4312    1.0000
       yhatc |   0.4312    1.0000    1.0000
```

```
. di "r2g = " r(rho)^2
r2g = .18593072
```

4.6.5 Prediction intervals in the log-linear model

A prediction interval in the log-linear model is constructed as

$$\left[\exp\left(\widehat{\ln(y)}-t_c\mathrm{se}(f)\right),\exp\left(\widehat{\ln(y)}+t_c\mathrm{se}(f)\right)\right]$$

It is based on the "natural" predictor and the standard error of the forecast constructed in Section 4.6.1 above. First, calculate the 97.5 percentile from the t-distribution with 998 degrees of freedom.

```
scalar tc = invttail(998,.025)
```

Generate the lower and upper prediction intervals of ln(wage)

```
gen lb_lwage = lwagehat - tc*sef
gen ub_lwage = lwagehat + tc*sef
```

Find the antilog using the exponential function exp.

```
gen lb_wage = exp(lb_lwage)
gen ub_wage = exp(ub_lwage)
```

List the values of the prediction interval for observation 1001.

```
list lb_wage ub_wage in 1001
```

```
. list lb_wage ub_wage in 1001
```

	lb_wage	ub_wage
1001.	5.260397	41.61581

Create a plot with wage data, the natural predictor and the interval predictor against education.

```
twoway (scatter wage educ, sort msize(small)) ///
       (line yhatn educ, sort lwidth(medthick) lpattern(solid)) ///
       (line ub_wage educ, sort lcolor(forest_green) lwidth(medthick) ///
       l      pattern(dash)) ///
       (line lb_wage educ, sort lcolor(forest_green) lwidth(medthick) ///
       lp     attern(dash))
```

```
graph save lwage_interval, replace
```

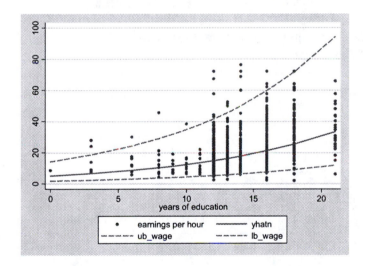

```
log close
```

4.7 A LOG-LOG MODEL

The log-log function, $\ln(y) = \beta_1 + \beta_2 \ln(x)$, is widely used to describe demand equations and production functions. The name "log-log" comes from the fact that the logarithm appears on both sides of the equation. In order to use this model all values of y and x must be positive. The slopes of these curves change at every point, but the elasticity is constant and equal to β_2. A useful way to think about the log-log function comes from closer inspection of its slope $dy/dx = \beta_2(y/x)$.

Rearrange this so that $\beta_2 = (dy/y)/(dx/x)$. Thus the slope of the log-log function exhibits constant *relative* change, whereas the linear function displays constant absolute change.

Open a new log file, and use the data *newbroiler.dta*.

```
log using chap04_loglog, replace text
use newbroiler, clear
describe
summarize
```

Variables of interest include

variable name	storage type	display format	value label	variable label
year	float	%9.0g		year
q	float	%9.0g		per capita consumption of boneless chicken, pounds
y	float	%9.0g		per capita real disposable income, 1996 = 100
p	float	%9.0g		real price (index) of fresh chicken

Create the logarithm of quantity and price and estimate the log-log model. Here we use the log function **ln** which is equivalent to **log**.

```
gen lq = ln(q)
gen lp = ln(p)
reg lq lp
```

```
. reg lq lp
```

Source	SS	df	MS		
Model	7.36410139	1	7.36410139	Number of obs =	52
Residual	.69608941	50	.013921788	F(1, 50) =	528.96
				Prob > F =	0.0000
				R-squared =	0.9136
				Adj R-squared =	0.9119
Total	8.0601908	51	.158042957	Root MSE =	.11799

lq	Coef.	Std. Err.	t	P>|t|	[95% Conf. Interval]
lp	-1.121358	.0487564	-23.00	0.000	-1.219288 -1.023428
_cons	3.716944	.0223594	166.24	0.000	3.672034 3.761854

The estimated elasticity is -1.12.

Obtain the corrected predictor and plot. The plot commands are a little long, so we wrapped them onto a second line here, but not in the do-file.

```
predict lqhat
scalar sig2 = e(rss)/e(df_r)
gen qhatc = exp(lqhat)*exp(sig2/2)
twoway (scatter q p, sort msize(small) lwidth(medthick) ///
        l       pattern(solid)) ///
```

```
(line qhatc p, sort lwidth(medthick)), ///
xtitle(Price of Chicken) ytitle(Quantity of Chicken) ///
title(Poultry Demand)
```

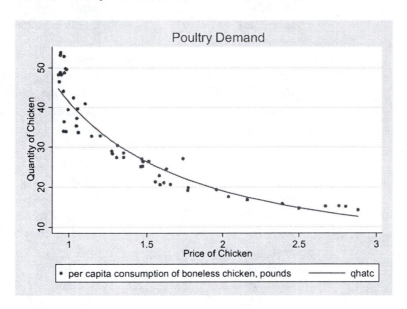

The generalized R^2 is given by

```
correlate q qhatc
di "r2g = " r(rho)^2
log close
```

```
. correlate q qhatc
(obs=52)
```

	q	qhatc
q	1.0000	
qhatc	0.9390	1.0000

```
. di "r2g = " r(rho)^2
r2g = .88177576
```

KEY TERMS

analysis of variance table	**histogram**	**predict**
chi2	**invchi2**	prediction
chi2tail	**invchi2tail**	prediction interval
connected	Jarque-Bera test	**regress**
correlate	kurtotsis	**replace**
correlations	**lcolor**	residual diagnostic plots
create	**lfit**	**return list**
data editor	**lincom**	R-squared
db scalar	linear-log model	**rvpplot**
drop	**list**	**scalar**
dydx	**ln**	**scatter**
edit	**log**	**set obs**
ereturn list	log-linear model	skewness
exponential function	log-log model	sort on x variable
expression builder	**lpattern**	standard error of forecast
factor variables	**lwidth**	**stdf**
gen	**margins**	**summarize**
generate	**msymbol**	**twoway**
goodness of fit	natural log	**yline**
graph editor	plot definition	

CHAPTER 4 DO-FILE [CHAP04.DO]

```
* file chap04.do for Using Stata for Principles of Econometrics, 4e

cd c:\data\poe4stata

* Stata Do-file
* copyright C 2011 by Lee C. Adkins and R. Carter Hill
* used for "Using Stata for Principles of Econometrics, 4e"
* by Lee C. Adkins and R. Carter Hill (2011)
* John Wiley and Sons, Inc.

* setup
version 11.1
capture log close
set more off

* open log
log using chap04_food, replace text

* open data
use food, clear

* add observation
edit
set obs 41
replace income=20 in 41

* estimate regression
quietly regress food_exp income
```

```
predict yhat
predict ehat, residuals
predict sef, stdf

* compute t-critical value
scalar define tc = invttail(38,.025)
di "t critical value 97.5 percentile = "  tc
gen lb = yhat - tc*sef
gen ub = yhat + tc*sef
list income lb yhat ub in 41
drop in 41

* R2
pwcorr food_exp income yhat

* effect of scaling

* create $ income and regress
gen inc_dollar = income*100
reg food_exp income
reg food_exp inc_dollar
log close

* Chapter 4.3.3 linear-log model
log using chap04_linlog, replace text

* open data
use food, clear

* log of income
gen lincome = ln(income)

* linear-log regression
reg food_exp lincome
predict lyhat
predict lehat, resid

* slope = beta2/x
summarize income
return list
scalar xbar = r(mean)
lincom lincome/xbar
lincom lincome/10
lincom lincome/20
lincom lincome/30

* fitted value plot
twoway (scatter food_exp income, sort)                    ///
      (line lyhat income, sort lwidth(medthick)),         ///
      xtitle(Income) ytitle(Food Expenditure) ylabel(0(100)600)  ///
      title(Linear Log Model)
graph save linlog, replace

* linear relationship
quietly reg food_exp income
predict yhat
predict ehat, resid

* linear and linear-log fitted lines
twoway (scatter food_exp income, sort)                    ///
      (line lyhat income, sort lwidth(medthick))          ///
      (line yhat income, sort lpattern(dash) lwidth(medthick)),  ///
      xtitle(Income) ytitle(Food Expenditure) ylabel(0(100)600)  ///
```

```
        title(Linear Log Model)
graph save linlog2, replace

* plot linear-log model residuals
twoway (scatter lehat income, sort) ,         ///
        xtitle(Income) ytitle(Residuals) ///
        title(Linear Log Model Residuals)
graph save linlog_residual, replace

* analyze residuals from original equation
histogram ehat, percent title(Linear Model Residuals)
graph save olsehat_hist, replace

* Jarque-Bera test of error normality
summarize ehat, detail
return list

scalar jb = (r(N)/6)*( (r(skewness)^2) + ((r(kurtosis)-3)^2)/4 )
di "Jarque-Bera Statistic = " jb
scalar chic = invchi2tail(2,.05)
di "Chi-square(2) 95th percentile = " chic
scalar pvalue = chi2tail(2,jb)
di "Jarque-Bera p-value = " pvalue
log close

* Polynomial model Chapter 4.4

* open new log
log using chap04_wheat, replace text

* open data and examine
use wa_wheat, clear
describe
summarize
gen yield = greenough
label variable yield "wheat yield greenough shire"

* plot data
twoway (scatter yield time, sort msymbol(circle)) ,        ///
        xtitle(Time) ylabel(0(.5)2.5) ytitle(Yield)        ///
        title(Wheat Yield)
graph save wawheat, replace

* regression
reg yield time
predict yhat
predict ehat, residuals

* plot fitted lines and data
twoway (scatter yield time, sort)                 ///
        (line yhat time, sort lwidth(medthick)) ,   ///
        xtitle(Time) ytitle(Yield) ylabel(0(.5)2.5)  ///
        title(Wheat Yield Fitted Linear Model)
graph save wheat_fit, replace

* plot residuals
twoway (scatter ehat time, sort) ,                ///
        xtitle(Time) ytitle(Residuals) yline(0)    ///
        title(Wheat Linear Model Residuals)
graph save wheat_ehat, replace

rvpplot time, recast(bar) yline(0)
graph save wheat_ehat_bar, replace
```

```
* Chapter 4.4.2 Cubic equation for yield

* create scaled cubic variable
generate time0=time/100
list yield time0 in 1/5
summarize time0

* cubic regression
reg yield c.time0#c.time0#c.time0
predict yhat3
predict ehat3, residuals

* slopes
margins, dydx(*) at(time=(0.15 0.30 0.45))

* plot fitted lines and data
twoway (scatter yield time, sort)                ///
       (line yhat3 time, sort lwidth(medthick)) ,  ///
       xtitle(Time) ytitle(Yield) ylabel(0(.5)2.5) ///
       title(Wheat Yield Fitted Cubic Model)
graph save wheat_cubic_fit, replace

* plot residuals
twoway (scatter ehat3 time, sort) ,                ///
       xtitle(Time) ytitle(Residuals) yline(0)     ///
       title("Residuals Wheat" "Cubic Specification")
graph save wheat_cube_ehat, replace

* Chapter 4.5 Log-linear Models

* wheat growth model
gen lyield = ln(yield)
reg lyield time
log close

* Wage Equation

* open new log file
log using chap04_lwage, replace text

* open cps4_small data
use cps4_small, clear

* summarize and plot
describe
summarize
tabulate educ

twoway (scatter wage educ, msize(small)) ,       ///
       xtitle(Education) ytitle(Wage)            ///
       title(Wage-Education Scatter)
graph save wage_educ, replace

* create log(wage) and plot
gen lwage = ln(wage)
twoway (scatter lwage educ, msize(small)),       ///
       xtitle(Education) ytitle(ln(Wage))        ///
       title(ln(Wage)-Education Scatter)
graph save lwage_educ, replace

* log-linear regression
* add one observation
```

```
edit
set obs 1001
replace educ=12 in 1001
reg lwage educ
predict lwagehat
predict ehat, residuals
predict sef, stdf

* calculate sigma-hat^2
ereturn list
scalar sig2 = e(rss)/e(df_r)
di "sigma-hat squared = " sig2

* Analyze resdiduals
histogram ehat, percent title(ln(Wage) Model Residuals)
graph save lwage_ehat, replace

summarize ehat, detail
scalar jb = (r(N)/6)*( (r(skewness)^2) + ((r(kurtosis)-3)^2)/4 )
di "Jarque-Bera Statistic = " jb
scalar chic = invchi2tail(2,.05)
di "Chi-square(2) 95th percentile = " chic
scalar pvalue = chi2tail(2,jb)
di "Jarque-Bera p-value = " pvalue
rvpplot educ, yline(0)

* compute natural and corrected predictor and plot
gen yhatn = exp(lwagehat)
di "correction factor = " exp(sig2/2)
gen yhatc = yhatn*exp(sig2/2)
twoway (scatter wage educ, sort msize(small))        ///
       (line yhatn educ, sort                        ///
        lwid     th(medthick) lpattern(dash))        ///
       (line yhatc educ, sort lwidth(medthick) lpattern(solid))
graph save lwage_predict, replace

* list predicted values
list educ yhatn yhatc in 1001
summarize wage if educ==12 in 1/1000

* R^2
correlate wage yhatn yhatc
di "r2g = " r(rho)^2

* prediction interval
scalar tc = invttail(998,.025)
gen lb_lwage = lwagehat - tc*sef
gen ub_lwage = lwagehat + tc*sef
gen lb_wage = exp(lb_lwage)
gen ub_wage = exp(ub_lwage)

* list and plot
list lb_wage ub_wage in 1001              .
twoway (scatter wage educ, sort msize(small))                       ///
       (line yhatn educ, sort lwidth(medthick) lpattern(solid))     ///
       (line ub_wage educ, sort lcolor(forest_green) lwidth(medthick)   ///
        lpat     tern(dash))              ///
       (line lb_wage educ, sort lcolor(forest_green) lwidth(medthick)   ///
        lpat     tern(dash))
graph save lwage_interval, replace
log close

* A log-log model example
```

```
log using chap04_loglog, replace text
use newbroiler, clear
describe
summarize

gen lq = ln(q)
gen lp = ln(p)
reg lq lp
predict lqhat
scalar sig2 = e(rss)/e(df_r)
gen qhatc = exp(lqhat)*exp(sig2/2)
twoway (scatter q p, sort msize(small) lwidth(medthick)          ///
        lpat        tern(solid))                    ///
      (line qhatc p, sort lwidth(medthick)),          ///
              xtitle(Price of Chicken) ytitle(Quantity of Chicken)    ///
        titl        e(Poultry Demand)

correlate q qhatc
di "r2g = " r(rho)^2
log close
```

CHAPTER **5**

The Multiple Regression Model

5.1 BIG ANDY'S BURGER BARN

In the simple linear regression the average value of a dependent variable is modeled as linear function of a constant and a single explanatory variable. The multiple linear regression model expands the number of explanatory variables. As such it is a simple but important extension that makes linear regression quite powerful.

The example used in this chapter is a model of sales for Big Andy's Burger Barn. Big Andy's hamburger sales depend on the price charged and the level of advertising. Thus, the model includes two explanatory variables and a constant:

$$SALES = \beta_1 + \beta_2 PRICE + \beta_3 ADVERT + e$$

where *SALES* is monthly sales in a given city and is measured in $1,000 increments, *PRICE* is price of a hamburger measured in dollars, *ADVERT* is the advertising expenditure also measured in thousands of dollars and $i = 1, 2, \ldots, N$.

First, start Stata and, from the command line, change the working directory to the location that contains your data files, or if you plan to use files stored at an internet address, the location to which you want to write the Stata log file. As in all of our examples, we choose

```
cd c:\data\poe4stata
```

Locate the file you wish to open, here *andy.dta*, and click **Open**. Before estimating any model, it is good practice to check that the data have been loaded into your software properly. In this case, check the summary statistics and list the first few observations. They should match those in table 5.1 of the textbook. Basically, you want to look at the summary statistics to see if they make sense. Do you have the desired number of observations? Do the ranges of the variables seem reasonable—in this instance, are the sales, prices and advertising expenditures positive?

Recall that the **summarize** command calls for the basic set of summary statistics and **list** prints the variables and observations in the data set. The **in 1/5** appended to list tells Stata to limit the printout to observations 1 through 5. The results are:

```
. summarize
```

Variable	Obs	Mean	Std. Dev.	Min	Max
sales	75	77.37467	6.488537	62.4	91.2
price	75	5.6872	.518432	4.83	6.49
advert	75	1.844	.8316769	.5	3.1

```
. list in 1/5
```

	sales	price	advert
1.	73.2	5.69	1.3
2.	71.8	6.49	2.9
3.	62.4	5.63	.8
4.	67.4	6.22	.7
5.	89.3	5.02	1.5

You may opt to estimate the regression from the command line, which usually saves time.

```
regress sales price advert
```

If you cannot recall the syntax, use the pull-down menus. Select **Statistics > Linear models and related > Linear regression**. This opens the **regress** dialog box shown in section 2.4. Enter **sales** as the dependent variable and **price** and **advert** as independent variables and click submit. Remember that Stata includes a constant variable that places an intercept into the model. Unless you have a good reason to omit the intercept from a model, you should always include one. Hence, this is the default for Stata. The output is given below:

Source	SS	df	MS
Model	1396.53893	2	698.269465
Residual	1718.94294	72	23.8742075
Total	3115.48187	74	42.1011063

```
Number of obs =      75
F( 2,    72) =   29.25
Prob > F      =  0.0000
R-squared     =  0.4483
Adj R-squared =  0.4329
Root MSE      =  4.8861
```

sales	Coef.	Std. Err.	t	P>|t|	[95% Conf. Interval]	
price	-7.907854	1.095993	-7.22	0.000	-10.09268	-5.723032
advert	1.862584	.6831955	2.73	0.008	.500659	3.22451
_cons	118.9136	6.351638	18.72	0.000	106.2519	131.5754

The parameter for the intercept is labeled **_cons** and those for the slopes β_2 and β_3 are labeled **price** and **advert**, respectively.

The variance-covariance matrix measures the precision with which the least squares estimator is able to measure the parameters of your model. The precision of least squares depends on a number of things, including the variability of your data (σ^2), the size of your sample, and the design of your 'experiment' implied by the numerical values of your independent variables. This information is summarized by the estimated variance-covariance matrix, which includes a measurement of the variance of the intercept, each slope and any covariances between them.

$$\text{cov}(b_1, b_2, b_3) = \begin{bmatrix} \text{var}(b_1) & \text{cov}(b_1, b_2) & \text{cov}(b_1, b_3) \\ \text{cov}(b_1, b_2) & \text{var}(b_2) & \text{cov}(b_2, b_3) \\ \text{cov}(b_1, b_3) & \text{cov}(b_2, b_3) & \text{var}(b_3) \end{bmatrix}$$

The variances of the least squares estimator fall on the diagonal and the covariance between each pair is in the lower triangle.

To print an estimate of the variance-covariance matrix following a regression use

```
. estat vce

Covariance matrix of coefficients of regress model
```

e(V)	price	advert	_cons
price	1.2012007		
advert	-.01974215	.46675606	
_cons	-6.7950641	-.7484206	40.343299

So, the estimated variance of b_2 is 1.20 and its estimated covariance with b_3 is −0.0197. Taking the square roots of the diagonal elements produces the least squares standard errors and, as one can easily verify, match the results in the regression table above.

A dialog box can be summoned using the pull-down menus by choosing **Statistics>Linear Models and related> Regression diagnostics>Specification tests, etc.**, which opens the estat-Postestimation statistics for regress dialog box. Use the scroll bar to select the Covariance matrix estimate (**vce**) option as shown below.

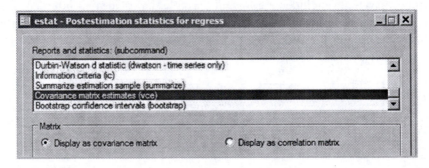

5.2 LEAST SQUARES PREDICTION

Prediction was touched upon in Chapter 2 and is revisited here. Suppose Big Andy wants to predict sales revenue for a price of $5.50 and an advertising expenditure of $1,200. This prediction is displayed using

```
di _b[_cons] + _b[price]*5.50 + _b[advert]*1.2
```

which is echoed to the **Results** window.

```
. di _b[_cons] + _b[price]*5.50 + _b[advert]*1.2
77.655513
```

In this example, predicted sales for the given price and advertising expenditure are 77.66.

One can also use the trick explored in Chapter 4 that adds observations to the data set and the predict command to generate conditional forecasts. Open the data editor **Data>Data editor** and add the desired values of the independent variables on a new data line (here, observation 76). This can be done from the **Command** window as well. First set the observations to 76 using **set obs 76**. Then use the **replace** command to enter the desired values of the independent variables for the new observation. This is done in the first three lines below.

```
set obs 76
replace price = 5.50 in 76
replace advert = 1.2 in 76
predict yhat
list yhat in 76
```

Once the desired values of **price** and **advert** are entered, Stata's **predict** command can be used to generate the prediction. The **predict** command assumes that the Big Andy regression was the last one estimated and it uses the default option, **xb** to get predicted values from the regression. Once again, the **list yhat** statement uses the conditional **in 76** to list the 76th observation of the data.

```
. list yhat in 76
```

	yhat
76.	77.65551

5.3 SAMPLING PRECISION

Many of the results needed to manually compute this and other statistics are stored internally by Stata. To view the contents of results produced from estimation use

```
ereturn list
```

which produces, in part

scalars:

```
          e(N) =  75
       e(df_m) =  2
       e(df_r) =  72
          e(F) =  29.24785947967357
         e(r2) =  .4482577622149436
       e(rmse) =  4.886123970679952
        e(mss) =  1396.538929773235
        e(rss) =  1718.942936893432
```

To estimate the equation's error variance, use the equation

$$\hat{\sigma}^2 = \frac{\sum\limits_{i=1}^{N} \hat{e}_i^2}{N-K}$$

Where the $\hat{e}_i^2$ are the squared least squares residuals. Essentially, the numerator is just the sum of squared errors from the regression, which is divided by the residual degrees of freedom.

The residual degrees of freedom is stored in **e(df_r)** and the sum-of-squared errors in **e(rss)**. So,

```
    scalar sighat2 = e(rss)/e(df_r)
    scalar list sighat2
```

produces:

```
. scalar list sighat2
  sighat2 =  23.874207
```

All of this information is available from the analysis of variance table produced by Stata, which is shown below.

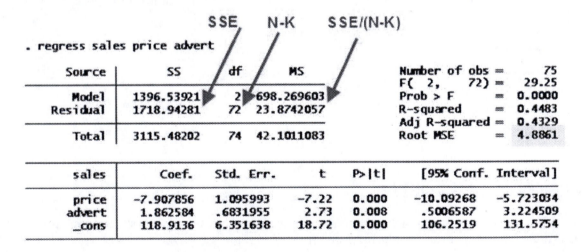

```
                           SSE      N-K    SSE/(N-K)

. regress sales price advert

     Source |      SS        df      MS              Number of obs =     75
------------+------------------------------           F( 2,    72) =  29.25
      Model | 1396.53921      2  698.269603           Prob > F      =  0.0000
   Residual | 1718.94281     72  23.8742057           R-squared     =  0.4483
------------+------------------------------           Adj R-squared =  0.4329
      Total | 3115.48202     74  42.1011083           Root MSE      =  4.8861

------------------------------------------------------------------------------
      sales |      Coef.   Std. Err.      t    P>|t|     [95% Conf. Interval]
------------+-----------------------------------------------------------------
      price |  -7.907856   1.095993    -7.22   0.000    -10.09268    -5.723034
     advert |   1.862584    .6831955    2.73   0.008      .5006587    3.224509
      _cons |   118.9136   6.351638    18.72   0.000     106.2519    131.5754
------------------------------------------------------------------------------
```

As you can see, the estimated variance is 23.874. Root MSE is the square root of this number and appears on the printout on the right-hand side of the table, highlighted in yellow.

5.4 CONFIDENCE INTERVALS

The regression table gives you the least squares estimates and the estimated standard errors. The given standard error is an estimate of how precisely least squares is able to measure the parameter of interest.

The confidence interval serves a similar purpose, though it is much more straightforward to interpret because it gives you upper and lower bounds between which the unknown parameter will lie with a given probability. Suppose one wants a 95% interval estimate for β_2, the response of sales revenue to a change in price at Big Andy's Burger Barn for a given level of advertising. The procedure is the same as that used in Chapter 3. This time, the t-distribution used to obtain the critical values will have $N - K = 75 - 3 = 72$ degrees of freedom.

The 95% confidence interval is based on equation (5.13) from the text:

$$P(-t_c < t_{(72)} < t_c) = .95$$

A critical value from the $t_{(72)}$-distribution, call it t_c, is needed that satisfies this equation. The constant t_c is the $\alpha/2$ critical value from the t-distribution and α is the total desired probability associated with the "rejection" area (the area outside of the confidence interval). The critical value, t_c, can be found in a statistical table or one can use the **invttail(df,α/2)** function in Stata to discover that the .025 critical value from $t_{(72)}$-distribution is 1.993. A little algebra yields the 95% interval estimator of β_2 based on its least squares estimator, b_2, and its estimated standard error, se(b_2):

$$\left[b_2 - 1.993 \times \text{se}(b_2), \ b_2 + 1.993 \times \text{se}(b_2)\right]$$

Below, you'll find the Stata commands to generate the lower and upper endpoints for the estimated confidence interval.

```
scalar lb = _b[price] - invttail(e(df_r),.025) * _se[price]
scalar ub = _b[price] + invttail(e(df_r),.025) * _se[price]
scalar list lb ub
```

```
. scalar list bL bU
       bL =  -10.092676
       bU =  -5.7230322
```

In this case, we've used several stored results from the Big Andy's regression. These include the least squares estimate of the coefficient on price, **_b[price]**, its estimated standard error, **_se[price]**, and the residual degrees for freedom from the regression ($N-K$), **e(df_r)**.

The 95% confidence intervals are computed by default whenever you estimate a linear regression model. The interval appears in the last two columns of the regression results. You can change the probabilities to 90% using the **level()** option after the regression. For example, to obtain the 90% intervals with your regression use

```
regress sales price advert, level(90)
```

The level can also be changed through the dialog system. Choose **Statistics > Linear models and related > Lin ear regression** from the pull-down menu to open the **regress—Linear regression** dialog box Choose the **Reporting** tab and change the confidence level to the one you desire as shown here:

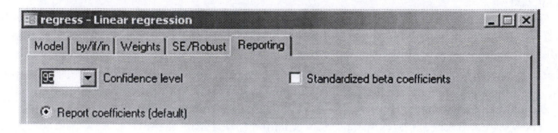

5.4.1 Confidence interval for a linear combination of parameters

Big Andy plans to increase advertising expenditure by $800 and drop the price by 40 cents. The change in expected sales is

$$\lambda = -0.4\beta_2 + 0.8\beta_3$$

which is a linear combination of parameters. Stata contains a built-in command **lincom** that computes various statistics for linear combination of parameters; **lincom** computes point estimates, standard errors, t or z statistics, p-values, and confidence intervals for linear combinations of coefficients after any estimation. To estimate λ using the least squares estimates of Big Andy's sales:

```
lincom -0.4*price+0.8*advert, level(90)
```

In this instance, the optional **level(90)** command is included in order to set the coverage probability for the confidence interval at 90%. The output is:

```
. lincom -0.4*price+0.8*advert, level(90)

 ( 1)   - .4*price + .8*advert = 0
```

sales	Coef.	Std. Err.	t	P>|t|	[90% Conf. Interval]
(1)	4.653209	.7096133	6.56	0.000	3.470785 5.835633

Stata echoes the command to the screen and reproduces the linear combination. The estimated value of λ is 4.65, its estimated standard error is 0.7096, and the 90% confidence interval is (3.471, 5.835).

One can use algebra and arithmetic to accomplish the same thing. Although Stata makes easy work of the computation, the user has to provide the algebra. Here, the estimated variances and covariances of the least estimator are used to compute standard error of $\hat{\lambda}$.

```
matrix cov=e(V)
scalar lambda = -0.4*_b[price]+0.8*_b[advert]
```

```
scalar var_lambda = (-0.4)^2*cov[1,1]+(0.8)^2*cov[2,2]+2* ///
    (-0.4)*(0.8)*cov[1,2]
```

The **matrix cov=e(V)** statement writes the variance covariance, which is saved in **e(V)**, to a matrix labeled **cov**. In the third and forth lines Stata's matrix indexing capabilities are used to select the desired elements from the covariance matrix to use in computing the variance of $\hat{\lambda}$. For instance **cov[1,1]** refers to the element that is in the first row and first column of **cov**—that is, the variance of b_2. Remember that Stata automatically places a constant at the end of an equation, hence b_2 is actually at the first element of coefficient vector.

Once the variance is computed, take its square root and divide the estimate of λ by the result to get the standard error. From there the confidence interval is computed in the usual way.

```
scalar se = sqrt(var_lambda)
scalar t = lambda/se
scalar lb = lambda-invttail(e(df_r),.05)*se
scalar ub = lambda+invttail(e(df_r),.05)*se
```

In the script, the **invttail(e(df_r),.05)** is used to get the 5% critical value from the t_{72} distribution. The results match those from **lincom** almost exactly.

```
. scalar list lambda var_lambda se t lb ub
      lambda =    4.6532091
  var_lambda =    .50355097
          se =    .70961325
           t =    6.5573876
          lb =    3.4707851
          ub =    5.8356332
```

5.5 HYPOTHESIS TESTS

5.5.1 Two-sided tests

The *t*-ratio of the test that $\beta_2 = 0$ against the two-sided alternative that $\beta_2 \neq 0$ is

$$t = \frac{b_2 - 0}{se(b_2)} \sim t_{(N-K)}$$

provided the null hypothesis that $\beta_2 = 0$ is true. The computed value is

$$t = \frac{-7.908}{1.096} = -7.215$$

Stata computes this easily from the command line. The *p*-value is obtained using the **tail(df,stat)** command, where **df** is the degrees of freedom and **stat** is the value of the test statistic. This function measures the tail area to the right of **stat** for the *t*-distribution with **df** degrees of freedom. For the two-sided test include the area to the left of the computed statistic (stat) by doubling the tail area of the positive value of t. Hence, use **2*ttail(72,abs(t1))**. The complete Stata code is:

```
scalar t1 = (_b[price]-0)/_se[price]
scalar p1 = 2*ttail(72,abs(t1))
scalar list t1 p1
```

The two-sided test that $\beta_3 = 0$ is performed similarly and the script is found at the end of this chapter.

5.5.2 One-sided tests

To test the null hypothesis that $\beta_2 \geq 0$ against the alternative $\beta_2 < 0$, use the same statistic

$$t = \frac{b_2 - 0}{se(b_2)} \sim t_{(N-K)}$$

Although the computation is the same, the critical value is now in the left tail of the t-distribution.

```
scalar t1 = (_b[price]-0)/_se[price]
scalar crit = -invttail(e(df_r),.05)
scalar pval = 1-ttail(e(df_r),t1)
```

The statement **ttail(e(df_r),t1)** computes the probability that a t-random variable with **df_r** degrees of freedom is larger that **t1**. Since the t-distribution is symmetric and we want the probability of being less than **t1,** we subtract **ttail(e(df_r),t1)** from 1.

If the p-value is less than the 5% significance level of the test, then reject the null hypothesis at that level of statistical significance. Otherwise, the null cannot be rejected at that level of significance.

The other way to conduct the test is to compare the statistic to the 5% critical value. Stata produces the critical value using the **invttail(e(df_r),.05)** function. The results of these computations are:

```
. scalar list t1 crit pval
       t1 = -7.2152415
     crit = -1.6662937
     pval =   2.212e-10
```

The test of advertising's effectiveness considers the null hypothesis that $\beta_3 \leq 1$ against the alternative $\beta_3 > 1$. The script is:

```
scalar t2 = (_b[advert]-1)/_se[advert]
scalar crit = invttail(e(df_r),.05)
scalar pval = ttail(e(df_r),t2)
```

Since the alternative is found in the right hand tail of the t-distribution the code is slightly more transparent. Again **invttail** computes the 5% right hand critical value for the t-distribution and **ttail** computes the area to the right of **t2**. These lines produce:

```
. scalar list t2 crit pval
       t2 =   1.2625732
     crit =   1.6662937
     pval =   .10540831
```

5.5.3 Testing a linear combination

Big Andy's marketing adviser claims that dropping the price by 20 cents will be more effective for increasing sales revenue than increasing advertising expenditure by \$500. In terms of the model, she thinks that $-0.2\,\beta_2 > 0.5\beta_3$. The null hypothesis is that $-0.2\,\beta_2 - 0.5\beta_3 \le 0$ and the alternative is $-0.2\,\beta_2 - 0.5\beta_3 > 0$

Once again, the `lincom` command is useful since it estimates the linear combination and its standard error. As a one-sided test, its best to compute the critical value or the p-value directly rather than rely on the printed output of `lincom`, which only gives you the p-value for a two-sided t-test.

First, use `lincom`

```
lincom -0.2*price-0.5*advert
```

which yields

```
( 1)   - .2*price - .5*advert = 0
```

sales	Coef.	Std. Err.	t	P>|t|	[95% Conf. Interval]	
(1)	.6502787	.4009846	1.62	0.109	-.1490694	1.449627

Dividing the estimated coefficient, 0.650, by the standard error, 0.400, yields the t-ratio 1.62. The one-sided p-value is half of the two-sided one, provided the estimated linear combination has the anticipated sign. To avoid confusion, we recommend computing the proper critical value or the p-value for one sided tests as is done below.

```
scalar t = r(estimate)/r(se)
scalar crit = invttail(r(df),.05)
scalar pval = ttail(r(df),t)
scalar list crit t pval
```

```
. scalar list crit t pval
     crit =   1.6662937
        t =   1.6217052
     pval =   .05461891
```

The new element involves **r(estimate)**, **r(df)** and **r(se)**. These are the estimated linear combination and standard error computed by `lincom`. Like the **e()** commands that are available after estimation, many other commands (e.g., **test** and `lincom`) also save results for further computation. Issuing

```
return list
```

yields

scalars:
```
        r(df) =  72
        r(se) =  .4009845529554849
  r(estimate) =  .65027873012098
```

This indicates that the degrees of freedom ($N-K$), the estimate and its standard error are saved from the prior use of the `lincom` command. When in doubt, use **ereturn list** or **return list** to verify what resides in the set of saved results.

5.6 POLYNOMIAL EQUATIONS

One way to allow for nonlinear relationships between independent and dependent variables is to introduce polynomials of the regressors into the model. In this example the marginal effect of an additional $1000 of advertising is expected to diminish as more advertising is used. The model becomes:

$$SALES = \beta_1 + \beta_2 PRICE + \beta_3 ADVERT + \beta_4 ADVERT^2 + e$$

There are two ways to estimate this. First, one can create the new variable $ADVERT^2$ add it to the model, and estimate the parameters. As in

```
generate a2 = advert*advert
reg sales price advert a2
```

which produces

```
. reg sales price advert a2
```

Source	SS	df	MS
Model	1583.39744	3	527.799145
Residual	1532.08443	71	21.5786539
Total	3115.48187	74	42.1011063

```
Number of obs =      75
F( 3,    71) =   24.46
Prob > F      = 0.0000
R-squared     = 0.5082
Adj R-squared = 0.4875
Root MSE      = 4.6453
```

sales	Coef.	Std. Err.	t	P>|t|	[95% Conf. Interval]	
price	-7.64	1.045939	-7.30	0.000	-9.725543	-5.554457
advert	12.15124	3.556164	3.42	0.001	5.060447	19.24203
a2	-2.767964	.9406241	-2.94	0.004	-4.643515	-.8924123
_cons	109.719	6.799045	16.14	0.000	96.16212	123.2759

The variable **a2**, which is created by multiplying **advert*advert**, is a simple example of what is sometimes referred to as an *interaction variable*. The simplest way to think about an interaction variable is that its effect on the dependent variable depends on another variable—the two variables interact to determine the average value of your dependent variable. In this case, the effect of advertising on average sales depends on the level of advertising itself.

When variables interact, the marginal effect of another unit of advertising ($1000) has to be computed manually based on the calculus. Taking the partial derivative of average sales with respect to advertising yields

$$\frac{\partial E(SALES)}{\partial ADVERT} = \beta_3 + 2\beta_4 ADVERT$$

The magnitude of the marginal effect depends on the parameters as well as on the level of advertising. In the example it is evaluated at two points, $ADVERT=.5$ and $ADVERT=2$. The code is:

```
scalar me1 = _b[advert]+2*(.5)*_b[a2]
scalar me2 = _b[advert]+2*(2)*_b[a2]
```

and listing the results produces

```
. scalar list me1 me2
      me1 =  9.3832736
      me2 =   1.079383
```

5.6.1 Optimal advertising: nonlinear combinations of parameters

The optimal level of advertising is defined in this example to be the amount maximizes net sales. Andy will advertise up to the point where another dollar of expenditure adds one dollar of sales—and no more. At this point the marginal effect is equal to one,

$$\beta_3 + 2\beta_4 ADVERT = 1$$

Solving $ADVERT$ in terms of the parameters

$$ADVERT_O = \frac{1 - \beta_3}{2\beta_4}$$

which is nonlinear in the parameters of the model. A consistent estimate of the optimal level of advertising can be obtained by substituting the least squares estimates for the parameters on the right-hand side. Estimating the standard error via the Delta method requires some calculus, but fortunately Stata includes a command **nlcom** that computes nonlinear combinations of parameters after estimation as well as the standard error, t-ratio, and confidence interval.

```
nlcom (1-_b[advert])/(2*_b[a2])
```

```
. nlcom (1-_b[advert])/(2*_b[a2])

    _nl_1:   (1-_b[advert])/(2*_b[a2])
```

sales	Coef.	Std. Err.	t	P>|t|	[95% Conf. Interval]	
_nl_1	2.01434	.128723	15.65	0.000	1.757673	2.271006

According to this estimate the optimal level of advertising is $2014.

5.6.2 Using factor variables for interactions

A better way to estimate models with interactions and evaluate marginal effects is to use Stata's *factor variables* and built-in **margins** command. Interacting variables in Stata is particularly easy, but some care must be taken to ensure that you are estimating what you intend. In Stata factor variables create indicator variables from categorical variables, interactions of indicators of categorical variables, interactions of categorical and continuous variables, and interactions of continuous variables (polynomials). They are allowed with most estimation and postestimation commands, along with a few other commands.

Factor-variables have their own operators in Stata:

Operator	Description
i.	unary operator to specify indicators
c.	unary operator to treat as continuous
#	binary operator to specify interactions
##	binary operator to specify factorial interactions

A *unary operator* is math-speak for a mathematical operation that affects only one number or variable—called an operand. An example would be a negative sign that appears before a number; when so used it takes the number and makes it negative. So, in the expression −2, the negative sign is a unary operator that operates on the number 2, making it negative. Binary operators operate on two variables. For example the − in the expression 1−2 operates on 1 and 2, subtracting 2 from 1.

Stata includes several unary operators that include **i.** and **c.** When used before a variable name these operators indicate to Stata that the variable is to be treated as continuous (e.g., **c.price**) or discrete (**i.price**). In the latter case, **i.price** will create an indicator variable for each different value of *PRICE*. Since the variable is continuous and each value in the data set is unique, Stata creates a set of N indicator variables to use in the model--probably not something you want to do ordinarily. On the other hand, it would be useful in creating sets if indicator variables for discrete variables in your data. Some examples of this are given elsewhere in this manual.

In the current case, *ADVERT* is continuous (equivalent to **c.advert**) and we want to interact it with itself (**c.advert**). The binary operator **#** is used to multiply two factor variables in Stata. In this way it creates the interaction of the two variables. So, the continuous variable $ADVERT^2$ is be created using **c.advert#c.advert**.

There are at least two reasons to specify variables in this way. First, there is no need to specifically generate the interaction variable to include in the data set; **c.advert#c.advert** can be added directly to the model by including it in the variable list of the **regress** command. Second, variables created this way can use Stata's built-in **margins** command to compute marginal effects. The use of **#** to multiply factor variables instead of the usual multiplication ***** indicates to Stata that the two variables that sandwich it have been interacted. This allows it to keep track of the marginal effects without you having to do any calculus. The key is to create the interactions using these factor variables and to use the proper options in **margins**.

To estimate the regression

```
regress sales price advert c.advert#c.advert
```

the results of which are:

```
. regress sales price advert c.advert#c.advert
```

Source	SS	df	MS
Model	1583.39741	3	527.799136
Residual	1532.08446	71	21.5786543
Total	3115.48187	74	42.1011063

```
Number of obs =      75
F( 3,    71) =   24.46
Prob > F      =  0.0000
R-squared     =  0.5082
Adj R-squared =  0.4875
Root MSE      =  4.6453
```

sales	Coef.	Std. Err.	t	P>|t|	[95% Conf. Interval]	
price	-7.64	1.045939	-7.30	0.000	-9.725543	-5.554457
advert	12.15124	3.556164	3.42	0.001	5.060446	19.24203
c.advert# c.advert	-2.767963	.940624	-2.94	0.004	-4.643514	-.892412
_cons	109.719	6.799045	16.14	0.000	96.16212	123.2759

Notice that the results from this regression are identical to those where **a2** was generated manually and included in the model. The coefficient on the interaction term is now identified as **c.advert#c.advert**. The payoff comes with the use of margins to compute the marginal effect. Evaluating the marginal effect at advertising levels of 0.5 and 2 is obtained:

```
. margins, dydx(advert) at(advert=(.5 2))
```

```
Average marginal effects                     Number of obs    =        75
Model VCE      : OLS

Expression     : Linear prediction, predict()
dy/dx w.r.t.   : advert

1._at          : advert           =          .5

2._at          : advert           =           2
```

		Delta-method				
	dy/dx	Std. Err.	z	P>|z|	[95% Conf. Interval]	
advert _at						
1	9.383273	2.636965	3.56	0.000	4.214916	14.55163
2	1.079383	.7019353	1.54	0.124	-.2963846	2.455151

The syntax for margins requires some explanation. The first option is **dydx(advert)**. This asks for the marginal effect of a one unit increase in the parenthesized variable **(advert)** on the mean of the dependent variable. The second option tells Stata at which values of **advert** to evaluate the marginal effect. In any event, margins produced the same result as the first method, and did so with virtually no programming and with no math. As a bonus, **margins** also produces an estimate of the standard error, *t*-ratio, two-sided *p*-value, and a confidence interval.

5.7 INTERACTIONS

Interaction among variables was introduced in the preceding section for creating polynomial terms. The concept is very general can be applied to any situation where the effect of a change in one variable on the mean of the dependent variable depends on another variable. The basic model considered is

$$PIZZA = \beta_1 + \beta_2 AGE + \beta_3 INCOME + e$$

It is proposed that as a person grows older, his or her marginal propensity to spend on pizza declines—this implies that the coefficient β_3 depends on a person's age.

$$\beta_3 = \beta_4 + \beta_5 AGE$$

Substituting this into the model produces

$$PIZZA = \beta_1 + \beta_2 AGE + \beta_4 INCOME + \beta_5 (INCOME \times AGE) + e$$

This introduces a new variable, $INCOME \times AGE$, which is an interaction variable. The marginal effect of unit increase in AGE in this model depends on $INCOME$ and the marginal effect of an increase in $INCOME$ depends on AGE.

The interaction could be created in Stata using the **generate** command, but a better choice is to use factor variables. This will permit one to evaluate marginal effects using the built-in margins command.

```
use pizza4, clear
regress pizza age income c.age#c.income
margins, dxdy(age) at(income=(25 90))
```

The output from the regression is

```
. regress pizza age income c.age#c.income
```

Source	SS	df	MS		
Model	367043.25	3	122347.75		
Residual	580608.65	36	16128.0181		
Total	947651.9	39	24298.7667		

```
Number of obs =      40
F( 3,    36) =    7.59
Prob > F      = 0.0005
R-squared     = 0.3873
Adj R-squared = 0.3363
Root MSE      =     127
```

pizza	Coef.	Std. Err.	t	P>|t|	[95% Conf. Interval]	
age	-2.977423	3.352101	-0.89	0.380	-9.775799	3.820952
income	6.979905	2.822768	2.47	0.018	1.255067	12.70474
c.age# c.income	-.1232394	.0667187	-1.85	0.073	-.2585512	.0120725
_cons	161.4654	120.6634	1.34	0.189	-83.25131	406.1822

And from the **margins** command:

```
. margins, dydx(age) at(income=(25 90))
```

Average marginal effects   Number of obs =   40
Model VCE   : OLS

Expression   : Linear prediction, predict()
dy/dx w.r.t. : age

1._at   : income   =   25

2._at   : income   =   90

		Delta-method					
		dy/dx	Std. Err.	z	P>|z|	[95% Conf.	Interval]
age							
	_at						
	1	-6.058407	2.390502	-2.53	0.011	-10.74371	-1.373109
	2	-14.06896	4.171058	-3.37	0.001	-22.24409	-5.893842

Another example introduces and interaction between education and experience into the wage model discussed in Chapter 4 that uses the *cps_small.dta* data set.

$$\ln(WAGE) = \beta_1 + \beta_2 EDUC + \beta_3 EXPER + \beta_4 (EDUC \times EXPER) + e$$

```
use cps4_small, clear
gen lwage = ln(wage)
regress lwage educ exper c.educ#c.exper
```

```
. regress lwage educ exper c.educ#c.exper
```

Source	SS	df	MS		Number of obs =	1000
					F(3, 996) =	80.23
Model	65.5449479	3	21.848316		Prob > F =	0.0000
Residual	271.235783	996	.272325084		R-squared =	0.1946
					Adj R-squared =	0.1922
Total	336.780731	999	.337117849		Root MSE =	.52185

lwage	Coef.	Std. Err.	t	P>|t|	[95% Conf.	Interval]
educ	.0949385	.0146246	6.49	0.000	.06624	.123637
exper	.0063295	.0066985	0.94	0.345	-.0068153	.0194743
c.educ#						
c.exper	-.0000364	.0004838	-0.08	0.940	-.0009858	.0009129
_cons	1.392318	.2066447	6.74	0.000	.986809	1.797827

And

```
regress lwage educ exper c.educ#c.exper c.exper#c.exper
```

```
. regress lwage educ exper c.educ#c.exper c.exper#c.exper
```

Source	SS	df	MS			
Model	82.3591698	4	20.5897924			
Residual	254.421562	995	.255700062			
Total	336.780731	999	.337117849			

```
Number of obs =    1000
F( 4,   995) =   80.52
Prob > F      =  0.0000
R-squared     =  0.2445
Adj R-squared =  0.2415
Root MSE      =  .50567
```

lwage	Coef.	Std. Err.	t	P>|t|	[95% Conf. Interval]	
educ	.1271953	.0147188	8.64	0.000	.0983118	.1560789
exper	.0629807	.0095361	6.60	0.000	.0442676	.0816938
c.educ#c.exper	-.0013224	.0004949	-2.67	0.008	-.0022935	-.0003513
c.exper#c.exper	-.0007139	.000088	-8.11	0.000	-.0008867	-.0005412
_cons	.5296774	.2267415	2.34	0.020	.084731	.9746237

Once again, the use of Stata's unary operators for factor variables makes estimating this regression particularly easy.

5.8 GOODNESS-OF-FIT

As we saw in Chapter 4 goodness-of-fit of the regression is based on statistics from the analysis of variance table. The R^2 measures the proportion of sample variation in the dependent variable accounted for by the regression. The same holds true for the multiple regression model. The only difference is that now there is more than one explanatory variable in the model. So, the relationship of Chapter 4 can be used. Decompose the total sum of squares of the dependent variable (*SST*) into explained (*SSR*) and unexplained (*SSE*) variation.

$$SST = SSR + SSE$$

Then the goodness-of-fit measure R^2 is

$$R^2 = \frac{SSR}{SST} = 1 - \frac{SSE}{SST}$$

You have to be careful when using Stata's analysis of variance table with the notation developed in *POE* and employed here. Stata refers to the explained variation as the *model sum of squares*. The text calls this the sum of squares regression or *SSR*. The unexplained variation in the dependent variable is captured in the least squares residuals. In your textbook this is called *the sum of squared errors, SSE*. Stata calls this unexplained variation the *residual sum of squares*.

Concept	POE	Stata
Unexplained variation	*SSE* (sum of squared errors)	Residual SS
Explained variation	*SSR* (sum of squares regression)	Model SS
Total variation	*SST*	Total SS

With that out of the way, you can get R^2 in a number of ways. The first is to use the analysis of variance table and compute it by hand. The second is to read it directly off of the regression output, since it is computed by default for linear regression. The third is to use the command line to compute it using saved results from the preceding regression. Certainly this option is easier than the first, but harder than the second! So, we will compute and display R^2 using the model sum of squares, which Stata saves in **e(mss)**, and residual sum of squares, saved in **e(rss)**. Note, the R^2 computed by default is also saved in Stata's memory and can be recalled using **e(r2)**.

```
use andy, clear
reg sales price advert
```

```
. reg sales price advert
```

Source	SS	df	MS
Model	1396.53893	2	698.269465
Residual	1718.94294	72	23.8742075
Total	3115.48187	74	42.1011063

Number of obs =	75
F(2, 72) =	29.25
Prob > F =	0.0000
R-squared =	0.4483
Adj R-squared =	0.4329
Root MSE =	4.8861

sales	Coef.	Std. Err.	t	P>|t|	[95% Conf. Interval]	
price	-7.907854	1.095993	-7.22	0.000	-10.09268	-5.723032
advert	1.862584	.6831955	2.73	0.008	.500659	3.22451
_cons	118.9136	6.351638	18.72	0.000	106.2519	131.5754

```
di "R-square " e(mss)/(e(mss)+e(rss))
di "R-square " 1-e(rss)/(e(mss)+e(rss))
```

```
. di "R-square " e(mss)/(e(mss)+e(rss))
R-square .44825776
```

```
. di "R-square " 1-e(rss)/(e(mss)+e(rss))
R-square .44825776
```

A disadvantage of R^2 as a measure of the goodness-of-fit is that adding regressors to the model always improves fit. A related measure of fit imposes a small penalty for adding regressors so that it is possible for the adjusted R^2 to get smaller as irrelevant independent variables are added to the model. The **adjusted R^2** is

$$\bar{R}^2 = 1 - \frac{SSE/(N-K)}{SST/(N-1)}$$

This statistic is also reported by default by Stata's **regress** command. Notice that *adjusted R-squared* is smaller than *R-squared*. In fact, R-squared will never be smaller than the adjusted R-Squared in multiple linear regression since the estimated fit is being penalized for adding explanatory variables.

KEY TERMS

#	**i.variable**	R^2
adjusted R^2	index	**regress**
binary operators	interaction variable	**replace**
c.variable	**invtail(df,alpha)**	**return list**
confidence interval	**level(90)**	Root MSE
di	**lincom**	**scalar**
dydx	**list**	**scalar list**
e(df_r)	marginal effect	**set obs**
e(mss)	**margins**	**test**
e(rss)	**matrix**	t-ratio
e(V)	multiple linear regression	**ttail(df,tstat)**
ereturn list	**nlcom**	unary operators
estat vce	prediction	variance
factor variables	p-value	variance covariance matrix

CHAPTER 5 DO-FILE [CHAP05.DO]

```
* file chap05.do for Using Stata for Principles of Econometrics, 4e

cd c:\data\poe4stata

* Stata Do-file
* copyright C 2011 by Lee C. Adkins and R. Carter Hill
* used for "Using Stata for Principles of Econometrics, 4e"
* by Lee C. Adkins and R. Carter Hill (2011)
* John Wiley and Sons, Inc.

* setup
version 11.1
capture log close
set more off

* open log
log using chap05_food, replace text

* open data
use andy, clear

* Summary Statistics
summarize

* List subset of observations
list in 1/5

* Least squares regression with covariance matrix
regress sales price advert
estat vce

* Predict sales when price is 5.50 and adv is 1200
di _b[_cons] + _b[price]*5.50 + _b[advert]*1.2

* Using the data editor to predict
set obs 76
```

```
replace price = 5.50 in 76
replace advert = 1.2 in 76
predict yhat
list yhat in 76

* Calculate sigma-hat square
ereturn list
scalar sighat2 = e(rss)/e(df_r)
scalar list sighat2

* Standard error of the regression
di sqrt(sighat2)

* Confidence Intervals
scalar bL = _b[price] - invttail(e(df_r),.025) * _se[price]
scalar bU = _b[price] + invttail(e(df_r),.025) * _se[price]

scalar list bL bU

* Using the level() command to change size of default intervals
regress sales price advert, level(90)

* Interval for a linear combination
* Easy way
lincom -0.4*price+0.8*advert, level(90)

* Hard way
matrix cov=e(V)
scalar lambda = -0.4*_b[price]+0.8*_b[advert]
scalar var_lambda = (-0.4)^2*cov[1,1]+(0.8)^2*cov[2,2]+2*(-0.4)*(0.8)*cov[1,2]
scalar se = sqrt(var_lambda)
scalar t = lambda/se
scalar lb = lambda-invttail(e(df_r),.05)*se
scalar ub = lambda+invttail(e(df_r),.05)*se
scalar list lambda var_lambda se t lb ub

* t-ratios
scalar t1 = (_b[price]-0)/_se[price]
scalar t2 = (_b[advert]-0)/_se[advert]
scalar list t1 t2

* pvalues
scalar p1 = 2*ttail(72,abs(t1))
scalar p2 = ttail(72,abs(t2))
scalar list p1 p2

* One sided significance test
scalar t1 = (_b[price]-0)/_se[price]
scalar crit = -invttail(e(df_r),.05)
scalar pval = 1-ttail(e(df_r),t1)
scalar list t1 crit pval

* One sided test of Advertising effectiveness
scalar t2 = (_b[advert]-1)/_se[advert]
scalar crit = invttail(e(df_r),.05)
scalar pval = ttail(e(df_r),t2)
scalar list t2 crit pval

* Linear combination
lincom -0.2*price-0.5*advert
scalar t = r(estimate)/r(se)
scalar crit = invttail(e(df_r),.05)
scalar pval = ttail(e(df_r),t)
```

```
scalar list crit t pval

return list

* Polynomial
generate a2 = advert*advert
reg sales price advert a2
scalar me1 = _b[advert]+2*(.5)*_b[a2]
scalar me2 = _b[advert]+2*(2)*_b[a2]
scalar list me1 me2

* Nonlinear combinations of variables
scalar advertt0 = (1-_b[advert])/(2*_b[a2])
scalar list advertt0

nlcom (1-_b[advert])/(2*_b[a2])

* Polynomial using factor variables
regress sales price advert c.advert#c.advert
margins, dydx(advert) at(advert=(.5 2))

* Interactions
use pizza4, clear
regress pizza age income c.age#c.income
margins, dydx(age) at(income=(25 90))

use cps4_small, clear
gen lwage = ln(wage)
regress lwage educ exper c.educ#c.exper
regress lwage educ exper c.educ#c.exper c.exper#c.exper

use andy, clear
reg sales price advert

di "R-square " e(mss)/(e(mss)+e(rss))
di "R-square " 1-e(rss)/(e(mss)+e(rss))
log close
```

CHAPTER **6**

Further Inference in the Multiple Regression Model

CHAPTER OUTLINE

6.1 THE *F*-TEST

The example used in this chapter is a model of sales for Big Andy's Burger Barn considered in Chapter 5. The model includes three explanatory variables and a constant:

$$SALES_i = \beta_1 + \beta_2 PRICE_i + \beta_3 ADVERT_i + \beta_4 ADVERT_i^2 + e_i$$

where $SALES_i$ is monthly sales in a given city and is measured in $1,000 increments, $PRICE_i$ is price of a hamburger measured in dollars, $ADVERT_i$ is the advertising expenditure also measured in thousands of dollars and $i=1, 2, \ldots, N$.

The null hypothesis is that advertising has no effect on average sales. For this marginal effect to be zero for all values of advertising requires $\beta_3 = 0$ and $\beta_4 = 0$. The alternative is $\beta_3 \neq 0$ or $\beta_4 \neq 0$. The parameters of the model under the null hypothesis are restricted to be zero and the parameters under the alternative are unrestricted.

The *F*-test compares the sum of squared errors from the unrestricted model to that of the restricted model. A large difference is taken as evidence that the restrictions are false. The statistic used to test the null hypothesis (restrictions) is

$$F = \frac{(SSE_R - SSE_U)/J}{SSE_U/(N-K)},$$

which has an F-distribution with J numerator and $N-K$ denominator degrees of freedom when the restrictions are true.

The statistic is computed by running two regressions. The first is unrestricted; the second has the restrictions imposed. Save the sum of squared errors from each regression, the degrees of freedom from the unrestricted regression ($N-K$), and the number of independent restrictions imposed (J). Then, compute the following:

$$F = \frac{(SSE_R - SSE_U)/J}{SSE_U/(N-K)} = \frac{(1896.391 - 1532.084)/2}{1532.084/(75-4)} = 8.44$$

To estimate this model load the data file *andy.dta*

```
use andy, clear
```

In Stata's variables window, you'll see that the data contain three variables: **sales, price**, and **advert**. These are used with the **regress** function to estimate the unrestricted model

```
regress sales price advert c.advert#c.advert
```

```
. regress sales price advert c.advert#c.advert
```

Source	SS	df	MS		Number of obs =	75
					F(3, 71) =	24.46
Model	1583.39741	3	527.799136		Prob > F =	0.0000
Residual	1532.08446	71	21.5786543		R-squared =	0.5082
					Adj R-squared =	0.4875
Total	3115.48187	74	42.1011063		Root MSE =	4.6453

sales	Coef.	Std. Err.	t	P>|t|	[95% Conf. Interval]	
price	-7.64	1.045939	-7.30	0.000	-9.725543	-5.554457
advert	12.15124	3.556164	3.42	0.001	5.060446	19.24203
c.advert#						
c.advert	-2.767963	.940624	-2.94	0.004	-4.643514	-.892412
_cons	109.719	6.799045	16.14	0.000	96.16212	123.2759

Save the sum of squared errors into a new scalar called **sseu** using **e(ssr)** and the residual degrees of freedom from the analysis of variance table into a variable called **df_unrest** using **e(df_r)**.

```
scalar sseu = e(ssr)
scalar df_unrest = e(df_r)
```

Next, impose the restriction on the model and reestimate it using least squares. Again, save the sum of squared errors and the residual degrees of freedom.

```
regress sales price
```

```
. regress sales price
```

Source	SS	df	MS
Model	1219.09103	1	1219.09103
Residual	1896.39084	73	25.9779567
Total	3115.48187	74	42.1011063

```
Number of obs =      75
F( 1,    73) =   46.93
Prob > F     =  0.0000
R-squared    =  0.3913
Adj R-squared = 0.3830
Root MSE     =  5.0969
```

sales	Coef.	Std. Err.	t	P>|t|	[95% Conf. Interval]	
price	-7.829074	1.142865	-6.85	0.000	-10.1068	-5.551348
_cons	121.9002	6.526291	18.68	0.000	108.8933	134.9071

```
scalar sser = e(ssr)
scalar df_rest = e(df_r)
```

The saved residual degrees of freedom from   the re stricted model can be used to obtain the number of restrictions imposed. Each unique restriction in a linear model reduces the number of parameters in the model by one. So, imposing one restriction on a three par ameter unrestricted model (e.g., Big Andy's) reduces the number of parameters in the restricted model to two. Let K_r be the number of regressors in the restricted model and K_u the number in the unrestricted model. Subtracting the degrees of freedom in the unrestricted m odel ($N-K_u$) from those of the restricted model ($N-K_r$) will yield the number of restrictions you've imposed, i.e., $(N-K_r) - (N-K_u) = (K_u-K_r) = J$. In Stata,

```
scalar J = df_rest - df_unrest
```

Then, the F-statistic can be computed

```
scalar fstat = ((sser-sseu)/J)/(sseu/(df_unrest))
```

The critical value from the $F_{(J,N-K)}$ distribution and th e p-value for the computed statistic can be computed in the usual way. In this case, **invFtail(J,N-K,α)** generates the α level critical value from the F-distribution with J numerator and $N-K$ denominator degrees of freedo m. The **Ftail(J,N-K,fstat)** function works si milarly to return the p-value for the co mputed statistic, **fstat**.

```
scalar crit1 = invFtail(J,df_unrest,.05)
scalar pvalue = Ftail(J,df_unrest,fstat)
scalar list sseu sser J df_unrest fstat pvalue crit1
```

The output for which is:

```
. scalar list sseu sser J df_unrest fstat pvalue crit1
      sseu =  1532.0845
      sser =  1896.3908
         J =          2
 df_unrest =         71
     fstat =    8.44136
    pvalue =  .00051416
     crit1 =  3.1257642
```

The dialog boxes can al so be used to t est restrictions on the parameters of the model. The first step is to estimate the model using **regress**. This proceeds just as it did in section 5.1 above. **Select Statistics > Linear models and related > Linear regression** from the pull-down menu. This reveals the **regress** dialog box. Using **sales** as the dependent variable and **price**, **advert**, and the interaction **c.advert#c.advertrt** as ind ependent variables in the **regress–Linear regression** dialog box, run the regression by clicking **OK**. Once the regression is estimated, post-estimation commands are used to test the hypothesis. From the pull-down menu select **Statistics > Postestimation > Tests > Test parameters**, which brings up the **testparm** dialog box:

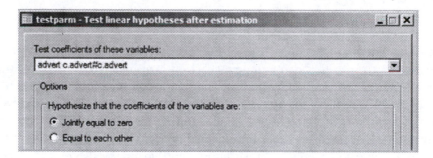

One can also use the test dialog box by selecting **Statistics > Postestimation > Tests > Test linear hypotheses**. The test dialog is harder to use. Each linear hypothesis must be entered as a *Specification*. F or *Specification 1 (required)* type in **advert=0** and make sure that either the *Coefficients are zero* or *Linear expressions are equal* radio butt on is selected. Then highlight *Specification 2* and type in **c.advert#c.advert=0** and click **Submit**. The d ialog box for this step is shown below:

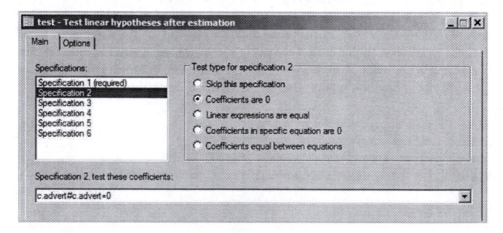

In both cases, the **Command** window is much easier to use. The **testparm** statement is the simplest to use for testing zero restrictions on the parameters. The syntax is

> testparm *varlist*

That means that one can simply list the variables that have zero coefficients under the null. It can also be coaxed into testing that coefficients are equal to one another using the **equal** option.

The **test** command can be used to test joint hypot heses about the param eters of the most recently fit model using a Wald test. There are several different ways to specify the hypotheses and a couple of these are explored here. The general syntax is

> test (hypothesis 1) (hypothesis 2)

Each of the joint hypotheses is enclosed in a set of parentheses. In a linear model the coefficients can be identified by their variable names, since their meaning is unam biguous. More generally, one can also use either parameter name, if pr eviously defined, or in the linear m odel the **_b[variable name]** syntax. Here are the three equivalent ways to test the joint null

```
regress sales price advert c.advert#c.advert
testparm advert c.advert#c.advert
test (advert=0)(c.advert#c.advert=0)
test (_b[advert]=0)(_b[c.advert#c.advert]=0)
```

```
. testparm advert c.advert#c.advert

 ( 1)   advert = 0
 ( 2)   c.advert#c.advert = 0

       F(  2,     71) =     8.44
            Prob > F =     0.0005

. test (advert=0)(c.advert#c.advert=0)

 ( 1)   advert = 0
 ( 2)   c.advert#c.advert = 0

       F(  2,     71) =     8.44
            Prob > F =     0.0005

. test (_b[advert]=0)(_b[c.advert#c.advert]=0)

 ( 1)   advert = 0
 ( 2)   c.advert#c.advert = 0

       F(  2,     71) =     8.44
            Prob > F =     0.0005
```

6.1.1 TESTING THE SIGNIFICANCE OF THE MODEL

In this applic ation of the F-test, you determine whether your m odel is signifi cant or not a t the desired level of statistical significance. Consider the general linear model with K regressors

$$y_i = \beta_1 + x_{i2}\beta_2 + x_{i3}\beta_3 + \cdots + x_{iK}\beta_K + e_i$$

If the explanatory variables have no effect on the average value of y then each of the slopes will be zero, leading to the null and alternative hypotheses:

$$H_0 : \beta_2 = 0, \ \beta_3 = 0, \ \cdots, \ \beta_K = 0$$
$$H_1 : At\ least\ one\ \text{of the}\ \beta_k\ \text{is nonzero for}\ k = 2,3,\ldots K$$

This amounts to $J=K-1$ restrictions. Again, estimate the model unrestricted, and restricted saving degrees of freedom for each. Then, use the Stata code from above to compute the test statistic:

$$F = \frac{(SST - SSE)/(K-1)}{SSE/(N-K)} = \frac{(3115.485 - 1532.084)/3}{1532.084/(75-4)} = 24.459$$

The Stata code is:

```
* Unrestricted Model (all variables)
regress sales price advert c.advert#c.advert
scalar sseu = e(rss)
scalar df_unrest = e(df_r)

* Restricted Model (no explanatory variables)
regress sales
scalar sser = e(rss)
scalar df_rest = e(df_r)
scalar J = df_rest - df_unrest

* F-statistic, critical value, pvalue
scalar fstat = ((sser -sseu)/J)/(sseu/(df_unrest))
scalar crit2 = invFtail(J,df_unrest,.05)
scalar pvalue = Ftail(J,df_unrest,fstat)

scalar list sseu sser J df_unrest fstat pvalue crit2
```

which produces:

```
. scalar list sseu sser J df_unrest fstat pvalue crit2
       sseu =   1532.0845
       sser =   3115.4819
          J =           3
  df_unrest =          71
      fstat =   24.459316
     pvalue =   5.600e-11
      crit2 =   2.7336472
```

This particular test of regression significance is important enough that it appears on the default output of every linear regression estimated using Stata. In the output below, the F-statistic for this test is 24.4595 and its p-value is well below 5%. Therefore, we reject the null hypothesis that the model is insignificant at the five percent level.

```
. regress sales price advert c.advert#c.advert
```

Source	SS	df	MS
Model	1583.39741	3	527.799136
Residual	1532.08446	71	21.5786543
Total	3115.48187	74	42.1011063

```
Number of obs =      75
F(  3,     71) =   24.46
Prob > F       =  0.0000
R-squared      =  0.5082
Adj R-squared  =  0.4875
Root MSE       =  4.6453
```

sales	Coef.	Std. Err.	t	P>|t|	[95% Conf. Interval]	
price	-7.64	1.045939	-7.30	0.000	-9.725543	-5.554457
advert	12.15124	3.556164	3.42	0.001	5.060446	19.24203
c.advert#c.advert	-2.767963	.940624	-2.94	0.004	-4.643514	-.892412
_cons	109.719	6.799045	16.14	0.000	96.16212	123.2759

6.1.2 Relationship between *t*- and *F*-tests

In this example, the equivalence of a t-test for   significance and an F-test is s hown. The basic model is

$$SALES_i = \beta_1 + \beta_2 PRICE_i + \beta_3 ADVERT_i + \beta_4 ADVERT_i^2 + e_i$$

The *t*-ratio for β_2 is equal to -7.30 (see the output at the end of section 6.1.2). The *F*-test can be used to test the hypothesi s that $\beta_2 = 0$ against the two-sided alternative that it is not zero. The restricted model is

$$SALES_i = \beta_1 + \beta_3 ADVERT_i + \beta_4 ADVERT_i^2 + e_i$$

Estimating the unrestricted model, the unrestricted model, and computing the *F*-statistic in Stata:

```
* Unrestricted Regression
regress sales price advert c.advert#c.advert
scalar sseu = e(rss)
scalar df_unrest = e(df_r)

scalar tratio = _b[price]/_se[price]
scalar t_sq = tratio^2

* Restricted Regression
regress sales advert c.advert#c.advert
scalar sser = e(rss)
scalar df_rest = e(df_r)
scalar J = df_rest - df_unrest

* F-statistic, critical value, pvalue
scalar fstat = ((sser -sseu)/J)/(sseu/(df_unrest))
scalar crit = invFtail(J,df_unrest,.05)
```

```
scalar pvalue = Ftail(J,df_unrest,fstat)

scalar list sseu sser J df_unrest fstat pvalue crit tratio t_sq
```

This produces the output:

```
. scalar list sseu sser J df_unrest fstat pvalue crit tratio t_sq
       sseu =    1532.0845
       sser =    2683.4109
          J =            1
  df_unrest =           71
      fstat =    53.354875
     pvalue =    3.236e-10
       crit =    3.9758102
     tratio =   -7.3044421
       t_sq =    53.354875
```

The F-statistic is 53.35. It is no coi ncidence that the square of the t-ratio is equal to the F: $-7.304^2 = 53.35$. The reason for this is the exact relationship between the t- and F-distributions. The square of a t random variable with df degrees of freedom is an F random variable with 1 degree of freedom in the numerator and df degrees of freedom in the denominator.

6.1.3 More General *F*-Tests

The F-test can also be used to t est hypotheses that are more general than ones involvi ng zero restrictions on the coefficients of regressors. Up to K conjectures involvin g linear hypotheses with equal signs can be tested. The test is performed in the same way by comparing the restricted sum of squar ed errors to i ts unrestricted value. To do this requires so me algebra by the user. Fortunately, Stata provides a couple of alternatives that avoid this.

The example considered is based on the optimal level of advertising first considered in Chapter 5. If the returns to advertising dim inish, then the optimal level of advertising will occur when the next dollar spent on adverti sing generates only one more dollar of sales. Setting the marginal effect of another (thousand) dollar on sales equal to 1:

$$\beta_3 + 2\beta_4 A_o = 1$$

and solving for A_O yields $\hat{A}_O = (1 - b_3)/2b_4$ where b_3 and b_4 are the least squares esti mates. Plugging in the results from the estimated model yields an estimated optimal level of adverti sing of 2.014 ($2014).

Suppose that Andy wants to test the conjecture that the optimal level of advertising is $1,900. Substituting 1.9 (remember, advertising in the data is measured in $1,000) l eads to null and alternative hypotheses:

$$H_0 : \beta_3 + 3.8\beta_4 = 1 \qquad H_1 : \beta_3 + 3.8\beta_4 \neq 1$$

The Stata commands to com pute the value of th is conjecture under the null hypothesis and its standard error are

```
lincom _b[advert]+3.8*_b[c.advert#c.advert]-1
```

Recall from previous chapters that the `lincomm` command computes linear com binations of parameters based on the regression that precedes it.

The output from **lincom** and the computation of the *t*-ratio is:

```
( 1)   advert + 3.8*c.advert#c.advert = 1
```

sales	Coef.	Std. Err.	t	P>|t|	[95% Conf. Interval]	
(1)	.6329759	.6541901	0.97	0.337	-.6714421	1.937394

Since the regression is linear, the simpler syntax can also be used to produce identical results:

```
lincom advert+3.8*c.advert#c.advert-1
```

In either case, an esti mate and standard e rror are generated and these quantities are saved in **r(estimate)** and **r(se)**, respectively. So, you can recall the m and use the **scalar** command to compute a *t*-ratio manually.

$$t = \frac{(b_3 + 3.8b_4) - 1}{se(b_3 + 3.8b_4)}$$

The commands to do this are:

```
scalar t = r(estimate)/r(se)
scalar pvalue2tail = 2*ttail(e(df_r),t)
scalar pvalue1tail = ttail(e(df_r),t)
scalar list t pvalue2tail pvalue1tail
```

The **ttail()** command is used to obtai n the one-sided *p*-value for the co mputed *t*-ratio. It uses **e(df_r)** which saves the residual degrees of fr eedom from the sales regression that precedes it s use.

The output is:

```
. scalar list t pvalue2tail pvalue1tail
          t =   .96757186
pvalue2tail =   .33654267
pvalue1tail =   .16827134
```

An algebraic trick can be used that wi ll enable y ou to rearr ange the model in terms of a new parameter that em bodies the desired restriction. Th is is useful if using software that does not contain something like the **lincom** command. Let $\theta = \beta_3 + 3.8\beta_4 - 1$, be the rest riction. Solve for $\beta_3 = \theta + 1 - 3.8\beta_4$, substitute this into the model and rearrange and you'll get

$$SALES_i - ADVERT_i = \beta_1 + \beta_2 PRICE_i + \theta ADVERT_i + \beta_4(ADVERT_i^2 - 3.8ADVERT_i) + e_i$$

The coefficient on advertising contains the complete restriction. Use a *t*-ratio on its coefficient, θ, to test w hether the restriction is true.   In Stata,   create   two   new   variables $x_i = ADVERT_i^2 - 3.8 ADVERT_i$ and $y_i = SALES_i - ADVERT_i$.

```
gen xstar = c.advert#c.advert-3.8*advert
gen ystar = sales - advert
```

These use these in a regression.

```
regress ystar price advert xstar
```

The *t*-ratio on the variable **advert** is the desired statistic. Its two-sided *p*-value is given in the output. If you want to compute this manually, try the following

```
scalar t = (_b[advert])/_se[advert]
scalar pvalue = ttail(e(df_r),t)
scalar list t pvalue
```

The output for the entire routine follows:

```
. regress ystar price advert xstar
```

Source	SS	df	MS
Model	1457.21493	3	485.738311
Residual	1532.08447	71	21.5786545
Total	2989.2994	74	40.3959379

Number of obs =	75
F(3, 71) =	22.51
Prob > F =	0.0000
R-squared =	0.4875
Adj R-squared =	0.4658
Root MSE =	4.6453

ystar	Coef.	Std. Err.	t	P>|t|	[95% Conf.	Interval]
price	-7.64	1.045939	-7.30	0.000	-9.725542	-5.554457
advert	.632976	.6541901	0.97	0.337	-.671442	1.937394
xstar	-2.767964	.9406241	-2.94	0.004	-4.643515	-.8924125
_cons	109.719	6.799046	16.14	0.000	96.16212	123.2759

```
. scalar t = (_b[advert])/_se[advert]

. scalar pvalue = ttail(e(df_r),t)

. scalar list t pvalue
        t =   .96757201
   pvalue =    .1682713
```

The *t*-ratio in the regression table is   0.97 and has a two-sided p-value of   0.337. The *t*-ratio computed using the scalar command is the same (though carried to more digits) and its one-sided *p*-value is half that of the two-sided one in the table. The results match.

    This section concludes with a joint test of   two of Big Andy's conjectures. In addition to proposing that the optimal level of m   onthly advertising expenditure is $ 1,900, Big A ndy is planning the staffing and purchasing of inputs on t he assumption that a price of *PRICE* = $6 and advertising expenditure of *ADVERT* =1.9 will, on average, y ield sales re venue of $80,000. The joint null hypothesis is

$$H_0: \quad \beta_3 + 3.8\beta_4 = 1 \quad \text{and} \quad \beta_1 + 6\beta_2 + 1.9\beta_3 + 3.61\beta_4 = 80$$

against the alternative that at least one of the c onjectures is not true. The Stata code for the joint test is:

```
regress sales price advert c.advert#c.advert
test (_b[advert]+3.8*_b[c.advert#c.advert]=1) (_b[_cons] + ///
6*_b[price] + 1.9*_b[advert]+3.61*_b[c.advert#c.advert]= 80)
```

This example uses the **test** command, which is followed by both restrictions, each contained in a separate set of parentheses. Notice that **test** uses the s aved coefficient estimates **_b[varname]** from the preceding regression. Once again, this can be simplified in a linear regression by using the variable names alone.

```
test (advert+3.8*c.advert#c.advert=1) (_cons + 6*price + ///
1.9*advert+3.61*c.advert#c.advert= 80)
```

The results are:

```
. test (_b[advert]+3.8*_b[c.advert#c.advert]=1) ///
>       (_b[_cons]+6*_b[price]+1.9*_b[advert]+3.61*_b[c.advert#c.advert]= 80)

 ( 1)   advert + 3.8*c.advert#c.advert = 1
 ( 2)   6*price + 1.9*advert + 3.61*c.advert#c.advert + _cons = 80

       F(  2,     71) =     5.74
            Prob > F =     0.0049
```

Since the p-value is 0.0049 and less than 5%, the null (joint) hypothesis is rejected at that level of significance.

6.2 Nonsample Information

Sometimes you have exact nonsam ple information that you want to use in the esti mation of the model. Using nonsample information improves the precision with which y ou can estimate the remaining parameters. In this example from *POE4*, the authors consider a model of beer sales as a function of beer prices, liquor prices, pr ices of other goods, and inco me. The variables appear in their natural logarithms

$$\ln(Q_t) = \beta_1 + \beta_2 \ln(PB_t) + \beta_3 \ln(PL_t) + \beta_4 \ln(PR_t) + \beta_5 \ln(I_t) + e_t$$

Economic theory suggests that

$$\beta_2 + \beta_3 + \beta_4 + \beta_5 = 0$$

The *beer.dta* data file is used to estimate the model. Open the data file:

```
use beer, clear
```

Then, generate the natural logarithm s of each variable for your dataset. The Stata function `log(variable)` is used to take the natural logarithm of `variable`. So, to generate natural logs of each variable, use:

```
use beer, clear
gen lq = ln(q)
gen lpb = ln(pb)
gen lpl = ln(pl)
gen lpr = ln(pr)
gen li = ln(i)
```

In order to impose linear restrictions you will use what Stata calls **constrained regression**. Stata calls the restriction a **constraint**, and the procedure it uses to impose those constraints on a linear regression model is **cnsreg**. The syntax looks like this:

```
constraint 1
constraint 2
cnsreg depvar indepvars [if] [in] [weight] , constraints(1 2)
```

Each of the restrictions (constraints) are listed first and given a unique number. Once these are in memory, the **cnsreg** command is used like **regress**; follow the regression model with a comma, and the list of constraint numbers **constraint(1 2 ...)** and Stata will impose the enumerated constraints and use least squares to esti mate the re maining parameters. The **constraint** command can be abbreviated **c(1 2)** as shown below. For the beer example the syntax is:

```
constraint 1 lpb+lpl+lpr+li=0
cnsreg lq lpb lpl lpr li, c(1)
```

The result is

```
. constraint 1 lpb+lpl+lpr+li=0

. cnsreg lq lpb lpl lpr li, c(1)
```

Constrained linear regression	Number of obs	=	30
	F(3, 26) =		36.46
	Prob > F	=	0.0000
	Root MSE	=	0.0617

(1)   lpb + lpl + lpr + li = 0

lq	Coef.	Std. Err.	t	P>|t|	[95% Conf. Interval]	
lpb	-1.299387	.1657377	-7.84	0.000	-1.640065	-.958708
lpl	.1868161	.2843833	0.66	0.517	-.3977422	.7713744
lpr	.1667424	.0770752	2.16	0.040	.0083121	.3251727
li	.9458282	.4270468	2.21	0.036	.0680209	1.823635
_cons	-4.797793	3.713905	-1.29	0.208	-12.43183	2.836247

The pull-down menus can also be used to obtain these results, though with m ore effort. First, the constraint must be defined. Select **Statistics > Other > Manage Constraints**

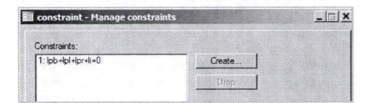

Click on the **Create** button to bring up the dialog box used to number and define the constraints.

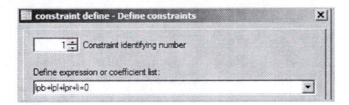

Choose the constraint nu mber and ty pe in the desired restri ction in the **Define expression** box. Click **OK** to accept the constraint and to close the box. To add constraints click **Create** again in the **constraint—Manage constraints** box. When finished, click **Close** to close the box. To estimate the restricted model, select **Statistics > Linear models and related > Constrained linear regression** from the pull-down menu as shown:

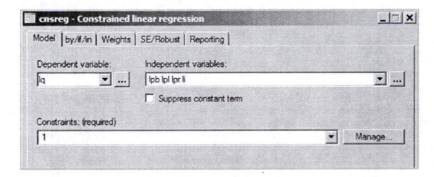

Click **OK** or **Submit** to estimate the constrained model.

6.3 MODEL SPECIFICATION

Three essential features of model choice are (1) choice of functional form , (2) choic e of explanatory variables (regressors) to be include d in the m odel, and (3) whether the m ultiple regression model assumptions MR1–MR6, listed in Chap ter 5, hold. In this sec tion the first two of these are explored.

6.3.1 Omitted Variables

If you omit relevant variables from your model, then least squares is biased. To introduce the **omitted variable problem**, we consider a sample of married couples where b oth husbands and wives work. The data are stored in the file *edu_inc.dta*.

Open the data file and clear any previously held data from Stata's memory

```
use edu_inc, clear
```

The first regression includes family income as the dependent variable (**faminc**) and husband's education (**he**) and wife's education (**we**) as explanatory variables. From the command line

```
regress faminc he we
```

The result is

```
. regress faminc he we
```

Source	SS	df	MS			Number of obs =	428
						F(2, 425) =	40.87
Model	1.3405e+11	2	6.7027e+10			Prob > F =	0.0000
Residual	6.9703e+11	425	1.6401e+09			R-squared =	0.1613
						Adj R-squared =	0.1574
Total	8.3109e+11	427	1.9463e+09			Root MSE =	40498

faminc	Coef.	Std. Err.	t	P>|t|	[95% Conf. Interval]	
he	3131.509	802.908	3.90	0.000	1553.344	4709.674
we	4522.641	1066.327	4.24	0.000	2426.711	6618.572
_cons	-5533.629	11229.53	-0.49	0.622	-27605.97	16538.71

Omitting wife's education (**we**) yields:

```
. regress faminc he
```

Source	SS	df	MS			Number of obs =	428
						F(1, 426) =	61.30
Model	1.0455e+11	1	1.0455e+11			Prob > F =	0.0000
Residual	7.2654e+11	426	1.7055e+09			R-squared =	0.1258
						Adj R-squared =	0.1237
Total	8.3109e+11	427	1.9463e+09			Root MSE =	41297

faminc	Coef.	Std. Err.	t	P>|t|	[95% Conf. Interval]	
he	5155.483	658.4574	7.83	0.000	3861.254	6449.713
_cons	26191.27	8541.108	3.07	0.002	9403.309	42979.23

Simple correlation analysis reveals that husband and wife's education levels are positively correlated. As suggested in the text, this implies that omitting **we** from the model is likely to cause positive bias in the **he** coefficient. This is borne out in the estimated models.

```
. correlate
(obs=428)
```

	faminc	he	we	k16	xtra_x5	xtra_x6
faminc	1.0000					
he	0.3547	1.0000				
we	0.3623	0.5943	1.0000			
k16	-0.0720	0.1049	0.1293	1.0000		
xtra_x5	0.2898	0.8362	0.5178	0.1487	1.0000	
xtra_x6	0.3514	0.8206	0.7993	0.1595	0.9002	1.0000

Including wife's education and number of preschool age children (**k16**) yields:

```
. regress faminc he we k16
```

Source	SS	df	MS
Model	1.4725e+11	3	4.9082e+10
Residual	6.8384e+11	424	1.6128e+09
Total	8.3109e+11	427	1.9463e+09

```
Number of obs =      428
F( 3,   424) =    30.43
Prob > F      =   0.0000
R-squared     =   0.1772
Adj R-squared =   0.1714
Root MSE      =    40160
```

faminc	Coef.	Std. Err.	t	P>|t|	[95% Conf.	Interval]
he	3211.526	796.7026	4.03	0.000	1645.547	4777.504
we	4776.907	1061.164	4.50	0.000	2691.111	6862.704
k16	-14310.92	5003.928	-2.86	0.004	-24146.52	-4475.326
_cons	-7755.33	11162.93	-0.69	0.488	-29696.91	14186.25

Notice that compared to the preceding regression, the coefficient estimates for **he** and **we** have not changed much. This occurs because **k16** is not strongly correlated with the either of the education variables. It implies that useful results can still be obtained even if a relevant variable is omitted. What is required is that that the omitted variable be uncorrelated with the included variables of interest, which in this example are the education variables. It this is the case, omitting a relevant variable will not affect the validity of the tests and confidence intervals involving **we** or **he**.

6.3.2 Irrelevant Variables

Including irrelevant variables in the model diminishes the precision of the least squares estimator. Least squares is unbiased, but the standard errors of the coefficients will be bigger than necessary. In this example, two irrelevant variables (**xtra_x5** and **xtra_x6**) are added to the model. These variables are correlated with **he** and **we**, but they are not related to the mean of family income. Estimate the model using linear regression to obtain:

```
. regress faminc he we k16 xtra_x5 xtra_x6
```

Source	SS	df	MS
Model	1.4776e+11	5	2.9553e+10
Residual	6.8332e+11	422	1.6192e+09
Total	8.3109e+11	427	1.9463e+09

Number of obs =	428
F(5, 422) =	18.25
Prob > F =	0.0000
R-squared =	0.1778
Adj R-squared =	0.1681
Root MSE =	40240

faminc	Coef.	Std. Err.	t	P>|t|	[95% Conf. Interval]	
he	3339.792	1250.039	2.67	0.008	882.7131	5796.871
we	5868.677	2278.067	2.58	0.010	1390.905	10346.45
k16	-14200.18	5043.72	-2.82	0.005	-24114.13	-4286.242
xtra_x5	888.8426	2242.491	0.40	0.692	-3519.001	5296.686
xtra_x6	-1067.186	1981.685	-0.54	0.590	-4962.389	2828.018
_cons	-7558.613	11195.41	-0.68	0.500	-29564.33	14447.1

Notice how much larger the estimated standard errors become compared to those in the preceding regression. If they had been uncorrelated with **he** and **we**, then we would expect to see very little effect on their standard errors.

6.3.3 Choosing the Model

Choosing the appropriate set of variables to include and a suitable functional form is as much art as science. Ideally, one you want to choose a functional form that captures the relevant features of the data and variables that allow consistent and efficient estimation of the parameters of interest.

In this section statistics that are often used for ad hoc variable selection and test the adequacy of functional form are considered.

Model Selection Criteria

Three model selection criteria are considered: adjusted-R^2, AIC, and SC (BIC). These statistics can be useful in deciding among alternative models, though their use is not without controversy. In any event, they should only be used when all other sources of model specification have been exhausted. That is use theory and common sense to the extent you can and resort to model selection rules only for additional information about the relative merits of alternative models. With that warning aside, let's proceed.

In Chapter 5, the adjusted R^2 was introduced as an alternative measure of least squares fit that overcomes a well-known problem with the usual R^2, namely that it never gets smaller when regressors are added to the model. The adjusted R^2 imposes a penalty on the fit from adding a regressor. If the improvement in fit is very small relative to the penalty, then the adjusted R^2 may get smaller when an irrelevant regressor is added to the model. The adjusted R^2 is:

$$\overline{R}^2 = 1 - \frac{SSE/(N-K)}{SST/(N-1)}$$

This statistic is reported by default by Stata's **regress** command.

The other model selection rules considered are the **Akaike information criterion** (AIC) given by

$$AIC = \ln\left(\frac{SSE}{N}\right) + 2\frac{K}{N}$$

and the Bayesian information criterion (SC) given by

$$SC = \ln\left(\frac{SSE}{N}\right) + 2\frac{K\ln(N)}{N}$$

The two statistics ar e very si milar and consist of two terms. The first is a   measure of fit; the better the fit, the smaller the SSE and the smaller its natural logarithm. Adding a regressor cannot increase the size of this term. The second term is a penalty imposed on the criterion for adding a regressor. As K increases , the penalty gets larg er. The idea is to pick the m odel among competing ones that m inimizes either AIC or SC.   They differ only in how large the penal ty is, with SC's being slightly larger.

These criteria are available in Stata, but are co mputed differently. Stata's versions wer e developed for use under a larger set of d ata generation processes than the one considered here, so by all means use them if the need arises.[1]

These criteria are used repeatedly in *Principles of Econometrics, 4ᵗʰ Edition* and one goal of this manual is to replicate their results. Therefore, it is a good idea to write a **program** to compute and display the three model selection rules; once written the program can be run multiple times to compare various model specifications. In Chapter 9, the model selection program is revisited and used within programming loops.

In Stata a program is a structure that allows one to execute blocks of code b y simply typing the program's name. In t he example below, a progra m called **modelsel** is created. Ea ch time **modelsel** is typed in t he **Command** window, the li nes of code within the pr ogram will run. I n this case, the program will compute AIC, SC, and print out the value of adjusted R^2, all based on the previously run regression.

Here's how programming works in Stata. A program starts by issu ing the **program** command and giving it a name, e.g., ***progname***. A block of Stata commands to be executed each time the program is run are then written. The program is closed by **end**. Here's the basic structure:

```
program progname
     Stata commands
end
```

After writing the program , it must be compiled. If the program is put in a sep arate .do file then just run the .do file in the usual way. If the pro gram resides alo ng with other code in a .do file, then highlight the pro gram code, and ex ecute the fragment in the u sual way. The program only needs to be compiled once. The program is executed by typing the program's name, ***progname,*** at Stata's dot prompt.

The **modelsel** program is:

```
program modelsel
   scalar aic = ln(e(rss)/e(N))+2*e(rank)/e(N)
```

---

[1] In fact, Stata's post-estimation command **estat ic** uses $AIC = -2\ln(L) + 2k$ and $BIC = -2\ln(L) + k\ln(N)$, where L is the value of the maximized likelihood function when the errors of the model are normally distributed.

```
        scalar bic = ln(e(rss)/e(N))+e(rank)*ln(e(N))/e(N)
        di "r-square = "e(r2) " and adjusted r_square " e(r2_a)
        scalar list aic bic
end
```

The program will reside in m emory until you end your Stata session or tell Stata to drop the program from memory. This is acco mplished in either of two way s. First, **program drop** *progname* will drop the gi ven program (i.e., *progname*) from memory. The other method is to drop all programs from memory using **program drop _all**. Only use this method if you want to clear all user defined programs from Stata's memory.

This particular program uses results that are produced and stored by Stata after a regression is run. Several of these will be fa miliar already. **e(rss)** contains the su m of squared errors and **e(N)** the sam ple size. The new res ult used is **e(rank),** which basically measures how many independent variables you have in t he model, excluding any that are perfectly collinear with the others. In an identified regression model, this ge nerally measures the number of coefficients in the model, K.

Within the body of the program the scalars **aic** and **bic** (sometimes called SC—the Schwartz criterion) are computed and a **display** command is issued to print out the value of adjusted R^2 in the model. Finally, the **scalar list** command is given to pri nt out the computed values of the scalars.

To estimate a model and compute the model selection rules derived from it run the **modelsel** program if you haven't already. Then, estimate the regression and type **modelsel**. For instance

```
    quietly regress faminc he
    di "Model 1 (he) "
    modelsel
    estimates store Model1
```

This produces:

```
. di "Model 1 (he) "
Model 1 (he)

. modelsel
r-square = .12580103 and adjusted r_square .12374892
      aic =  21.261776
      bic =  21.280744
```

To use the model selection rules, run **modelsel** after each model and choose the one that either has the largest adjusted R^2 (usually a bad idea) or the smallest AIC or BIC (better, but not a great idea).

```
    quietly regress faminc he we
    di "Model 2 (he, we) "
    modelsel
    estimates store Model2
    quietly regress faminc he we k16
    di "Model 3 (he, we, k16) "
    modelsel
    estimates store Model3
```

```
        quietly regress faminc he we k16 xtra_x5 xtra_x6
        di "Model 4 (he, we, k16. x5, x6) "
        modelsel
        estimates store Model4

. di "Model 2 (he, we) "
Model 2 (he, we)

. modelsel
r-square = .16130044 and adjusted r_square .15735362
       aic =  21.224993
       bic =  21.253445

. di "Model 3 (he, we, k16) "
Model 3 (he, we, k16)

. modelsel
r-square = .17717332 and adjusted r_square .17135143
       aic =  21.210559
       bic =  21.248495

. di "Model 4 (he, we, k16. x5, x6) "
Model 4 (he, we, k16. x5, x6)

. modelsel
r-square = .17779646 and adjusted r_square .16805472
       aic =  21.219148
       bic =  21.276051
```

In the example, Stata's **estimates store** command is issued after each model and the results are accumulated using the **estimates table** command

```
    estimates table Model1 Model2 Model3 Model4, b(%9.3f) stfmt(%9.3f) ///
              se stats(N r2 r2_a aic bic)
```

Variable	Model1	Model2	Model3	Model4
he	5155.483	3131.509	3211.526	3339.792
	658.457	802.908	796.703	1250.039
we		4522.641	4776.907	5868.677
		1066.327	1061.164	2278.067
k16			-1.43e+04	-1.42e+04
			5003.928	5043.720
xtra_x5				888.843
				2242.491
xtra_x6				-1067.186
				1981.685
_cons	26191.270	-5533.629	-7755.330	-7558.613
	8541.108	11229.533	11162.935	11195.411
N	428	428	428	428
r2	0.126	0.161	0.177	0.178
r2_a	0.124	0.157	0.171	0.168
aic	10314.652	10298.909	10292.731	10296.407
bic	10322.770	10311.086	10308.967	10320.761

legend: b/se

In this table produced by Stata, Stata's versions of the **aic** and **bic** statistics computed for each regression are used. Obviously, Stata is using a different computation! No worries though, both sets of computations are valid and lead to the sa me conclusion. The largerst $\overline{R}^2$ is from Model 3 as are the smallest **aic** and **bic** statistics. It is clear that Model 3 is the preferred specificati on in this example.

Functional Form

Although theoretical considerations should be your primary guide to functional form selection, there are many instances when economic theory or common sense isn't enough. This is where the RESET test is useful. RESET can be used as a crude check to determine whether you've made an obvious error in specifying the functi onal form. It is NOT really a test for omitted variables; instead it is a test of the adequacy of your functional form.

The test is simple. The null hypothesis is that your functional form is adequate; the alternative is that it is not. Estim ate the regression assu ming that functional form is corre ct and obtain the predicted values. Square a nd cube these, add the m back to the m odel, reestimate the regression and perform a joint test of the significance of $\hat{y}^2$ and $\hat{y}^3$.

There are actually several variants of this test. The first adds only $\hat{y}^2$ to the m odel and tests its significance using either an F-test or the equivalent t-test. The second add both $\hat{y}^2$ and $\hat{y}^3$ and then does a j oint test of t heir significance. We'll refer to these as RESET(1) and RESET (2), respectively.

The example is again based on the fa mily income regression. Estimate the model using least squares and use the **predict** statement to save the linear predictions from the regression

```
regress faminc he we k16
predict yhat
```

Recall that the syntax to obtain the in-sample predicted values from a regression, $\hat{y}_i$, is **predict yhat, xb.** In this command **yhat** is a name that you designate. We can safely omit the **xb** option since this is Stata's default setting. Now, generate the squares and cubes of $\hat{y}_i$ using

```
gen yhat2 = yhat^2
gen yhat3 = yhat^3
```

Estimate the original regression with **yhat2** added to the model. Test **yhat2**'s significance using a t-test or an *F*-test. For the latter use Stata's **test** command as shown.

```
regress faminc he we k16 yhat2
test yhat2
```

The test result is

```
. test yhat2

 ( 1)   yhat2 = 0
        Constraint 1 dropped

        F(  0,   423) =         .
            Prob > F =               .
```

Obviously there is a problem with this formulation. Stata tells us that the constraint was dropped leaving nothing to test! The problem is that the data are **ill-conditioned**. For the computer to be able to do the arithmetic, it needs the variables to be of a similar magnitude in the dataset. Take a look at the summary statistics for the variables in the model.

```
. summarize faminc he we k16
```

Variable	Obs	Mean	Std. Dev.	Min	Max
faminc	428	91213	44117.35	9072	344146.3
he	428	12.61215	3.035163	4	17
we	428	12.65888	2.285376	5	17
k16	428	.1401869	.3919231	0	2

The magnitude of **faminc** is 1,000s of times larger than the other variables. The predictions from a linear regression will be of similar scale. When these are squared and cubed as required by the RESET tests, the conditioning worsens to the point that your computer can't do the arithmetic. The solution is to rescale **faminc** so that its magnitude is more in line with that of the other variables. Recall that in linear regression, rescaling dependent and independent variables only affects the magnitudes of the coefficients, not any of the substantive outcomes of the regression. So, drop the ill-conditioned predictions from the data and rescale **faminc** by dividing it by 10,000.

```
drop yhat yhat2 yhat3
gen faminc_sc = faminc/10000
```

Now, estimate the model, save the predictions and generate the squares and cubes.

```
regress faminc_sc he we k16
```

```
. regress faminc_sc he we k16
```

Source	SS	df	MS
Model	1472.46499	3	490.821663
Residual	6838.40844	424	16.1283218
Total	8310.87343	427	19.4634038

```
Number of obs =      428
F( 3,   424) =    30.43
Prob > F      =   0.0000
R-squared     =   0.1772
Adj R-squared =   0.1714
Root MSE      =    4.016
```

faminc_sc	Coef.	Std. Err.	t	P>|t|	[95% Conf. Interval]	
he	.3211526	.0796703	4.03	0.000	.1645547	.4777504
we	.4776908	.1061164	4.50	0.000	.2691111	.6862704
k16	-1.431092	.5003928	-2.86	0.004	-2.414652	-.4475326
_cons	-.775533	1.116293	-0.69	0.488	-2.969691	1.418625

```
predict yhat
gen yhat2 = yhat^2
gen yhat3 = yhat^3
```

For RESET(1) add **yhat2** to the model and test its significance using its t-ratio or an F-test.

```
. regress faminc_sc he we k16 yhat2
```

Source	SS	df	MS
Model	1567.85524	4	391.963811
Residual	6743.01819	423	15.9409413
Total	8310.87343	427	19.4634038

Number of obs = 428
F(4, 423) = 24.59
Prob > F = 0.0000
R-squared = 0.1887
Adj R-squared = 0.1810
Root MSE = 3.9926

faminc_sc	Coef.	Std. Err.	t	P>|t|	[95% Conf. Interval]	
he	-.2381465	.2419692	-0.98	0.326	-.7137582	.2374653
we	-.4235108	.383214	-1.11	0.270	-1.176752	.32973
k16	1.088733	1.143928	0.95	0.342	-1.159757	3.337224
yhat2	.099368	.0406211	2.45	0.015	.0195237	.1792123
_cons	8.724297	4.03894	2.16	0.031	.785406	16.66319

```
. test yhat2

 ( 1)  yhat2 = 0

        F(  1,   423) =     5.98
             Prob > F =    0.0148
```

Once again, the squared value of the t-ratio is equal to the F-statistic and they have the same p-value. For RESET(2), add **yhat3** and test the joint significance of the squared and cubed predictions:

```
. regress faminc_sc he we k16 yhat2 yhat3
```

Source	SS	df	MS
Model	1572.19036	5	314.438072
Residual	6738.68307	422	15.9684433
Total	8310.87343	427	19.4634038

Number of obs = 428
F(5, 422) = 19.69
Prob > F = 0.0000
R-squared = 0.1892
Adj R-squared = 0.1796
Root MSE = 3.9961

faminc_sc	Coef.	Std. Err.	t	P>|t|	[95% Conf. Interval]	
he	-.8451478	1.189891	-0.71	0.478	-3.184	1.493704
we	-1.301625	1.72841	-0.75	0.452	-4.698991	2.095741
k16	3.741007	5.217535	0.72	0.474	-6.514588	13.9966
yhat2	.3234728	.4320297	0.75	0.454	-.5257254	1.172671
yhat3	-.0085692	.0164465	-0.52	0.603	-.0408965	.023758
_cons	15.01857	12.73868	1.18	0.239	-10.0206	40.05774

```
. test yhat2 yhat3

 ( 1)  yhat2 = 0
 ( 2)  yhat3 = 0

        F(  2,   422) =     3.12
             Prob > F =    0.0451
```

Both RESET(1) and RESET(2) are significant at the 5% level and you can conclude that the original linear functional form is not adequate to model this relationship.

Stata includes a post-estimation command that will perform a RESET(3) test after a regression. The syntax is

```
regress faminc he we k16
estat ovtest
```

```
. estat ovtest
```

```
Ramsey RESET test using powers of the fitted values of faminc
        Ho:   model has no omitted variables
                F(3, 421) =        2.15
                 Prob > F =       0.0931
```

This version of RESET adds $\hat{y}^2$, $\hat{y}^3$, and $\hat{y}^4$ to the model and tests their joint significance. Technically there is nothing wrong wit h this. However, includin g this many powers of $\hat{y}$ is not often recommended since the RESET loses statistical power rapidly as powers of $\hat{y}$ are added.

6.4 POOR DATA, COLLINEARITY AND INSIGNIFICANCE

In the preceding section we mentioned that one of Stata's computations fails due to poor conditioning of the data. This is si milar to wh at collinearity does to a regression. Collinearit y makes it difficult or im possible to compute the pa rameter estimates and variou s other statistics with much precision. In a statistical model collinearity arises because of p oor experimental design, or in our case, because of data that don' t vary enough to permit precise measurement of the parameters. Unfortunately, there is no simple cure for this; rescaling the data has no effect on the linear relationships contained therein.

The example here uses *cars.dta*. Load the cars data, clearing any previous data out of memory

```
use cars, clear
```

A look at the summary statistics (**summarize**) reveals reasonable variation in the data

```
. summarize
```

Variable	Obs	Mean	Std. Dev.	Min	Max
mpg	392	23.44592	7.805007	9	46.6
cyl	392	5.471939	1.705783	3	8
eng	392	194.412	104.644	68	455
wgt	392	2977.584	849.4026	1613	5140

Each of the variables contains variation as measured by their ra nge and standard deviatio ns. Simple correlations (**corr**) reveal a potential problem.

```
. corr
(obs=392)
```

	mpg	cyl	eng	wgt
mpg	1.0000			
cyl	-0.7776	1.0000		
eng	-0.8051	0.9508	1.0000	
wgt	-0.8322	0.8975	0.9330	1.0000

Notice that among the potential explanatory variables (cyl, eng, wgt), the correlations are very high; the smallest occurs between cyl and wgt and it is nearly 0.9. Estimating independent effects of each of these variables on miles per gallon will prove challenging.

First, estimate a simple model of miles per gallon (mpg) as a function of the number of cylinders (cyl) in the engine.

regress mpg cyl

. regress mpg cyl

Source	SS	df	MS
Model	14403.0831	1	14403.0831
Residual	9415.91039	390	24.14336
Total	23818.9935	391	60.9181419

Number of obs =   392
F(1,   390) = 596.56
Prob > F   = 0.0000
R-squared   = 0.6047
Adj R-squared = 0.6037
Root MSE   = 4.9136

mpg	Coef.	Std. Err.	t	P>|t|	[95% Conf. Interval]	
cyl	-3.558078	.1456755	-24.42	0.000	-3.844486	-3.271671
_cons	42.91551	.8348668	51.40	0.000	41.2741	44.55691

Add the car's engine displacement in cubic inches (eng) weight (wgt) to the model.

regress mpg cyl eng wgt

. regress mpg cyl eng wgt

Source	SS	df	MS
Model	16656.4443	3	5552.1481
Residual	7162.54916	388	18.4601782
Total	23818.9935	391	60.9181419

Number of obs =   392
F(3,   388) = 300.76
Prob > F   = 0.0000
R-squared   = 0.6993
Adj R-squared = 0.6970
Root MSE   = 4.2965

mpg	Coef.	Std. Err.	t	P>|t|	[95% Conf. Interval]	
cyl	-.2677968	.4130673	-0.65	0.517	-1.079927	.5443336
eng	-.012674	.0082501	-1.54	0.125	-.0288944	.0035465
wgt	-.0057079	.0007139	-8.00	0.000	-.0071115	-.0043043
_cons	44.37096	1.480685	29.97	0.000	41.45979	47.28213

Now, test a series of hypotheses. The first is for the significance of cyl, the second for the significance of eng, and the third is of their joint significance.

test cyl
test eng
test cyl eng

The results are:

```
. test cyl

 ( 1)   cyl = 0

        F(  1,    388) =      0.42
                Prob > F =    0.5172

. test eng

 ( 1)   eng = 0

        F(  1,    388) =      2.36
                Prob > F =    0.1253

. test eng cyl

 ( 1)   eng = 0
 ( 2)   cyl = 0

        F(  2,    388) =      4.30
                Prob > F =    0.0142
```

Essentially, neither of the variables is individually significant, but they are jointly significant at the 5% level. This can happen because you were not able to measure their separate influences precisely enough. As revealed by the simple correlations, the independent variables **cyl**, **eng**, and **wgt** are highly correlated with one another. This can be verified by estimating several auxiliary regressions where each of the independent variables is regressed on all of the others.

```
        regress cyl eng wgt
           scalar r1 = e(r2)
        regress eng wgt cyl
           scalar r2 = e(r2)
        regress wgt eng cyl
           scalar r3 = e(r2)
```

An R^2 above 0.8 indicates strong collinearity which may adversely affect the precision with which you can estimate the parameters of a model that contains all the variables. In the example, the R^2s are 0.93, 0.90, and 0.87, all well above the 0.8 threshold. This is further confirmation that it will be difficult to differentiate the individual contributions of displacement and number of cylinders to a car's gas mileage.

```
. scalar list r1 r2 r3
         r1 =   .90490236
         r2 =   .93665456
         r3 =   .87160914
```

The advantage of using auxiliary regressions instead of simple correlations to detect collinearity is not that obvious in this particular example. Collinearity may be hard to detect using correlations when there are many variables in the regression. Although no two variables may be highly correlated, several variables may be linearly related in ways that are not apparent. Looking at the R^2 from the auxiliary multiple regressions will be more useful in these situations.

KEY TERMS

adjusted R^2	F-statistic	**regress**
AIC	functional form	RESET
BIC	**invFtail(J,N_K,alpha)**	restricted regression
cnsreg	**invttail(df,alpha)**	restricted sum of squares
collinearity	**irrelevant variables**	Schwartz criterion
constraint	joint significance test	**test (hypoth 1)(hypoth 2)**
e(df_r)	**lincom**	**testparm varlist**
e(r2)	Manage constraints	t-ratio
e(r2_a)	model selection	**ttail(df,tstat)**
e(rank)	omitted variables	unrestricted sum of squares
e(rss)	overall F-test	
estat ovtest	**predict, xb**	
estimates store	**program**	
estimates table	**program drop** *progname*	
Ftail(J,N-K,fstat)	**program drop _all**	

CHAPTER 6 DO-FILE [CHAP06.DO]

```
* file chap06.do for Using Stata for Principles of Econometrics, 4e

cd c:\data\poe4stata

* Stata Do-file
* copyright C 2011 by Lee C. Adkins and R. Carter Hill
* used for "Using Stata for Principles of Econometrics, 4e"
* by Lee C. Adkins and R. Carter Hill (2011)
* John Wiley and Sons, Inc.

* setup
version 11.1
capture log close
set more off

* open log
log using chap06, replace text

use andy, clear

* -------------------------------------------
* The following block estimates Andy's sales
* and uses the difference in SSE to test
* a hypothesis using an F-statistic
* -------------------------------------------

* Unrestricted Model
regress sales price advert c.advert#c.advert
scalar sseu = e(rss)
scalar df_unrest = e(df_r)

* Restricted Model
```

```
regress sales price
scalar sser = e(rss)
scalar df_rest = e(df_r)
scalar J = df_rest - df_unrest

* F-statistic, critical value, pvalue
scalar fstat = ((sser -sseu)/J)/(sseu/(df_unrest))
scalar crit1 = invFtail(J,df_unrest,.05)
scalar pvalue = Ftail(J,df_unrest,fstat)

scalar list sseu sser J df_unrest fstat pvalue crit1

* -------------------------------------------
* Here, we use Stata's test statement
* to test hypothesis using an F-statistic
* Note: Three versions of the syntax
* -------------------------------------------

regress sales price advert c.advert#c.advert
testparm advert c.advert#c.advert
test (advert=0)(c.advert#c.advert=0)
test (_b[advert]=0)(_b[c.advert#c.advert]=0)

* -------------------------------------------
* Overall Significance of the Model
* Uses same Unrestricted Model as above
* -------------------------------------------

* Unrestricted Model (all variables)
regress sales price advert c.advert#c.advert
scalar sseu = e(rss)
scalar df_unrest = e(df_r)

* Restricted Model (no explanatory variables)
regress sales
scalar sser = e(rss)
scalar df_rest = e(df_r)
scalar J = df_rest - df_unrest

* F-statistic, critical value, pvalue
scalar fstat = ((sser -sseu)/J)/(sseu/(df_unrest))
scalar crit2 = invFtail(J,df_unrest,.05)
scalar pvalue = Ftail(J,df_unrest,fstat)

scalar list sseu sser J df_unrest fstat pvalue crit2

* -------------------------------------------
* Relationship between t and F
* -------------------------------------------

* Unrestricted Regression
regress sales price advert c.advert#c.advert
scalar sseu = e(rss)
scalar df_unrest = e(df_r)

scalar tratio = _b[price]/_se[price]
scalar t_sq = tratio^2

* Restricted Regression
regress sales advert c.advert#c.advert
scalar sser = e(rss)
scalar df_rest = e(df_r)
scalar J = df_rest - df_unrest
```

```
* F-statistic, critical value, pvalue
scalar fstat = ((sser -sseu)/J)/(sseu/(df_unrest))
scalar crit = invFtail(J,df_unrest,.05)
scalar pvalue = Ftail(J,df_unrest,fstat)

scalar list sseu sser J df_unrest fstat pvalue crit tratio t_sq

* -------------------------------------------
* Optimal Advertising
* Uses both sets of syntax for test
* -------------------------------------------

* Equivalent to Two sided t-test
regress sales price advert c.advert#c.advert
test _b[advert]+3.8*_b[c.advert#c.advert]=1
test advert+3.8*c.advert#c.advert=1

* t stat for Optimal Advertising (use lincom)
lincom _b[advert]+3.8*_b[c.advert#c.advert]-1
lincom advert+3.8*c.advert#c.advert-1
scalar t = r(estimate)/r(se)
scalar pvalue2tail = 2*ttail(e(df_r),t)
scalar pvalue1tail = ttail(e(df_r),t)
scalar list t pvalue2tail pvalue1tail

* t stat for Optimal Advertising (alternate method)
gen xstar = c.advert#c.advert-3.8*advert
gen ystar = sales - advert
regress ystar price advert xstar
scalar t = (_b[advert])/_se[advert]
scalar pvalue = ttail(e(df_r),t)
scalar list t pvalue

* One-sided t-test
regress sales price advert c.advert#c.advert
lincom advert+3.8*c.advert#c.advert-1
scalar tratio = r(estimate)/r(se)
scalar pval = ttail(e(df_r),tratio)
scalar crit = invttail(e(df_r),.05)

scalar list tratio pval crit

*  Joint Test
regress sales price advert c.advert#c.advert
test (_b[advert]+3.8*_b[c.advert#c.advert]=1) ///
    (_b[_cons]+6*_b[price]+1.9*_b[advert]+3.61*_b[c.advert#c.advert]= 80)

* -------------------------------------------
*  Nonsample Information
* -------------------------------------------

use beer, clear
gen lq = ln(q)
gen lpb = ln(pb)
gen lpl = ln(pl)
gen lpr = ln(pr)
gen li = ln(i)

constraint 1 lpb+lpl+lpr+li=0
cnsreg lq lpb lpl lpr li, c(1)

* -------------------------------------------
```

```
* MROZ Examples
* -------------------------------------------

use edu_inc, clear
regress faminc he we
regress faminc he

* correlations among regressors
correlate

regress faminc he we kl6

* Irrelevant variables
regress faminc he we kl6 xtra_x5 xtra_x6

* Model selection
program modelsel
  scalar aic = ln(e(rss)/e(N))+2*e(rank)/e(N)
  scalar bic = ln(e(rss)/e(N))+e(rank)*ln(e(N))/e(N)
  di "r-square = "e(r2) " and adjusted r_square " e(r2_a)
  scalar list aic bic
end

quietly regress faminc he
di "Model 1 (he) "
modelsel
estimates store Model1
quietly regress faminc he we
di "Model 2 (he, we) "
modelsel
estimates store Model2
quietly regress faminc he we kl6
di "Model 3 (he, we, kl6) "
modelsel
estimates store Model3
quietly regress faminc he we kl6 xtra_x5 xtra_x6
di "Model 4 (he, we, kl6. x5, x6) "
modelsel
estimates store Model4


estimates table Model1 Model2 Model3 Model4, b(%9.3f) stfmt(%9.3f) se stats(N r2 r2_a aic
bic)

* RESET
regress faminc he we kl6
predict yhat
gen yhat2=yhat^2
gen yhat3=yhat^3

summarize faminc he we kl6

*-------------------------------
* Data are ill-conditioned
* Reset test won' work here
* Try it anyway!
*-------------------------------

regress faminc he we kl6 yhat2
test yhat2
regress faminc he we kl6 yhat2 yhat3
test yhat2 yhat3
```

```
*-------------------------------------------
* Drop the previously defined predictions
* from the dataset
*-------------------------------------------

drop yhat yhat2 yhat3

*--------------------------------
* Recondition the data by
* scaling FAMINC by 10000
* -------------------------------
gen faminc_sc = faminc/10000
regress faminc_sc he we k16
predict yhat
gen yhat2 = yhat^2
gen yhat3 = yhat^3

summarize faminc_sc faminc he we k16 yhat yhat2 yhat3

regress faminc_sc he we k16 yhat2
test yhat2
regress faminc_sc he we k16 yhat2 yhat3
test yhat2 yhat3


* ---------------------------------------------
* Stata uses the estat ovtest following
* a regression to do a RESET(3) test.
* ---------------------------------------------

regress faminc he we k16
estat ovtest


* ---------------------------------------------
* Cars Example
* ---------------------------------------------

use cars, clear

summarize
corr

regress mpg cyl
regress mpg cyl eng wgt
test cyl
test eng
test eng cyl

* Auxiliary regressions for collinearity
* Check: r2 >.8 means severe collinearity
regress cyl eng wgt
scalar r1 = e(r2)
regress eng wgt cyl
scalar r2 = e(r2)
regress wgt eng cyl
scalar r3 = e(r2)
scalar list r1 r2 r3

log close
program drop modelsel
```

CHAPTER 7

Using Indicator Variables

CHAPTER OUTLINE

7.1 INDICATOR VARIABLES

Indicator, or dummy, variables are binary 0/1 variables that indicate the presence or absence of a characteristic. In this section we explore the use of indicator variables in a real estate example. Open a new log file, and open the data file *utown.dta*.

```
log using chap07_utown, replace text
use utown, clear
describe
summarize
```

Summarize the data and list the first six observations

```
list in 1/6
list in 501/506
```

. list in 1/6

	price	sqft	age	utown	pool	fplace
1.	205.452	23.46	6	0	0	1
2.	185.328	20.03	5	0	0	1
3.	248.422	27.77	6	0	0	0
4.	154.69	20.17	1	0	0	0
5.	221.801	26.45	0	0	0	1
6.	199.119	21.56	6	0	0	1

. list in 501/506

	price	sqft	age	utown	pool	fplace
501.	314.65	29.28	24	1	1	0
502.	288.556	24.48	4	1	0	1
503.	302.834	27.02	1	1	0	1
504.	247.82	21.26	2	1	0	1
505.	269.971	22.76	4	1	0	0
506.	292.926	26	17	1	0	1

7.1.1 Creating indicator variables

In many examples in POE indicator variables hav e already been creat ed and are r eady to use. There are several features in Stata that facilitate creating new indicator variables. The **generate** command (or **gen**) can be used to generate indicator va riables that are based on values of other variables.

Compute the detailed summary statistics for **price** and **sqft**.

```
summarize price sqft, detail
```

To create an indicator variable to indicate larg e houses, more than 2500 square feet in si ze, use **generate** along with a statement of the condition ($SQFT > 25$).

```
gen large = (sqft > 25)
```

If the house is such that $SQFT > 25$ then the statement is "true ," and the **generate** function creates the value 1. Otherwise the statement is not true and large = 0.

> **Remark**: The textbook data we provide has no missing values. Using the "logical operators" described above is ri   sky if dat a has missing values. For example, if t here are some missing sqft values, they would be clas sified as "large" which may not be an outcome you desire. Be careful with these automatic commands.

To create an indicator variable that is 1 for "mid-price" houses use

```
gen midprice = (215 < price) & (price < 275)
```

The "&" is a logical operator. If the conditi ons, $PRICE > 215$ **and** $PRICE < 275$ are both true, then the variable *MIDPRICE* will be 1. List a few observations to see the outcomes
.

```
list sqft price large midprice in 1/5
```

. list sqft price large midprice in 1/5

	sqft	price	large	midprice
1.	23.46	205.452	0	0
2.	20.03	185.328	0	0
3.	27.77	248.422	1	1
4.	20.17	154.69	0	0
5.	26.45	221.801	1	1

7.1.2 Estimating an indicator variable regression

Actually estimating a model with indicator variables is no diffe rent from any other regre ssion. Consider the model

$$PRICE = \beta_1 + \delta_1 UTOWN + \beta_2 SQFT + \gamma(SQFT \times UTOWN)$$

$$+ \beta_3 AGE + \delta_2 POOL + \delta_3 FPLACE + e$$

Using factor variable notation the model is

```
reg price i.utown sqft i.utown#c.sqft age i.pool i.fplace
```

Notice that the regression command, **regress** has been shortened to **reg**. This is just one example where Stata accepts abbreviated forms of commo nly used commands (e.g ., **gen** can be used instead of **generate**). The factor variable notation f or a continuous variable **c.** is required o nly when the continuous variable is used in an interaction term.

The term **i.utown#c.sqft** is the interaction between *UTOWN* and *SQFT*. Since the equation contains *UTOWN* and *SQFT* and its interaction, we can use t he "A##B" operator which Stata interprets to mean A, B and A#B.

```
reg price i.utown##c.sqft age i.pool i.fplace
```

The output denotes the indicator variable *UTOWN* as **1.utown** and the coefficient o f the interaction term $SQFT \times UTOWN$ as **utown#c.sqft**.

```
. reg price i.utown##c.sqft age i.pool i.fplace
```

Source	SS	df	MS
Model	1548261.71	6	258043.619
Residual	230184.426	993	231.807076
Total	1778446.14	999	1780.22637

Number of obs = 1000
F(6, 993) = 1113.18
Prob > F = 0.0000
R-squared = 0.8706
Adj R-squared = 0.8698
Root MSE = 15.225

price	Coef.	Std. Err.	t	P>|t|	[95% Conf. Interval]	
1.utown	27.45295	8.422582	3.26	0.001	10.92485	43.98106
sqft	7.612177	.2451765	31.05	0.000	7.131053	8.0933
utown#c.sqft						
1	1.299405	.3320478	3.91	0.000	.6478091	1.951001
age	-.1900864	.0512046	-3.71	0.000	-.2905681	-.0896048
1.pool	4.377163	1.196692	3.66	0.000	2.028828	6.725498
1.fplace	1.649176	.9719568	1.70	0.090	-.2581495	3.556501
_cons	24.49998	6.191721	3.96	0.000	12.34962	36.65035

7.1.3 Testing the significance of the indicator variables

Testing hypotheses about coefficients of indicator variables is no different than testing hypotheses about any other coefficients. To test the significance of the University Town location we test the joint null hypothesis $H_0 : \delta_1 = 0, \gamma = 0$ against the alternative that one of these coefficients is not zero. The F-test of this hypothesis can be carried out using a **post-estimation** command. On the Stata menu follow the path **Statistics > Postestimation > Tests > Test linear hypotheses** or following the regression enter **db test** to open a testing dialog box. The Stata command is

```
test 1.utown 1.utown#c.sqft
```

```
. test 1.utown 1.utown#c.sqft

 ( 1)   1.utown = 0
 ( 2)   1.utown#c.sqft = 0

       F(  2,    993) = 1954.83
            Prob > F =    0.0000
```

Based on the test result, with p-value 0.0000, we reject the null hypothesis that location has no effect at significance level $\alpha = 0.05$ or even $\alpha = 0.001$.

7.1.4 Further calculations

The estimated regression function for the houses near the university is

$$\widehat{PRICE} = (24.5 + 27.453) + (7.6122 + 1.2994)SQFT - .1901AGE$$
$$+ 4.3772POOL + 1.6492FPLACE$$

$$= 51.953 + 8.9116SQFT - .1901AGE + 4.3772POOL + 1.6492FPLACE$$

Use **lincom** to calculate the esti   mated regression slope and intercept for houses near the university.

```
lincom _cons + 1.utown
lincom c.sqft + 1.utown#c.sqft
```

The results shows not only the estimates but their 95% interval estimate as well

```
. lincom _cons + 1.utown

 ( 1)   1.utown + _cons = 0
```

price	Coef.	Std. Err.	t	P>|t|	[95% Conf. Interval]	
(1)	51.95294	5.767235	9.01	0.000	40.63557	63.2703

```
. lincom c.sqft + 1.utown#c.sqft

 ( 1)   sqft + 1.utown#c.sqft = 0
```

price	Coef.	Std. Err.	t	P>|t|	[95% Conf. Interval]	
(1)	8.911581	.2247944	39.64	0.000	8.470455	9.352708

7.1.5 Computing average marginal effects

Another advantage of using factor variable not   ation is that marginal eff   ects are computed correctly using the **margins** command. To compute the marginal effects, denoted **dy/dx**, of all variables averaged over all observations use

```
margins, dydx(*)
```

```
. margins, dydx(*)

Average marginal effects                          Number of obs   =       1000
Model VCE    : OLS

Expression   : Linear prediction, predict()
dy/dx w.r.t. : 1.utown sqft age 1.pool 1.fplace
```

	dy/dx	Delta-method Std. Err.	z	P>|z|	[95% Conf. Interval]	
1.utown	60.21049	.9646176	62.42	0.000	58.31988	62.10111
sqft	8.286568	.1661803	49.86	0.000	7.96086	8.612275
age	-.1900864	.0512046	-3.71	0.000	-.2904456	-.0897272
1.pool	4.377163	1.196692	3.66	0.000	2.031691	6.722636
1.fplace	1.649176	.9719568	1.70	0.090	-.2558247	3.554176

Note: dy/dx for factor levels is the discrete change from the base level.

Now it is just a   matter of figuring out what the **average marginal effects** reported b y Stata actually are. For *AGE*, *POOL* and *FPLACE* it is no mystery. For *AGE* it is the marginal effect of

AGE on *PRICE*, the estimated coefficient. Since *POOL* and *FPLACE* are indicator variables their marginal effect is not a derivative, but a discrete change in *PRICE* between having a pool or not, in the first place, and between having a fireplace or not, in the s econd place. For **1.utown** and **sqft** however it is not that simple.

The difference in expected *PRICE* between the two neighborhoods is

$$\left(E(PRICE)|UTOWN=1\right)-\left(E(PRICE)|UTOWN=0\right)=\delta_1+\gamma SQFT$$

Stata computes

$$AME(UTOWN)=\frac{1}{N}\sum_{i=1}^{N}\left(\delta_1+\gamma SQFT_i\right)=\delta_1+\gamma\overline{SQFT}$$

The variance of the estimated marginal effect is

$$\text{var}\left(\widehat{AME}(UTOWN)\right)=\text{var}\left(\hat{\delta}_1+\hat{\gamma}\overline{SQFT}\right)=\text{var}\left(\hat{\delta}_1\right)+\overline{SQFT}^2\text{var}\left(\hat{\gamma}\right)+2\overline{SQFT}\text{cov}\left(\hat{\delta}_1,\hat{\gamma}\right)$$

To see that this is true execute the following

```
quietly summarize sqft
scalar asqft = r(mean)
lincom 1.utown+c.sqft#1.utown*asqft
```

```
. quietly summarize sqft

. scalar asqft = r(mean)

. lincom 1.utown+c.sqft#1.utown*asqft

 ( 1)  1.utown + 25.20965*1.utown#c.sqft = 0
```

price	Coef.	Std. Err.	t	P>|t|	[95% Conf. Interval]	
(1)	60.21049	.9646176	62.42	0.000	58.31757	62.10342

Similarly, the marginal effect of *SQFT* is

$$\frac{\partial E(PRICE)}{\partial SQFT}=\beta_2+\gamma UTOWN$$

Stata computes

$$AME(SQFT)=\frac{1}{N}\sum_{i=1}^{N}\beta_2+\gamma UTOWN_i=\beta_2+\gamma\overline{UTOWN}$$

To see that this is so, execute

```
quietly summarize utown
scalar autown = r(mean)
lincom c.sqft+c.sqft#1.utown*autown
```

. quietly summarize utown

. scalar autown = r(mean)

. lincom c.sqft+c.sqft#1.utown*autown

 (1)   sqft + .519*1.utown#c.sqft = 0

price	Coef.	Std. Err.	t	P>|t|	[95% Conf. Interval]	
(1)	8.286568	.1661803	49.86	0.000	7.960463	8.612673

```
log close
```


7.2 APPLYING INDICATOR VARIABLES

In this section we illustrat e a variety of applicati ons of indicator variables. Open the data file *cps4_small.dta*. Start a new log and examine the data.

```
log using chap07_cps4, replace text
use cps4_small, clear
describe
```

```
Contains data from cps4_small.dta
  obs:          1,000
  vars:            12
  size:        23,000 (99.9% of memory free)
```

variable name	storage type	display format	value label	variable label
wage	double	%10.0g		earnings per hour
educ	byte	%8.0g		years of education
exper	byte	%8.0g		post education years experience
hrswk	byte	%8.0g		usual hours worked per week
married	byte	%8.0g		= 1 if married
female	byte	%8.0g		= 1 if female
metro	byte	%8.0g		= 1 if lives in metropolitan area
midwest	byte	%8.0g		= 1 if lives in midwest
south	byte	%8.0g		= 1 if lives in south
west	byte	%8.0g		= 1 if lives in west
black	byte	%8.0g		= 1 if black
asian	byte	%8.0g		= 1 if asian

```
summarize
```

```
. summarize
```

Variable	Obs	Mean	Std. Dev.	Min	Max
wage	1000	20.61566	12.83472	1.97	76.39
educ	1000	13.799	2.711079	0	21
exper	1000	26.508	12.85446	2	65
hrswk	1000	39.952	10.3353	0	90
married	1000	.581	.4936423	0	1
female	1000	.514	.5000541	0	1
metro	1000	.78	.4144536	0	1
midwest	1000	.24	.4272968	0	1
south	1000	.296	.4567194	0	1
west	1000	.24	.4272968	0	1
black	1000	.112	.3155243	0	1
asian	1000	.043	.2029586	0	1

7.2.1 Interactions between qualitative factors

First, we consider an interaction between two indicator variables, black and female in the model

$$WAGE = \beta_1 + \beta_2 EDUC + \delta_1 BLACK + \delta_2 FEMALE + \gamma (BLACK \times FEMALE) + e$$

Using the factor variable operator "**##**" the regression is

```
reg wage educ i.black##i.female
```

```
. reg wage educ i.black##i.female
```

Source	SS	df	MS
Model	34370.7606	4	8592.69016
Residual	130194.667	995	130.848912
Total	164565.428	999	164.730158

Number of obs =	1000
F(4, 995) =	65.67
Prob > F =	0.0000
R-squared =	0.2089
Adj R-squared =	0.2057
Root MSE =	11.439

wage	Coef.	Std. Err.	t	P>|t|	[95% Conf. Interval]
educ	2.070391	.1348781	15.35	0.000	1.805712	2.335069
1.black	-4.169077	1.774714	-2.35	0.019	-7.651689	-.6864656
1.female	-4.784607	.7734139	-6.19	0.000	-6.302317	-3.266898
black#female						
1 1	3.844294	2.327653	1.65	0.099	-.7233779	8.411966
_cons	-5.281159	1.900468	-2.78	0.006	-9.010544	-1.551774

We estimate the wage difference between white males and black females using

```
lincom 1.black + 1.female + 1.black#1.female
```

```
. lincom 1.black + 1.female + 1.black#1.female

 ( 1)  1.black + 1.female + 1.black#1.female = 0
```

wage	Coef.	Std. Err.	t	P>|t|	[95% Conf. Interval]
(1)	-5.10939	1.510567	-3.38	0.001	-8.073652 -2.145128

Carry out an F-test of joint significance of *FEMALE, BLACK* and their interaction using

test 1.female 1.black 1.black#1.female

The result is

```
. test 1.female 1.black 1.black#1.female

 ( 1)  1.female = 0
 ( 2)  1.black = 0
 ( 3)  1.black#1.female = 0

       F( 3,   995) =    14.21
            Prob > F =    0.0000
```

The marginal effects are computed using the **margins** command.

margins, dydx(*)

```
. margins, dydx(*)

Average marginal effects                      Number of obs   =        1000
Model VCE     : OLS

Expression    : Linear prediction, predict()
dy/dx w.r.t.  : educ 1.black 1.female
```

	dy/dx	Delta-method Std. Err.	z	P>|z|	[95% Conf. Interval]
educ	2.070391	.1348781	15.35	0.000	1.806034 2.334747
1.black	-2.19311	1.160919	-1.89	0.059	-4.468469 .0822488
1.female	-4.354046	.7313539	-5.95	0.000	-5.787474 -2.920619

```
Note: dy/dx for factor levels is the discrete change from the base level.
```

Recall that the model is

$$WAGE = \beta_1 + \beta_2 EDUC + \delta_1 BLACK + \delta_2 FEMALE + \gamma (BLACK \times FEMALE) + e$$

So

$$E(WAGE \mid FEMALE = 1) = \beta_1 + \beta_2 EDUC + \delta_1 BLACK + \delta_2 + \gamma BLACK$$
$$= (\beta_1 + \delta_2) + \beta_2 EDUC + (\delta_1 + \gamma) BLACK$$

and $E(WAGE \mid FEMALE = 0) = \beta_1 + \beta_2 EDUC + \delta_1 BLACK$. The difference is

$$E(WAGE \mid FEMALE = 1) - E(WAGE \mid FEMALE = 0) = \delta_2 + \gamma BLACK$$

Stata reports the average over the sample of the estimated counterpart

$$AME(FEMALE) = \frac{1}{N} \sum_{i=1}^{N} \left(\hat{\delta}_2 + \hat{\gamma} BLACK_i \right) = \hat{\delta}_2 + \hat{\gamma} \overline{BLACK}$$

The calculation of the **Average marginal effect** of **female** is verified using

```
quietly summarize black
scalar ablack = r(mean)
lincom 1.female + 1.black#1.female*ablack
```

. lincom 1.female + 1.black#1.female*ablack

 (1)   1.female + .112*1.black#1.female = 0

wage	Coef.	Std. Err.	t	P>|t|	[95% Conf. Interval]
(1)	-4.354046	.7313539	-5.95	0.000	-5.789219 -2.918873

7.2.2 Adding regional indicators

Next add indicator variables with several categories, regional dummies. The model of interest is

$$WAGE = \beta_1 + \beta_2 EDUC + \beta_3 BLACK + \beta_4 FEMALE + \beta_5 \left(BLACK \times FEMALE \right)$$
$$+ \delta_1 SOUTH + \delta_2 MIDWEST + \delta_3 WEST + e$$

Because the regional indicator variables are already defined in the data file, we simply add them to the regression model

```
reg wage educ i.black##i.female i.south i.midwest i.west
```

A portion of the output is

wage	Coef.	Std. Err.	t	P>|t|	[95% Conf. Interval]
educ	2.071231	.1344687	15.40	0.000	1.807355 2.335106
1.black	-3.905465	1.786258	-2.19	0.029	-7.410743 -.4001873
1.female	-4.744129	.7698381	-6.16	0.000	-6.254827 -3.233431
black#female					
1 1	3.625021	2.318375	1.56	0.118	-.9244618 8.174504
1.south	-.4499056	1.025024	-0.44	0.661	-2.46137 1.561558
1.midwest	-2.608406	1.059644	-2.46	0.014	-4.687807 -.5290049
1.west	.9866332	1.059815	0.93	0.352	-1.093104 3.06637
_cons	-4.80621	2.028691	-2.37	0.018	-8.787229 -.8251912

To test the joint significance of these regional dummies we use the **test** statement

```
test 1.south 1.midwest 1.west
```

```
. test 1.south 1.midwest 1.west

 ( 1)   1.south = 0
 ( 2)   1.midwest = 0
 ( 3)   1.west = 0

        F(  3,    992) =      4.25
              Prob > F =    0.0054
```

Calculate and display the critical values from   the F-distribution with 3 numerator and 992 denominator degrees of freedom.

```
di "F(3,992,.95) = " invFtail(3,992,.05)
di "F(3,992,.90) = " invFtail(3,992,.10)
```

```
. di "F(3,992,.95) = " invFtail(3,992,.05)
F(3,992,.95) = 2.6138755
```

```
. di "F(3,992,.90) = " invFtail(3,992,.10)
F(3,992,.90) = 2.0893205
```

7.2.3 Testing the equivalence of two regressions

To test the equivalence of the wage equations for the southern region versus the remainder of the country (i.e., not south) we create interaction va riable for each variable in the regression model with the indicator variable south. The equation we wish to test is

$$WAGE = \beta_1 + \beta_2 EDUC + \delta_1 BLACK + \delta_2 FEMALE + \gamma (BLACK \times FEMALE) + e$$

The model with indicator variable interactions included is

$$WAGE = \beta_1 + \beta_2 EDUC + \delta_1 BLACK + \delta_2 FEMALE + \gamma (BLACK \times FEMALE) +$$

$$\theta_1 SOUTH + \theta_2 (EDUC \times SOUTH) + \theta_3 (BLACK \times SOUTH) +$$

$$\theta_4 (FEMALE \times SOUTH) + \theta_5 (BLACK \times FEMALE \times SOUTH) + e$$

We have interacted *SOUTH* with each variable in the regres sion model, including the intercept. Use the St ata operator **##** to create all the interactions. First, to create *BLACK, FEMALE,* and their interaction we use use **i.black##i.female**. Then the fully interacted model is

```
reg wage i.south##(c.educ i.black##i.female)
```

```
. reg wage i.south##(c.educ i.black##i.female)
```

Source	SS	df	MS
Model	34581.0189	9	3842.33543
Residual	129984.409	990	131.297383
Total	164565.428	999	164.730158

Number of obs =	1000
F(9, 990) =	29.26
Prob > F =	0.0000
R-squared =	0.2101
Adj R-squared =	0.2030
Root MSE =	11.459

wage	Coef.	Std. Err.	t	P>|t|	[95% Conf. Interval]	
1.south	3.94391	4.048453	0.97	0.330	-4.000625	11.88845
educ	2.172554	.1664639	13.05	0.000	1.845891	2.499216
1.black	-5.08936	2.64306	-1.93	0.054	-10.276	.0972837
1.female	-5.005078	.8990074	-5.57	0.000	-6.769257	-3.240899
black#female						
1 1	5.305574	3.497267	1.52	0.130	-1.557333	12.16848
south#c.educ						
1	-.308541	.2857343	-1.08	0.280	-.8692554	.2521734
south#black						
1 1	1.704396	3.633327	0.47	0.639	-5.42551	8.834302
south#female						
1 1	.9011198	1.772665	0.51	0.611	-2.577492	4.379732
south#black#female						
1 1 1	-2.935834	4.787647	-0.61	0.540	-12.33094	6.459268
_cons	-6.605572	2.336628	-2.83	0.005	-11.19088	-2.02026

To test the hypothesis that there is "no difference" between the model for the south and rest of the country we test the joint hypothesis $H_0 : \theta_1 = \theta_2 = \theta_3 = \theta_4 = \theta_5 = 0$ using a **test** statement.

```
test 1.south 1.south#c.educ 1.south#1.black 1.south#1.female ///
        1.south#1.black#1.female
```

```
. test 1.south 1.south#c.educ 1.south#1.black 1.south#1.female ///
>       1.south#1.black#1.female

 ( 1)   1.south = 0
 ( 2)   1.south#c.educ = 0
 ( 3)   1.south#1.black = 0
 ( 4)   1.south#1.female = 0
 ( 5)   1.south#1.black#1.female = 0

       F( 5,   990) =     0.32
            Prob > F =    0.9009
```

From the fully interacted model we can obtain the combined effect of *BLACK* and *SOUTH* using

```
lincom 1.black + 1.black#1.south
```

```
. lincom 1.black + 1.black#1.south

( 1)   1.black + 1.south#1.black = 0
```

wage	Coef.	Std. Err.	t	P>|t|	[95% Conf. Interval]	
(1)	-3.384964	2.49305	-1.36	0.175	-8.277233	1.507305

Similarly, the combined effect of *FEMALE* and *SOUTH* is obtained using

> **lincom 1.female + 1.female#1.south**

```
. lincom 1.female + 1.female#1.south

( 1)   1.female + 1.south#1.female = 0
```

wage	Coef.	Std. Err.	t	P>|t|	[95% Conf. Interval]	
(1)	-4.103958	1.527785	-2.69	0.007	-7.102027	-1.105889

7.2.4 Estimating separate regressions

Instead of using the fully interacted model approach in the previous section, the *F*-statistic can be computed using the restricted and unrestricted   sum of squared residuals. The   sum of squared residuals for the full model is the sum of the *SSE* from the two separate regressions

$$SSE_{full} = SSE_{non-south} + SSE_{south} = 89088.5 + 40895.9 = 129984.4$$

The estimations on the t wo regions c an be efficiently carried out using the standard **regress** command with **bysort**, which allows Stata commands to be repeated on subsets of the data. Enter **help bysort**. To use the **by** prefix the data must be sorted by grouping variable, or variables. If this has not already been done, then **by** and **sort** are combined into **bysort**. The sy ntax for the commands is

> **by varlist: stata_cmd**

> **bysort varlist: stata_cmd**

To implement regressions for the two regions we have

> **bysort south: reg wage educ i.black##i.female**

That is, we f irst sort acco rding to the values of *SOUTH* and then im plement the regression for each group of observations.

```
. bysort south: reg wage educ i.black##i.female
```

```
-> south = 0
```

Source	SS	df	MS		Number of obs =	704
					F(4, 699) =	49.72
Model	25346.0083	4	6336.50209		Prob > F =	0.0000
Residual	89088.4615	699	127.451304		R-squared =	0.2215
					Adj R-squared =	0.2170
Total	114434.47	703	162.780185		Root MSE =	11.289

wage	Coef.	Std. Err.	t	P>|t|	[95% Conf.	Interval]
educ	2.172554	.1640077	13.25	0.000	1.850547	2.49456
1.black	-5.08936	2.604061	-1.95	0.051	-10.20208	.0233585
1.female	-5.005078	.8857423	-5.65	0.000	-6.744112	-3.266044
black#female						
1 1	5.305574	3.445664	1.54	0.124	-1.459516	12.07066
_cons	-6.605572	2.30215	-2.87	0.004	-11.12553	-2.085615

```
-> south = 1
```

Source	SS	df	MS		Number of obs =	296
					F(4, 291) =	16.43
Model	9234.26014	4	2308.56503		Prob > F =	0.0000
Residual	40895.9474	291	140.535902		R-squared =	0.1842
					Adj R-squared =	0.1730
Total	50130.2075	295	169.932907		Root MSE =	11.855

wage	Coef.	Std. Err.	t	P>|t|	[95% Conf.	Interval]
educ	1.864013	.2402682	7.76	0.000	1.391129	2.336896
1.black	-3.384964	2.579268	-1.31	0.190	-8.46135	1.691422
1.female	-4.103958	1.580621	-2.60	0.010	-7.214857	-.993059
black#female						
1 1	2.36974	3.382739	0.70	0.484	-4.287995	9.027476
_cons	-2.661662	3.420413	-0.78	0.437	-9.393547	4.070223

The two *SSE* come from the analysis of variance table from the separate regressions.

7.2.5 Indicator variables in log-linear models

The calculation of the e xact effect of an i ndicator variable in a lo g-linear model seems complicated, but Stata's command **nlcom** makes it much easier.

Create **ln(wage)** and estimate the equation

$$\ln(WAGE) = \beta_1 + \beta_2 EDUC + \delta FEMALE$$

```
gen lwage = ln(wage)
reg lwage educ i.female
```

The results are

```
. reg lwage educ i.female
```

Source	SS	df	MS
Model	74.5420655	2	37.2710328
Residual	262.238666	997	.263027749
Total	336.780731	999	.337117849

```
Number of obs =    1000
F( 2,   997) =  141.70
Prob > F      =  0.0000
R-squared     =  0.2213
Adj R-squared =  0.2198
Root MSE      = .51286
```

lwage	Coef.	Std. Err.	t	P>|t|	[95% Conf. Interval]	
educ	.0962484	.0060365	15.94	0.000	.0844026	.1080942
1.female	-.243214	.0327275	-7.43	0.000	-.3074367	-.1789913
_cons	1.653868	.0843786	19.60	0.000	1.488288	1.819448

The exact effect of the indicator variable female is

$$100\left(e^{\delta} - 1\right)\%$$

This is a nonlinear function of the parameters that requires the use of **nlcom**.

```
nlcom 100*(exp(_b[1.female]) - 1)
```

The result is

```
. nlcom 100*(exp(_b[1.female]) - 1)

    _nl_1:  100*(exp(_b[1.female]) - 1)
```

lwage	Coef.	Std. Err.	t	P>|t|	[95% Conf. Interval]	
_nl_1	-21.58963	2.566176	-8.41	0.000	-26.62535	-16.5539

That is, holding all else constant, we estimate that female workers earn 21.6% less than their male counterparts.

Similarly we can calculate other nonlinear marginal effects. Consider the model

$$\ln(WAGE) = \beta_1 + \beta_2 EDUC + \beta_3 EXPER + \gamma(EDUC \times EXPER)$$

The approximate marginal effect is

$$100(\beta_3 + \gamma EDUC)\%$$

Create the interaction of education and experience and add it to the regression model

    reg lwage c.educ##c.exper

The estimation results are

```
. reg lwage c.educ##c.exper
```

Source	SS	df	MS
Model	65.5449479	3	21.848316
Residual	271.235783	996	.272325084
Total	336.780731	999	.337117849

Number of obs =	1000
F(3, 996) =	80.23
Prob > F =	0.0000
R-squared =	0.1946
Adj R-squared =	0.1922
Root MSE =	.52185

lwage	Coef.	Std. Err.	t	P>|t|	[95% Conf.	Interval]
educ	.0949385	.0146246	6.49	0.000	.06624	.123637
exper	.0063295	.0066985	0.94	0.345	-.0068153	.0194743
c.educ# c.exper	-.0000364	.0004838	-0.08	0.940	-.0009858	.0009129
_cons	1.392318	.2066447	6.74	0.000	.986809	1.797827

For using **lincom** or **nlcom** the coefficient names, in the form **_b[variable]**, are sometimes not immediately evident when using factor notati   on. These can be revealed by specify   ing the **regress** command with the option **coeflegend**, which display s the coefficien ts' legend rather than the coefficient table.

    reg, coeflegend

```
. reg, coeflegend
```

Source	SS	df	MS
Model	65.5449479	3	21.848316
Residual	271.235783	996	.272325084
Total	336.780731	999	.337117849

Number of obs =	1000
F(3, 996) =	80.23
Prob > F =	0.0000
R-squared =	0.1946
Adj R-squared =	0.1922
Root MSE =	.52185

lwage	Coef.	Legend
educ	.0949385	_b[educ]
exper	.0063295	_b[exper]
c.educ# c.exper	-.0000364	_b[c.educ#c.exper]
_cons	1.392318	_b[_cons]

The approximate and exact effects are calculated using

```
lincom 100*(exper+ c.educ#c.exper*16)
```

```
. lincom 100*(exper+ c.educ#c.exper*16)

 ( 1)   100*exper + 1600*c.educ#c.exper = 0
```

lwage	Coef.	Std. Err.	t	P>|t|	[95% Conf. Interval]	
(1)	.574639	.174402	3.29	0.001	.2324014	.9168765

```
nlcom 100*(exp( _b[exper]+_b[c.educ#c.exper]*16) - 1)
```

```
. nlcom 100*(exp( _b[exper]+_b[c.educ#c.exper]*16) - 1)

    _nl_1:  100*(exp( _b[exper]+_b[c.educ#c.exper]*16) - 1)
```

lwage	Coef.	Std. Err.	t	P>|t|	[95% Conf. Interval]	
_nl_1	.5762932	.1754071	3.29	0.001	.2320833	.920503

```
log close
```

7.3 THE LINEAR PROBABILITY MODEL

When modeling choice between two alternatives, an indicator variable will b e the **dependent** variable rather than an independent variable in a regression model. Suppose

$$y = \begin{cases} 1 & \text{if first alternative is chosen} \\ 0 & \text{if second alternative is chosen} \end{cases}$$

If p is the pr obability that the first alternative is chosen, then $P[y = 1] = p$, then the expe cted value of y is $E(y) = p$ and its variance is $\text{var}(y) = p(1-p)$.

We are interested in identify ing factors that m ight affect the probabilit y p using a linear regression function, or in this context a **linear probability model**,

$$E(y) = p = \beta_1 + \beta_2 x_2 + \cdots + \beta_K x_K$$

The linear probability regression model is

$$y = \beta_1 + \beta_2 x_2 + \cdots + \beta_K x_K + e$$

The variance of the error term e is

$$\text{var}(e) = (\beta_1 + \beta_2 x_2 + \cdots + \beta_K x_K)(1 - \beta_1 - \beta_2 x_2 - \cdots - \beta_K x_K)$$

This error is not homoscedastic and will be treated in Chapter 8.

As an illustration consider the choice between Coke and Pepsi. Open *coke.dta* and check its contents.

```
log using chap07_coke, replace text
use coke, clear
describe
summarize
```

variable name	storage type	display format	value label	variable label
coke	byte	%8.0g		=1 if coke chosen, =0 if pepsi chosen
pr_pepsi	double	%10.0g		price of 2 liter bottle of pepsi
pr_coke	double	%10.0g		price of 2 liter bottle of coke
disp_pepsi	byte	%8.0g		= 1 if pepsi is displayed at time of purchase, otherwise = 0
disp_coke	byte	%8.0g		= 1 if coke is displayed at time of purchase, otherwise = 0
pratio	double	%10.0g		price of coke relative to price of pepsi

To estimate the linear probability model for choosing Coke using the least squares regression

```
reg coke pratio disp_coke disp_pepsi
```

. reg coke pratio disp_coke disp_pepsi

Source	SS	df	MS
Model	33.8378078	3	11.2792693
Residual	248.004297	1136	.218313642
Total	281.842105	1139	.247446976

```
Number of obs =    1140
F(  3,  1136) =   51.67
Prob > F      =  0.0000
R-squared     =  0.1201
Adj R-squared =  0.1177
Root MSE      =  .46724
```

coke	Coef.	Std. Err.	t	P>|t|	[95% Conf. Interval]
pratio	-.4008614	.0613494	-6.53	0.000	-.5212324 -.2804904
disp_coke	.0771745	.0343919	2.24	0.025	.0096956 .1446533
disp_pepsi	-.1656637	.0355997	-4.65	0.000	-.2355122 -.0958152
_cons	.8902151	.0654849	13.59	0.000	.7617301 1.0187

A concern with the linear regression approach is that the predicted probabilities can be outside the interval [0, 1]. Obtain the predicted values, which are in this case probabilities, and **summarize**.

```
predict phat
summarize phat
```

```
. summarize phat
```

Variable	Obs	Mean	Std. Dev.	Min	Max
phat	1140	.4473684	.1723611	-.2073211	.7680784

We see that the minimum value is less than zero, but none of the predicted probabilities are greater than one. To see how many predicted probabilities are negative, **summarize** just those, using

> **summarize phat if phat<=0**

```
. summarize phat if phat<=0
```

Variable	Obs	Mean	Std. Dev.	Min	Max
phat	16	-.0183585	.0523201	-.2073211	-.0002385

We see that 16 of the 1140 observations have negative predicted probabilities.

> **log close**

7.4 TREATMENT EFFECTS

In order to understand the measurement of treatment effects, consider a simple regression model in which the explanatory variable is a dummy variable, indicating whether a particular individual is in the treatment or control group. Let y be the outcome variable, the measured characteristic the treatment is designed to affect. Define the indicator variable d as

$$d_i = \begin{cases} 1 & \text{individual in treatment group} \\ 0 & \text{individual in control group} \end{cases}$$

The effect of the treatment on the outcome can be modeled as

$$y_i = \beta_1 + \beta_2 d_i + e_i, \quad i = 1, \dots, N$$

where e_i represents the collection of other factors affecting the outcome. The regression functions for the treatment and control groups are

$$E(y_i) = \begin{cases} \beta_1 + \beta_2 & \text{if in treatment group, } d_i = 1 \\ \beta_1 & \text{if in control group, } d_i = 0 \end{cases}$$

The **treatment effect** that we wish to measure is β_2. The least squares estimator of β_2 is

$$b_2 = \frac{\sum_{i=1}^{N}(d_i - \bar{d})(y_i - \bar{y})}{\sum_{i=1}^{N}(d_i - \bar{d})^2} = \bar{y}_1 - \bar{y}_0$$

where $\bar{y}_1 = \sum_{i=1}^{N_1} y_i / N_1$ is the sample mean of the N_1 observations on y for the treatment group (d = 1) and $\bar{y}_0 = \sum_{i=1}^{N_0} y_i / N_0$ is the sample mean of the N_0 observations on y for the control group (d = 0). In this treatment/control framework the estimator b_2 is called the **difference estimator** because it is the difference between the sample means of the treatment and control groups.

To illustrate, we use the data from project STAR described in *Principles of Econometrics*, 4th edition, Chapter 7.5.3.

```
log using chap07_star, replace text
use star, clear
describe
```

variable name	storage type	display format	value label	variable label
id	int	%8.0g		student id
schid	long	%12.0g		school id
tchid	long	%12.0g		teacher id
tchexper	byte	%8.0g		teacher years of experience
absent	byte	%8.0g		days absent
readscore	int	%8.0g		reading score
mathscore	int	%8.0g		math score
totalscore	float	%9.0g		combined math and reading score
boy	float	%9.0g		male student
white_asian	float	%9.0g		white or asian student
black	float	%9.0g		black student
tchwhite	float	%9.0g		white teacher
tchmasters	float	%9.0g		teacher with masters degree
freelunch	float	%9.0g		free lunch provided
schurban	float	%9.0g		school urban or inner city
schrural	float	%9.0g		school rural
small	byte	%8.0g		small class
regular	byte	%8.0g		regular class
aide	byte	%8.0g		regular class with aide

To examine the effect of small versus regular size classes drop the observations for classes of regular size with a teacher aide.

```
drop if aide==1
summarize
```

We find that 3743 observations remain. The core model of interest is

$$TOTALSCORE_i = \beta_1 + \beta_2 SMALL_i + e_i$$

Which we may augment with additional control variables such as

$$TOTALSCORE_i = \beta_1 + \beta_2 SMALL_i + \beta_3 TCHEXPER_i + e_i$$

It is convenient when estimating alternative specifications of models to define lists of variables that can be inserted into the Stata code with the prefix **$**. To do this we use a **global** declaration. Below we give the name **x1list** to the single variable, **small**. The list denoted **x2list** contains the first list, denoted $ **x1list**, plus the variable **tchexper**. Similarly, we create **x3list** containing the contents of **$x2list** plus the additional variables **boy**, **freelunch**, and **white_asian**.

```
global x1list small
global x2list $x1list tchexper
global x3list $x2list boy freelunch white_asian
global x4list $x3list tchwhite tchmasters schurban schrural
```

We can use these lists in Stata commands, for example

```
summarize totalscore $x4list if regular==1
```

The output is

```
. summarize totalscore $x4list if regular==1
```

Variable	Obs	Mean	Std. Dev.	Min	Max
totalscore	2005	918.0429	73.13799	635	1229
small	2005	0	0	0	0
tchexper	2005	9.068329	5.724446	0	24
boy	2005	.513217	.49995	0	1
freelunch	2005	.4738155	.4994385	0	1
white_asian	2005	.6812968	.4660899	0	1
tchwhite	2005	.798005	.4015887	0	1
tchmasters	2005	.3650873	.4815747	0	1
schurban	2005	.3012469	.4589142	0	1
schrural	2005	.4997506	.5001247	0	1

Similarly

```
summarize totalscore $x4list if small==1
```

```
. summarize  totalscore $x4list if small==1
```

Variable	Obs	Mean	Std. Dev.	Min	Max
totalscore	1738	931.9419	76.35863	747	1253
small	1738	1	0	1	1
tchexper	1738	8.995397	5.731568	0	27
boy	1738	.5149597	.49992	0	1
freelunch	1738	.4718067	.4993482	0	1
white_asian	1738	.6846951	.4647709	0	1
tchwhite	1738	.8624856	.3444887	0	1
tchmasters	1738	.3176064	.4656795	0	1
schurban	1738	.306099	.461004	0	1
schrural	1738	.4626007	.4987428	0	1

We observe that the average test score for students in small classes is higher.

If students are assigned random ly to classes of alternative sizes, then there should be no correlation between class size and any ot her variables. The correlations for the group of variables **x3list** is

```
pwcorr $x3list
```

	small	tchexper	boy	freelu~h	white_~n
small	1.0000				
tchexper	-0.0064	1.0000			
boy	0.0017	-0.0341	1.0000		
freelunch	-0.0020	-0.0969	0.0066	1.0000	
white_asian	0.0036	0.1286	0.0231	-0.4378	1.0000

Note in the first column that the correlations between small and the other factors are nearly zero.

The experiment took place in 79 schools. We will control f or school effects by including an indicator variable for each. That is, we can introduce 78 new indicators

$$SCHOOL\_j = \begin{cases} 1 & \text{if student is in school } j \\ 0 & \text{otherwise} \end{cases}$$

To create these use **tabulate** with the **generate** option.

```
tabulate schid, gen(school)
```

. tabulate schid, gen(school)

school id	Freq.	Percent	Cum.
112038	33	0.88	0.88
123056	34	0.91	1.79

In the Variables window we find that we have indicator variables **school1**, **school2** and so on.

Name	Label
regular	regular class
aide	regular class with ...
school1	schid==112038.0...
school2	schid==123056.0...
school3	schid==128068.0...
school4	schid==128076.0...

We now are in the position to estim   ate the alte rnative models. We will esti mate four models, suppressing the output using **quietly** and reporting the results in a convenient table.

```
quietly reg totalscore $x1list
estimates store model1

quietly reg totalscore $x2list
estimates store model2
```

```
quietly reg totalscore $x3list
estimates store model3

quietly reg totalscore $x4list
estimates store model4
```

Enter **help estimates table** for a summary of the features, or **help estout** for a complete suite of commands to make regression tables which are stored preferably using **eststo**. The command is

```
estimates table model1 model2 model3 model4, b(%12.3f)
        se stats(N r2 F bic)
```

This will create a table o f results with columns the different models. The esti mates will be reported in a decimal format (enter **help format**) with three places after the deci mal. Below the estimates are the standard errors, and at the bottom the sample size, R^2, F and the *BIC*.

While perfectly satisfactory we prefer the user-written co mmand **esttab**. Enter **findit esttab**. Click the blue link st0085_1. You must have administrator privileges to install.

```
esttab model1 model2 model3 model4 , se(%12.3f) b(%12.3f) ///
star(* 0.10 ** 0.05 *** 0.01) gaps ar2 bic scalars(rss) ///
title("Project Star: Kindergarden")
```

A portion of that table is

Project Star: Kindergarden

	(1) totalscore	(2) totalscore	(3) totalscore	(4) totalscore
small	13.899*** (2.447)	13.983*** (2.437)	13.870*** (2.338)	13.358*** (2.352)
tchexper		1.156*** (0.212)	0.703*** (0.206)	0.781*** (0.213)
boy			-15.345*** (2.335)	-15.287*** (2.330)

The model including indicator variables for each school is

$$TOTALSCORE_i = \beta_1 + \beta_2 SMALL_i + \beta_3 TCHEXPER_i + \sum_{j=2}^{79} \delta_j SCHOOL\_j_i + e_i$$

This regression with school fixed effects can be estimated the "hard way" using

```
reg totalscore $x2list school2-school79
```

However, if we do so the results will be clutt ere d with 78 additional coefficients in which we are really not interested. It is more convenient to use a modified regression command, **areg**. The help information shows that this is a linear regression with a large dummy-variable (indicator variable) set. The option absorb suppresses the school-specific intercept terms.

```
help areg                                    dialog:  areg
                                             also see: areg postestimation
────────────────────────────────────────────────────────────────────────
Title

    [R] areg — Linear regression with a large dummy-variable set

Syntax

        areg depvar [indepvars] [if] [in] [weight], absorb(varname) [options]

    options                    description
    ────────────────────────────────────────────────────────────────────
    Model
  * absorb(varname)            categorical variable to be absorbed
```

For example, applying areg to estimate the model with explanatory variable **small**, and absorbing the indicator effects represented by **schild**, we have

```
        areg totalscore $x1list, absorb(schid)
        estimates store amodel1
```

```
. areg totalscore $x1list, absorb(schid)

Linear regression, absorbing indicators       Number of obs =      3743
                                               F( 1,  3663) =      51.80
                                               Prob > F      =    0.0000
                                               R-squared     =    0.2377
                                               Adj R-squared =    0.2213
                                               Root MSE      =    66.151
```

totalscore	Coef.	Std. Err.	t	P>|t|	[95% Conf. Interval]	
small	15.99778	2.222846	7.20	0.000	11.63964	20.35592
_cons	917.0684	1.494793	613.51	0.000	914.1377	919.9991
schid	F(78, 3663) =		14.118	0.000	(79 categories)	

Note that at the bottom of the output the F-test of significance of the indicator variables shows that there is a significant difference among the school indicator variables. We estimate the remainder of the specifications and include them in a table.

```
        areg totalscore $x2list, absorb(schid)
        estimates store amodel2

        quietly areg totalscore $x3list, absorb(schid)
        estimates store amodel3

        quietly areg totalscore $x4list, absorb(schid)
        estimates store amodel4

        esttab amodel1 amodel2 amodel3 amodel4 , se(%12.3f) b(%12.3f) ///
            star(* 0.10 ** 0.05 *** 0.01) gaps ar2 bic scalars(rss) ///
```

title("Project Star: Kindergarden, with school effects")

The table is

Project Star: Kindergarden, with school effects

	(1) totalscore	(2) totalscore	(3) totalscore	(4) totalscore
small	15.998*** (2.223)	16.066*** (2.218)	16.055*** (2.127)	16.265*** (2.140)
tchexper		0.913*** (0.226)	0.821*** (0.217)	0.893*** (0.223)
boy			-13.457*** (2.095)	-13.356*** (2.093)
freelunch			-36.335*** (2.505)	-36.102*** (2.504)
white_asian			25.261*** (4.415)	25.148*** (4.413)
tchwhite				-9.642** (4.270)
tchmasters				-4.508 (2.903)
schurban				.
schrural				.
_cons	917.068*** (1.495)	908.786*** (2.532)	916.477*** (4.375)	925.168*** (5.528)
N	3743	3743	3743	3743
adj. R-sq	0.221	0.225	0.287	0.289
BIC	41938.575	41930.098	41635.780	41643.497
rss	16028908.368	15957533.543	14653879.350	14619709.135

Standard errors in parentheses
* p<0.10, ** p<0.05, *** p<0.01

The variables **schurban** and **schrural** in **x4list** are redundant, exactly collinear, with the school effects and thus are dropped in column (4).

The class sizes were assigned randomly within schools. Above we computed the correlations between small and other variables. However correlations are only measure pairwise associations, so it is important to check for associations between small and other variables using a linear probability model, with and without school fixed effects.

```
reg small boy white_asian tchexper freelunch
areg small boy white_asian tchexper freelunch, absorb(schid)
```

```
. areg small boy white_asian tchexper freelunch, absorb(schid)
```

```
Linear regression, absorbing indicators        Number of obs =      3743
                                                F(  4,  3660) =      0.08
                                                Prob > F      =    0.9894
                                                R-squared     =    0.0488
                                                Adj R-squared =    0.0275
                                                Root MSE      =   .49189
```

small	Coef.	Std. Err.	t	P>|t|	[95% Conf. Interval]	
boy	.002337	.0162813	0.14	0.886	-.0295843	.0342584
white_asian	.0094167	.0343154	0.27	0.784	-.0578626	.076696
tchexper	-.0007506	.0016829	-0.45	0.656	-.0040501	.0025488
freelunch	.0012833	.0194693	0.07	0.947	-.0368884	.039455
_cons	.4628762	.0331314	13.97	0.000	.3979184	.5278341
schid	F(78, 3660) =		2.405	0.000	(79 categories)	

The linear p robability model is reco nsidered in Chapter 8, and altern atives to the li near probability model are given in Chapter 16.

7.5 DIFFERENCES-IN-DIFFERENCES ESTIMATION

Natural experiments mimic randomized control experiments and are useful for e valuating policy changes. There is a treatment group that is affected by a policy change and a control group that is similar but which is not af fected by the policy change. The situation is illustr ated in the figure below. The treatment effect is the change $\overline{CD}$.

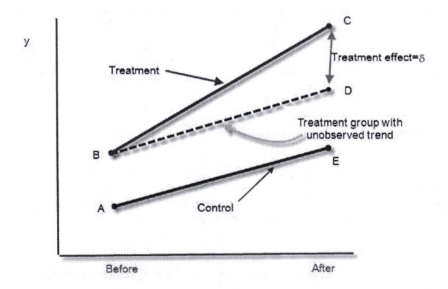

The treatment effect is estimated as

$$\hat{\delta} = \left(\hat{C} - \hat{E}\right) - \left(\hat{B} - \hat{A}\right) = \left(\bar{y}_{Treatment,After} - \bar{y}_{Control,After}\right) - \left(\bar{y}_{Treatment,Before} - \bar{y}_{Control,Before}\right)$$

Where $\bar{y}$ denotes the various sample means. The estimator is called a **differences-in-differences** (abbreviated as D-in-D, DD, or DID) estimator of the treatment effect.

The DID estimator can be conveniently calculated using a simple regression. Define y_{it} to be the observed outcome for individual i in period t. Let $AFTER_t$ be an indicator variable that equals 1 in the period after the policy change ($t = 2$) and equals 0 in the period before the policy change ($t = 1$). Let $TREAT_i$ be an indicator variable that equals 1 if individual i is in the treatment group, and equals 0 if the individual is in the control (non-treatment) group. Consider the regression model

$$y_{it} = \beta_1 + \beta_2 TREAT_i + \beta_3 AFTER_t + \delta\left(TREAT_i \times AFTER_t\right) + e_{it}$$

The example in *Principles of Econometrics*, 4th edition, is from Card and Kruegar (199 4)[1]. On April 1, 1992, New Jersey's minimum wage was increased from \$4.25 to \$5.05 per hour, while the minimum wage in Pennsylvania stayed at \$4.25 per hour. Card and Krueger collected data on 410 fast food restaurants in New Jersey (the treatment group) and eastern Pennsylvania (the control group). The "before" period is February, 1992, and the "after" period is November, 1992. Using these data they estimate the effect of the "treatment," raising the New Jersey minimum wage on employment at fast food restaurants in New Jersey.

We open a new log and *njmin3.dta*.

```
log using chap07_nj, replace text
use njmin3, clear
describe
```

The key variables are

variable name	storage type	display format	value label	variable label
nj	byte	%8.0g		= 1 if new jersey
d	byte	%8.0g		= 1 if after nj min wage increase
d_nj	byte	%8.0g		nj*d interaction
fte	double	%10.0g		full time-equivalent employees

The summary statistics for the key variables are

```
summarize
```

Full-time equivalent employment is not observed for all franchises, so there are so me missing values in the data.

---

[1] David Card and Alan Krueger (1994) "Minimum Wages and Employment: A Case Study of the Fast Food Industry in New Jersey and Pennsylvania," *The American Economic Review*, 84, 316-361.

```
. summarize nj d d_nj fte
```

Variable	Obs	Mean	Std. Dev.	Min	Max
nj	820	.8073171	.3946469	0	1
d	820	.5	.5003052	0	1
d_nj	820	.4036585	.49093	0	1
fte	794	21.02651	9.422746	0	85

The various means for the DID estimator are computed using

```
bysort nj d: summarize fte
```

```
. bysort nj d: summarize fte
```

-> nj = 0, d = 0

Variable	Obs	Mean	Std. Dev.	Min	Max
fte	77	23.33117	11.85628	7.5	70.5

-> nj = 0, d = 1

Variable	Obs	Mean	Std. Dev.	Min	Max
fte	77	21.16558	8.276732	0	43.5

-> nj = 1, d = 0

Variable	Obs	Mean	Std. Dev.	Min	Max
fte	321	20.43941	9.106239	5	85

-> nj = 1, d = 1

Variable	Obs	Mean	Std. Dev.	Min	Max
fte	319	21.02743	9.293024	0	60.5

Using the regression approach we can compute the means using **lincom**.

```
reg fte nj d d_nj
estimates store did
```

```
. reg fte nj d d_nj
```

Source	SS	df	MS
Model	521.116463	3	173.705488
Residual	69887.878	790	88.4656683
Total	70408.9944	793	88.7881393

Number of obs =	794
F(3, 790) =	1.96
Prob > F =	0.1180
R-squared =	0.0074
Adj R-squared =	0.0036
Root MSE =	9.4056

fte	Coef.	Std. Err.	t	P>|t|	[95% Conf. Interval]	
nj	-2.891761	1.193524	-2.42	0.016	-5.234614	-.5489079
d	-2.165584	1.515853	-1.43	0.154	-5.14116	.8099912
d_nj	2.753606	1.688409	1.63	0.103	-.560693	6.067905
_cons	23.33117	1.07187	21.77	0.000	21.22712	25.43522

The average FTE in New Jersey before the policy change is

```
        lincom _cons + nj
```

```
. lincom _cons + nj
```

```
 ( 1)  nj + _cons = 0
```

fte	Coef.	Std. Err.	t	P>|t|	[95% Conf. Interval]	
(1)	20.43941	.5249705	38.93	0.000	19.40891	21.46991

Similarly the other values are estimated using

```
        lincom _cons + d
        lincom _cons + nj + d  + d_nj
        lincom (_cons + nj + d + d_nj)-(_cons + d)-((_cons + nj)-_cons)
```

```
. lincom _cons + d
```

```
 ( 1)  d + _cons = 0
```

fte	Coef.	Std. Err.	t	P>|t|	[95% Conf. Interval]	
(1)	21.16558	1.07187	19.75	0.000	19.06153	23.26963

```
. lincom _cons + nj + d  + d_nj
```

```
 ( 1)  nj + d + d_nj + _cons = 0
```

fte	Coef.	Std. Err.	t	P>|t|	[95% Conf. Interval]	
(1)	21.02743	.5266136	39.93	0.000	19.9937	22.06116

```
. lincom (_cons + nj + d + d_nj)-(_cons + d)-((_cons + nj)-_cons)

 ( 1)   d_nj = 0
```

fte	Coef.	Std. Err.	t	P>|t|	[95% Conf. Interval]
(1)	2.753606	1.688409	1.63	0.103	-.560693 6.067905

Add other control variables and create a table using

```
reg fte nj d d_nj kfc roys wendys co_owned
estimates store did2

reg fte nj d d_nj kfc roys wendys co_owned southj centralj pa1
estimates store did3

esttab did did2 did3, b(%10.4f) se(%10.3f) t(%10.3f) r2 ar2 ///
title("Difference in Difference Regressions")
```

A portion of the table is

Difference in Difference Regressions

	(1) fte	(2) fte	(3) fte
nj	-2.8918*	-2.3766*	-0.9080
	(1.194)	(1.079)	(1.272)
d	-2.1656	-2.2236	-2.2119
	(1.516)	(1.368)	(1.349)
d_nj	2.7536	2.8451	2.8149
	(1.688)	(1.523)	(1.502)

If we used only paired observations

```
reg fte nj d d_nj if !missing(demp)
```

```
. reg fte nj d d_nj if !missing(demp)
```

Source	SS	df	MS
Model	528.354829	3	176.118276
Residual	69115.6953	764	90.4655698
Total	69644.0502	767	90.8005869

```
Number of obs =      768
F( 3,   764) =     1.95
Prob > F      =   0.1206
R-squared     =   0.0076
Adj R-squared =   0.0037
Root MSE      =   9.5113
```

fte	Coef.	Std. Err.	t	P>|t|	[95% Conf. Interval]
nj	-2.949417	1.224327	-2.41	0.016	-5.352862 -.5459732
d	-2.283333	1.553195	-1.47	0.142	-5.33237 .7657035
d_nj	2.75	1.73146	1.59	0.113	-.6489834 6.148983
_cons	23.38	1.098275	21.29	0.000	21.22401 25.53599

The variable **demp** is missing if employment figures were not available both before and after the policy change. The Stata logical operator " != " is "not equal to," so the `if` qualifier uses only observations for which **demp** is not a missing value.

KEY TERMS

!missing	factor variables	**margins, dydx**
areg	fixed effects	missing value
areg varlist, absorb(var)	F-test	**nlcom**
average marginal effect	F-test critical value	not equal to !=
by	**generate**	pairwise correlations
bysort	**global**	**pwcorr**
Chow test	**if**	**quietly**
delta method	indicator variables	regional indicator variables
DID	interaction variables	**regress, coeflegend**
difference estimator	**invFtail**	**tabulate**
differences-in-differences	**lincom**	**tabul varname, gen()**
dummy variables	linear probability model	**test**
estimates store	log-linear model	treatment effects
estimates table	marginal effect	
esttab	**margins**	

CHAPTER 7 DO-FILE

```
* file chap07.do for Using Stata for Principles of Econometrics, 4e

cd c:\data\poe4stata

* Stata Do-file
* copyright C 2011 by Lee C. Adkins and R. Carter Hill
* used for "Using Stata for Principles of Econometrics, 4e"
* by Lee C. Adkins and R. Carter Hill (2011)
* John Wiley and Sons, Inc.

* setup
version 11.1
capture log close
set more off

* Chapter 7.1 Indicator Variables in Real Estate Example

* open log
log using chap07_utown, replace text

* open data
use utown, clear

* summarize and examine
describe
summarize
list in 1/6
```

```
list in 501/506

* examples creating indicator variables
summarize price sqft, detail
gen large = (sqft > 25)
gen midprice = (215 < price) & (price < 275)
list sqft price large midprice in 1/5

* estimate dummy variable regression
reg price i.utown sqft i.utown#c.sqft age i.pool i.fplace
reg price i.utown##c.sqft age i.pool i.fplace

* test significance of utown
test 1.utown 1.utown#c.sqft

* use lincom for utown slope and intercept
lincom _cons + 1.utown
lincom c.sqft + 1.utown#c.sqft

* ame
margins, dydx(*)

* ame for utown
quietly summarize sqft
scalar asqft = r(mean)
lincom 1.utown+c.sqft#1.utown*asqft

* ame for sqft
quietly summarize utown
scalar autown = r(mean)
lincom c.sqft+c.sqft#1.utown*autown

/*******************************/
/* A matrix approach           */
/* Not included in text material*/
/*******************************/

matrix list e(b)
matrix list e(V)
matrix vbols = e(V)

*---------------------------------
* for utown
*---------------------------------
* extract variances and covariance
scalar vb2=vbols[2,2]
scalar vb5=vbols[5,5]
scalar cov52 = vbols[5,2]

* mean of _cons and sqft
quietly summarize sqft
scalar asqft = r(mean)
scalar aconst = 1

* delta method for ame of utown
scalar vame=(aconst^2)*vb2+(asqft^2)*vb5+2*asqft*aconst*cov52
scalar seame = sqrt(vame)
di "Delta-method standard error for utown " seame

*---------------------------------
* for sqft
*---------------------------------
* delta method se for sqft ame
```

```
quietly summarize utown
scalar autown = r(mean)
scalar vb3=vbols[3,3]
scalar cov53 = vbols[5,3]

* delta method
scalar vame=(aconst^2)*vb3+(autown^2)*vb5+2*autown*aconst*cov53
scalar seame = sqrt(vame)
di "Delta-method standard error for sqft " seame

log close

* Chapter 7.2 in POE4: Applying indicator variables

* open new log
log using chap07_cps4, replace text

* open data
use cps4_small, clear
describe
summarize

* estimate model with black-female interaction
reg wage educ i.black##i.female

* estimate wage difference between black-female and white-male
lincom 1.black + 1.female + 1.black#1.female

* F-test of joint significance
test 1.female 1.black 1.black#1.female

* Average marginal effects
margins, dydx(*)

quietly summarize black
scalar ablack = r(mean)
lincom 1.female + 1.black#1.female*ablack

* Chapter 7.2.2 Add regional indicators
reg wage educ i.black##i.female i.south i.midwest i.west
test 1.south 1.midwest 1.west

di "F(3,992,.95) = " invFtail(3,992,.05)
di "F(3,992,.90) = " invFtail(3,992,.10)

* Chapter 7.2.3 Testing the equivalence of two regressions
reg wage i.south##(c.educ i.black##i.female)
test 1.south 1.south#c.educ 1.south#1.black 1.south#1.female ///
        1.south#1.black#1.female

* constructing estimates in separate regressions from fully interacted model
lincom 1.black + 1.black#1.south
lincom 1.female + 1.female#1.south

* Estimate separate regressions
bysort south: reg wage educ i.black##i.female

* Chapter 7.3 Log-linear models

gen lwage = ln(wage)

* estimate regression
reg lwage educ i.female
```

```
* use nlcom to obtain exact effect of dummy variable
nlcom 100*(exp(_b[1.female]) - 1)

* using nlcom with interaction variables
reg lwage c.educ##c.exper
reg, coeflegend

lincom 100*(exper+ c.educ#c.exper*16)
nlcom 100*(exp( _b[exper]+_b[c.educ#c.exper]*16) - 1)
log close

* Chapter 7.4 Linear Probability Model

* open new log
log using chap07_coke, replace text

* open data and examine
use coke, clear
describe
summarize

* estimate regression
reg coke pratio disp_coke disp_pepsi
predict phat
summarize phat
summarize phat if phat<=0
log close

* Chapter 7.5 Treatment Effects

* open new log
log using chap07_star, replace text

* open data and examine
use star, clear
describe

drop if aide==1
summarize

* create lists
global x1list small
global x2list $x1list tchexper
global x3list $x2list boy freelunch white_asian
global x4list $x3list tchwhite tchmasters schurban schrural

* summarize for regular and small classes
summarize totalscore $x4list if regular==1
summarize  totalscore $x4list if small==1

* correlations
pwcorr $x3list

* create school indicators
tabulate schid, gen(school)

* regressions
quietly reg totalscore $x1list
estimates store model1

quietly reg totalscore $x2list
estimates store model2
```

```
quietly reg totalscore $x3list
estimates store model3

quietly reg totalscore $x4list
estimates store model4

* create simple tables
estimates table model1 model2 model3 model4, b(%12.3f) se stats(N r2 F bic)

* create better tables: enter findit esttab
esttab model1 model2 model3 model4 , se(%12.3f) b(%12.3f) ///
        star(* 0.10 ** 0.05 *** 0.01) gaps ar2 bic scalars(rss) ///
        title("Project Star: Kindergarden")

* regressions with fixed effects
* the hard way
reg totalscore $x2list school2-school79

* using areg
areg totalscore $x1list, absorb(schid)
estimates store amodel1

areg totalscore $x2list, absorb(schid)
estimates store amodel2

quietly areg totalscore $x3list, absorb(schid)
estimates store amodel3

quietly areg totalscore $x4list, absorb(schid)
estimates store amodel4

esttab amodel1 amodel2 amodel3 amodel4 , se(%12.3f) b(%12.3f) ///
        star(* 0.10 ** 0.05 *** 0.01) gaps ar2 bic scalars(rss) ///
        title("Project Star: Kindergarden, with school effects")

* create Table 7.7
esttab model1 model2 amodel1 amodel2 , se(%14.4f) b(%14.4f) ///
        star(* 0.10 ** 0.05 *** 0.01) gaps ar2 scalars(rss) ///
            title("Project Star: Kindergarden")

* Chapter 7.5.4b Check randomness of treatment

* checking using linear probability models
reg small boy white_asian tchexper freelunch
areg small boy white_asian tchexper freelunch, absorb(schid)

/* The following are not discussed in the Chapter */
* adding robust covariance: see chapter 8
reg small boy white_asian tchexper freelunch, vce(robust)
areg small boy white_asian tchexper freelunch, absorb(schid) vce(robust)

* checking randomness using probit: see Chapter 16
probit small boy white_asian tchexper freelunch
probit small boy white_asian tchexper freelunch school2-school79
log close

* Chapter 7.5.6 Differences in Differences Estimators

* open new log file
log using chap07_nj, replace text

* open data file
```

```
use njmin3, clear
describe
summarize nj d d_nj fte

* DID estimation using sample means
bysort nj d: summarize fte

* DID estimation using regression
reg fte nj d d_nj
estimates store did

lincom _cons + nj
lincom _cons + d
lincom _cons + nj + d  + d_nj
lincom (_cons + nj + d + d_nj)-(_cons + d)-((_cons + nj)-_cons)

* add owner controls
reg fte nj d d_nj kfc roys wendys co_owned
estimates store did2

* add location controls
reg fte nj d d_nj kfc roys wendys co_owned southj centralj pa1
estimates store did3

esttab did did2 did3, b(%10.4f) se(%10.3f) t(%10.3f) r2 ar2 ///
title("Difference in Difference Regressions")

* DID regression using only balanced sample
reg fte nj d d_nj if !missing(demp)

log close
```

CHAPTER **8**

Heteroskedasticity

8.1 THE NATURE OF HETEROSKEDASTICITY

The simple linear regression models of Chapters 3 and 4 and the multiple regression model in Chapters 5 and 6 can be generalized in several ways. For instance, there is no guarantee that the random variables of these models (either the y_i or the e_i) have the same inherent variability across observations. That is, some observations may have a larger variance than others. This describes the condition referred to as **heteroskedasticity**. The simple linear regression model is shown below.

$$y_i = \beta_1 + \beta_2 x_i + e_i$$

where y_i is your dependent variable, x_i i^{th} observation on the independent variable, e_i is random error, and β_1 and β_2 are the parameters you want to estimate. The errors have zero mean for any value of x_i and are uncorrelated with one another. The difference in this model is that the variance of the errors now depends on the observation to which it belongs. So, the error variance is now referenced with the observation subscript, $i=1, 2, \ldots, N$.

The error assumptions are summarized

$$E(e_i) = 0 \quad \text{var}(e_i) = \sigma_i^2 \quad \text{cov}(e_i, e_j) = 0$$

In this chapter, several w ays to detect heterosk edasticity are considered. Also, statistically valid ways of estimating the parameters of the linear regression model and testing hypotheses about the parameters when the data are heteroskedastic are explored.

The least squares estimator can be used to estimate the linear model even when the errors are heteroskedastic; it is unbiased and consi stent even when MR3, $\text{var}(y_i) = \text{var}(e_i) = \sigma^2$, is violated. The problem with using least squar es in a hetero skedastic model is that the usual measure of precision (estimated variance-covariance matrix) is not consistent. There are several w ays to tackle this problem. The first is to use least squa res along with an estimator of its covariance that *is* consistent whether errors are heterosk edastic or not. This is the so-called **robust** estimator of covariance that Stata uses . This is discussed in Section 8.2 below. Another is to m odel the heteroskedasticity and use weighted least squares. This option is discussed in Section 8.3.

In the first exam ple, the food expenditure data is used to esti mate the model using least squares. Change your working directory to the one containing the *food.dta* data set and load the data set.

```
cd c:\data\poe4stata
use food, clear
```

Start by estimating the food expenditure model using least squares.

```
regress food_exp income
```

It can be useful to plot the data and the estimated regression line. In Stata

```
graph twoway (scatter food_exp income) (lfit food_exp income)
```

produces two scatter plots in the same graph. The co mmands to generate e ach plot are contained in the two sets of parentheses. The f irst graph is a **twoway** scatter plot of **food_exp** against **income**. T he second uses **lfit** to esti mate the si mple regression of **food_exp** onto **income**. Deviations between the re gression line and the actual values of **food_exp** are the least squ ares residuals.

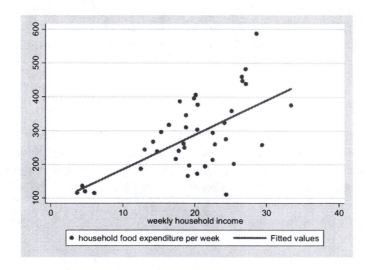

The graph looks very similar to Figure 8.2 in *Principles of Econometrics*, 4th Edition (*POE4*).

8.2 DETECTING HETEROSKEDASTICITY

There are a num ber of graphical and statistical way s to detect heteroskedasticity in a m odel. In this section, several are discussed.

8.2.1 Residual Plots

One way to get a f eeling for whether t he errors are heteroskedastic is to plot them against the sorted value of the independent variabl e. A couple of exam ples were given in the preceding section. Another way to visualize the relationship is to estimate the model, save the residuals, and use **graph twoway** to plot the two:

```
regress food_exp income
predict ehat, res
graph twoway scatter ehat income, yline(0)
```

The graph is

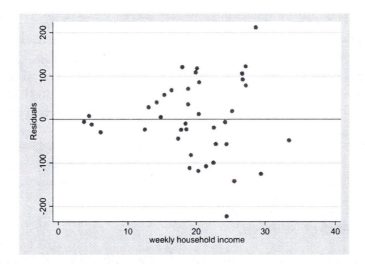

The **yline(0)** option was added to plot the red horizontal line at zero. From the graph it appears that the residuals are l arger for larger values of income. This can be conf irmed statistically using one or more of the tests below.

Another graphical method that shows the relationship between the magnitude of the residuals and the independent variable is shown below:

```
generate abs_e = abs(ehat)
twoway (scatter abs_e income) (lowess abs_e income, lw(thick))
```

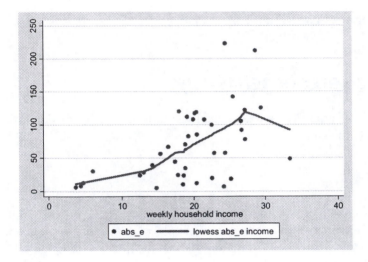

To generate this graph two things have been done. First, the absolute value of the least squares residuals have been saved to a new variable called **abs_e**. Then these are plotted against **income** as a scatter and as a locally weighted, s moothed scatterplot estimated by process called **lowess**. From Stata documentation we learn that the basic idea behind **lowess** is to create a new variable (**newvar**) that, for each value of the dependent variable, y_i, contains the corresponding smoothed value. The smoothed values are obtained by running a regression of y on x by using only the data $(x_i; y_i)$ and a few o f the data ne ar this poi nt. In **lowess**, the regression is weighted so that the central point $(x_i; y_i)$ gets the hi ghest weight and points that are f arther away (based on the distance $|x_j - x_i|$) receive less weight. The estimated regre ssion line is then used to predict the smoothed value $\hat{y}_i$ for y_i only. The procedure is repeat ed to obtain the rem aining smoothed values, which means that a separate weighted regression is performed for every point in the data. Obviously, if your data set is large, this can take a while. **Lowess** is said to be a desirable smoother because of it tends to follow t he data. Polynomial smoothing methods, for instance, are global in that what happens on the extreme left of a scatterplot can affect the fitt ed values on the extreme right.

One can see from the gra ph that the re siduals tend to get larger as income rises, reaching a maximum at 28. The residual for an observation having the largest income is relatively small and the locally smoothed prediction causes the line to start trending downward.

8.2.2 Lagrange Multiplier Tests

There are many tests of the n ull hypothesis of homoskedasticity that hav e been prop osed elsewhere. Two of these, based on Lagrange multipliers, are particularly simple to do and u seful. The first is sometimes referred to as the Breusch-Pagan (BP) test or in Stata, the Breusch-Godfrey test. The second test is credited to White.

The null and alternative hypotheses for the Breusch-Pagan test are

$$H_0 : \sigma_i^2 = \sigma^2 \qquad H_1 : \sigma_i^2 = \sigma^2 h(\alpha_2 z_{i2} + ... + \alpha_s z_{is})$$

The null h ypothesis is that the data are ho moskedastic. The alternative is that the data are heteroskedastic in a way that depends upon t he variables z_{i2}, z_{i3}, ..., $z_{is,}$, which are exogenou s variables that are correlated with the model's variances. The function $h()$, is not specified. It could be anything that depends on its argument, i.e., the linear function of the variables in z.

Here are the steps:

- Estimate the regression model
- Save the residuals
- Square the residuals
- Regress the squared residuals on $z_{i2}, z_{i3}, ..., z_{is}$
- Compute NR^2 from this regression and compare it to α level critical value from the $\chi^2(S-1)$ distribution.

In Stata the test for heteroskedasticity dependent on income in the food expenditure model is:

```
use food, clear
quietly regress food_exp income
predict ehat, residual
gen ehat2=ehat^2
quietly regress ehat2 income
di "NR2 = " e(N)*e(r2)
di "5% critical value = " invchi2tail(e(df_m),.05)
di "P-value = " chi2tail(e(df_m),e(N)*e(r2))
```

The result

```
NR2 = 7.3844244
5% critical value = 3.8414588
P-value = .00657911
```

Notice that Stata saves the sample size, R^2, and the degrees of freedom from the auxilia ry regression in **e(N)**, **e(r2)**, and **e(df_m)**, respectively. As usual, **invchi2tail** is used to obtain the 5% critical value and **chi2tail** the *p*-value associated with the computed value of the *LM* statistic.

White's test is in fact just a minor variation on the Breusch-Pagan test. The null and alternative hypotheses are

$$H_0 : \sigma_i^2 = \sigma^2 \qquad H_1 : \sigma_i^2 \neq \sigma_j^2$$

for at least one $i \neq j$. This is a composite alternative that captures every possibility other than the one covered by the null. If you know nothing about the nature of heteroskedasticity in your data, then this is a good place to start. Th e test is very similar to the BP test. In this test, the heteroskedasticity related variables ($z_{i2}, z_{i3}, ..., z_{is}$) include each non-redundant regressor and its square, and all cross products between regresso rs. See your t ext for detai ls. In the f ood expenditure model there is only one continuous regressor and an intercept. So, the constant squared and the cross product between the consta nt and income are redundant. This leaves only one unique variable to add to the m odel, income squared. In Stata genera te the squared value of income and regress the squared residuals from the model on income and its square. Compute NR^2 from this regression and compare it to α level critical value fro m the $\chi^2(S-1)$ distribution. As is the case in all the *LM* tests considered in this book, *N* is the number of observations in the second or auxiliary regression.

```
quietly regress ehat2 income c.income#c.income
di "NR2 = " e(N)*e(r2)
di "5% critical value = " invchi2tail(e(df_m),.05)
di "P-value = " chi2tail(e(df_m),e(N)*e(r2))
```

The result

```
NR2 = 7.5550786
5% critical value = 5.9914645
P-value = .02287892
```

Fortunately, Stata has built in functions to compute both of these test statistics and their *p*-values. They are a little hard to find, but here's how. The first thing to do is estimate the linear regression. Then select **Statistics > Linear models and related > Regression Diagnostics > Specification tests, etc** from the pull-down menu. Then for the *LM* test, use the scroll wheel on the right side of the box to select **Tests for heteroskedasticity (hettest)** from the list. In the next fly-out menu, choose **N*R2 version of the score test**; this adds the **iid** option to the command **estat hottest** command. Click the radio button for **Use the following variables**, then type in or select the desired variable(s) from the fly-out list. Click **OK**.

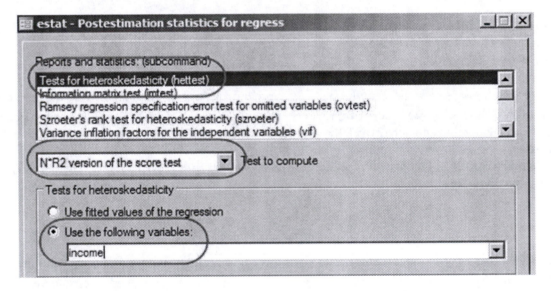

This yields

```
. estat hettest income, iid

Breusch-Pagan / Cook-Weisberg test for heteroskedasticity
         Ho: Constant variance
         Variables: income

         chi2(1)      =       7.38
         Prob > chi2  =     0.0066
```

which is the same result obtained manually using Stata commands.

White's test can be performed using the same dialog box. This time select *Information matrix test* (**imtest**) as highlighted and check the *Perform White's original heteroskedasticity test* box as shown below.

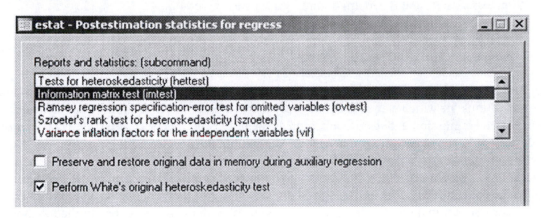

The result is

```
. estat imtest, white

White's test for Ho: homoskedasticity
        against Ha: unrestricted heteroskedasticity

        chi2(2)      =         7.56
        Prob > chi2  =       0.0229
```

The best of both worlds can be accomplished via the **Command** window using

```
quietly regress food_exp income
estat hettest income, iid
estat imtest, white
```

8.2.3 The Goldfeld-Quandt test

The Goldfeld-Quandt test is easy to perform when you suspect that the variance depends on a specific variable. To illustrate this test an example is used where average wages are estimated as a linear function of education and experience. In addition, a dummy variable is included that is equal to one if a person lives in a metropolitan area. This is an "intercept" dummy variable, which means that folks living in the metro areas are expected to respond similarly to changes in education and experience (same slopes), but that they earn a premium relative to those in rural areas (different intercept).

The test compares the estimated variances from two partitions of the data. In this example it is hypothesized that the error variance for the metro subsample is equal to that of the rural one.

$$H_0 : \sigma_M^2 = \sigma_R^2 \qquad \text{against} \qquad H_0 : \sigma_M^2 \neq \sigma_R^2$$

The two partitions are estimated via least squares and the estimated variances, $\hat{\sigma}_M^2$ and $\hat{\sigma}_R^2$, are obtained. The test statistic is $F = \hat{\sigma}_M^2 / \hat{\sigma}_R^2$ which has an $F_{(NM\text{-}KM,\ NR\text{-}KR)}$ distribution if the null hypothesis is true. ($N_M - K_M$) is just the degrees of freedom from the metro partition and ($N_R - K_R$) is that from the rural partition.

First, the entire sa mple from the *cps2.dta* data set is used to esti mate the wage model using education, experience, and the metro dummy variable as regressors.

```
use cps2, clear
regress wage educ exper metro
```

The rural subsample is estimated using the **if metro==0** qualifier. Stata is instructed to use only the observations for which **metro** is equal to zero or one using an **if** qualifier; the **if** qualifier is used *after* the regression and *before* any regression options. In this case the st atement **if metro == 0** uses only the observations that satisfy the conditional (metro equal to zero). The d ouble equal sign is necessary, otherwise Stata thinks that you are trying to assign the variable **metro** the value of 0; in a single instance = i s Stata's assignment operator. It assigns val ue that lies t o its right to the nam e given on its left; **x=2** *assigns* the value 2 to the variable **x**. That is not what i s wanted here, so use two equal signs. Estimate the model with the observations limited to those for which **metro == 0** and save $\hat{\sigma}$ and the degrees of freedom for later use.

```
regress wage educ exper if metro == 0
scalar rmse_r = e(rmse)
scalar df_r = e(df_r)
```

Repeat for the metro subsample

```
regress wage educ exper if metro == 1
scalar rmse_m = e(rmse)
scalar df_m = e(df_r)
```

Now form the Goldfeld-Quandt ratio, get the 5% critical value and the *p*-value of GQ.

```
scalar GQ = rmse_m^2/rmse_r^2
scalar crit = invFtail(df_m,df_r,.05)
scalar pvalue = Ftail(df_m,df_r,GQ)
scalar list GQ pvalue crit
```

And the result from Stata is:

```
. scalar list GQ pvalue crit
       GQ =   2.0877623
   pvalue =   1.567e-09
     crit =   1.2150333
```

The homoskedasticity null hypothesis is rejected at any reasonable level of si gnificance (5% or 10%) in favor of the alternative.

Food Expenditure Example

Another example uses the food expenditure m odel. In this example the variance is thought t o be an increasing function of income. So, we first sort the data by income (ascending) and then repeat the Goldfeld-Quandt test. The fort y observations are broken into t wo equal size partitions. Then the same steps used above are repeated to obtain the result. First load the food dataset and sort by income

```
use food, clear
sort income
```

Then regress **food_exp** on **income** and a constant using the first 20 observations, saving the estimated variance and de grees of free dom. The st atement **in 1/20** is a conditional statement similar to the **if** qualifier used in Section 8.3. In thi s case, **in** instructs Stat a to use a range of observations and **1/20** is the syntax used to indicate observations 1 to 20.

```
regress food_exp income in 1/20
scalar s_small = e(rmse)^2
scalar df_small = e(df_r)
```

Now, regress **food_exp** on **income** and a constant using observatio ns 21 through 40 (**in 21/40**), saving the estimated variance and degrees of freedom.

```
regress food_exp income in 21/40
scalar s_large = e(rmse)^2
scalar df_large = e(df_r)
```

Now, compute the Goldfeld-Quandt statistic, its 5% critical value and p-value.

```
scalar GQ = s_large/s_small
scalar crit = invFtail(df_large,df_small,.05)
scalar pvalue = Ftail(df_large,df_small,GQ)
scalar list GQ pvalue crit
```

The results are

```
. scalar list GQ pvalue crit
       GQ =  3.6147557
   pvalue =  .00459643
     crit =  2.2171971
```

Once again, the hom   oskedasticity null hypothesi s is reject ed at any reasonable level of significance in favor of the alternative.

8.3 HETEROSKEDASTIC-CONSISTENT STANDARD ERRORS

The least squares estimator can be used to esti mate the linear model even w hen the error s are heteroskedastic with good results. As mentioned above, the problem with using least squares in a heteroskedastic model is that the usual esti   mator of precision (esti mated variance-covariance matrix) is not consistent. The si   mplest way to t ackle this proble m is to use   least squar es to estimate the intercept and slopes and   use an estimator of l east squares covariance that *is* consistent whether errors are heterosked astic or not. This is t he so-called **heteroskcedasticity robust** estimator of covariance that Stata uses.

In this example, the food expenditure da ta is used to estimate the model using least squares. Change your working directory to the one containing the *food.dta* data set and the data set.

```
use food, clear
```

Start by estimating the f ood expenditure model using least sq uares and st ore the esti mates (Usual). Re-estimate the m odel using the **vce(robust)** option and store the results (**store White**). Then use the estimates table command to print both sets of results to the screen.

```
quietly regress food_exp income
estimates store Usual

quietly reg food_exp income, vce(robust)
estimates store White

estimates table Usual White, b(%7.4f) se(%7.3f) stats(F)
```

. estimates table Usual White, b(%7.4f) se(%7.3f) stats(F)

Variable	Usual	White
income	10.2096	10.2096
	2.093	1.809
_cons	83.4160	83.4160
	43.410	27.464
F	23.7888	31.8498

legend: b/se

Notice that t he coefficient estimates are the same, but that the esti mated standard errors are different. Interestingly enough, the robust standard errors are actually smaller than the usual ones!

The level of the confidence interval can be changed to 90% by using the **level(90)** option in the regress statement.

```
reg food_exp income, vce(robust) level(90)
```

Linear regression

```
Number of obs =      40
F(  1,    38) =   31.85
Prob > F      =  0.0000
R-squared     =  0.3850
Root MSE      =  89.517
```

food_exp	Coef.	Robust Std. Err.	t	P>|t|	[90% Conf. Interval]	
income	10.20964	1.809077	5.64	0.000	7.159622	13.25966
_cons	83.416	27.46375	3.04	0.004	37.11337	129.7186

Or, the confidence intervals can be computed manually using saved results from the regression as shown in the .do-file at the end of this chapter.

The dialog boxes can be used to obtain the sa me results. Select **Statistics > Linear models and related > Linear reg ression** to open the fam iliar **regress – Linear regre ssion** dialog box. Fill in the dependent and independent variables as you usually would. Before leaving the dialog, select the tab labeled **SE/Robust**.

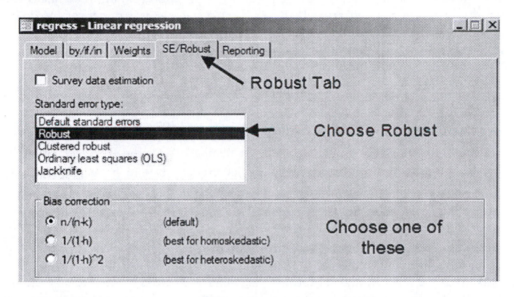

Choose the **Robust** option in the *standard error type* box and s elect one of the options fo r bias correction using the radio buttons. Here, we have left it at the default value. All are consistent, but each gives slightly different results in small samples. Now click **OK**.

These robust standard errors are obtained from what is often referred to as t he heteroskedasticity-consistent covariance matrix estimator (**HCCME**) that was proposed by Huber and rediscovered by White. In econometrics, the HCCME standard errors may be referred to as White's standard errors or Huber/White standard errors.

Since least squares is inefficient in heteroskedastic models, you'd think that t here might be another unbiased esti mator that is m ore precise. And, there is. The **generalized least square s** (GLS) estimator is, at least in principle, easy to obtain. Essentially, with the GLS esti mator of the heteroskedastic model, the different error variances are used to rew eight the data so that they are all have the same (homoskedastic) variance. If the data are equally variable, then least squares is efficient!

8.4 THE GENERALIZED LEAST SQUARES ESTIMATOR

If $\text{var}(e_i) = \sigma_i^2$, then dividing e_i by σ_i will give all the errors the sam e variance (equal to 1). That is,

$$\text{var}(e_i / \sigma_i) = 1/\sigma_i^2 \, \text{var}(e_i) = (1/\sigma_i^2)\sigma_i^2 = 1$$

To transform your model weight the observations using σ_i. For the food ex penditure model this becomes

$$\frac{y_i}{\sigma_i} = \beta_1 \frac{1}{\sigma_i} + \beta_2 \frac{x_i}{\sigma_i} + \frac{e_i}{\sigma_i}$$

Each observation, y_i, constant, and x_i is being weighted by the reciprocal of the standard deviation associated with that observation's error. It sounds complicated, but it is rather easy to do in Stata, provided you know the part of σ_i that varies.

Assume that the variance in the food expenditure model is proportional to x_i:

$$\text{var}(e_i) = \sigma_i^2 = \sigma^2 x_i$$

So, to give each observa tion the same variance, d ivide y_i, the constant, and x_i by $\sqrt{x_i}$. Stata includes a way to work with weighted data in a number of its procedures, including li near regression. To estimate the food expenditure model the data sh ould be weighted by $1/\sqrt{x_i}$, which is done using *analytic weights* in Stata. The analytic weights are <u>*inversely*</u> proportional to the *variance* of an observation. So, the syntax used to reweight the food expenditure model is

```
regress food_exp income [aweight=1/income]
```

where **aweight** is the Stata co mmand for analytic weights. There is no need to take the sq uare root of the weight to get s tandard deviation; St ata expects the variance. To divide observations by $\sqrt{x_i}$, then set the **aweight** to $1/x_i$.

The dialogs are e asy to use in this case as well. Select **Statistics > Linear models and related > Linear regression** to open t he now familiar **regress – Linear regression** dialog box. Fill in the dependent and independent variables as you usually would. Before leaving the dialog, select the tab labeled **Weights**.

Click the *Analytic weights* button and enter the desired analy tic weight in the box as shown below. In this case, we've used the reciprocal of **income**.

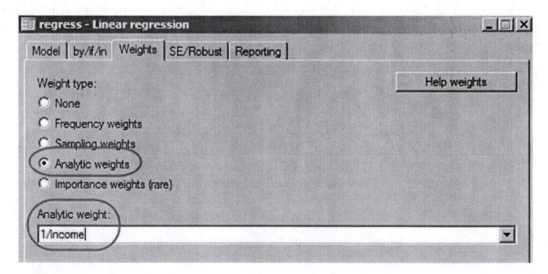

Click **OK** and you get:

```
. regress food_exp income [aweight = 1/income]
(sum of wgt is    2.6616e+00)
```

Source	SS	df	MS
Model	300459.464	1	300459.464
Residual	200775.783	38	5283.57325
Total	501235.248	39	12852.1858

Number of obs = 40
F(1, 38) = 56.87
Prob > F = 0.0000
R-squared = 0.5994
Adj R-squared = 0.5889
Root MSE = 72.688

food_exp	Coef.	Std. Err.	t	P>|t|	[95% Conf. Interval]
income	10.45101	1.385891	7.54	0.000	7.645419 13.2566
_cons	78.68408	23.78872	3.31	0.002	30.52633 126.8418

You can see that the GLS estimated standard error for the income coefficient (1.386) is substantially smaller than the one produced for least squares by the HCCME (1.809).

8.4.1 GLS using Grouped Data

The example consists of estimating wages as a function of education and experience and is based on the *cps2.dta* used in the Goldfeld-Quandt test example. The strategy for combining these partitions and estimating the parameters using generalized least squares is the fairly simple. Each subsample will be used to estimate the model and the standard error of the regression (e(rmse)) will be saved. Then each subsample is weighted by its estimated variance (which is the squared value of the e(rmse).

There are a couple of ways to estimate each subsample. The first was used in the Goldfeld-Quandt test example where the metro subsample was chosen using the if metro==1 qualifier and the rural one chosen with if metro==0. Grouped GLS using this method can be found in the .do file at the end of the chapter and will not be repeated here. The other uses a trick whereby subsamples of the data can be taken using analytical weights (i.e., the aweight command). Weighting variables by 0 or 1 is a handy way of taking subsamples. Weighting an observation by 0 drops it from the computation of the estimator, whereas ones weighted by 1 are included in its computation.

After loading the data, create an indicator variable for rural households (1 if rural, 0 otherwise) by subtracting metro from one. The run the two subset regressions using the analytical weights, saving the root mean square error of each. Here is the complete code:

```
use cps2, clear
gen rural = 1 - metro
regress wage educ exper [aweight = rural]
scalar sr = e(rmse)^2
regress wage educ exper [aweight = metro]
scalar sm = e(rmse)^2
```

The saved values of the root MSEs are combined into a single weight that can be used to reweight all observations.

```
gen wtall=(sr*rural) + (sm*metro)
regress wage educ exper metro [aweight = 1/wtall]
```

The last line uses the entire sample to estimate the model by GLS. This results in:

```
. regress wage educ exper metro [aweight = 1/wt]
(sum of wgt is   3.7986e+01)
```

Source	SS	df	MS		Number of obs =	1000
					F(3, 996) =	123.75
Model	9797.06665	3	3265.68888		Prob > F =	0.0000
Residual	26284.1489	996	26.3897077		R-squared =	0.2715
					Adj R-squared =	0.2693
Total	36081.2155	999	36.1173329		Root MSE =	5.1371

wage	Coef.	Std. Err.	t	P>|t|	[95% Conf. Interval]	
educ	1.195721	.068508	17.45	0.000	1.061284	1.330157
exper	.1322088	.0145485	9.09	0.000	.1036595	.160758
metro	1.538803	.3462856	4.44	0.000	.8592702	2.218336
_cons	-9.398362	1.019673	-9.22	0.000	-11.39931	-7.397408

In this model, the coefficients of experience and years of schooling are the same for urban and rural wage earners. The indicator variable, **metro**, allows for a shift in the intercept, which is positive for urban workers.

8.4.2 Feasible GLS – a more general case

In the example above, the observation's standard error σ_i (or what it is proportional to) is known. In most cases this information will not be known to you and you will have to estimate it using the data. This turns generalized least squares (GLS) into something slightly different, namely estimated or *feasible* generalized least squares (FGLS).

The first step is to choose a model for the variance that is a function of some independent variables. You'll need some variables that are thought to be correlated with the change in variance and you'll have to specify a functional relationship between the variance and these variables. A common model of the variance uses the exponential function

$$\sigma_i^2 = \exp(\alpha_1 + \alpha_2 z_{i2} + \cdots + \alpha_s z_{iS})$$

where the z_{is} are independent variables and the α_i are parameters. Taking the natural logarithm, substituting the squared least squares residuals for the unobservable σ_i^2, and adding an error term gives you a regression model that can be used to estimate the α_i. For simplicity, assume only one heteroskedasticity related variable z_i and you have

$$\ln(\hat{e}_i^2) = \ln(\sigma_i^2) + v_i = \alpha_1 + \alpha_2 z_i + v_i$$

where the $\hat{e}_i^2$ are from least squares estimation of your original heteroskedastic regression model. Let $z_i = \ln(\text{income})$ and the Stata code to estimate the α_i is

```
gen z = ln(income)
regress food_exp income
predict ehat, residual
```

```
gen ln_ehat_sq = ln(ehat*ehat)
reg ln_ehat_sq z
```

The natural logarithm of **income** is generated, **food_exp** is regressed on **income** and a constant, the residuals saved and the natural logarithm of th e squares is taken. Finall y, these are regressed on **z** and a constant.

This regression yields:

```
. reg ln_ehat_sq z
```

Source	SS	df	MS		
Model	54.8255435	1	54.8255435	Number of obs =	40
Residual	112.530968	38	2.96134126	F(1, 38) =	18.51
				Prob > F =	0.0001
				R-squared =	0.3276
				Adj R-squared =	0.3099
Total	167.356512	39	4.2911926	Root MSE =	1.7209

ln_ehat_sq	Coef.	Std. Err.	t	P>|t|	[95% Conf. Interval]	
z	2.329239	.5413358	4.30	0.000	1.233362	3.425116
_cons	.9377961	1.583106	0.59	0.557	-2.267034	4.142626

To obtain weights for FGLS y   ou need the antil ogs of the predicted values fro   m the last regression. That is, get the linear predictions from this regression **lnsig2** and generate weights using the exponential function **exp(lnsig2)**.

```
predict lnsig2, xb
gen wt = exp(lnsig2)
```

Now, use its reciprocal in **aweight** to reweigh the observations for the regression

```
regress food_exp income [aweight = 1/wt]
```

The result of which is:

```
. regress food_exp income [aweight=(1/wt)]
(sum of wgt is    6.1600e-02)
```

Source	SS	df	MS		
Model	186108.089	1	186108.089	Number of obs =	40
Residual	59033.089	38	1553.50234	F(1, 38) =	119.80
				Prob > F =	0.0000
				R-squared =	0.7592
				Adj R-squared =	0.7529
Total	245141.178	39	6285.67122	Root MSE =	39.414

food_exp	Coef.	Std. Err.	t	P>|t|	[95% Conf. Interval]	
income	10.63349	.9715143	10.95	0.000	8.666763	12.60022
_cons	76.05379	9.71349	7.83	0.000	56.38986	95.71773

8.5 HETEROSKEDASTICITY IN THE LINEAR PROBABILITY MODEL

In Chapter 7.4 we introduced the linear proba bility model for explaining choi ce between two alternatives. This choice can be repr esented by an indicator variable y that takes the value one with probability p if the first alternative is chosen, and the value zero with probability $1-p$ if the second alternative is chosen.

The regression function for the ith observation is

$$y_i = E(y_i) + e_i = \beta_1 + \beta_2 x_{i2} + \ldots + \beta_k x_{iK} + e_i$$

and $E(y_i) = p_i$, which is the probability that the a lternative is chosen by individual i. It can be shown that

$$\text{var}(y_i) = p_i(1 - p_i)$$

which makes the model heteroskedastic. The feasible GLS estimator is easy to compute. First, a linear regression is esti mated and predictions $\hat{y}_i = \hat{p}_i$ are obtained. These are substituted into the variance equation

$$\widehat{\text{var}(y_i)} = \hat{p}_i(1 - \hat{p}_i)$$

Finally, these are used as analytical weights in the regression. Sometimes this fails because one or more of the predicted probabilities lies outside of the (0,1) interval.

The example is based on the data in *coke.dta*. The independent variable, **coke**, takes the value of 1 if the in dividual purchases Coca-Cola and is 0 if not. The de cision to purchase Coca-Cola depends on the ratio of th e price relative to Peps i, and whether display s for Coca-Cola or Pepsi were present. The variables **disp_coke**=1 if a Coca-Cola display was present, otherwise 0; **disp_pepsi** =1 if a Pepsi display was present, otherwise zero.

First, the data are loaded and the summary statistics are provided.

```
use coke, clear
summarize
```

```
. summarize
```

Variable	Obs	Mean	Std. Dev.	Min	Max
coke	1140	.4473684	.4974404	0	1
pr_pepsi	1140	1.202719	.3007257	.68	1.79
pr_coke	1140	1.190088	.2999157	.68	1.79
disp_pepsi	1140	.3640351	.4813697	0	1
disp_coke	1140	.3789474	.4853379	0	1
pratio	1140	1.027249	.286608	.497207	2.324675

Next, the model is estimated by least squares a nd predictions are generated and checked for any negative values (or values greater than one).

```
quietly regress coke pratio disp_coke disp_pepsi
predict p, xb
gen var = p*(1-p)
summarize p var
```

```
. summarize p var
```

Variable	Obs	Mean	Std. Dev.	Min	Max
p	1140	.4473684	.1723611	-.2073211	.7680784
var	1140	.2175476	.0529915	-.2503031	.2499397

Since the minimum is negative, some additional thought has to be given to how one should proceed. One possibility is to omit the observations for which **p**<0 and estimate the model.

```
reg coke pratio disp_coke disp_pepsi [aweight=1/var] if  p > 0
```

Another is to replace all values of **p** less than a small positive threshold with the threshold. Letting the threshold be 0.01 give us

```
replace p = .01 if p < .01
replace var = p*(1-p)
reg coke pratio disp_coke disp_pepsi [aweight=1/var]
```

Here, the **replace** command is used to set **p=0.01** when it actually falls below that value. There are 16 values of **p** that fall below the threshold. The final possibility is to estimate the model using least squares and use the HCCME standard errors. Inferences will be valid if not efficient.

```
reg coke pratio disp_coke disp_pepsi, vce(robust)
```

Each of these regressions were computed and assembled into a table (see the do-file at the end of the chapter for details).

```
. estimates table LS Robust Trunc Omit, b(%7.4f) se(%7.4f) stats(F N)
```

Variable	LS	Robust	Trunc	Omit
pratio	-0.4009	-0.4009	-0.1652	-0.3859
	0.0613	0.0604	0.0444	0.0527
disp_coke	0.0772	0.0772	0.0940	0.0760
	0.0344	0.0339	0.0399	0.0353
disp_pepsi	-0.1657	-0.1657	-0.1314	-0.1587
	0.0356	0.0344	0.0354	0.0360
_cons	0.8902	0.8902	0.6505	0.8795
	0.0655	0.0653	0.0568	0.0594
F	51.6654	57.0701	36.9728	105.6006
N	1140	1140	1140	1124

legend: b/se

The first column, labeled **LS**, contains the least squares estimates along with the usual (inconsistent) standard errors. The next column contains the least squares estimates with heteroskedasticity-consistent standard errors delivered via the **robust** command. The column labeled **Trunc** contains the estimates where the observations less than the 0.01 threshold were truncated to be 0.01. The last column shows the results when the observations producing negative predictions are omitted from the model. The results are reasonably consistent across models except for **Trunc**.

Although the model is theoretically heteroskedastic, it may be worth verifying that the sample is heteroskedastic via White's test discussed earlier in this chapter.

```
quietly regress coke pratio disp_coke disp_pepsi
imtest, white
```

```
. imtest, white

White's test for Ho: homoskedasticity
         against Ha: unrestricted heteroskedasticity

        chi2(7)       =      25.82
        Prob > chi2   =      0.0005
```

The *p*-value is well below 5% and therefore we conclude that the data are heteroskedastic at that level of significance.

KEY TERMS

analytic weights	**graph twoway**	**lowess**
aweight	groupwise heteroskedastic.	**replace**
Breusch-Pagan test	HCCME	residual plots
chi2tail(df,stat)	heteroskedasticity	robust standard errors
drop	**imtest, white**	subsample
e(df_r)	**invchi2tail(df,alpha)**	**twoway**
e(rmse)	**invFtail(J,N-K,alpha)**	**vce(robust)**
estat hettest	Lagrange multiplier	Weighted Least Squares
Ftail(J,N-K,fstat)	**lfit**	White's standard errors
Generalized Least Squares	linear probability model	White's test
Goldfeld-Quandt test	*LM* test	**yline(0)**

CHAPTER 8 DO-FILE [CHAP06.DO]

```
* file chap08.do for Using Stata for Principles of Econometrics, 4e

cd c:\data\poe4stata

* Stata Do-file
* copyright C 2011 by Lee C. Adkins and R. Carter Hill
* used for "Using Stata for Principles of Econometrics, 4e"
* by Lee C. Adkins and R. Carter Hill (2011)
* John Wiley and Sons, Inc.

* setup
version 11.1
capture log close
set more off

* open log
```

```
log using chap08, replace text

* ----------------------------------------
* food expenditure example
* OLS, OLS with White's std errors, GLS
* ----------------------------------------
use food, clear

regress food_exp income
predict ehat, res

graph twoway (scatter food_exp income) (lfit food_exp income, lw(thick))

* ----------------------------------------
* Graph relationship between size of errors and income
* ----------------------------------------
generate abs_e = abs(ehat)
twoway (scatter abs_e income) (lowess abs_e income, lw(thick))

* ----------------------------------------
* Graph relationship between errors and income
* ----------------------------------------
graph twoway scatter ehat income, yline(0)
drop ehat

* ----------------------------------------
* Breusch-Pagan and White tests
* ----------------------------------------

quietly regress food_exp income
predict ehat, residual
gen ehat2=ehat^2
quietly regress ehat2 income
di "NR2 = " e(N)*e(r2)
di "5% critical value = " invchi2tail(e(df_m),.05)
di "P-value = " chi2tail(e(df_m),e(N)*e(r2))

quietly regress ehat2 income c.income#c.income
di "NR2 = " e(N)*e(r2)
di "5% critical value = " invchi2tail(e(df_m),.05)
di "P-value = " chi2tail(e(df_m),e(N)*e(r2))

quietly regress food_exp income
estat hettest income, iid
estat imtest, white

* ----------------------------------------
* Goldfeld Quandt test
* ----------------------------------------
use cps2, clear
regress wage educ exper metro

* ----------------------------------------
* Rural subsample regression
* ----------------------------------------

regress wage educ exper if metro == 0
scalar rmse_r = e(rmse)
scalar df_r = e(df_r)

* ----------------------------------------
* Urban subsample regression
* ----------------------------------------
```

```
regress wage educ exper if metro == 1
scalar rmse_m = e(rmse)
scalar df_m = e(df_r)

scalar GQ = rmse_m^2/rmse_r^2
scalar crit = invFtail(df_m,df_r,.05)
scalar pvalue = Ftail(df_m,df_r,GQ)
scalar list GQ pvalue crit


* -------------------------------------------
* Goldfeld Quandt test for food
* expenditure example
* -------------------------------------------
use food, clear
sort income

regress food_exp income in 1/20
scalar s_small = e(rmse)^2
scalar df_small = e(df_r)

regress food_exp income in 21/40
scalar s_large = e(rmse)^2
scalar df_large = e(df_r)

scalar GQ = s_large/s_small
scalar crit = invFtail(df_large,df_small,.05)
scalar pvalue = Ftail(df_large,df_small,GQ)
scalar list GQ pvalue crit


* -------------------------------------------
* HCCME
* -------------------------------------------

use food, clear
quietly reg food_exp income
estimates store Usual
scalar bL = _b[income] - invttail(e(df_r),.025) * _se[income]
scalar bU = _b[income] + invttail(e(df_r),.025) * _se[income]
scalar list bL bU

quietly reg food_exp income, vce(robust)
estimates store White
scalar bL = _b[income] - invttail(e(df_r),.025) * _se[income]
scalar bU = _b[income] + invttail(e(df_r),.025) * _se[income]
scalar list bL bU

estimates table Usual White,  b(%7.4f) se(%7.3f) stats(F)

reg food_exp income, vce(robust) level(90)
* -------------------------------------------
* GLS
* -------------------------------------------

regress food_exp income [aweight = 1/income]
scalar bL = _b[income] - invttail(e(df_r),.025) * _se[income]
scalar bU = _b[income] + invttail(e(df_r),.025) * _se[income]
scalar list bL bU


* -------------------------------------------
* cps example
* -------------------------------------------
```

```
use cps2, clear
regress wage educ exper

* --------------------------------------------
* Groupwise heteroskedastic regression using FGLS
* --------------------------------------------

gen rural = 1 - metro
gen wt=(rmse_r^2*rural) + (rmse_m^2*metro)
regress wage educ exper metro [aweight = 1/wt]

* --------------------------------------------
* subsample regressions using dummy variables
* for weights
* --------------------------------------------

regress wage educ exper [aweight = rural]
scalar sr = e(rmse)^2
regress wage educ exper [aweight = metro]
scalar sm = e(rmse)^2
scalar df_r = e(df_r)

* --------------------------------------------
* Groupwise heteroskedastic regression using FGLS
* --------------------------------------------

gen wtall=(sr*rural) + (sm*metro)
regress wage educ exper metro [aweight = 1/wtall]

regress wage educ exper metro
predict ehat, residual

twoway (scatter ehat metro)
more

twoway (scatter ehat wage)
more

* --------------------------------------------
* Heteroskedastic regression using FGLS
* --------------------------------------------

use food, clear
gen z = ln(income)
reg food_exp income
predict ehat, residual
gen ln_ehat_sq = ln(ehat^2)
reg ln_ehat_sq z
predict sighat, xb
gen wt = exp(sighat)
regress food_exp income [aweight=(1/wt)]

* --------------------------------------------
* FGLS with Linear Probability Model
* --------------------------------------------
use coke, clear
summarize
* OLS with inconsistent std errors
quietly regress coke pratio disp_coke disp_pepsi
estimates store LS

predict p, xb
gen var = p*(1-p)
```

```
summarize p var

predict ehat, res
gen ehat2=ehat^2

* White's test
quietly imtest
scalar NR2 = r(chi2_h)
scalar crit05 = invchi2tail(r(df_h),.05)
scalar pval = chi2tail(r(df_h),r(chi2_h))
scalar list NR2 crit05 pval

* White's test manually
quietly regress ehat2 pratio disp_coke disp_pepsi i.disp_coke#i.disp_pepsi
i.disp_coke#c.pratio i.disp_pepsi#c.pratio c.pratio#c.pratio
di "NR2 = " e(N)*e(r2)

* OLS with HCCME std errors
quietly reg coke pratio disp_coke disp_pepsi, vce(robust)
estimates store Robust

* OLS, omitting observations with negative variances
quietly reg coke pratio disp_coke disp_pepsi [aweight=1/var] if  p > 0
estimates store Omit

* OLS, where all p<.01 are truncated to be equal .01
replace p = .01 if p < .01
replace var = p*(1-p)
quietly reg coke pratio disp_coke disp_pepsi [aweight=1/var]
estimates store Trunc

estimates table LS Robust Trunc Omit, b(%7.4f) se(%7.4f) stats(F N)

* Test for heteroskedasticity
quietly regress coke pratio disp_coke disp_pepsi
imtest, white

log close
```

CHAPTER 9

Regression with Time-Series Data: Stationary Variables

CHAPTER OUTLINE

9.1 INTRODUCTION

As in Chapter 9 of *Principles of Econometrics, 4*[th] *Edition*, three ways in which dynamics can enter a regression relationship are considered —through lagged values of the explanatory variable, lagged values of the dependent variable, and lagged values of the error term.

In time series regressions the data need to be stationary in order for the usual econometric procedures to have the proper statistical properties. Basically this requires that the means, variances and covariances of the time series data cannot depend on the time period in which they are observed. For instance, the mean and variance of GDP in the third quarter of 1973 cannot be different from those of the 4th quarter of 2006. Methods to deal with this problem have provided a rich field of research for econometricians in recent years and several of these techniques are explored later in Chapter 12.

One of the first diagnostic tools used is a sim ple time series plot of the data. A tim e series plot will reveal potential problem s with the data and suggest way s to proceed statistically. As seen in earlier chapters, time series plots are simple to generate in Stata and a few new tricks will be explored below.

Finally, since this chapter deals wit h time-series observations the usual num ber of observations, N, is replaced by the m ore commonly used T. In later chapters, where both time-series and cross sectional data are used, both N and T are used.

9.1.1 Defining Time-Series in Stata

In order to take advantage of Stata's many built-in functions for analyzing time-series data, one has to declare the data in the set to be a time-series. Since time-series are ordered in time their position relative to the other observations must be maintained. It is, after all, their temporal relationships that make analysis of this kind of data different from cross-sectional analysis.

If the data you have do not already have a proper date to identify the time period in which the observation was collected, then adding one is a good idea. This makes identification of historical periods easier and enhances the infor mation content of graphs considerably. The data set s distributed with your book have not been declared to be time series and m ost do not contain the relevant dates in the set of variables. S o, the first order of busine ss is to add this inform ation to the data set and then to us e the dates to iden tify the observations as ti me-series and indicates the period of time that separates the individual observati ons (e.g., daily, m onthly, quarterly, yearly). In analyzing the time dependencies in the data, this is vital information as will be explained below.

Before getting to the specific exam ples from the text, som ething should be said about how Stata handles dates and times. Ba sically, Stata treats each time period as an integer. The integer records the num ber of ti me units (what ever you define them to be) that have passed from an agreed-upon base, which for Stata is 1960.

For example, for 100 quarterly data observations that start in 1961 we could generate Stata dates using

```
set obs 100
generate date = tq(1961q1) + _n-1
```

The `tq(1961q1)` is referred to as a pseudofunction. They are called pseudofunctions because they translate what you type into integer equivalent s. The integer equivalent of 1961q1 is 4—that is how many quarters have passed since the first one in 1960. The second quarter is set to 5 and so on. Adding `_n-1` is done t o increment the observations b y 1. Listing the first 5 observations of date reveals:

```
. list date in 1/5
```

	date
1.	4
2.	5
3.	6
4.	7
5.	8

which is exactly what we expect.

To make this meaningful for people, these need to be formatted as strings in order to make it easy for us to tell what date is 20 quarters from 1960. This is done using a **format** command.

```
format %tq date
```

The **format** command just changes the way the integer dates are displayed.

```
. list date in 1/5
```

	date
1.	1961q1
2.	1961q2
3.	1961q3
4.	1961q4
5.	1962q1

As you can see the **format %tq date** tells Stata to display the integers 4, 5, 6, and 7 contained in the variable **date** as 1961q1, 1961q2, and so on. Finally, the observations are declared to be time-series using the **tsset** command followed by the variable name that identifies the time variable.

```
tsset date
```

```
. tsset date
        time variable:  date, 1961q1 to 1985q4
                delta:  1 quarter
```

Once the data are declared to be time-series, Stata prints out important information about the period covered and the measurement interval. It identifies the name of the time variable, the dates it covers, and the **delta** or the period of time that elapses between observations. Check this carefully whenever generating dates to make sure that those created match what is desired.

Stata includes other functions and pseudofunctions for defining weekly (**tw**), monthly (**tm**), yearly (**ty**) and others. Again, these create sets of integers that indicate the number of elapsed time periods since **1960q1**. To display the integers as dates the corresponding formats are (**%tw**), (**%tm**), and (**%ty**), respectively. To see other options and to learn more about how they operate type

```
help dates and times
```

at the **Command** window and Stata open a **viewer** window and carry you to the relevant information.

Once the dates have been created and the data set declared to be time series, save the data set so that this process will not have to be repeated for these data. Stata saves the new variable, desired display format, and time-series information along with the data set.

```
save new.dta, replace
```

The replace option will cause Stata to overwrite an existing data set of the same name, so be careful with this option.

Okun data set

The first thing to do is t o change the directory to the one containing your data and load the data. In this exercise we'll be using the *okun.dta* data.

```
use okun, clear
```

This data set contains two variables, **g** and **u**, that are quarterly observations on the percentage change in Gross Do mestic Product and the unem ployment rate for the U.S. from 1985q2 to 2009q3, respectively. Once the data are loaded, a date is assigned using the generate co mmand. Stata includes special functions for creating da   tes which translate the way Stata treats da   tes (integers) and the way people do (days, months, years, etc.).

The quarterly data begin i n the second quarter of 1985. To establish dates and convert all o f the variables to a time series use:

```
generate date = tq(1985q2) + _n-1
list date in 1
format %tq date
list date in 1
tsset date
```

. generate date = tq(1985q2) + _n-1

. list date in 1

	date
1.	101

.

. format %tq date

. list date in 1

	date
1.	1985q2

.

. tsset date
```
        time variable:   date, 1985q2 to 2009q3
                delta:   1 quarter
```

The two **list in 1** commands were added to dem onstrate what Stata is do ing—they are not necessary in practice. Still, they reveal that 1985q2 is 101 quarters ahead of 1960q1. The for mat command tells Stata to display the integer date 101 as 1985q2.

9.1.2 Time-Series Plots

Once the data are loaded, the tim e variable generated, form atted and the variables declar ed as time-series, you are ready to begi n the initial phase s of anal ysis. With tim e-series, there is no better place to start than plotting the variables against time. This will reveal important features of the data (e.g., stationarity, trends, structural breaks, etc.).

To plot the unemployment rate and GDP growth rates the `tsline` plot is used. In order to get the labels of both pl ots on the sam e graph, the l abels are shortened using the `label var` commands. Then `tsline`, which is an abbreviation of `graph twoway tsline`, plots both series in the same graph.

```
label var u "% Unemployed"
label var g "% GDP growth"
tsline u g, lpattern(solid dash)
```

The two time-serie s graphs are overla id since each of the series to be graphe d are enclose d in parentheses. Other options can be used, but we will keep it simple at this point.

The Stata graphs appear below:

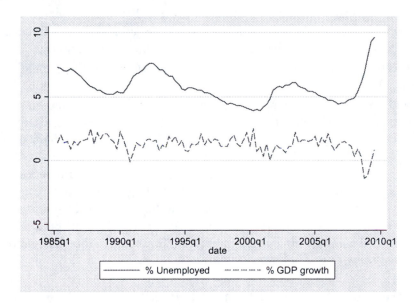

The unemployment series (solid) shows a wider ra nge of variation than GDP growth, but less variance from one time period to the next. There ar e no obvious trends, breaks, or other fe atures that would suggest that either of the variabl es is nonstationary. Therefore, these variables ar e probably well-suited for the traditional regression techniques discussed in this chapter. In Chapter 12 more formal tests are developed to explore the possible nonstationarity of the series. For now it is assumed that they are stationary.

9.1.3 Stata's Lag and Difference Operators

As seen before, the list command is used to print variables from the data set to the screen. In this case it is used with **in 1/5** and **96/98** to limit the observations. The variables that are printed use another instance of Stata's unary operators that were first explored in Chapter 5.

Stata includes special unary operators that can be used to make taking lags and differences of time-series data very easy and efficient. These operators are documented in the *Stata User's Manual* under the headin g **Time-series varlists.** Here is a partial list of operators and their meanings:

```
Operator   Meaning
------------------------------------------------------------
L.         lag (x_t-1)
L2.        2-period lag (x_t-2)
...
D.         difference (x_t - x_t-1)
D2.        difference of difference (x_t - 2x_t-1 + x_t-2)
------------------------------------------------------------
```

These (unary) operators operate on the variable that follows the period. For instance, L.u takes the variable u and lags it one period. Similarly, D.u takes the one period time difference $u_t - u_{t-1}$

The lag and difference operators are linear and can be used together in any order. For instance to take the lagged difference between the observations in u (i.e., $ldu_t = u_{t-1} - u_{t-2}$) one can use L.D.u. This works right to left: take the difference of u and then lag it one pe riod. Linearity in operations implies this is equivalent to D.L.u—lag u one period and then difference. It is also true L.L=L2. To lag the variable u two periods, then use L.L.u or, more simply, L2.u. The number following L indicates how many periods in the past to lag the va riable. Thus L2.u lags u two periods (i.e., = u_{t-2}).

There are additional time-series operators that create leads (F) and seasonal differences (S). Just as in the case of the unary operators for factor variables, these time-series operators save one from having to separatel y generate variables to include in a m odel. There are several other shortcuts that will be discussed below.

To demonstrate the use of these operators the variables, lags and differences are listed below for observations at the beginnin g and end of the da ta set. In general, it is often goo d practice to print a few observations to ensure that the conten ts of the se ries make sense and that the t ime periods have been assigne d to the correct variables. Below the d ate, u, the change in u, g, and several lags are printed using the time-series operators. These match the observations in Table 9.1 in *Principles of Econometrics, 4th Edition (POE4)*.

```
list date u L.u D.u g L1.g L2.g L3.g in 1/5
list date u L.u D.u g L1.g L2.g L3.g in 96/98
```

. list date u L.u D.u g L1.g L2.g L3.g in 1/5

			L.	D.		L.	L2.	L3.
	date	u	u	u	g	g	g	g
1.	1985q2	7.3	.	.	1.4	.	.	.
2.	1985q3	7.2	7.3	-.1	2	1.4	.	.
3.	1985q4	7	7.2	-.2	1.4	2	1.4	.
4.	1986q1	7	7	0	1.5	1.4	2	1.4
5.	1986q2	7.2	7	.2	.9	1.5	1.4	2

```
. list date u L.u D.u g L1.g L2.g L3.g in 96/98
```

			L.	D.		L.	L2.	L3.
	date	u	u	u	g	g	g	g
96.	2009q1	8.1	6.9	1.2	-1.2	-1.4	.3	.9
97.	2009q2	9.3	8.1	1.2	-.2	-1.2	-1.4	.3
98.	2009q3	9.6	9.3	.3	.8	-.2	-1.2	-1.4

The time-series operators have another feature that makes t hem easy to use. Stata also understands **operator(**_numlist_**)**.

```
A numlist is a list of numbers with blanks or commas in between.  There are a number of
shorthand conventions to reduce the amount of typing necessary.  For instance:

    2                       just one number
    1 2 3                   three numbers
    3 2 1                   three numbers in reversed order
    .5 1 1.5                three different numbers
    1 3 -2.17 5.12          four numbers in jumbled order

    1/3                     three numbers: 1, 2, 3
    3/1                     the same three numbers in reverse order
    5/8                     four numbers: 5, 6, 7, 8
    -8/-5                   four numbers: -8, -7, -6, -5
    -5/-8                   four numbers: -5, -6, -7, -8
    -1/2                    four numbers: -1, 0, 1, 2

    1 2 to 4                four numbers: 1, 2, 3, 4
    4 3 to 1                four numbers: 4, 3, 2, 1
    10 15 to 30             five numbers: 10, 15, 20, 25, 30

    1 2:4                   same as 1 2 to 4
    4 3:1                   same as 4 3 to 1
    10 15:30                same as 10 15 to 30

    1(1)3                   three numbers: 1, 2, 3
    1(2)9                   five numbers: 1, 3, 5, 7, 9
    1(2)10                  the same five numbers: 1, 3, 5, 7, 9
    9(-2)1                  five numbers: 9, 7, 5, 3, and 1
    -1(.5)2.5               the numbers: -1, -.5, 0, .5, 1, 1.5, 2, 2.5

    1[1]3                   same as 1(1)3
    1[2]9                   same as 1(2)9
    1[2]10                  same as 1(2)10
    9[-2]1                  same as 9(-2)1
    -1[.5]2.5               same as -1(.5)2.5

    1 2 3/5 8(2)12          eight numbers: 1, 2, 3, 4, 5, 8, 10, 12
    1,2,3/5,8(2)12          the same eight numbers
    1 2 3/5 8 10 to 12      the same eight numbers
    1,2,3/5,8,10 to 12      the same eight numbers
    1 2 3/5 8 10:12         the same eight numbers
```

As you can see, a _numlist_ is very flexible. It allows you to specify ranges, sequences, as well as lists of speci fic numbers. These c an include nega tive numbers and their order can be easily reversed. Using this syntax the **list** commands can be shortened to

```
list date L(0/1).u D.u L(0/3).g in 1/5
list date L(0/1).u D.u L(0/3).g in 96/98
```

The command **L(0/1).u** is equivalent to **u L.u** and **L(0/3).g** is the same as **g L.g L2.g L3.g**.

9.2 FINITE DISTRIBUTED LAGS

Finite distributed lag models contain independent variables and their lags as regressors.

$$y_t = \alpha + \beta_0 x_t + \beta_1 x_{t-1} + \beta_2 x_{t-2} + \cdots + \beta_q x_{t-q} + e_t, \qquad t = q+1, \ldots, T$$

The particular example considered here is an examination of Okun's Law. In this model the change in the unemployment rate from one period to the next depends on the rate of growth of output in the economy.

$$U_t - U_{t-1} = -\gamma(G_t - G_N)$$

where U_t is the unemployment rate, G_t is GDP growth, G_N is the normal rate of GDP growth. The regression model is

$$DU_t = \alpha + \beta_0 G + e_t$$

where D is the difference operator, $\alpha = \gamma G_N$, $\beta_0 = -\gamma$ and an error term has been added to the model. Recognizing that changes in output are likely to have a distributed-lag effect on unemployment—not all of the effect will take place instantaneously—lags are added to the model to produce:

$$DU_t = \alpha + \beta_0 G_t + \beta_1 G_{t-1} + \beta_2 G_{t-2} + \cdots + \beta_q G_{t-q} + e_t, \qquad t = q+1, \ldots, T$$

The two time series can be plotted using

```
tsline D.u g
```

and this will produce a single graph that looks like those in Figure 9.4 of *POE4*.

To estimate a finite distributed lag model in Stata is quite simple using the time-series operators. Letting q=3 and

```
regress D.u L(0/3).g
```

yields

```
. regress D.u L(0/3).g
```

Source	SS	df	MS
Model	5.13367789	4	1.28341947
Residual	2.73516422	90	.030390714
Total	7.86884211	94	.083711086

Number of obs = 95
F(4, 90) = 42.23
Prob > F = 0.0000
R-squared = 0.6524
Adj R-squared = 0.6370
Root MSE = .17433

D.u	Coef.	Std. Err.	t	P>|t|	[95% Conf. Interval]	
g						
--.	-.2020526	.0330131	-6.12	0.000	-.267639	-.1364663
L1.	-.1645352	.0358175	-4.59	0.000	-.2356929	-.0933774
L2.	-.071556	.0353043	-2.03	0.046	-.1416941	-.0014179
L3.	.003303	.0362603	0.09	0.928	-.0687345	.0753405
_cons	.5809746	.0538893	10.78	0.000	.4739142	.688035

Once again the L(*numlist*) syntax is used to place the contemporaneous and 3 lagged values of **g** into the model.

Re-estimating the model using a lag length of two produces

```
. regress D.u L(0/2).g
```

Source	SS	df	MS
Model	5.17925206	3	1.72641735
Residual	2.74074794	92	.029790739
Total	7.92	95	.083368421

Number of obs = 96
F(3, 92) = 57.95
Prob > F = 0.0000
R-squared = 0.6539
Adj R-squared = 0.6427
Root MSE = .1726

D.u	Coef.	Std. Err.	t	P>|t|	[95% Conf. Interval]	
g						
--.	-.2020216	.0323832	-6.24	0.000	-.2663374	-.1377059
L1.	-.1653269	.0335368	-4.93	0.000	-.2319339	-.0987198
L2.	-.0700135	.0331	-2.12	0.037	-.1357529	-.0042741
_cons	.5835561	.0472119	12.36	0.000	.4897892	.6773231

There is virtually no change in the model fit as a consequence of dropping the statistically insignificant third lag on **g**.

9.3 SERIAL CORRELATION

Another complication in time-series regression occurs when the errors of the regression model are correlated with one another. This violates one of the basic assumptions of the Gauss-Markov theorem and has a substantial effect on the properties of least squares estimation of the parameters.

In economics, serial correlation happens when the duration of economic shocks exceed the sampling frequency of the data. This causes the shock to bleed over into subsequent time periods, causing errors to be positively correlated. In most cases this implies a failure to model the time structure of the regression properly—either lagged variables are omitted that are correlated with included regressors or if there is so me persistence in the depen dent variable that has not been properly modeled. The solution is to properly specify the regression function so that $E(e_t \mid \text{all regressors}_t) = 0$. That satisfies the necessary condit ion for least squares to be cons istent for the intercept and slopes.

Detecting autocorrelation in the least squares residuals is important because least squares may be inconsistent in this case. The first t ool used is to produce a scatter graph of **g** and **L.g**. Horizontal and vertical lines are placed approximately at the mean.

```
summarize g
scatter g L.g, xline(`r(mean)') yline(`r(mean)')
```

which yields

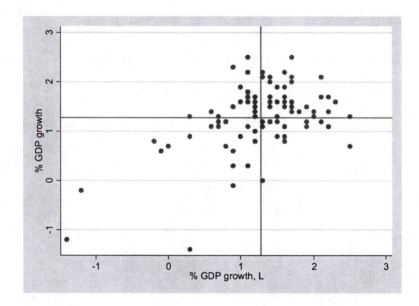

The **summarize** command that precede s scatter is neces sary because the mean of GDP growth needs to be computed to draw the lines shown in the graph. The mean of **g** is among the saved results, which can be viewed using the usual **return list** command.

```
. summarize g
```

Variable	Obs	Mean	Std. Dev.	Min	Max
g	98	1.276531	.6469279	-1.4	2.5

```
. return list

scalars:
                  r(N) =  98
              r(sum_w) =  98
               r(mean) =  1.276530612244898
                r(Var) =  .4185156743109615
                 r(sd) =  .6469278741180978
                r(min) =  -1.4
                r(max) =  2.5
                r(sum) =  125.1
```

To access the mean, its macro name, **r(mean),** must be enclosed in single quotes, i.e., **`r(mean)'**. The first quo te is the left single quote (`--upper left of m ost keyboards) and the second is the right single quote ('--located under the double quote " on most keyboards).

A numerical approach is to look at the co mputed sample autocorrelations. These are summoned using

```
ac g, lags(12) generate(ac_g)
list ac_g in 1/12
```

The command **ac** computes sample autocorrelations for the variable that follows (**g**) and the **lags(12)** option tells Stata to co mpute autocorrelations for **g** up to 12 periods apart. The output consists of a graph, though the autocorrelations are saved using the **generate** option in a variable named **ac_g**. The graph is

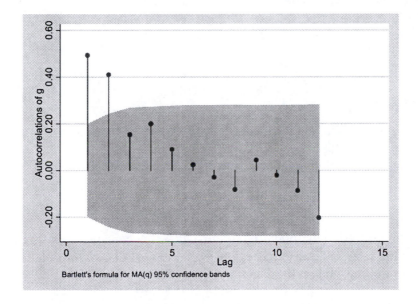

Bartlett's formula for MA(q) 95% confidence bands

The 95% confidence band appears in the shad ed area. No tice that only the first two autocorrelations are significantly different from zero at the 5% level.

Approximate 95% confidence bands are computed using the fact that $\sqrt{T} r_k \overset{a}{\sim} N(0,1)$. Use **gen z=sqrt(e(N))*ac_g** to generate the b oundary. If a ny of the nu mbers are less than -1.96 or greater than 1.96, it lies o utside of the approximate 95% confidence interval and is statistically significant at the 5% level. Stata's **ac** function uses a different method (Bartlett's) and the results may differ from those based on this simple approximation.

The values of the autocorrelations stored in **ac_g** and the boundaries, **z**, are

```
. list ac_g z in 1/12
```

	ac_g	z
1.	.49425676	4.842708
2.	.4107073	4.024093
3.	.1544205	1.513006
4.	.20043788	1.963882
5.	.09038538	.8855922
6.	.02447111	.239767
7.	-.03008434	-.2947652
8.	-.08231978	-.8065658
9.	.04410661	.4321548
10.	-.02128483	-.2085479
11.	-.08683463	-.8508022
12.	-.20404326	-1.999207

Phillips Curve

The second example is based on the Phillips curve, which expresses the relationship between inflation and unemployment.

The simple regression relating inflation and the change in unemployment is

$$INF_t = \beta_1 + \beta_2 DU_t + e_t$$

The model is estimated using the *phillips_aus.dta* data which contains the quarterly inflation rate and unemployment rates for Australia beginning in 1987q1. Load the data, generate a date, format the date to a string, and set the data set as time series.

```
use phillips_aus, clear
generate date = tq(1987q1) + _n-1
format %tq date
tsset date
```

First, plot the inflation rate and the change in unemployment

```
tsline inf
tsline D.u
```

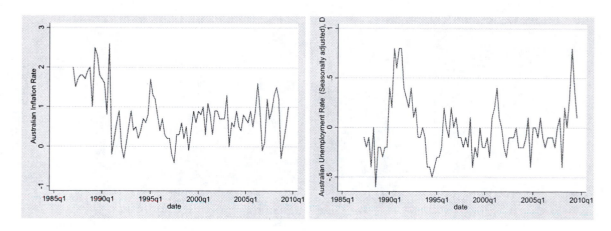

Next, estimate the model using least squares and save the residual.

```
reg inf D.u
predict ehat, res
```

. reg inf D.u

Source	SS	df	MS		
Model	2.04834633	1	2.04834633		
Residual	34.0445426	88	.386869802		
Total	36.0928889	89	.405538077		

Number of obs	=	90		
F(1, 88)	=	5.29		
Prob > F	=	0.0238		
R-squared	=	0.0568		
Adj R-squared	=	0.0460		
Root MSE	=	.62199		

inf	Coef.	Std. Err.	t	P>|t|	[95% Conf. Interval]
u D1.	-.5278638	.2294049	-2.30	0.024	-.9837578 -.0719699
_cons	.7776213	.0658249	11.81	0.000	.646808 .9084345

The residuals will be ex amined for autocorrelation using the residual **correlogram**. A residual correlogram is a graph that plots series of autocorrelations between $\hat{e}_t$ and $\hat{e}_{t-j}$ against the time interval between the observations, $j=1, 2, ..., m$. The sample autocorrelations are saved in a variable called **rk**, the first five are printed, and then dropped from the data set since they are no longer needed.

```
ac ehat, lags(12) generate(rk)
list rk in 1/5
```

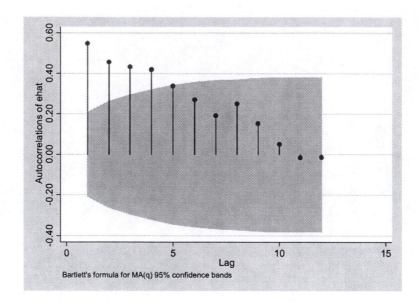

```
. list rk in 1/5
```

	rk
1.	.54865864
2.	.45573248
3.	.43321579
4.	.42049358
5.	.33903419

It is rather obvious that there are a number of significant autocorrelations and that they are relatively large.

Stata contains a **corrgram** function, of which th e **ac** command is a subset. **corrgram** produces a table of the aut ocorrelations (as well as partial autocorrelations, and Portmanteau (Q) statistics). It also display s a character-based plot of the autocorrelations. An other feature of **corrgram** is that each of these statistics are saved as **r( )**. To save and print the first five autocorrelations using **corrgram**

```
corrgram ehat, lags(5)
```

```
. corrgram ehat, lags(5)
```

LAG	AC	PAC	Q	Prob>Q	-1 0 1 [Autocorrelation]	-1 0 1 [Partial Autocor]
1	0.5487	0.5498	28.006	0.0000	⊢—	⊢—
2	0.4557	0.2297	47.548	0.0000	⊢—	⊢
3	0.4332	0.1926	65.409	0.0000	⊢—	⊢
4	0.4205	0.1637	82.433	0.0000	⊢—	⊢
5	0.3390	0.0234	93.63	0.0000	⊢—	⊢

Printing the first three sample autocorrelations

```
. di "rho1 = " r(ac1) " rho2 = " r(ac2) " rho3 = " r(ac3)
rho1 = .54865864 rho2 = .45573248 rho3 = .43321579
```

Type **return list** to view other statistics that are stored after executing **corrgram**.

9.4 OTHER TESTS FOR SERIAL CORRELATION

A second test for serial correlation is based on the Lagran ge multiplier test princip le discussed in the context of heteroskedasticity in Chapter 8. The test statistic is based on TR^2 from an auxiliary regression. For autocorrelation, this test is based on an auxiliary regression where you regress least squares residuals on lagged least squares residuals and the original regressors. If the regressors, which in cludes $\hat{e}_{t-1}$, explain sufficient variation i n $\hat{e}_t$, then there must be autocorrelation due to $\hat{e}_{t-1}$. For a regression model

$$y_t = \beta_1 + \beta_2 x_t + e_t,$$

estimate the parameters using leas t squares and save the residuals, $\hat{e}_t$. Lag the residuals to get $\hat{e}_{t-1}$. Then, estimate a second 'a uxiliary' regression with $\hat{e}_t$ as the dependent variable and the lagged value $\hat{e}_{t-1}$ as an independent variable. Include all of the other independent variables from the original regression as well. For a simple linear regression the auxiliary regression is

$$\hat{e}_t = \gamma_1 + \gamma_2 x_t + \rho \hat{e}_{t-1} + residual$$

TR^2 from this regression has a $\chi^2(1)$ distribution if the null hypothesis of no autocorrelation is true, where T is the nu mber of observations in the a uxiliary regression. Rejecti on leads to t he conclusion that there is significant autocorrelation. For the Phillips curve example, assuming that **ehat** was saved from the original regression,

```
quietly regress ehat D.u L.ehat
di "Observations = " e(N) " and TR2 = " e(N)*e(r2)
```

yields

```
. di "Observations = " e(N) " and TR2 = " e(N)*e(r2)
Observations = 89 and TR2 = 27.608808
```

In *Principles of Econo metrics, 4th Edition*, this statistic is co mputed using all available observations. Since a lagged value, $\hat{e}_{t-1}$, appears in the model, one would nor mally lose an observation when estimating the auxiliary regression. In this case, the m issing value for the first residual can be replaced with a zero. This is per missible in the current context because th at is what its expected value is (i.e., $E(e_1)=0$). Technically setting $\hat{e}_1 = 0$ is unnecessary to obtain a valid test statistic; however, to replicate the result in the text it is done here. Then,

```
replace ehat = 0 in 1
quietly regress inf D.u L.ehat
di "Observations = " e(N) " and TR2 = " e(N)*e(r2)
```

yields

```
. di "Observations = " e(N) " and TR2 = " e(N)*e(r2)
Observations = 90 and TR2 = 27.592347
```

This matches the result in the text.

Testing for higher order a utocorrelation is simple. To test for AR(4), then include 4 lagge d least squares residuals as regressors and compute TR^2. The degrees of freedom for the chi-square equal the order of the autocorrelation under the alternative (in this case, 4).

The code to do this is:

```
quietly regress ehat D.u L(1/4).ehat
```

which results in

```
. di "Observations = " e(N) " and TR2 = " e(N)*e(r2)
Observations = 86 and TR2 = 33.385269
```

Manually replicating the r esults in *POE4* requires som e work. The m issing values of **ehat** that occur from taking lags are set to zero (i. e., $\hat{e}_{-3} = 0$, $\hat{e}_{-2} = 0$, $\hat{e}_{-1} = 0$, $\hat{e}_0 = 0$). This allows use of the entire sample. It turns out that this is n ot particularly straightforward to program in Stata so we will skip that discussion here. However, the code to do so can be found in the do-file at the end of this chapter.

The results *can* be repli cated easily using the built-in post-estimation command **estat bgodfrey**.

```
regress inf D.u
estat bgodfrey, lags(1)
estat bgodfrey, lags(4)
```

The command uses an option that indicates how many lagged residuals to include as regressors in the model. In the AR(1) exam ple, the alternative hypothesis is th at the model's errors have first order autocorrelation; lags(1) is used. The result

```
. estat bgodfrey, lags(1)
```

Breusch-Godfrey LM test for autocorrelation

lags(p)	chi2	df	Prob > chi2
1	27.592	1	0.0000

HO: no serial correlation

For the AR(4) alternative

```
. estat bgodfrey, lags(4)
```

Breusch-Godfrey LM test for autocorrelation

lags(p)	chi2	df	Prob > chi2
4	36.672	4	0.0000

H0: no serial correlation

In each case there is clear evidence of autocorrelation in the residuals of the simple regression.

9.5 ESTIMATION WITH SERIALLY CORRELATED ERRORS

As long as the regression model does not contain lags of the dependent variable as regressors, the least squares estimator is consistent even if the errors follow an AR(q) model. It is no longer efficient (asymptotically), when the least squares assumption MR4, $\text{cov}(e_t, e_s) = 0$ for $t \neq s$ is violated. Unfortunately, the usual standard errors are no longer correct, leading to statistically invalid hypothesis tests and confidence intervals.

9.5.1 Least squares and HAC standard errors

Although the usual least squares standard errors are not the correct, we can compute consistent standard errors just as we did in heteroskedastic models using an estimator proposed by Newey and West. Newey-West standard errors (also known as HAC--heteroskedasticity and autocorrelation consistent standard errors) are analogous to the heteroskedasticity consistent standard errors introduced in Chapter 8. They have the advantage of being consistent for autocorrelated errors that are not necessarily AR(1), and do not require specification of the dynamic error model that would be needed to get an estimator with a lower variance.

HAC is not as automatic in use as the heteroskedasticity robust standard error estimator in Chapter 8. To be robust with respect to autocorrelation one has to specify how far away in time the residual autocorrelation is likely to be significant. Essentially, the autocorrelated errors over the chosen time window are averaged in the computation of HAC; the number of periods over which to average and how much weight to assign each residual in that average has to be set by the user.

The weighted average is accomplished using what is called a **kernel** and the number of errors to average using the weighting scheme (kernel) is called **bandwidth**. To be quite honest, these terms reveal little about what they do to the average user. Just think of the kernel as another name for weighted average and bandwidth as the term for number of terms to average. Stata offers no way to choose a kernel; the Bartlett is the only one available. However, a bandwidth **must** be selected.

There are several methods to help choose a suitable bandwidth and two are given here. In both cases, the bandwidth depends on the sample size, T. The first uses $B = 0.75 T^{1/3}$. The other popular choice is $B = 4(T/100)^{2/9}$. This one appears to be the default in other programs like *EViews* and it is the one used here to obtain the results in the text.

Implicitly there is a trade-off to consider. A larger bandwidth reduces bias (good) as well as precision (bad). A smaller bandwidth excludes more relevant autocorrelations (and hence is more biased), but has a smaller variance. The general principle is to choose a bandwidth that is large enough to contain the largest autocorrelations.

To compute a bandwidth use the command

```
scalar B = round(4*(e(N)/100)^(2/9))
scalar list B
```

This returns the value 4 i n the *phillips_aus.dta* data set. The r esult is rounded because S tata requires a whole number to be used to specify the number of lags in the HAC's computation.

The only kernel available in Stata is the Bartlett. This is the one u sed by Newey and West in their research on this issue. Consequently, Stata refers to the procedure that c omputes HAC as **newey**. It is basically a replacement for **regress**, and it requires the specification of a bandwidth. Then, to estimate the model by least squares with Newey-West standard errors and a ban dwidth of 4 use the following command

```
newey inf D.u, lag(4)
```

In the exam ple the m odel is esti mated using least squares with t he usual least squares standard errors and th e HAC standard errors. T he results ap pear below, with the HAC standard errors appearing below the estimates in the right-hand column.

```
esttab Wrong_SE HAC_4, compress se(%12.3f) b(%12.5f) gaps ///
    scalars(r2_a rss aic) title("Dependent Variable: inf") ///
    mtitles("LS" "HAC(4)")
```

Dependent Variable: inf

	(1) LS	(2) HAC(4)
D.u	-0.52786* (0.229)	-0.52786 (0.318)
_cons	0.77762*** (0.066)	0.77762*** (0.112)
N	90	90
r2_a	0.04603	
rss	34.04454	
aic	171.91634	.

Standard errors in parentheses
* p<0.05, ** p<0.01, *** p<0.001

The **compress** option is used to reduce the vertical space between lines, the **gaps** option adds empty rows (or, m ore generally, additional vertical space) between coeffici ents, and **scalars** option allows you to print various stati stics that are stored along with the regression results. In this case, the adjusted R^2, the regression sum of squares error, and Stata's calculation of t he AIC criterion. In addition, the **mtitle** option is used to give each col umn a meaningful name; when this option is used the default colum n name, which is the nam e of the dependent variabl e, is replaced by whatever y ou place in each set of double quotes. The **title** option is used to let readers know that the dep endent variable used in each case is in f. In this exam ple, the HAC standard errors are substantially larger than the usual (inconsistent) ones.

9.5.2 Nonlinear Least Squares

As you can see, HAC standard errors suffer at least two disadvantages: 1) they are not automatic since they require specification of a bandwidth and 2) they are larger than standard errors of more estimators that are more efficient than ordinary linear regression. In this section, no nlinear least squares is used to efficiently estimate the parameters of the AR(1) model.

In your text book the authors start with the AR (1) regression model and, using a little algebra, arrive at

$$y_t = \beta_1(1-\rho) + \beta_2 x_t + \rho y_{t-1} - \rho\beta_2 x_{t-1} + v_t$$

This model is nonlinear in the parameters, but ha s an additive white noise error. These features make the model suitable for nonlinear least squa res estimation. Nonlinear l east squares uses numerical methods to find the values of the parameters that minimize the sum of squared errors. To estimate the model use Stata's generic nonlinear least squares command, **nl**:

```
nl (inf = {b1}*(1-{rho}) + {b2}*D.u + {rho}*L.inf - {rho}*{b2}*(L.D.u)), ///
variables(inf D.u L.inf L.D.u)
```

The syntax is fairly simple, but requires some explanation. The basic syntax is:

```
nl (depvar=<sexp>) [if] [in] [weight] [, options]
```

The systematic portion of the model is included in side the first set of parentheses. Param eters must be enclosed in braces {}. The **if, in,** and **weight** statements are used in the same way as in a linear regression. However, because the variables that have been lagged, missing values will be created for the first observation on t he lagged variab les in the data set. For this to work, the sample must be limited to only those observations that are co mplete. There are two ways to do this. First, you could use **(depvar=<sexp>) in 2/34.** Or, you can list the variables as done here using the option **variables(inf D.u L.inf L.D.u).**

The results of the estimation are

Source	SS	df	MS
Model	12.3860433	2	6.19302165
Residual	23.1986758	86	.269752044
Total	35.5847191	88	.404371808

Number of obs = 89
R-squared = 0.3481
Adj R-squared = 0.3329
Root MSE = .5193766
Res. dev. = 132.9069

inf	Coef.	Std. Err.	t	P>|t|	[95% Conf. Interval]	
/b1	.7608716	.1245311	6.11	0.000	.513312	1.008431
/rho	.5573922	.0901546	6.18	0.000	.3781709	.7366136
/b2	-.694388	.247894	-2.80	0.006	-1.187185	-.201591

Parameter b1 taken as constant term in model & ANOVA table

The coefficient estimates match those in the text. The minimum of the sum of squares function is reached at the same parameter estimates. There are some small differences in estimated standard errors, though. This happens because there are different ways of estimating these consistently in nonlinear models; in small samples like the one in this example, those differences may be exaggerated. In larger samples the differences will usually be small and in fact vanish according to theory as the sample size grows. The *t*-ratio on the parameter ρ is equal to 6.18, which has a *p*-value less than 0.001. This means that at any reasonable level of significance (e.g., 5%) there is evidence of first order autocorrelation among the residuals.

After estimating the model a couple of scalars are computed to be used in the next section.

```
scalar delta = _b[b1:_cons]*(1-_b[rho:_cons])
scalar delta1 = - _b[rho:_cons]*_b[b2:_cons]
```

The scalar called **delta** is $\hat{\beta}_1(1-\hat{\rho})$ and **delta1** is $-\hat{\rho}\hat{\beta}_2$. The reasons for these will be discussed in the next section. However, note that the estimates are referred to a bit differently than in the linear regression. The **_b[varname]** convention used in linear models has been replaced by **_b[paramname:_cons]**. The **coeflegend** option can be used after the **nl** command to find the proper names for the parameters. To verify that you have identified the parameters correctly, run the nonlinear least squares regression again using the **coeflegend** option. This suppresses much of the output that you ordinarily want, but it does produce a legend that identifies Stata's names for each of the parameters. There is an example of this contained in the do-file at the end of the chapter.

9.5.3 A More General Model

A more general form of the model is considered

$$y_t = \delta + \delta_0 x_t + \delta_1 x_{t-1} + \theta_1 y_{t-1} + v_t$$

which is linear in the parameters and can be estimated by linear regression. This model is related to the previous model by the relationships

$$\delta = \beta_1(1-\rho) \qquad \delta_0 = \beta_2 \qquad \delta_1 = -\rho\beta_2 \qquad \theta_1 = \rho$$

The linear model can be estimated by (linear) least squares and a hypothesis test of the implied restriction can be conducted. The null hypothesis implied by the restriction is $H_0 : \delta_1 = -\theta_1\delta_0$ against the alternative that it is not equal. The first step is to estimate the model using least squares

```
regress inf L.inf D.u L.D.u
```

```
. regress inf L.inf D.u L.D.u
```

Source	SS	df	MS
Model	12.4166337	3	4.13887791
Residual	23.1680854	85	.27256571
Total	35.5847191	88	.404371808

```
Number of obs =        89
F(  3,     85) =     15.18
Prob > F       =    0.0000
R-squared      =    0.3489
Adj R-squared  =    0.3260
Root MSE       =    .52208
```

inf	Coef.	Std. Err.	t	P>|t|	[95% Conf. Interval]	
inf						
L1.	.5592676	.0907962	6.16	0.000	.3787403	.7397948
u						
D1.	-.6881852	.2498704	-2.75	0.007	-1.184994	-.191376
LD.	.3199526	.257504	1.24	0.217	-.1920343	.8319396
_cons	.3336325	.0899028	3.71	0.000	.1548817	.5123834

The scalars computed at the end of the previous section correspond to δ and δ_1 above. The computed values were

```
. scalar list delta delta1
     delta =  .33676767
    delta1 =  .38704645
```

The more general estimates obtained from the linear regression are $\hat{\delta} = 0.334$ and $\hat{\delta}_1 = 0.320$. Both values are fairly close to the ones implied by the more restrictive nonlinear model estimated by **nl**.

To actually test the nonlinear hypothesis $H_0 : \delta_1 = -\theta_1\delta_0$ use the Stata's built in function for testing nonlinear functions of the paramters, **testnl**.

```
        testnl _b[L.D.u]=-_b[L.inf]*_b[D.u]
```

```
. testnl _b[L.D.u]=-_b[L.inf]*_b[D.u]

  (1)  _b[L.D.u] = -_b[L.inf]*_b[D.u]

              F(1, 85) =         0.11
              Prob > F =       0.7384
```

The large p-value of 0.74 suggests that the AR(1) model estimated by nonlinear least squares in not overly restrictive.

The various linear specifications of the models considered are compared using the **esttab** command:

```
. esttab General No_LDu Original, compress se(%12.3f) b(%12.5f) ///
>        gaps scalars(r2_a rss aic)
```

	(1) inf	(2) inf	(3) inf
L.inf	0.55927*** (0.091)	0.52825*** (0.085)	
D.u	-0.68819** (0.250)	-0.49086* (0.192)	-0.52786* (0.229)
LD.u	0.31995 (0.258)		
_cons	0.33363*** (0.090)	0.35480*** (0.088)	0.77762*** (0.066)
N	89	90	90
r2_a	0.32595	0.33137	0.04603
rss	23.16809	23.59054	34.04454
aic	140.78946	140.90217	171.91634

```
Standard errors in parentheses
* p<0.05, ** p<0.01, *** p<0.001
```

The **compress** option is used to reduce the vertical space between lines, the **gaps** option adds empty rows (or, m ore generally, additional vertical space) between coeffici ents, and **scalars** option allows you to print various stati stics that are stored along with the regression results. In this case, the adjusted R^2, the regression sum of squares error, and Stata's calculation of t he AIC criterion.

9.6 AUTOREGRESSIVE DISTRIBUTED LAG MODELS

A model that combines finite distributed lags and is autoregressive is considered. This is the so-called autoregressive distributed lag model (ARDL). The ARDL(p,q) model has the general form

$$y_t = \delta + \theta_1 y_{t-1} + \cdots + \theta_p y_{t-p} + \delta_0 x_t + \delta_1 x_{t-1} + \cdots + \delta_q x_{t-q} + v_t$$

As regressors, it has p lags of the dependent variable, y_t, and q lags of the independent variable, x_t. The ARDL(1,1) and ARDL(1,0) m odels of inflati on can be estim ated using least squares. The estimates are stored and printed in a table below.

```
regress inf L.inf L(0/1).D.u        .
estimates store AR1_DL1
regress inf L.inf D.u
estimates store AR1_DL0
```

```
. esttab AR1_DL1 AR1_DL0, compress se(%12.3f) b(%12.5f) ///
>        gaps scalars(r2_a rss aic)
```

	(1) inf	(2) inf
L.inf	0.55927***	0.52825***
	(0.091)	(0.085)
D.u	-0.68819**	-0.49086*
	(0.250)	(0.192)
LD.u	0.31995	
	(0.258)	
_cons	0.33363***	0.35480***
	(0.090)	(0.088)
N	89	90
r2_a	0.32595	0.33137
rss	23.16809	23.59054
aic	140.78946	140.90217

Standard errors in parentheses
* p<0.05, ** p<0.01, *** p<0.001

Choosing between these models can be done in several way s. First, if the t-ratio on DU_{t-1} is insignificant, then the evidence suggests that o mitting it may not adversely impact the properties of the least squares estimator of the restricted model.

Another possibility is to use one of the model selection rules discussed in Chapter 6. Recall that we wrote a program called **modelsel** that computes the AIC and SC m odel selection rules. Here, the program is modified slightly by om itting the displa y of the adj usted R^2 and instead printing the number of o bservations in the model. Refer to Chapter 6 for m ore details on the program structure in Stata.

To choose between the ARDL(1,1) and ARDL(1,0) using the AIC or SC create and run the following program called **modelsel**.

```
program modelsel
  scalar aic = ln(e(rss)/e(N))+2*e(rank)/e(N)
  scalar sc = ln(e(rss)/e(N))+e(rank)*ln(e(N))/e(N)
  scalar obs = e(N)
  scalar list aic sc obs
end
```

Now estimate each model, checking the selection criteria as indicated below. This produce s the output:

```
. quietly regress inf L.inf L(0/1).D.u

. modelsel
        aic =  -1.255973
         sc = -1.1441242
        obs =         89

. quietly regress inf L.inf L.D.u

. modelsel
        aic = -1.1929642
         sc = -1.1090776
        obs =         89
```

The ARDL(1,0) minimizes both AIC and SC and is the preferred model. One problem with this analysis is that the residuals may still be autocorrelated or that longer lags than the ones considered here have been omitted. In the next section this is considered more carefully.

9.6.1 Phillips Curve

First, the errors of the ARDL(1,0) should be checked for autocorrelation. This can be done by looking at the correlogram

```
quietly regress inf L.inf D.u
predict ehat, res
ac ehat, lags(12)
```

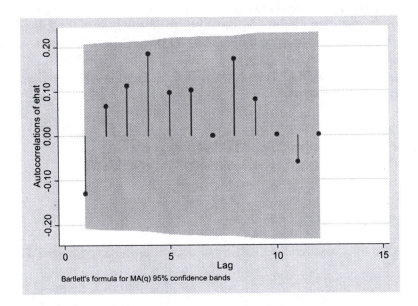

or by the *LM* (Breusch-Godfrey) test, which in this case includes statistics for lags 1-5.

```
. estat bgodfrey, lags(1 2 3 4 5)
```

Breusch-Godfrey LM test for autocorrelation

lags(p)	chi2	df	Prob > chi2
1	4.130	1	0.0421
2	5.123	2	0.0772
3	5.221	3	0.1563
4	9.554	4	0.0486
5	12.485	5	0.0287

HO: no serial correlation

The results from the two procedures give different impressions about the possible existence of autocorrelation in the residuals of the ARDL(1 ,0). None of the autocorrelations in the correlogram lie outside of the 95% confidence interval, but the *LM* statistics for models having 1, 4, or 5 lags are statistically significant at the 5% level. The latter suggests that the model selection rules should be applied to a wider set of models that include more autocorrelation terms. This means estimating twelve models; the AR terms are varied from 1 to 6 and the DL from 0 to 1 with every combination estimated. The AIC and SC statistics are computed for each model and searched for the overall minima. The Stata code to estimate each of these models for time periods after 1988q3 is provided at the end of this chapter in a do-file. The complete code can be used to reproduce the results found in Table 9.4 of *POE4*. Below, a code snippet is given and its syntax explained.

The following code estimates the ARDL(1,1) model for data beginning in the third quarter of 1983. The regression is estimated using the **quietly** command, abbreviated in Stata **qui**, to suppress the actual regression results; our interest is in the values of the model selection rules only at this point. To limit the sample to certain dates, the pseudofunction **tq(1988q3)** is used. Recall from earlier in this chapter that this pseudofunction translates the date 1988q3 into a number that Stata understands. For quarterly data, this is the proper syntax

```
qui reg L(0/1).inf L(0/1).D.u if date>= tq(1988q3)
di "p=1   q=1"
modelsel
```

The lag operators are being used to their fullest advantage by specifying the dependent variable and autoregressive independent variables in one statement, **L(0/1).inf**. The first variable in this statement is the zero lag of inflation, **L(0).inf,** which is just **inf**. So, the statement **L(0/1).inf** is equivalent to **inf L.inf** Since **inf** appears first after **regress**, Stata recognizes it as the dependent variable.

The result from this snippet is

```
. di "p=1   q=0"
p=1   q=0

. modelsel
        aic = -1.2466292
         sc =  -1.160418
        obs =         85
```

Using loops can make model selection much easier. As an example, let's search over all possible models for p=1, 2, 3, 4, 5, and 6 q=0 and 1. A n ested loop can be form ed using **forvalues** command, which loops over consecutive values.

The basic structure would be

```
forvalues q=0/1 {
    forvalues p=1/6 {
    [statements to compute and print]
    }
}
```

The loop is executed as long as calculated values of **q** and **p** are within the given range (e.g., 0 and 1 for **q** and between 1 and 6 inclusive for **p**). In this form the values of **p** and **q** will increment in steps of 1. Braces must be specified with **forvalues**, and

1. the open brace must appear on the same line as **forvalues**;
2. nothing may follow the open brace except, of course, comments; the first command to be executed must appear on a new line;
3. the close brace must appear on a line by itself.

For the ARDL(p,q) of Okun's Law the code looks is:

```
forvalues q=0/1 {
    forvalues p=1/6 {
        quietly regress L(0/`p').inf L(0/`q').D.u if date >= tq(1988q3)
        display "p=`p'  q=`q'"
        modelsel
        }
    }
```

Notice a couple of things about the statements that are being computed within the loops. First, the **p** and **q** are now referred to by their macro names. That means that they when they are referred to they need to be enclosed in single q uotes (left and right as we did above). Second, the dependent variable and autoregressive independe nt variables are once again includ ed in one statement, **L(0/`p').inf**. As **p** increments from 1 to 6, lags are added and the **modelsel** program is executed after printing the current values of **p** and **q** to the screen. Henc e, in a few s hort statements many models can be considered and the orders of the autoregressive and distributed lags can easily be changed.

When loops are nested this way, the **q** loop starts at zero and then the **p** loop iterates from 1 to 6. Once the **p** loop is finis hed, the **q** loop increments by 1 and the **p** loop starts over again. You can change the order of these if desired.

9.6.2 Okun's Law

Okun's Law provides anot her opportunity to search for an adequ ate specification of t he time-series model. Load the *okun.dta* data, generate dates beginnin g at 1985q2, format them to be printed as strings, and declare the data to be time series.

```
use okun, clear
generate date = tq(1985q2) + _n-1
```

```
format %tq date
tsset date
```

The model estimated in section 9.2 was an ARDL(0,2) that related the change in the unemployment rate to G DP growth. Below the model is estim ated by least squares, the correlogram is obtained, and *LM* statistics for models containing up to 5 autoc orreleted residuals are produced.

```
reg D.u g L(1/2).g L.D.u
predict ehat, res
ac ehat, lags(12)
drop ehat
estat bgodfrey, lags(1 2 3 4 5)
```

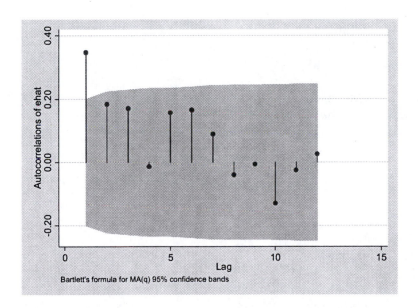

. estat bgodfrey, lags(1 2 3 4 5)

Breusch-Godfrey LM test for autocorrelation

lags(p)	chi2	df	Prob > chi2
1	12.364	1	0.0004
2	12.894	2	0.0016
3	13.754	3	0.0033
4	15.228	4	0.0043
5	19.648	5	0.0015

HO: no serial correlation

The correlogram has one significant autocorrelation and each of the LM statistics is significant at the 5% level. This suggests that the ARDL(0,2) is misspecified. In the do-file at the end of the chapter code is given to estimate a series of models using the Okun data set. The sam ple is limited as in the previous example, this time for observations beginning in the first quarter of 1986.

The autocorrelations are varied from 0 to 2 and distributed lags are varied from 1 to 3; this results in 9 models to estimate.

```
forvalues q=1/3 {
    forvalues p=0/2 {
        quietly regress L(0/`p').D.u L(0/`q').g if date >= tq(1986q1)
        display "p=`p'  q=`q'"
        modelsel
        }
    }
```

This produces:

```
p=0   q=1
        aic = -3.4362364
         sc = -3.3555876
        obs =          95
p=1   q=1
        aic = -3.5879866
         sc =   -3.480455
        obs =          95
p=2   q=1
        aic = -3.5693074
         sc = -3.4348928
        obs =          95
p=0   q=2
        aic = -3.4633827
         sc =   -3.355851
        obs =          95
p=1   q=2
        aic = -3.5675498
         sc = -3.4331352
        obs =          95
p=2   q=2
        aic = -3.5483196
         sc = -3.3870221
        obs =          95
p=0   q=3
        aic = -3.4424223
         sc = -3.3080077
        obs =          95
p=1   q=3
        aic = -3.5611594
         sc = -3.3998619
        obs =          95
p=2   q=3
```

```
aic = -3.5490965
 sc = -3.3609161
obs =         95
```

The model that minimizes both AIC and SC is the ARDL(1,1). This model is estimated using the entire sample and the errors are checked for any remaining autocorrelation using the LM statistic. This is done using:

```
reg D.u L.D.u L(0/1).g
estat bgodfrey
```

which results in

Source	SS	df	MS
Model	5.49727601	3	1.83242534
Residual	2.42272399	92	.026333956
Total	7.92	95	.083368421

Number of obs = 96
F(3, 92) = 69.58
Prob > F = 0.0000
R-squared = 0.6941
Adj R-squared = 0.6841
Root MSE = .16228

D.u	Coef.	Std. Err.	t	P>|t|	[95% Conf. Interval]	
u LD.	.3501158	.084573	4.14	0.000	.1821466	.518085
g --.	-.1840843	.0306984	-6.00	0.000	-.245054	-.1231146
L1.	-.0991552	.0368244	-2.69	0.008	-.1722917	-.0260187
_cons	.3780104	.0578398	6.54	0.000	.2631356	.4928853

. estat bgodfrey

Breusch-Godfrey LM test for autocorrelation

lags(p)	chi2	df	Prob > chi2
1	0.170	1	0.6804

H0: no serial correlation

There appears to be no remaining autocorrelation in the model's residuals (p-value=0.68), suggesting that the ARDL(1,1) model is adequate.

9.6.3 Autoregressive Models

Autoregressive models can be thought of as special cases of the ARDL(p,q). Basically, an AR(p) model is equivalent to an ARDL(p,0). The data on U.S. GDP growth found in *okun.dta* was examined for autocorrelation in Section 9.3. In the correlogram of **g**, there was evidence of correlation among the observations of the time-series.

To examine this further, an AR(2) model is estimated for GDP growth and the correlogram of the residuals is drawn. The autoregression is estimated, the residuals saved, and autocorrelations produced for the first 12 lags:

```
reg g L(1/2).g
predict ehat, res
ac ehat, lags(12)
```

which produces

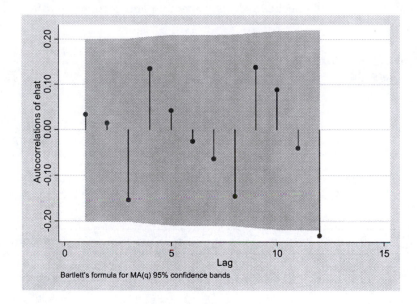

The AR(2) model appears to be adequate since most of the residual autocorrelations are small and insignificant. To explore this further, the order of the autoregression is varied from 1 to 5 and the model selection rules are used to select the preferred model, again with the model producing the smallest value of AIC or SC:

```
forvalues p=1/5 {
  qui reg L(0/`p').g if date> tq(1986q2)
  display "p=`p'
  modelsel
  }
```

which produces

```
p=1
          aic = -1.0935183
           sc = -1.0390538
          obs =          93
p=2
          aic =  -1.130582
           sc = -1.0488852
          obs =          93
p=3
          aic = -1.1242025
           sc = -1.0152735
          obs =          93
```

```
p=4
        aic = -1.1331587
         sc = -.99699743
        obs =          93
p=5
        aic = -1.1116622
         sc = -.94826871
        obs =          93
```

The model producing the smallest value of AIC is the AR(4) wh ere AIC = −1.133. The model producing the smallest SC is the AR(2) where SC =   −1.049. This illustrates an i mportant difference between the two m odel selection rules: the SC criteri on imposes a larger penalt y for adding a regressor and ten ds to choose sm aller models than the AIC. This is well-known an d understood among practitioners.

9.7 FORECASTING

In this Section we consider forecasting using 3 di fferent models, an AR model, an ARDL model, and an exponential smoothing model. The examples focus on short-term forecasting, typically up to 3 periods into the future.

9.7.1 Forecasting with an AR Model

Suppose that it is the 3 rd quarter in 20 09 and have estimated the AR(2) model of GDP gro wth using data up to and including 20 09q3. In this sec tion the use of an AR(2) model to forecast the next three periods is discussed and forecast confidence intervals are generated.

The AR(2) model in terms of its unknown coefficients

$$G_t = \delta + \theta_1 G_{t-1} + \theta_2 G_{t-2} + v_t$$

Denoting the last sample observation as G_T, the task is to forecast G_{T+1}, G_{T+2} and G_{T+3}. The value of the next observation beyond the available sample is

$$G_{T+1} = \delta + \theta_1 G_T + \theta_2 G_{T-1} + v_{T+1}$$

Growth rates for the 2 most recent quarters are $G_T = G_{2009q3} = 0.8$, and $G_{T-1} = G_{2009q2} = -0.2$, which with the estimated values of the parameters is used to make a forecast of $G_{T+1} = G_{2009q4}$.

$$\hat{G}_{T+1} = \hat{\delta} + \hat{\theta}_1 G_T + \hat{\theta}_2 G_{T-1}$$
$$= 0.46573 + 0.37700 \times 0.8 + 0.24624 \times (-0.2)$$
$$= 0.7181$$

Once the model is estimated in Stata this is easy to compute. Estimate the AR(2) model

```
reg g L(1/2).g
```

Then compute the scalar forecast using

```
scalar ghat1 = _b[_cons]+_b[L1.g]*g[98]+ _b[L2.g]*g[97]
```

Stata's indexing capabiliti es are used to get the last two observations on G from the data set. Since the data consist of 98 observation s that end in 2009q3, **g[98]** refers to the 98th observation on G_{2009q3}. Similarly, **g[97]** refers to the observation on G from 2009q2.

The next forecast

$$\hat{G}_{T+2} = \hat{\delta} + \hat{\theta}_1 \hat{G}_{T+1} + \hat{\theta}_2 G_T$$

is produced using

```
scalar ghat2 = _b[_cons]+_b[L1.g]*ghat1+ _b[L2.g]*g[98]
```

Notice that forecast of **ghat1** is used to estimate $\hat{G}_{T+1}$. G_T is actually observed and is located in the data set at observation 98.

```
scalar ghat2 = _b[_cons]+_b[L1.g]*ghat1+ _b[L2.g]*g[98]
```

Finally, the last forecast

$$\hat{G}_{T+3} = \hat{\delta} + \hat{\theta}_1 \hat{G}_{T+2} + \hat{\theta}_2 \hat{G}_{T+1}$$

is generated with

```
scalar ghat3 = _b[_cons]+_b[L1.g]*ghat2+ _b[L2.g]*ghat1
```

The forecast **ghat2** is used to estimate $\hat{G}_{T+2}$ and this forecast depend s completely on previous forecasts.

The complete set of forecasts generated in this way is:

```
. scalar list ghat1 ghat2 ghat3
     ghat1 =   .71807948
     ghat2 =   .93343472
     ghat3 =   .99445191
```

As shown in *POE4*, the forecast error variances are

$$\sigma_1^2 = \text{var}(u_1) = \sigma_v^2$$

$$\sigma_2^2 = \text{var}(u_2) = \sigma_v^2 \left(1 + \theta_1^2\right)$$

$$\sigma_3^2 = \text{var}(u_3) = \sigma_v^2 \left(\left(\theta_1^2 + \theta_2\right)^2 + \theta_1^2 + 1\right)$$

which are estimated by substituting in estimates from the AR(2) model

```
scalar var = e(rmse)^2
scalar se1 = sqrt(var)
scalar se2 = sqrt(var*(1+(_b[L1.g])^2))
scalar se3 = sqrt(var*((_b[L1.g]^2+_b[L2.g])^2+1+_b[L1.g]^2))
scalar list se1 se2 se3
```

```
. scalar list se1 se2 se3
      se1 =  .55268751
      se2 =  .59065984
      se3 =  .62845236
```

The 95% forecast confidence intervals are constructed in the usual way. They are centered at the forecast and extend approximately 2 standard deviations in either direction. More precisely, they are computed using the 2.5% critical value from the *t*-distribution and use the forecast standard errors computed above.

```
scalar f1L = ghat1 - invttail(e(df_r),.025)*se1
scalar f1U = ghat1 + invttail(e(df_r),.025)*se1

scalar f2L = ghat2 - invttail(e(df_r),.025)*se2
scalar f2U = ghat2 + invttail(e(df_r),.025)*se2

scalar f3L = ghat3 - invttail(e(df_r),.025)*se3
scalar f3U = ghat3 + invttail(e(df_r),.025)*se3

scalar list f1L f1U f2L f2U f3L f3U
```

In Stata the computation of the exact critical value uses the `invttail` function. The results follow.

```
. scalar list f1L f1U f2L f2U f3L f3U
     f1L = -.37944839
     f1U =  1.8156073
     f2L = -.23949866
     f2U =  2.1063681
     f3L = -.25352994
     f3U =  2.2424338
```

9.7.2 Exponential Smoothing

Another popular model used for predicting the future value of a variable based on its history is exponential smoothing. Like forecasting with an AR model, forecasting using exponential smoothing does not use information from any other variable.

The basic idea is that the forecast for next period is a weighted average of the forecast for the current period and the actual realized value in the current period.

$$\hat{y}_{T+1} = \alpha y_T + (1-\alpha)\hat{y}_T$$

The exponential smoothing method is a versatile forecasting tool, but one needs a value for the smoothing parameter α and a value for $\hat{y}_T$ to generate the forecast $\hat{y}_{T+1}$. The value of α can reflect one's judgment about the relative weight of current information; alternatively, it can be estimated from historical information by obtaining **within-sample forecasts**

$$\hat{y}_t = \alpha y_{t-1} + (1-\alpha)\hat{y}_{t-1} \quad t = 2,3,\ldots,T$$

and choosing that value of α that minimizes the sum of squares of the **one-step forecast errors**

$$v_t = y_t - \hat{y}_t = y_t - \left(\alpha y_{t-1} + (1-\alpha)\hat{y}_{t-1}\right)$$

Smaller values of α result in more smoothing of the forecast. Stata contains a routine that performs various forms of smoothing for time-series called **tssmooth**. **tssmooth** creates new variable *newvar* and fills it in by passing the variable through the requested smoother. There are several smoothers available, including the exponential. Once can specify the desired value of the smoothing parameter, α, or its value can be chosen automatically to minimize the in-sample sum-of-squared prediction errors as discussed in *POE4*.

Below, the *okun.dta* data are used to obtain the exponentially smoothed forecast values of GDP growth. First the data are opened, the dates generated, reformatted, and the variables are set as time-series.

```
use okun, clear
generate date = tq(1985q2) + _n-1
format %tq date
tsset date
```

The first thing to do before smoothing **g** is to add an (empty) observation to the time-series. Doing this before smoothing will allow Stata to fill that observation with the one-step ahead forecast.

```
tsappend, add(1)
```

The command to exponentially smooth the series **g** is:

```
tssmooth exponential sm1=g, parms(.38)
```

The syntax for **tssmooth**, which appears below, deserves some explanation.

<u>Syntax</u>

```
    tssmooth smoother [type] newvar = exp [if] [in] [, ...]
```

Smoother category	smoother
Moving average	
with uniform weights	ma
with specified weights	ma
Recursive	
exponential	exponential
double exponential	dexponential
nonseasonal Holt-Winters	hwinters
seasonal Holt-Winters	shwinters
Nonlinear filter	nl

The first thing to specify i s the desired type of smoothing. Here, we choose ex ponential. Next a new variable name must be created and set equal to the series that is to be smoothed (**sm1=g**). This is followed by some options. The first, **parms(.38)**, sets the value of the sm oothing parameter. If this option is not specified, then **tssmooth** chooses the one that m inimizes the sum-of-squared errors.

This produces the output

```
. tssmooth exponential sm1=g, parms(.38)

exponential coefficient  =        0.3800
sum-of-squared residuals =        31.122
root mean squared error  =        .56354
```

The new variable **sm1** contains the exponentially smoothed series and it is added to t he data set. Once the smoothed series is generated, it can be compared to the unsm oothed version in a time-series plot. In the line that follows, the t wo series are plotted and the lege nd is relabeled so that everything fits on the graph a little better.

```
tsline sm1 g, legend(lab (1 "G") lab(2 "Ghat")) title(alpha=.38) \\\
lpattern(solid dash)
```

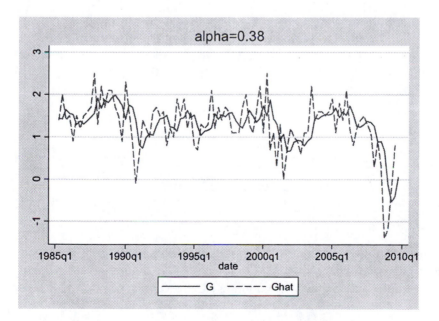

The forecast for the next period is generated a   nd listed. Also, the inform ation is com puted automatically by **tssmooth** for 1 period. If more are desired then Stata offers options for that. The manually generated and the automatic forecast from Stata match.

```
scalar f1 = .38*g[98]+(1-.38)*sm1[98]
scalar list f1
list sm1 in 99
```

```
. scalar list f1
        f1 =   .05356533
```

```
. list sm1 in 99
```

	sm1
99.	.0535653

The exercise is repeated for a smoothing parameter of $\alpha = 0.8$. The code and results are below.

```
tssmooth exponential sm2=g, parms(.8)
tsline sm2 g, legend(lab (1 "G") lab(2 "Ghat")) title(alpha=.8) \\\
lpattern(solid dash)
scalar f2 = .8*g[98]+(1-.8)*sm2[98]
scalar list f2
```

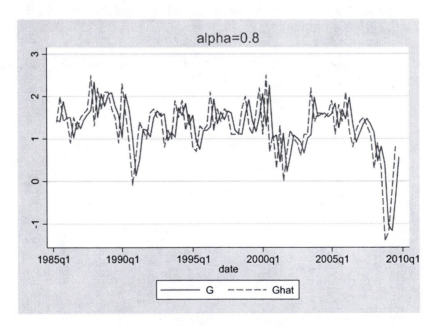

The larger value of $\alpha = 0.8$ results in less sm oothing; the exponentially smoothed series is much closer to the original that when $\alpha = 0.38$. The forecast, **f2**, is 0.56128444, which is much larger than the one generated with the larger smoothing parameter.

Finally, if the specific value of the sm oothing parameter is o mitted as an option, Stat a chooses the value that m inimizes the in-sam ple sum-of-squared prediction errors. Th is is estimated in Stata using

```
tssmooth exponential sm3=g
scalar f3 = r(alpha)*g[98]+(1-r(alpha))*sm3[98]
scalar list f3
```

which yields

```
computing optimal exponential  coefficient (0,1)

optimal exponential coefficient =        0.3803
sum-of-squared residuals        =       31.122043
root mean squared error         =       .56353515

. scalar f3 = r(alpha)*g[98]+(1-r(alpha))*sm3[98]

. scalar list f3
        f3 =   .05367152
```

By this accounting, the fixed choice o f 0.38 was an informed one! Note that the value of the smoothing parameter is saved as **r(alpha)** after sm oothing and that it can be used to generate forecasts just as easily as with a fixed value.

9.8 MULTIPLIER ANALYSIS

Multiplier analysis refers to the effect, and the tim ing of the effect, of a change i n one variable on the outcome of another variable. The si mplest form of multiplier analysis is based on a finite distributed lag model

$$y_t = \alpha + \beta_0 x_t + \beta_1 x_{t-1} + \beta_2 x_{t-2} + \cdots + \beta_q x_{t-q} + e_t$$

The estimated coefficients from this model can be used to pr oduce **impact, delay** and **interim** multipliers. The impact multiplier is the impact of a one unit change in x_t on the mean of y_t. Since x and y are in the same time period the effect is contemporaneous and therefore equal to the initial impact of the change. The s-period *delay multiplier* is

$$\frac{\partial E(y_t)}{\partial x_{t-s}} = \beta_s$$

is the effect of a change in x s-periods in the past on the average v alue of the dependent variable in the current period. If x_t is increased by 1 unit and then m aintained at its new level in subsequent periods $(t+1),(t+2),\ldots.$, then one can co mpute the interi m multiplier. An *interim multiplier* simply adds the immediat e effect (i mpact multiplier), β_0, to su bsequent delay multipliers to measure the cu mulative effect. So in period $t+1$ the interi m effect is $\beta_0 + \beta_1$. In period $t+2$, it will be $\beta_0 + \beta_1 + \beta_2$, and so on. The **total multiplier** is the final effect on y of the sustained increase after q or more periods have elapsed; it is given by $\sum_{s=0}^{q}\beta_s$.

The ARDL model adds lagged values of the dependent variable to the AR model.

$$y_t = \delta + \theta_1 y_{t-1} + \cdots + \theta_p y_{t-p} + \delta_0 x_t + \delta_1 x_{t-1} + \cdots + \delta_q x_{t-q} + v_t$$

and this makes the multiplier analysis a little harder. Basically, this needs to be transformed into an infinite distributed lag model using the properties of the lag operator, L, which works just as the Stata commands based on it do. That is, $L^i x_t = x_{t-i}$. This puts the model into the familiar AR form and the usual definitions of the multipliers can be applied. This is discussed in detail in *POE4* and will not be replicated here.

For the ARDL(1,1) model used to describe Okun's law we have

$$DU_t = \delta + \theta_1 DU_{t-1} + \delta_0 G_t + \delta_1 G_{t-1} + v_t$$

or, written with the lag operator, L

$$(1-\theta_1 L)DU_t = \delta + (\delta_0 + \delta_1 L)G_t + v_t$$

$$DU_t = (1-\theta_1 L)^{-1}\delta + (1-\theta_1 L)^{-1}(\delta_0 + \delta_1 L)G_t + (1-\theta_1 L)^{-1}v_t$$

$$DU_t = \alpha + \beta_0 G_t + \beta_1 G_{t-1} + \beta_2 G_{t-2} + \beta_3 G_{t-3} + \cdots + e_t$$

$$= \alpha + (\beta_0 + \beta_1 L + \beta_2 L^2 + \beta_3 L^3 + \cdots)G_t + e_t$$

This is just an infinite distributed lag model. The coefficients for the multipliers involve the βs, which must be solved for in terms of the estimated parameters of the ARDL.

The solutions given in *POE4* are

$$\beta_0 = \delta_0$$
$$\beta_1 = \delta_1 + \beta_0 \theta_1$$
$$\beta_j = \beta_{j-1}\theta_1 \quad \text{for } j \geq 2$$

The Stata code to estimate the impact and first few interim multipliers based on the ARDL(1,1) for the Okun model is:

```
regress D.u L.D.u L(0/1).g
scalar b0 = _b[g]
scalar b1 = _b[L1.D.u]*b0+_b[L1.g]
scalar b2 = b1*_b[L1.D.u]
scalar b3 = b2*_b[L1.D.u]
```

and so on.

Stata provides a slick way to get these into a data set so that they can be graphed. After the regression generate a new variable called **mult** and place the estimated coefficient β_0 into the first observation

```
gen mult = _b[g] in 1
```

For the second o bservation where $\beta_1 = \delta_1 + \beta_0\theta_1$, use the replace command to put the computed value into the second observation:

```
replace mult = L.mult*_b[L1.D.u]+_b[L1.g] in 2
```

Notice that **L.mult** is used for the esti mate of β_0. The rest of the multipliers are computed based on $\beta_j = \beta_{j-1}\theta_1$, which can be estimated using a single line

```
replace mult = L.mult*_b[L1.D.u] in 3/8
list mult in 1/8
```

In this case **L.mult** is the lagged value of the vari able **mult** that contains the multipliers. You could easily compute these up to T if desired, though we've ch osen to only do eight. Finally, create a new variable call ed **lag** that contains integers to be used as the lag weights (1 to 8). Finally, you can plot them.

```
gen lag = _n-1 in 1/8
line mult lag in 1/8
```

The multipliers are:

```
. list mult in 1/8
```

	mult
1.	-.1840843
2.	-.163606
3.	-.057281
4.	-.020055
5.	-.0070216
6.	-.0024584
7.	-.0008607
8.	-.0003013

and the graph:

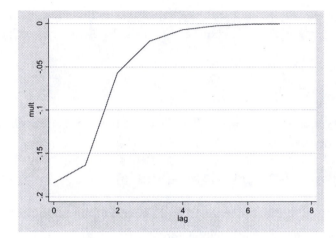

It appears that the initial impact is negative, but converges to zero as time passes. By the 6th period the effect of a one unit change in GDP growth on unemployment is virtually zero.

9.9 APPENDIX

9.9.1 Durbin-Watson Test

The Durbin-Watson statistic is easily produced using **estat dwatson** after a regression. For the Phillips dataset the DW statistic is produced using the code:

```
* Durbin Watson test
use phillips_aus, clear
generate date = tq(1987q1) + _n-1
format %tq date
tsset date

regress inf D.u
estat dwatson
```

which produces

```
. estat dwatson

Durbin-Watson d-statistic(  2,    90) =   .8872891
```

Note, the **dwatson** test in Stata requires you to looks up the upper and lower bounds in a table. The exact p-value obtained by integrating the distribution function of DW is not performed at this point in time.

9.9.2 Prais-Winsten FGLS

The feasible GLS estimator of the AR(1) model can be estimated using the Stata procedure called **prais**. The **prais** command operates much like **regress** and uses similar syntax. There are a few additional options that may be worth explorin g if you are interested. The biggest lim itation of **prais** is t hat it will onl y estimate models with first-order autoc orrelation. For more complex models, see the **arima** command which estimates more general models using m aximum likelihood. Two-step FGLS estimation of a linear regression model with AR(1) errors is estimated

```
* Prais-Winsten FGLS estimator
prais inf D.u, twostep
```

If the **twostep** option is not given, the esti mator iterates until a stable solution is found. Both estimators have the same asymptotic properties so there is really no need to iterate.

```
prais inf D.u
```

This produces:

```
. esttab _2step Iterate, compress se(%12.3f) b(%12.5f) gaps scalars(rss rho) //
> /
>          mtitle("2-step" "Iterated") title("Dependent Variable: inf")
```

Dependent Variable: inf

	(1) 2-step	(2) Iterated
D.u	-0.69943** (0.243)	-0.70236** (0.243)
_cons	0.78584*** (0.120)	0.78619*** (0.122)
N	90	90
rss	23.50157	23.49538
rho	0.54988	0.55825

```
Standard errors in parentheses
* p<0.05, ** p<0.01, *** p<0.001
```

The first column contains the two-step FGLS re sults and the second are the on es from iteration. The results are very similar.

The maximum likelihood estimator derived via the **arima** command is estimated using

```
arima inf D.u, ar(1)
```

which produces

```
ARIMA regression

Sample:  1987q2 - 2009q3                    Number of obs    =        90
                                            Wald chi2(2)     =     44.96
Log likelihood =   -67.4559                 Prob > chi2      =    0.0000
```

inf	Coef.	OPG Std. Err.	z	P>|z|	[95% Conf. Interval]	
inf						
u						
D1.	-.7025681	.3167053	-2.22	0.027	-1.323299	-.0818371
_cons	.7861493	.1398032	5.62	0.000	.51214	1.060159
ARMA						
ar						
L1.	.5588218	.0873961	6.39	0.000	.3875285	.7301151
/sigma	.5109273	.0277513	18.41	0.000	.4565358	.5653188

The first block contains the estimates of the regression. The intercept is estimated to be 0.786 and the slope on the change in unemployment is −0.7023. The autocorrelation parameter is in the box labeled ARMA and is estimated to be 0.559. These results are very similar to the FGLS estimates obtained using **prais**.

KEY TERMS

%tq	**estat dwatson**	**nl**
ac	**exponential smoothing**	**nonlinear least squares**
AIC criterion	**finite distributed lag**	Prais-Winsten
AR(1) error	forecast error	**prais**
AR(p) model	forecast standard error	**program**
ARDL(p,q) model	forecasting	pseudofunctions
arima	format	replace
autocorrelation	forvalues	sample autocorrelations
autoregressive	HAC standard errors	**SC criterion**
autoregressive error	**impact multiplier**	**serial correlation**
autoregressive model	**infinite distributed lag**	TR^2 form of LM test
bandwidth	interim multiplier	**total multiplier**
BIC criterion	kernel	tsline
correlogram	L(0/4).varname	tsset
corrgram	**L.** operator	tssmooth
D. operator	lag length	tsvarlist
delay multiplier	**lag operator**	within-sample forecasts
difference operator	lagged dependent variable	
distributed lags	LM test	
e(df_r)	macro	
e(N)	**multiplier analysis**	
e(r2)	**newey**	
estat bgodfrey	Newey-West standard errors	

CHAPTER 9 DO-FILE [CHAP09.DO]

```
* file chap09.do for Using Stata for Principles of Econometrics, 4e

cd c:\data\poe4stata

* Stata Do-file
* copyright C 2011 by Lee C. Adkins and R. Carter Hill
* used for "Using Stata for Principles of Econometrics, 4e"
* by Lee C. Adkins and R. Carter Hill (2011)
* John Wiley and Sons, Inc.

* setup
version 11.1
capture log close
set more off

* dates
clear
set obs 100
generate date = tq(1961q1) + _n-1
list date in 1/5
format %tq date
list date in 1/5
tsset date
save new.dta, replace

* open log
log using chap09, replace text
use okun, clear
generate date = tq(1985q2) + _n-1
list date in 1

format %tq date
list date in 1

tsset date

label var u "% Unemployed"
label var g "% GDP growth"
tsline u g, lpattern(solid dash)

list date u L.u D.u g L1.g L2.g L3.g in 1/5
list date u L.u D.u g L1.g L2.g L3.g in 96/98

regress D.u L(0/3).g
regress D.u L(0/2).g

summarize g
return list

scatter g L.g, xline(`r(mean)') yline(`r(mean)')
ac g, lags(12) generate(ac_g)

* approximate z scores
gen z=sqrt(e(N))*ac_g
list ac_g z in 1/12

use phillips_aus, clear
generate date = tq(1987q1) + _n-1
format %tq date
tsset date
```

```
tsline inf
tsline D.u

reg inf D.u
predict ehat, res

ac ehat, lags(12) generate(rk)
list rk in 1/5

* -----------------------------------------------------
* Corrgram
* -----------------------------------------------------
corrgram ehat, lags(5)
di "rho1 = " r(ac1) " rho2 = " r(ac2) " rho3 = " r(ac3)
drop rk ehat

* LM tests for AR(1) and AR(4) alternatives
reg inf D.u
predict ehat, res
regress inf D.u L.ehat
test L.ehat
* LM test for AR(1)
quietly regress ehat D.u L.ehat
di "Observations = " e(N) " and TR2 = " e(N)*e(r2)
* LM test for AR(4)
quietly regress ehat D.u L(1/4).ehat
di "Observations = " e(N) " and TR2 = " e(N)*e(r2)
drop ehat

* Using the built-in bgodfrey command to test the
* AR(1) and AR(4) alternatives
regress inf D.u
predict ehat, res
estat bgodfrey, lags(1)
estat bgodfrey, lags(4)

* Replacing ehat(1) with zero and computing LM
replace ehat = 0 in 1
regress inf D.u L.ehat
test L.ehat
quietly regress ehat D.u L.ehat
di "Observations = " e(N) " and TR2 = " e(N)*e(r2)
drop ehat

* Getting Stata to use 90 observations for the LM test
reg inf D.u
predict ehat, res

* Using all observations for bgodfrey test
set obs 94                               // add 3 observations to data
gsort -date                              // moves missing observations to end
replace date = date[_n-1] - 1 if missing(date) // creates dates for missing obs
replace ehat = 0 if missing(ehat)        // puts zeros in for missing ehats
sort date                                // re-sort data into ascending order
regress ehat D.u L(1/4).ehat
di "Observations = " e(N) " and TR2 = " e(N)*e(r2)

use phillips_aus, clear
generate date = tq(1987q1) + _n-1
format %tq date
tsset date
```

```
scalar B = round(4*(e(N)/100)^(2/9))
scalar list B

regress inf D.u
estimates store Wrong_SE
newey inf D.u, lag(4)
estimates store HAC_4

esttab Wrong_SE HAC_4, compress se(%12.3f) b(%12.5f) gaps ///
       scalars(r2_a rss aic) title("Dependent Variable: inf") ///
       mtitles("LS" "HAC(4)")

* ---------------------------------------------------
* Nonlinear least squares of AR(1) regression model
* ---------------------------------------------------

nl (inf = {b1}*(1-{rho}) + {b2}*D.u + {rho}*L.inf - {rho}*{b2}*(L.D.u)), ///
         variables(inf D.u L.inf L.D.u)
* To see the coefficient legend use coeflegend option
nl (inf = {b1}*(1-{rho}) + {b2}*D.u + {rho}*L.inf - {rho}*{b2}*(L.D.u)), ///
         variables(inf D.u L.inf L.D.u) coeflegend
scalar delta = _b[b1:_cons]*(1-_b[rho:_cons])
scalar delta1 = - _b[rho:_cons]*_b[b2:_cons]


   * ---------------------------------------------------
   * More general model
   * ---------------------------------------------------

regress inf L.inf D.u L.D.u
estimates store General
scalar list delta delta1

testnl _b[L.D.u]=-_b[L.inf]*_b[D.u]

regress inf L.inf D.u
estimates store No_LDu

regress inf D.u
estimates store Original
esttab General No_LDu Original, compress se(%12.3f) b(%12.5f) ///
       gaps scalars(r2_a rss aic)

* ARDL
regress inf L.inf L(0/1).D.u
estimates store AR1_DL1
regress inf L.inf D.u
estimates store AR1_DL0
esttab AR1_DL1 AR1_DL0, compress se(%12.3f) b(%12.5f) ///
       gaps scalars(r2_a rss aic)

* Model selection program computes aic and sc
* To remove it from memory use:
* program drop modelsel
capture program drop modelsel

program modelsel
  scalar aic = ln(e(rss)/e(N))+2*e(rank)/e(N)
  scalar sc = ln(e(rss)/e(N))+e(rank)*ln(e(N))/e(N)
  scalar obs = e(N)
  scalar list aic sc obs
end

quietly regress inf L.inf L(0/1).D.u
```

```
modelsel
quietly regress inf L.inf L.D.u
modelsel


* ---------------------------------------------------
* Residual correlogram and graph
* ---------------------------------------------------

quietly regress inf L.inf D.u
predict ehat, res
corrgram ehat, lags(12)
ac ehat, lags(12)
estat bgodfrey, lags(1 2 3 4 5)
drop ehat

* Table 9.4 AIC and SC Values for Phillips Curve ARDL model
* Note that regress can be abreviated to reg and quietly to qui

quietly reg L(0/1).inf D.u if date>= tq(1988q3)
di "p=1  q=0"
modelsel
quietly regress L(0/2).inf D.u if date>= tq(1988q3)
di "p=2  q=0"
modelsel
quietly regress L(0/3).inf D.u if date>= tq(1988q3)
di "p=3  q=0"
modelsel
quietly regress L(0/4).inf D.u if date>= tq(1988q3)
di "p=4  q=0"
modelsel
quietly regress L(0/5).inf D.u if date>= tq(1988q3)
di "p=5  q=0"
modelsel
quietly regress L(0/6).inf D.u if date>= tq(1988q3)
di "p=6  q=0"
modelsel

qui reg L(0/1).inf L(0/1).D.u if date>= tq(1988q3)
di "p=1  q=1"
modelsel
qui reg L(0/2).inf L(0/1).D.u if date>= tq(1988q3)
di "p=2  q=1"
modelsel
qui reg L(0/3).inf L(0/1).D.u if date>= tq(1988q3)
di "p=3  q=1"
modelsel
qui reg L(0/4).inf L(0/1).D.u if date>= tq(1988q3)
di "p=4  q=1"
modelsel
qui reg L(0/5).inf L(0/1).D.u if date>= tq(1988q3)
di "p=5  q=1"
modelsel
qui reg L(0/6).inf L(0/1).D.u if date>= tq(1988q3)
di "p=6  q=1"
modelsel

* Table 9.4 AIC and SC Values for Phillips Curve ARDL model
* Here is the entire thing again, using nested loops
forvalues q=0/1 {
    forvalues p=1/6 {
        quietly regress L(0/`p').inf L(0/`q').D.u if date >= tq(1988q3)
        display "p=`p'  q=`q'"
        modelsel
```

```
        }
    }

* Using var to estimate ARDL
* Disadvantage:  No estat after the procedure

var inf in 7/91, lags(1/3) exog(L(0/1).D.u)

* ARDL models
use okun, clear
generate date = tq(1985q2) + _n-1
format %tq date
tsset date

* Estimate the ARDL(0,2)
* Generate the correlogram and test for autocorrelation
reg D.u L(0/2).g
predict ehat, res
ac ehat, lags(12)
drop ehat
estat bgodfrey, lags(1 2 3 4 5)

* Model Selection for Okun's Law model
forvalues q=1/3 {
    forvalues p=0/2 {
        quietly regress L(0/`p').D.u L(0/`q').g if date >= tq(1986q1)
        display "p=`p'  q=`q'"
        modelsel
        }
    }

reg D.u L.D.u L(0/1).g
estat bgodfrey

* Figure 9.11
reg g L(1/2).g
predict ehat, res
ac ehat, lags(12)

* Table 9.6
forvalues p=1/5 {
  qui reg L(0/`p').g if date> tq(1986q2)
  display "p=`p'
  modelsel
  }


* Forecasting using -arima- instead of -regress-
* which, of course, yields different predictions
arima g, ar(1/2)
tsappend, add(3)
predict ghat, y // for the point estimates
predict ghatse, mse // for the standard error of prediction

* Forecasting with an AR model

reg g L(1/2).g
scalar ghat1 = _b[_cons]+_b[L1.g]*g[98]+ _b[L2.g]*g[97]
scalar ghat2 = _b[_cons]+_b[L1.g]*ghat1+ _b[L2.g]*g[98]
scalar ghat3 = _b[_cons]+_b[L1.g]*ghat2+ _b[L2.g]*ghat1
scalar list ghat1 ghat2 ghat3

scalar var = e(rmse)^2
```

```
scalar se1 = sqrt(var)
scalar se2 = sqrt(var*(1+(_b[L1.g])^2))
scalar se3 = sqrt(var*((_b[L1.g]^2+_b[L2.g])^2+1+_b[L1.g]^2))
scalar list se1 se2 se3

scalar f1L = ghat1 - invttail(e(df_r),.025)*se1
scalar f1U = ghat1 + invttail(e(df_r),.025)*se1

scalar f2L = ghat2 - invttail(e(df_r),.025)*se2
scalar f2U = ghat2 + invttail(e(df_r),.025)*se2

scalar f3L = ghat3 - invttail(e(df_r),.025)*se3
scalar f3U = ghat3 + invttail(e(df_r),.025)*se3

scalar list f1L f1U f2L f2U f3L f3U


* --------------------------------------------------
* Impact and Delay Multipliers from Okun's ARDL(1,1) model
* --------------------------------------------------

regress D.u L.D.u L(0/1).g

scalar b0 = _b[g]
scalar b1 = _b[L1.D.u]*b0+_b[L1.g]
scalar b2 = b1*_b[L1.D.u]
scalar list b0 b1 b2

* An alternative method: Exploiting variable creation
regress D.u L.D.u L(0/1).g
gen mult = _b[g] in 1
replace mult = L.mult*_b[L1.D.u]+_b[L1.g] in 2
replace mult = L.mult*_b[L1.D.u] in 3/8
list mult in 1/8
gen lag = _n-1 in 1/8
line mult lag in 1/8


* --------------------------------------------------
* Exponential Smoothing
* --------------------------------------------------

use okun, clear
generate date = tq(1985q2) + _n-1
format %tq date
tsset date

tsappend, add(1)
tssmooth exponential sm1=g, parms(.38)
tsline sm1 g, legend(lab (1 "G") lab(2 "Ghat")) title(alpha=0.38) lpattern(solid dash)
scalar f1 = .38*g[98]+(1-.38)*sm1[98]
scalar list f1
list sm1 in 99

tssmooth exponential sm2=g, parms(.8)
tsline sm2 g, legend(lab (1 "G") lab(2 "Ghat")) title(alpha=0.8) lpattern(solid dash)
scalar f2 = .8*g[98]+(1-.8)*sm2[98]
scalar list f2

tssmooth exponential sm3=g
scalar f3 = r(alpha)*g[98]+(1-r(alpha))*sm3[98]
scalar list f3
list sm3 in 99

program drop modelsel
```

```
drop sm1 sm2 sm3

* appendix
* Durbin Watson test
use phillips_aus, clear
generate date = tq(1987q1) + _n-1
format %tq date
tsset date

regress inf D.u
estat dwatson

* Prais-Winsten FGLS estimator
prais inf D.u, twostep
estimates store _2step
prais inf D.u
estimates store Iterate
esttab _2step Iterate, compress se(%12.3f) b(%12.5f) gaps scalars(rss rho) ///
        mtitle("2-step" "Iterated") title("Dependent Variable: inf")

* AR(1) using arima
arima inf D.u, ar(1)
log close
```

CHAPTER **10**

Random Regressors and Moment-Based Estimation

CHAPTER OUTLINE

10.1 Least squares estimation of a wage equation
10.2 Two-stage least squares
10.3 IV estimation with surplus instruments
    10.3.1 Illustrating partial correlations
10.4 The Hausman test for endogeneity
10.5 Testing the validity of surplus instruments

10.6 Testing for weak instruments
10.7 Calculating the Cragg-Donald F-statistic
10.8 A simulation experiment
Key Terms
Chapter 10 Do-file

10.1 LEAST SQUARES ESTIMATION OF A WAGE EQUATION

The example in Chapter 10 of *Principles of Econometrics, 4th Edition*, uses Thomas Mroz's data on labor force experiences of married women. Open a log file, the data file *mroz.dta*, and examine the data

```
log using chap10_wage, replace text
use mroz, clear
describe
summarize
```

We will use the wage data on working women to estimate the log-linear wage equation

$$\ln(WAGE) = \beta_1 + \beta_2 EDUC + \beta_3 EXPER + \beta_4 EXPER^2 + e$$

To eliminate non-working women in the data file we use the **drop** statement. The variable identifying labor force participation is **lfp** which is 1 if a woman is in the labor force and 0 if she is not. Then **summarize** the key variables **wage**, **educ** and experience (**exper**).

```
drop if lfp==0
```

```
summarize wage educ exper
```

. summarize wage educ exper

variable	Obs	Mean	Std. Dev.	Min	Max
wage	428	4.177682	3.310282	.1282	25
educ	428	12.65888	2.285376	5	17
exper	428	13.03738	8.055923	0	38

Create the variables ln(wage) and experience squared.

```
gen lwage = ln(wage)
gen exper2 = exper^2
```

Estimate regression model using least squares

```
reg lwage educ exper exper2
```

. reg lwage educ exper exper2

Source	SS	df	MS
Model	35.0222967	3	11.6740989
Residual	188.305145	424	.444115908
Total	223.327442	427	.523015086

```
Number of obs =     428
F( 3,   424) =   26.29
Prob > F      =  0.0000
R-squared     =  0.1568
Adj R-squared =  0.1509
Root MSE      =  .66642
```

lwage	Coef.	Std. Err.	t	P>|t|	[95% Conf. Interval]	
educ	.1074896	.0141465	7.60	0.000	.0796837	.1352956
exper	.0415665	.0131752	3.15	0.002	.0156697	.0674633
exper2	-.0008112	.0003932	-2.06	0.040	-.0015841	-.0000382
_cons	-.5220406	.1986321	-2.63	0.009	-.9124667	-.1316144

For later purposes we will save these regression results using the **estimates store** command. This **post-estimation** command saves the results in Stata's memory and can be recalled for later use. Save the estimates under the name "**ls**" for "least squares." The command is

```
estimates store ls
```

Should you forget the syntax click **Statistics > Postestimation**. Then select **Manage estimation results > Store in memory**

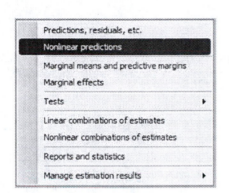

In the resulting dialog box enter a name, "**ls**" for the saved results.

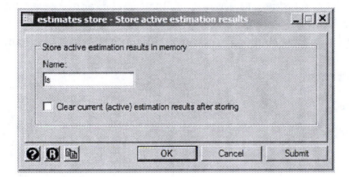

10.2 TWO-STAGE LEAST SQUARES

In this example we might consider the education variable **educ** to be endogenous because it may be correlated with ability and other factors in the regression error term. Instrumental variables estimation is also known as two-stage least squares because the estimates can be obtained in two steps. Estimate the first-stage equation for education, **educ**, including on the right-hand side as explanatory variables the included exogenous variables **exper** and **exper2** and the instrumental variable **mothereduc** which is not included in the model.

```
reg educ exper exper2 mothereduc
```

```
. reg educ exper exper2 mothereduc
```

Source	SS	df	MS		Number of obs =	428
					F(3, 424) =	25.47
Model	340.537834	3	113.512611		Prob > F =	0.0000
Residual	1889.65843	424	4.45674158		R-squared =	0.1527
					Adj R-squared =	0.1467
Total	2230.19626	427	5.22294206		Root MSE =	2.1111

educ	Coef.	Std. Err.	t	P>|t|	[95% Conf. Interval]	
exper	.0488615	.0416693	1.17	0.242	-.0330425	.1307655
exper2	-.0012811	.0012449	-1.03	0.304	-.003728	.0011659
mothereduc	.2676908	.0311298	8.60	0.000	.2065029	.3288787
_cons	9.775103	.4238886	23.06	0.000	8.941918	10.60829

A key element in the first-stage regression is that **mothereduc** is a statistically significant explanatory variable, with a t-statistic > 3.3 or an F-value > 10. More will be said about critical values for the F-test in Section 10.6 of this chapter. The F-test values is obtained using

```
        test mothereduc
```

```
. test mothereduc
```

```
 ( 1)  mothereduc = 0

       F( 1,   424) =   73.95
            Prob > F =    0.0000
```

Obtain the fitted value from the first stage equation, and use it as an explanatory variable in the ln(wage) equation in place of **educ**.

```
        predict educ_hat
        reg lwage educ_hat exper exper2
```

The resulting coefficient estimates are proper *IV/2SLS* estimates, but the reported standard errors, t-statistics, p-values and interval estimates reported below are not correct.

```
. reg lwage educhat exper exper2
```

Source	SS	df	MS		Number of obs =	428
					F(3, 424) =	6.75
Model	10.181204	3	3.39373467		Prob > F =	0.0002
Residual	213.146238	424	.502703391		R-squared =	0.0456
					Adj R-squared =	0.0388
Total	223.327442	427	.523015086		Root MSE =	.70902

lwage	Coef.	Std. Err.	t	P>|t|	[95% Conf. Interval]	
educhat	.0492629	.0390562	1.26	0.208	-.0275049	.1260308
exper	.0448558	.0141644	3.17	0.002	.0170147	.072697
exper2	-.0009221	.000424	-2.17	0.030	-.0017554	-.0000887
_cons	.1981861	.4933427	0.40	0.688	-.7715157	1.167888

When carrying out instrumental variable estimation always use software designed for this purpose. In Stata 11 this command is `ivregress`. For a full description of the capabilities of this powerful command enter `help ivregress`. To implement `ivregress` using a dialog box follow the path

Statistics > Endogenous covariates > Single-equation instrumental-variables regression

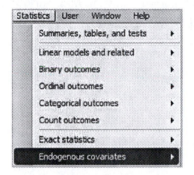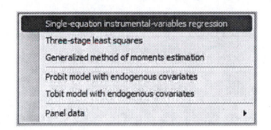

Alternatively enter **db ivregress** in the **Command** window. Fill in as shown and press OK.

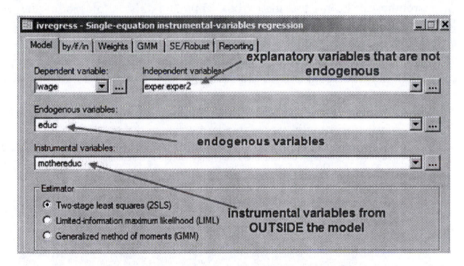

```
. ivregress 2sls lwage exper exper2 (educ = mothereduc)
```

Instrumental variables (2SLS) regression

Number of obs	=	428
Wald chi2(3)	=	22.25
Prob > chi2	=	0.0001
R-squared	=	0.1231
Root MSE	=	.67642

lwage	Coef.	Std. Err.	z	P>|z|	[95% Conf. Interval]	
educ	.049263	.0372607	1.32	0.186	-.0237666	.1222925
exper	.0448558	.0135132	3.32	0.001	.0183704	.0713413
exper2	-.0009221	.0004045	-2.28	0.023	-.0017148	-.0001293
_cons	.1981861	.4706623	0.42	0.674	-.7242952	1.120667

```
Instrumented:  educ
Instruments:   exper exper2 mothereduc
```

The implied Stata command is

```
ivregress 2sls lwage exper exper2 (educ=mothereduc)
```

After **ivregress** use the option **2sls**, which is required for instrumental variables estimation. The dependent variable **lwage** follows, which is then followed by the explanatory variables. Endogenous variables are placed in parentheses with the list of instrumental variables from outside the model, as in **(educ=mothereduc)**. For any explanatory variable that is **endogenous** we have the statement in parentheses, which is

```
(varlist2 = varlist_iv)
```

where

> **varlist2** is a list of all the right-hand size endogenous variables
> **varlist_iv** is a list of all the instrumental variables that are **not** in the model

Explanatory variables that are not endogenous would be listed either before or after the expression in parentheses. Using the dialog-box approach this is placed at the end of the command, but it can appear anywhere after the dependent variable.

The coefficient estimates are the *IV* estimates, and the standard errors are properly computed. The reported test statistics are labeled "z" because *IV* estimators have asymptotic properties, and in large samples the *t*-statistics converge to the standard normal distribution, and *Z*–statistics are appropriate.

To take a more "conservative" approach we compute *t*-statistics, which correct for the degrees of freedom, producing slightly larger standard errors and thus slightly larger *p*-values. In the dialog box use the **Reporting** tab and choose option for **degrees-of-freedom adjustments**.

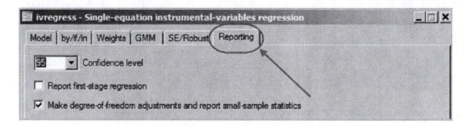

Equivalently, in the command, we add the option **small**

```
ivregress 2sls lwage (educ=mothereduc) exper exper2, small
```

Note that in this command we have placed **(educ=mothereduc)** after the dependent variable. As noted this placement is at the discretion of the programmer.

```
. ivregress 2sls lwage (educ=mothereduc) exper exper2, small
```

Instrumental variables (2SLS) regression

Source	SS	df	MS		
Model	27.4983827	3	9.16612758		
Residual	195.829059	424	.461860988		
Total	223.327442	427	.523015086		

Number of obs =	428
F(3, 424) =	7.35
Prob > F =	0.0001
R-squared =	0.1231
Adj R-squared =	0.1169
Root MSE =	.6796

lwage	Coef.	Std. Err.	t	P>|t|	[95% Conf. Interval]	
educ	.049263	.037436	1.32	0.189	-.0243204	.1228463
exper	.0448558	.0135768	3.30	0.001	.0181696	.0715421
exper2	-.0009221	.0004064	-2.27	0.024	-.0017208	-.0001233
_cons	.1981861	.4728772	0.42	0.675	-.7312895	1.127662

Instrumented: educ
Instruments: exper exper2 mothereduc

Note that now *t*-statistics are reported in the usual fashion, along with an analysis of variance table. The usual formulas for the explained sum of squares (due to regression) do not hold with *IV* estimation. However the sums of squares add up because Stata defines **SS_Model = SS_Total − SS_Residual**. Such details may be found by reading the full Stata documentation. This material is advanced and uses matrix algebra.

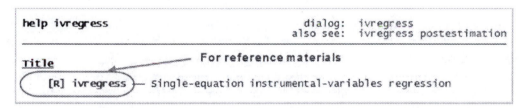

For cross sectional data, such as the Mroz data, we may also be concerned about heteroskedasticity in the data. Instrumental variables standard errors can be made "robust" to heteroskedasticity, using the White heteroskedasticity correction, by adding the option **vce(robust)** to **ivregress**. In the **ivregress** dialog box on the **SE/Robust** Tab choose **Robust**.

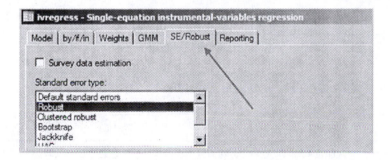

In the command line enter

```
ivregress 2sls lwage (educ=mothereduc) exper exper2, vce(robust) small
```

```
. ivregress 2sls lwage (educ=mothereduc) exper exper2, vce(robust) small
```

```
Instrumental variables (2SLS) regression        Number of obs =      428
                                                 F( 3,   424) =     5.50
                                                 Prob > F     =   0.0010
                                                 R-squared    =   0.1231
                                                 Adj R-squared =  0.1169
                                                 Root MSE     =    .6796
```

lwage	Coef.	Robust Std. Err.	t	P>|t|	[95% Conf. Interval]	
educ	.049263	.0380396	1.30	0.196	-.0255067	.1240326
exper	.0448558	.0156038	2.87	0.004	.0141853	.0755264
exper2	-.0009221	.0004319	-2.14	0.033	-.001771	-.0000732
_cons	.1981861	.4891462	0.41	0.686	-.7632673	1.159639

```
Instrumented:  educ
Instruments:   exper exper2 mothereduc
```

The standard errors are now labeled **Robust Std. Err.** Note that the robust standard errors are slightly larger than the usual standard errors, which is the usual outcome. The overall *F*-test is also based on the robust covariance matrix.

10.3 IV ESTIMATION WITH SURPLUS INSTRUMENTS

Increasing the number of instruments requires a simple modification to the syntax of **ivregress**. Suppose that in addition to **mothereduc** we use **fathereduc** as an instrument. To test whether our instruments are adequately correlated with education estimate the first-stage equation. Test the significance of the instruments from outside the model. Because we have only one endogenous explanatory variable we require only one instrumental variable. If we consider **mothereduc** and **fathereduc** individually we can use *t*-tests to test their significance. Recall that mere significance is not enough. For *t*-tests we look for values in excess of 3.3.

```
    reg educ exper exper2 fathereduc
```

```
. reg educ exper exper2 fathereduc
```

Source	SS	df	MS		Number of obs =	428
					F(3, 424) =	30.09
Model	391.477157	3	130.492386		Prob > F =	0.0000
Residual	1838.7191	424	4.33660166		R-squared =	0.1755
					Adj R-squared =	0.1697
Total	2230.19626	427	5.22294206		Root MSE =	2.0825

educ	Coef.	Std. Err.	t	P>|t|	[95% Conf. Interval]	
exper	.0468243	.0411074	1.14	0.255	-.0339754	.127624
exper2	-.0011504	.0012286	-0.94	0.350	-.0035652	.0012645
fathereduc	.2705061	.0288786	9.37	0.000	.2137431	.3272691
_cons	9.887034	.3956078	24.99	0.000	9.109438	10.66463

If we use both instruments together we will examine their individual and joint significance.

```
reg educ exper exper2 mothereduc fathereduc
test mothereduc fathereduc
```

```
. test mothereduc fathereduc

 ( 1)  mothereduc = 0
 ( 2)  fathereduc = 0

      F(  2,   423) =   55.40
           Prob > F =    0.0000
```

Or, making this test robust to heteroskedasticity

```
reg educ exper exper2 mothereduc fathereduc, vce(robust)
test mothereduc fathereduc
```

```
. test mothereduc fathereduc

 ( 1)  mothereduc = 0
 ( 2)  fathereduc = 0

      F(  2,   423) =   49.53
           Prob > F =    0.0000
```

In a joint test of significance the alternative hypothesis is that at least one of the variables is significant, and one is all we require when there is one endogenous variable. For an F-test, the minimum threshold value for an adequate instrument is about 10. Assured that our instruments are strong, we can now carry out *IV* estimation with two instrumental variables using

```
ivregress 2sls lwage (educ=mothereduc fathereduc) exper exper2, small
estimates store iv
```

```
. ivregress 2sls lwage (educ=mothereduc fathereduc) exper exper2 , small
```

Instrumental variables (2SLS) regression

Source	SS	df	MS		
Model	30.3074259	3	10.1024753	Number of obs =	428
Residual	193.020016	424	.455235886	F(3, 424) =	8.14
				Prob > F =	0.0000
				R-squared =	0.1357
				Adj R-squared =	0.1296
Total	223.327442	427	.523015086	Root MSE =	.67471

lwage	Coef.	Std. Err.	t	P>|t|	[95% Conf. Interval]	
educ	.0613966	.0314367	1.95	0.051	-.0003945	.1231878
exper	.0441704	.0134325	3.29	0.001	.0177679	.0705729
exper2	-.000899	.0004017	-2.24	0.026	-.0016885	-.0001094
_cons	.0481003	.4003281	0.12	0.904	-.7387745	.834975

Instrumented: educ
Instruments: exper exper2 mothereduc fathereduc

Note that we have stored the instrumental variables estimates for future use. The post-estimation command **estat firststage** produces the first-stage *F*-statistic value. In the **ivregress** dialog box select this option on the **Reporting** tab.

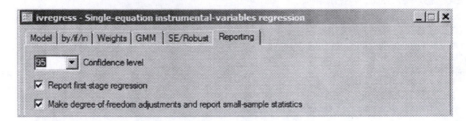

The post-estimation command is

    estat firststage

. estat firststage

First-stage regression summary statistics

variable	R-sq.	Adjusted R-sq.	Partial R-sq.	F(2,423)	Prob > F
educ	0.2115	0.2040	0.2076	55.4003	0.0000

Minimum eigenvalue statistic = 55.4003

| Critical Values Ho: Instruments are weak | # of endogenous regressors: | 1 |
| | # of excluded instruments: | 2 |

	5%	10%	20%	30%
2SLS relative bias		(not available)		

	10%	15%	20%	25%
2SLS Size of nominal 5% Wald test	19.93	11.59	8.75	7.25
LIML Size of nominal 5% Wald test	8.68	5.33	4.42	3.92

The *F*-value is given the name **Minimum eigenvalue statistic** . This terminology and the usefulness of the **Critical Values** given below the statistic will be explained in Section 10.6 of this chapter.

The *IV* estimation can be made robust to heteroskedasticity using

    ivregress 2sls lwage (educ=mothereduc fathereduc) exper exper2,
        vce(robust) small

```
. ivregress 2sls lwage (educ=mothereduc fathereduc) exper exper2 , vce(robust)
> small
```

```
Instrumental variables (2SLS) regression        Number of obs =      428
                                                 F(  3,    424) =     6.15
                                                 Prob > F       =   0.0004
                                                 R-squared      =   0.1357
                                                 Adj R-squared  =   0.1296
                                                 Root MSE       =  .67471
```

lwage	Coef.	Robust Std. Err.	t	P>|t|	[95% Conf. Interval]	
educ	.0613966	.0333386	1.84	0.066	-.0041329	.1269261
exper	.0441704	.0155464	2.84	0.005	.0136128	.074728
exper2	-.000899	.0004301	-2.09	0.037	-.0017443	-.0000536
_cons	.0481003	.4297977	0.11	0.911	-.7966992	.8928998

```
Instrumented:  educ
Instruments:   exper exper2 mothereduc fathereduc
```

```
        estat firststage
```

```
. estat firststage
```

```
   First-stage regression summary statistics
```

Variable	R-sq.	Adjusted R-sq.	Partial R-sq.	Robust F(2,423)	Prob > F
educ	0.2115	0.2040	0.2076	49.5266	0.0000

After robust *IV* estimation, the automatic first stage command, **estat firststage**, does not report the **Critical Values** because they are not valid under heteroskedasticity.

10.3.1 Illustrating partial correlations

One of the phrases heard during discussions of instrument strength is "partial correlations." What does this mean? To simplify let us consider the case in which we have a single instrumental variable, **mothereduc**. Examine part of the output of **estat firststage** following **ivregress**.

```
        ivregress 2sls lwage (educ=mothereduc) exper exper2, small
        estat firststage
```

```
. estat firststage
```

```
   First-stage regression summary statistics
```

Variable	R-sq.	Adjusted R-sq.	Partial R-sq.	F(1,424)	Prob > F
educ	0.1527	0.1467	0.1485	73.9459	0.0000

The partial correlation of interest is the correlation between the endogenous variable **educ** and the instrumental variable **mothereduc** after removing the effects of the other exogenous variables, **exper** and **exper2**. Instrument strength can be measured by the partial correlation between the endogenous variable and a single instrument. The effects of **exper** and **exper2** are removed by regressing **educ** and **mothereduc** on these variables and computing the least squares residuals. The residuals contain what is left after removing the effects of **exper** and **exper2**.

```
reg educ exper exper2
predict v1, r

reg mothereduc exper exper2
predict v2, r
```

The option "r" in the predict statements is short for **residuals**. The correlation between these residuals is

```
correlate v1 v2
```

```
. correlate v1 v2
(obs=428)
```

	v1	v2
v1	1.0000	
v2	0.3854	1.0000

The square of this correlation is obtained by first using **return list** to see what has been saved after **correlate**.

```
return list
```

```
. return list

scalars:
                r(N) =   428
              r(rho) =   .3853595047039399
```

The square of the correlation is then displayed with

```
di "partial correlation = "r(rho)^2
```

```
. di "partial correlation = "r(rho)^2
partial correlation = .14850195
```

In the output of **estat firststage** this is called the **Partial R-sq**. Why is it called a called an R-squared? Regress **v1** on **v2**, with no constant since the average value of the residuals **v1** is zero.

```
reg v1 v2, noconstant
```

```
. reg v1 v2, noconstant
```

Source	SS	df	MS
Model	329.557956	1	329.557956
Residual	1889.65843	427	4.42542958
Total	2219.21639	428	5.18508502

```
Number of obs =     428
F(  1,    427) =   74.47
Prob > F      =  0.0000
R-squared     =  0.1485
Adj R-squared =  0.1465
Root MSE      =  2.1037
```

v1	Coef.	Std. Err.	t	P>|t|	[95% Conf. Interval]
v2	.2676908	.0310202	8.63	0.000	.2067194 .3286622

Note that the **R-squared** from this regression, which does not include a constant, is 0.1485.

The relation between correlations and covariance helps us understand the regression coefficient above. The sample covariance between **v1** and **v2** is obtained using

```
correlate v1 v2, covariance
return list
```

```
. correlate v1 v2, covariance
(obs=428)
```

	v1	v2
v1	5.19723	
v2	2.88317	10.7705

```
. return list

scalars:
             r(N) =  428
        r(cov_12) =  2.883171450907586
         r(Var_2) =  10.77052844798386
         r(Var_1) =  5.197228071400259
```

From these values we can compute the regression coefficient and the correlation.

```
di "partial LS coefficient = " r(cov_12)/r(Var_2)
di "partial correlation = " r(cov_12)/sqrt(r(Var_2)*r(Var_1))
```

```
. di "partial LS coefficient = " r(cov_12)/r(Var_2)
partial LS coefficient = .26769081
```

```
. di "partial correlation = " r(cov_12)/sqrt(r(Var_2)*r(Var_1))
partial correlation = .3853595
```

10.4 THE HAUSMAN TEST FOR ENDOGENEITY

We do not always know whether there might be an endogenous regressor among our explanatory variables. The Hausman procedure is a way to empirically test whether an explanatory variable is endogenous or not.

In the regression $y = \beta_1 + \beta_2 x + e$ we wish to know whether x is correlated with e. Let z_1 and z_2 be instrumental variables for x. At a minimum one instrument is required for each variable that might be correlated with the error term. Then carry out the following steps:

1. Estimate the model $x = \gamma_1 + \theta_1 z_1 + \theta_2 z_2 + v$ by ordinary (i.e., not *2SLS*) least squares, and obtain the residuals $\hat{v} = x - \hat{\gamma}_1 - \hat{\theta}_1 z_1 - \hat{\theta}_2 z_2$. If there is more than one explanatory variable that are being tested for endogeneity, repeat this estimation for each one, using all available instrumental variables in each regression.
2. Include the residuals computed in step 1 as an explanatory variable in the original regression, $y = \beta_1 + \beta_2 x + \delta\hat{v} + e$. Estimate this "artificial regression" by least squares, and employ the usual *t*-test for the hypothesis of significance

$$H_0 : \delta = 0 \,(\text{no correlation between } x \text{ and } e)$$
$$H_1 : \delta \neq 0 \,(\text{correlation between } x \text{ and } e)$$

To test whether **educ** is endogenous, and correlated with the regression error term, we use the regression based Hausman test described above. To implement the test estimate the first stage equation for **educ** using least squares, including all exogenous variables, including the instrumental variables **mothereduc** and **fathereduc**, on the right-hand side. Save the residuals

```
reg educ exper exper2 mothereduc fathereduc
predict vhat, residuals
```

Add the computed residuals to the ln(wage) equation as an additional explanatory variable, and test its significance using a standard *t*-test.

```
reg lwage educ exper exper2 vhat
```

. reg lwage exper exper2 educ vhat

Source	SS	df	MS
Model	36.2573098	4	9.06432745
Residual	187.070132	423	.442246175
Total	223.327442	427	.523015086

```
Number of obs =     428
F( 4,   423) =   20.50
Prob > F      =  0.0000
R-squared     =  0.1624
Adj R-squared =  0.1544
Root MSE      =  .66502
```

lwage	Coef.	Std. Err.	t	P>|t|	[95% Conf. Interval]	
exper	.0441704	.0132394	3.34	0.001	.0181471	.0701937
exper2	-.000899	.0003959	-2.27	0.024	-.0016772	-.0001208
educ	.0613966	.0309849	1.98	0.048	.000493	.1223003
vhat	.0581666	.0348073	1.67	0.095	-.0102502	.1265834
_cons	.0481003	.3945753	0.12	0.903	-.7274721	.8236727

If heteroskedasticity is suspected, then compute robust standard errors by adding the **vce(robust)** option.

> reg lwage educ exper exper2 vhat, vce(robust)

. reg lwage exper exper2 educ vhat, vce(robust)

Linear regression

```
Number of obs =     428
F( 4,   423) =   21.52
Prob > F      =  0.0000
R-squared     =  0.1624
Root MSE      =  .66502
```

lwage	Coef.	Robust Std. Err.	t	P>|t|	[95% Conf. Interval]	
exper	.0441704	.0151219	2.92	0.004	.0144469	.0738939
exper2	-.000899	.0004152	-2.16	0.031	-.0017152	-.0000828
educ	.0613966	.0326667	1.88	0.061	-.0028127	.125606
vhat	.0581666	.0364135	1.60	0.111	-.0134073	.1297405
_cons	.0481003	.4221019	0.11	0.909	-.7815781	.8777787

These tests indicate that **educ** is endogenous at about the 10% level of significance.

We prefer the regression based test in most circumstances. To implement Stata's "automatic" Hausman test, we contrast the previously saved instrumental variables (**iv**) and least squares (**ls**) estimates. Using **help hausman** we find the syntax.

```
help hausman                                              dialog:  hausman


Title

    [R] hausman —— Hausman specification test


Syntax

        hausman name-consistent [name-efficient] [, options]
```

To use the dialog-box approach, enter **db hausman**, or follow the path **Statistics > Postestimation > Tests > Hausman specification test**.

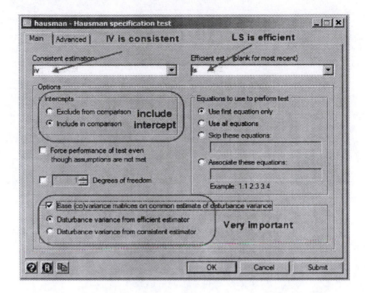

The automatic test is a **contrast test** between the least squares estimator, which is best linear unbiased and efficient if the assumptions listed in Section 10.1 of *POE4*. If a regressor is endogenous, then the least squares estimator is inconsistent, but the instrumental variables estimator is consistent. This contrast test is not valid under heteroskedasticity, because the test is predicated upon the least squares estimator being efficient. If heteroskedasticity is present least squares is not efficient because the Gauss-Markov theorem does not hold. This is one advantage of the regression based test, which can be applied with heteroskedastic data. In the **Consistent estimation** drop-down list select "**iv**" and in the **Efficient estimation** list select "**ls**".

The other choices we show are so that this contrast test will work as well as possible. Include the intercept in the comparison and, <u>most importantly</u>, base the estimator variances on a common estimate of the error variance, the estimate of σ^2 based on the least squares estimates and residuals. This estimator is valid if the null hypothesis of "no endogeneity" is true.

In the Stata **Result** window there are lots of words you do not understand, and which are beyond the scope of this book. The key result from your point of view is that the Hausman test is a chi-square statistic with 1 degree of freedom. The chi-square value is given, along with its *p*-value. Based on this version of the test we also conclude that **educ** is correlated with the regression error at the 10% level of significance.

```
chi2(1) = (b-B)'[(V_b-V_B)^(-1)](b-B)
        =          2.78
Prob>chi2 =      0.0954
```

The implied Stata command is

```
hausman iv ls, constant sigmamore
```

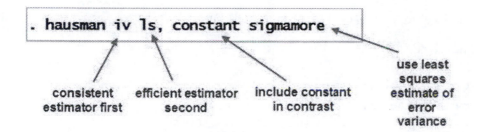

The option **constant** is added so that the contrast will include the intercept term. The option **sigmamore** is included to force Stata to use the least squares residuals in the estimation of the error variance for both estimators. This ensures that Stata will calculate the correct number of degrees of freedom for the Hausman test, which is the number of endogenous variables on the right-hand side of the regression.

10.5 TESTING THE VALIDITY OF SURPLUS INSTRUMENTS

An *LM* test for the validity of the surplus, or overidentifying, instruments is computed as NR^2 from an artificial regression with the *IV/2SLS* residuals as the dependent variable and all instrumental and exogenous variables as explanatory variables. For that purpose compute the *IV/2SLS* residuals from this estimation.

```
quietly ivregress 2sls lwage (educ=mothereduc fathereduc) exper exper2,
        small
predict ehat, residuals
```

Because we have already seen it, we can suppress the estimation output by adding the Stata command **quietly** before **ivregress**. Now regress **ehat** on all exogenous variables and instrumental variables.

```
reg ehat exper exper2 mothereduc fathereduc
```

Use **ereturn list** to recall what elements are saved from the regression. Then compute NR^2

```
ereturn list
scalar nr2 = e(N)*e(r2)
```

Also compute the chi-square(1) 95th percentile using **invchi2tail**, which will be the 0.05 critical value for the test of the validity of the surplus instruments. Surplus instruments are also called "overidentifying restrictions" in the literature. The number of degrees of freedom here is 1 because there is one surplus instrument.

```
scalar chic = invchi2tail(1,.05)
```

Compute the *p*-value of the test using **chi2tail**.

```
scalar pvalue = chi2tail(1,nr2)
```

Then display the results using

```
di "R^2 from artificial regression = " e(r2)
di "NR^2 test of overidentifying restriction  = " nr2
di "Chi-square critical value 1 df, .05 level = " chic
di "p value for overidentifying test 1 df, .05 level = " pvalue
```

```
. di "R^2 from artificial regression = " e(r2)
R^2 from artificial regression = .00088334

. di "NR^2 test of overidentifying restriction  = " nr2
NR^2 test of overidentifying restriction  = .37807151

. di "Chi-square critical value 1 df, .05 level = " chic
Chi-square critical value 1 df, .05 level = 3.8414588

. di "p value for overidentifying test 1 df, .05 level = " pvalue
p value for overidentifying test 1 df, .05 level = .53863714
```

Using Stata we can produce this same *LM* test. Obtain the *IV/2SLS* estimates, again using **quietly** because we have already inspected these results, followed by **estat overid**.

```
quietly ivregress 2sls lwage (educ=mothereduc fathereduc) exper
        exper2, small
estat overid
```

The resulting Sargan (score) test is the *LM* test, NR^2, from above.

```
. quietly ivregress 2sls lwage (educ=mothereduc fathereduc) exper exper2, small

. estat overid

Tests of overidentifying restrictions:

Sargan (score) chi2(1) =   .378071  (p = 0.5386)
Basmann chi2(1)        =   .373985  (p = 0.5408)
```

Remark: *Principles of Econometrics, 4th Edition*, Appendix 10F includes fully worked examples using a simulated data set. We will not discuss those examples, although complete code is provided in the do-file for this chapter, which is listed at the end of this chapter.

10.6 TESTING FOR WEAK INSTRUMENTS

The *F*-test for weak instruments is not adequate for models with more than one endogenous variable on the right side of the equation. For example, suppose there we have two endogenous variables and two instrumental variables. For instrumental variables estimation we required two external instrumental variables. Using the first stage *F*-test approach, we would estimate two first stage equations and test the joint significance of the two instrumental variables. The first stage F-tests has as the alternative hypothesis that <u>at least</u> one of the instruments is a relevant, strong instrument. Suppose however that of our two instruments only one is actually related to the endogenous variables. So in truth we have one instrument. The F-test will reject the joint null hypothesis, leading us to believe we have two instruments, when we do not.

Using **canonical correlations** there is a solution to the problem of identifying weak instruments when an equation has more than one endogenous variable. Canonical correlations are a generalization of the usual concept of a correlation between two variables and attempt to describe the association between two **sets** of variables. A detailed discussion of canonical correlations is beyond the scope of this work. Consult a book on multivariate analysis, but explanations will involve matrix algebra. Let N denote the sample size, B the number of right-hand side endogenous variables, G the number of exogenous variables included in the equation (including the intercept), L the number of "external" instruments that are not included in the model. If we have two variables in the first set of variables and two variables in the second set then there are two canonical correlations, r_1 and r_2. If we have B variables in the first group (the endogenous variables with the effects of the exogenous variables $x_1 \equiv 1, x_2, \ldots, x_G$ removed) and $L \geq B$ variables in the second group (the group of instruments with the effects of $x_1 \equiv 1, x_2, \ldots, x_G$ removed), then there are B possible canonical correlations, $r_1 \geq r_2 \geq \cdots \geq r_B$, with r_B being the minimum canonical correlation. A test for weak identification, the situation that arises when the instruments are correlated with the endogenous regressors but only weakly, is based on the **Cragg-Donald F-test statistic**

$$\text{Cragg} - \text{Donald } F = \left[(N - G - B)/L \right] \times \left[r_B^2 / (1 - r_B^2) \right]$$

The Cragg-Donald statistic reduces to the usual weak instruments F-test when the number of endogenous variables is $B = 1$. Critical values for this test statistic have been tabulated by James Stock and Motohiro Yogo (2005)[1], so that we can test the null hypothesis that the instruments are weak, against the alternative that they are not, for two particular consequences of weak instruments.

> **Relative Bias:** In the presence of weak instruments the amount of bias in the IV estimator can become large. Stock and Yogo consider the bias when estimating the coefficients of the endogenous variables. They examine the maximum IV estimator bias relative to the bias of the least squares estimator. Stock and Yogo give the illustration of estimating the return to education. If a researcher believes that the least squares estimator suffers a maximum bias of 10%, and if the relative bias is 0.1, then the maximum bias of the IV estimator is 1%.

> **Rejection Rate (Test Si ze):** When estimating a model with endogenous regressors, testing hypotheses about the coefficients of the endogenous variables is frequently of interest. If we choose the $\alpha = 0.05$ level of significance we expect that a true null hypothesis is rejected 5% of the time in repeated samples. If instruments are weak, then the actual rejection rate of the null hypothesis, also known as the **test size**, may be larger. Stock and Yogo's second criterion is the maximum rejection rate of a true null hypothesis if we choose $\alpha = 0.05$. For example, we may be willing to accept a maximum rejection

---

[1] "Testing for Weak Instruments in Linear IV Regression," in *Identification and Inference for Econometric Models Essays in Honor of Thomas Rothenberg*, eds, Donald W. K. Andrews and James H. Stock, *Cambridge University Press*, Chapter 5.

rate of 10% for a test at the 5% level, but we may not be willing to accept a rejection rate of 20% for a 5% level test.

To test the null hypothesis that instruments are weak, against the alternative that they are not, we compare the Cragg-Donald F-test statistic to a critical value. The values given in Tables 10E.1 and Table 10E.2 in *POE4* are built into Stata. When `estat firststage` is used after `ivregress` these critical values are reported, as shown in Section 10.3 of this chapter. The steps are

1. **First** choose either the maximum relative bias or maximum test size criterion. You must also choose the maximum relative bias or maximum test size you are willing to accept.
2. Reject the null hypothesis that the instruments are weak if the Cragg-Donald F-test statistic is larger than the tabled critical value. If the F-test statistic is not larger than the critical value, then do not reject the null hypothesis that the instruments are weak.

Using Mroz's data consider the following *HOURS* supply equation specification

$$HOURS = \beta_1 + \beta_2 MTR + \beta_3 EDUC + \beta_4 KIDSL6 + \beta_5 NWIFEINC + e$$

The variable $NWIFEINC = (FAMINC - WAGE \times HOURS)/1000$ is household income attributable to sources other than the wife's income. The variable *MTR* is the marginal tax rate facing the wife, including social security taxes. In this equation we expect the signs of coefficients on *MTR*, *KIDSL6* and *NWIFEINC* to be negative and the coefficient on *EDUC* is of uncertain sign.

Treat both marginal tax rate *MTR* and education *EDUC* as endogenous, so that $B = 2$. Use mother's and father's education, *MOTHEREDUC* and *FATHEREDUC*, as instruments, so that $L = 2$. To begin, open the data and create the required variables.

```
use mroz, clear
drop if lfp==0
gen lwage=ln(wage)
gen nwifeinc = (faminc-wage*hours)/1000
gen exper2 = exper^2
```

The first stage equations and tests for *MTR* and *EDUC* are obtained using

```
reg mtr mothereduc fathereduc kidsl6 nwifeinc
test mothereduc fathereduc
```

```
. test mothereduc fathereduc

 ( 1)  mothereduc = 0
 ( 2)  fathereduc = 0

       F(  2,   423) =      8.14
            Prob > F =    0.0003
```

```
reg educ mothereduc fathereduc kidsl6 nwifeinc
test mothereduc fathereduc
```

```
. test mothereduc fathereduc

 ( 1)   mothereduc = 0
 ( 2)   fathereduc = 0

       F(  2,    423) =    49.02
              Prob > F =    0.0000
```

The test results show that the instruments are strong for *EDUC* as we have earlier seen, with the first stage weak instrument F-test statistic 49.02. For *MTR* these two instruments are less strong. *FATHEREDUC* is significant at the 5% level, and the first stage weak instrument F-test statistic is 8.14, which has a p-value of 0.0003. While this does not satisfy the $F > 10$ rule of thumb, it is "close," and we may have concluded that these two instruments were adequately strong.

The instrumental variables estimates and first stage statistics are obtained using

```
ivregress 2sls hours (mtr educ =  mothereduc fathereduc) kids16
         nwifeinc, small
     estat firststage
```

The instrumental variables estimates are

```
. ivregress 2sls hours (mtr educ =  mothereduc fathereduc) kids16 nwifeinc, smal
> l


Instrumental variables (2SLS) regression
```

Source	SS	df	MS		Number of obs =	428
					F(4, 423) =	0.79
Model	-1.0343e+09	4	-258577372		Prob > F =	0.5329
Residual	1.2916e+09	423	3053476.37		R-squared =	.
					Adj R-squared =	.
Total	257311020	427	602601.92		Root MSE =	1747.4

hours	Coef.	Std. Err.	t	P>|t|	[95% Conf. Interval]	
mtr	29709.47	90487.78	0.33	0.743	-148152.2	207571.2
educ	258.559	846.0142	0.31	0.760	-1404.356	1921.474
kids16	-1144.478	2510.194	-0.46	0.649	-6078.485	3789.529
nwifeinc	149.2325	470.5173	0.32	0.751	-775.6108	1074.076
_cons	-24491.6	79689.72	-0.31	0.759	-181128.8	132145.6

```
Instrumented:  mtr educ
Instruments:   kids16 nwifeinc mothereduc fathereduc
```

The first stage results are

```
. estat firststage
```

Shea's partial R-squared

Variable	Shea's Partial R-sq.	Shea's Adj. Partial R-sq.
mtr	0.0005	-0.0066
educ	0.0024	-0.0046

Minimum eigenvalue statistic = .100568

Critical Values Ho: Instruments are weak	# of endogenous regressors: 2 # of excluded instruments: 2			
	5%	10%	20%	30%
2SLS relative bias		(not available)		
	10%	15%	20%	25%
2SLS Size of nominal 5% Wald test	7.03	4.58	3.95	3.63
LIML Size of nominal 5% Wald test	7.03	4.58	3.95	3.63

Suppose that we are willing to accept a maximum test size of 15% for a 5% test. Stata shows the critical value for the weak instrument test when using *2SLS* is 4.58. Ignore the critical values for *LIML*. These values will be explained in Chapter 11. See also Table 10E.1 in *POE4*. The Cragg-Donald *F*-test statistic value is only 0.101, which is far below the critical value 4.58 for 15% maximum test size (for a 5% test on *MTR* and *EDUC*). We cannot reject the null hypothesis that the instruments are **weak**, despite the favorable first stage *F*-test values. The estimates of the *HOURS* supply equation shows parameter estimates that are wildly different from those in Model (1) and Model (2), given in Table 10E.4, *POE4*, page 439, and the very small *t*-statistic values imply very large standard errors, another consequence for instrumental variables estimation in the presence of weak instruments. Other models are illustrated in the Chapter 10 do-file at the end of this chapter.

10.7 CALCULATING THE CRAGG-DONALD F-STATISTIC

To illustrate the calculation of the Cragg-Donald *F*-statistic use the model illustrated in Section 10.6 above, with **mothereduc** and **fathereduc** as instruments. Save the degrees of freedom, $N-G-B$ using **ereturn list** to show which results are saved post-estimation.

```
ivregress 2sls hours (mtr educ =  mothereduc fathereduc) kids16
     nwifeinc, small
ereturn list
scalar df_r = e(df_r)
```

Partial out the effects of **kids16** and **nwifeinc** from the endogenous variables and from the instruments, using the procedure outlined in Section 10.3.1 above.

```
reg mtr kids16 nwifeinc
```

```
predict mtrr, r
reg educ kids16 nwifeinc
predict educr, r

reg mothereduc kids16 nwifeinc
predict mothereducr, r

reg fathereduc kids16 nwifeinc
predict fathereducr, r
```

Canonical correlations are computed by Stata using the command **canon**. See **help canon**.

```
help canon                                    dialog:  canon
                                              also see:  canon postestimation

Title

    [MV] canon — Canonical correlations

Syntax

         canon (varlist1) (varlist2) [if] [in] [weight] [, options]
```

To use the dialog box, click on the link above or follow

> **Statistics > Multivariate analysis > MANOVA, multivariate regression, and
> related > Canonical correlations**

The command to find the canonical correlations from the two endogenous variables and two instruments, from which we have removed the effects of the other exogenous variables, is

```
canon (mtrr educr) (mothereducr fathereducr)
```

While there is other output the canonical correlations are shown to be

```
Canonical correlations:
  0.4356   0.0218
```

The saved results and minimum canonical correlation are extracted using

```
ereturn list
matrix r2=e(ccorr)
di "Calculation of Cragg-Donald statistic "
di "The canonical correlations "
matrix list r2
scalar mincc = r2[1,2]
di "The minimum canonical correlation = " mincc
```

```
. di "The minimum canonical correlation = " mincc
The minimum canonical correlation = .02180077
```

The calculation of the Cragg-Donald F-statistic is then straightforward and identical to the automatic calculation using **estat firststage** following **ivregress**. The "2" in denominator is the number of instrumental variables, L.

```
        scalar cd = df_r*(mincc^2)/(2*(1-mincc^2))
        di "The Cragg-Donald F-statistic = " cd

. di "The Cragg-Donald F-statistic = " cd
The Cragg-Donald F-statistic = .10056813
```

10.8 A SIMULATION EXPERIMENT

In *Principles of Econometrics, 4th Edition*, Appendix 10F.2, a simulation experiment is performed to illustrate the sampling properties of the *IV/2SLS* estimator. In the simulation we use the data generation process $y = x + e$, so that the intercept parameter is 0 and the slope parameter is 1. The first stage regression is $x = \pi z_1 + \pi z_2 + \pi z_3 + v$. Note that we have $L = 3$ instruments, each of which has an independent standard normal $N(0,1)$ distribution. The parameter π controls the instrument strength. If $\pi = 0$ the instruments are not correlated with x and instrumental variables estimation will fail. The larger π becomes the stronger the instruments become. Finally, we create the random errors e and v to have standard normal distributions with correlation ρ, which controls the endogeneity of x. If $\rho = 0$, then x is not endogenous. The larger ρ becomes the stronger the endogeneity. We create 10,000 samples of size $N = 100$ and then try out least squares (*LS*) and *IV/2SLS* under several scenarios. We let $\pi = 0.1$ (weak instruments) and $\pi = 0.5$ (strong instruments). We let $\rho = 0$ (x exogenous) and $\rho = 0.8$ (x highly endogenous).

The simulation begins by clearing all memory, and specifying global constants that control the simulation.

```
        clear all
        global numobs 100    // number of simulated sample observations
        global pi      0.1    // first stage parameter controls IV strength
        global rho     0.8    // rho controls endogeneity
        set seed 1234567      // random number seed
        set obs $numobs
```

The **seed** set above will ensure that when we repeat the code we will obtain the same sequences of pseudo-random numbers and thus the same results. For an explanation of pseudo-random numbers and seed values, see *POE4*, Appendix B. A key component in the simulation experiment is the correlation between the error terms e and v. Creating correlated random numbers is achieved using the Stata command **drawnorm**. From **help drawnorm** we find the basic syntax and options.

```
help drawnorm                                              dialog:   drawnorm

Title

    [D] drawnorm — Draw sample from multivariate normal distribution

Syntax

        drawnorm newvarlist [, options]
```

Among the options are

```
n(#)                      # of observations to be generated
cov(matrix|vector)        covariance matrix
```

That is, we can specify the number of observations, and covariances and variances to be anything we choose. We will use a covariance matrix that is

$$\Sigma = \begin{bmatrix} \text{var}(e) & \text{cov}(e,v) \\ \text{cov}(e,v) & \text{var}(v) \end{bmatrix} = \begin{bmatrix} 1 & \rho \\ \rho & 1 \end{bmatrix}$$

Specify this matrix using

```
matrix sig = (1, $rho \ $rho, 1)          // corr(e,v)
drawnorm e v, n($numobs) corr(sig)        // e & v values
```

For the instruments we use 3 independent normal random variables.

```
gen z1 = rnormal()
gen z2 = rnormal()
gen z3 = rnormal()
```

Using the data generation process noted above, we create x and y. The error terms are correlated with correlation $rho.

```
generate x = $pi*z1 + $pi*z2 + $pi*z3 + v
generate y = x + e
correlate x e
```

The 100 random values we have drawn have sample correlation

```
. correlate x e
(obs=100)
```

	x	e
x	1.0000	
e	0.7960	1.0000

The first stage regression using the simulated data shows that the instruments are weak, since we have set $pi = 0.1

```
reg x z1 z2 z3
```

. reg x z1 z2 z3

Source	SS	df	MS
Model	1.69113235	3	.563710782
Residual	115.728748	96	1.20550779
Total	117.419881	99	1.1860594

Number of obs = 100
F(3, 96) = 0.47
Prob > F = 0.7056
R-squared = 0.0144
Adj R-squared = -0.0164
Root MSE = 1.098

x	Coef.	Std. Err.	t	P>|t|	[95% Conf. Interval]	
z1	.1141584	.098892	1.15	0.251	-.0821408	.3104575
z2	.03231	.1214898	0.27	0.791	-.2088453	.2734652
z3	.0217676	.1132988	0.19	0.848	-.2031288	.2466641
_cons	.0174734	.1106386	0.16	0.875	-.2021425	.2370893

The following least squares estimate of the slope is far from the true value because the x variable we generated is strongly endogenous.

```
reg y x
```

. reg y x

Source	SS	df	MS
Model	369.721081	1	369.721081
Residual	40.7364595	98	.415678159
Total	410.45754	99	4.14603576

Number of obs = 100
F(1, 98) = 889.44
Prob > F = 0.0000
R-squared = 0.9008
Adj R-squared = 0.8997
Root MSE = .64473

y	Coef.	Std. Err.	t	P>|t|	[95% Conf. Interval]	
x	1.77446	.0594987	29.82	0.000	1.656387	1.892534
_cons	.1243801	.0644743	1.93	0.057	-.003567	.2523272

Since we have weak instruments, we see that the *IV/2SLS* estimate of the slope is not especially close to the true value either.

```
ivregress 2sls y (x=z1 z2 z3), small
```

```
. ivregress 2sls y (x=z1 z2 z3), small
```

Instrumental variables (2SLS) regression

Source	SS	df	MS
Model	353.009983	1	353.009983
Residual	57.4475569	98	.586199561
Total	410.45754	99	4.14603576

```
Number of obs =      100
F(  1,    98) =     5.63
Prob > F      =   0.0196
R-squared     =   0.8600
Adj R-squared =   0.8586
Root MSE      =  .76564
```

y	Coef.	Std. Err.	t	P>|t|	[95% Conf. Interval]
x	1.397208	.5887541	2.37	0.020	.2288449 2.565572
_cons	.1268431	.0766601	1.65	0.101	-.0252863 .2789726

```
Instrumented:  x
Instruments:   z1 z2 z3
```

We use a program to serve as the basis for the simulation. In the first portion of the program we have the same data generation process, controlled by global macros.

```
program ch10sim, rclass
    version 11.1
    drop _all

    set obs $numobs
    matrix sig = (1, $rho \ $rho, 1)
    drawnorm e v, n($numobs) corr(sig)
      gen z1 = rnormal()
      gen z2 = rnormal()
      gen z3 = rnormal()

    * DGP
    generate x = $pi*z1 + $pi*z2 + $pi*z3 + v
    generate y = x + e                     // structural equation

    * first stage regression using all IV
    reg x z1 z2 z3
```

During the execution of this program the values are "returned" from the post-estimation results

```
    return scalar rsq = e(r2)      // first stage r^2
    return scalar F=e(F)           // first stage F
    predict vhat, r
```

The least squares slope estimate (**bols**) and t-value (**tols**) for a 5% test of the true null hypothesis that the slope is 1, are returned, as is the outcome (**rols**) of the test. The value of **rols** is 1 if the null hypothesis is rejected, and **rols** is 0 otherwise. Under the assumptions of the linear regression model in Chapter 10.1 of *POE4* the test should reject the true null hypothesis 5% of the time.

```
* OLS
reg y x
return scalar bols =_b[x]
return scalar seols = _se[x]
return scalar tols = (_b[x]-1)/_se[x]
return scalar rols = abs(return(tols))>invttail($numobs-2,.025)
```

The regression-based Hausman test statistic is **haust**. The outcome of the 5% test is **haus**, which takes the value 1 if the null hypothesis of no endogeneity is rejected.

```
* Hausman
reg y x vhat
return scalar haust = _b[vhat]/_se[vhat]
return scalar haus = abs(return(haust))>invttail($numobs-3,.025)
```

The *IV/2SLS* slope estimate (**b2sls**), the t-value for the test of the true null hypothesis that the slope is 1, and the test outcome (**r2sls**) are returned. The test outcome **r2sls** is 1 if the null hypothesis is rejected and is zero otherwise. The test should reject the true null hypothesis 5% of the time if the instruments are relevant and valid.

```
* 2sls
ivregress 2sls y (x=z1 z2 z3), small
return scalar b2sls =_b[x]
return scalar se2sls = _se[x]
return scalar t2sls = (_b[x]-1)/_se[x]
return scalar r2sls = abs(return(t2sls))>invttail($numobs-2,.025)
```

```
end
```

The program concludes with **end**. The simulation is actually carried out using Stata's **simulate** command.

```
simulate rsqf = r(rsq) Fr=r(F) bolsr=r(bols) seolsr=r(seols) ///
    rolsr=r(rols) b2slsr=r(b2sls) se2slsr=r(se2sls) ///
    t2slsr=r(t2sls) r2slsr=r(r2sls) hausr=r(haus),  ///
    reps(10000) nodots nolegend seed(1234567): ch10sim
```

The variable names assigned to the returned values are **rsqf**, **Fr**, **bolsr**, etc. There are 10,000 experimental replications of the program **ch10sim**. After the simulation we display the global parameter values, for record keeping purposes.

```
di " Simulation parameters"
di " rho   " $rho
di " N     " $numobs
di " pi    " $pi
```

```
. di " Simulation parameters"
 Simulation parameters

. di " rho = " $rho
 rho = .8

. di " N = " $numobs
 N = 100

. di " pi = " $pi
 pi = .1
```

We are interested in the average first-stage F-value, which is an indicator of instrument strength.

```
di " average first stage F"
mean Fr
```

```
Mean estimation                         Number of obs    =    10000
```

	Mean	Std. Err.	[95% Conf. Interval]	
rsqf	.0576316	.000391	.0568652	.0583981

For each estimator we compute its average value and standard deviation using the Stata command **tabstat**. This is a convenient alternative to **summarize** as is permits specification of the statistics to report in a nice table. For a dialog box follow

> **Statistics > Summaries, tables, and tests > Tables > Table of summary statistics (tabstat)**

The syntax and important options are given by **help tabstat**.

```
help tabstat                                          dialog: tabstat

Title

    [R] tabstat — Display table of summary statistics

Syntax

        tabstat varlist [if] [in] [weight] [, options]

    options                        description

    Main
      by(varname)                  group statistics by variable
      statistics(statname [...])   report specified statistics
```

The average estimate value should be close to the true value, 1, if the estimator is unbiased. The average of the rejection rate variable (**rols**) indicates the actual rejection rate of the true null hypothesis. The average of **mseols** is the "mean squared error" of estimation. This is the empirical analog of

$$MSE = E\left[\left(b_2 - \beta_2 \right)^2 \right] = \operatorname{var}\left(b_2 \right) + \left[\operatorname{bias}\left(b_2 \right) \right]^2$$

Mean squared error answers the question of how close, on average, are the estimates to the true parameter value. Finally we examine the average rejection rate of the Hausman test.

```
di " OLS"
gen mseols = (bolsr-1)^2
tabstat bolsr seolsr rolsr mseols hausr, stat(mean sd)
```

. tabstat bolsr seolsr rolsr mseols hausr, stat(mean sd)

stats	bolsr	seolsr	rolsr	mseols	hausr
mean	1.776194	.0612667	1	.6061978	.3841
sd	.0609983	.0061937	0	.0947578	.4864061

The average value of the least squares estimates is 1.776 which is not close to the true value of 1. The t-test of the true null hypothesis rejects 100% of the time instead of the nominal 5% rate. The Hausman regression based test rejects the (false) null hypothesis of no endogeneity 38% of the time.

```
di " 2sls"
gen mse2sls = (b2slsr-1)^2
tabstat b2slsr se2slsr r2slsr mse2sls, stat(mean sd)
```

Similar values for the *IV/2SLS* estimator are

. tabstat b2slsr se2slsr r2slsr mse2sls, stat(mean sd)

stats	b2slsr	se2slsr	r2slsr	mse2sls
mean	1.331058	.8850129	.2886	1.008766
sd	.9482915	35.54677	.4531342	58.61448

If we increase the instrument strength by setting $pi to 0.5, for the least squares estimates we find not any improvement.

. tabstat bolsr seolsr rolsr mseols hausr, stat(mean sd)

stats	bolsr	seolsr	rolsr	mseols	hausr
mean	1.456824	.0608191	1	.2124129	1
sd	.0610322	.0061183	0	.0560244	0

However for the *IV/2SLS* estimator we find a great deal of improvement, thanks to the stronger instrumental variables.

. tabstat b2slsr se2slsr r2slsr mse2sls, stat(mean sd)

stats	b2slsr	se2slsr	r2slsr	mse2sls
mean	1.011116	.11695	.0636	.0139068
sd	.1174081	.0274133	.2440512	.0227001

KEY TERMS

2SLS

canon

canonical correlations

chi2tail(n,x)

correlate

Cragg-Donald F-test

drawnorm

drop

endogenous covariates

ereturn list

estat firststage

estat overid

estimates store

first stage regression

F-test

global

Hausman test

Hausman test, regression based

heteroskedasticity robust

instrumental variables estimation

invchi2tail(n,p)

ivregress

LM test

matrix

mean squared error

minimum eigenvalue statistic

MSE

option, sigmamore

option, small

overidentifying instruments

partial correlation

quietly

random regressors

rejection rate criterion

relative bias criterion

return list

rnormal()

robust standard errors

Sargan statistic

seed

Stock-Yogo critical values

strong instruments

surplus instruments

tabstat

two-stage least squares

valid instruments

vce(robust)

Wald chi-square test

weak instruments

CHAPTER 10 DO-FILE [CHAP10.DO]

```
* file chap10.do for Using Stata for Principles of Econometrics, 4e

cd c:\data\poe4stata

* Stata do-file
* copyright C 2011 by Lee C. Adkins and R. Carter Hill
* used for "Using Stata for Principles of Econometrics, 4e"
* by Lee C. Adkins and R. Carter Hill (2011)
* John Wiley and Sons, Inc.

* setup
version 11.1
capture log close
set more off

************* POE4 Chapter 10.2.4: A Wage Equation
* open log
log using chap10_wage, replace text

* open data and examine
use mroz, clear
describe
summarize

* drop nonworking women and summarize
drop if lfp==0
summarize wage educ exper

* create variables
gen lwage = ln(wage)
gen exper2 = exper^2
```

```
* Least squares estimation
reg lwage educ exper exper2
estimates store ls

********** POE4 Chapter 10.3.6: IV estimation of wage equation
* using only mothereduc as IV

* first stage regression
reg educ exper exper2 mothereduc

* test IV strength
test mothereduc

* obtain predicted values
predict educhat

* 2sls using 2-stages
reg lwage educhat exper exper2

* IV estimation using automatic command
ivregress 2sls lwage (educ=mothereduc) exper exper2
ivregress 2sls lwage (educ=mothereduc) exper exper2, small
ivregress 2sls lwage (educ=mothereduc) exper exper2, vce(robust) small

********** Add fathereduc as an IV
* Test fathereduc alone
reg educ exper exper2 fathereduc

* joint first stage regression F-test for weak instruments
reg educ exper exper2 mothereduc fathereduc
test mothereduc fathereduc

reg educ exper exper2 mothereduc fathereduc, vce(robust)
test mothereduc fathereduc

* IV estimation with surplus instruments
ivregress 2sls lwage (educ=mothereduc fathereduc) exper exper2, small
estimates store iv

* Testing for weak instruments using estat
estat firststage

* IV estimation with robust standard errors

ivregress 2sls lwage (educ=mothereduc fathereduc) exper exper2, vce(robust) small
estat firststage

********** Chapter 10.3.7: Illustrate partial correlation
ivregress 2sls lwage (educ=mothereduc) exper exper2, small
estat firststage

* partial out exper and exper^2
reg educ exper exper2
predict v1, r

reg mothereduc exper exper2
predict v2, r

* partial correlation
correlate v1 v2
return list
di "partial correlation = "r(rho)^2
```

```
* effect of mothereduc on educ controlling for exper and exper^2
reg v1 v2, noconstant

* partial correlation
correlate v1 v2, covariance
return list

* calculate partial least squares regression coefficient
di "partial LS coefficient = " r(cov_12)/r(var_2)

* calculate partial correlation
di "partial correlation = " r(cov_12)/sqrt(r(var_2)*r(var_1))

********** Chapter 10.4.3: Hausman test

* reduced form
reg educ exper exper2 mothereduc fathereduc
predict vhat, residuals

* augment wage equation with reduced form residuals
reg lwage exper exper2 educ vhat
reg lwage exper exper2 educ vhat, vce(robust)

* Hausman test automatic
hausman iv ls, constant sigmamore

********** Testing surplus moment conditions

* obtain 2sls residuals
quietly ivregress 2sls lwage (educ=mothereduc fathereduc) exper exper2, small
predict ehat, residuals

* regress 2sls residuals on all IV
reg ehat exper exper2 mothereduc fathereduc
ereturn list

* NR^2 test
scalar nr2 = e(N)*e(r2)
scalar chic = invchi2tail(1,.05)
scalar pvalue = chi2tail(1,nr2)
di "R^2 from artificial regression = " e(r2)
di "NR^2 test of overidentifying restriction  = " nr2
di "Chi-square critical value 1 df, .05 level = " chic
di "p value for overidentifying test 1 df, .05 level = " pvalue

* Using estat
quietly ivregress 2sls lwage (educ=mothereduc fathereduc) exper exper2, small
estat overid

log close

*********** Chapter 10E: Testing for Weak Instruments

* open new log
log using chap10_weakiv, replace text

* open data & create variables
use mroz, clear
drop if lfp==0
gen lwage=ln(wage)
gen nwifeinc = (faminc-wage*hours)/1000
gen exper2 = exper^2
```

```
********** 2SLS with various instrument sets

* B=1, L=1
ivregress 2sls hours (mtr = exper) educ kids16 nwifeinc, small
estat firststage
estimates store m11

* first stage
reg mtr exper educ kids16 nwifeinc
estimates store r11
test exper

* B=1, L=2
ivregress 2sls hours (mtr =  exper exper2) educ kids16  nwifeinc, small
estat firststage
estimates store m12

* first stage
reg mtr exper exper2 educ kids16 nwifeinc
estimates store r12
test exper exper2

* B=1, L=3
ivregress 2sls hours (mtr = exper exper2 largecity) educ kids16  nwifeinc, small
estat firststage
estimates store m13

* first stage
reg mtr exper exper2 largecity educ  kids16  nwifeinc
estimates store r13
test exper exper2 largecity

* B=1, L=4
ivregress 2sls hours (mtr = exper exper2 largecity unemployment) educ  kids16  nwifeinc,
small
estat firststage
estimates store m14

* first stage
reg mtr exper exper2 largecity unemployment educ kids16 nwifeinc
estimates store r14
test exper exper2 largecity unemployment

* B=2, L=2
ivregress 2sls hours (mtr educ =  mothereduc fathereduc) kids16 nwifeinc, small
estat firststage
estimates store m22

* first stage
reg mtr mothereduc fathereduc kids16 nwifeinc
test mothereduc fathereduc
estimates store r22a

* first stage
reg educ mothereduc fathereduc kids16 nwifeinc
test mothereduc fathereduc
estimates store r22b

* B=2, L=3
ivregress 2sls hours (mtr educ =  mothereduc fathereduc exper) kids16 nwifeinc, small
estat firststage
estimates store m23
```

```
* first stage
reg mtr mothereduc fathereduc exper kidsl6 nwifeinc
test mothereduc fathereduc exper
estimates store r23a

* first stage
reg educ mothereduc fathereduc exper kidsl6 nwifeinc
test mothereduc fathereduc exper
estimates store r23b

* B=2, L=4
ivregress 2sls hours (mtr educ =  mothereduc fathereduc exper exper2) kidsl6 nwifeinc,
small
estat firststage
estimates store m24

* create tables
esttab r11 r13 r22a r22b r23a r23b, compress t(%12.2f) b(%12.5f) nostar ///
        gaps scalars(r2_a rss) title("First Stage Equations")

esttab m11 m13 m22 m23, t(%12.4f) b(%12.4f) nostar ///
        gaps title("IV estimations")

********** Appendix 10E Calculating Cragg-Donald Statistic

ivregress 2sls hours (mtr educ =  mothereduc fathereduc) kidsl6 nwifeinc, small
ereturn list
scalar df_r = e(df_r)

* partial out kidsl6 and nwifeinc
reg mtr kidsl6 nwifeinc
predict mtrr, r

reg educ kidsl6 nwifeinc
predict educr, r

reg mothereduc kidsl6 nwifeinc
predict mothereducr, r

reg fathereduc kidsl6 nwifeinc
predict fathereducr, r

* canonical correlations
canon (mtrr educr) (mothereducr fathereducr)
ereturn list
matrix r2=e(ccorr)
di "Calculation of Cragg-Donald statistic "
di "The canonical correlations "
matrix list r2
scalar mincc = r2[1,2]
di "The minimum canonical correlation = " mincc
scalar cd = df_r*(mincc^2)/(2*(1-mincc^2))
di "The Cragg-Donald F-statistic = " cd

log close

********** Chapter 10F.1 Using Simulated Data

* open new log file
log using chap10_AppF, replace text

* open data
```

```
use ch10, clear
summarize

* Least squares estimation
reg y x
estimates store ls

* IV estimation
reg x z1
predict xhat
reg y xhat

* IV estimation using automatic command
ivregress 2sls y (x=z1)
ivregress 2sls y (x=z1), small
ivregress 2sls y (x=z2), small
ivregress 2sls y (x=z3), small

* IV estimation with surplus instruments
ivregress 2sls y (x=z1 z2), small
estimates store iv

* Hausman test regression based
reg x z1 z2
predict vhat, residuals
reg y x vhat

* Hausman test automatic contrast
hausman iv ls, constant sigmamore

* Testing for weak instrument
reg x z1
reg x z2

* Joint test for weak instrument
reg x z1 z2
test z1 z2

* Testing for weak iv using estat
ivregress 2sls y (x=z1 z2), small
estat firststage

* Testing surplus moment conditions
predict ehat, residuals
reg ehat z1 z2
scalar nr2 = e(N)*e(r2)
scalar chic = invchi2tail(1,.05)
scalar pvalue = chi2tail(1,nr2)
di "NR^2 test of overidentifying restriction  = " nr2
di "Chi-square critical value 1 df, .05 level = " chic
di "p value for overidentifying test 1 df, .05 level = " pvalue

* Testing for weak iv using estat
quietly ivregress 2sls y (x=z1 z2), small
estat overid

* Testing surplus moment conditions
ivregress 2sls y (x=z1 z2 z3), small
predict ehat2, residuals
reg ehat2 z1 z2 z3
scalar nr2 = e(N)*e(r2)
scalar chic = invchi2tail(2,.05)
scalar pvalue = chi2tail(2,nr2)
```

```
di "NR^2 test of overidentifying restriction  = " nr2
di "Chi-square critical value 2 df, .05 level = " chic
di "p value for overidentifying test 2 df, .05 level = " pvalue


* Testing surplus moments using estat
quietly ivregress 2sls y (x=z1 z2 z3)
estat overid

log close

********** Chapter 10F.2: Repeated Sampling Properties of IV/2SLS

* open log file and clear all
log using chap10_sim, text replace
clear all

* specify constants to control simulation
*-------------------------------------------------------------------
global numobs 100      // number of simulated sample observations
global pi     0.1      // reduced form parameter controls IV strength
global rho    0.8      // rho controls endogeneity
*-------------------------------------------------------------------

set obs $numobs
set seed 1234567     // random number seed

* correlation between e and v controls endogeneity
matrix sig = (1, $rho \ $rho, 1)            // corr(e,v)
drawnorm e v, n($numobs) corr(sig)       // e & v values

* create 3 uncorrelated standard normal variables
gen z1 = rnormal()
gen z2 = rnormal()
gen z3 = rnormal()

* DGP
generate x = $pi*z1 + $pi*z2 + $pi*z3 + v
generate y = x + e
correlate x e

* first stage regression using all IV
reg x z1 z2 z3

* OLS
reg y x

* 2sls
ivregress 2sls y (x=z1 z2 z3), small

* program used for simulation

program ch10sim, rclass
    version 11.1
    drop _all

    set obs $numobs
    matrix sig = (1, $rho \ $rho, 1)
    drawnorm e v, n($numobs) corr(sig)

        gen z1 = rnormal()
        gen z2 = rnormal()
        gen z3 = rnormal()
```

```
        * DGP
        generate x = $pi*z1 + $pi*z2 + $pi*z3 + v
        generate y = x + e                          // structural equation

        * first stage regression using all IV
        reg x z1 z2    z3
        return scalar rsq = e(r2)              // first stage r^2
        return scalar F=e(F)                   // first stage F
        predict vhat, r

        * OLS
        reg y x
    return scalar bols =_b[x]
    return scalar seols = _se[x]
    return scalar tols = (_b[x]-1)/_se[x]
    return scalar rols = abs(return(tols))>invttail($numobs-2,.025)

        * Hausman
        reg y x vhat
    return scalar haust = _b[vhat]/_se[vhat]
    return scalar haus = abs(return(haust))>invttail($numobs-3,.025)

        * 2sls
        ivregress 2sls y (x=z1 z2 z3), small
        return scalar b2sls =_b[x]
    return scalar se2sls = _se[x]
    return scalar t2sls = (_b[x]-1)/_se[x]
    return scalar r2sls = abs(return(t2sls))>invttail($numobs-2,.025)

end

simulate rsqf = r(rsq) Fr=r(F) bolsr=r(bols) seolsr=r(seols) ///
        rolsr=r(rols) b2slsr=r(b2sls) se2slsr=r(se2sls) ///
            t2slsr=r(t2sls) r2slsr=r(r2sls) hausr=r(haus),  ///
        reps(10000) nodots nolegend seed(1234567): ch10sim

di " Simulation parameters"
di " rho = " $rho
di " N = " $numobs
di " pi = " $pi
di " average first stage r-square"
mean rsqf

di " average first stage F"
mean Fr

* For each estimator compute
* avg and standard deviation estimate beta
* avg nominal standard error
* avg percent rejection 5% test

di " OLS"
gen mseols = (bolsr-1)^2
tabstat bolsr seolsr rolsr mseols hausr, stat(mean sd)

di " 2sls"
gen mse2sls = (b2slsr-1)^2
tabstat b2slsr se2slsr r2slsr mse2sls, stat(mean sd)

log close
```

CHAPTER **11**

Simultaneous Equations Models

CHAPTER OUTLINE

11.1 TRUFFLE SUPPLY AND DEMAND

Consider a supply and demand model for truffles:

$$\text{Demand: } Q = \alpha_1 + \alpha_2 P + \alpha_3 PS + \alpha_4 DI + e_d$$

$$\text{Supply: } Q = \beta_1 + \beta_2 P + \beta_3 PF + e_s$$

In the demand equation Q is the quantity of truffles traded in a particular French market place, P is the market price of truffles, PS is the market price of a substitute for real truffles (another fungus much less highly prized), and DI is per capita monthly disposable income of local residents. The supply equation contains the market price and quantity supplied. Also it includes the price of a factor of production, PF, which in this case is the hourly rental price of truffle-pigs used in the search process. In this model we assume that P and Q are endogenous variables. The exogenous variables are PS, DI, PF and the intercept variable.

The data for this example are in the data file *truffles.dta*. Execute the usual beginning commands, start a log and open the data file

```
use truffles, clear
describe
```

Examine the data by listing the first 5 observations, and computing summary statistics.

```
list in 1/5
```

```
. list in 1/5
```

	p	q	ps	di	pf
1.	29.64	19.89	19.97	2.103	10.52
2.	40.23	13.04	18.04	2.043	19.67
3.	34.71	19.61	22.36	1.87	13.74
4.	41.43	17.13	20.87	1.525	17.95
5.	53.37	22.55	19.79	2.709	13.71

```
summarize
```

Variable	Obs	Mean	Std. Dev.	Min	Max
p	30	62.724	18.72346	29.64	105.45
q	30	18.45833	4.613088	6.37	26.27
ps	30	22.022	4.077237	15.21	28.98
di	30	3.526967	1.040803	1.525	5.125
pf	30	22.75333	5.329654	10.52	34.01

11.2 ESTIMATING THE REDUCED FORM EQUATIONS

The reduced form equations express each endogenous variable, P and Q, in terms of the exogenous variables PS, DI, PF and the intercept variable, plus an error term. They are:

$$Q = \pi_{11} + \pi_{21}PS + \pi_{31}DI + \pi_{41}PF + v_1$$

$$P = \pi_{12} + \pi_{22}PS + \pi_{32}DI + \pi_{42}PF + v_2$$

We can estimate these equations by least squares since the right-hand side variables are exogenous and uncorrelated with the random errors. The reduced form for $QUANTITY$ is obtained using

```
reg q ps di pf
```

Source	SS	df	MS
Model	430.382604	3	143.460868
Residual	186.754213	26	7.18285434
Total	617.136817	29	21.2805799

```
Number of obs =      30
F( 3,    26) =    19.97
Prob > F      =  0.0000
R-squared     =  0.6974
Adj R-squared =  0.6625
Root MSE      =  2.6801
```

q	Coef.	Std. Err.	t	P>|t|	[95% Conf.	Interval]
ps	.6564021	.1425376	4.61	0.000	.3634118	.9493923
di	2.167156	.7004738	3.09	0.005	.727311	3.607
pf	-.5069823	.1212617	-4.18	0.000	-.7562392	-.2577254
_cons	7.895099	3.243422	2.43	0.022	1.228151	14.56205

The reduced form for *PRICE* is

```
reg p ps di pf
```

Source	SS	df	MS
Model	9034.77551	3	3011.59184
Residual	1131.69721	26	43.5268157
Total	10166.4727	29	350.568025

```
Number of obs =        30
F( 3,     26) =     69.19
Prob > F      =    0.0000
R-squared     =    0.8887
Adj R-squared =    0.8758
Root MSE      =    6.5975
```

p	Coef.	Std. Err.	t	P>|t|	[95% Conf. Interval]	
ps	1.708147	.3508806	4.87	0.000	.9869017	2.429393
di	7.602491	1.724336	4.41	0.000	4.058068	11.14691
pf	1.353906	.2985062	4.54	0.000	.7403175	1.967494
_cons	-32.51242	7.984235	-4.07	0.000	-48.92425	-16.10059

For later use, we obtain the fitted or predicted values of price using the **predict** post-estimation command. Name the variable **phat**, to remind us of $\hat{P}$.

```
predict phat
```

11.3 2SLS ESTIMATES OF TRUFFLE DEMAND

Two-stage least squares (2SLS) estimates can be obtained by replacing the endogenous variable on the right-hand side of the structural equations by the fitted value from the reduced form and then applying least squares. The two-stage least squares estimates of the demand equation obtained using this approach are

```
reg q phat ps di
```

Source	SS	df	MS
Model	430.382596	3	143.460865
Residual	186.754221	26	7.18285466
Total	617.136817	29	21.2805799

```
Number of obs =        30
F( 3,     26) =     19.97
Prob > F      =    0.0000
R-squared     =    0.6974
Adj R-squared =    0.6625
Root MSE      =    2.6801
```

q	Coef.	Std. Err.	t	P>|t|	[95% Conf. Interval]	
phat	-.374459	.0895643	-4.18	0.000	-.5585611	-.1903569
ps	1.296033	.1930944	6.71	0.000	.8991219	1.692944
di	5.013976	1.241414	4.04	0.000	2.462213	7.56574
_cons	-4.27947	3.013834	-1.42	0.168	-10.47449	1.915554

The standard errors, *t*-statistics and 95% confidence intervals in this output are incorrect because the error variance is based on least squares residuals. It is always better to use software commands for 2SLS.

Stata has a built in command for 2SLS estimation called **ivregress**, which stands for "instrumental variables regression." For a complete explanation of why 2SLS is called an instrumental variables estimator see Chapter 10 in *Principles of Econometrics, 4th Edition*, and in Chapter 10 of this manual. Enter **help ivregress** for Stata help.

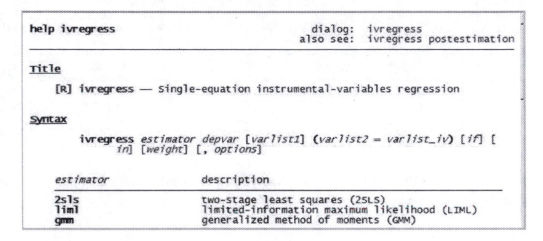

It is available through the pull-down menus. Select

Statistics > Endogenous covariates > Single-equation instrumental-variables regression.

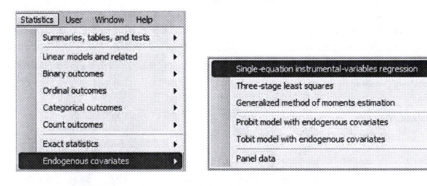

The naming conventions in Stata appeal to a broad segment of statistical practitioners. **"Covariates"** is another term used for regression explanatory variables. **"Endogenous covariates"** means that right-hand side explanatory variables are endogenous, and correlated with the error term. Within this category there are several choices, but we are working with a single equation and want to use instrumental variables estimation, so that choice is clear.

The dialog box can be accessed by entering **db ivregress** into the **Command** line, or clicking in the help box **dialog: ivregress**. The "instrument variables" in the dialog box (on next page) are the exogenous variables that are not in the demand equation. In this case that variable is **pf** which is the price of a factor of production, which appears in the supply equation, not the demand equation. The "independent variables" in the dialog box are the right-hand side variables that are not endogenous. We choose the 2SLS option and click OK.

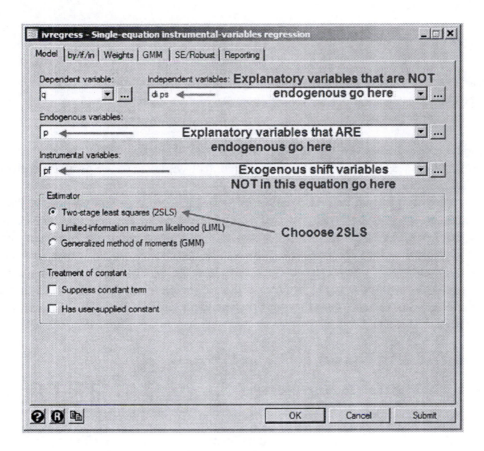

The Stata command shown in the Results window is

```
ivregress 2sls q di ps (p = pf)
```

. ivregress 2sls q di ps (p = pf)

Instrumental variables (2SLS) regression

Number of obs =   30
Wald chi2(3)   =   20.43
Prob > chi2   =   0.0001
R-squared   =   .
Root MSE   =   4.5895

q	Coef.	Std. Err.	z	P>|z|	[95% Conf. Interval]	
p	-.3744591	.1533755	-2.44	0.015	-.6750695	-.0738486
di	5.013977	2.125875	2.36	0.018	.847339	9.180615
ps	1.296033	.3306669	3.92	0.000	.6479381	1.944128
_cons	-4.279471	5.161076	-0.83	0.407	-14.39499	5.836052

Instrumented: p
Instruments: di ps pf

After the command **ivregress** we must specify which estimator we want, which in this case is
2sls. The regression model specification is standard, with the dependent variable **q** coming first.
For any explanatory variable that is endogenous we have the statement in parentheses, which is

```
(varlist2 = varlist_iv)
```

where

> **varlist2** is a list of all the right-hand size endogenous variables
> **varlist_iv** is a list of all the exogenous variables that are not
>   in the model

Explanatory variables that are not endogenous would be listed either before or after the expression in parentheses. Also, the order of independent variables in the printed results depends on their order of entry in the dialog box.

The IV regression output reports z-values because IV regression has properties that depend upon having large samples, and we know that in large samples the t-distribution converges to the standard normal $N(0,1)$ distribution. Thus t-statistics become z-statistics. In large samples it does not matter if critical values for tests come from one distribution or the other, but in smaller samples it can matter. It is our preference to always base inferences on the t-distribution. This is achieved in Stata by using the **small** option. In the following command, also note that we have placed the endogenous variable **(p=pf)** after the dependent variable to make the point that it does not have to appear at the end.

```
ivregress 2sls q (p=pf) ps di, small
```

```
Instrumental variables (2SLS) regression
```

Source	SS	df	MS		
Model	-14.780326	3	-4.92677534	Number of obs =	30
Residual	631.917143	26	24.3045055	F(3, 26) =	5.90
				Prob > F =	0.0033
				R-squared =	.
				Adj R-squared =	.
Total	617.136817	29	21.2805799	Root MSE =	4.93

q	Coef.	Std. Err.	t	P>|t|	[95% Conf. Interval]	
p	-.3744591	.1647517	-2.27	0.032	-.713111	-.0358071
ps	1.296033	.3551932	3.65	0.001	.5659232	2.026143
di	5.013977	2.283556	2.20	0.037	.3200608	9.707893
_cons	-4.279471	5.543884	-0.77	0.447	-15.67509	7.116147

```
Instrumented:  p
Instruments:   ps di pf
```

The output will be different in two regards. In the previous estimation the overall test of model significance was based on the Wald chi-square test. With the **small** option the overall test is reported as an F-test. The second difference is that t-values are reported, and the p-values and interval estimates are based on the t-distribution.

Stata also includes an option that will display the first stage (the reduced form) of two stage least squares. It is an option called **first**.

```
ivregress 2sls q (p=pf) ps di, small first
```

First-stage regressions
_____

```
                                    Number of obs   =         30
                                    F(   3,    26) =      69.19
                                    Prob > F        =     0.0000
                                    R-squared       =     0.8887
                                    Adj R-squared   =     0.8758
                                    Root MSE        =     6.5975
```

p	Coef.	Std. Err.	t	P>|t|	[95% Conf. Interval]	
ps	1.708147	.3508806	4.87	0.000	.9869017	2.429393
di	7.602491	1.724336	4.41	0.000	4.058068	11.14691
pf	1.353906	.2985062	4.54	0.000	.7403175	1.967494
_cons	-32.51242	7.984235	-4.07	0.000	-48.92425	-16.10059

The additional output is the first-stage regressions. In this case, since there is one right-hand side endogenous variable, *PRICE* (**p**), Stata reports its reduced form. The reason is that in this reduced form there must be evidence that the instrument, **pf**, is actually a significant explanatory variable. We see that its *t*-statistic is 4.54. There is a rule of thumb in this literature that for two-stage least squares estimation to be reliable the *t*-statistic must be greater than about 3.3, or the *F*-value for testing the instruments greater than 10. For much more detail on this issue see *Principles of Econometrics, 4th Edition*, Chapter 10, Appendix E, and Chapter 10.6 of this manual.

There is a "post-estimation" command called **estat firststage** that carries out this test of instrument validity. It is located on the pull-down Stata menu by selecting **Statistics > Postestimation > Reports and statistics**. From the resulting list select the first item.

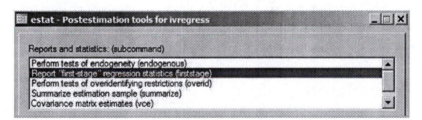

There is quite a bit of output and most you will not understand, but the key item is the value of the *F*-statistic. Since there is a single external instrument this value, 20.5717 is the square of the t-statistic from the reduced form.

```
. estat firststage
```

First-stage regression summary statistics

Variable	R-sq.	Adjusted R-sq.	Partial R-sq.	F(1,26)	Prob > F
p	0.8887	0.8758	0.4417	20.5717	0.0001

In the lower portion of the output, shown on the next page, from **estat firststage** are the Stock-Yogo critical values for the test of whether or not instruments are strong. The rule of thumb value for the first stage *F*-test is 10, but this has been refined. For an explantion of how to use these critical values, see Chapter 10.6 of this manual.

```
Minimum eigenvalue statistic = 20.5717
```

Critical Values Ho: Instruments are weak	# of endogenous regressors: 1 # of excluded instruments: 1			
2SLS relative bias	5% (not	10% available)	20%	30%
	10%	15%	20%	25%
2SLS Size of nominal 5% Wald test	16.38	8.96	6.66	5.53
LIML Size of nominal 5% Wald test	16.38	8.96	6.66	5.53

The Stata command is

```
estat firststage
```

11.4 2SLS ESTIMATES OF TRUFFLE SUPPLY

The two-stage least squares estimates of the supply equation are similarly obtained. Note that there are two exogenous shift variables for this estimation, **ps** and **di**, which are variables in the demand equation.

```
ivregress 2sls q (p=ps di) pf, small first
```

The first stage estimation results are shown below. In this estimation, at least one of the external instruments, the shift variables **ps** and **di**, must be significant.

```
First-stage regressions
```

```
                                      Number of obs   =         30
                                      F(   3,     26) =      69.19
                                      Prob > F        =     0.0000
                                      R-squared       =     0.8887
                                      Adj R-squared   =     0.8758
                                      Root MSE        =     6.5975
```

p	Coef.	Std. Err.	t	P>|t|	[95% Conf. Interval]	
pf	1.353906	.2985062	4.54	0.000	.7403175	1.967494
ps	1.708147	.3508806	4.87	0.000	.9869017	2.429393
di	7.602491	1.724336	4.41	0.000	4.058068	11.14691
_cons	-32.51242	7.984235	-4.07	0.000	-48.92425	-16.10059

The 2SLS estimates of the supply equation are

```
Instrumental variables (2SLS) regression
```

Source	SS	df	MS
Model	556.582251	2	278.291126
Residual	60.5545652	27	2.24276167
Total	617.136817	29	21.2805799

```
Number of obs =       30
F( 2,    27) =    95.26
Prob > F      =   0.0000
R-squared     =   0.9019
Adj R-squared =   0.8946
Root MSE      =   1.4976
```

q	Coef.	Std. Err.	t	P>|t|	[95% Conf. Interval]
p	.3379816	.0249196	13.56	0.000	.2868509 .3891123
pf	-1.000909	.0825279	-12.13	0.000	-1.170243 -.831576
_cons	20.0328	1.223115	16.38	0.000	17.52318 22.54243

```
Instrumented:  p
Instruments:   pf ps di
```

To check the joint significance of the shift variables we use

estat firststage

```
First-stage regression summary statistics
```

Variable	R-sq.	Adjusted R-sq.	Partial R-sq.	F(2,26)	Prob > F
p	0.8887	0.8758	0.7614	41.4873	0.0000

The key figure is the F-statistic. The value 41.4873 is greater than the rule of thumb threshold of 10, reassuring us that the first-stage coefficient of at least one of the shift variables **ps** and **di** is significantly different than from zero.

11.5 SUPPLY AND DEMAND OF FISH

The second example of a simultaneous equations model is from the Fulton Fish Market in New York City. Let us specify the demand equation for this market as

$$\ln(QUAN_t) = \alpha_1 + \alpha_2 \ln(PRICE_t) + \alpha_3 MON_t + \alpha_4 TUE_t + \alpha_5 WED_t + \alpha_6 THU_t + e_t^d$$

where $QUAN_t$ is the quantity sold, in pounds, and $PRICE_t$ the average daily price per pound. Note that we are using the subscript "t" to index observations for this relationship because of the time series nature of the data. The remaining variables are indicator variables for the days of the week, with Friday being omitted. The coefficient α_2 is the price elasticity of demand, which we expect to be negative. The daily indicator variables capture day to day shifts in demand. The supply equation is

$$\ln(QUAN_t) = \beta_1 + \beta_2 \ln(PRICE_t) + \beta_3 STORMY_t + e_t^s$$

The coefficient β_2 is the price elasticity of supply. The variable *STORMY* is an indicator variable indicating stormy weather during the previous three days. This variable is important in the supply equation because stormy weather makes fishing more difficult, reducing the supply of fish brought to market.

Open a new log file, and open and examine the data file *fultonfish.dta*.

```
use fultonfish, clear
describe
```

Examine the data by listing the first 5 observations for the variables in the system.

```
list lquan lprice mon tue wed thu stormy in 1/5
```

	lquan	lprice	mon	tue	wed	thu	stormy
1.	8.994421	-.4307829	1	0	0	0	1
2.	7.707063	0	0	1	0	0	1
3.	8.350194	.0723207	0	0	1	0	0
4.	8.656955	.247139	0	0	0	1	1
5.	7.844241	.6643268	0	0	0	0	1

Now obtain the summary statistics for these variables

```
summarize lquan lprice mon tue wed thu stormy
```

Variable	Obs	Mean	Std. Dev.	Min	Max
lquan	111	8.52343	.741672	6.194406	9.981374
lprice	111	-.1936811	.3819346	-1.107745	.6643268
mon	111	.1891892	.3934351	0	1
tue	111	.2072072	.4071434	0	1
wed	111	.1891892	.3934351	0	1
thu	111	.2072072	.4071434	0	1
stormy	111	.2882883	.4550202	0	1

11.6 REDUCED FORMS FOR FISH PRICE AND QUANTITY

It is very important to estimate the reduced form equations for each endogenous variable in a system of simultaneous equations. The reduced form equations can be estimated by least squares because all the right-hand side variables are exogenous. The reduced form equation for $\ln(QUAN)$ is obtained using

```
reg lquan mon tue wed thu stormy
```

Because $\ln(PRICE)$ is the right-hand side explanatory variable let us examine its reduced form equation more closely. It is estimated using

```
reg lprice mon tue wed thu stormy
```

Source	SS	df	MS		
Model	2.87047878	5	.574095757		
Residual	13.1756621	105	.125482496		
Total	16.0461409	110	.145874008		

Number of obs = 111
F(5, 105) = 4.58
Prob > F = 0.0008
R-squared = 0.1789
Adj R-squared = 0.1398
Root MSE = .35424

lprice	Coef.	Std. Err.	t	P>|t|	[95% Conf. Interval]	
mon	-.1129225	.1072918	-1.05	0.295	-.3256623	.0998174
tue	-.0411493	.1045087	-0.39	0.695	-.2483707	.1660721
wed	-.011825	.1069299	-0.11	0.912	-.2238473	.2001973
thu	.0496456	.1044582	0.48	0.636	-.1574758	.256767
stormy	.3464055	.0746776	4.64	0.000	.1983337	.4944774
_cons	-.2717054	.076389	-3.56	0.001	-.4231706	-.1202402

The concept of identification is discussed in *POE4*. To use 2SLS there must be $M - 1$ (M is the number of equations) exogenous variables that are excluded from the equation—these are the instrumental variables. However, not only must they be omitted from the equation in question, but they must be statistically significant in the reduced form.

In the demand equation, the variable **stormy** is not included, because storms affect supply and not demand. In the reduced form for $\ln(PRICE)$ the variable **stormy** must be very significant for 2SLS to work well. Note that the t-statistic for stormy is 4.64 and the p-value is very small. This is very good. The key "rule of thumb" threshold for the t-statistic value of the shift variable is 3.3. If the t-statistic is lower than this value, 2SLS may not work very well.

In the supply equation, the variables omitted are the days of the week, **mon**, **tue**, **wed** and **thu**. In order to use 2SLS to estimate the supply equation at least one of these variables must be (very) significant. The t-values are small. The F-statistic of the joint null hypothesis that all these variables have no effect is obtained using

```
test mon tue wed thu
```

This particular syntax is another simplification of that used in our discussion of the **test** statement in Chapter 6. Since each coefficient is zero under the null hypothesis, you can simply list the variables after test. The result is

```
. test mon tue wed thu

 ( 1)   mon = 0
 ( 2)   tue = 0
 ( 3)   wed = 0
 ( 4)   thu = 0

       F(  4,    105) =     0.62
            Prob > F =     0.6501
```

In order to use 2SLS for the supply equation we would look for a very significant test outcome, with an F-value greater than 10. Clearly this is not the case. Thus in practical terms the supply equation is not identified, and thus we should not rely on the 2SLS estimates for this equation.

11.7 2SLS ESTIMATES OF FISH DEMAND

To obtain the 2SLS estimates of the demand equation we again use the Stata command **ivregress**. The exogenous shift variable is **stormy**. It appears in the parentheses along with the right-hand side endogenous variable **lprice**, with other explanatory variables listed either before or after. We use the option **small** so that t-statistics will be displayed rather than z-statistics, and we use the option **first** to obtain the first stage regression which is the reduced form for **lprice**.

```
ivregress 2sls lquan (lprice=stormy) mon tue wed thu, small first
```

The reduced form equation is

```
First-stage regressions
```

				Number of obs	=	111
				F(5, 105)	=	4.58
				Prob > F	=	0.0008
				R-squared	=	0.1789
				Adj R-squared	=	0.1398
				Root MSE	=	0.3542

lprice	Coef.	Std. Err.	t	P>|t|	[95% Conf. Interval]	
mon	-.1129225	.1072918	-1.05	0.295	-.3256623	.0998174
tue	-.0411493	.1045087	-0.39	0.695	-.2483707	.1660721
wed	-.011825	.1069299	-0.11	0.912	-.2238473	.2001973
thu	.0496456	.1044582	0.48	0.636	-.1574758	.256767
stormy	.3464055	.0746776	4.64	0.000	.1983337	.4944774
_cons	-.2717054	.076389	-3.56	0.001	-.4231706	-.1202402

Note that stormy is significant with a t-value of 4.64, which is larger than the rule of thumb value 3.3. It should also be mentioned that the small option alters the computation of p-values and the confidence intervals, which are also based on the t-distribution. The two-stage least squares, instrumental variables, estimates are

```
Instrumental variables (2SLS) regression
```

Source	SS	df	MS		
Model	8.41819623	5	1.68363925		
Residual	52.0903208	105	.496098293		
Total	60.508517	110	.550077427		

```
Number of obs =      111
F( 5,    105) =     4.72
Prob > F      =   0.0006
R-squared     =   0.1391
Adj R-squared =   0.0981
Root MSE      =   .70434
```

lquan	Coef.	Std. Err.	t	P>|t|	[95% Conf. Interval]	
lprice	-1.119417	.428645	-2.61	0.010	-1.969341	-.269493
mon	-.0254022	.2147742	-0.12	0.906	-.4512596	.4004553
tue	-.5307694	.2080001	-2.55	0.012	-.9431951	-.1183437
wed	-.5663511	.2127549	-2.66	0.009	-.9882047	-.1444975
thu	.1092673	.2087866	0.52	0.602	-.3047179	.5232525
_cons	8.505911	.1661669	51.19	0.000	8.176433	8.83539

```
Instrumented:  lprice
Instruments:   mon tue wed thu stormy
```

The post-estimation command **estat firststage** can also be used to test the validity of the instrument **stormy**.

```
    estat firststage
```

```
First-stage regression summary statistics
```

Variable	R-sq.	Adjusted R-sq.	Partial R-sq.	F(1,105)	Prob > F
lprice	0.1789	0.1398	0.1701	21.5174	0.0000

```
Minimum eigenvalue statistic = 21.5174
```

Critical Values Ho: Instruments are weak	# of endogenous regressors: 1 # of excluded instruments: 1			
	5%	10%	20%	30%
2SLS relative bias		(not available)		
	10%	15%	20%	25%
2SLS Size of nominal 5% Wald test	16.38	8.96	6.66	5.53
LIML Size of nominal 5% Wald test	16.38	8.96	6.66	5.53

Once again we point out that the lower portion the output contains the Stock-Yogo critical values for the first-stage F-test, and the use of these critical values is explained in *POE4*, Chapter 10, Appendix E, and in Chapter 10.6 of this manual.

11.8 2SLS ALTERNATIVES

There has always been great interest in alternatives to the standard IV/2SLS estimator. See *Principles of Econometrics, 4* [th] *Edition*, Appendix E. The limited information maximum likelihood (LIML) estimator was first derived by Anderson and Rubin in 1949.[1] There is renewed interest in LIML in the presence of weak instruments. Several modifications of LIML have been suggested by Fuller (1977) and others. These estimators are unified in a common framework, along with 2SLS, using the idea of a **k-class** of estimators. LIML suffers less from test size aberrations than the 2SLS estimator, and the Fuller modification suffers less from bias.

In a system of M simultaneous equations let the endogenous variables be $y_1, y_2, \ldots, y_M$. Let there be K exogenous variables $x_1, x_2, \ldots, x_K$. Suppose the first structural equation within this system is

$$y_1 = \alpha_2 y_2 + \beta_1 x_1 + \beta_2 x_2 + e_1$$

The endogenous variable y_2 has reduced form $y_2 = \pi_{12} x_1 + \pi_{22} x_2 + \cdots + \pi_{K2} x_K + v_2 = E(y_2) + v_2$. The parameters of the reduced form equation are consistently estimated by least squares, so that

$$\widehat{E(y_2)} = \hat{\pi}_{12} x_1 + \hat{\pi}_{22} x_2 + \cdots + \hat{\pi}_{K2} x_K$$

The reduced form residuals are

$$\hat{v}_2 = y_2 - \widehat{E(y_2)}$$

The two-stage least squares estimator is an IV estimator using $\widehat{E(y_2)}$ as an instrument. A *k-class* estimator is an IV estimator using instrumental variable $y_2 - k\hat{v}_2$. The LIML estimator uses $k = \hat{\ell}$ where $\hat{\ell}$ is the minimum ratio of the sum of squared residuals from two regressions. The explanation is given on pages 468-469 of *POE4*. A modification suggested by Wayne Fuller (1977)[2] uses the *k-class* value

$$k = \hat{\ell} - \frac{a}{N - K}$$

where K is the total number of instrumental variables (included and excluded exogenous variables) and N is the sample size. The value of a is a constant—usually 1 or 4.

With the Mroz data we estimate the *HOURS* supply equation

$$HOURS = \beta_1 + \beta_2 MTR + \beta_3 EDUC + \beta_4 KIDSL6 + \beta_5 NWIFEINC + e$$

This example was used in Chapter 10.6 of this manual. The example we consider has endogenous variables **educ** and **mtr** and *IV* **mothereduc** and **fathereduc** and experience, **exper**. The code for other *POE4* examples is given in the Chapter 11 do-file, but we will not discuss them here.

Open a new log, and re-open the Mroz data, clearing memory. Create variables used in the example.

[1] Anderson, T.W. and H. Rubin (1949) "Estimation of the Parameters of a Single Equation in a Complete System of Stochastic Equations," *Annals of Mathematical Statistics*, 21, pp. 46-63.

[2] "Some Properties of a Modification of the Limited Information Estimator," *Econometrica*, 45, pp. 939-953.

```
use mroz, clear
drop if lfp==0
gen lwage=ln(wage)
gen nwifeinc = (faminc-wage*hours)/1000
gen exper2 = exper^2
```

The LIML estimates are obtained using **ivregress**. Using the dialog box, **db ivregress**, click the radio button for Limited-information maximum likelihood (LIML).

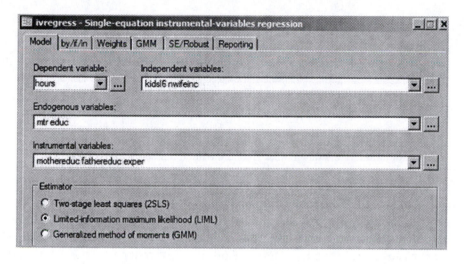

The Stata command is

> **ivregress liml hours kids16 nwifeinc (mtr educ = mothereduc fathereduc exper)**

```
. ivregress liml hours kids16 nwifeinc (mtr educ = mothereduc fathereduc exper)
```

```
Instrumental variables (LIML) regression        Number of obs =      428
                                                 Wald chi2(4)  =    36.52
                                                 Prob > chi2   =   0.0000
                                                 R-squared     =        .
                                                 Root MSE      =   852.35
```

hours	Coef.	Std. Err.	z	P>|z|	[95% Conf.	Interval]
mtr	-19196.52	3980.227	-4.82	0.000	-26997.62	-11395.42
educ	-197.2591	64.24267	-3.07	0.002	-323.1724	-71.34579
kids16	207.5531	162.2957	1.28	0.201	-110.5406	525.6469
nwifeinc	-104.9415	20.56548	-5.10	0.000	-145.2491	-64.63395
_cons	18587.91	3662.026	5.08	0.000	11410.47	25765.35

```
Instrumented:  mtr educ
Instruments:   kids16 nwifeinc mothereduc fathereduc exper
```

The test for weak instruments is obtained using

> **estat firststage**

```
. estat firststage

Shea's partial R-squared
```

Variable	Shea's Partial R-sq.	Shea's Adj. Partial R-sq.
mtr	0.0618	0.0529
educ	0.1042	0.0957

```
Minimum eigenvalue statistic = 8.60138

Critical Values                    # of endogenous regressors:    2
Ho: Instruments are weak           # of excluded instruments:     3
```

	5%	10%	20%	30%
2SLS relative bias		(not available)		

	10%	15%	20%	25%
2SLS Size of nominal 5% Wald test	13.43	8.18	6.40	5.45
LIML Size of nominal 5% Wald test	5.44	3.81	3.32	3.09

Using the maximum size of 10%, for a nominal 5% test of a hypothesis concerning the coefficient of the endogenous variable, the critical value is given in the Stata output as 5.44. We reject the null hypothesis that the instruments are weak using the Cragg-Donald F-test statistic (called **Minimum eigenvalue statistic** by Stata) of 8.60. If we were using the 2SLS/IV estimator, we would have not rejected the hypothesis that the instruments are weak because the critical value is 13.43. For more understanding of this test you are referred to Chapter 10.6 of this manual, and Chapter 11, Appendix B in *Principles of Econometrics, 4th Edition*.

The Stata command **ivregress** does not have an option for Fuller's modified k-class estimator. However there is a user-written routine to use. In the Stata command window enter **findit ivreg2**. In the resulting help window, locate

```
SJ-7-4  st0030_3 . . . .  Enhanced routines for IV/GMM estimation and testing
. . . . . . . . . . .  C. F. Baum, M. E. Schaffer, and S. Stillman
(help ivactest, ivendog, ivhettest, ivreg2, ivreset,
overid, ranktest if installed)
Q4/07   SJ 7(4):465--506
extension of IV and GMM estimation addressing hetero-
skedasticity- and autocorrelation-consistent standard
errors, weak instruments, LIML and k-class estimation,
tests for endogeneity and Ramsey's regression
specification-error test, and autocorrelation tests
for IV estimates and panel-data IV estimates
```

Click on st0030_3. In the resulting viewer you can install this package if you have administrative privileges on the computer.

```
package st0030_3 from http://www.stata-journal.com/software/sj7-4

TITLE
      SJ7-4 st0030_3.  Update: Instrumental variables and GMM:...

DESCRIPTION/AUTHOR(S)
      Update: Instrumental variables and GMM:  Estimation and
         testing

      by Christopher F. Baum, Boston College
         Mark E. Schaffer, Heriot-Watt University
         Steven Stillman, Motu Economic Public Policy Research
      Support:  baum@bc.edu, m.e.schaffer@hw.ac.uk,
              stillman@motu.org.nz
      After installation, type help ivactest, ivendog, ivhettest,
                                ivreg2, overid, and ranktest

                                          (click here to install)
INSTALLATION FILES
      st0030_3/ivactest.ado
```

The syntax of the command is much like **ivregress**.

> **ivreg2 hours (mtr educ = mothereduc fathereduc exper) kids16 nwifeinc,**
> **fuller(1) small**

In the option **fuller(1)**, the **1** indicates setting the constant $a = 1$. At the top of the output we find the parameter estimates and the k-value used in estimation, as well as the value of $\hat{\ell}$.

```
LIML estimation
───────────────
k                   =1.00051
lambda              =1.00288
Fuller parameter=1

Estimates efficient for homoskedasticity only
Statistics consistent for homoskedasticity only
```

			Number of obs	=	428
			F(4, 423)	=	9.22
			Prob > F	=	0.0000
Total (centered) SS	=	257311019.9	Centered R2	=	-0.1746
Total (uncentered) SS	=	983895094	Uncentered R2	=	0.6928
Residual SS	=	302240888.2	Root MSE	=	845.3

hours	Coef.	Std. Err.	t	P>|t|	[95% Conf. Interval]	
mtr	-18730.16	3870.958	-4.84	0.000	-26338.87	-11121.45
educ	-191.1248	62.73944	-3.05	0.002	-314.4446	-67.80487
kids16	193.2295	159.1413	1.21	0.225	-119.5767	506.0358
nwifeinc	-102.629	20.03279	-5.12	0.000	-142.0052	-63.25276
_cons	18156.78	3560.13	5.10	0.000	11159.04	25154.53

In addition to the estimates we are automatically given many diagnostics. For current purposes we report only the weak instrument test results. The Cragg-Donald F-statistic is reported along with critical values for the criteria based on relative bias. See Appendix 10.6 of this manual for a description of the relative bias criterion.

```
weak identification test (Cragg-Donald Wald F statistic):        8.601
Stock-Yogo weak ID test critical values:   5% maximal Fuller rel. bias    10.83
                                           10% maximal Fuller rel. bias     8.96
                                           20% maximal Fuller rel. bias     7.18
                                           30% maximal Fuller rel. bias     6.15
                                            5% Fuller maximum bias         10.00
                                           10% Fuller maximum bias          8.39
                                           20% Fuller maximum bias          6.79
                                           30% Fuller maximum bias          5.88
NB: Critical values based on Fuller parameter=1
Source: Stock-Yogo (2005).  Reproduced by permission.
```

11.9 MONTE CARLO SIMULATION RESULTS

In Chapter 10.8 of this manual we explained the Monte Carlo simulation experiment used in Chapter 10, Appendix 10F.2 of *Principles of Econometrics, 4 [th] Edition*. The Monte Carlo simulation explores the properties of the IV/2SLS estimators. Here we employ the same experiment, adding aspects of the LIML and k-class estimators.

The code is completely given in the Chapter 11 do-file at the end of this chapter. The structure is explained in Chapter 10.8 in this manual. The first portion, the global control parameters and data generation process are unchanged.

```
clear all
set more off
global numobs 100
global pi     0.5        // reduced form parameter controls IV strength
global rho    0.8        // rho controls endogeneity
set seed 1234567         // random number seed
set obs $numobs
matrix sig = (1, $rho \ $rho, 1)        // corr(e1,v2)
drawnorm e v, n($numobs) corr(sig)      // e1 & v2 values
generate z1 = rnormal()
generate z2 = rnormal()
generate z3 = rnormal()
generate x = $pi*z1 + $pi*z2 + $pi*z3 + v      // reduced form
generate y = x + e
correlate x e
regress x z1 z2      z3
regress y x
ivregress 2sls y (x=z1 z2 z3), small
```

The first new element is the application of the LIML estimator to the simulated data. The command and output are given below. Note that the LIML estimates are close to the true values because we have set the global variable $pi = 0.5$ so that the instruments are strong.

```
ivregress liml y (x=z1 z2 z3), small
```

. ivregress liml y (x=z1 z2 z3), small

Instrumental variables (LIML) regression

Source	SS	df	MS
Model	356.810445	1	356.810445
Residual	112.041511	98	1.14328073
Total	468.851956	99	4.73587834

```
Number of obs =      100
F(  1,     98) =    51.15
Prob > F       =   0.0000
R-squared      =   0.7610
Adj R-squared  =   0.7586
Root MSE       =   1.0692
```

y	Coef.	Std. Err.	t	P>|t|	[95% Conf. Interval]	
x	.9951923	.1391497	7.15	0.000	.7190542	1.27133
_cons	.1290802	.1074206	1.20	0.232	-.0840924	.3422528

Instrumented: x
Instruments: z1 z2 z3

Next, we introduce the Fuller-modified k-class estimator with $a = 1$ and $a = 4$.

ivreg2 y (x=z1 z2 z3), small fuller(1)

. ivreg2 y (x=z1 z2 z3), small fuller(1)

LIML estimation

```
k            =0.99954
lambda       =1.00996
Fuller parameter=1
```

Estimates efficient for homoskedasticity only
Statistics consistent for homoskedasticity only

```
                                       Number of obs =      100
                                       F(  1,     98) =    55.25
                                       Prob > F       =   0.0000
Total (centered) SS   = 468.8519559    Centered R2    =   0.7671
Total (uncentered) SS = 469.1579693    Uncentered R2  =   0.7672
Residual SS           = 109.2043273    Root MSE       =    1.056
```

y	Coef.	Std. Err.	t	P>|t|	[95% Conf. Interval]	
x	1.010894	.1359953	7.43	0.000	.7410159	1.280772
_cons	.130244	.106042	1.23	0.222	-.0801929	.3406808

ivreg2 y (x=z1 z2 z3), small fuller(4)

```
. ivreg2 y (x=z1 z2 z3), small fuller(4)

LIML estimation
```
```
k                =0.96829
lambda           =1.00996
Fuller parameter=4
```

Estimates efficient for homoskedasticity only
Statistics consistent for homoskedasticity only

```
                                          Number of obs =        100
                                          F( 1,    98) =      68.37
                                          Prob > F      =     0.0000
Total (centered) SS    = 468.8519559      Centered R2   =     0.7829
Total (uncentered) SS  = 469.1579693      Uncentered R2 =     0.7830
Residual SS            = 101.7893518      Root MSE      =      1.019
```

y	Coef.	Std. Err.	t	P>|t|	[95% Conf. Interval]	
x	1.054443	.1275256	8.27	0.000	.801373	1.307514
_cons	.1334717	.1023524	1.30	0.195	-.0696432	.3365867

The program used for the simulation is similar in structure to the one used in Chapter 10.8 of this manual.

```
program ch11sim, rclass
version 11.1
drop _all
set obs $numobs

matrix sig = (1, $rho \ $rho, 1)        // cov(e1,v2)
drawnorm e v, n($numobs) corr(sig)      // e1 & v2 values
generate z1 = rnormal()
generate z2 = rnormal()
generate z3 = rnormal()
generate x = $pi*z1 + $pi*z2 + $pi*z3 + v
generate y = x + e

ivregress 2sls y (x=z1 z2 z3), small
return scalar b2sls =_b[x]
return scalar se2sls = _se[x]
return scalar t2sls = (_b[x]-1)/_se[x]
return scalar r2sls = abs(return(t2sls))>invttail($numobs-2,.025)
```

We introduced LIML and Fuller-modified k-class with returns the same as 2SLS.

```
ivregress liml y (x=z1 z2 z3), small
return scalar bliml =_b[x]
return scalar seliml = _se[x]
return scalar tliml = (_b[x]-1)/_se[x]
return scalar rliml = abs(return(tliml))>invttail($numobs-2,.025)
```

```
ivreg2 y (x=z1 z2 z3), small fuller(1)
return scalar bfull =_b[x]
return scalar sefull = _se[x]
return scalar tfull = (_b[x]-1)/_se[x]
return scalar rfull = abs(return(tfull))>invttail($numobs-2,.025)

ivreg2 y (x=z1 z2 z3), small fuller(4)
return scalar bfull4 =_b[x]
return scalar sefull4 = _se[x]
return scalar tfull4 = (_b[x]-1)/_se[x]
return scalar rfull4 = abs(return(tfull4))>invttail($numobs-2,.025)

end
```

The simulate command has more elements but the same structure as in Chapter 10.8 of this manual.

```
simulate b2slsr=r(b2sls) se2slsr=r(se2sls) t2slsr=r(t2sls) ///
    r2slsr=r(r2sls) blimlr=r(bliml) selimlr=r(seliml) ///
    tlimlr=r(tliml) rlimlr=r(rliml) bfullr=r(bfull) ///
    sefullr=r(sefull) tfullr=r(tfull) rfullr=r(rfull) ///
    bfull4r=r(bfull4) sefull4r=r(sefull4) tfull4r=r(tfull4) ///
    rfull4r=r(rfull4), reps(10000) nodots nolegend seed(1234567):
    ch    11sim
```

The first display and results for 2SLS are the same as in Chapter 10.8 of this manual.

```
di " Simulation parameters"
di " rho = " $rho
di " N = " $numobs
di " pi = " $pi
```

```
. di " Simulation parameters"
 Simulation parameters

. di " rho = " $rho
 rho = .8

. di " N = " $numobs
 N = 100

. di " pi = " $pi
 pi = .5
```

```
di " 2sls"
gen mse2sls = (b2slsr-1)^2
tabstat b2slsr se2slsr r2slsr mse2sls, stat(mean sd)
```

```
. tabstat b2slsr se2slsr r2slsr mse2sls, stat(mean sd)
```

stats	b2slsr	se2slsr	r2slsr	mse2sls
mean	1.011116	.11695	.0636	.0139068
sd	.1174081	.0274133	.2440512	.0227001

Note in the above that the two-stage least squares estimates averaged over 10,000 simulations are very close to the true slope parameter value of 1, and the t-test of the true null hypothesis rejects about 5% of the time, as it should.

```
di " liml"
gen mseliml = (blimlr-1)^2
tabstat blimlr selimlr rlimlr mseliml, stat(mean sd)
```

```
. tabstat blimlr selimlr rlimlr mseliml, stat(mean sd)
```

stats	blimlr	selimlr	rlimlr	mseliml
mean	.9881047	.1210493	.0509	.0153914
sd	.1234965	.029831	.2198045	.0276647

The LIML results, above, are similar in this strong IV example.

```
di " fuller(1)"
gen msefull = (bfullr-1)^2
tabstat bfullr sefullr rfullr msefull, stat(mean sd)
```

```
. tabstat bfullr sefullr rfullr msefull, stat(mean sd)
```

stats	bfullr	sefullr	rfullr	msefull
mean	.999965	.1189061	.0553	.0141615
sd	.1190081	.0283846	.2285763	.0239569

The Fuller-modified k-class estimator with $a = 1$ is designed to produce an estimator that is nearly unbiased, and the results above are consistent with that objective.

```
di " fuller(4)"
gen msefull4 = (bfull4r-1)^2
tabstat bfull4r sefull4r rfull4r msefull4, stat(mean sd)
```

```
. tabstat bfull4r sefull4r rfull4r msefull4, stat(mean sd)
```

stats	bfull4r	sefull4r	rfull4r	msefull4
mean	1.033343	.1130738	.0812	.0126647
sd	.1074901	.0247115	.2731557	.0177391

The Fuller-modified *k*-class estimator with $a = 4$ is designed to have a small mean squared error, and the results above show that it does have lower MSE than the other estimators. Recall that the mean squared error is computed for each estimator as

$$\text{mse}\left(\hat{\beta}_2\right) = \sum_{m=1}^{10000} \left(\hat{\beta}_{2m} - \beta_2\right)^2 \Big/ 10000$$

KEY TERMS

2sls	instrument variables	**regress**
correlate	**ivreg2**	**rnormal()**
demand equation	**ivregress**	**seed**
drawnorm	k-class estimator	**simulate**
endogenous variables	LIML	simultaneous equations
esttab	**list**	Stock-Yogo critical value
exogenous variables	**matrix**	**summarize**
findit	mean squared error	supply equation
F-test	Monte Carlo simulation	**test**
global	**predict**	two-stage least squares
identification	reduced form equations	Wald test

CHAPTER 11 DO-FILE [CHAP11.DO]

```
* file chap11.do for Using Stata for Principles of Econometrics, 4e

cd c:\data\poe4stata

* Stata do-file
* copyright C 2011 by Lee C. Adkins and R. Carter Hill
* used for "Using Stata for Principles of Econometrics, 4e"
* by Lee C. Adkins and R. Carter Hill (2011)
* John Wiley and Sons, Inc.

* setup
version 11.1
capture log close
set more off

********** Chapter 11.6 Truffle Supply and Demand

* open log file
log using chap11_truffles, replace text

* open data
use truffles, clear

* examine data
describe
list in 1/5
summarize
```

```
* reduced form equations
reg q ps di pf
reg p ps di pf
predict phat

* 2sls of demand
reg q phat ps di

* IV/2sls of demand equation
ivregress 2sls  q (p=pf) ps di
ivregress 2sls  q (p=pf) ps di, small
ivregress 2sls  q (p=pf) ps di, small first
estat firststage

* 2sls of supply using least squares
reg q phat pf

* IV/2sls of supply equation
ivregress 2sls q (p=ps di) pf, small first
estat firststage

********* 2sls using REG3
********* This is not discussed in the chapter.
********* Enter help reg3

reg3 (q p ps di) (q p pf), endog(q p) 2sls
log close

********** Chapter 11.7 Fulton Fish Market

* open log
log using chap11_fish, replace text

* open data
use fultonfish, clear

* examine data
describe
list lquan lprice mon tue wed thu stormy in 1/5
summarize lquan lprice mon tue wed thu stormy

* estimate reduced forms
reg lquan mon tue wed thu stormy
reg lprice mon tue wed thu stormy
test mon tue wed thu

* IV/2sls
ivregress 2sls lquan (lprice=stormy) mon tue wed thu, small first
estat firststage

log close

********** Chapter 11B.2.3a

log using chap11_liml, replace text
use mroz, clear
drop if lfp==0
gen lwage=ln(wage)
gen nwifeinc =  (faminc-wage*hours)/1000
gen exper2 = exper^2

* B=1, L=1
```

```
ivregress liml hours (mtr = exper) educ kids16 nwifeinc, small
estat firststage
estimates store m11

* B=1, L=2
ivregress liml hours (mtr =  exper exper2) educ kids16 nwifeinc, small
estat firststage
estimates store m12

*********** View LIML as IV estimator

* save liml k-value
scalar kvalue=e(kappa)

* reduced form residuals
reg mtr exper exper2 educ kids16 nwifeinc
predict vhat, r

* create purged endogenous variable
gen emtr = mtr - kvalue*vhat

* apply 2sls with IV = purged endogenous variable
ivregress 2sls hours (mtr = emtr) educ kids16 nwifeinc, small

* B=1, L=3
ivregress liml hours (mtr = exper exper2 largecity) educ kids16 nwifeinc, small
estat firststage
estimates store m13

* B=1, L=4
ivregress liml hours (mtr = exper exper2 largecity unemployment) educ kids16  nwifeinc,
small
estat firststage
estimates store m14

* B=2, L=2
ivregress liml hours (mtr educ =  mothereduc fathereduc) kids16 nwifeinc, small
estat firststage
estimates store m22

* B=2, L=3
ivregress liml hours (mtr educ =  mothereduc fathereduc exper) kids16 nwifeinc, small
estat firststage
estimates store m23

* B=2, L=4
ivregress liml hours (mtr educ =  mothe reduc fathereduc exper exper2) kids16  nwifeinc,
small
estat firststage
estimates store m24

********** Table 11B.3

esttab m11 m13 m22 m23, t(%12.2f) b(%12.4f) nostar ///
        gaps scalars(kappa) title("LIML estimations")
log close

********** Chapter 11B.2.3b Fuller modified LIML
********** Estimation using IVREG2 a user written command
********** In the command line type FINDIT IVREG2 and click to install
********** You must have administrative power to install

* open log file
```

```
log using chap11_fuller, text replace

* open data
use mroz, clear
drop if lfp==0
gen lwage=ln(wage)
gen nwifeinc = (faminc-wage*hours)/1000
gen exper2 = exper^2

* B=1, L=1
ivreg2 hours (mtr = exper) educ kids16 nwifeinc, fuller(1) small
estimates store m11

* B=1, L=2
ivreg2 hours (mtr = exper exper2) educ kids16 nwifeinc, fuller(1) small
estimates store m12

* B=1, L=3
ivreg2 hours (mtr = exper exper2 largecity) educ kids16 nwifeinc, ///
        fuller(1) small
estimates store m13

* B=1, L=4
ivreg2 hours (mtr = exper exper2 largecity unemployment) educ kids16 nwifeinc, ///
        fuller(1) small
estimates store m14

* B=2, L=2
ivreg2 hours (mtr educ = mothereduc fathereduc) kids16 nwifeinc, ///
        fuller(1) small
estimates store m22

* B=2, L=3
ivreg2 hours (mtr educ =  mothereduc fathereduc exper) kids16 nwifeinc, ///
        fuller(1) small
estimates store m23

* B=2, L=4
ivreg2 hours (mtr educ =  mothereduc fathereduc exper exper2) kids16 ///
        nwifeinc, fuller(1) small
estimates store m24

esttab  m11 m13 m22 m23, t(%12.2f) b(%12.4f) nostar ///
        gaps scalars(kclass fuller widstat) title("fuller(1) estimations")
log close

********** Chapter 11B.3 Monte Carlo simulation

* open log
log using chap11_sim, replace text

* clear memory
clear all
set more off

* set experiment parameters
global numobs 100
global pi      0.5                      // reduced form parameter controls IV strength
global rho     0.8                      // rho controls endogeneity

set seed 1234567                        // random number seed
set obs $numobs
```

```
* draw correlated e and v
matrix sig = (1, $rho \ $rho, 1)                  // corr(e1,v2)
drawnorm e v, n($numobs) corr(sig)                // e1 & v2 values

* draw 3 uncorrelated standard normals
generate z1 = rnormal()
generate z2 = rnormal()
generate z3 = rnormal()

* DGP
generate x = $pi*z1 + $pi*z2 + $pi*z3 + v         // reduced form
generate y = x + e

* correlation between x and e
correlate x e

* reduced form regression
regress x z1 z2       z3

* OLS
regress y x

* 2sls

ivregress 2sls y (x=z1 z2 z3), small

* liml
ivregress liml y (x=z1 z2 z3), small

* fuller(1)
ivreg2 y (x=z1 z2 z3), small fuller(1)

* fuller(4)
ivreg2 y (x=z1 z2 z3), small fuller(4)

* program to carry out simulation

program ch11sim, rclass
        version 11.1
        drop _all

        set obs $numobs
        matrix sig = (1, $rho \ $rho, 1)                  // cov(e1,v2)
        drawnorm e v, n($numobs) corr(sig)     // e1 & v2 values

        generate z1 = rnormal()
        generate z2 = rnormal()
        generate z3 = rnormal()

        * DGP
        generate x = $pi*z1 + $pi*z2 + $pi*z3 + v
        generate y = x + e

        * 2sls
        ivregress 2sls y (x=z1 z2 z3), small
        return scalar b2sls =_b[x]
        return scalar se2sls = _se[x]
        return scalar t2sls = (_b[x]-1)/_se[x]
        return scalar r2sls = abs(return(t2sls))>invttail($numobs-2,.025)

        * liml
        ivregress liml y (x=z1 z2 z3), small
        return scalar bliml =_b[x]
```

```
      return scalar seliml = _se[x]
      return scalar tliml = (_b[x]-1)/_se[x]
      return scalar rliml = abs(return(tliml))>invttail($numobs-2,.025)

      * fuller a=1
      ivreg2 y (x=z1 z2 z3), small fuller(1)
      return scalar bfull =_b[x]
      return scalar sefull = _se[x]
      return scalar tfull = (_b[x]-1)/_se[x]
      return scalar rfull = abs(return(tfull))>invttail($numobs-2,.025)

      * fuller a=4
      ivreg2 y (x=z1 z2 z3), small fuller(4)
      return scalar bfull4 =_b[x]
      return scalar sefull4 = _se[x]
      return scalar tfull4 = (_b[x]-1)/_se[x]
      return scalar rfull4 = abs(return(tfull4))>invttail($numobs-2,.025)
end

simulate b2slsr=r(b2sls) se2slsr=r(se2sls) t2slsr=r(t2sls) ///
      r2slsr=r(r2sls) blimlr=r(bliml) selimlr=r(seliml) ///
      tlimlr=r(tliml) rlimlr=r(rliml) bfullr=r(bfull) ///
      sefullr=r(sefull) tfullr=r(tfull) rfullr=r(rfull) ///
      bfull4r=r(bfull4) sefull4r=r(sefull4) tfull4r=r(tfull4) ///
      rfull4r=r(rfull4), reps(10000) nodots nolegend ///
      seed(1234567): ch11sim

di " Simulation parameters"
di "  rho = " $rho
di "  N = " $numobs
di "  pi = "  $pi

* For each estimator compute
* avg and standard deviation estimate beta
* avg nominal standard error
* avg percent rejection 5% test

di " 2sls"
gen mse2sls = (b2slsr-1)^2
tabstat b2slsr se2slsr r2slsr mse2sls, stat(mean sd)

di " liml"
gen mseliml = (blimlr-1)^2
tabstat blimlr selimlr rlimlr mseliml, stat(mean sd)

di " fuller(1)"
gen msefull = (bfullr-1)^2
tabstat bfullr sefullr rfullr msefull, stat(mean sd)

di " fuller(4)"
gen msefull4 = (bfull4r-1)^2
tabstat bfull4r sefull4r rfull4r msefull4, stat(mean sd)

log close
```

CHAPTER **12**

Regression with Time-Series Data: Nonstationary Variables

CHAPTER OUTLINE

12.1 Stationary and nonstationary data

    12.1.1 Review: generating dates in Stata

    12.1.2 Extracting dates

    12.1.3 Graphing the data

12.2 Spurious regressions

12.3 Unit root tests for stationarity

12.4 Integration and cointegration

    12.4.1 Engle-Granger test

    12.4.2 Error-correction model

Key Terms

Chapter 12 Do-file

12.1 STATIONARY AND NONSTATIONARY DATA

The main purpose of this chapter is to show you how to use Stata to explore the time series properties of your data. One of the fundamental principles in econometrics is that the statistical properties of estimators, and consequently their usefulness for research, depend on how the data behave. For instance, in a linear regression model where errors are correlated with regressors, the least squares estimator is no longer consistent and it should not be used for either estimation or subsequent testing.

In time series regressions the data need to be stationary in order for the usual econometric procedures to have the proper statistical properties. Basically this requires that the means, variances and covariances of the time series data cannot depend on the time period in which they are observed. For instance, the mean and variance of GDP in the third quarter of 1973 cannot be different from those of the 4th quarter of 2006. Methods to deal with this problem have provided a rich field of research for econometricians in recent years and several of these techniques are explored here.

One of the first diagnostic tools used is a simple time series plot of the data. A time series plot will reveal potential problems with the data and suggest ways to proceed statistically. As we've seen in earlier chapters time series plots are simple to generate in Stata and a few new tricks will be explored below.

The first thing to do is to change the directory to the one containing the data and load it into memory. In this exercise we'll be using the *usa.dta* data.

```
cd c:\data\poe4stata
use usa, clear
```

This dataset includes four variables (**gdp**, **inf**, **f**, and **b**) but no time variables. In order to use Stata's built in time series functions we'll have to create a time variable and then declare the data to be time series using **tsset**. To make the graphs more meaningful, go the extra mile to create a set of dates to match those from the actual dataset. The definition files distributed with the data indicate that the data are quarterly, begin in the first quarter of 1984 (1984q1), and end in the third quarter of 2009 (2009q3). A more complete discussion of generating proper dates in Stata was given in Chapter 9 and it is suggested that you review that material now if you have not done so already.

12.1.1 Review: Generating Dates in Stata

Essentially, the first thing to do is to enter a series of integers that mark the desired dates. Recall from Chapter 9 that Stata records the passage of time as the number of time units that pass from the baseline date (1960). Therefore, date creation must include a function to indicate the time unit and the starting date. Thus, **q(1984q1)** means that the increment is quarterly (and that the series of integers starts in the first quarter of 1984. To verify this, type

```
display q(1984q1)
```

which reveals

```
. di q(1984q1)
96
```

This tells one that the 1ˢᵗ quarter of 1984 is 96 quarters beyond 1960q1. To increment the numbers by rows of the data set add **_n-1** to this number. **_n** is Stata's method of identifying the observation number. So at observation number 1 this is equal to zero. The first observation is 1984q1 which is equal to 96. For observation number 2 (**_n=2**), and date will be equal to 97, and so on. This variable is written to date using the **generate** command.

```
gen date = q(1984q1) + _n - 1
```

Next, the format command is used to convert the integers into strings using the display format **%tq**. That is, 96 is displayed as 1984q1 to make it easier for someone to identify what the date actually is. Finally, the new variable is declared to be a time-series using the **tsset** command.

```
format %tq date
tsset date
```

12.1.2 Extracting Dates

There are situations where having separate year and quarter variables can be useful. Once the time series have been generated, formatted, and declared this is very simple to do. To extract the quarter and year information contained in the usa.dta requires a couple of steps. First, the date needs to be given a new format. In our case, the **%tq** formatted dates need to be changed into the **%td** format. The **%td** format is the mother format in Stata and this is the only one from which month, day, year etc can be extracted from the date information. The function to convert **%tq** quarterly data to **%td** format is **dofq()**. This reads as "daily of quarterly". The argument must contain the dates in quarterly format. Once the format has been changed, then the year and quarter can be extracted using very clear syntax as shown below.

```
gen newdate = dofq(newdate)
gen y = year(newdate)
gen q = quarter(newdate)
```

To convert **%tm** to **%td**, use **dofm()**. For others type **help dates** at the **Command** window and see the sections on *Converting and Extracting date and time values*.

With the date information correctly in the dataset, it's a good idea to save your data. This puts the new date information into the dataset permanently, saving you the trouble of manually typing it in each time you want to use it. Either **File > Save** or keyboard command **Ctrl+S** will save the current information into *usa.dta*.

12.1.3 Graphing the Data

Use the **graph** command to graph the **gdp** series. The complete syntax to graph time-series is

```
graph twoway (tsline gdp)
```

The first argument is **twoway** followed by **tsline** (which stands for time series line) and it can be used instead of the variable date to measure the time dimension of the variable **gdp** on the x-axis. To graph the first differences, use Stata's built in difference operator, **D.** (or **D1**). Like the lag operator **L** the difference operator is used as a prefix and will difference the data very easily. It can be used either in generate statement or directly in all of Stata's the time series commands. For more information on other time series operators, search for **tsvarlist** in the online help or in the viewer.

This can be abbreviated to

```
tsline gdp
```

foregoing the **graph twoway** altogether. This is the convention we will follow below.

A graph of the differenced series is obtained using

```
tsline D.gdp
```

An easy way to combine graph is name them using the **name(*graph_name*)** option as done below. Graphs of **gdp** and its differences are created, given names, and then combined using the **graph combine** command. The Stata code is

```
qui tsline gdp, name(gdp, replace)
qui tsline D.gdp, name(dgdp, replace)
graph combine gdp dgdp
```

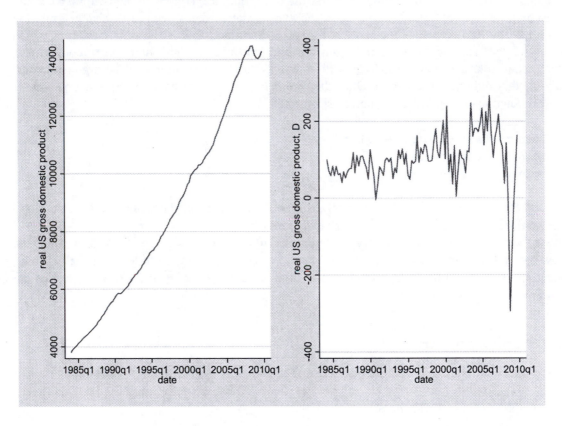

The panel on the left is the level of U.S. GDP and the quarterly change is on the right. To remove graphs from memory that were created and named, issue the **graph drop** *graph_name* command.

If you want to save the graph, then use the **saving(***graph_name***)** option. This can be handy if you want to save the graphs to paste into another program. To erase graphs that have been created and saved using the **saving(***graph_name***)** option, use Stata's **shell** command to gain direct access to the command line for your operating system. My current system is operated by Microsoft's Windows XP. Using **shell** opens a Windows XP command window. From there standard operating system commands can be issued for the computer.

Next, a set of graphs for the inflation rate, the Fed funds rate, and the 3-year bond rate are combined along-side their changes.

```
qui tsline inf, name(inf, replace)
qui tsline D.inf, name(dinf, replace) yline(0)
qui tsline f, name(f, replace)
qui tsline D.f, name(df, replace) yline(0)
qui tsline b, name(b, replace)
qui tsline D.b, name(db, replace) yline(0)

graph combine inf dinf f df b db, cols(2)
```

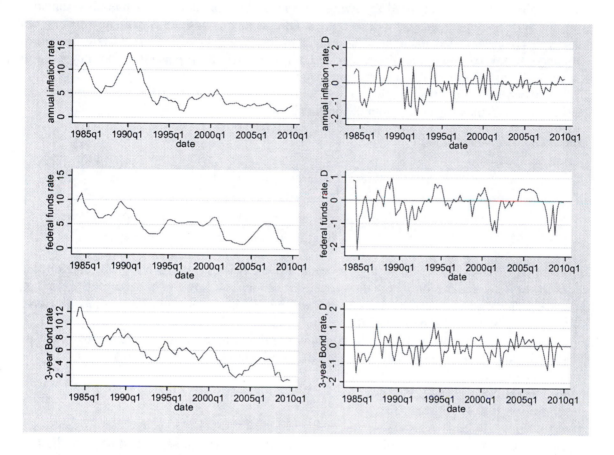

Horizontal lines were placed at zero using the `yline(0)` option for each of the series measured in changes. This is useful so that negative and positive values can easily be identified. Also, the `graph combine` command employs the `cols(2)` option so that the graphs for each series and difference appear side-by-side.

Next, create a set of summary statistics. In this case, *Principles of Econometrics, 4th Edition (POE4)* has you produce summary statistics for subsamples of the data. The first subsample consists of the 52 observations from 1984q1 to 1996q4. The second contains 52 observations and continues from 1996q4 to 2009q4. The `summarize` command is used to obtain the summary statistics using the conditional `if` statement. The trick will be to condition the subsample to the desired period.

There are a couple of ways to do this. First, we could limit the sample dates using a standard `if` statement. The subsample starts at the beginning of the dataset and ends at 1996q4. The syntax is

```
summarize if date<=q(1996q4)
```

This summarizes all the data up to and including 1996q4. The dates are stored in the variable **date**, `q(1996q4)` tells Stata that the date is quarterly using `q()`, and that the relevant date is 1996q4. The `<=` operator is mathematically equivalent to "less than or equal to". The second subsample starts in the first quarter of 1997 and extends to the end of the data set. The syntax is

```
summarize if date>=q(1997q1)
```

If the variable names are not listed following the **summarize** command, then summary statistics for all the variables in the data set will be printed. Of course, this will not contain any differences unless you have generated them first and put them into the data set using separate **generate** commands. In this example, the differences had not previously been generated and they have to be specifically listed after the summarize command.

The other way to limit the sample is to use the built-in **tin()** function, but this only works for time-series. The syntax for **tin()** from the on-line help is

```
Time-series function

    tin(d1, d2)
        Domain d1:    data or time literals recorded in units of t previously tsset
        Domain d2:    data or time literals recorded in units of t previously tsset
        Range:        0 and 1, 1 means true
        Description:  true if d1 ≤ t ≤ d2, where t is the time variable previously tsset.

                      You must have previously tsset the data to use tin(). When you tsset
                      the data, you specify a time variable t, and the format on t states how
                      it is recorded. You type d1 and d2 according to that format.
```

The name "tin" reads "t in" which suggests what it does. It is essentially a logical function that checks to see if an observation within the specified time window between its arguments **d1** and **d2** (inclusive). The arguments can be dates or integers, but in either case the data set must be **tsset** as a time series in order for this function to work.

If you want the sample to start at the beginning of the sample, simply leave the argument **d1** blank. To include observations to the end, omit **d2**. Here is the syntax using **tin()**:

```
summarize if tin(,1996q4)
summarize if tin(1997q1,)
```

To actually replicate the numbers in Table 12.1 of *POE4*, **d1** has to be specified because the first observation is dropped. The first observation used in the computation of the table is from 1984q2 so the command

```
summarize gdp inf b f D.gdp D.inf D.b D.f if tin(1984q2,1996q4)
```

The result for the first subsample is

Variable	Obs	Mean	Std. Dev.	Min	Max
gdp	51	5813.02	1204.604	3906.3	8023
inf	51	6.903725	3.337811	1.28	13.55
b	51	7.343137	1.939775	4.32	12.64
f	51	6.417255	2.130539	2.99	11.39
gdp D1.	51	82.65882	29.33348	-4.6	161.8
inf D1.	51	-.1605882	.8320058	-1.8	1.43
b D1.	51	-.1029412	.6312822	-1.54	1.45
f D1.	51	-.0864706	.5860711	-2.12	.97

and for the second

```
. summarize gdp inf b f D.gdp D.inf D.b D.f if tin(1997q1,)
```

Variable	Obs	Mean	Std. Dev.	Min	Max
gdp	52	11458.19	2052.135	8137	14484.9
inf	52	3.219423	1.116619	1.45	6.04
b	52	3.977115	1.564322	1.27	6.56
f	52	3.4875	2.025269	.12	6.52
gdp D1.	52	120.275	92.91987	-293.7	267.9
inf D1.	52	.0251923	.4617422	-.93	1.52
b D1.	52	-.0875	.4788502	-1.33	.81
f D1.	52	-.0992308	.5142893	-1.43	.59

These match the results from Table 12.1.

12.2 SPURIOUS REGRESSIONS

It is possible to estimate a regression and find a statistically significant relationship even if none exists. In time series analysis this is actually a common occurrence when data are not stationary. This example uses two data series, *rw1* and *rw2*, that were generated as independent random walks.

$$rw_1: \ y_t = y_{t-1} + v_{1t}$$

$$rw_2: \ x_t = x_{t-1} + v_{2t}$$

The errors are independent standard normal random deviates generated using a pseudo-random number generator. As you can see, x_t and y_t are not related in any way. To explore the empirical relationship between these unrelated series, load the *spurious.dta* data, create a time variable, and declare the data to be time series.

```
use spurious, clear
gen time = _n
tsset time
```

Since the data are artificial, there is no need to take the time to create actual dates. In this case a simple period counter is sufficient and one is created that is equal to the observation number using _n. This simple way to create a time variable can be used for any series that is recorded at regular intervals (i.e., the elapsed time between observations is equal).

The first thing to do is to plot the data using a time series plot. Simply use

```
tsline rw1 rw2, name(g1, replace)
```

to produce the following plot:

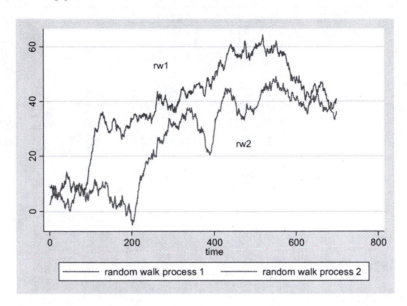

A scatter plot reveals a potentially spurious relationship between the variables:

```
scatter rw1 rw2, name(g2, replace)
```

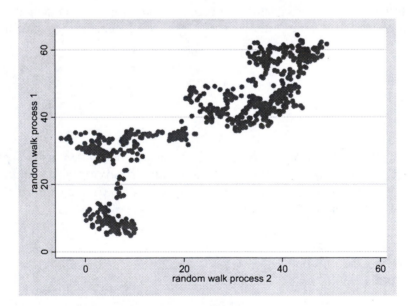

The **name( )** option is not necessary, but convenient when running these commands in a batch file. This gives each graph a name and will open all of them in separate windows.

A linear regression confirms the *appearance of a linear relationship* between these two unrelated time series.

```
regress rw1 rw2
```

yields the result

```
. regress rw1 rw2
```

Source	SS	df	MS
Model	122116.557	1	122116.557
Residual	51112.3314	698	73.2268359
Total	173228.888	699	247.823874

```
Number of obs =      700
F(  1,   698) = 1667.65
Prob > F      =   0.0000
R-squared     =   0.7049
Adj R-squared =   0.7045
Root MSE      =   8.5573
```

rw1	Coef.	Std. Err.	t	P>|t|	[95% Conf. Interval]	
rw2	.8420412	.0206196	40.84	0.000	.8015572	.8825251
_cons	17.81804	.6204776	28.72	0.000	16.59981	19.03627

The coefficient on *rw2* is positive (.842) and significant ($t = 40.84 > 1.96$). However, these variables are actually **not** related! The observed relationship is purely *spurious*. The cause of the spurious result is the nonstationarity of the two series. This is why you must check your data for stationarity whenever you use time series in a regression.

A quick check of the residuals for the possibility of autocorrelation can be done using the LM test (see Chapter 9).

```
. estat bgodfrey
```

Breusch-Godfrey LM test for autocorrelation

lags(p)	chi2	df	Prob > chi2
1	682.958	1	0.0000

H0: no serial correlation

The *p*-value is very, very small and is evidence of misspecification in the model. Further investigation is warranted.

12.3 UNIT ROOT TESTS FOR STATIONARITY

The (augmented) **Dickey-Fuller tests** can be used to test for the stationarity of your data. To perform this test, a few decisions have to be made regarding the time series. Sometimes these choices can be made based on visual inspection of the time series plots. By inspecting the plots you try to determine whether the time series have a nonzero mean or if they have a linear or quadratic trend. If the trend in the series is quadratic then the differenced version of the series will have a linear trend in them. In the graphs of the Fed Funds rate above you can see that **F** appears to be trending downward and its difference (**D.f**) appears to wander around some constant amount. Bonds behave similarly. This suggests that the **Augmented Dickey-Fuller** (ADF) test regressions for each of the series should contain a constant, but not a time trend.

The GDP series in appears to be slightly quadratic in time. The differenced version of the series that appears below it has a slight upward drift and hence you would choose an ADF test that included a constant and a time trend. As you can tell, judgment is required and there is something of an art to using it wisely. Our goal is to reduce some of the uncertainty using formal tests whenever we can, but realize that choosing the appropriate test specification requires some judgment by the econometrician.

The next decision is to pick the number of lags to include in the ADF regressions. Again, this is a judgment call, but the residuals from the ADF regression should not be autocorrelated; include enough lagged differences in the model to ensure that the residuals are white noise.

In this section two ways to estimate the Dickey-Fuller tests for stationarity will be explored. One is manual. In this case you estimate an appropriate model using least squares, find the t-ratio for the test, and compare it to tabled values in your text. Recall, the t-ratio on lagged value of your series does not have a t-distribution. The correct distribution is complex and we have to rely on established tables or simulation to get the right critical values for testing.

The second method uses one of Stata's built-in functions. The advantage here is that Stata generates the correct critical values for the test and you won't have to refer to an external source (i.e., a table) to get them. Stata also provides you with an approximate p-value.

First, here is the basic taxonomy of the Dickey-Fuller regressions

Series Characteristics	Regression Model
No Constant and No Trend	$\Delta y_t = \gamma y_{t-1} + v_t$
Constant, but No Trend	$\Delta y_t = \alpha + \gamma y_{t-1} + v_t$
Constant and Trend	$\Delta y_t = \alpha + \gamma y_{t-1} + \lambda t + v_t$

In each case, the null and alternative hypotheses are $H_0 : \gamma = 0$ and $H_1 : \gamma < 0$. Basically, the regressions are estimated, the t-ratio on γ computed, and compared to the tabled critical value in the text or, better yet, to the one provided by Stata.

The augmented version of the Dickey-Fuller test adds lagged differences to the model. For the model with a constant and no trend this would be:

$$\Delta y_t = \alpha + \gamma y_{t-1} + \sum_{s=1}^{m} a_s \Delta y_{t-s} + v_t$$

You have to pick the number of lags to include. Essentially, one should include just enough lags of Δy_{t-s} to ensure that the residuals uncorrelated. An example of this appears later in this manual.

The number of lagged terms can also be determined by examining the autocorrelation function (ACF) of the residuals v_t , or the significance of the estimated lag coefficients a_s .

In the example, the Federal Funds rate (**f**) and the 3-year Bond rate (**b**) are considered. The series plots show that the data wander about, indicating that they may be nonstationary. To perform the Dickey-Fuller tests, first decide whether to use a constant and/or a trend. Since the series fluctuates around a nonzero mean we include a constant. There doesn't appear to be a linear or quadratic trend so we adopt the constant, no trend formulation. Then decide on how many lagged difference terms to include on the right-hand side of the equation. Using the model selection rules described in Chapter 9, we find that the inclusion of one lagged difference term is sufficient to eliminate autocorrelation in the residuals in both cases.

Reload the *usa.dta* data, clearing any previous data held in Stata's memory.

```
use usa, clear
```

If the *usa.dta* data were not saved after creating the time variables and declaring the data in the first example, then recreate the **date** variable now

```
use usa, clear
gen date = q(1984q1) + _n - 1
format %tq date
tsset date
```

The regressions in Stata are

```
regress D.f L.f L.D.f
regress D.b L.b L.D.b
```

The difference operator is used to create the changes in **f** and **b** on the left-hand side of the equation. The lag operator **L.** operator is used to obtain the first lagged level of **f** and **b**. The last variable uses both operators, **L.D.f** and **L.D.b**. The linearity of these operators allows them to be combined and used in any order (commutative). So, **L.D.f** takes the lagged value of **D.f**, which in turn is the first differenced value of **f**. The commutative property also means that we can reverse the order using **D.L.f** and get the same result.

```
. regress D.f L.f L.D.f
```

Source	SS	df	MS		Number of obs	=	102
					F(2, 99)	=	25.45
Model	10.0957158	2	5.0478579		Prob > F	=	0.0000
Residual	19.6353195	99	.198336561		R-squared	=	0.3396
					Adj R-squared	=	0.3262
Total	29.7310353	101	.294366686		Root MSE	=	.44535

D.f	Coef.	Std. Err.	t	P>|t|	[95% Conf. Interval]	
f						
L1.	-.0446213	.0178142	-2.50	0.014	-.0799685	-.0092741
LD.	.5610582	.0809827	6.93	0.000	.4003708	.7217455
_cons	.1725221	.1002333	1.72	0.088	-.0263625	.3714067

```
. regress D.b L.b L.D.b
```

Source	SS	df	MS		Number of obs	=	102
					F(2, 99)	=	8.32
Model	4.20542707	2	2.10271354		Prob > F	=	0.0005
Residual	25.0098641	99	.25262489		R-squared	=	0.1439
					Adj R-squared	=	0.1267
Total	29.2152912	101	.289260309		Root MSE	=	.50262

D.b	Coef.	Std. Err.	t	P>|t|	[95% Conf. Interval]	
b						
L1.	-.0562412	.0208081	-2.70	0.008	-.097529	-.0149534
LD.	.2903078	.0896069	3.24	0.002	.1125084	.4681072
_cons	.236873	.1291731	1.83	0.070	-.0194345	.4931804

The *t*-ratios on the lagged values of **f** and **b** are circled in the figure above. These are the relevant values for conducting the Dickey-Fuller test.

The lag operators also support *numlist* and this can shorten the syntax further.

```
reg L(0/1).D.f L.f
```

```
reg L(0/1).D.b L.b
```

In this case **regress** is abbreviated as **reg** and **L(0/1).D.f** replaces **D.f L.D.f**. The latter does not actually save any characters in this instance, but would if more lags of the difference in **f** were added to the model. As shown below, it is also useful for using loops for model lag selection.

Stata has built-in commands to do Dickey-Fuller regressions. The command is **dfuller** and the syntax from the online help is

<u>Syntax</u>
```
        dfuller varname [if] [in] [, options]

    options          description
    ─────────────────────────────────────────────────────────
    Main
      noconstant     suppress constant term in regression
      trend          include trend term in regression
      drift          include drift term in regression
      regress        display regression table
      lags(#)        include # lagged differences
    ─────────────────────────────────────────────────────────
    You must tsset your data before using dfuller; see [TS] tsset.
    varname may contain time-series operators; see tsvarlist.
```

For options you can choose whether to include a constant, a trend, drift (trend squared) and specify the number of lags. If you use the **regress** option, then the complete regression results will be printed. For the sake of comparison, we'll use this option below:

```
dfuller f, regress lags(1)
```

produces the Dickey-Fuller test statistic, critical values, and the regression results when the **regress** option is used. The approximate *p*-value for the test is given as well, making the test quite easy to carry out. In this case, the *p*-value is greater than 0.10 and the unit root null hypothesis cannot be rejected at that level of significance.

```
. dfuller f, regress lags(1)

Augmented Dickey-Fuller test for unit root        Number of obs   =       102
```

	Test Statistic	1% Critical Value	5% Critical Value	10% Critical Value
		—— Interpolated Dickey-Fuller ——		
Z(t)	-2.505	-3.509	-2.890	-2.580

MacKinnon approximate p-value for Z(t) = 0.1143

D.f	Coef.	Std. Err.	t	P>|t|	[95% Conf. Interval]
f					
L1.	-.0446213	.0178142	-2.50	0.014	-.0799685 -.0092741
LD.	.5610582	.0809827	6.93	0.000	.4003708 .7217455
_cons	.1725221	.1002333	1.72	0.088	-.0263625 .3714067

The test for the bond yield series is

```
. dfuller b, regress lags(1)
```

Augmented Dickey-Fuller test for unit root   Number of obs   =   102

	Test Statistic	Interpolated Dickey-Fuller		
		1% Critical Value	5% Critical Value	10% Critical Value
z(t)	-2.703	-3.509	-2.890	-2.580

MacKinnon approximate p-value for Z(t) = 0.0735

D.b	Coef.	Std. Err.	t	P>|t|	[95% Conf. Interval]	
b						
L1.	-.0562412	.0208081	-2.70	0.008	-.097529	-.0149534
LD.	.2903078	.0896069	3.24	0.002	.1125084	.4681072
_cons	.236873	.1291731	1.83	0.070	-.0194345	.4931804

The approximate *p*-value for this test is greater than 5% and the nonstationary null hypothesis is not rejected at that level.

Notice that the Dickey-Fuller statistic is given (called **z(t)**) and that the 1%, 5%, and 10% critical values for the test are given in the accompanying table. These numbers differ a little from the ones in your text, probably due to the interpolation that Stata does for you. In any event, the test statistics do not fall within the rejection region and we conclude that the levels of the data are nonstationary, at least at the 5% level of significance.

The Dickey-Fuller tests are repeated for the differenced series. The differenced series contain neither a trend nor a constant. No lags are needed so the code becomes:

> **dfuller D.f, noconstant lags(0)**
> **dfuller D.b, noconstant lags(0)**

The regression results are omitted this time and we obtain

```
. dfuller D.f, noconstant lags(0)
```

Dickey-Fuller test for unit root   Number of obs   =   102

	Test Statistic	Interpolated Dickey-Fuller		
		1% Critical Value	5% Critical Value	10% Critical Value
z(t)	-5.487	-2.600	-1.950	-1.610

```
. dfuller D.b, noconstant lags(0)
```

Dickey-Fuller test for unit root   Number of obs   =   102

	Test Statistic	Interpolated Dickey-Fuller		
		1% Critical Value	5% Critical Value	10% Critical Value
z(t)	-7.662	-2.600	-1.950	-1.610

In this case, we reject the nonstationary null hypothesis and conclude that both series are stationary in their differences (Integrated of order 1, i.e., I(1)).

The dialog boxes for the Dickey-Fuller test are found be selecting **Statistics > Time series > Tests > Augmented Dickey-Fuller unit root tests**. This brings up the following dialog box

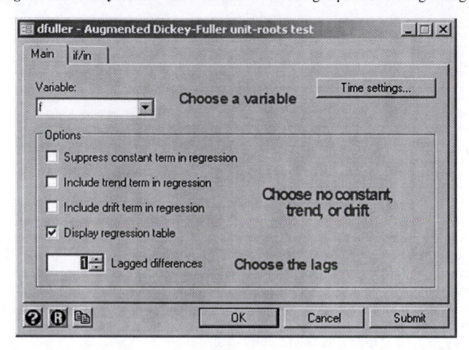

Once again, the **dfuller** dialog simply generates the commands discussed above. Choose the variable you wish to test, select **noconstant**, **trend**, or **drift** from the list of options, and choose the number of lags with which to augment the Dickey-Fuller regression. You can also check the box to display the regression results as done here.

There are other tests for nonstationarity in Stata that you may find useful. The first is the DF-GLS test. **dfgls** tests for a unit root in a time series. It performs the modified Dickey–Fuller t test (known as the DF-GLS test) proposed by Elliott, Rothenberg, and Stock (1996). Essentially, the test is an augmented Dickey–Fuller test, similar to the test performed by Stata's **dfuller** command, except that the time series is transformed via a generalized least squares (GLS) regression before performing the test. Elliott, Rothenberg, and Stock and later studies have shown that this test has significantly greater power than the previous versions of the augmented Dickey–Fuller test. Consequently, it is not unusual for this test to reject the null of nonstationarity when the usual augmented Dickey-Fuller test does not.

dfgls performs the DF-GLS test for the series of models that include 1 to k lags of the first differenced, detrended variable, where k can be set by the user or by the method described in Schwert (1989). As discussed above and in *POE4*, the augmented Dickey–Fuller test involves fitting a regression of the form

$$\Delta y_t = \alpha + \beta y_{t-1} + \delta t + \zeta_1 \Delta y_{t-1} + \ldots + \zeta_k \Delta y_{t-k} + u_t$$

and then testing the null hypothesis Ho: $\beta = 0$. The DF-GLS test is performed analogously but on GLS-detrended data. The null hypothesis of the test is that y_t is a random walk, possibly with drift. There are two possible alternative hypotheses: y_t is stationary about a linear time trend or y_t is stationary with a possibly nonzero mean but with no linear time trend. The default is to use the former. To specify the latter alternative, use the **notrend** option.

For the levels of the Fed funds and 3-year bond rates:

```
dfgls f
dfgls b
```

The results are:

```
. dfgls f
```

DF-GLS for f   Number of obs =   91
Maxlag = 12 chosen by Schwert criterion

[lags]	DF-GLS tau Test Statistic	1% Critical Value	5% Critical Value	10% Critical Value
12	-3.035	-3.575	-2.753	-2.479
11	-3.025	-3.575	-2.783	-2.508
10	-2.905	-3.575	-2.813	-2.537
9	-3.107	-3.575	-2.842	-2.565
8	-3.097	-3.575	-2.870	-2.591
7	-3.602	-3.575	-2.898	-2.617
6	-3.732	-3.575	-2.924	-2.641
5	-3.436	-3.575	-2.949	-2.664
4	-3.290	-3.575	-2.972	-2.686
3	-3.793	-3.575	-2.994	-2.706
2	-3.499	-3.575	-3.014	-2.723
1	-3.278	-3.575	-3.031	-2.739

```
Opt Lag (Ng-Perron seq t) =  1 with RMSE  .3535111
Min SC   = -1.980541 at lag  1 with RMSE  .3535111
Min MAIC = -1.808821 at lag  1 with RMSE  .3535111
```

```
. dfgls b
```

DF-GLS for b   Number of obs =   91
Maxlag = 12 chosen by Schwert criterion

[lags]	DF-GLS tau Test Statistic	1% Critical Value	5% Critical Value	10% Critical Value
12	-2.556	-3.575	-2.753	-2.479
11	-2.571	-3.575	-2.783	-2.508
10	-2.265	-3.575	-2.813	-2.537
9	-2.787	-3.575	-2.842	-2.565
8	-3.270	-3.575	-2.870	-2.591
7	-2.896	-3.575	-2.898	-2.617
6	-3.185	-3.575	-2.924	-2.641
5	-3.206	-3.575	-2.949	-2.664
4	-2.995	-3.575	-2.972	-2.686
3	-3.392	-3.575	-2.994	-2.706
2	-2.924	-3.575	-3.014	-2.723
1	-3.095	-3.575	-3.031	-2.739

```
Opt Lag (Ng-Perron seq t) =  3 with RMSE  .4644163
Min SC   = -1.371452 at lag  1 with RMSE  .4793635
Min MAIC = -1.216796 at lag  1 with RMSE  .4793635
```

One of the benefits of using **dfgls** is readily obvious. The Schwert criterion sets a maximum lag length of 12 and models are searched from lags 1 to 12. The model that minimizes SC, the MAIC, and the Ng-Perron statistic are given. For **f**, the lag selection is unambiguously equal to 1 and the nonstationarity hypothesis is rejected at the 5% level. For **b**, two of the criteria choose lags of 1 and these are significant at 5% as well.

The greater efficiency of the GLS estimator has led to a set of ambiguous results. The levels of the series may actually be stationary. One more test is sometimes recommended. The Phillips-Perron (1988) test also has the null hypothesis that the time-series is non-stationary against the alternative that it is stationary. **pperron** uses Newey–West standard errors discussed in Chapter 9 to account for serial correlation, whereas the augmented Dickey–Fuller test implemented in **dfuller** uses additional lags of the first-differenced variable. The advantage of this test is that one does not need to consider a model selection process to help decide how to augment the regression. Consequently, the **regress** option can be used to print the regression results. The disadvantage is that the results depend on the choice of bandwidth. Unlike the **newey** procedure discussed in Chapter 9, the **pperron** test automatically will choose one of the choices suggested there, namely $4(T/100)^{2/9}$. You have the option to add a trend or to remove the constant. In this example, a trend is included since the time-series graphs show a downward trend.

For the levels of the two time series we have

```
pperron b, regress trend
pperron f, regress trend
```

The results

```
. pperron f, regress trend
```

Phillips-Perron test for unit root

```
                                              Number of obs   =        103
                                              Newey-West lags =          4
```

	Test Statistic	1% Critical Value	5% Critical Value	10% Critical Value
		— Interpolated Dickey-Fuller —		
Z(rho)	-13.209	-27.420	-20.712	-17.510
Z(t)	-2.560	-4.039	-3.450	-3.150

MacKinnon approximate p-value for Z(t) = 0.2985

f	Coef.	Std. Err.	t	P>|t|	[95% Conf. Interval]	
f						
L1.	.9460524	.0326592	28.97	0.000	.8812574	1.010847
_trend	-.0035557	.0027713	-1.28	0.202	-.0090539	.0019426
_cons	.3633958	.2941354	1.24	0.220	-.2201604	.9469521

and

```
. pperron b, regress trend
```

```
Phillips-Perron test for unit root                Number of obs   =      103
                                                  Newey-West lags =        4
```

	Test Statistic	1% Critical Value	Interpolated Dickey-Fuller 5% Critical Value	10% Critical Value
Z(rho)	-16.361	-27.420	-20.712	-17.510
Z(t)	-2.978	-4.039	-3.450	-3.150

```
MacKinnon approximate p-value for Z(t) = 0.1382
```

b	Coef.	Std. Err.	t	P>|t|	[95% Conf. Interval]	
b						
L1.	.8924541	.0429605	20.77	0.000	.8072218	.9776865
_trend	-.0069282	.0035347	-1.96	0.053	-.013941	.0000845
_cons	.8823205	.4187536	2.11	0.038	.0515253	1.713116

This set of results supports those from the usual augmented Dickey-Fuller regressions. The **z(rho)** statistic is not in the rejection region of either test, supporting the nonstationarity of both **b** and **f**. The trend term in **f** is not significant and could possibly be dropped. It is significant in the other series, providing evidence of its inclusion.

12.4 INTEGRATION AND COINTEGRATION

Two nonstationary time series are **cointegrated** if they tend to move together through time. For instance, we have established that the levels of the Fed Funds rate and the 3-year bond rate are nonstationary, whereas their differences are stationary. In the opaque terminology used in the time series literature, each series is said to be "**integrated of order 1** " or **I(1)**. If the two nonstationary series move together through time then we say they are "cointegrated." Economic theory would suggest that they should be tied together via arbitrage, but that is no guarantee, so we perform a formal statistical test.

The test procedure is very simple. Regress one I(1) variable on another using least squares. Then test the residuals for nonstationarity using the (augmented) Dickey-Fuller test. If the series are cointegrated, the Dickey-Fuller test statistic will be statistically significant. The null hypothesis is that the residuals are nonstationary. Rejection of this leads to the conclusion that the residuals are stationary and the series are cointegrated.

12.4.1 Engle-Granger Test

The test described in the preceding section is commonly referred to as the Engle-Granger test. Regress **b** on **f** and a constant, save the residuals then use these in an augmented Dickey-Fuller regression. Manually, this is done

```
regress b f
```

```
. regress b f
```

Source	SS	df	MS
Model	568.17396	1	568.17396
Residual	66.9519745	102	.656391907
Total	635.125935	103	6.16627121

```
Number of obs =      104
F(  1,    102) =  865.60
Prob > F       =  0.0000
R-squared      =  0.8946
Adj R-squared  =  0.8936
Root MSE       =  .81018
```

b	Coef.	Std. Err.	t	P>|t|	[95% Conf. Interval]	
f	.9144114	.0310801	29.42	0.000	.8527641	.9760587
_cons	1.13983	.1740833	6.55	0.000	.7945362	1.485123

```
        predict ehat, residual
        regress D.ehat L.ehat L.D.ehat, noconstant

. regress D.ehat L.ehat L.D.ehat, noconstant
```

Source	SS	df	MS
Model	3.53907328	2	1.76953664
Residual	17.4123657	100	.174123657
Total	20.951439	102	.205406265

```
Number of obs =      102
F(  2,    100) =   10.16
Prob > F       =  0.0001
R-squared      =  0.1689
Adj R-squared  =  0.1523
Root MSE       =  .41728
```

D.ehat	Coef.	Std. Err.	t	P>|t|	[95% Conf. Interval]	
ehat						
L1.	-.2245093	.0535039	-4.20	0.000	-.3306595	-.1183592
LD.	.2540448	.0937006	2.71	0.008	.0681454	.4399442

The t-ratio on the lagged value of $\hat{e}$ is -4.20. The critical value has to be obtained from the proper table e.g., Table 12.4 in *POE4*. The 5% critical value for a cointegrating regression containing an intercept is -3.37 and the t-ratio is less than this. The null hypothesis of no cointegration is rejected when $t \le t_c$, and not rejected when $t > t_c$. The t-statistic in this case is $-4.196 < -3.37$ and the null hypothesis that the least squares residuals are nonstationary is rejected; the residuals are stationary. This implies that the bond rate and the federal funds rate are cointegrated.

Once can use the built-in **dfuller** command to obtain the t-ratio, but the critical values printed by Stata will not be correct. Those still have to come from a table of values suitable for a cointegrating equation; these are not the same as those for a conventional Dickey-Fuller regression.

```
. dfuller ehat, noconstant lags(1)
```

Augmented Dickey-Fuller test for unit root   Number of obs   =   102

	Test Statistic	Interpolated Dickey-Fuller		
		1% Critical Value	5% Critical Value	10% Critical Value
Z(t)	-4.196	-2.600	-1.950	-1.610

Once again, be careful not to use the critical values from this table when testing the stationarity of *residuals*; the given critical values are computed under the assumption that the time series being tested has not been estimated.

12.4.2 The Error Correction Model

Cointegration is a relationship between two nonstationary, I(1), variables. These variables share a common trend and tend to move together in the long-run. In this section, a dynamic relationship between I(0) variables which embeds a cointegrating relationship known as the short-run error correction model is examined.

Start with an ARDL(1,1)

$$y_t = \delta + \theta_1 y_{t-1} + \delta_0 x_t + \delta_1 x_{t-1} + v_t$$

after some manipulation (see POE4 for details)

$$\Delta y_t = -(1 - \theta_1)(y_{t-1} - \beta_1 - \beta_2 x_{t-1}) + \delta_0 \Delta x_t + \delta_1 \Delta x_{t-1} + v_t$$

The term in the second set of parentheses is a cointegrating relationship. The levels of y and x are linearly related. Let $\alpha = (1 - \theta_1)$ and the equation's parameters can be estimated by nonlinear least squares.

```
gen Db=D.b
nl (Db = -{alpha}*(L.b-{beta1}-beta2}*L.f)+ ///
{delta0}*D.f+{delta1}*D.L.f), variables(L.b L.f D.L.f)
```

The only trick here is that the time-series operator **D.** cannot be used in the formation of the dependent variable. It has to be generated separately before it can be used in **nl**. The lag and difference operators can be used on the right-hand side of the equation if listed in the variables option. The results are:

Source	SS	df	MS		
Model	15.0345905	4	3.75864763	Number of obs =	102
Residual	14.1807005	97	.146192788	R-squared =	0.5146
				Adj R-squared =	0.4946
				Root MSE =	.3823517
Total	29.215291	101	.289260307	Res. dev. =	88.20819

Db	Coef.	Std. Err.	t	P>|t|	[95% Conf. Interval]	
/alpha	.1418774	.0496561	2.86	0.005	.0433237	.240431
/beta1	1.429188	.6246253	2.29	0.024	.18948	2.668897
/beta2	.7765569	.1224753	6.34	0.000	.5334773	1.019637
/delta0	.8424631	.0897482	9.39	0.000	.6643378	1.020588
/delta1	-.3268445	.0847928	-3.85	0.000	-.4951347	-.1585544

Parameter beta1 taken as constant term in model & ANOVA table

To estimate θ_1

```
        scalar theta1 = 1-_b[alpha:_cons]
        scalar list theta1
```

```
. scalar list theta1
    theta1 =  .85812265
```

Finally, obtain the residuals and perform the ADF test for stationarity

```
        gen ehat = L.b - _b[beta1:_cons]-_b[beta2:_cons]*L.f
        reg D.ehat L.ehat L.D.ehat, noconst
        di di _b[L.ehat]/_se[L.ehat]
```

```
. di _b[L.ehat]/_se[L.ehat]
-3.9108174
```

As before, the null is that (y, x) are not cointegrated. Since the cointegrating relationship includes a constant term, the critical value is -3.37. Comparing the calculated value (-3.912) with the critical value, we reject the null hypothesis and conclude that (y, x) are cointegrated.

KEY TERMS

augmented DF test	**estat bgodfrey**	stationary
cointegration	**format %tm**	**time series plots**
combine graph	**format %tq**	tin(d1,d2)
date functions	integration	trend
dfuller	lag operator, **L.**	**tsline**
Dickey-Fuller (DF) test	**nl**	**tsvarlist**
difference operator, **D.**	**noconstant**	
dofq	**q(1996q4)**	
dofm	**name(graph, replace)**	
drift	nonstationary	
Engle-Granger test	**shell**	

CHAPTER 12 DO-FILE [CHAP12.DO]

```
* file chap12.do for Using Stata for Principles of Econometrics, 4e

* cd c:\data\poe4stata

* Stata Do-file
* copyright C 2011 by Lee C. Adkins and R. Carter Hill
* used for "Using Stata for Principles of Econometrics, 4e"
* by Lee C. Adkins and R. Carter Hill (2011)
* John Wiley and Sons, Inc.

* setup
version 11.1
capture log close
set more off
```

```
* open log
log using chap12, replace text
use usa, clear


* -------------------------------------
* Create dates and declare time-series
* -------------------------------------

generate date = q(1984q1) + _n-1
format date %tq
tsset date


* -------------------------------------
* Extract dates with year and quarter
* -------------------------------------

gen double newdate = dofq(date)
gen y = year(newdate)
gen q = quarter(newdate)

list date y q in 1/9


* -------------------------------------
* Graph time-series
* Graphs are named with replace option
* and combined.
* -------------------------------------

qui tsline gdp, name(gdp, replace)
qui tsline D.gdp, name(dgdp, replace)
graph combine gdp dgdp

qui tsline inf, name(inf, replace)
qui tsline D.inf, name(dinf, replace) yline(0)
qui tsline f, name(f, replace)
qui tsline D.f, name(df, replace) yline(0)
qui tsline b, name(b, replace)
qui tsline D.b, name(db, replace) yline(0)

graph combine inf dinf f df b db, cols(2)

* Two ways to limit dates
summarize if date<=q(1996q4)
summarize if date>=q(1997q1)

summarize if tin(,1996q4)
summarize if tin(1997q1,)

* To get summary stats for all variables and differences without generate
summarize gdp inf b f D.gdp D.inf D.b D.f if tin(1984q2,1996q4)
summarize gdp inf b f D.gdp D.inf D.b D.f if tin(1997q1,)
summarize


* -------------------------------------
* Spurious Regression
* -------------------------------------

use spurious, clear
gen time = _n
tsset time

regress rw1 rw2
```

```
estat bgodfrey

tsline rw1 rw2, name(g1, replace)
scatter rw1 rw2, name(g2, replace)

regress rw1 rw2
estat bgodfrey

* ---------------------------------------
* Unit root tests and cointegration
* ---------------------------------------

use usa, clear
gen date = q(1984q1) + _n - 1
format %tq date
tsset date

* Augmented Dickey Fuller Regressions
regress D.f L.f L.D.f
regress D.b L.b L.D.b

* Augmented Dickey Fuller Regressions with built in functions
dfuller f, regress lags(1)
dfuller b, regress lags(1)

* ADF on differences
dfuller D.f, noconstant lags(0)
dfuller D.b, noconstant lags(0)

* DF-GLS tests
dfgls f
dfgls b

* Phillips-Perron tests
pperron f, regress trend
pperron b, regress trend

* Engle Granger cointegrations test
regress b f
predict ehat, residual
regress D.ehat L.ehat L.D.ehat, noconstant

* Using the built-in Stata commands
dfuller ehat, noconstant lags(1)
drop ehat

gen Db=D.b
nl (Db = -{alpha}*(L.b-{beta1}-{beta2}*L.f)+{delta0}*D.f+{delta1}*D.L.f), ///
variables(L.b L.f D.L.f)
scalar theta1 = 1-_b[alpha:_cons]
scalar list theta1

gen ehat = L.b - _b[beta1:_cons]-_b[beta2:_cons]*L.f
qui reg D.ehat L.ehat L.D.ehat, noconst
di _b[L.ehat]/_se[L.ehat]
log close
```

CHAPTER **13**

Vector Error Correction and Vector Autoregressive Models

CHAPTER OUTLINE
13.1 VEC and VAR models
13.2 Estimating a VEC Model
13.3 Estimating a VAR

13.4 Impulse responses and variance
    decompositions
Key Terms
Chapter 13 do-file

13.1 VEC AND VAR MODELS

The vector autoregressive (VAR) model is a general framework used to describe the dynamic interrelationship among stationary variables. So, the first step in time-series analysis should be to determine whether the levels of the data are stationary. If not, take the first differences of the series and try again. Usually, if the levels (or log-levels) of your time series are not stationary, the first differences will be.

If the time series are not stationary then the VAR framework needs to be modified to allow consistent estimation of the relationships among the series. The vector error correction (VEC) model is just a special case of the VAR for variables that are stationary in their differences (i.e., I(1)). The VEC can also take into account any cointegrating relationships among the variables.

Consider two time-series variables, y_t and x_t. Generalizing the discussion about dynamic relationships in Chapter 9 to these two interrelated variables yields a system of equations:

$$y_t = \beta_{10} + \beta_{11} y_{t-1} + \beta_{12} x_{t-1} + v_t^y$$

$$x_t = \beta_{20} + \beta_{21} y_{t-1} + \beta_{22} x_{t-1} + v_t^x$$

The equations describe a system in which each variable is a function of its own lag, and the lag of the other variable in the system. In this case, the system contains two variables y and x. Together the equations constitute a system known as a vector autoregression (VAR). In this example, since the maximum lag is of order one, we have a VAR(1).

If y and x are stationary, the system can be estimated using least squares applied to each equation. If y and x are not stationary in their levels, but stationary in differences (i.e., I(1)), then take the differences and estimate:

$$\Delta y_t = \beta_{11}\Delta y_{t-1} + \beta_{12}\Delta x_{t-1} + v_t^{\Delta y}$$

$$\Delta x_t = \beta_{21}\Delta y_{t-1} + \beta_{22}\Delta x_{t-1} + v_t^{\Delta x}$$

using least squares.

If y and x are I(1) and cointegrated, then the system of equations can be modified to allow for the cointegrating relationship between the I(1) variables. Introducing the cointegrating relationship leads to a model known as the vector error correction (VEC) model.

13.2 ESTIMATING A VEC MODEL

In the first example, data on the Gross Domestic Product of Australia and the U.S. are used to estimate a VEC model. We decide to use the vector error correction model because (1) the time series are not stationary in their levels but are in their differences (2) the variables are cointegrated. Our initial impressions are gained from looking at plots of the two series.

To get started, change the directory to the one containing your data and load your data. In this exercise we'll be using the *gdp.dta* data.

```
cd c:\data\poe4stata
use gdp, clear
```

The data contain two quarterly time series: Australian and U.S. GDP from 1970q1 to 2004q4. Just as you did in Chapter 13, create a sequence of quarterly dates:

```
gen date = q(1970q1) + _n - 1
format %tq date
tsset date
```

Plotting the levels and differences of the two GDP series suggests that the data are nonstationary in levels, but stationary in differences. In this example, we used the **tsline** command with an optional *scheme*. A scheme holds saved graph preferences for later use. You can create your own or use one of the ones installed with Stata. At the command line you can use determine which schemes are installed on your computer by typing

```
graph query, schemes
```

In this example I used a scheme called **sj,** which stands for *Stata Journal*. This produces graphs that look just like the ones published there. In this case, it produces a grayscale line graph with two different line definitions: solid lines for *aus* and dashed ones for *usa*. The complete syntax for the graphs with optional scheme is:

```
tsline aus usa, scheme(sj)
tsline D.aus D.usa, scheme(sj)
```

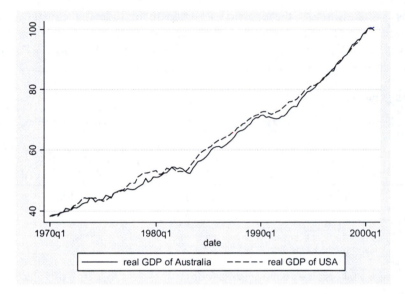

Neither series looks stationary in its levels. They appear to have a common trend, an indication that they may be cointegrated.

Unit root tests are performed using the procedures discussed in Chapter 12. Augmented Dickey-Fuller regressions require some judgment about specification. User has to decide whether to include a constant, trend or drift, and lag lengths for the differences that augment the regular Dickey-Fuller regressions. The differences are graphed and this gives some clues about specification. The graph below shows little evidence of trend or drift.

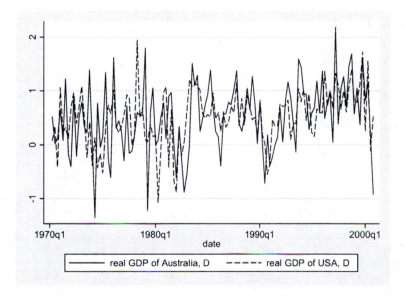

Lag lengths can be chosen using model selection rules or by starting at a maximum lag length, say 4, and eliminating lags one-by-one until the *t*-ratio on the last lag becomes significant.

```
dfuller aus, regress lags(1)
dfuller usa, regress lags(3)
```

Through process of elimination the decision is made to include the constant (though it looks unnecessary) and to include 1 lag for *aus* and 3 for the *usa* series. In none of the ADF regressions I estimated was either ADF statistic even close to being significant at the 5% level. Satisfied that the series are nonstationary in levels, their cointegration is explored.

```
. dfuller aus, regress lags(1)

Augmented Dickey-Fuller test for unit root         Number of obs    =       122

                         ──────── Interpolated Dickey-Fuller ────────
                Test      1% Critical      5% Critical     10% Critical
            Statistic        Value            Value           Value
─────────────────────────────────────────────────────────────────────
 Z(t)          2.658          -3.503          -2.889          -2.579
─────────────────────────────────────────────────────────────────────
MacKinnon approximate p-value for Z(t) = 0.9991

. dfuller usa, regress lags(3)

Augmented Dickey-Fuller test for unit root         Number of obs    =       120

                         ──────── Interpolated Dickey-Fuller ────────
                Test      1% Critical      5% Critical     10% Critical
            Statistic        Value            Value           Value
─────────────────────────────────────────────────────────────────────
 Z(t)          1.691          -3.503          -2.889          -2.579
─────────────────────────────────────────────────────────────────────
MacKinnon approximate p-value for Z(t) = 0.9981
```

In each case, the null hypothesis of nonstationarity cannot be rejected at any reasonable level of significance. Notice that both lagged differences are significant in the U.S. equation and the 3rd lag in the Australia equation are significant; significant lag coefficients provide some evidence that the lagged variables should be included.

Next, estimate the cointegrating equation using least squares. Notice that the cointegrating relationship does not include a constant.

regress aus usa, noconst

```
. reg aus usa, noconst

      Source |       SS       df       MS              Number of obs =     124
─────────────┼──────────────────────────────           F(  1,   123) =       .
       Model | 526014.204      1   526014.204           Prob > F      =  0.0000
    Residual | 182.885542    123   1.48687433           R-squared     =  0.9997
─────────────┼──────────────────────────────           Adj R-squared =  0.9996
       Total | 526197.09     124   4243.52492           Root MSE      =  1.2194

─────────────────────────────────────────────────────────────────────────────
         aus |      Coef.   Std. Err.      t    P>|t|     [95% Conf. Interval]
─────────────┼───────────────────────────────────────────────────────────────
         usa |   .9853495   .0016566   594.79   0.000     .9820703    .9886288
─────────────────────────────────────────────────────────────────────────────
```

The residuals are saved in order to conduct an Engle-Granger test of cointegration and plotted.

```
predict ehat, residual
tsline ehat
```

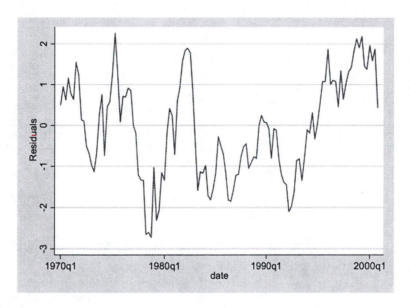

The residuals have an intercept of zero and show little evidence of trend. Finaly, the saved residuals are used in an auxiliary regression

$$\Delta\hat{e}_t = \phi\hat{e}_{t-1} + v_t$$

The Stata command is:

regress D.ehat L.ehat, noconstant

```
. reg D.ehat L.ehat, noconst
```

Source	SS	df	MS
Model	2.99032657	1	2.99032657
Residual	43.7006336	122	.358201914
Total	46.6909601	123	.379601302

```
Number of obs =      123
F(  1,    122) =     8.35
Prob > F       =   0.0046
R-squared      =   0.0640
Adj R-squared  =   0.0564
Root MSE       =    .5985
```

D.ehat	Coef.	Std. Err.	t	P>|t|	[95% Conf. Interval]
ehat L1.	-.1279366	.0442792	-2.89	0.005	-.2155916 -.0402816

The t-ratio is equal to −2.89. The 5% critical value for a cointegrating relationship with no intercept is −2.76 and so this falls within the rejection region of the test. The null hypothesis of no cointegration is rejected at the 5% level of significance.

To measure the one quarter response of real GDP to economic shocks we estimate the parameters of the vector error correction model by least squares.

```
regress D.aus L1.ehat
regress D.usa L1.ehat
```

The error correction model results the Australian GDP are:

Source	SS	df	MS		Number of obs =	123
					F(1, 121) =	4.32
Model	1.77229686	1	1.77229686		Prob > F =	0.0399
Residual	49.697821	121	.410725793		R-squared =	0.0344
					Adj R-squared =	0.0265
Total	51.4701178	122	.421886212		Root MSE =	.64088

D.aus	Coef.	Std. Err.	t	P>|t|	[95% Conf. Interval]	
ehat L1.	-.0987029	.0475158	-2.08	0.040	-.1927729	-.0046329
_cons	.4917059	.0579095	8.49	0.000	.3770587	.606353

The significant negative coefficient on $\hat{e}_{t-1}$ indicates that Australian GDP responds to a temporary disequilibrium between the U.S. and Australia. For the U.S.:

Source	SS	df	MS		Number of obs =	123
					F(1, 121) =	0.62
Model	.166467786	1	.166467786		Prob > F =	0.4312
Residual	32.2879333	121	.266842424		R-squared =	0.0051
					Adj R-squared =	-0.0031
Total	32.4544011	122	.266019681		Root MSE =	.51657

D.usa	Coef.	Std. Err.	t	P>|t|	[95% Conf. Interval]	
ehat L1.	.0302501	.0382992	0.79	0.431	-.0455732	.1060734
_cons	.5098843	.0466768	10.92	0.000	.4174752	.6022934

The U.S. does not appear to respond to a disequilibrium between the two economies; the *t*-ratio on $\hat{e}_{t-1}$ is insignificant. These results support the idea that economic conditions in Australia depend on those in the U.S. more than conditions in the U.S. depend on Australia. In a simple model of two economy trade, the U.S. is a large closed economy and Australia is a small open economy.

13.3 ESTIMATING A VAR

The vector autoregressive model (VAR) is actualy simpler to estimate than the VEC model. It is used when there is no cointegration among the variables and it is estimated using time series that have been transformed to their stationary values.

In the example from *POE4*, we have macroeconomic data log of real personal disposable income (denoted as *Y*) and log of real personal consumption expenditure (denoted as *C*) for the U.S. economy over the period 1960:1 to 2009:4 that are found in the *fred.dta* dataset. As in the previous example, the first step is to determine whether the variables are stationary. If they are not, then difference them, checking to make sure that the differences are stationary (i.e., integrated). Next, test for cointegration. If they are cointegrated, estimate the VEC model. If not, use the differences and lagged differences to estimate a VAR. model.

First, change the directory to the one containing your data and load your data. In this exercise we'll be using the *fred.dta* data.

```
cd c:\data\poe4stata
use fred, clear
```

The data are quartery and begin in 1960q1 and extend to 2009q4. Just as we did in Chapter 12 and in the example above, sequences of quartery dates:

```
gen date = q(1960q1) + _n - 1
format %tq date
tsset date
```

The first step is to plot the series in order to identify whether constants or trends should be included in the tests of nonstationarity. Both the levels and differences are plotted.

```
tsline c y, legend(lab (1 "ln(Consumption)") lab(2 "ln(PDI)"))
tsline D.c D.y, legend(lab (1 "D.ln(Consumption)") lab(2 "D.ln(PDI)"))
```

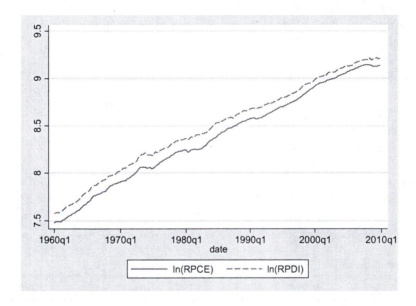

The levels series appear to be trending together. The differences show no obvious trend, but the mean of the series appears to be greater than zero, suggesting that a constant be included in the ADF regressions.

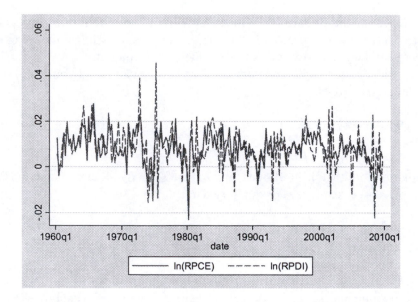

The other decision that needs to be made is the number of lagged differences to include in the augmented Dickey-Fuller regressions. The principle to follow is to include just enough so that the residuals of the ADF regression are not autocorrelated. So, start out with a basic regression that contains no lags, estimate the DF regression, then use the LM test discussed in chapter 9 to determine whether the residuals are autocorrelated. Add enough lags to eliminate the autocorrelation among residuals. If this strategy is pursued in Stata, then the ADF regressions will have to be explicity estimated; the **estat bgodfrey** command will not be based on the proper regression if issued after **dfuller**.

The regressions for the ADF tests are

```
qui reg L(0/1).D.c L.c
estat bgodfrey, lags(1 2 3)
qui reg L(0/2).D.c L.c
estat bgodfrey, lags(1 2 3)
qui reg L(0/3).D.c L.c
estat bgodfrey, lags(1 2 3)
```

The test results for the last two regressions appear below.

Breusch-Godfrey LM test for autocorrelation

lags(p)	chi2	df	Prob > chi2
1	2.077	1	0.1495
2	2.539	2	0.2810
3	2.542	3	0.4677

H0: no serial correlation

Breusch-Godfrey LM test for autocorrelation

lags(p)	chi2	df	Prob > chi2
1	0.157	1	0.6916
2	1.271	2	0.5297
3	2.098	3	0.5523

H0: no serial correlation

It is clear that the residuals of the ADF(2) are autocorrelated and those of the ADF(3) are not. The resulting ADF statistic is obtained using:

dfuller c, lags(3)

where the indicated number of lags is used.

. dfuller c, lags(3)

Augmented Dickey-Fuller test for unit root   Number of obs   =   196

| | Test Statistic | Interpolated Dickey-Fuller | | |
		1% Critical Value	5% Critical Value	10% Critical Value
z(t)	-1.995	-3.478	-2.884	-2.574

MacKinnon approximate p-value for Z(t) = 0.2886

Note also that this regression contains a constant and that the test statistic is -1.995. The unit root hypothesis is not rejected at the 5% level.

A Stata loop is used to perform the same procedure for **y**.

```
forvalues p = 1/3 {
    qui reg L(0/`p').D.y L.y
    di "Lags =" `p'
    estat bgodfrey, lags(1 2 3)
}
```

The loop increments the macro **p** from 1 to 3. The **quietly** option is used for the regression to suppress output. The abbreviated coding for the linear regression is used, which combines the dependent variable **D.y** with the lagged regressors in one statement, i.e., **reg L(0/`p').D.y**. For **p=1** this is equivalent to **reg D.y L.D.y**. I've instructed Stata to print the current value of **p** before printing the results from the *LM* test. The output is:

Lags =1

Breusch-Godfrey LM test for autocorrelation

lags(p)	chi2	df	Prob > chi2
1	0.208	1	0.6487
2	2.853	2	0.2401
3	2.880	3	0.4105

H0: no serial correlation

Lags =2

Breusch-Godfrey LM test for autocorrelation

lags(p)	chi2	df	Prob > chi2
1	2.077	1	0.1495
2	2.539	2	0.2810
3	2.542	3	0.4677

HO: no serial correlation

Lags =3

Breusch-Godfrey LM test for autocorrelation

lags(p)	chi2	df	Prob > chi2
1	0.157	1	0.6916
2	1.271	2	0.5297
3	2.098	3	0.5523

HO: no serial correlation

There is no evidence that lagged differences of **y** need to be included as regressors (i.e., the regular Dickey-Fuller regression). The Dickey-Fuller test yields:

. dfuller y, lags(0)

Dickey-Fuller test for unit root   Number of obs   =   199

	Test Statistic	1% Critical Value	5% Critical Value	10% Critical Value
Z(t)	-2.741	-3.477	-2.883	-2.573

MacKinnon approximate p-value for Z(t) = 0.0673

Recall that the cointegrating relationship can be estimated using least squares.

$$C_t = \beta_1 + \beta_2 Y_t + v_t$$

The residuals from this regression are obtained and their changes are regressed on the lagged value

$$\Delta \hat{e}_t = \gamma \hat{e}_{t-1} + \delta \Delta \hat{e}_{t-1} + v_t$$

The Stata code for this procedure is:

```
reg c y
predict ehat, res
reg D.ehat L.ehat D.L.ehat, noconst
di _b[L.ehat]/_se[L.ehat]
```

and the results,

```
. di _b[L.ehat]/_se[L.ehat]
-2.8728997
```

Note that an intercept term has been included here to capture the component of (log) consumption that is independent of disposable income. The 5% critical value of the test for stationarity in the cointegrating residuals is −3.37. Since the unit root t-value of −2.873 is greater than −3.37, it indicates that the errors are not stationary, and hence that the relationship between C (i.e., ln*(RPCE)*) and Y (i.e., ln*(RPDI)*) is spurious—that is, we have no cointegration. In this case, estimate the coefficients of the model using a VAR in differences.

The VAR is simple to estimate in Stata. The easiest route is to use the **varbasic** command. **varbasic** fits a basic vector autoregressive (VAR) model and graphs the impulse-response functions (IRFs) and the forecast-error variance decompositions (FEVDs).

The basic structure of the VAR that is stationary in differences is given in the equations below:

$$\Delta y_t = \beta_{11}\Delta y_{t-1} + \beta_{12}\Delta x_{t-1} + v_t^{\Delta y}$$

$$\Delta x_t = \beta_{21}\Delta y_{t-1} + \beta_{22}\Delta x_{t-1} + v_t^{\Delta x}$$

The variables x_t and y_t are nonstationary, but the differences are stationary. Each difference is a linear function of it own lagged differences and of lagged differences of each of the other variables in the system. The equations are linear and least squares can be used to estimate the parameters. The **varbasic** command simplifies this. You need to specify the variables in the system (Δy_t and Δx_t) and the number of lags to include on the right-hand-side of the model. In our example, only 1 lag is included and the syntax to estimate the VAR is:

varbasic D.c D.y, lags(1/1) step(12) nograph

The syntax **lags(1/1)** tells Stata to include lags from the first number to the last, which in this case is lag 1 to lag 1. If your VAR is longer than 1 lag then you'll change that. Also added is the **step(12)** option. This option is used to limit the number of lagged periods for which to compute impulse responses (IRF) and forecast error variance decompositions (FEVD) —when used it can make the graphs easier to interpret and it conserves space in the tables that Stata can generate. Finally, the **nograph** option is used to suppress the graphs of the IRFs and the FEVDs. These can be called later in separate statements as is done below. The output from this is:

```
. varbasic D.c D.y, lags(1/1) step(12) nograph

Vector autoregression

Sample:  1960q3 - 2009q4                        No. of obs     =        198
Log likelihood =    1400.444                    AIC            =   -14.0853
FPE            =    2.62e-09                     HQIC           =  -14.04496
Det(Sigma_ml)  =    2.46e-09                     SBIC           =  -13.98565

Equation          Parms    RMSE      R-sq     chi2      P>chi2
-----------------------------------------------------------------
D_c                  3     .006575   0.1205   27.12459  0.0000
D_y                  3     .008562   0.1118   24.92656  0.0000
-----------------------------------------------------------------
```

		Coef.	Std. Err.	z	P>|z|	[95% Conf. Interval]	
D_c							
c	LD.	.2156068	.0741801	2.91	0.004	.0702164	.3609972
y	LD.	.1493798	.0572953	2.61	0.009	.0370832	.2616765
_cons		.0052776	.0007516	7.02	0.000	.0038046	.0067507
D_y							
c	LD.	.4754276	.0965863	4.92	0.000	.286122	.6647332
y	LD.	-.2171679	.0746013	-2.91	0.004	-.3633839	-.070952
_cons		.0060367	.0009786	6.17	0.000	.0041187	.0079547

In light of the fact that longer lags were used in the Dickey-Fuller regressions it is likely that the VAR should also have longer lags. In practice, it would probably be a good idea to test the residuals of the VAR for autocorrelation. The Stata command **varlmar** issued after **varbasic** will perform a *LM* test of the residuals similar to the ones that were performed for autocorrelation.

```
. varlmar
```

Lagrange-multiplier test

lag	chi2	df	Prob > chi2
1	9.5086	4	0.04957
2	5.6784	4	0.22449

H0: no autocorrelation at lag order

There is evidence of autocorrelation in the residuals since the *p*-value at lag 1 is less than 5%. Extending the lag length to 3 removes the ambiguity.

Stata includes another procedure that makes selecting lag lengths in VAR models very easy. The **varsoc** command reports the final prediction error (FPE), Akaike's information criterion (AIC), Schwarz's Bayesian information criterion (SC), and the Hannan and Quinn information criterion (HQIC) lag-order selection statistics for a series of vector autoregressions. This can be used to find lag lengths for VAR or VEC models of unknown order. For the example above Stata yields:

```
. varsoc D.c D.y, maxlag(4)
```

Selection-order criteria
Sample: 1961q2 - 2009q4   Number of obs   =   195

lag	LL	LR	df	p	FPE	AIC	HQIC	SBIC
0	1355.02				3.2e-09	-13.8772	-13.8636	-13.8436
1	1379.09	48.129	4	0.000	2.6e-09	-14.083	-14.0422*	-13.9823*
2	1383.92	9.6655*	4	0.046	2.6e-09	-14.0915	-14.0235	-13.9237
3	1388.24	8.6379	4	0.071	2.6e-09*	-14.0948*	-13.9996	-13.8598
4	1391.6	6.7149	4	0.152	2.6e-09	-14.0882	-13.9659	-13.7861

The AIC selects a lag order of 3 while the SC (labeled by Stata, SBIC) chooses 1.

The dialog box for **varbasic** is found **Statistics > Mutivariate time series > Basic VAR**

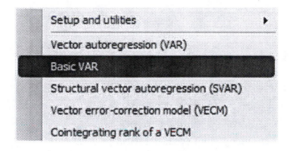

This dialog box is

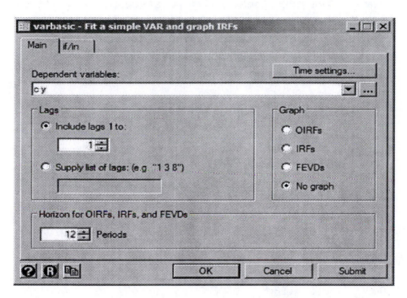

List both **c** and **y** as dependent variables and click the radio button labeled **Include lags 1 to:**
The number in the box below this button should be set to 1 to produce the results in *POE4*,
though we've set it to three in this example. At the bottom left of the box, we have chosen a 12
period **horizon** for impulse responses and the forecast error variance decompositions. Click **OK**.

13.4 IMPULSE RESPONSES AND VARIANCE DECOMPOSITIONS

Impulse response functions show the effects of shocks on the adjustment path of the variables.
Forecast error variance decompositions measure the contribution of each type of shock to the
forecast error variance. Both computations are useful in assessing how shocks to economic
variables reverberate through a system.

Impulse response functions (IRFs) and forecast error variance decompositions (FEVD) can be
produced after using the **varbasic** command. The results can be presented in a table or a graph.
In this example we illustrate both. After the **varbasic** command, we use the **irf table**
command to generate IRFs and FEVDs:

```
irf table irf
irf table fevd
```

The syntax for `irf table` is:

```
irf table [stat] [, options]
```

where **stat** can be any of the following:

```
irf       impulse-response function
oirf      orthogonalized impulse-response function
dm        dynamic-multiplier function
cirf      cumulative impulse-response function
coirf     cumulative orthogonalized impulse-response function
cdm       cumulative dynamic-multiplier function
fevd      Cholesky forecast-error variance decomposition
sirf      structural impulse-response function
sfevd     structural forecast-error variance decomposition
```

The results from the IRF table are:

step	(1) irf	(1) Lower	(1) Upper	(2) irf	(2) Lower	(2) Upper
0	1	1	1	0	0	0
1	.215607	.070216	.360997	.475428	.286122	.664733
2	.117506	.042463	.192549	-.000742	-.088665	.087181
3	.025224	-.014994	.065442	.056027	.007234	.104819
4	.013808	-.003806	.031422	-.000175	-.020898	.020548
5	.002951	-.004713	.010615	.006603	-.002593	.015799
6	.001623	-.001478	.004723	-.000031	-.003694	.003632
7	.000345	-.000905	.001595	.000778	-.000719	.002275
8	.000191	-.000295	.000676	-4.9e-06	-.000581	.000571
9	.00004	-.000148	.000228	.000092	-.000134	.000317
10	.000022	-.000049	.000094	-7.2e-07	-.000086	.000084
11	4.7e-06	-.000022	.000032	.000011	-.000022	.000043
12	2.6e-06	-7.4e-06	.000013	-1.0e-07	-.000012	.000012

step	(3) irf	(3) Lower	(3) Upper	(4) irf	(4) Lower	(4) Upper
0	0	0	0	1	1	1
1	.14938	.037083	.261676	-.217168	-.363384	-.070952
2	-.000233	-.027858	.027392	.118181	.043031	.193332
3	.017604	-.000946	.036153	-.025776	-.066356	.014804
4	-.000055	-.006566	.006456	.013967	-.003818	.031752
5	.002075	-.001028	.005177	-.003059	-.010845	.004726
6	-9.7e-06	-.001161	.001141	.001651	-.001506	.004807
7	.000244	-.000241	.00073	-.000363	-.001642	.000916
8	-1.5e-06	-.000182	.000179	.000195	-.000303	.000693
9	.000029	-.000043	.000101	-.000043	-.000237	.000151
10	-2.2e-07	-.000027	.000026	.000023	-.000051	.000097
11	3.4e-06	-6.9e-06	.000014	-5.1e-06	-.000033	.000023
12	-3.2e-08	-3.8e-06	3.7e-06	2.7e-06	-7.7e-06	.000013

```
95% lower and upper bounds reported
(1) irfname = varbasic, impulse = D.c, and response = D.c
(2) irfname = varbasic, impulse = D.c, and response = D.y
(3) irfname = varbasic, impulse = D.y, and response = D.c
(4) irfname = varbasic, impulse = D.y, and response = D.y
```

The results appear in four quadrants and a key is given at the bottom of the table. In quadrant one (northwest) is the response in ln*(RCPE)* to a shock in itself. You'll remember that this series is stationary and therefore shocks are not persistent; their effects eventually die out. Shocks to ln*(RPDI)* are not persistent either. More interesting is how ln*(RPDI)* responds to shocks in the ln*(RCPE)*, and vice versa. Quadrant 2 (northeast) shows a shocks to ln*(RCPE)* affects ln*(RPDI)* for one period, but dies out very quickly. Shocks to the ln*(RRDI)* create a smaller, but significant response in ln*(RCPE)* (quadrant 3), though once again if falls to zero very quickly.

A separate command called **irf graph** basically does the same thing as **irf table**, except the results appear as a graph rather than in tabular form.

irf graph

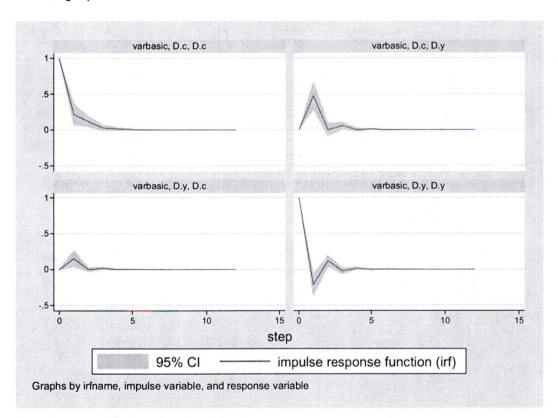

This is merely the data produced by **irf table** in graphical form.

Like the impulse responses, the FEVDs can be produced in either tabular or graphical form. The commands are, respectively:

```
irf table fevd
irf graph fevd
```

The results are arranged in the same way, by quadrant with a key at the bottom.

step	(1) fevd	(1) Lower	(1) Upper	(2) fevd	(2) Lower	(2) Upper
0	0	0	0	0	0	0
1	1	1	1	.198552	.099067	.298037
2	.97297	.932729	1.01321	.2438	.146908	.340692
3	.973298	.933619	1.01298	.243198	.145308	.341087
4	.972967	.93271	1.01322	.243752	.145393	.34211
5	.972972	.932723	1.01322	.243743	.145351	.342135
6	.972967	.932709	1.01323	.24375	.145347	.342153
7	.972967	.932709	1.01323	.24375	.145346	.342154
8	.972967	.932709	1.01323	.24375	.145346	.342154
9	.972967	.932709	1.01323	.24375	.145346	.342154
10	.972967	.932709	1.01323	.24375	.145346	.342154
11	.972967	.932709	1.01323	.24375	.145346	.342154
12	.972967	.932709	1.01323	.24375	.145346	.342154

step	(3) fevd	(3) Lower	(3) Upper	(4) fevd	(4) Lower	(4) Upper
0	0	0	0	0	0	0
1	0	0	0	.801448	.701963	.900933
2	.02703	-.013212	.067271	.7562	.659308	.853092
3	.026702	-.012977	.066381	.756802	.658913	.854692
4	.027033	-.013225	.06729	.756248	.65789	.854607
5	.027028	-.01322	.067277	.756257	.657865	.854649
6	.027033	-.013225	.067291	.75625	.657847	.854653
7	.027033	-.013225	.067291	.75625	.657846	.854654
8	.027033	-.013225	.067291	.75625	.657846	.854654
9	.027033	-.013225	.067291	.75625	.657846	.854654
10	.027033	-.013225	.067291	.75625	.657846	.854654
11	.027033	-.013225	.067291	.75625	.657846	.854654
12	.027033	-.013225	.067291	.75625	.657846	.854654

```
95% lower and upper bounds reported
(1) irfname = varbasic, impulse = D.c, and response = D.c
(2) irfname = varbasic, impulse = D.c, and response = D.y
(3) irfname = varbasic, impulse = D.y, and response = D.c
(4) irfname = varbasic, impulse = D.y, and response = D.y
```

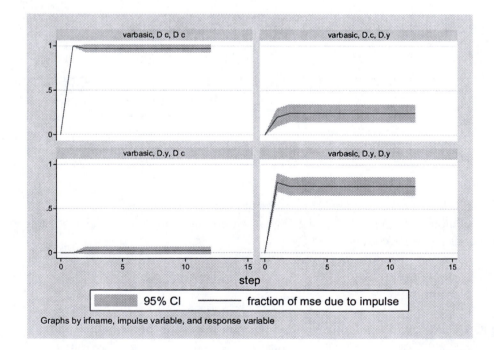

Graphs by irfname, impulse variable, and response variable

The tabulation and graphing functions in Stata for IRFs and FEVDs are really very flexible. You can combine tables, overlay graphs, and do many other things using either the language or the dialog boxes. Choose **Statistics > Multivariate time series > IRF and FEVD analysis** to reveal the final box:

Here you have a number of choices including the ones we've just discussed. However, you can also use these dialogs to overlay graphs, combine graphs, or select specific portions of the tables or graphs to use in your output. Feel free to experiment!

KEY TERMS

ADF test

cointegration

dfuller

drift

Engle-Granger test

estat bgodfrey

forecast error variance
decomposition (FEVD)

impulse response function

IRF

irf graph

irf table

lags

LM test

multivariate time series

scheme

trend

tsline

varbasic

varlmar

varsoc

vector autoregressive model

vector error correction model

CHAPTER 13 DO-FILE

```
* file chap13.do for Using Stata for Principles of Econometrics, 4e

* cd c:\data\poe4stata

* Stata do-file
* copyright C 2011 by Lee C. Adkins and R. Carter Hill
* used for "Using Stata for Principles of Econometrics, 4e"
* by Lee C. Adkins and R. Carter Hill (2011)
* John Wiley and Sons, Inc.

* setup
version 11.1
capture log close
set more off

* open log
log using chap13, replace text
```

```
*------------------------------------------
* Estimating a VECM
* Load the data and create a time variable
*------------------------------------------

use gdp, clear
gen date = q(1970q1) + _n - 1
format %tq date
tsset date


*------------------------------------------
* Plot the series to identify constants
* and trends.
*------------------------------------------

tsline aus usa, scheme(sj) name(level, replace)
tsline D.aus D.usa, scheme(sj) name(difference, replace)

* Test for Unit Roots
* Experiment with noconst, trend, drift, and lag length
dfuller aus, regress lags(1)
dfuller usa, regress lags(3)

* Cointegrating regression
reg aus usa, noconst
predict ehat, res
tsline ehat, name(C1, replace)

* Engle-Granger Test for Cointegration
reg D.ehat L.ehat, noconst
dfuller ehat, lags(0) noconst


*------------------------------------------
* VECM
*------------------------------------------

regress D.aus L.ehat
regress D.usa L.ehat
drop ehat


*------------------------------------------
* VAR Estimation
*------------------------------------------

use fred, clear
gen date = q(1960q1) + _n - 1
format %tq date
tsset date


*------------------------------------------
* Plot the series to identify constants
* and trends.
*------------------------------------------

tsline c y, legend(lab (1 "ln(RPCE)") lab(2 "ln(RPDI)")) ///
       name(l1, replace) lpattern(solid dash)
tsline D.c D.y, legend(lab (1 "ln(RPCE)") lab(2 "ln(RPDI)")) ///
       name(d1, replace) lpattern(solid dash)

* Stationarity Analysis
* Brute force, 1 equation at a time
qui reg L(0/1).D.c L.c
```

```
di "Lags = 1"
estat bgodfrey, lags(1 2 3)
qui reg L(0/2).D.c L.c
di "Lags = 2"
estat bgodfrey, lags(1 2 3)
qui reg L(0/3).D.c L.c
di "Lags = 3"
estat bgodfrey, lags(1 2 3)
dfuller c, lags(3)

* Use the loop to compute stats for y
forvalues p = 1/3 {
    qui reg L(0/`p').D.y L.y
    di "Lags =" `p'
    estat bgodfrey, lags(1 2 3)
}
dfuller y, lags(0)

* Cointegration Test: Case 2
reg c y
predict ehat, res
reg D.ehat L.ehat D.L.ehat, noconst
di _b[L.ehat]/_se[L.ehat]

reg D.c D.L.c D.L.y
reg D.y D.L.c D.L.y

varbasic D.c D.y, lags(1/1) step(12) nograph

*------------------------------------------
* Test residuals for autocorrelation
*------------------------------------------
varlmar

* Try extending lags to 3 and repeat
quietly varbasic D.c D.y, lags(1/3) step(12)
varlmar
* There is evidence of autocorrelation so extend the lag to 3

* Selecting lags using model selection criteria
varsoc D.c D.y, maxlag(4)

* Impulse responses and variance decompositions
qui varbasic D.c D.y, lags(1/1) step(12)
irf table irf
irf table fevd

irf graph irf, name(g1, replace)
irf graph fevd, name(g2, replace)

* Combining irf and fevd in a single table
irf table irf fevd, title("Combined IRF/FEVD for C and Y")

log close
```

CHAPTER **14**

Time-Varying Volatility and ARCH Models

CHAPTER OUTLINE

14.1 ARCH model and time-varying volatility
14.2 Estimating, testing, and forecasting
14.3 Extensions
   14.3.1 GARCH

14.3.2 T-GARCH
14.3.3 GARCH-in-mean
Key Terms
Chapter 14 Do-file

14.1 ARCH MODEL AND TIME-VARYING VOLATILITY

In this chapter we'll use Stata to estimate several models in which the variance of the dependent variable changes over time. These are broadly referred to as ARCH (autoregressive conditional heteroskedasticity) models and there are many variations upon the theme.

    The first thing to do is illustrate the problem graphically using data on stock returns. The data are stored in the Stata dataset *returns.dta*. Change the directory to the one containing the data and load it into memory.

```
cd c:\data\poe4stata
use returns, clear
```

The data contain four monthly stock price indices: U.S. Nasdaq (**nasdaq**), the Australian All Ordinaries (**allords**), the Japanese Nikkei (**nikkei**) and the U.K. FTSE (**ftse**). The data are recorded monthly beginning in 1988m1 and ending in 2009m7.

```
gen date = m(1988m1) + _n - 1
format date %tm
tsset date
```

Plots of the s eries in their levels are generated using **twoway(tsline varname)**, which can be abbreviated **tsline varname**. As done previously, each graph is given a **name** with a **replace** option. Then the graphs are combined.

```
qui tsline nasdaq, name(nas, replace)
qui tsline allords, name(a, replace)
qui tsline ftse, name(f, replace)
qui tsline nikkei, name(nk, replace)
graph combine nas a f nk, cols(2) name(all1, replace)
```

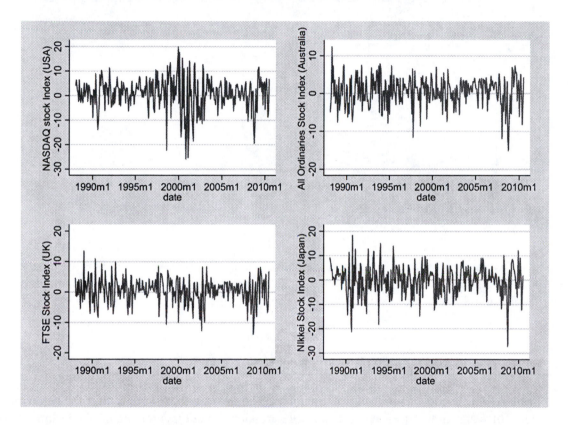

The series are characterized by random, rapid changes and are said to be **volatile**. The volatility seems to ch ange over time as well.   For instance the U.S. stock returns index (NASD   AQ) experiences a relatively sedate period from 1992 to 1996. Then, stock returns become much more volatile until early 2004. Volatility increases again at the end of the sam   ple. The other series exhibit similar periods of relative calm followed by increased volatility.

Next, the **histogram** command is used to generate graphs   of the empirical distribution of returns. A curve from a normal distribution is overlaid using the **normal** option.

```
qui histogram nasdaq, normal name(nas, replace)
qui histogram allords, normal name(a, replace)
qui histogram ftse, normal name(f, replace)
qui histogram nikkei, normal name(nk, replace)
graph combine nas a f nk, cols(2) name(all2, replace)
```

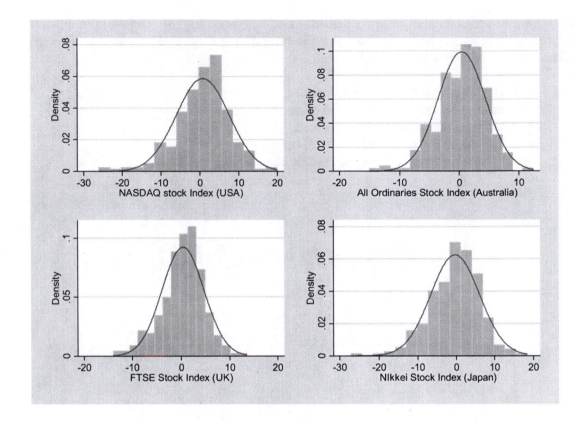

These series are leptokurtic. That means they have lots of observations around the average and a relatively large number of observations that are fa r from average; the center of the histogram has a high peak and the tails are relatively heavy compared to the normal.

14.2 TESTING, ESTIMATING, AND FORECASTING

The basic ARCH models consist of two equations. The **mean equation** describes the behavior of the mean of y our time series; it is a linear re gression function that contains a constan t and possibly some explanatory variables. In the cas es considered below, the mean function contains only an intercept.

$$y_t = \beta + e_t$$

In this case we expect th e time series to vary randomly about i ts mean, β. If the mean of y our time series drifts over time or is explained by other variables, you'd add them to this equation just as you would in the usual regression model. The error of the regression is normally distributed and heteroskedastic. The variance of the current period's error depends on information that is revealed in t he preceding period. The variance of e_t is given the sy mbol h_t. The **variance equation** describes how the error variance behaves.

$$h_t = \alpha + \alpha_1 e_{t-1}^2$$

Notice that h_t depends on the squared error in the preceding time period. The parameters in this equation have to be positive to ensure that the variance, h_t, is positive.

A Lagrange Multiplier (*LM*) test can be used to test for the presence of ARCH effects (i.e., whether $\alpha>0$). To perform this test, first estimate the mean equation. Save and square the estimated residuals, $\hat{e}_t^2$. You will use these in an auxiliary regression from which you'll use the sample size and goodness-of-fit measure to compute a test statistic. For first order ARCH, regress $\hat{e}_t^2$ on the lagged residuals $\hat{e}_{t-1}^2$ and a constant:

$$\hat{e}_t^2 = \gamma_0 + \gamma_1 \hat{e}_{t-1}^2 + v_t$$

where v_t is a random term. The null and alternative hypotheses are:

$$H_0 : \gamma_1 = 0$$

$$H_1 : \gamma_1 \neq 0$$

The test statistic is TR^2, where T is the number of observations in the auxiliary regression. It has a $\chi^2(1)$ distribution is the null hypothesis is true. Compare the *p*-value from this statistic to the desired test level (α) and reject the null if the *p*-value is smaller. If you suspect a higher order ARCH(q) error variance process, then include q lags of $\hat{e}_t^2$ as regressors, compute TR^2, and use the $\chi^2(q)$ distribution to obtain the *p*-value.

In the first ARCH example the *byd.dta* data are used. Load the data using the clear option to remove any previous data from Stata's memory.

```
use byd, clear
```

This dataset contains a single undated time series. Generate a time variable in the easiest way possible and declare the data to be time series.

```
gen time = _n
tsset time
```

In this instance, a time counter equal to the observation number is created using **_n** and this is set equal to the variable **time**. Then the **tsset** command is used to declare it a time series.

The first thing to do is plot the time series using

```
tsline r, name(g1, replace)
```

This yields

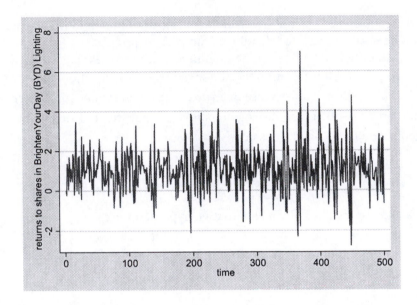

There is visual evidence of time varying volatility. Towards the end of the time series, returns for BYD appear to become more volatile. An ARCH(1) model is proposed and the ARCH(1) model is tested against the null hypothesis of no ARCH using the LM test discussed above. The first step is to estimate a regression that contains only an intercept. Obtain the residuals, which we call **ehat**, and square them.

```
regress r
predict ehat, residual
gen ehat2 = ehat * ehat
```

The auxiliary regression $\hat{e}_t^2 = \gamma_0 + \gamma_1 \hat{e}_{t-1}^2 + v_t$ uses the lag operator **L.** to take a single lag to include as a regressor in the auxiliary model.

```
regress ehat2 L.ehat2
```

The test statistic is TR^2 from this regression. The p-value is computed using the **chi2tail** function. Remember, the first argument of **chi2tail** is the degrees of freedom for your test (equal to q) and the second argument is the computed value of your statistic. Reject no arch if the p-value is less than the desired significance level, α. The Stata code is:

```
scalar TR2 = e(N)*e(r2)
scalar pvalue = chi2tail(1,TR2)
scalar crit = invchi2tail(1,.05)
scalar list TR2 pvalue crit
```

This yields the result:

```
. scalar list TR2 pvalue crit
       TR2 =  62.159504
    pvalue =  3.167e-15
      crit =  3.8414588
```

Stata also includes a built-in function to compute this test statistic. Using it will provide identical results. First estimate the regression then use the post-estimation command **archlm** as shown below:

```
. regress r
```

Source	SS	df	MS
Model	0	0	.
Residual	700.737278	499	1.40428312
Total	700.737278	499	1.40428312

Number of obs =	500
F(0, 499) =	0.00
Prob > F =	.
R-squared =	0.0000
Adj R-squared =	0.0000
Root MSE =	1.185

r	Coef.	Std. Err.	t	P>|t|	[95% Conf. Interval]
_cons	1.078294	.0529959	20.35	0.000	.9741716 1.182417

Then use the post-estimation command **archlm** as shown below.

```
estat archlm, lags(1)
```

As we know, post-estimation commands begin with **estat**, after which the **archlm** command is issued. The **archlm** command uses the **lags(q)** option, where **q** is the order of the ARCH process you wish to include in the alternative hypothesis. In this example $q=1$.

The results from the **archlm** command are:

```
. estat archlm, lags(1)
LM test for autoregressive conditional heteroskedasticity (ARCH)
```

lags(p)	chi2	df	Prob > chi2
1	62.160	1	0.0000

HO: no ARCH effects   vs.   H1: ARCH(p) disturbance

This is a particularly useful alternative to the manual process of computing TR^2 from an auxiliary regression. The null and alternative hypotheses are clearly stated, the statistic and its distribution are given, and the p-value is computed and shown in the default output. That means that Stata is generating all the information you need to properly conduct the test. Excellent!

The **archlm** test can be accessed through the dialogs, but the process is fairly convoluted. Just in case you haven't weaned yourself from using the pull-down menus yet here is how. First you need to estimate the mean equation using regression. Select **Statistics > Linear models and related > Linear regression**. Choose **r** as the dependent variable (with no independent variables) and click **OK**. Then, choose **Statistics > Time series > Tests < Time-series tests after regress**.

This reveals the **estat** dialog box that we've seen before.

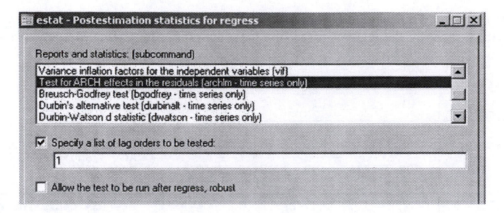

In this case, scroll down to the option **Test for ARCH effects in the residuals (archlm – time series only)** and then specify the number of lags to be tested (1 as shown). Click **OK**.

In this example, the no ARCH e ffects hypothesis is rejected at the 5% level and we proceed to estimation of the model.

The basic ARCH model and all the variants considered below are esti mated using the **arch** command. The syntax is shown below:

arch depvar [indepvars] [if] [in] [weight] [, options]

After issuing the **arch** command, list the dependent variable, independent variables (if you have any), and any conditionals or weights y ou may wish to use. Then, list the desired options. These options are what make Stata's arch command very flexible and powerful.

For the ARCH(1) model of BYD, th e option to use is sim ply **arch(1)**. The complete command syntax for an ARCH(1) model of BYD's returns is

arch r, arch(1)

which produces this output:

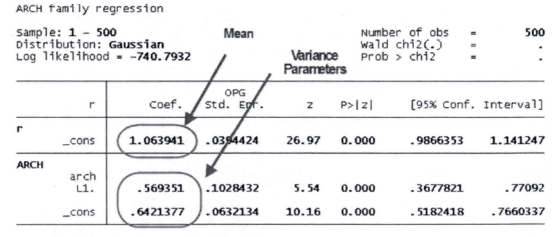

```
ARCH family regression

Sample: 1 - 500                    Mean              Number of obs   =        500
Distribution: Gaussian                               wald chi2(.)    =          .
Log likelihood = -740.7932              Variance     Prob > chi2     =          .
                                        Parameters
```

r	Coef.	OPG Std. Err.	z	P>|z|	[95% Conf. Interval]
r						
_cons	1.063941	.0384424	26.97	0.000	.9866353	1.141247
ARCH						
arch L1.	.569351	.1028432	5.54	0.000	.3677821	.77092
_cons	.6421377	.0632134	10.16	0.000	.5182418	.7660337

In the Stata output (but not shown) is a list of ite rations; this gives a clue as to how this magic is being performed. **Iterations** indicate that a nonlin ear numerical optimization is being us ed to obtain estimates, in this case to maxi mize the likelihood function (see Section C.8 of *Principles* *of Econometrics*). The log likelihood should be getting larger as the iterations proceed. If the numerical optimization somehow fails, an erro r message will appear just after the (many) iterations.

The parameter estimates follow the iteration su mmary. In this case they match those in *POE4*, but the standard errors are a little different.   Don't worry about this, they are valid if the ARCH(1) model is appropriate. So, in the BYD example, the average return is a bout 1.06%. The ARCH term's *t*-ratio is statistically significant and y   ou conclude that the varian   ce is autoregressive conditionally hete roskedastic (which for good m easure should be repeated out loud three times).

To   arrive at these results through   the dialogs choose   **Statistics > Time series > ARCH/GARCH > ARCH and GAR CH models** from the pull-down m enu. This reveals the **arch – Autoregres sive conditional heteroskedasticity family of estimators** dialog box sho wn below:

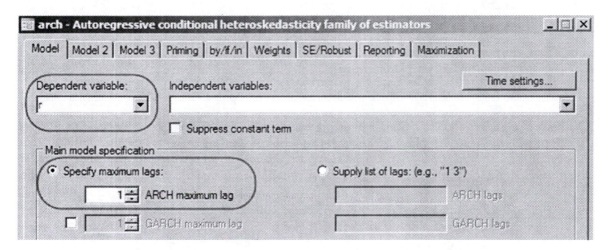

In this box choose **r** as the dependent variable and select a single lag in the **ARCH maximum lag** box. Click **OK** and you are done. Note, you can cho ose longer maximum ARCH lags (i.e., *q*) or even specify a list of lags in this dialog. The di alog is also used t o estimate a generalization of ARCH that is considered in the next section. Before moving on though, let's graph the estimated future return r_{t+1} and the conditional volatility h_{t+1}.

The forecasted return is just a constant in this case, since no explanatory variables other than a constant was included in the regression portion of the ARCH model

$$\hat{r}_{t+1} = \hat{\beta}_0 = 1.063$$

The forecasted error variance is essentially an in-sample prediction model based on the estimated variance function.

$$\hat{h}_{t+1} = \hat{\alpha}_0 + \hat{\alpha}_1 \left(r_t - \hat{\beta}_0 \right)^2 = 0.642 + 0.569 \left(r_t - 1.063 \right)^2$$

Stata generates this whenever it estimates an ARCH model and saves the result to a variable using the **predict** command with option **variance**. Here the ARCH(1) model is esti mated and the variance is generated and placed into a variable called **htarch**.

```
arch r, arch(1)
predict htarch, variance
```

This could be generated manually using saved results from the estimated ARCH model

```
gen ht_1 = _b[ARCH:_cons]+_b[ARCH:L1.arch]*(L.r-_b[r:_cons])^2
list htarch ht_1 in 496/500
```

which produces:

```
. list htarch ht_1 in 496/500
```

	htarch1	ht_1
496.	1.412281	1.412281
497.	.8093833	.8093833
498.	1.968768	1.968768
499.	1.614941	1.614941
500.	2.122526	2.122526

The built-in computation from Stata's **predict** command is confirmed by our manual calculation. Then **tsline** is used to plot the forecast error variance against time.

```
tsline htarch, name(g2, replace)
```

This produces the time series plot

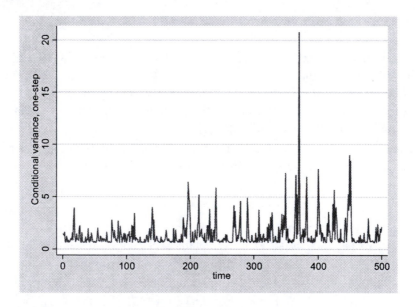

Obviously, there is a lot more volatility towards the end of the sample.

14.3 EXTENTIONS

An important extension of the ARCH(1) is the ARCH(q) model. Here, additional lags of the squared residuals are added as determinants of the equation's variance, h_t:

$$h_t = \alpha_0 + \alpha_1 e_{t-1}^2 + \alpha_2 e_{t-2}^2 ... + \alpha_q e_{t-q}^2$$

14.3.1 GARCH

Another extension is the **Generalized ARCH or GARCH** model. The GARCH model adds up to p lags of the variance, h_{t-p}, to the standard ARCH. A GARCH(1,1) model would look like this:

$$h_t = \delta + \alpha_1 e_{t-1}^2 + \beta_1 h_{t-1}$$

It has one lag of the regression model's squared residual (one ARCH t erm) and one lag of the variance (one GARCH term). Additional ARCH or GARCH terms can be added to obtai n the GARCH(p,q), where p is the number of lags for h_t and q is the n umber of lags of e_t included in the model.

Estimating a GARCH(1,1) m odel for BYD is simple. Basically, you just add a single GARCH term to the existing ARCH model, so the command is

```
arch r, arch(1) garch(1)
```

The syntax is interpreted this way . We have an **arch** regression m odel that includes **r** as a dependent variable and h as no i ndependent variables other than a constant. The first opt ion **arch(1)** tells Stata to add a single lagged value of e_t to the modeled variance; the second op tion **garch(1)** tells Stata to add a single lag of the variance, h_t, to the modeled variance. The result is:

```
ARCH family regression
```

Sample: 1 - 500   Number of obs   =   500
Distribution: Gaussian   Wald chi2(.)   =   .
Log likelihood = -736.0281   Prob > chi2   =   .

r	Coef.	OPG Std. Err.	z	P>|z|	[95% Conf. Interval]	
r						
_cons	1.049856	.0404623	25.95	0.000	.9705517	1.129161
ARCH						
arch L1.	.4911796	.1015995	4.83	0.000	.2920482	.6903109
garch L1.	.2379837	.1114836	2.13	0.033	.0194799	.4564875
_cons	.4009868	.0899182	4.46	0.000	.2247505	.5772232

The estimate of α_1 is 0.491 and the e stimated coefficient on the lagged variance, β_1 is 0.238. Again, there are a few minor differences between these results and those in the text, but that is to be expected when coefficient estim ates have to be s olved for via numerical methods rather than analytical ones.

As in the ARCH model, the predicted forecast variance can be saved and plotted:

```
predict htgarch, variance
tsline htgarch
```

which yields the time series plot:

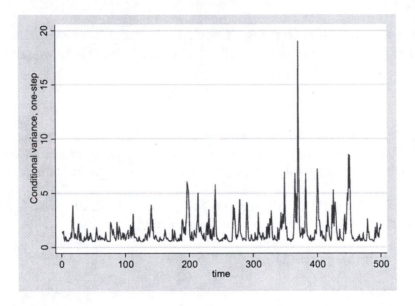

14.3.2 Threshold GARCH

The **threshold GARCH** model, or T-GARCH, is another generalization of the GARCH model where positive and negati ve news are treated asymmetrically. In the T-GARCH version of the model, the specification of the conditional variance is:

$$h_t = \delta + \alpha_1 e_{t-1}^2 + \gamma d_{t-1} e_{t-1}^2 + \beta_1 h_{t-1}$$

$$d_t = \begin{cases} 1 & e_t < 0 \text{ (bad news)} \\ 0 & e_t \geq 0 \text{ (good news)} \end{cases}$$

In Stata this just means that another opti on is added to the **arch r** regression model. The option to add asy mmetry of this sort is **tarch()** where t he argument tells St ata how many lagged asymmetry terms to add. This can be less than the number of ARCH terms, q, but not greater.

Here is a T-GARCH model for BYD.

```
arch r, arch(1) garch(1) tarch(1)
predict httgarch, variance
tsline httgarch
```

Once again, the variance is saved and plotted using a time series plot. The threshold GARCH result is:

```
ARCH family regression

Sample: 1 - 500                              Number of obs    =        500
Distribution: Gaussian                       Wald chi2(.)     =          .
Log likelihood =  -730.554                   Prob > chi2      =          .
```

	r	Coef.	OPG Std. Err.	z	P>|z|	[95% Conf. Interval]	
r							
	_cons	.9948399	.0429174	23.18	0.000	.9107234	1.078956
ARCH							
	arch L1.	.754298	.2003852	3.76	0.000	.3615501	1.147046
	tarch L1.	-.4917071	.2045045	-2.40	0.016	-.8925285	-.0908856
	garch L1.	.2873	.1154888	2.49	0.013	.0609462	.5136538
	_cons	.3557296	.0900538	3.95	0.000	.1792274	.5322318

and the plotted predicted error variances are:

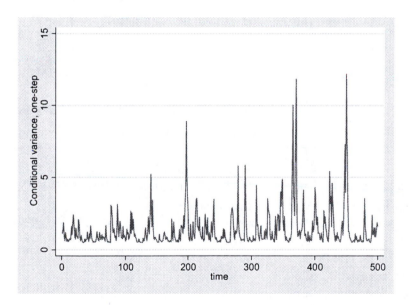

14.3.3 GARCH-in-mean

A final variation of the ARCH model is called **GARCH-in-mean (MGARCH)**. In this model, the variance, h_t, is added to the regression function.

$$y_t = \beta_0 + \theta h_t + e_t$$

If its parameter, θ, is positive then higher variances will cause the average return $E(y)$ to increase. This seems reasonable: more risk, higher average reward! To add a GARCH-in-mean to the BYD example, we simply add another option to the growing list in the **arch** statement. The command becomes:

```
arch r, archm arch(1) garch(1) tarch(1)
```

In this case, the option **archm** (which stands for arch in m ean) is added to the others, **arch(1) garch(1)** and **tarch(1)**. These are retained since these terms are included in the BYD example from the text. The results are

```
ARCH family regression
```

```
Sample: 1 - 500                              Number of obs   =         500
Distribution: Gaussian                       Wald chi2(1)    =        8.51
Log likelihood = -724.6549                   Prob > chi2     =      0.0035
```

r	Coef.	OPG Std. Err.	z	P>|z|	[95% Conf. Interval]	
r						
_cons	.8181453	.0711579	11.50	0.000	.6786783	.9576122
ARCHM						
sigma2	.1958843	.067164	2.92	0.004	.0642453	.3275233
ARCH						
arch L1.	.6160302	.1634603	3.77	0.000	.2956538	.9364066
tarch L1.	-.321069	.1621927	-1.98	0.048	-.6389608	-.0031772
garch L1.	.2783425	.1039073	2.68	0.007	.074688	.481997
_cons	.3705214	.0818646	4.53	0.000	.2100698	.5309731

You can see that the coefficient on the GARC H-in-mean term $\hat{\theta} = 0.1959$, is positive and statistically significant at the 5% level in this instance.

Finally, the p redicted mean and varian ce functions are saved an d plotted using time series plots.

```
predict m_mgarch, xb
predict htmgarch, variance
qui tsline m_mgarch, name(g5, replace)
qui tsline htmgarch, name(g6, replace)
graph combine g5 g6, cols(1)
```

In this case, the mean and variance are plotted in the same graph in a single column:

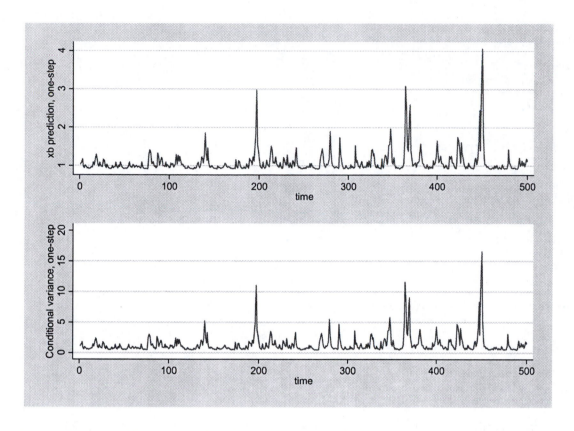

The predictions of the mean and variance follow very similar patterns.

KEY TERMS

arch()	**garch()**	threshold GARCH
ARCH	generalized ARCH (GARCH)	**tarch()**
format %tm	**histogram**	**tsline**
arch y, options	*LM* test	**variance equation**
archlm, lags()	mean equation	volatility
archm	**predict ehat, residual**	**%tm**
autoregressive conditional		
heteroskedastic	**predict yhat, xb**	
GARCH in Mean (MGARCH)	returns	

CHAPTER 14 DO-FILE

```
* file chap14.do for Using Stata for Principles of Econometrics, 4e

* cd c:\data\poe4stata

* Stata Do-file
* copyright C 2011 by Lee C. Adkins and R. Carter Hill
* used for "Using Stata for Principles of Econometrics, 4e"
```

```
* by Lee C. Adkins and R. Carter Hill (2011)
* John wiley and Sons, Inc.

* setup
version 11.1
capture log close
set more off

* open log
log using chap14, replace text
use returns, clear

* -----------------------------------------------
* Create dates and declare time series
* -----------------------------------------------

gen date = m(1988m1) + _n - 1
format date %tm
tsset date

* -----------------------------------------------
* Time series plots and histograms
* -----------------------------------------------

qui tsline nasdaq, name(nas, replace)
qui tsline allords, name(a, replace)
qui tsline ftse, name(f, replace)
qui tsline nikkei, name(nk, replace)
graph combine nas a f nk, cols(2) name(all1, replace)

qui histogram nasdaq, normal name(nas, replace)
qui histogram allords, normal name(a, replace)
qui histogram ftse, normal name(f, replace)
qui histogram nikkei, normal name(nk, replace)
graph combine nas a f nk, cols(2) name(all2, replace)

* -----------------------------------------------
* Load byd, create dates and declare time series
* -----------------------------------------------
use byd, clear
gen time = _n
tsset time

tsline r, name(g1, replace)

* -----------------------------------------------
* LM test for ARCH(1)
* -----------------------------------------------

regress r
predict ehat, residual

gen ehat2 = ehat * ehat
qui reg ehat2 L.ehat2
scalar TR2 = e(N)*e(r2)
scalar pvalue = chi2tail(1,TR2)
scalar crit = invchi2tail(1,.05)
scalar list TR2 pvalue crit

* -----------------------------------------------
* Built-in LM Test for ARCH(1)
* -----------------------------------------------
```

```
regress r
estat archlm, lags(1)


* -------------------------------------------------
* ARCH(1)
* -------------------------------------------------

arch r, arch(1)
predict htarch1, variance
tsline htarch, name(g2, replace)

gen ht_1 = _b[ARCH:_cons]+_b[ARCH:L1.arch]*(L.r-_b[r:_cons])^2
list htarch ht_1 in 496/500

* -------------------------------------------------
* GARCH(1,1)
* -------------------------------------------------

arch r, arch(1) garch(1)
predict htgarch, variance
tsline htgarch, name(g3, replace)


* -------------------------------------------------
* Threshold GARCH
* -------------------------------------------------

arch r, arch(1) garch(1) tarch(1)
predict httgarch, variance
tsline httgarch, name(g4, replace)


* -------------------------------------------------
* GARCH in mean
* -------------------------------------------------

arch r, archm arch(1) garch(1) tarch(1)
predict m_mgarch, xb
predict htmgarch, variance
qui tsline m_mgarch, name(g5, replace)
qui tsline htmgarch, name(g6, replace)
graph combine g5 g6, cols(1)

summarize m_mgarch r, detail
histogram m_mgarch, normal

log close
```

CHAPTER **15**

Panel Data Models

CHAPTER OUTLINE

15.1 A MICROECONOMETRIC PANEL

The data file *nls_panel.dta* contains a panel of data for 716 women for 5 years. Open the data file and obtain the summary statistics on key variables.

```
use nls_panel, clear
```

To take advantage of the cross section and time series nature of the data we must define the variables identifying the individual and time. To use any of Stata's powerful "**xt**" commands we must identify the variables that indicate the cross section observations (**i**) and the time series observations (**t**). The Stata command for this task is **xtset**.

```
xtset id year
```

```
. xtset id year
       panel variable:  id (strongly balanced)
        time variable:  year, 82 to 88, but with gaps
                delta:  1 unit
```

The data are strongly balanced, which means that for each individual we have the same number of time series observations, here 5, though the years, 1982, 1983, 1985, 1987 and 1988 are not evenly spaced. This is called a "balanced panel" and it was created by the authors from a larger data set, *nls.dta*, which is not balanced. Most panel data sets have large numbers of missing observations. This one does not have missing values for the key variables. The Stata command **xtdescribe** provides more information about the panel.

```
. xtdescribe

        id:  1, 2, ..., 716                              n =        716
      year:  82, 83, ..., 88                             T =          5
             Delta(year) = 1 unit
             Span(year)  = 7 periods
             (id*year uniquely identifies each observation)

Distribution of T_i:    min      5%     25%     50%     75%     95%     max
                          5       5       5       5       5       5       5

      Freq.   Percent    Cum. |  Pattern
     -------------------------+-----------
        716    100.00  100.00 |  11.1.11
     -------------------------+-----------
        716    100.00         |  XX.X.XX
```

If we **summarize** the data we find that the key variables have the same numbers of observations.

```
summarize lwage educ south black union exper tenure
```

```
. summarize lwage educ south black union exper tenure

    Variable |       Obs        Mean    Std. Dev.       Min         Max
-------------+----------------------------------------------------------
       lwage |      3580    1.918238    .4646068    .137109    4.254619
        educ |      3580    13.02235     2.44402          4          18
       south |      3580    .4240223    .4942627          0           1
       black |      3580    .2821229    .4500957          0           1
       union |      3580    .2642458    .4409924          0           1
-------------+----------------------------------------------------------
       exper |      3580    12.02858    3.862796   1.057692     27.1923
      tenure |      3580    6.947439    5.171849          0       24.75
```

If we list the first few observations we can see how they are stacked by individual.

```
list id year lwage educ south black union exper tenure in 1/10
```

. list id year lwage educ south black union exper tenure in 1/10

	id	year	lwage	educ	south	black	union	exper	tenure
1.	1	82	1.808289	12	0	1	1	7.666667	7.666667
2.	1	83	1.863417	12	0	1	1	8.583333	8.583333
3.	1	85	1.789367	12	0	1	1	10.17949	1.833333
4.	1	87	1.84653	12	0	1	1	12.17949	3.75
5.	1	88	1.856449	12	0	1	1	13.62179	5.25
6.	2	82	1.280933	17	0	0	0	7.576923	2.416667
7.	2	83	1.515855	17	0	0	0	8.384615	3.416667
8.	2	85	1.93017	17	0	0	0	10.38461	5.416667
9.	2	87	1.919034	17	0	0	1	12.03846	.3333333
10.	2	88	2.200974	17	0	0	1	13.21154	1.75

The fixed effects model is a model for pooling data. It permits cross-section heterogeneity by allowing the intercept to vary across individuals.

15.2 A POOLED MODEL

A pooled model is one where individuals are simply pooled together with no provision for individual or time differences.

$$y_{it} = \beta_1 + \beta_2 x_{2it} + \beta_3 x_{3it} + e_{it}$$

A basic regression specification is

> **reg lwage educ exper exper2 tenure tenure2 black south union**

. reg lwage educ exper exper2 tenure tenure2 black south union

Source	SS	df	MS
Model	251.535043	8	31.4418803
Residual	521.026186	3571	.145904841
Total	772.561229	3579	.215859522

```
Number of obs =     3580
F(  8,  3571) =   215.50
Prob > F      =   0.0000
R-squared     =   0.3256
Adj R-squared =   0.3241
Root MSE      =   .38197
```

lwage	Coef.	Std. Err.	t	P>|t|	[95% Conf. Interval]	
educ	.0714488	.0026894	26.57	0.000	.0661759	.0767217
exper	.0556851	.0086072	6.47	0.000	.0388096	.0725605
exper2	-.0011475	.0003613	-3.18	0.002	-.0018559	-.0004392
tenure	.01496	.0044073	3.39	0.001	.006319	.023601
tenure2	-.000486	.0002577	-1.89	0.059	-.0009913	.0000192
black	-.1167139	.0157159	-7.43	0.000	-.1475269	-.0859008
south	-.1060026	.0142008	-7.46	0.000	-.1338451	-.07816
union	.1322432	.0149616	8.84	0.000	.102909	.1615774
_cons	.4766	.0561559	8.49	0.000	.3664993	.5867008

15.2.1 Cluster-robust standard errors

Panel data has several observations per individual. The individual's error term may have some common components that are present for each time period. For example, if we are estimating a wage equation, the unobserved characteristics of any individual, such as ability, are present in each time period. The error terms for each individual may show an intercorrelation within the "cluster" of observations specific to the individual. To relax the usual assumption of zero error correlation over time for the same individual we write

$$cov(e_{it}, e_{is}) = \psi_{ts}$$

Notice that this alternative assumption also relaxes the assumption of homoskedasticity because, when $t = s$, we have

$$cov(e_{it}, e_{it}) = var(e_{it}) = \psi_{tt}$$

The error variance can be different in different time periods, but is constant over individuals. To avoid confusion with different σ^2's that will be used later, we have introduced another Greek letter "psi" (ψ) to denote the variances and covariances.

Under these assumptions the least squares estimator is unbiased and consistent, but the usual least squares estimator variance formulas no longer hold. It is much the same as in Chapters 8 and 9, where we used a "robust" covariance matrix for the least squares estimator. Similarly, in this case, we have "robust-cluster" standard errors. The concept and procedures are explained in *Principles of Econometrics, 4*[th] *Edition*, Appendix 15A on pages 581-583. Stata implements robust standard errors with a simple option

```
reg lwage educ exper exper2 tenure tenure2 black south union,
       vce(cluster id)
```

The option **vce(cluster id)** requires the variable **id** to be specified so that we can identify which observational error terms may be intercorrelated.

```
                            (Std. Err. adjusted for 716 clusters in id)
```

lwage	Coef.	Robust Std. Err.	t	P>|t|	[95% Conf. Interval]	
educ	.0714488	.0054995	12.99	0.000	.0606517	.0822459
exper	.0556851	.0113101	4.92	0.000	.03348	.0778901
exper2	-.0011475	.0004925	-2.33	0.020	-.0021144	-.0001807
tenure	.01496	.0071232	2.10	0.036	.0009752	.0289448
tenure2	-.000486	.0004102	-1.18	0.236	-.0012914	.0003194
black	-.1167139	.0281342	-4.15	0.000	-.1719493	-.0614784
south	-.1060026	.0270616	-3.92	0.000	-.1591322	-.052873
union	.1322432	.0270747	4.88	0.000	.0790878	.1853986
_cons	.4766	.0845629	5.64	0.000	.3105787	.6426213

Note that the output now shows **Robust Std. Err.** and a message that the standard errors are **adjusted for 716 clusters**, which corresponds to the number of individuals in the sample. Compared to the incorrect standard errors provided using **regress** with no correction, these robust standard errors are slightly larger.

15.3 THE FIXED EFFECTS MODEL

The fixed effects model allows for differences in the intercept parameter for each individual. The model is

$$y_{it} = \beta_{1i} + \beta_2 x_{2it} + \beta_3 x_{3it} + e_{it}, \quad i = 1, \dots, N$$

Note that the intercept now includes a subscript i which means that it is individual specific. We have in effect introduced N new parameters, one intercept parameter for each individual. To accomplish this we can create N indicator variables such as

$$D_{1i} = \begin{cases} 1 & i=1 \\ 0 & \text{otherwise} \end{cases} \qquad D_{2i} = \begin{cases} 1 & i=2 \\ 0 & \text{otherwise} \end{cases} \qquad D_{3i} = \begin{cases} 1 & i=3 \\ 0 & \text{otherwise} \end{cases}$$

If N is not too large then these indicator variables can be added to the regression model as additional variables. This is called the least squares dummy variable model.

$$y_{it} = \beta_{11} D_{1i} + \beta_{12} D_{2i} + \cdots + \beta_{1,10} D_{10i} + \beta_2 x_{2it} + \beta_3 x_{3it} + e_{it}$$

To illustrate, we have created a smaller version of *nls_panel.dta* with only 10 individuals. Open and examine the data set *nls_panel10.dta*.

```
use nls_panel10, clear
summarize
```

```
. summarize lwage educ exper exper2 tenure tenure2 black south union
```

Variable	Obs	Mean	Std. Dev.	Min	Max
lwage	50	2.197666	.3770917	1.280933	3.579129
educ	50	14.2	1.678191	12	17
exper	50	12.50923	2.827552	7.576923	19.04487
exper2	50	164.316	73.05605	57.40976	362.7071
tenure	50	6.498334	5.357182	0	19
tenure2	50	70.35375	96.20069	0	361
black	50	.1	.3030458	0	1
south	50	0	0	0	0
union	50	.44	.5014265	0	1

Note that among these 10 individuals none lived in the south, so that variable *SOUTH* will be omitted from the analysis in this section.

Rather than actually creating 10 indicator variables for the individuals, we use Stata's factor variable notation. In this case we want all levels of the variable **id** to have a unique indicator variable. Enter **help factor variables** and locate the discussion of "Base levels." A particular group can be specified as the base using **ib#.** where # is the desired base. That is, **ib2.group** would indicate that the 2nd group was the base group. Here, we do not wish a base group at all, so we specify **ibn.group** to indicate there is no base level.

The least squares dummy variable model is then estimated using

```
reg lwage ibn.id exper exper2 tenure tenure2 union, noconstant
```

We suppress the automatic constant term as its inclusion would create exact collinearity.

```
. reg lwage ibn.id exper exper2 tenure tenure2 union, noconstant
```

Source	SS	df	MS
Model	245.787227	15	16.3858151
Residual	2.66718984	35	.076205424
Total	248.454417	50	4.96908834

```
Number of obs =      50
F( 15,    35) =  215.02
Prob > F      =  0.0000
R-squared     =  0.9893
Adj R-squared =  0.9847
Root MSE      =  .27605
```

lwage	Coef.	Std. Err.	t	P>|t|	[95% Conf. Interval]	
id						
1	.1519055	1.096745	0.14	0.891	-2.074606	2.378417
2	.1868944	1.071485	0.17	0.863	-1.988335	2.362124
3	-.0630423	1.350917	-0.05	0.963	-2.805549	2.679464
4	.185626	1.343498	0.14	0.891	-2.54182	2.913072
5	.9389866	1.09778	0.86	0.398	-1.289625	3.167598
6	.7944846	1.111771	0.71	0.480	-1.462531	3.0515
7	.5811988	1.235914	0.47	0.641	-1.92784	3.090237
8	.537925	1.097498	0.49	0.627	-1.690114	2.765964
9	.4183341	1.084049	0.39	0.702	-1.782401	2.61907
10	.614558	1.090176	0.56	0.577	-1.598618	2.827734
exper	.2379985	.1877565	1.27	0.213	-.1431675	.6191646
exper2	-.0081882	.0079048	-1.04	0.307	-.0242358	.0078595
tenure	-.01235	.0341433	-0.36	0.720	-.0816647	.0569646
tenure2	.0022961	.0026885	0.85	0.399	-.0031617	.007754
union	.1135435	.1508628	0.75	0.457	-.1927244	.4198113

The analysis of variance table includes the usual information and shows that we have estimated 15 parameters.

For later use we save the sum of squared residuals, the degrees of freedom $N - K$, and the estimated error variance.

```
scalar sse_u = e(rss)
scalar df_u = e(df_r)
scalar sig2u = sse_u/df_u
```

To test the equality of the intercepts form the null and alternative hypotheses.

$$H_0 : \beta_{11} = \beta_{12} = \cdots = \beta_{1N}$$

$$H_1 : \text{the } \beta_{1i} \text{ are not all equal}$$

Use Stata's **test** statement with 9 pairs of equalities.

```
test (1.id=2.id) (2.id=3.id) (3.id=4.id) (4.id=5.id) ///
     (5.id=6.id) (6.id=7.id) (7.id=8.id) (8.id=9.id)(9.id=10.id)
```

```
. test (1.id=2.id) (2.id=3.id) (3.id=4.id) (4.id=5.id) ///
>      (5.id=6.id) (6.id=7.id) (7.id=8.id) (8.id=9.id)(9.id=10.id)

 ( 1)  1bn.id - 2.id = 0
 ( 2)  2.id - 3.id = 0
 ( 3)  3.id - 4.id = 0
 ( 4)  4.id - 5.id = 0
 ( 5)  5.id - 6.id = 0
 ( 6)  6.id - 7.id = 0
 ( 7)  7.id - 8.id = 0
 ( 8)  8.id - 9.id = 0
 ( 9)  9.id - 10.id = 0

      F( 9,     35) =     4.13
            Prob > F =    0.0011
```

In this case we find no significant differences, due primarily to the fact that we have only 10 individuals in the sample.

Alternatively we can estimated the "restricted model" and compute the F-statistic using

$$F = \frac{(SSE_R - SSE_U)/J}{SSE_U/(NT - K)}$$

Estimate the restricted model and save restricted sum of squared residuals SSE_R

```
reg lwage exper exper2 tenure tenure2 union
scalar sse_r = e(rss)
```

Use these values to compute the F-statistic, critical value and p-value.

```
scalar f = (sse_r - sse_u)/(9*sig2u)
scalar fc = invFtail(9,df_u,.05)
scalar pval = Ftail(9,df_u,f)
di "F test of equal intercepts = " f
di "F(9,df_u,.95) = " fc
di "p value = " pval
```

The results of these commands are

```
. di "F test of equal intercepts = " f
F test of equal intercepts = 4.1339667

. di "F(9,df_u,.95) = " fc
F(9,df_u,.95) = 2.1608293

. di "p value = " pval
p value = .00108357
```

15.3.1 The fixed effects estimator

The above approach works for small N. If we have thousands of individuals it is inconvenient to introduce indicator variables for each. Fixed effects estimation can be carried out using a single command that we will discuss below. First, however, we will consider an alternative approach using data that is in deviations from the mean form. To proceed, first find individual averages of the regression data for each individual.

$$\bar{y}_i = \frac{1}{T}\sum_{t=1}^{T} y_{it} = \beta_{1i} + \beta_2 \frac{1}{T}\sum_{t=1}^{T} x_{2it} + \beta_3 \frac{1}{T}\sum_{t=1}^{T} x_{3it} + \frac{1}{T}\sum_{t=1}^{T} e_{it}$$

$$= \beta_{1i} + \beta_2 \bar{x}_{2i} + \beta_3 \bar{x}_{3i} + \bar{e}_i$$

The "bar" notation $\bar{y}_i$ indicates that we have averaged the values of y_{it} over time. Then, subtract this averaged equation from

$$y_{it} = \beta_{1i} + \beta_2 x_{2it} + \beta_3 x_{3it} + e_{it} \quad t = 1, \ldots, T$$

to obtain

$$y_{it} = \beta_{1i} + \beta_2 x_{2it} + \beta_3 x_{3it} + e_{it}$$

$$\underline{- \quad (\bar{y}_i = \beta_{1i} + \beta_2 \bar{x}_{2i} + \beta_3 \bar{x}_{3i} + \bar{e}_i)}$$

$$y_{it} - \bar{y}_i = \beta_2(x_{2it} - \bar{x}_{2i}) + \beta_3(x_{3it} - \bar{x}_{3i}) + (e_{it} - \bar{e}_i)$$

Least squares applied to this equation will produce the fixed effects estimates. The data set *nls_panel_devn.dta* contains the data in deviation from the mean form. Open this data set and **summarize**.

```
use nls_panel_devn, clear
summarize
```

```
. summarize

    Variable |        Obs        Mean    Std. Dev.        Min         Max
-------------+--------------------------------------------------------------
      lw_dev |         50     2.83e-18    .2643443   -.8445444    1.055708
     exp_dev |         50    -1.48e-17     2.26546   -3.092308    3.369232
    exp2_dev |         50     2.58e-16    58.50121   -93.17334    111.1935
     ten_dev |         50    -4.86e-18    2.130799   -3.583334    3.383334
    ten2_dev |         50    -3.42e-16    39.09372   -91.27776    111.3819
-------------+--------------------------------------------------------------
   union_dev |         50            0    .2857143         -.6          .8
```

Note that the Mean of each variable is zero, because it is in deviation about the mean form.
List a few of the values.

```
list lw_dev exp_dev union_dev in 1/10
```

```
. list lw_dev exp_dev union_dev in 1/10
```

	lw_dev	exp_dev	union_~v
1.	-.0245214	-2.779487	0
2.	.0306066	-1.862821	0
3.	-.0434434	-.266664	0
4.	.0137196	1.733336	0
5.	.0236386	3.175636	0
6.	-.4884602	-2.7423066	-.4
7.	-.2535382	-1.9346146	-.4
8.	.1607768	.0653804	-.4
9.	.1496408	1.7192304	.6
10.	.4315808	2.8923104	.6

Try to use the data and summary statistics from *nls_panel10.dta* to create a few of these values by hand. The regression using these data is

reg lw_dev exp_dev exp2_dev ten_dev ten2_dev union_dev, noconstant

```
. reg lw_dev exp_dev exp2_dev ten_dev ten2_dev union_dev, noconstant
```

Source	SS	df	MS
Model	.756828872	5	.151365774
Residual	2.66718984	45	.059270885
Total	3.42401872	50	.068480374

```
Number of obs =      50
F(  5,    45) =    2.55
Prob > F      =  0.0407
R-squared     =  0.2210
Adj R-squared =  0.1345
Root MSE      =  .24346
```

lw_dev	Coef.	Std. Err.	t	P>|t|	[95% Conf. Interval]
exp_dev	.2379985	.1655857	1.44	0.158	-.0955082 .5715052
exp2_dev	-.0081882	.0069714	-1.17	0.246	-.0222293 .0058529
ten_dev	-.01235	.0301116	-0.41	0.684	-.0729979 .0482978
ten2_dev	.0022961	.002371	0.97	0.338	-.0024793 .0070716
union_dev	.1135435	.1330485	0.85	0.398	-.15443 .381517

Compare the estimated coefficients to those from the estimation including the 10 indicator variables. They are the same. The standard errors here are a little off, because their calculation using **regress** does not recognize that we have taken the deviations about the mean. A correct calculation would have the Residual degrees of freedom equal to 35.

Let us create the deviations ourselves. Open again the *nls_panel10.dta* file, clear memory and use **xtset**.

```
use nls_panel10, clear
xtset id year
```

We can use the dialog boxes for **extensions to functions** to accomplish the calculation of the group means. From the drop down menus select **Data > Create or change variables > Create new variable (extended)**.

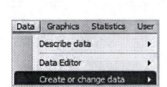

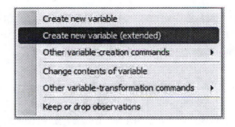

The dialog box can also be opened using the link from **help egen**

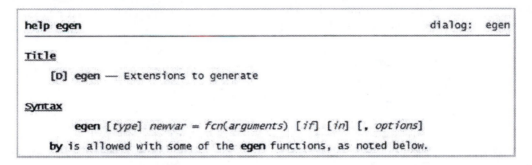

Alternatively enter **db egen**. Fill in the **Generate variable** box with a variable name. Select **mean** in the **egen function** drop down list. Enter the **expression** on which the function will operate, here simply the variable **lwage**

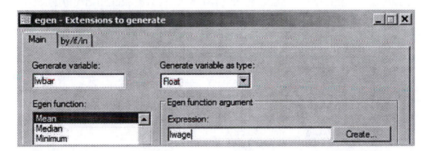

Click on the **by/if/in** tab.

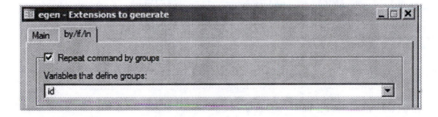

Enter the variable defining the groups (individuals) and click the **Repeat command by groups** box. Equivalently use the Stata commands. **Sort** the data by individual **id**, using the **stable** option, and then use extensions to generate commands (**egen**) with the **by** command.

```
sort id, stable
```

To save ourselves some typing, and reduce the odds of a typing error, we will use a loop in order to create deviations about means for each variable. First, create a list containing the variables we wish to transform.

```
global v1list lwage exper exper2 tenure tenure2 union
```

The **foreach** loop control has much the same structure as the **forvalues** loop used in Chapter 9. For each of the variables in the global v1list we will use **egen** to create the mean, and then **generate** the deviation about the mean. The **foreach** statement line ends in a left brace "{" and concludes with a single right brace "}". The statements in between are performed repeatedly using the `var` to designate the variable name in the list.

```
foreach var of varlist $v1list {
        by i: egen `var'bar = mean(`var')
        gen `var'_dev = `var' - `var'bar
        }
```

List the data, and apply least squares to these data, with no constant, produce the fixed effects estimates.

```
list id year lwage lwagebar lwage_dev in 1/10
```

We see that **lwbar** is constant across each time observation for each individual.

```
. list id year lwage lwagebar lwage_dev in 1/10
```

	id	year	lwage	lwagebar	lwage_dev
1.	1	82	1.808289	1.83281	-.0245214
2.	1	83	1.863417	1.83281	.0306066
3.	1	85	1.789367	1.83281	-.0434434
4.	1	87	1.84653	1.83281	.0137196
5.	1	88	1.856449	1.83281	.0236386
6.	2	82	1.280933	1.769393	-.4884602
7.	2	83	1.515855	1.769393	-.2535382
8.	2	85	1.93017	1.769393	.1607768
9.	2	87	1.919034	1.769393	.1496408
10.	2	88	2.200974	1.769393	.4315808

Apply least squares estimation to the data in deviation from mean form.

```
reg lwage_dev exper_dev exper2_dev tenure_dev tenure2_dev union_dev,
        noconstant
```

```
. reg lwage_dev exper_dev exper2_dev tenure_dev tenure2_dev union_dev, noconst
> ant
```

Source	SS	df	MS		Number of obs =	50
					F(5, 45) =	2.55
Model	.756828858	5	.151365772		Prob > F =	0.0407
Residual	2.66718982	45	.059270885		R-squared =	0.2210
					Adj R-squared =	0.1345
Total	3.42401868	50	.068480374		Root MSE =	.24346

lwage_dev	Coef.	Std. Err.	t	P>|t|	[95% Conf. Interval]	
exper_dev	.2379985	.1655857	1.44	0.158	-.0955082	.5715052
exper2_dev	-.0081882	.0069714	-1.17	0.246	-.0222293	.0058529
tenure_dev	-.01235	.0301116	-0.41	0.684	-.0729979	.0482978
tenure2_dev	.0022961	.002371	0.97	0.338	-.0024793	.0070716
union_dev	.1135435	.1330485	0.85	0.398	-.15443	.3815169

The standard errors from this least squares regression are not correct. This is because the estimate of the error variance used by the least squares software is $\hat{\sigma}_{e*}^2 = SSE/(NT-5)$, which neglects the fact that we have used N individual means to center the data. The centering process uses up a degree of freedom for each individual. When what is required is $\hat{\sigma}_e^2 = SSE/(NT-N-5)$. It is better to use the automatic software for fixed effects, so this calculation will be done correctly.

15.3.2 The fixed effects estimator using xtreg

Fixed effects estimation is accomplished using the **xtreg** command with the option **fe**. Stata help, **help xtreg**, shows the syntax for this estimation.

```
help xtreg                                          dialog:  xtreg
                                                    also see:  xtreg postestimation


Title

    [XT] xtreg — Fixed-, between-, and random-effects, and population-averaged linear models


Syntax

    GLS random-effects (RE) model

        xtreg depvar [indepvars] [if] [in] [, re RE_options]


    Between-effects (BE) model

        xtreg depvar [indepvars] [if] [in] , be [BE_options]


    Fixed-effects (FE) model

        xtreg depvar [indepvars] [if] [in] [weight] , fe [FE_options]
```

```
xtreg lwage exper exper2 tenure tenure2 union, fe
```

```
. xtreg lwage exper exper2 tenure tenure2 union, fe

Fixed-effects (within) regression              Number of obs      =          50
Group variable: id                             Number of groups   =          10

R-sq:  within  = 0.2210                         Obs per group: min =           5
       between = 0.0226                                        avg =         5.0
       overall = 0.0742                                        max =           5

                                                F(5,35)            =        1.99
corr(u_i, Xb)  = -0.3986                        Prob > F           =      0.1050
```

lwage	Coef.	Std. Err.	t	P>|t|	[95% Conf. Interval]
exper	.2379985	.1877565	1.27	0.213	-.1431675 .6191646
exper2	-.0081882	.0079048	-1.04	0.307	-.0242358 .0078595
tenure	-.01235	.0341433	-0.36	0.720	-.0816647 .0569646
tenure2	.0022961	.0026885	0.85	0.399	-.0031617 .007754
union	.1135435	.1508628	0.75	0.457	-.1927244 .4198113
_cons	.4346871	1.14518	0.38	0.707	-1.890152 2.759526
sigma_u	.3161662				
sigma_e	.2760533				
rho	.56742384	(fraction of variance due to u_i)			

```
F test that all u_i=0:      F(9, 35) =      4.13             Prob > F = 0.0011
```

There are some familiar, and some unfamiliar, contents. The familiar items are the coefficients and standard errors of the estimated coefficients. One unfamiliar item is the coefficient labeled **_cons**. Stata reports the average of the 10 indicator variable coefficients. We explore this below. The F-test statistic for the null hypothesis that there is no significant difference between the individual intercepts is located at the bottom of the output.

15.3.3 Fixed effects using the complete panel

Now we use the complete panel data set to estimate the wage equation. Open *nls_panel.dta* and use **xtset**.

```
use nls_panel, clear
xtset id year
```

Create a variable list that we will use repeatedly and then apply the fixed effects estimator.

```
global x1list exper exper2 tenure tenure2 south union
xtreg lwage $x1list, fe
```

```
. xtreg lwage $x1list, fe
```

```
Fixed-effects (within) regression          Number of obs     =       3580
Group variable: id                         Number of groups  =        716

R-sq:  within  = 0.1430                     Obs per group: min =          5
       between = 0.1162                                    avg =        5.0
       overall = 0.1170                                    max =          5

                                           F(6,2858)         =      79.46
corr(u_i, Xb)  = 0.0952                     Prob > F          =     0.0000
```

lwage	Coef.	Std. Err.	t	P>|t|	[95% Conf.	Interval]
exper	.0410832	.00662	6.21	0.000	.0281027	.0540637
exper2	-.0004091	.0002733	-1.50	0.135	-.000945	.0001269
tenure	.0139089	.0032778	4.24	0.000	.0074818	.0203361
tenure2	-.0008962	.0002059	-4.35	0.000	-.0012999	-.0004926
south	-.0163224	.036149	-0.45	0.652	-.0872031	.0545584
union	.0636972	.0142538	4.47	0.000	.0357485	.091646
_cons	1.450034	.04014	36.12	0.000	1.371328	1.52874

sigma_u	.40231926					
sigma_e	.19511039					
rho	.80959194	(fraction of variance due to u_i)				

```
F test that all u_i=0:      F(715, 2858) =      19.66          Prob > F = 0.0000
```

The overall *F*-test for 715 individual differences, labeled by Stata **F test that all u_i=0:**, shows that there are significant differences between at least some individuals.

If heteroskedasticity is anticipated, or if we anticipate unobserved heterogeneity to persist through time for individuals, then we can make adjustment using cluster corrected standard errors.

```
xtreg lwage $x1list, fe vce(cluster id)
```

(Std. Err. adjusted for 716 clusters in id)

lwage	Coef.	Robust Std. Err.	t	P>|t|	[95% Conf.	Interval]
exper	.0410832	.0082404	4.99	0.000	.0249049	.0572615
exper2	-.0004091	.0003299	-1.24	0.215	-.0010568	.0002387
tenure	.0139089	.0042154	3.30	0.001	.0056329	.022185
tenure2	-.0008962	.0002495	-3.59	0.000	-.0013861	-.0004064
south	-.0163224	.05848	-0.28	0.780	-.1311355	.0984907
union	.0636972	.0168605	3.78	0.000	.0305952	.0967993
_cons	1.450034	.055029	26.35	0.000	1.341996	1.558072

These commands can be obtained using the pull-down menus. Follow the path

Statistics > Longitudinal/panel data > Linear models > Linear regression (FE, RE, PA, BE)

Alternatively enter **db xtreg**. In the dialog box choose the dependent and independent variables, and choose the **Fixed-effects** button. Click OK.

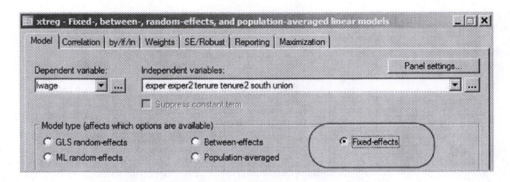

To obtain the fixed effects, from the **Statistics > Postestimation** drop down menu select **Predictions, residuals, etc.**

In the dialog box name the variable and select the option shown. Click OK.

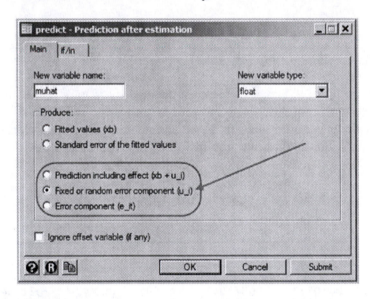

Alternatively, to compute the indicator variable coefficients for each individual, follow the estimation of the fixed effects model with the post-estimation command

```
predict muhat, u
```

Here **muhat** is a variable name, and the option **u** with predict in this case estimates the fixed effects. To obtain the indicator variable coefficients **add these values to the average value** given by **_cons**. Compute the sum of the **muhat** values

```
tabstat muhat if year==82, stat(sum)
```

variable	sum
muhat	-1.12e-07

It should be noted that including the variables for race (**black**) and years of education (**educ**) leads to exact collinearity of a particular form. The variable **black** is an indicator variable equal to 1 for a black person and 0 for white. In this data set only two races are included for simplicity. In larger data sets there may be indicators for other races. In this case, for each person the indicator **black** does not change over time. It is said to be time invariant. Similarly, in this sample, the variable **educ** does not change across time for any of the women in the sample. This is because they had all completed their education before the data collection began. Thus when we create deviations about the means, as in Section 15.3.1 above, we obtain a string of 5 zeroes for both of these variables. The variables **black** and **educ** in deviation about the mean form are all zeroes, and thus offer no variation to use in the estimation process. The fixed effects estimation including these variables is

```
global x2list educ black $x1list
xtreg lwage $x2list, fe
```

lwage	Coef.	Std. Err.	t	P>|t|	[95% Conf. Interval]	
educ	(omitted)					
black	(omitted)					
exper	.0410832	.00662	6.21	0.000	.0281027	.0540637
exper2	-.0004091	.0002733	-1.50	0.135	-.000945	.0001269
tenure	.0139089	.0032778	4.24	0.000	.0074818	.0203361
tenure2	-.0008962	.0002059	-4.35	0.000	-.0012999	-.0004926
south	-.0163224	.036149	-0.45	0.652	-.0872031	.0545584
union	.0636972	.0142538	4.47	0.000	.0357485	.091646
_cons	1.450034	.04014	36.12	0.000	1.371328	1.52874
sigma_u	.40231926					
sigma_e	.19511039					
rho	.80959194	(fraction of variance due to u_i)				

In the results note that the variables **black** and **educ** have been dropped by Stata. Look at the few listed observations in Section 15.1 of this chapter, and you can see that this is true, for these few observations. A better check is provided using the Stata command **xtsum**, which summarizes cross section and time series data.

```
xtsum educ
```

Variable		Mean	Std. Dev.	Min	Max	Observations	
educ	overall	13.02235	2.44402	4	18	N =	3580
	between		2.445387	4	18	n =	716
	within		0	13.02235	13.02235	T =	5

Note that the **within standard deviation** is zero. That means that within the observations on each individual there is no variation, or that **educ** is constant for each individual. The fixed effects transformation eliminates such variables. While Stata drops variables that are time invariant from the fixed effects estimation, it is better to specify the model correctly. See the estimation results at the beginning of Section 15.3.3.

Chapter 15

15.4 RANDOM EFFECTS ESTIMATION

The random effects model treats the heterogeneity across individuals as a random component. The model is

$$y_{it} = \overline{\beta}_1 + \beta_2 x_{2it} + \beta_3 x_{3it} + \left(e_{it} + u_i \right)$$

$$= \overline{\beta}_1 + \beta_2 x_{2it} + \beta_3 x_{3it} + v_{it}$$

where the combined error is

$$v_{it} = u_i + e_{it}$$

The key properties of this new error term is that it is homoskedastic

$$\sigma_v^2 = \text{var}\left(v_{it} \right) = \text{var}\left(u_i + e_{it} \right) = \sigma_u^2 + \sigma_e^2$$

but serially correlated in a special way. For individual i

$$\text{cov}\left(v_{it}, v_{is} \right) = \sigma_u^2$$

The correlation of these observations is

$$\rho = \text{corr}(v_{it}, v_{is}) = \frac{\text{cov}(v_{it}, v_{is})}{\sqrt{\text{var}(v_{it}) \text{var}(v_{is})}} = \frac{\sigma_u^2}{\sigma_u^2 + \sigma_e^2}$$

This intra-individual correlation is very important. For two individuals i and j

$$\text{cov}\left(v_{it}, v_{js} \right) = 0$$

The model's parameters are estimated by (feasible) generalized least squares. This estimation is implemented by **xtreg** in the same way fixed effects estimation is carried out. Random effects estimation is accomplished by simply changing the **xtreg** option to **re**. We continue with the data file *nls_panel.dta* used in the previous section.

```
xtreg lwage $x2list, re theta
```

The option **theta** is present to have Stata print the transformation parameter used in the GLS estimation. We will say more about this below.

```
Random-effects GLS regression              Number of obs    =      3580
Group variable: id                         Number of groups =       716

R-sq:  within  = 0.1411                    Obs per group: min =         5
       between = 0.3543                                    avg =       5.0
       overall = 0.3191                                    max =         5

Random effects u_i ~ Gaussian              Wald chi2(8)     =    860.08
corr(u_i, X)        = 0 (assumed)           Prob > chi2      =    0.0000
theta               = .74368295
```

lwage	Coef.	Std. Err.	z	P>|z|	[95% Conf. Interval]	
educ	.0732536	.0053308	13.74	0.000	.0628055	.0837017
exper	.043617	.0063576	6.86	0.000	.0311564	.0560776
exper2	-.000561	.0002626	-2.14	0.033	-.0010757	-.0000463
tenure	.0141541	.0031666	4.47	0.000	.0079478	.0203605
tenure2	-.0007553	.0001947	-3.88	0.000	-.001137	-.0003737
black	-.1167366	.0302087	-3.86	0.000	-.1759446	-.0575286
south	-.0818117	.0224109	-3.65	0.000	-.1257363	-.0378871
union	.0802353	.0132132	6.07	0.000	.0543379	.1061327
_cons	.5339294	.0798828	6.68	0.000	.377362	.6904968

sigma_u	.32904965	
sigma_e	.19511039	
rho	.73986872	(fraction of variance due to u_i)

In the estimation output, note several items. First the coefficients of educ and black can be estimated by random effects. Second, the estimated value of $\rho = 0.74$. The error components estimates are

$$\hat{\sigma}_u = .3290$$

$$\hat{\sigma}_e = .1951$$

The random effects estimator's standard errors can be made robust to cluster effects.

```
xtreg lwage $x2list, re vce(cluster id)
```

We might do such a thing if we believe that there is heteroskedasticity across individual, or there is serial correlation in the overall error term over time.

15.4.1 The GLS transformation

The process of implementing generalized least squares in the random effects model is discussed in *Principles of Econometrics, 4th edition*, Chapter 15, Appendix B. The random effects model is

$$y_{it} = \bar{\beta}_1 + \beta_2 x_{2it} + \beta_3 x_{3it} + (u_i + e_{it})$$

where u_i is the individual specific error and e_{it} is the usual regression error. We will discuss the case for a balanced panel, with T time series observations for each of N individuals. To implement generalized least squares estimation we need to consistently estimate σ_u^2, the variance of the individual specific error component, and σ_e^2, the variance of the regression error.

We obtain the generalized least squares estimator in the random effects model by applying least squares to a transformed model. The transformed model is

$$y_{it}^* = \beta_1 x_{1it}^* + \beta_2 x_{2it}^* + \beta_3 x_{3it}^* + v_{it}^*$$

where the transformed variables are

$$y_{it}^* = y_{it} - \alpha \overline{y}_i, \quad x_{1it}^* = 1 - \alpha, \quad x_{2it}^* = x_{2it} - \alpha \overline{x}_{2i}, \quad x_{3it}^* = x_{3it} - \alpha \overline{x}_{3i}$$

The variables $\overline{y}_i$, $\overline{x}_{2i}$ and $\overline{x}_{3i}$ are the individual means. The transformed error term is $v_{it}^* = v_{it} - \alpha \overline{v}_i$. The key transformation parameter α (which is called **theta** by Stata) is defined as

$$\alpha = 1 - \frac{\sigma_e}{\sqrt{T\sigma_u^2 + \sigma_e^2}}$$

The regression error variance σ_e^2 comes from the fixed effects estimator. The panel data regression in "deviation about the individual mean" form is

$$y_{it} - \overline{y}_i = \beta_2 \left(x_{2it} - \overline{x}_{2i} \right) + \beta_3 \left(x_{3it} - \overline{x}_{3i} \right) + \left(e_{it} - \overline{e}_i \right)$$

A consistent estimator of σ_e^2 is obtained by dividing SSE_{DV} by the appropriate degrees of freedom, which is $NT - N - K_{slopes}$, where K_{slopes} is the number of parameters that are present in the transformed

$$\hat{\sigma}_e^2 = \frac{SSE_{DV}}{NT - N - K_{slopes}}$$

The estimator of σ_u^2 requires a bit more work. We begin with the time averaged observations

$$\overline{y}_i = \beta_1 + \beta_2 \overline{x}_{2i} + \beta_3 \overline{x}_{3i} + u_i + \overline{e}_i \qquad i = 1, 2, \ldots, N$$

The least squares estimator of this model is called the **between estimator**. The error term in this model is $u_i + \overline{e}_i$; it is uncorrelated across individuals, and has homoskedastic variance

$$\mathrm{var} \left(u_i + \overline{e}_i \right) = \sigma_u^2 + \frac{\sigma_e^2}{T}$$

We can estimate this variance by estimating the between regression and dividing the sum of squared errors, SSE_{BE}, by the degrees of freedom $N - K_{BE}$, where K_{BE} is the total number of parameters in the between regression, including the intercept parameter. Then

$$\widetilde{\sigma_u^2 + \frac{\sigma_e^2}{T}} = \frac{SSE_{BE}}{N - K_{BE}}$$

With this estimate in hand we can estimate σ_u^2 as

$$\hat{\sigma}_u^2 = \widetilde{\sigma_u^2 + \frac{\sigma_e^2}{T}} - \frac{\hat{\sigma}_e^2}{T} = \frac{SSE_{BE}}{N - K_{BE}} - \frac{SSE_{DV}}{T\left(NT - N - K_{slopes}\right)}$$

While Stata shows us the theta parameter used in the GLS estimation, **theta = .74368295**, it is good to be able to replicate this value for ourselves.

First, obtain the fixed effects estimate and save the estimated error variance.

```
quietly xtreg lwage $x2list, fe
scalar sig2e =( e(sigma_e))^2
```

The between estimator is another option within **xtreg**. Use **ereturn list** to see what is saved.

```
xtreg lwage $x2list, be
ereturn list
```

Obtain the estimated error variance and carry out the calculation of the transformation parameter.

```
scalar sig2b = e(rss)/e(df_r)
scalar sig2u = sig2b - sig2e/e(Tbar)
scalar sigu = sqrt(sig2u)
scalar theta = 1-sqrt(sig2e/(e(Tbar)*sig2u+sig2e))
di "Components of variance"
di "sig2e   = " sig2e " variance of overall error e(it)"
di "sige    = " sqrt(sig2e) " standard deviation of e(it)"
di "sig2b   = " sig2b " variance from between regression "
di "sig2u   = " sig2u " derived variance mu(i) "
di "sigu    = " sigu  " standard deviation mu(i) "
di "theta   = " theta " transformation parameter "
```

The displayed information shows that we have obtained the same value as Stata.

```
Components of variance
sig2e   = .03806806 variance of overall error e(it)
sige    = .19511039 standard deviation of e(it)
sig2b   = .11588729 variance from between regression
sig2u   = .10827367 derived variance mu(i)
sigu    = .32904965 standard deviation mu(i)
theta   = .74368295 transformation parameter
```

The transformation of the data is accomplished in the same way as the fixed effects transformation, subtracting a scalar times the time averaged variables, including the intercept. First compute the time averages and then the partial differences.

```
gen one = 1
sort id, stable

global v2list lwage one $x2list

foreach var of varlist $v2list {
      by i: egen `var'bar = mean(`var')
      gen `var'd = `var' - theta*`var'bar
      }
```

Applying least squares to the transformed data we have

```
reg lwaged educd blackd experd exper2d tenured tenure2d southd uniond
    oned, noconstant
```

Source	SS	df	MS
Model	898.326385	9	99.8140427
Residual	136.490642	3571	.038221966
Total	1034.81703	3580	.289055035

Number of obs =	3580
F(9, 3571) =	2611.43
Prob > F =	0.0000
R-squared =	0.8681
Adj R-squared =	0.8678
Root MSE =	.1955

lwaged	Coef.	Std. Err.	t	P>|t|	[95% Conf. Interval]	
educd	.0732536	.0053308	13.74	0.000	.0628019	.0837052
blackd	-.1167366	.0302087	-3.86	0.000	-.1759646	-.0575085
experd	.043617	.0063576	6.86	0.000	.0311521	.0560818
exper2d	-.000561	.0002626	-2.14	0.033	-.0010758	-.0000461
tenured	.0141541	.0031666	4.47	0.000	.0079457	.0203626
tenure2d	-.0007553	.0001947	-3.88	0.000	-.0011371	-.0003736
southd	-.0818117	.0224109	-3.65	0.000	-.1257512	-.0378722
uniond	.0802353	.0132132	6.07	0.000	.0543291	.1061415
oned	.5339295	.0798828	6.68	0.000	.377309	.6905499

Compare these estimates to the estimates obtained using **xtreg** with the option **re**. They are the same, as are the standard errors.

15.4.2 The Breusch-Pagan test

To test for the presence of random effects we use the Breusch-Pagan test statistic

$$LM^2 = \frac{NT}{2(T-1)} \left\{ \frac{\left[\sum_{i=1}^{N} \left(\sum_{t=1}^{T} \hat{e}_{it} \right) \right]^2}{\sum_{i=1}^{N} \sum_{t=1}^{T} \hat{e}_{it}^2} - 1 \right\}^2$$

If the null hypothesis $H_0 : \sigma_u^2 = 0$ is true, i.e., there are no random effects, then $LM \sim N(0,1)$ in large samples. Thus, we reject H_0 at significance level α and accept the alternative $H_1 : \sigma_u^2 > 0$ if $LM > z_{(1-\alpha)}$, where $z_{(1-\alpha)}$ is the $100(1-\alpha)$ percentile of the standard normal $[N(0,1)]$ distribution. This critical value is 1.645 if $\alpha = 0.05$ and 2.326 if $\alpha = 0.01$. Rejecting the null hypothesis leads us to conclude that random effects are present.

The original LM test due to Breusch and Pagan used LM^2 with the distribution under H_0 as $\chi_{(1)}^2$. Subsequent authors pointed out that the alternative hypothesis for using LM^2 is $H_1 : \sigma_u^2 \neq 0$, and that we can do better by using LM as a one-sided $N(0,1)$ test with alternative hypothesis $H_1 : \sigma_u^2 > 0$. Some software, for example Stata, reports LM^2. The danger from using LM^2 is that $LM < 0$ is possible and should not be taken as evidence that $\sigma_u^2 > 0$. The adjustment for a chi-square test at significance α is to use the $100(1 - 2\alpha)$ percentile of the χ^2-distribution. This critical value for an $\alpha = 0.05$ test is 2.706 which is 1.645^2. It should only be used for $LM > 0$.

To implement this test in Stata use the post estimation command **xttest0**. Obtain the random effects estimates again quietly, since **xttest0** operates on the previous estimation.

```
quietly xtreg lwage $x2list, re
xttest0
```

```
Breusch and Pagan Lagrangian multiplier test for random effects

        lwage[id,t] = Xb + u[id] + e[id,t]

        Estimated results:
                      |      Var       sd = sqrt(Var)
                ------+-------------------------------
                lwage |   .2158595        .4646068
                    e |   .0380681        .1951104
                    u |   .1082737        .3290497

        Test:    Var(u) = 0
                              chi2(1) =    3859.28
                          Prob > chi2 =     0.0000
```

15.4.3 The Hausman test

To check for any correlation between the error component u_i and the regressors in a random effects model we can use a Hausman test. The test compares the coefficient estimates from the random effects model to those from the fixed effects model. The idea underlying Hausman's test is that both the random effects and fixed effects estimators are consistent if there is no correlation between u_i and the explanatory variables x_{kit}. If both estimators are consistent then they should converge to the true parameter values β_k in large samples. That is, in large samples the random effects and fixed effects estimates should be similar. On the other hand, if u_i is correlated with any x_{kit} the random effects estimator is inconsistent, while the fixed effects estimator remains consistent. Thus in large samples the fixed effects estimator converges to the true parameter values, but the random effects estimator converges to some other value that is not the value of the true parameters. In this case, we expect to see differences between the fixed and random effects estimates.

To implement the test obtain the fixed effects and random effects estimates and save them.

```
quietly xtreg lwage $x2list, fe
estimates store fe

quietly xtreg lwage $x2list, re
estimates store re
```

The Hausman contrast test is carried out using the post estimation command

```
hausman fe re
```

When using the **hausman** command the consistent fixed effects estimator (**fe**) is listed first, and the efficient random effects estimator (**re**) is listed second.

| | ——— Coefficients ——— | | | |
	(b) fe	(B) re	(b-B) Difference	sqrt(diag(V_b-V_B)) S.E.
exper	.0410832	.043617	-.0025338	.0018455
exper2	-.0004091	-.000561	.0001519	.0000758
tenure	.0139089	.0141541	-.0002452	.0008468
tenure2	-.0008962	-.0007553	-.0001409	.0000668
south	-.0163224	-.0818117	.0654893	.0283637
union	.0636972	.0802353	-.0165381	.0053462

```
                        b = consistent under Ho and Ha; obtained from xtreg
            B = inconsistent under Ha, efficient under Ho; obtained from xtreg

    Test:  Ho:  difference in coefficients not systematic

             chi2(6) = (b-B)'[(V_b-V_B)^(-1)](b-B)
                     =        20.73
            Prob>chi2 =      0.0021
```

The output of the test shows the **Coefficients** common to both models and their estimated **Difference**. The column labeled **S.E.** is the standard error of the difference, so calculation of the t-statistic for the coefficient on south is

$$t = \frac{b_{FE,k} - b_{RE,k}}{\left[se\left(b_{FE,k}\right)^2 - se\left(b_{RE,k}\right)^2 \right]^{1/2}} = \frac{-.0163 - (-.0818)}{\left[(.0361)^2 - (.0224)^2 \right]^{1/2}} = \frac{.0654893}{.0283637} = 2.3137$$

This test statistic is asymptotically normal when the null hypothesis is true, and the critical value 1.96 is exceeded by the test statistic value, thus we reject the equality of the two coefficients.

At the bottom of the panel is the chi-square statistic comparing all 6 coefficients, which has a small p-value again leading us to reject the hypothesis that the coefficient estimates are equal to one another. This difference suggests that the random effects estimator is inconsistent. It may be the result of an endogenous variable, such as education, or some other misspecification.

An alternative testing approach due to Yair Mundlak and described, for example, in Wooldridge (2010, p. 332)[1]. The idea is that if there is a systematic relation between u_i and x_{kit} it may show up as a relationship between u_i and the time averages of time-varying explanatory variables. To implement the test we augment the original model with the time average, estimate the model by random effects, and test the significance of the augmenting variables. If there is no relation between u_i and x_{kit} we should find no significance.

```
global xlist3 experbar exper2bar tenurebar tenure2bar southbar ///
        unionbar educ exper exper2 tenure tenure2 black south union

xtreg lwage $xlist3, re
test experbar exper2bar tenurebar tenure2bar southbar unionbar
```

```
( 1)   expbar = 0
( 2)   exp2bar = 0
( 3)   tenbar = 0
( 4)   ten2bar = 0
( 5)   southbar = 0
( 6)   unionbar = 0

        chi2(  6) =     20.44
      Prob > chi2 =    0.0023
```

The advantages of this test include avoidance of sometimes negative Hausman statistic, and the ability to make this test robust.

```
xtreg lwage $xlist3, re vce(cluster id)
test experbar exper2bar tenurebar tenure2bar southbar unionbar
```

```
. test experbar exper2bar tenurebar tenure2bar southbar unionbar

( 1)   experbar = 0
( 2)   exper2bar = 0
( 3)   tenurebar = 0
( 4)   tenure2bar = 0
( 5)   southbar = 0
( 6)   unionbar = 0

        chi2(  6) =     17.26
      Prob > chi2 =    0.0084
```

Another possible option, if we think the year effect might be significant, is to add a year indicator variable prior to the test.

```
tabulate year, generate (d)
xtreg lwage $xlist3 d2-d5, re vce(cluster id)
test expbar exp2bar tenbar ten2bar southbar unionbar
```

[1] Econometric Analysis of Cross Section and Panel Data, MIT Press.

```
. test experbar exper2bar tenurebar tenure2bar southbar unionbar

 ( 1)   experbar = 0
 ( 2)   exper2bar = 0
 ( 3)   tenurebar = 0
 ( 4)   tenure2bar = 0
 ( 5)   southbar = 0
 ( 6)   unionbar = 0

          chi2(  6) =    16.29
        Prob > chi2 =     0.0123
```

Using all these test variations we reject the null hypothesis that the random effect is uncorrelated with the regressors, casting doubt on random effects estimation.

15.4.4 The Hausman-Taylor model

The outcome from our comparison of the fixed and random effects estimates of the wage equation poses a dilemma. Correlation between the explanatory variables and the random effects means the random effects estimator will be inconsistent. We can overcome the inconsistency problem by using the fixed effects estimator, but doing so means we can no longer estimate the effects of the time invariant variables *EDUC* and *BLACK*. The wage return to an extra year of education, and whether or not there is wage discrimination on the basis of race might be two important questions that we would like to answer.

The **Hausman-Taylor estimator** is an instrumental variables estimator applied to the random effects model, to overcome the problem of inconsistency caused by correlation between the random effects and some of the explanatory variables. This model is discussed in Wooldridge (2010, Chapter 11.3). To explain how it works consider the regression model

$$y_{it} = \beta_1 + \beta_2 x_{it,exog} + \beta_3 x_{it,endog} + \beta_3 w_{i,exog} + \beta_4 w_{i,endog} + u_i + e_{it}$$

We have divided the explanatory variables into 4 categories:

$x_{it,exog}$: exogenous variables that vary over time and individuals

$x_{it,endog}$: endogenous variables that vary over time and individuals

$w_{i,exog}$: time-invariant exogenous variables

$w_{i,endog}$: time-invariant endogenous variables

The model equation is written as if there is one variable of each type, but in practice there could be more than one. For the Hausman-Taylor estimator to work the number of exogenous time-varying variables $\left(x_{it,exog} \right)$ must be at least as great as the number of endogenous time-invariant variables $\left(w_{i,endog} \right)$.

To implement the estimation in Stata we use **xthtaylor**. The wage equation is specified as usual, but with options **endog()** to identify which variables might be endogenous, and the option **constant()** identifying variables that are time-invariant. Enter **help xthtaylor**

```
help xthtaylor                                      dialog:  xthtaylor
                                                   also see: xthtaylor postestimation
```

Title

    [XT] **xthtaylor** — Hausman-Taylor estimator for error-components models

Syntax

    xthtaylor *depvar indepvars* [*if*] [*in*] [*weight*] , **endog**(*varlist*) [*options*]

options	description
Main	
noconstant	suppress constant term
* **endog**(*varlist*)	explanatory variables in *indepvars* to be treated as endogenous
constant(*varlist_ti*)	independent variables that are constant within panel
varying(*varlist_tv*)	independent variables that are time varying within panel
amacurdy	fit model based on Amemiya and MaCurdy estimator

In the example used in *Principles of Econometrics, 4th Edition*, page 560-562 the variables **south** and **educ** are treated as potentially endogenous. The variable **south** is time varying, but **educ** is time invariant.

        xthtaylor lwage $x2list, endog(south educ) constant(educ black)

The output is arranged into the 4 parts identified above.

```
Random effects u_i ~ i.i.d.                Wald chi2(8)      =     609.26
                                           Prob > chi2       =     0.0000
```

lwage	Coef.	Std. Err.	z	P>|z|	[95% Conf. Interval]	
TVexogenous						
exper	.0399079	.0064745	6.16	0.000	.027218	.0525977
exper2	-.0003913	.0002676	-1.46	0.144	-.0009159	.0001332
tenure	.0143257	.0031597	4.53	0.000	.0081328	.0205186
tenure2	-.0008526	.0001974	-4.32	0.000	-.0012395	-.0004657
union	.0719692	.0134545	5.35	0.000	.045599	.0983395
TVendogenous						
south	-.0317122	.0348474	-0.91	0.363	-.1000118	.0365874
TIexogenous						
black	-.0359136	.0600681	-0.60	0.550	-.1536449	.0818177
TIendogenous						
educ	.1705081	.0444628	3.83	0.000	.0833626	.2576535
_cons	-.7507694	.5862357	-1.28	0.200	-1.89977	.3982314
sigma_u	.44986996					
sigma_e	.1949059					
rho	.84195987	(fraction of variance due to u_i)				

Note: TV refers to time varying; TI refers to time invariant.

15.5 SETS OF REGRESSION EQUATIONS

In this section we will examine investment data from two firms, General Electric (GE) and Westinghouse (WE). These are two firms among 10 in Grunfeld's classic data. To begin, issue the usual initial commands. Open the data file *grunfeld2.dta* and examine its contents.

```
use grunfeld2, clear
describe
summarize
```

For each of the 10 firms in Grunfeld's data there are 20 time series observations. The data file *grunfeld2.dta* omits all the data on firms other than GE or WE.

The equations we consider first are two investment models. If the models have the same parameters we can estimate a pooled regression model using all 40 observations

$$INV_{GE,t} = \beta_1 + \beta_2 V_{GE,t} + \beta_3 K_{GE,t} + e_{GE,t} \quad t = 1,\ldots,20$$

$$INV_{WE,t} = \beta_1 + \beta_2 V_{WE,t} + \beta_3 K_{WE,t} + e_{WE,t} \quad t = 1,\ldots,20$$

To obtain pooled regression estimates with the abbreviated form of regress use

```
reg inv v k
```

If the firm parameters are not identical the models will be

$$INV_{GE,t} = \beta_{1,GE} + \beta_{2,GE} V_{GE,t} + \beta_{3,GE} K_{GE,t} + e_{GE,t} \quad t = 1,\ldots,20$$

$$INV_{WE,t} = \beta_{1,WE} + \beta_{2,WE} V_{WE,t} + \beta_{3,WE} K_{WE,t} + e_{WE,t} \quad t = 1,\ldots,20$$

To test whether we should pool the data or not, estimate a dummy variable model

$$INV_{it} = \beta_{1,GE} + \delta_1 D_i + \beta_{2,GE} V_{it} + \delta_2 D_i \times V_{it} + \beta_{3,GE} K_{it} + \delta_3 D_i \times K_{it} + e_{it}$$

where $D = 1$ for Westinghouse observations. Create this dummy variable and its interactions

```
tabulate firm, generate(d)
gen vd1 = v*d1
gen kd1 = k*d1
gen vd2 = v*d2
gen kd2 = k*d2
```

Use regress to estimate the model with dummy variables, using GE as the base when the indicator variables are zero.

```
reg inv v k d2 vd2 kd2
```

```
. reg inv v k d2 vd2 kd2
```

Source	SS	df	MS		Number of obs =	40
					F(5, 34) =	32.70
Model	72079.4011	5	14415.8802		Prob > F =	0.0000
Residual	14989.8218	34	440.877111		R-squared =	0.8278
					Adj R-squared =	0.8025
Total	87069.2229	39	2232.54418		Root MSE =	20.997

inv	Coef.	Std. Err.	t	P>|t|	[95% Conf. Interval]	
v	.0265512	.011722	2.27	0.030	.0027291	.0503733
k	.1516939	.0193564	7.84	0.000	.1123568	.1910309
d2	9.446918	28.80535	0.33	0.745	-49.0926	67.98643
vd2	.0263429	.0343527	0.77	0.448	-.0434701	.096156
kd2	-.0592874	.1169464	-0.51	0.615	-.2969511	.1783764
_cons	-9.956307	23.62636	-0.42	0.676	-57.97086	38.05824

Test the significance of the coefficients of the indicator and slope-indicator variables.

>   **test d2 vd2 kd2**

```
. test d2 vd2 kd2

 ( 1)   d2 = 0
 ( 2)   vd2 = 0
 ( 3)   kd2 = 0

       F( 3,     34) =      1.19
            Prob > F =    0.3284
```

If this is the form of the regression you wish to report, then we can achieve the same without creating the indicator variables using factor variable notation. The factor variable **ib1.firm** is 1 for firm 2 but zero otherwise, as we have declared the base group to be the first, GE.

>   **reg inv v k ib1.firm ib1.firm#(c.v c.k)**

```
. reg inv v k ib1.firm ib1.firm#(c.v c.k)
```

Source	SS	df	MS		Number of obs =	40
					F(5, 34) =	32.70
Model	72079.4012	5	14415.8802		Prob > F =	0.0000
Residual	14989.8217	34	440.877109		R-squared =	0.8278
					Adj R-squared =	0.8025
Total	87069.2229	39	2232.54418		Root MSE =	20.997

inv	Coef.	Std. Err.	t	P>|t|	[95% Conf. Interval]	
v	.0265512	.011722	2.27	0.030	.0027291	.0503733
k	.1516939	.0193564	7.84	0.000	.1123568	.1910309
2.firm	9.446916	28.80535	0.33	0.745	-49.0926	67.98643
firm#c.v						
2	.0263429	.0343527	0.77	0.448	-.0434701	.096156
firm#c.k						
2	-.0592874	.1169464	-0.51	0.615	-.2969511	.1783764
_cons	-9.956306	23.62636	-0.42	0.676	-57.97086	38.05824

The corresponding test statement is

```
    test 2.firm 2.firm#c.v 2.firm#c.k
```

```
. test 2.firm 2.firm#c.v 2.firm#c.k

 ( 1)   2.firm = 0
 ( 2)   2.firm#c.v = 0
 ( 3)   2.firm#c.k = 0

       F(  3,     34) =      1.19
            Prob > F =     0.3284
```

Instead of using one firm as the base we could include separate intercepts and slopes for each firm.

```
    reg inv d1 d2 vd1 vd2 kd1 kd2, noconstant
```

Source	SS	df	MS		
Model	282856.08	6	47142.6801		
Residual	14989.8218	34	440.877113		
Total	297845.902	40	7446.14756		

		Number of obs =	40
		F(6, 34) =	106.93
		Prob > F =	0.0000
		R-squared =	0.9497
		Adj R-squared =	0.9408
		Root MSE =	20.997

inv	Coef.	Std. Err.	t	P>|t|	[95% Conf. Interval]	
d1	-9.956306	23.62636	-0.42	0.676	-57.97086	38.05824
d2	-.5093887	16.47857	-0.03	0.976	-33.99786	32.97909
vd1	.0265512	.011722	2.27	0.030	.0027291	.0503733
vd2	.0528941	.0322909	1.64	0.111	-.0127288	.1185171
kd1	.1516939	.0193564	7.84	0.000	.1123568	.1910309
kd2	.0924065	.1153334	0.80	0.429	-.1419792	.3267922

To test for significant difference in the coefficients of GE and WE test the joint null hypothesis that the dummy variable coefficients are zero,

```
    test (d1=d2) (vd1=vd2) (kd1=kd2)
```

```
. test (d1=d2) (vd1=vd2) (kd1=kd2)

 ( 1)   d1 - d2 = 0
 ( 2)   vd1 - vd2 = 0
 ( 3)   kd1 - kd2 = 0

       F(  3,     34) =      1.19
            Prob > F =     0.3284
```

If this second approach is what you wish, using factor variables makes creation of the indicator variables and their interactions unnecessary.

```
    reg inv ibn.firm ibn.firm#(c.v c.k), noconstant
    test (1.firm=2.firm) (1.firm#c.v=2.firm#c.v) (1.firm#c.k=2.firm#c.k)
```

```
. reg inv ibn.firm ibn.firm#(c.v c.k), noconstant
```

Source	SS	df	MS
Model	282856.081	6	47142.6801
Residual	14989.8217	34	440.877109
Total	297845.902	40	7446.14756

Number of obs =	40
F(6, 34) =	106.93
Prob > F =	0.0000
R-squared =	0.9497
Adj R-squared =	0.9408
Root MSE =	20.997

inv	Coef.	Std. Err.	t	P>|t|	[95% Conf. Interval]	
firm						
1	-9.956306	23.62636	-0.42	0.676	-57.97086	38.05824
2	-.5093902	16.47857	-0.03	0.976	-33.99786	32.97908
firm#c.v						
1	.0265512	.011722	2.27	0.030	.0027291	.0503733
2	.0528941	.0322909	1.64	0.111	-.0127288	.1185171
firm#c.k						
1	.1516939	.0193564	7.84	0.000	.1123568	.1910309
2	.0924065	.1153334	0.80	0.429	-.1419792	.3267922

```
. test (1.firm=2.firm) (1.firm#c.v=2.firm#c.v) (1.firm#c.k=2.firm#c.k)

 ( 1)  1bn.firm - 2.firm = 0
 ( 2)  1bn.firm#c.v - 2.firm#c.v = 0
 ( 3)  1bn.firm#c.k - 2.firm#c.k = 0

       F( 3,    34) =    1.19
            Prob > F =    0.3284
```

There is no strong evidence that the coefficients are different in these two regressions. However, we should also test for differences in variances. Use the Goldfeld-Quandt test discussed in Chapter 8. We estimate two separate regressions using the **regress** command with the **if** qualifier. Also, for later use we will save the *SSE*. Recall that **ereturn list** will display the items saved after a regression

```
        reg inv v k if firm==1
        scalar sse_ge = e(rss)

        reg inv v k if firm==2
        scalar sse_we = e(rss)

        * Goldfeld-Quandt test
        scalar GQ = sse_ge/sse_we
        scalar fc95 = invFtail(17,17,.05)
        di "Goldfeld-Quandt Test statistic = " GQ
        di "F(17,17,.95) = " fc95

. di "Goldfeld-Quandt Test statistic = " GQ
Goldfeld-Quandt Test statistic = 7.4533808

. di "F(17,17,.95) = " fc95
F(17,17,.95) = 2.2718929
```

We have strong evidence that the error variances of the two equations are different. Recall that if you do not remember the syntax for a scalar, type **db scalar** and use the dialog box.

15.5.1 Seemingly unrelated regressions

Seemingly unrelated regressions (SUR) permits equation coefficients and variances to differ, and also allows for contemporaneous correlation between the errors,

$$\text{cov}\left(e_{GE,t}, e_{WE,t}\right) = \sigma_{GE,WE}$$

The SUR estimator is a generalized least squares estimator, and because the data are stacked, one firm atop the other, is implemented in Stata using **xtgls**. Later we will see how the estimation is carried out with data in "wide form." The command **xtgls** is very powerful with many options. Enter **help xtgls** to see the syntax and some of the options listed.

```
help xtgls                                          dialog:  xtgls
                                                    also see:  xtgls postestimation

Title

    [XT] xtgls — Fit panel-data models by using GLS

Syntax

        xtgls depvar [indepvars] [if] [in] [weight] [, options]

    options                     description

    Model
      noconstant                suppress constant term
      panels(iid)               use i.i.d. error structure
      panels(heteroskedastic)   use heteroskedastic but uncorrelated error structure
      panels(correlated)        use heteroskedastic and correlated error structure
      corr(independent)         use independent autocorrelation structure
      corr(ar1)                 use AR1 autocorrelation structure
      corr(psar1)               use panel-specific AR1 autocorrelation structure
      rhotype(calc)             specify method to compute autocorrelation parameter; see Options for
                                   details; seldom used
      igls                      use iterated GLS estimator instead of two-step GLS estimator
      force                     estimate even if observations unequally spaced in time

    SE
      nmk                       normalize standard error by N-k instead of N
```

The option **panels(correlated)** is the SUR model. The errors are heteroskedastic across equations and have a correlated error structure. To implement the estimation use **xtset** to which we add the option **yearly** to indicate annual data.

```
    xtset firm year, yearly
```

The model is

```
    xtgls inv ibn.firm ibn.firm#(c.v c.k), noconstant panels(correlated) nmk
```

We add the option **nmk** to obtain the degrees of freedom correction $N - K$ when computing the error variances and covariance.

```
. xtgls inv ibn.firm ibn.firm#(c.v c.k), noconstant panels(correlated) nmk

Cross-sectional time-series FGLS regression

Coefficients:  generalized least squares
Panels:        heteroskedastic with cross-sectional correlation
Correlation:   no autocorrelation

Estimated covariances      =         3      Number of obs      =         40
Estimated autocorrelations =         0      Number of groups   =          2
Estimated coefficients     =         6      Time periods       =         20
                                            Wald chi2(6)       =     424.35
                                            Prob > chi2        =     0.0000
```

inv	Coef.	Std. Err.	z	P>|z|	[95% Conf. Interval]	
firm						
1	-27.71932	29.32122	-0.95	0.344	-85.18785	29.74922
2	-1.251988	7.545217	-0.17	0.868	-16.04034	13.53637
firm#c.v						
1	.0383102	.0144152	2.66	0.008	.010057	.0665634
2	.0576298	.0145463	3.96	0.000	.0291196	.08614
firm#c.k						
1	.1390363	.0249856	5.56	0.000	.0900654	.1880072
2	.0639781	.0530406	1.21	0.228	-.0399796	.1679357

The Chow-like test for equal coefficients in the two equations is

```
    test (1.firm=2.firm) (1.firm#c.v=2.firm#c.v) (1.firm#c.k=2.firm#c.k)

. test (1.firm=2.firm) (1.firm#c.v=2.firm#c.v) (1.firm#c.k=2.firm#c.k)

 ( 1)   1bn.firm - 2.firm = 0
 ( 2)   1bn.firm#c.v - 2.firm#c.v = 0
 ( 3)   1bn.firm#c.k - 2.firm#c.k = 0

        chi2(  3) =       8.77
      Prob > chi2 =     0.0326
```

In passing we note that **xtgls** offers many more options. You should try the following. First, if we think that the variances are different for the two regressions we might use the grouped or partitioned heteroskedasticity model from Chapter 8. If there is no contemporaneous covariance use

```
    * pooled model GLS with group hetero
    xtgls inv v k, panels(heteroskedastic) nmk
```

If we choose to pool the regressions, but wish to retain the SUR assumptions of cross-equation heteroskedasticity and contemporaneous covariance use

```
    * pooled model GLS with sur assumptions
    xtgls inv v k, panels(correlated) nmk
```

SUR models can be iterated. This means that after the SUR estimates are obtained, they can be used to obtain new equation residuals. These residuals are used to estimate the variances of the two equations and covariance and a new set of SUR estimates. The process can be repeated until convergence. Here we illustrate the iterated process with a pooled model by adding the option igls.

```
* pooled model GLS with sur assumptions iterated
xtgls inv v k, panels(correlated) nmk igls
```

We may consider estimation of the SUR model incorporating first order serial correlation between the errors for each equation. That is, we assume

$$e_{GE,t} = \rho_{GE} e_{GE,t-1} + v_{GE,t}$$

$$e_{WE,t} = \rho_{WE} e_{WE,t-1} + v_{WE,t}$$

The option corr(ar1) implements this estimation under the assumption that $\rho_{GE} = \rho_{WE}$.

```
* pooled model GLS with sur assumptions and common ar(1)
xtgls inv v k, panels(correlated) corr(ar1) nmk
```

The details of all these models are beyond the scope of this work. However see the complete documentation for xtgls as well as Cameron and Trivedi (2010, pp. 273-278)[2].

When equations are numerous, and the number of time observations is not, implementation of SUR estimation using GLS is often not recommended. Instead it has been suggested by Beck and Katz (1995) that we are often better off using least squares with a robust standard errors that account for SUR-type assumptions. These are called "panel-corrected standard errors." To implement this in Stata use xtpcse. If we apply this to the pooled regression model we use

```
xtpcse inv v k, nmk
```

Linear regression, correlated panels corrected standard errors (PCSEs)

Group variable:	firm		Number of obs	=	40
Time variable:	year		Number of groups	=	2
Panels:	correlated (balanced)		Obs per group: min =		20
Autocorrelation:	no autocorrelation		avg =		20
			max =		20
Estimated covariances	=	3	R-squared	=	0.8098
Estimated autocorrelations	=	0	Wald chi2(2)	=	176.16
Estimated coefficients	=	3	Prob > chi2	=	0.0000

inv	Coef.	Panel-corrected Std. Err.	z	P>|z|	[95% Conf.	Interval]
v	.0151926	.006932	2.19	0.028	.0016062	.0287791
k	.1435792	.0246476	5.83	0.000	.0952707	.1918876
_cons	17.872	4.690806	3.81	0.000	8.678191	27.06581

[2] Microeconometrics Using Stata, Revised Edition, Stata Press.

15.5.2 SUR with wide data

To estimate an SUR model in Stata (and most software) the data should be in "wide form" rather than "stacked form" such as we have with *grunfeld2.dta*. It is possible to make this conversion in Stata quite easily.

```
use grunfeld2, clear
reshape wide inv v k, i(year) j(firm)
```

The reshape command shows us

```
. reshape wide inv v k, i(year) j(firm)
(note: j = 1 2)
```

Data	long	->	wide
Number of obs.	40	->	20
Number of variables	5	->	7
j variable (2 values)	firm	->	(dropped)
xij variables:			
	inv	->	inv1 inv2
	v	->	v1 v2
	k	->	k1 k2

Take a look at the data using

```
describe
summarize
list in 1/5
```

The variable descriptions are

```
. describe

Contains data
  obs:            20
  vars:            7
  size:        1,080  (99.9% of memory free)
```

variable name	storage type	display format	value label	variable label
year	int	%8.0g		year
inv1	double	%10.0g		1 inv
v1	double	%10.0g		1 v
k1	double	%10.0g		1 k
inv2	double	%10.0g		2 inv
v2	double	%10.0g		2 v
k2	double	%10.0g		2 k

```
Sorted by:  year
```

Instead of the variables **inv**, **v** and **k** in *grunfeld2.dta*, we now have variables for each firm in a data set containing 20 observations. The summary statistics are

```
. summarize
```

Variable	Obs	Mean	Std. Dev.	Min	Max
year	20	1944.5	5.91608	1935	1954
inv1	20	102.29	48.5845	33.1	189.6
v1	20	1941.325	413.8433	1170.6	2803.3
k1	20	400.16	250.6188	97.8	888.9
inv2	20	42.8915	19.11019	12.93	90.08
v2	20	670.91	222.3919	191.5	1193.5
k2	20	85.64	62.26494	.8	213.5

A few of the observations are

```
. list in 1/5
```

	year	inv1	v1	k1	inv2	v2	k2
1.	1935	33.1	1170.6	97.8	12.93	191.5	1.8
2.	1936	45	2015.8	104.4	25.9	516	.8
3.	1937	77.2	2803.3	118	35.05	729	7.4
4.	1938	44.6	2039.7	156.2	22.89	560.4	18.1
5.	1939	48.1	2256.2	172.6	18.84	519.9	23.5

With data in wide-form the SUR model is estimated using **sureg**.

```
help sureg                                    dialog:  sureg
                                            also see:  sureg postestimation

Title
    [R] sureg — Zellner's seemingly unrelated regression

Syntax
    Basic syntax
        sureg (depvar1 varlist1) (depvar2 varlist2) ...  (depvarN varlistN) [if] [in] [weight]
```

With the data in wide form the estimation command is

```
sureg (inv1 v1 k1) (inv2 v2 k2), corr dfk small
```

. sureg (inv1 v1 k1) (inv2 v2 k2), corr dfk small

Seemingly unrelated regression

Equation	Obs	Parms	RMSE	"R-sq"	F-Stat	P
inv1	20	2	28.47948	0.6926	20.92	0.0000
inv2	20	2	10.29363	0.7404	25.27	0.0000

	Coef.	Std. Err.	t	P>|t|	[95% Conf. Interval]	
inv1						
v1	.0383102	.0144152	2.66	0.012	.0090151	.0676053
k1	.1390363	.0249856	5.56	0.000	.0882594	.1898131
_cons	-27.71932	29.32122	-0.95	0.351	-87.3072	31.86857
inv2						
v2	.0576298	.0145463	3.96	0.000	.0280682	.0871914
k2	.0639781	.0530406	1.21	0.236	-.0438134	.1717695
_cons	-1.251988	7.545217	-0.17	0.869	-16.58571	14.08174

Correlation matrix of residuals:

```
          inv1      inv2
inv1    1.0000
inv2    0.7290    1.0000
```

Breusch-Pagan test of independence: chi2(1) =   10.628, Pr = 0.0011

Each separate equation is enclosed in parentheses, with the dependent variable first in the list, as always. The following options are:

- **dfk** requests that the estimated error variances and the contemporaneous covariance be corrected for degrees of freedom, as in

$$\hat{\sigma}_{GE,WE} = \frac{1}{\sqrt{T-K_{GE}}\sqrt{T-K_{WE}}}\sum_{t=1}^{20}\hat{e}_{GE,t}\hat{e}_{WE,t} = \frac{1}{T-3}\sum_{t=1}^{20}\hat{e}_{GE,t}\hat{e}_{WE,t}$$

- **corr** requests that the correlations between residuals of the different equations be reported, and that the *LM* test of "no correlation" be displayed,

$$LM = T\sum_{i=2}^{M}\sum_{j=1}^{i-1}r_{ij}^{2}$$

This LM statistic has a χ^2-distribution with $M(M-1)/2$ degrees of freedom, in large samples.

- **small** requests that tests be based on *t*-statistics and *F*-statistics rather than *z*-statistics and χ^2-statistics.

To see the estimated variances and covariance use

```
matrix list e(Sigma)
```

```
symmetric e(Sigma)[2,2]
            inv1        inv2
inv1  777.44634
inv2  207.58713   104.30788
```

15.6 MIXED MODELS[3]

The random effects model allows for random individual heterogeneity that is constant over time, and which is captured by the intercept. A natural question to ask is "If the intercept can vary randomly across individuals, what about slopes and other parameters?" That is an excellent question. One way to approach such questions is through the use of mixed models. These models incorporate not only random intercepts but also random slopes. Furthermore, multiple layers of group effects can be captured. For example, if we sampling school children, we may allow individual heterogeneity, but there also may be a school effect, and children are within a school. Stata's **xtmixed** is designed for such problems. See the help for syntax and links to further documentation, examples and a dialog-box.

```
help xtmixed                                   dialog:  xtmixed
                                            also see:  xtmixed postestimation

Title

    [XT] xtmixed — Multilevel mixed-effects linear regression

Syntax

        xtmixed depvar [fe_equation] [|| re_equation] [|| re_equation ...] [, options]
```

Another excellent source is the previously cited Cameron and Trivedi (2010, Chapters 9.5 and 9.6).

Our approach is to illustrate the use of xtmixed using simulated data. By seeing the data generation process and estimation command you will have a better idea of when the various options should be used. The simulated data will have group and individual effects. First we generate some data.

```
clear

* set random number seed
set seed 1234567
```

First we generate two group effects **u1** and **u2** for 10 groups which are correlated with correlation 0.5.

```
set obs 10          // number of groups
```

[3] Contains some advanced material.

```
* random group effects with correlation sgrp
matrix sgrp = (1, .5 \ .5, 1)
drawnorm u1 u2, corr(sgrp)
```

The tricky part of the data generation process is keeping group and individual heterogeneity components constant over sets of observations. Create a group id variable, **grp**, and then replicate these observations 20 times, for 20 individuals per group.

```
gen grp = _n          // assign group id
expand 20             // number of individuals per group
```

Next we create two random individual effects, **u3** and **u4**, with correlation 0.7.

```
* random individual effects with correlation sind
matrix sind = (1, .7 \ .7, 1)
drawnorm u3 u4, corr(sind)
```

Assign a person id, **id**, and replicate these individual observations 10 times, so that we have 10 time series observations, or occasions, in which we observe the individual.

```
gen id = _n           // assign individual id
expand 10             // number of observations per individual
```

Arrange the data by group and individual.

```
sort grp id           // arrange by group and person
```

Create a counter **t** = 1-10 for the occasions.

```
by grp id: gen t = _n
```

Now randomly create an uncorrelated x variable and an overall disturbance e.

```
matrix sigxe = (1, 0 \ 0,1)
drawnorm x e, corr(sigxe)
```

For convenience change the order of variables and list some observations.

```
order grp id t u1 u2 u3 u4 x e
list in 1/20
```

	grp	id	t	u1	u2	u3	u4	x	e
1.	1	1	1	1.071039	.8732365	-.2009179	1.186175	.2388448	.1548654
2.	1	1	2	1.071039	.8732365	-.2009179	1.186175	-1.448084	-1.003928
3.	1	1	3	1.071039	.8732365	-.2009179	1.186175	-.5339671	-.045241
4.	1	1	4	1.071039	.8732365	-.2009179	1.186175	-1.477673	.5904121
5.	1	1	5	1.071039	.8732365	-.2009179	1.186175	.3947991	-.891265
6.	1	1	6	1.071039	.8732365	-.2009179	1.186175	-.1993113	-1.329407
7.	1	1	7	1.071039	.8732365	-.2009179	1.186175	.6081262	-.9055414
8.	1	1	8	1.071039	.8732365	-.2009179	1.186175	-.0429053	1.274183
9.	1	1	9	1.071039	.8732365	-.2009179	1.186175	-.6466608	-1.245
10.	1	1	10	1.071039	.8732365	-.2009179	1.186175	-.1450447	1.576772
11.	2	2	1	1.729758	-.0415373	.6692421	1.480754	-.3922293	.4159981
12.	2	2	2	1.729758	-.0415373	.6692421	1.480754	-.4346218	.1466878
13.	2	2	3	1.729758	-.0415373	.6692421	1.480754	-.0884378	1.965032
14.	2	2	4	1.729758	-.0415373	.6692421	1.480754	.2971053	-.0706769
15.	2	2	5	1.729758	-.0415373	.6692421	1.480754	-1.087195	.2557569
16.	2	2	6	1.729758	-.0415373	.6692421	1.480754	-.875877	1.194646
17.	2	2	7	1.729758	-.0415373	.6692421	1.480754	-.812617	-.8523542
18.	2	2	8	1.729758	-.0415373	.6692421	1.480754	1.365633	-.952275
19.	2	2	9	1.729758	-.0415373	.6692421	1.480754	-2.571998	-.2759298
20.	2	2	10	1.729758	-.0415373	.6692421	1.480754	.5481977	1.791418

These are observations for group 1, and individuals 1 and 11, with time observations 1-10. The group and individual effects are constant across group and time, respectively.

Using this structure we can generate and estimate a variety of models. First, generate a variable **y** that has a random intercept, as in the random effects model. The true intercept is 10 and the slope is 5. Note that we multiply the random error term by 3 so that $\sigma_e = 3$ and the random effect has standard deviation $\sigma_{u1} = 1.0$.

```
gen y = (10 + u3) + 5*x + 3*e

xtset id t
xtreg y x, re
```

```
Random effects u_i ~ Gaussian          Wald chi2(1)        =    5751.83
corr(u_i, X)        = 0 (assumed)       Prob > chi2         =     0.0000
```

y	Coef.	Std. Err.	z	P>|z|	[95% Conf. Interval]	
x	4.984971	.0657294	75.84	0.000	4.856144	5.113798
_cons	10.01111	.0969605	103.25	0.000	9.821075	10.20115
sigma_u	1.0010396					
sigma_e	2.9607527					
rho	.10258664	(fraction of variance due to u_i)				

Testing for the random effect we of course find it since we have generated the data this way.

```
xttest0
```

```
Breusch and Pagan Lagrangian multiplier test for random effects

     y[id,t] = Xb + u[id] + e[id,t]

     Estimated results:
                             Var       sd = sqrt(Var)
                    ──────────────────────────────────
                 y │   36.40073        6.033302
                 e │    8.766056        2.960753
                 u │    1.00208         1.00104

    Test:    Var(u) = 0
                             chi2(1) =      94.07
                        Prob > chi2 =       0.0000
```

Next, generate an outcome with both random intercept and slope, with intercept and slope correlated.

```
     gen y2 = (10 + u3) + (5 + u4)*x + 3*e
     xtmixed y2 x || id: x
```

The **xtmixed** command specifies the regression part as usual. The presence of random intercept and slope, varying randomly across individuals, is indicated by **|| id: x**. The double vertical bar **||** denotes a group level; **id:** denotes the individual level, and the following **x** indicates that the slope is random, with the randomness of the intercept being implicit. The output is quite complicated. The first set of estimates are for the intercept and slope.

```
. xtmixed y2 x || id: x

Performing EM optimization:

Performing gradient-based optimization:

Iteration 0:    log restricted-likelihood = -5162.5524
Iteration 1:    log restricted-likelihood = -5162.5522

Computing standard errors:

Mixed-effects REML regression              Number of obs      =        2000
Group variable: id                         Number of groups   =         200

                                           Obs per group: min =          10
                                                          avg =        10.0
                                                          max =          10

                                           Wald chi2(1)       =     2299.45
Log restricted-likelihood = -5162.5522     Prob > chi2        =      0.0000
```

y2	Coef.	Std. Err.	z	P>|z|	[95% Conf. Interval]	
x	4.944701	.1031165	47.95	0.000	4.742596	5.146805
_cons	9.999877	.0989142	101.10	0.000	9.806009	10.19375

These are followed by the estimates of the standard deviations of the random components and the overall disturbance. The likelihood-ratio test is said to be conservative because it ignores the one-tail character of the alternative hypothesis, $\sigma_{u3} > 0$ and/or $\sigma_{u4} > 0$.

Random-effects Parameters	Estimate	Std. Err.	[95% Conf. Interval]	
id: Independent				
sd(x)	1.080571	.0974925	.905431	1.289589
sd(_cons)	1.01991	.0969353	.8465669	1.228748
sd(Residual)	2.946652	.0516848	2.847074	3.049714

LR test vs. linear regression: chi2(2) =   148.14   Prob > chi2 = 0.0000

Note: LR test is conservative and provided only for reference.

Next consider a model in which there are random individual (**u3** and **u4**) and group effects (**u1** and **u2**), and that these effects can be correlated. The group level is **|| grp: x, cov(un)** with the option **cov(un)** indicating that the covariance of the group effects is unstructured. Similarly, **||id: x, cov(un)** specifies the individual effects with unstructured covariance.

```
gen y3 = (10 + u3 + 2*u1) + (5 + u4 + 2*u2)*x + 3*e
xtmixed y3 x || grp: x, cov(un) ||id: x, cov(un)
```

The first part of the output, above, reports the estimated slope and intercept. The estimation procedure is called restricted maximum likelihood (REML). The underlying assumptions are normality and homoscedasticity for the random effects.

Mixed-effects REML regression   Number of obs   =   2000

Group Variable	No. of Groups	Observations per Group		
		Minimum	Average	Maximum
grp	10	200	200.0	200
id	200	10	10.0	10

Log restricted-likelihood = -5172.5486   Wald chi2(1)   =   58.29
                                                   Prob > chi2   =   0.0000

y3	Coef.	Std. Err.	z	P>|z|	[95% Conf. Interval]	
x	4.654365	.6096052	7.64	0.000	3.459561	5.849169
_cons	9.898466	.7274034	13.61	0.000	8.472782	11.32415

The lower part of the output shows the estimates for the standard deviations of the random effects and their estimated correlation.

Random-effects Parameters	Estimate	Std. Err.	[95% Conf.	Interval]
grp: Unstructured				
sd(x)	1.901634	.4607021	1.182795	3.057345
sd(_cons)	2.280183	.5469646	1.424904	3.648832
corr(x,_cons)	.3811047	.2914015	-.2606752	.7892862
id: Unstructured				
sd(x)	1.027574	.0993964	.8501143	1.242079
sd(_cons)	.9615468	.0987601	.7862195	1.175972
corr(x,_cons)	.6619854	.1118354	.3852072	.8294962
sd(Residual)	2.948056	.0517184	2.848413	3.051185

LR test vs. linear regression: chi2(6) =   1172.43   Prob > chi2 = 0.0000

Note: <u>LR test is conservative</u> and provided only for reference.

KEY TERMS

between estimator	**ib1.group**	**sureg**
Breusch-Pagan test	**ibn.group**	**tabstat**
by	**invFtail**	**tabulate**
corr	LM test	**test**
dfk	matrix	**theta**
drawnorm	mixed models	**vce(cluster id)**
dummy variables	Mundlak test	wide data
egen	**noconstant**	**xtdescribe**
estimates store	**order**	**xtgls**
expand	panel data	**xtmixed**
fe	pooled model	**xtpcse**
fixed effects	random effects	**xtreg**
foreach	**re**	**xtset**
global macro	**reshape**	**xtsum**
GLS	**robust cluster**	**xttest0**
Goldfeld-Quandt test	seemingly unrelated	
group effects	**small**	
Hausman test	**sort**	
Hausman-Taylor model	SUR	

CHAPTER 15 DO-FILE [CHAP15.DO]

```
* file chap15.do for Using Stata for Principles of Econometrics, 4e

cd c:\data\poe4stata

* Stata do-file
* copyright C 2011 by Lee C. Adkins and R. Carter Hill
* used for "Using Stata for Principles of Econometrics, 4e"
* by Lee C. Adkins and R. Carter Hill (2011)
* John Wiley and Sons, Inc.
```

```
* setup
version 11.1
capture log close
set more off

*********** A Microeconomic Panel

* open log file
log using chap15_nls, replace text

* Open and examine the data
use nls_panel, clear
xtset id year
describe
summarize lwage educ south black union exper tenure
list id year lwage educ south black union exper tenure in 1/10

*********** Pooled OLS

* OLS
reg lwage educ exper exper2 tenure tenure2 black south union

* OLS with cluster robust standard errors
reg lwage educ exper exper2 tenure tenure2 black south union, vce(cluster id)

********** LSDV estimator for small N
use nls_panel10, clear
summarize lwage educ exper exper2 tenure tenure2 black south union

* LSDV for wage equation
reg lwage ibn.id exper exper2 tenure tenure2 union, noconstant

scalar sse_u = e(rss)
scalar df_u = e(df_r)
scalar sig2u = sse_u/df_u

test (1.id=2.id) (2.id=3.id) (3.id=4.id) (4.id=5.id) ///
     (5.id=6.id) (6.id=7.id) (7.id=8.id) (8.id=9.id)(9.id=10.id)


* Pooled model
reg lwage exper exper2 tenure tenure2 union
scalar sse_r = e(rss)

* F-test: using sums of squared residuals

scalar f = (sse_r - sse_u)/(9*sig2u)
scalar fc = invFtail(9,df_u,.05)
scalar pval = Ftail(9,df_u,f)
di "F test of equal intercepts = " f
di "F(9,df_u,.95) = " fc
di "p value = " pval

********** Use data in deviation from mean form

use nls_panel_devn, clear
summarize
list lw_dev exp_dev union_dev in 1/10
reg lw_dev exp_dev exp2_dev ten_dev ten2_dev union_dev, noconstant

* Create deviation from mean data
use nls_panel10, clear
```

```
xtset id year
sort id, stable

* Sort data and create group means
global v1list lwage exper exper2 tenure tenure2 union

foreach var of varlist $v1list {
        by i: egen `var'bar = mean(`var')
        gen `var'_dev = `var' - `var'bar
        }

list id year lwage lwagebar lwage_dev in 1/10

* OLS regression on data in deviations from mean
reg lwage_dev exper_dev exper2_dev tenure_dev tenure2_dev union_dev, noconstant

* Using fixed effects software
xtreg lwage exper exper2 tenure tenure2 union, fe

* Fixed effects using complete NLS panel
use nls_panel, clear
xtset id year

global x1list exper exper2 tenure tenure2 south union
xtreg lwage $x1list, fe

* FE with robust cluster-corrected standard errors
xtreg lwage $x1list, fe vce(cluster id)

* Recover individual differences from mean
predict muhat, u
tabstat muhat if year==82, stat(sum)

* Using time invariant variables
global x2list educ black $x1list
xtreg lwage $x2list, fe
xtsum educ

********** Random Effects

xtreg lwage $x2list, re theta

* RE with robust cluster-corrected standard errors
xtreg lwage $x2list, re vce(cluster id)

* Calculation of RE transformation parameter
quietly xtreg lwage $x2list, fe
scalar sig2e =( e(sigma_e))^2

* Automatic Between estimator
xtreg lwage $x2list, be
ereturn list

* Save sigma2_between and compute theta
scalar sig2b = e(rss)/e(df_r)
scalar sig2u = sig2b - sig2e/e(Tbar)
scalar sigu = sqrt(sig2u)
scalar theta = 1-sqrt(sig2e/(e(Tbar)*sig2u+sig2e))
di "Components of variance"
di "sig2e  = " sig2e " variance of overall error e(it)"
di "sige   = " sqrt(sig2e) " standard deviation of e(it)"
di "sig2b  = " sig2b " variance from between regression "
di "sig2u  = " sig2u " derived variance mu(i) "
```

```
di "sigu    = " sigu  " standard deviation mu(i) "
di "theta   = " theta " transformation parameter "

* transform data including intercept
gen one = 1
sort id, stable
global v2list lwage one $x2list

foreach var of varlist $v2list {
        by i: egen `var'bar = mean(`var')
        gen `var'd = `var' - theta*`var'bar
        }

* RE is ols applied to transformed data
reg lwaged educd blackd experd exper2d tenured tenure2d southd uniond oned, noconstant

* Breusch-Pagan test
quietly xtreg lwage $x2list, re
xttest0

* Hausman contrast test
quietly xtreg lwage $x2list, fe
estimates store fe

quietly xtreg lwage $x2list, re
estimates store re

hausman fe re

* Regression based Hausman test
global xlist3 experbar exper2bar tenurebar tenure2bar southbar ///
        unionbar educ exper exper2 tenure tenure2 black south union

xtreg lwage $xlist3, re
test experbar exper2bar tenurebar tenure2bar southbar unionbar

* Hausman test with robust VCE
xtreg lwage $xlist3, re vce(cluster id)
test experbar exper2bar tenurebar tenure2bar southbar unionbar

* Add year specific indicator variable
tabulate year, generate (d)
xtreg lwage $xlist3 d2-d5, re vce(cluster id)
test experbar exper2bar tenurebar tenure2bar southbar unionbar

* Hausman-Taylor Model
xthtaylor lwage $x2list, endog(south educ) constant(educ black)

log close

********** Seemingly Unrelated Regressions

* open log
log using chap15_sur, replace text

* Open Grunfeld GE & WE data
use grunfeld2, clear
describe
summarize

* pooled least squares
reg inv v k
```

```
* Create slope and intercept indicators
tabulate firm, generate(d)
gen vd1 = v*d1
gen kd1 = k*d1
gen vd2 = v*d2
gen kd2 = k*d2

* model with indicator and slope-indicator variables
reg inv v k d2 vd2 kd2
test d2 vd2 kd2

reg inv v k ib1.firm ib1.firm#(c.v c.k)
test 2.firm 2.firm#c.v 2.firm#c.k

* model with firm specific variables
reg inv d1 d2 vd1 vd2 kd1 kd2, noconstant
test (d1=d2) (vd1=vd2) (kd1=kd2)

* use factor variable notation
reg inv ibn.firm ibn.firm#(c.v c.k), noconstant
test (1.firm=2.firm) (1.firm#c.v=2.firm#c.v) (1.firm#c.k=2.firm#c.k)

* Separate regressions allow different variances
reg inv v k if firm==1
scalar sse_ge = e(rss)

reg inv v k if firm==2
scalar sse_we = e(rss)

* Goldfeld-Quandt test
scalar GQ = sse_ge/sse_we
scalar fc95 = invFtail(17,17,.05)
di "Goldfeld-Quandt Test statistic = " GQ
di "F(17,17,.95) = " fc95

* SUR using XTGLS
xtset firm year, yearly
xtgls inv ibn.firm ibn.firm#(c.v c.k), noconstant panels(correlated) nmk
test (1.firm=2.firm) (1.firm#c.v=2.firm#c.v) (1.firm#c.k=2.firm#c.k)

* pooled model GLS with group hetero
xtgls inv v k, panels(heteroskedastic) nmk

* pooled model GLS with sur assumptions
xtgls inv v k, panels(correlated) nmk

* pooled model GLS with sur assumptions iterated
xtgls inv v k, panels(correlated) nmk igls

* pooled model GLS with sur assumptions and common ar(1)
xtgls inv v k, panels(correlated) corr(ar1) nmk

* pooled ols with sur cov matrix
xtpcse inv v k, nmk

* Convert long data to wide data and use SUREG
use grunfeld2, clear
reshape wide inv v k, i(year) j(firm)
describe
summarize
list in 1/5

sureg (inv1 v1 k1) (inv2 v2 k2), corr dfk small
```

```
matrix list e(Sigma)

log close

********** Mixed models

log using chap15_mixed, replace text
clear

* set random number seed
set seed 1234567

* generate some panel data

set obs 10                      // number of groups

* random group effects with correlation sgrp
matrix sgrp = (1, .5 \ .5, 1)
drawnorm u1 u2, corr(sgrp)

gen grp = _n                    // assign group id
expand 20                       // number of individuals per group

* random individual effects with correlation sind
matrix sind = (1, .7 \ .7, 1)
drawnorm u3 u4, corr(sind)

gen id = _n                     // assign individual id
expand 10                       // number of observations per individual
sort grp id                     // arrange by group and person

* generate time or occasion counter for each id
by grp id: gen t = _n

* generate uncorrelated x and e
matrix sigxe = (1, 0 \ 0,1)
drawnorm x e, corr(sigxe)

* change variable order
order grp id t u1 u2 u3 u4 x e
list grp id t u1 u2 u3 u4 x e in 1/20

* random individual intercept dgp
gen y = (10 + u3) + 5*x + 3*e

xtset id t
xtreg y x, re
xttest0

* random individual intercept and random slope
gen y2 = (10 + u3) + (5 + u4)*x + 3*e
xtmixed y2 x || id: x

* random intercept and slope: person and group effect
gen y3 = (10 + u3 + 2*u1) + (5 + u4 + 2*u2)*x + 3*e
xtmixed y3 x || grp: x, cov(un) ||id: x, cov(un)
log close
```

CHAPTER **16**

Qualitative and Limited Dependent Variable Models

CHAPTER OUTLINE

16.1 MODELS WITH BINARY DEPENDENT VARIABLES

We will illustrate binary choice models using an important problem from transportation economics. How can we explain an individual's choice between driving (private transportation) and taking the bus (public transportation) when commuting to work, assuming, for simplicity, that these are the only two alternatives? We represent an individual's choice by the dummy variable

$$y = \begin{cases} 1 & \text{individual drives to work} \\ 0 & \text{individual takes bus to work} \end{cases}$$

If we collect a random sample of workers who commute to work, then the outcome y will be unknown to us until the sample is drawn. Thus, y is a random variable. If the probability that an individual drives to work is p, then $P[y=1]=p$. It follows that the probability that a person uses public transportation is $P[y=0]=1-p$. Define the explanatory variable

$$x = (\text{commuting time by bus} - \text{commuting time by car})$$

Let Z be a standard normal random variable, with probability density function

$$\phi(z) = \frac{1}{\sqrt{2\pi}} e^{-5z^2}$$

This function is computed using the Stata function **normalden**. The cumulative distribution function of Z is

$$\Phi(z) = P[Z \leq z] = \int_{-\infty}^{z} \frac{1}{\sqrt{2\pi}} e^{-5u^2} du$$

The Stata function that computes this value is **normal**.

The **probit** statistical model expresses the probability p that y takes the value 1 to be

$$p = P[y = 1] = P[Z \leq \beta_1 + \beta_2 x] = \Phi(\beta_1 + \beta_2 x)$$

Sample data on automobile and public transportation travel times and the alternative chosen for $N = 21$ individuals are contained in the data file *transport.dta*. In this table the variable *DTIME* = (bus time − auto time) and the dependent variable *AUTO* = 1 if automobile transportation is chosen.

Issue the standard opening commands, open the data file, and examine the data

```
use transport, clear
describe
summarize
```

. summarize

Variable	Obs	Mean	Std. Dev.	Min	Max
autotime	21	49.34762	32.43491	.2	99.1
bustime	21	48.12381	34.63082	1.6	91.5
dtime	21	-.122381	5.691037	-9.07	9.1
auto	21	.4761905	.5117663	0	1

Estimation of the probit model is by a Stata command with the same syntax as other estimation commands.

```
probit auto dtime
```

The first variable after **probit** is the binary dependent variable, followed by the explanatory variables. The commands and options for **probit** are available from the Stata menus. Select **Statistics > Binary outcomes > Probit regression** or enter **db probit**.

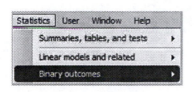
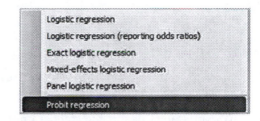

The **probit dialog box** is similar to others. A problem with the menu approach is that you may be confronted with many unfamiliar choices, especially for advanced models, thus for the most part we will stick with the simple command approach.

In the output you will notice a series of Iterations. These are a record of the steps Stata is taking to maximize the log-likelihood function. See Appendix C in *Principles of Econometrics, 4th Edition* for more on maximum likelihood estimation.

```
. probit auto dtime

Iteration 0:   log likelihood = -14.532272
Iteration 1:   log likelihood = -6.2074807
Iteration 2:   log likelihood =  -6.165583
Iteration 3:   log likelihood = -6.1651585
Iteration 4:   log likelihood = -6.1651585

Probit regression                               Number of obs   =         21
                                                LR chi2(1)      =      16.73
                                                Prob > chi2     =     0.0000
Log likelihood = -6.1651585                     Pseudo R2       =     0.5758
```

auto	Coef.	Std. Err.	z	P>|z|	[95% Conf. Interval]	
dtime	.2999898	.1028673	2.92	0.004	.0983735	.5016061
_cons	-.0644338	.3992438	-0.16	0.872	-.8469372	.7180696

In the output we see the estimated coefficients, standard errors and *z* values. The properties of the probit estimator are all asymptotic, which is why the normal distribution is used for test statistic critical values. Also reported is an overall test of model significance called **LR chi2(1)** and its *p*-value. This test is a joint test that all the variable coefficients, other than the intercept, are zero, analogous to the overall *F*-test of model significance in regression.

Predicted probabilities are based on the probit model estimates, so

$$\hat{p} = \Phi(\tilde{\beta}_1 + \tilde{\beta}_2 x)$$

These predicted probabilities for sample values are obtained using the post-estimation **predict** command.

```
predict phat
```

Suppose that we wish to estimate the marginal effect of increasing public transportation time, given that travel via public transportation currently takes 20 minutes longer [**dtime** = 2] than auto travel. It is calculated as

$$\frac{dP[AUTO=1]}{dDTIME} = \phi(\tilde{\beta}_1 + \tilde{\beta}_2 DTIME)\tilde{\beta}_2 = \phi(-0.0644 + 0.3000 \times 2)(0.3000)$$

$$= \phi(.5355)(0.3000) = 0.3456 \times 0.3000 = 0.1037$$

In this expression $\phi(\cdot)$ is the standard normal probability density function (*pdf*) evaluated at the argument, which we evaluate using the Stata function **normalden**. To compute $\tilde{\beta}_1 + \tilde{\beta}_2 DTIME$ for **dtime** = 2 we can use **lincom**

```
lincom _b[_cons]+_b[dtime]*2
```

(1)   2*[auto]dtime + [auto]_cons = 0

auto	Coef.	Std. Err.	z	P>|z|	[95% Conf. Interval]
(1)	.5355458	.4505849	1.19	0.235	-.3475843 1.418676

The value of $\phi(\tilde{\beta}_1 + \tilde{\beta}_2 DTIME)$ is then computed using **nlcom**, because the normal *pdf* is a nonlinear function.

```
nlcom (normalden(_b[_cons]+_b[dtime]*2))
```

_nl_1:   normalden(_b[_cons]+_b[dtime]*2)

auto	Coef.	Std. Err.	z	P>|z|	[95% Conf. Interval]
_nl_1	.3456449	.0834072	4.14	0.000	.1821699 .50912

The marginal effect is $\phi(\tilde{\beta}_1 + \tilde{\beta}_2 DTIME)\tilde{\beta}_2$. The **nlcom** command to compute the marginal effect at **dtime** = 2 is

```
nlcom (normalden(_b[_cons]+_b[dtime]*2)*_b[dtime] )
```

_nl_1:   normalden(_b[_cons]+_b[dtime]*2)*_b[dtime]

auto	Coef.	Std. Err.	z	P>|z|	[95% Conf. Interval]
_nl_1	.10369	.0326394	3.18	0.001	.0397179 .167662

The above steps are used to compute the marginal effect when **dtime** = 2. Another representative value is the average time difference **dtime** = −0.122381.

```
lincom _b[_cons]+_b[dtime]*(-.122381)
nlcom (normalden(_b[_cons]+_b[dtime]*(-.122381)))
nlcom (normalden(_b[_cons]+_b[dtime]*(-.122381))*_b[dtime] )
```

The results from these commands are

```
. lincom _b[_cons]+_b[dtime]*(-.122381)
  ( 1)  - .122381*[auto]dtime + [auto]_cons = 0
```

auto	Coef.	Std. Err.	z	P>|z|	[95% Conf. Interval]	
(1)	-.1011468	.3993423	-0.25	0.800	-.8838433	.6815496

```
. nlcom (normalden(_b[_cons]+_b[dtime]*(-.122381)))
     _nl_1:  normalden(_b[_cons]+_b[dtime]*(-.122381))
```

auto	Coef.	Std. Err.	z	P>|z|	[95% Conf. Interval]	
_nl_1	.3969068	.0160319	24.76	0.000	.3654847	.4283288

```
. nlcom (normalden(_b[_cons]+_b[dtime]*(-.122381))*_b[dtime] )
     _nl_1:  normalden(_b[_cons]+_b[dtime]*(-.122381))*_b[dtime]
```

auto	Coef.	Std. Err.	z	P>|z|	[95% Conf. Interval]	
_nl_1	.119068	.0409982	2.90	0.004	.038713	.199423

Similarly we can calculate a predicted probability, such as

$$\hat{p} = \Phi(\tilde{\beta}_1 + \tilde{\beta}_2 DTIME) = \Phi(-0.0644 + 0.3000 \times 3) = 0.7983$$

The function $\Phi(\cdot)$ is the standard normal cumulative distribution function (*cdf*). The Stata function **normal** returns the value of the standard normal *cdf*. Using **nlcom** we compute

```
nlcom (normal(_b[_cons]+_b[dtime]*3) )
     _nl_1:  normal(_b[_cons]+_b[dtime]*3)
```

auto	Coef.	Std. Err.	z	P>|z|	[95% Conf. Interval]	
_nl_1	.7982919	.1425387	5.60	0.000	.5189211	1.077663

16.1.1 Average marginal effects

Rather than compute the marginal effect, or a prediction, at a specific point, such as the means, a trend is to find the average marginal effect using each data point in the sample. We can do this manually by generating a variable that is the marginal effect for each sample value of **dtime**.

```
gen ame = normalden(_b[_cons]+_b[dtime]*dtime)*_b[dtime]
```

Find the summary statistics for this quantity.

```
tabstat ame, stat(n mean sd min max)
```

variable	N	mean	sd	min	max
ame	21	.0484069	.0364573	.0024738	.1152559

This value is

$$\widehat{AME} = \frac{1}{N} \sum_{i=1}^{N} \phi(\tilde{\beta}_1 + \tilde{\beta}_2 DTIME_i) \tilde{\beta}_2$$

The average marginal effect has become a popular alternative to computing the marginal effect at the mean as it summarizes the response of individuals in the sample to a change in the value of an explanatory variable. For the current example, 0.0484 is the average estimated increase in probability given a 10 minute increase in bus travel time relative to auto travel time.

The standard deviation **sd** reported by **tabstat** is the sample standard deviation of the individual values. It gives us measure of how much variation there is in the marginal effect from person to person.

Stata uses the **margins** command to compute marginal effect, predictions, and average marginal effects for most models. You may study **help margins** and the Stata documentation, but it is very massive, and somewhat overwhelming. We hope that introducing it to you in bits will be useful. The marginal effect of *DTIME* is

$$\frac{\widehat{dP(AUTO=1)}}{dDTIME} = \phi(\tilde{\beta}_1 + \tilde{\beta}_2 DTIME) \tilde{\beta}_2 = g(\tilde{\beta}_1, \tilde{\beta}_2)$$

The marginal effect is an estimator, since it is a function of the estimators $\tilde{\beta}_1$ and $\tilde{\beta}_2$. The discussion of the "delta method" in *Principles of Econometrics, 4th Edition*, Appendix 5B.5, is relevant because the marginal effect is a **nonlinear** function of $\tilde{\beta}_1$ and $\tilde{\beta}_2$.

To compute the marginal effect of *DTIME* at the variable means use

```
margins, dydx(dtime) atmeans
```

```
Conditional marginal effects                    Number of obs   =         21
Model VCE    : OIM

Expression   : Pr(auto), predict()
dy/dx w.r.t. : dtime
at           : dtime          =    -.122381 (mean)
```

	dy/dx	Delta-method Std. Err.	z	P>|z|	[95% Conf. Interval]	
dtime	.119068	.0409982	2.90	0.004	.038713	.199423

The output shows that we have computed a **Conditional** marginal effect, **dy/dx**, with respect to dtime at dtime = **-.122381 (mean)**. The standard error is described as **Delta-method Std.**

Err. The 95% interval estimate is based on the standard normal distribution, with critical values ± 1.96. Because there are only 21 observations we may want to use critical values from the *t*-distribution.

The average marginal effect is the default with `margins`.

```
margins, dydx(dtime)
```

```
Average marginal effects                          Number of obs   =          21
Model VCE     : OIM

Expression   : Pr(auto), predict()
dy/dx w.r.t. : dtime
```

	dy/dx	Delta-method Std. Err.	z	P>|z|	[95% Conf. Interval]	
dtime	.0484069	.003416	14.17	0.000	.0417116	.0551022

The **Average marginal effects** are calculated and the value 0.0484 is the same as we calculated manually. The **Delta-method standard error** is not the standard deviation of the marginal effects that we computed above. This quantity is explained in *Principles of Econometrics, 4th Edition*, Appendix 16A.2. Rather than rely on the standard normal based interval estimate we can instead use the *t*-distribution for the calculation.

```
scalar t975 = invttail(19,.025)
di "0.975 critical value 19 df " t975

scalar lbame =    .0484069    - t975*.003416
scalar ubame =    .0484069    + t975*.003416
di "95% interval estimate AME"
di "lbame = " lbame " ubame = " ubame
```

The returned interval is slightly wider than the standard normal based interval because it uses critical value 2.0930241.

```
lbame = .04125713 ubame = .05555667
```

In the previous section we manually computed the marginal effect of *DTIME* at the value *DTIME* = 2. Using Stata's `margins` command we can do this automatically using

```
margins, dydx(dtime) at(dtime=2)
```

```
Conditional marginal effects                    Number of obs    =        21
Model VCE      : OIM

Expression   : Pr(auto), predict()
dy/dx w.r.t. : dtime
at           : dtime            =        2
```

	dy/dx	Delta-method Std. Err.	z	P>|z|	[95% Conf. Interval]
dtime	.1036899	.0326394	3.18	0.001	.0397179 .167662

This is a conditional marginal effect because it is evaluated at a specific point.

The **margins** command can also compute predicted values, as we did manually in the previous section, for us.

> **margins, predict(pr) at(dtime=3)**

```
Adjusted predictions                            Number of obs    =        21
Model VCE      : OIM

Expression   : Pr(auto), predict(pr)
at           : dtime            =        3
```

	Margin	Delta-method Std. Err.	z	P>|z|	[95% Conf. Interval]
_cons	.7982919	.1425387	5.60	0.000	.5189211 1.077663

We have the predicted probability that we computed above as

$$\hat{p} = \Phi(\tilde{\beta}_1 + \tilde{\beta}_2 DTIME) = \Phi(-0.0644 + 0.3000 \times 3) = 0.7983$$

The Delta-method standard error is required because the normal *cdf* $\Phi(\cdot)$ is a nonlinear function.

The average value of the predictions at each observation is obtained using

> **margins, predict(pr)**

```
Predictive margins                              Number of obs    =        21
Model VCE      : OIM

Expression   : Pr(auto), predict(pr)
```

	Margin	Delta-method Std. Err.	z	P>|z|	[95% Conf. Interval]
_cons	.4863133	.0647176	7.51	0.000	.3594693 .6131574

Recall that we computed these predictions and called them **phat**. Finding the summary statistics we observe that the mean or average is the quantity reported by Stata's **margins** command.

> **summarize phat**

variable	Obs	Mean	Std. Dev.	Min	Max
phat	21	.4863133	.4116046	.0026736	.996156

16.1.2 Probit marginal effects: details[1]

Consider the probit model $p = \Phi(\beta_1 + \beta_2 x)$. The marginal effect of a continuous x, evaluated at a specific point $x = x_0$ is

$$\left.\frac{dp}{dx}\right|_{x=x_0} = \phi(\beta_1 + \beta_2 x_0)\beta_2 = g(\beta_1, \beta_2)$$

The estimator of the marginal effect is $g(\tilde{\beta}_1, \tilde{\beta}_2)$, where $\tilde{\beta}_1$ and $\tilde{\beta}_2$ are the maximum likelihood estimators of the unknown parameters. The variance of this estimator was developed in *Principles of Econometrics, 4th Edition*, Appendix 5B.5, in equation (5B.8), and is given by

$$\text{var}\left[g(\tilde{\beta}_1, \tilde{\beta}_2)\right] \cong \left[\frac{\partial g(\beta_1, \beta_2)}{\partial \beta_1}\right]^2 \text{var}(\tilde{\beta}_1) + \left[\frac{\partial g(\beta_1, \beta_2)}{\partial \beta_2}\right]^2 \text{var}(\tilde{\beta}_2)$$

$$+ 2\left[\frac{\partial g(\beta_1, \beta_2)}{\partial \beta_1}\right]\left[\frac{\partial g(\beta_1, \beta_2)}{\partial \beta_2}\right]\text{cov}(\tilde{\beta}_1, \tilde{\beta}_2)$$

(16.1)

The variances and covariance of the estimators come from maximum likelihood estimation. The essence of these calculations is given in *POE4*, Appendix C.8.2. To implement the delta method we require the derivative

$$\frac{\partial g(\beta_1, \beta_2)}{\partial \beta_1} = \frac{\partial\left[\phi(\beta_1 + \beta_2 x_0)\beta_2\right]}{\partial \beta_1}$$

$$= \left\{\frac{\partial \phi(\beta_1 + \beta_2 x_0)}{\partial \beta_1} \times \beta_2\right\} + \phi(\beta_1 + \beta_2 x_0) \times \frac{\partial \beta_2}{\partial \beta_1}$$

$$= -\phi(\beta_1 + \beta_2 x_0) \times (\beta_1 + \beta_2 x_0) \times \beta_2$$

To obtain the final result we used $\partial \beta_2 / \partial \beta_1 = 0$ and

$$\frac{\partial \phi(\beta_1 + \beta_2 x_0)}{\partial \beta_1} = -\phi(\beta_1 + \beta_2 x_0) \times (\beta_1 + \beta_2 x_0)$$

Using similar steps we obtain the other key derivative,

---

[1] This section contains advanced material. It shows Stata code for *Principles of Econometrics, 4th Edition*, Appendix 16A.1.

$$\frac{\partial g\left(\beta_1,\beta_2\right)}{\partial \beta_2} = \phi\left(\beta_1 + \beta_2 x_0\right)\left[1 - \left(\beta_1 + \beta_2 x_0\right) \times \beta_2 x_0\right]$$

From the maximum likelihood estimation results using the transportation data example we obtain the estimator variances and covariance[2]

$$\begin{bmatrix} \widehat{\mathrm{var}\left(\tilde{\beta}_1\right)} & \widehat{\mathrm{cov}\left(\tilde{\beta}_1,\tilde{\beta}_2\right)} \\ \widehat{\mathrm{cov}\left(\tilde{\beta}_1,\tilde{\beta}_2\right)} & \widehat{\mathrm{var}\left(\tilde{\beta}_2\right)} \end{bmatrix} = \begin{bmatrix} 0.1593956 & 0.0003261 \\ 0.0003261 & 0.0105817 \end{bmatrix}$$

To obtain these values in Stata, estimate the probit model and list the matrix **e(v)**. Estimation returns are viewed with **ereturn list**.

```
        probit auto dtime
        ereturn list

        matrix list e(v)

symmetric e(v)[2,2]
                   auto:         auto:
                   dtime         _cons
auto:dtime    .01058169
auto:_cons    .0003261    .15939558
```

Note that Stata places the intercept estimator last among the coefficients.

The marginal effect of **dtime** on the probability of choosing auto travel, when **dtime** = 2, is obtained using

```
        margins, dydx(dtime) at(dtime=2)

Conditional marginal effects                      Number of obs    =         21
Model VCE    : OIM

Expression   : Pr(auto), predict()
dy/dx w.r.t. : dtime
at           : dtime              =         2
```

	dy/dx	Delta-method Std. Err.	z	P>|z|	[95% Conf. Interval]	
dtime	.1036899	.0326394	3.18	0.001	.0397179	.167662

To confirm this calculation the derivatives must be evaluated at the maximum likelihood estimates. For **dtime** = 2 ($x_0 = 2$), the calculated values of the derivatives are

$$\frac{\widehat{\partial g\left(\beta_1,\beta_2\right)}}{\partial \beta_1} = -0.055531 \quad \text{and} \quad \frac{\widehat{\partial g\left(\beta_1,\beta_2\right)}}{\partial \beta_2} = 0.2345835$$

---

[2] Using minus the inverse matrix of second derivatives.

We compute these values using **nlcom**:

```
nlcom (-normalden(_b[_cons]+_b[dtime]*2)*(_b[_cons]+_b[dtime]*2)
       *_b[dtime])
```

auto	Coef.	Std. Err.	z	P>|z|	[95% Conf. Interval]	
_nl_1	-.0555307	.0454006	-1.22	0.221	-.1445142	.0334528

```
nlcom (normalden(_b[_cons]+_b[dtime]*2)*(1-(_b[_cons]+_b[dtime]*2)*
       _b[dtime]*2))
```

auto	Coef.	Std. Err.	z	P>|z|	[95% Conf. Interval]	
_nl_1	.2345835	.1710668	1.37	0.170	-.1007013	.5698683

Carrying out the required multiplication for equation (16.1) above we obtain the estimated variance and standard error of the marginal effect

$$\widehat{\text{var}\left[g\left(\tilde{\beta}_1,\tilde{\beta}_2\right)\right]} = 0.0010653 \text{ and } \text{se}\left[g\left(\tilde{\beta}_1,\tilde{\beta}_2\right)\right] = 0.0326394$$

16.1.3 Standard error of average marginal effect[3]

Consider the probit model $p = \Phi(\beta_1 + \beta_2 x)$. For the transportation data example the explanatory variable $x = DTIME$. The average marginal effect of this continuous variable is

$$AME = \frac{1}{N}\sum_{i=1}^{N}\phi(\beta_1 + \beta_2 DTIME_i)\beta_2 = g_2\left(\beta_1,\beta_2\right)$$

This is calculated using

```
margins, dydx(dtime)
```

```
Average marginal effects                    Number of obs   =          21
Model VCE    : OIM

Expression   : Pr(auto), predict()
dy/dx w.r.t. : dtime
```

	dy/dx	Delta-method Std. Err.	z	P>|z|	[95% Conf. Interval]	
dtime	.0484069	.003416	14.17	0.000	.0417116	.0551022

---

[3] This section contains advanced material. It explains the calculations used in Principles of Econometrics, 4th Edition, Chapter 16, Appendix 16A.2.

The estimator of the average marginal effect is $g_2\left(\tilde{\beta}_1,\tilde{\beta}_2\right)$. To apply the delta method to find $\text{var}\left[g_2\left(\tilde{\beta}_1,\tilde{\beta}_2\right)\right]$ we require the derivatives

$$\frac{\partial g_2\left(\beta_1,\beta_2\right)}{\partial \beta_1} = \frac{1}{N}\sum_{i=1}^{N}\frac{\partial}{\partial \beta_1}\left[\phi(\beta_1 + \beta_2 DTIME_i)\beta_2\right]$$

$$= \frac{1}{N}\sum_{i=1}^{N}\frac{\partial g\left(\beta_1,\beta_2\right)}{\partial \beta_1}$$

The term $\partial g\left(\beta_1,\beta_2\right)/\partial \beta_1$ we evaluated in the previous section. Similarly, the derivative

$$\frac{\partial g_2\left(\beta_1,\beta_2\right)}{\partial \beta_2} = \frac{1}{N}\sum_{i=1}^{N}\frac{\partial}{\partial \beta_2}\left[\phi(\beta_1 + \beta_2 DTIME_i)\beta_2\right]$$

$$= \frac{1}{N}\sum_{i=1}^{N}\frac{\partial g\left(\beta_1,\beta_2\right)}{\partial \beta_2}$$

For the transportation data we compute

$$\frac{\widetilde{\partial g_2\left(\beta_1,\beta_2\right)}}{\partial \beta_1} = -0.00185 \text{ and } \frac{\widetilde{\partial g_2\left(\beta_1,\beta_2\right)}}{\partial \beta_2} = -0.032366$$

To calculate these values use

```
gen dg21 = -normalden(_b[_cons]+_b[dtime]*dtime)* ///
           (_b[_cons]+_b[dtime]*dtime)*_b[dtime]

gen dg22 = normalden(_b[_cons]+_b[dtime]*dtime)* ///
           (1-(_b[_cons]+_b[dtime]*dtime)*_b[dtime]*dtime)

summarize dg21 dg22
```

Variable	Obs	Mean	Std. Dev.	Min	Max
dg21	21	-.00185	.0538807	-.0724431	.0725776
dg22	21	-.0323657	.1530839	-.1792467	.3620589

Using (16.1) above, with g replaced by g_2, and carrying out the required multiplication, we obtain the estimated variance and standard error of the average marginal effect

$$\text{var}\left[g_2\left(\tilde{\beta}_1,\tilde{\beta}_2\right)\right] = 0.0000117 \text{ and } \text{se}\left[g_2\left(\tilde{\beta}_1,\tilde{\beta}_2\right)\right] = 0.003416$$

16.2 THE LOGIT MODEL FOR BINARY CHOICE

We use the choice between Coke and Pepsi as an example to illustrate more about the linear probability model, probit and the logit model for binary choice. Open the data file *coke.dta* and examine its contents.

```
use coke, clear
describe
```

variable name	storage type	display format	value label	variable label
coke	byte	%8.0g		=1 if coke chosen, =0 if pepsi chosen
pr_pepsi	double	%10.0g		price of 2 liter bottle of pepsi
pr_coke	double	%10.0g		price of 2 liter bottle of coke
disp_pepsi	byte	%8.0g		= 1 if pepsi is displayed at time of purchase, otherwise = 0
disp_coke	byte	%8.0g		= 1 if coke is displayed at time of purchase, otherwise = 0
pratio	double	%10.0g		price of coke relative to price of pepsi

```
summarize
```

Variable	Obs	Mean	Std. Dev.	Min	Max
coke	1140	.4473684	.4974404	0	1
pr_pepsi	1140	1.202719	.3007257	.68	1.79
pr_coke	1140	1.190088	.2999157	.68	1.79
disp_pepsi	1140	.3640351	.4813697	0	1
disp_coke	1140	.3789474	.4853379	0	1
pratio	1140	1.027249	.286608	.497207	2.324675

The variable *COKE*

$$COKE = \begin{cases} 1 & \text{if Coke is chosen} \\ 0 & \text{if Pepsi is chosen} \end{cases}$$

The expected value of this variable is $E(COKE) = P(COKE = 1) = p_{COKE}$ probability that Coke is chosen. As explanatory variables we use the relative price of Coke to Pepsi (*PRATIO*), as well as *DISP_COKE* and *DISP_PEPSI*, which are indicator variables taking the value 1 if the respective store display is present and 0 if it is not present. We expect that the presence of a Coke display will increase the probability of a Coke purchase, and the presence of a Pepsi display will decrease the probability of a Coke purchase.

The cumulative distribution function for a logistic random variable is

$$\Lambda(l) = P[L \le l] = \frac{1}{1 + e^{-l}}$$

In the logit model the probability p that the observed value y takes the value 1 is

$$p = P[L \le \beta_1 + \beta_2 x] = \Lambda(\beta_1 + \beta_2 x) = \frac{1}{1 + e^{-(\beta_1 + \beta_2 x)}}$$

The probit and logit models for the choice are the same except for the cumulative distribution function. The two models are

$$p_{COKE} = E(COKE) = \Phi(\beta_1 + \beta_2 PRATIO + \beta_3 DISP\_COKE + \beta_4 DISP\_PEPSI)$$

$$p_{COKE} = E(COKE) = \Lambda(\gamma_1 + \gamma_2 PRATIO + \gamma_3 DISP\_COKE + \gamma_4 DISP\_PEPSI)$$

Let us examine the alternative models and model results obtained using logit, probit, and the linear probability model. Begin with the linear probability model. Use **regress** with robust standard errors. Save the estimates for later and obtain the linear predictions.

```
regress coke pratio disp_coke disp_pepsi, vce(robust)
estimates store lpm
predict phat
```

Using the margins command we can calculate the predicted value at a specific point.

```
margins, predict(xb) at(pratio=1.1 disp_coke=0 disp_pepsi=0)
```

```
Adjusted predictions                          Number of obs   =        1140
Model VCE     : Robust

Expression    : Linear prediction, predict(xb)
at            : pratio         =         1.1
                disp_coke      =           0
                disp_pepsi     =           0
```

	Margin	Delta-method Std. Err.	z	P>|z|	[95% Conf. Interval]	
_cons	.4492675	.0202031	22.24	0.000	.4096702	.4888648

To predict the choice outcomes compare the predicted choice probabilities to 0.5 and tabulate these results.

```
generate p1 = (phat >=.5)
tabulate p1 coke,row
```

```
┌─────────────────────┐
│ Key                 │
├─────────────────────┤
│     frequency       │
│   row percentage    │
└─────────────────────┘
```

	=1 if coke chosen, =0 if pepsi chosen		
p1	0	1	Total
0	507	263	770
	65.84	34.16	100.00
1	123	247	370
	33.24	66.76	100.00
Total	630	510	1,140
	55.26	44.74	100.00

The successful predictions are on the diagonal.
  Obtain the probit estimates and store them.

```
probit coke pratio disp_coke disp_pepsi
estimates store probit
```

The post-estimation command **estat** will create a classification table like the one we created for the linear probability model, along with quite a bit of other information.

```
estat classification
```

Probit model for coke

Classified	True		Total
	D	~D	
+	247	123	370
-	263	507	770
Total	510	630	1140

Classified + if predicted Pr(D) >= .5

Using margins calculate the average marginal effect of a change in the price-ratio variable.

```
margins, dydx(pratio)
```

Average marginal effects   Number of obs   =   1140
Model VCE   : OIM

Expression   : Pr(coke), predict()
dy/dx w.r.t. : pratio

	dy/dx	Delta-method Std. Err.	z	P>|z|	[95% Conf. Interval]	
pratio	-.4096951	.0616434	-6.65	0.000	-.530514	-.2888761

Using `margins` we can also compute marginal effects at specific values.

> `margins, dydx(pratio) at(pratio=1.1 disp_coke=0 disp_pepsi=0)`

```
Conditional marginal effects                    Number of obs   =      1140
Model VCE      : OIM

Expression    : Pr(coke), predict()
dy/dx w.r.t.  : pratio
at            : pratio          =           1.1
                disp_coke       =           0
                disp_pepsi      =           0
```

	dy/dx	Delta-method Std. Err.	z	P>|z|	[95% Conf. Interval]
pratio	-.4518877	.0702839	-6.43	0.000	-.5896417 -.3141338

Furthermore, using `margins` we can compute predictions at specific values.

> `margins, predict(pr) at(pratio=1.1 disp_coke=0 disp_pepsi=0)`

```
Adjusted predictions                            Number of obs   =      1140
Model VCE      : OIM

Expression    : Pr(coke), predict(pr)
at            : pratio          =           1.1
                disp_coke       =           0
                disp_pepsi      =           0
```

	Margin	Delta-method Std. Err.	z	P>|z|	[95% Conf. Interval]
_cons	.4393966	.0218425	20.12	0.000	.3965861 .4822071

16.2.1 Wald tests

Hypothesis tests concerning individual coefficients in probit and logit models are carried out in the usual way based on an "asymptotic-t" test. If the null hypothesis is $H_0 : \beta_k = c$, then the test statistic using the probit model is

$$t = \frac{\tilde{\beta}_k - c}{\text{se}(\tilde{\beta}_k)} \overset{a}{\sim} t_{(N-K)}$$

where $\tilde{\beta}_k$ is the parameter estimator, N is the sample size, and K is the number of parameters estimated. The test is asymptotically justified, and if N is large the critical values from the $t_{(N-K)}$ distribution will be very close to those from the standard normal distribution. In smaller samples, however, the use of the t-distribution critical values can make minor differences and is the more "conservative" choice.

The t-test is based on the **Wald principle**. This testing principle is discussed in *Principles of Econometrics, 4th Edition*, Appendix C.8.4b. Stata has "built in" Wald test statements that are convenient to use. To illustrate, using the probit model, consider the two hypotheses

Hypothesis (1) $H_0 : \beta_3 = -\beta_4$, $H_1 : \beta_3 \neq -\beta_4$

Hypothesis (2) $H_0 : \beta_3 = 0, \beta_4 = 0$, $H_1 :$ either β_3 or β_4 is not zero

Hypothesis (1) is that the coefficients on the display variables are equal in magnitude but opposite in sign, or that the effect of the Coke and Pepsi displays have an equal but opposite effect on the probability of choosing Coke. A t-test is calculated using

```
lincom disp_coke + disp_pepsi
```

(1)   [coke]disp_coke + [coke]disp_pepsi = 0

coke	Coef.	Std. Err.	z	P>|z|	[95% Conf. Interval]	
(1)	-.2301101	.0989868	-2.32	0.020	-.4241207	-.0360994

Automatic **test** commands usually generate the chi-square distribution version of the test, which in this case is the square of the t-statistic, $W = 5.4040$. If the null hypothesis is true the Wald test statistic has an asymptotic $\chi^2_{(1)}$ distribution.

```
test disp_coke + disp_pepsi=0
```

(1)   [coke]disp_coke + [coke]disp_pepsi = 0

```
       chi2( 1) =     5.40
     Prob > chi2 =   0.0201
```

The link between the t and chi-square test is fully explained in *POE4*, Appendix C.8.4b.

A generalization of the Wald statistic is used to test the joint null hypothesis (2) that neither the Coke nor Pepsi display affects the probability of choosing Coke. Here we are testing 2 hypotheses, so that the Wald statistic has an asymptotic $\chi^2_{(2)}$ distribution.

```
test disp_coke disp_pepsi
```

(1)   [coke]disp_coke = 0
(2)   [coke]disp_pepsi = 0

```
       chi2( 2) =    19.46
     Prob > chi2 =   0.0001
```

16.2.2 Likelihood ratio tests

When using maximum likelihood estimators, such as probit and logit, tests based on the likelihood ratio principle are generally preferred. Appendix C.8.4a in *POE4* contains a discussion of this methodology. One test component is the log-likelihood function value in the unrestricted, full model (call it $\ln L_U$) evaluated at the maximum likelihood estimates. The second ingredient is the log-likelihood function value from the model that is "restricted" by imposing the condition that the null hypothesis is true (call it $\ln L_R$). The likelihood ratio test statistic is $LR = 2(\ln L_U - \ln L_R)$. If the null hypothesis is true, the statistic has an asymptotic chi-square distribution with degrees of freedom equal to the number of hypotheses being tested. The null hypothesis is rejected if the value LR is larger than the chi-square distribution critical value.

To illustrate, first the overall test of model significance. After a probit or logit model estimation the value of the log-likelihood function is saved as **e(11)**. If all the parameters are zero except the intercept the probit model is $p_{COKE} = \Phi(\beta_1)$. The log-likelihood for this model is saved as **e(11_0)**. Then the likelihood ratio test of probit model significance is calculated using

```
scalar lnlu = e(11)
scalar lnlr = e(11_0)
scalar lr_test = 2*(lnlu-lnlr)
di "lnlu    =" lnlu
di " lnlr    =" lnlr
di " lr_test =" lr_test
```

```
. di "lnlu      = " lnlu
lnlu      = -710.94858

. di " lnlr     = " lnlr
 lnlr     = -783.86028

. di " lr_test = " lr_test
 lr_test = 145.82341
```

The **probit** estimation automatically reports this value following estimation.

```
Probit regression                         Number of obs   =        1140
                                          LR chi2(3)      =      145.82
                                          Prob > chi2     =      0.0000
```

We can test other hypotheses using this principle. Hypothesis (1) on the previous page is tested by first imposing the hypothesis as a restriction on the model. If this hypothesis is true then

$$P(COKE = 1) = \Phi\left(\beta_1 + \beta_2 PRATIO + \beta_4 \left(DISP\_PEPSI - DISP\_COKE\right)\right)$$

Create a variable equal to the difference of displays, and estimate the resulting "restricted model.

```
gen disp = disp_pepsi-disp_coke
probit coke pratio disp
estimates store probitr
```

Stata has an automatic command to compute a likelihood ratio test given an unrestricted and a restricted model. Using the saved model results we have

```
lrtest probit probitr
```

```
Likelihood-ratio test                                  LR chi2(1)  =      5.42
(Assumption: probitr nested in probit)                 Prob > chi2 =    0.0199
```

To test Hypothesis (2) that the display variables are not significant, we estimate the restricted model $P(COKE=1)=\Phi(\beta_1+\beta_2 PRATIO)$ and repeat.

```
        probit coke pratio
        estimates store probitr
        lrtest probit probitr
```

```
Likelihood-ratio test                                  LR chi2(2)  =     19.55
(Assumption: probitr nested in probit)                 Prob > chi2 =    0.0001
```

16.2.3 Logit estimation

The syntax and analysis for logit models is the same as for the probit model.

```
        logit coke pratio disp_coke disp_pepsi
        estimates store logit
```

```
Logistic regression                          Number of obs   =       1140
                                             LR chi2(3)      =     148.83
                                             Prob > chi2     =     0.0000
Log likelihood = -709.44614                  Pseudo R2       =     0.0949
```

coke	Coef.	Std. Err.	z	P>|z|	[95% Conf. Interval]	
pratio	-1.995742	.3145873	-6.34	0.000	-2.612322	-1.379162
disp_coke	.3515994	.1585398	2.22	0.027	.0408671	.6623316
disp_pepsi	-.7309859	.1678376	-4.36	0.000	-1.059941	-.4020303
_cons	1.922972	.3258328	5.90	0.000	1.284352	2.561593

```
        estat classification
```

```
Logistic model for coke
```

	True		
Classified	D	~D	Total
+	247	123	370
-	263	507	770
Total	510	630	1140

```
Classified + if predicted Pr(D) >= .5
```

```
        margins, dydx(pratio)
```

```
Average marginal effects                        Number of obs   =        1140
Model VCE     : OIM

Expression    : Pr(coke), predict()
dy/dx w.r.t.  : pratio
```

	dy/dx	Delta-method Std. Err.	z	P>|z|	[95% Conf. Interval]
pratio	-.4332631	.0639434	-6.78	0.000	-.5585899 -.3079363

margins, dydx(pratio) at(pratio=1.1 disp_coke=0 disp_pepsi=0)

```
Conditional marginal effects                    Number of obs   =        1140
Model VCE     : OIM

Expression    : Pr(coke), predict()
dy/dx w.r.t.  : pratio
at            : pratio          =          1.1
                disp_coke       =            0
                disp_pepsi      =            0
```

	dy/dx	Delta-method Std. Err.	z	P>|z|	[95% Conf. Interval]
pratio	-.489797	.0753207	-6.50	0.000	-.6374228 -.3421711

margins, predict(pr) at(pratio=1.1 disp_coke=0 disp_pepsi=0)

```
Adjusted predictions                            Number of obs   =        1140
Model VCE     : OIM

Expression    : Pr(coke), predict(pr)
at            : pratio          =          1.1
                disp_coke       =            0
                disp_pepsi      =            0
```

	Margin	Delta-method Std. Err.	z	P>|z|	[95% Conf. Interval]
_cons	.4323318	.0224204	19.28	0.000	.3883885 .476275

16.2.4 Out-of-sample prediction

Evaluating the predictive ability of choice models in new data, not used in the estimation, is of interest. Use the first 1000 observations for estimation of the linear probability, probit and logit models, then predict the remaining 140 outcomes.

```
regress coke pratio disp_coke disp_pepsi in 1/1000
predict phat2
generate p2 = (phat2 >=.5)
tabulate p2 coke in 1001/1140,row
```

```
┌─────────────────────────┐
│ Key                     │
├─────────────────────────┤
│     frequency           │
│   row percentage        │
└─────────────────────────┘
```

```
                  │ =1 if coke chosen, =0
                  │  if pepsi chosen
        p2        │    0            1   │   Total

         0        │   51           45   │      96
                  │ 53.13        46.88  │  100.00

         1        │    6           38   │      44
                  │ 13.64        86.36  │  100.00

       Total      │   57           83   │     140
                  │ 40.71        59.29  │  100.00
```

> probit coke pratio disp_coke disp_pepsi in 1/1000
> estat classification in 1001/1140

Probit model for coke

```
                  ──────── True ────────
Classified    │       D            ~D    │   Total

     +        │      38             6    │     44
     -        │      45            51    │     96

   Total      │      83            57    │    140
```

Classified + if predicted Pr(D) >= .5

> logit coke pratio disp_coke disp_pepsi in 1/1000
> estat classification in 1001/1140

Logistic model for coke

```
                  ──────── True ────────
Classified    │       D            ~D    │   Total

     +        │      38             6    │     44
     -        │      45            51    │     96

   Total      │      83            57    │    140
```

Classified + if predicted Pr(D) >= .5

We find no difference between logit and probit predictions in this example.

16.3 MULTINOMIAL LOGIT

Suppose that a decision maker must choose between several distinct alternatives. Let us focus on a problem with $J = 3$ alternatives. An example might be the choice facing a high school graduate. Shall I attend a 2-year college, a 4-year college, or not go to college? The factors affecting this choice might include household income, the student's high school grades, family size, race, the student's gender, and the parent's education. As in the logit and probit models, we try to explain the probability that the ith person will choose alternative j,

$$p_{ij} = P[\text{individual } i \text{ chooses alternative } j]$$

In our example there are $J = 3$ alternatives, denoted by $j = 1, 2,$ or 3. These numerical values have no meaning because the alternatives in general have no particular ordering, and are assigned arbitrarily. You can think of them as categories A, B and C.

If we assume a single explanatory factor, x_i, then, in the multinomial logit specification, the probabilities of individual i choosing alternatives $j = 1, 2, 3$ are:

$$p_{i1} = \frac{1}{1 + \exp(\beta_{12} + \beta_{22} x_i) + \exp(\beta_{13} + \beta_{23} x_i)}, \quad j = 1$$

$$p_{i2} = \frac{\exp(\beta_{12} + \beta_{22} x_i)}{1 + \exp(\beta_{12} + \beta_{22} x_i) + \exp(\beta_{13} + \beta_{23} x_i)}, \quad j = 2$$

$$p_{i3} = \frac{\exp(\beta_{13} + \beta_{23} x_i)}{1 + \exp(\beta_{12} + \beta_{22} x_i) + \exp(\beta_{13} + \beta_{23} x_i)}, \quad j = 3$$

Because the model is such a complicated nonlinear function of the β-parameters, it will not surprise you to learn that the β-parameters are not "slopes." In these models the marginal effect is the effect of a change in x, everything else held constant, on the probability that an individual chooses alternative $m = 1, 2,$ or 3. It can be shown that

$$\left. \frac{\Delta p_{im}}{\Delta x_i} \right|_{\text{all else constant}} = \frac{\partial p_{im}}{\partial x_i} = p_{im} \left[\beta_{2m} - \sum_{j=1}^{3} \beta_{2j} p_{ij} \right]$$

Estimation of such models is by maximum likelihood. To illustrate use the data file *nels_small.dta*. We have 1000 observations on students who choose, upon graduating from high school, either no college (*PSECHOICE*=1), a 2-year college (*PSECHOICE*=2), or a 4-year college (*PSECHOICE*=3). For illustration purposes we focus on the explanatory variable *GRADES*, which is an index ranging from 1.0 (highest level, A+ grade) to 13.0 (lowest level, F grade) and represents combined performance in English, Math and Social Studies.[4] Open the data file and examine its contents.

```
use nels_small, clear
describe
```

---

[4] The indexing for grades is a bit awkward since higher grades correspond to smaller numbers. While we could have reversed this, we have chosen to stay with the original indexing.

variable name	storage type	display format	value label	variable label
psechoice	byte	%8.0g		no college = 1, 2 = 2-year college, 3 = 4-year college
hscath	byte	%8.0g		= 1 if catholic high school graduate
grades	double	%10.0g		average grade on 13 point scale with 1 = highest
faminc	float	%9.0g		gross 1991 family income (in $1000)
famsiz	byte	%8.0g		number of family members
parcoll	byte	%8.0g		= 1 if most educated parent graduated from college or had an advanced degree
female	byte	%8.0g		= 1 if female
black	byte	%8.0g		= 1 if black

Obtain detailed summary statistics for *GRADES*.

```
summarize grades, detail
```

Note that the median of *GRADES* (50th percentile) is 6.64, and the 5th percentile mark is 2.635. We will use these values in calculations below.

average grade on 13 point scale with 1 = highest

	Percentiles	Smallest		
1%	2.02	1.74		
5%	2.635	1.85		
10%	3.375	1.96	Obs	1000
25%	4.905	2	Sum of Wgt.	1000
50%	6.64		Mean	6.53039
		Largest	Std. Dev.	2.265855
75%	8.24	11.46		
90%	9.525	11.53	Variance	5.134097
95%	10.105	11.77	Skewness	-.0909654
99%	11.13	12.33	Kurtosis	2.243896

Within the 1000 observations tabulate *PSECHOICE* to see the distribution of choices.

```
tab psechoice
```

no college = 1, 2 = 2-year college, 3 = 4-year college	Freq.	Percent	Cum.
1	222	22.20	22.20
2	251	25.10	47.30
3	527	52.70	100.00
Total	1,000	100.00	

To estimate this model we use the **mlogit** command. For this command the dependent variable must take values 1, 2, ..., *m*, representing different categories facing the decision maker. They are unordered alternatives. We attach an option **baseoutcome(1)** to indicate that we want the first category, *PSECHOICE* = 1 (no college) to be the "base category".

```
mlogit psechoice grades, baseoutcome(1)
```

On the Stata menu you can locate the **mlogit** dialog box by entering the command **db mlogit**, or by following **Statistics > Categorical outcomes > Multinomial logistic regression**

Because estimation is by maximum likelihood, there will be an iteration history, showing the steps that Stata has taken.

```
Iteration 0:   log likelihood = -1018.6575
Iteration 1:   log likelihood = -881.68524
Iteration 2:   log likelihood = -875.36084
Iteration 3:   log likelihood = -875.31309
Iteration 4:   log likelihood = -875.31309
```

The algorithm used converges to a solution in 4 steps. Note that the value of the log-likelihood is increasing with each iteration.

The estimation results are

```
Multinomial logistic regression              Number of obs   =       1000
                                             LR chi2(2)      =     286.69
                                             Prob > chi2     =     0.0000
Log likelihood = -875.31309                  Pseudo R2       =     0.1407
```

psechoice	Coef.	Std. Err.	z	P>|z|	[95% Conf. Interval]	
1	(base outcome)					
2						
grades	-.3087889	.0522849	-5.91	0.000	-.4112654	-.2063125
_cons	2.506421	.4183848	5.99	0.000	1.686402	3.32644
3						
grades	-.7061967	.0529246	-13.34	0.000	-.809927	-.6024664
_cons	5.769876	.4043229	14.27	0.000	4.977417	6.562334

In the results there are estimated coefficients for *PSECHOICE* = 2 and = 3. These are $\tilde{\beta}_{12}$, $\tilde{\beta}_{22}$, $\tilde{\beta}_{13}$, and $\tilde{\beta}_{23}$. The other coefficients relate to the first alternative, $\beta_{11} = \beta_{21} = 0$, and are set to zero because of the identification problem. The coefficients themselves have little direct meaning, but the coefficients of *GRADES* are statistically significant. At the top of the results is the **LR chi2(2)** which is the result of a joint test that the coefficients of *GRADES* are zero. This is the test of overall model significance.

Use the post-estimation command **predict** to obtain predicted probabilities of every choice for each observation in the sample. Because there are 3 choices, 3 names must be provided for the predictions.

```
predict ProbNo ProbCC ProbColl
```

If we summarize these predicted probabilities we find that their mean is the same as the percentage of choices in the original data (see results of tabulate command above). This is a characteristic of the logit model.

```
summarize ProbNo ProbCC ProbColl
```

Variable	Obs	Mean	Std. Dev.	Min	Max
ProbNo	1000	.222	.1739746	.009808	.7545629
ProbCC	1000	.251	.0784017	.0702686	.3314252
ProbColl	1000	.527	.2388916	.0399892	.9199234

The probabilities and marginal effects are complicated algebraic expressions, but luckily the **margins** post-estimation command will do the calculations. There is one additional required option in the command. Because there are 3 choices, we must indicate the outcome for which the predictions or marginal effects are desired. Also, as in probit, if we want to specify the values of the explanatory variables at which the derivative are calculated we can do so with an **at** option. Some examples of using margins to compute predicted probabilities are:

```
margins, predict(outcome(1)) at(grades=6.64)
```

```
Adjusted predictions                          Number of obs   =        1000
Model VCE      : OIM

Expression     : Pr(psechoice==1), predict(outcome(1))
at             : grades         =        6.64
```

	Margin	Delta-method Std. Err.	z	P>|z|	[95% Conf. Interval]
_cons	.181006	.0148743	12.17	0.000	.151853 .2101591

Other predictions are obtained similarly, and for these we omit the output.

```
margins, predict(outcome(2)) at(grades=6.64)
margins, predict(outcome(3)) at(grades=6.64)
margins, predict(outcome(1)) at(grades=2.635)
margins, predict(outcome(2)) at(grades=2.635)
margins, predict(outcome(3)) at(grades=2.635)
```

To compute the derivatives of probability with respect to individual explanatory variables we again using **margins**.

```
margins, dydx(grades) at(grades=6.64)
```

```
Conditional marginal effects                  Number of obs   =        1000
Model VCE      : OIM

Expression     : Pr(psechoice==1), predict()
dy/dx w.r.t.   : grades
at             : grades         =        6.64
```

	dy/dx	Delta-method Std. Err.	z	P>|z|	[95% Conf. Interval]
grades	.0841445	.0063047	13.35	0.000	.0717875 .0965015

Above, since we did not specify the outcome of interest, Stata computes the change in the probability of the base outcome, alternative 1, given a unit change in grades.

If we omit the conditioning level of *GRADES*, then Stata computes the **Average marginal effect** over all individuals in the sample. That is, it finds the marginal effect on the probability of the first outcome at the grade level of each student, as computed in the previous command, and then finds the average of those marginal effects.

```
margins, dydx(grades)
```

Average marginal effects   Number of obs   =   1000
Model VCE   : OIM

Expression   : Pr(psechoice==1), predict()
dy/dx w.r.t. : grades

	dy/dx	Delta-method Std. Err.	z	P>|z|	[95% Conf. Interval]
grades	.0743738	.0052076	14.28	0.000	.064167 .0845805

The marginal effects for the other choices at the two chosen percentiles are obtained using similar commands. We omit the output.

```
margins, dydx(grades) predict(outcome(2)) at(grades=6.64)
margins, dydx(grades) predict(outcome(2)) at(grades=2.635)
margins, dydx(grades) predict(outcome(3)) at(grades=6.64)
margins, dydx(grades) predict(outcome(3)) at(grades=2.635)
```

16.4 CONDITIONAL LOGIT

Suppose that a decision maker must choose between several distinct alternatives, just as in the multinomial logit model. In a marketing context, suppose our decision is between three types ($J = 3$) of soft drinks, say Pepsi, 7-Up and Coke Classic, in 2-liter bottles. Shoppers will visit their supermarkets and make a choice, based on prices of the products and other factors. With the advent of supermarket scanners at checkout, data on purchases (what brand, how many units, and the price paid) are recorded. Of course we also know the prices of the products that the consumer did not buy on a particular shopping occasion. The key point is that if we collect data on soda purchases from a variety of supermarkets, over a period of time, we observe consumer choices from the set of alternatives and we know the prices facing the shopper on each trip to the supermarket.

Let y_{i1}, y_{i2} and y_{i3} be indicator variables that indicate the choice made by individual i. If alternative 1 (Pepsi) is selected, then $y_{i1} = 1$, $y_{i2} = 0$ and $y_{i3} = 0$. If alternative 2 (7-Up) is selected then $y_{i1} = 0$, $y_{i2} = 1$ and $y_{i3} = 0$. If alternative 3 (Coke) is selected then $y_{i1} = 0$, $y_{i2} = 0$ and $y_{i3} = 1$. The price facing individual i for brand j is $PRICE_{ij}$. That is, the price of Pepsi, 7-Up and Coke is potentially different for each customer who purchases soda. Remember, different customers can shop at different supermarkets and at different times. Variables like price are to be individual and alternative specific, because they vary from individual to individual and are different for each choice the consumer might make.

Our objective is to understand the factors that lead a consumer to choose one alternative over another, and we will construct a model for the probability that individual i chooses alternative j

$$p_{ij} = P[\text{individual } i \text{ chooses alternative } j]$$

The conditional logit model specifies these probabilities as

$$p_{ij} = \frac{\exp(\beta_{1j} + \beta_2 PRICE_{ij})}{\exp(\beta_{11} + \beta_2 PRICE_{i1}) + \exp(\beta_{12} + \beta_2 PRICE_{i2}) + \exp(\beta_{13} + \beta_2 PRICE_{i3})}$$

Note that unlike the probabilities for the multinomial logit model, there is only one parameter β_2 relating the effect of each price to the choice probability p_{ij}. We have also included alternative specific constants (intercept terms). These cannot all be estimated, and one must be set to zero. We will set $\beta_{13} = 0$.

Estimation of the unknown parameters is by maximum likelihood. How a change in price affects the choice probability is different for "own price" changes and "cross price" changes. Specifically it can be shown that the own-price effect is

$$\frac{\partial p_{ij}}{\partial PRICE_{ij}} = p_{ij}(1 - p_{ij})\beta_2$$

The sign of β_2 indicates the direction of the own-price effect.

The change in probability of alternative j being selected if the price of alternative k changes $(k \neq j)$ is

$$\frac{\partial p_{ij}}{\partial PRICE_{ik}} = -p_{ij} p_{ik} \beta_2$$

The cross-price effect is in the opposite direction of the own-price effect. Examining the marginal effects, we can see that if we have estimates of the coefficients and predicted values, we can compute them.

We observe 1822 purchases, covering 104 weeks and 5 stores, in which a consumer purchased either two-liter bottles of Pepsi (34.6%), 7-Up (37.4%) or Coke Classic (28%). These data are in the file *cola.dta*. Open this data file. Compute summary statistics.

```
use cola, clear
describe
```

variable name	storage type	display format	value label	variable label
id	int	%8.0g		customer id
choice	byte	%8.0g		= 1 if brand chosen
price	double	%10.0g		price of 2 liter soda
feature	byte	%8.0g		= 1 featured item at the time of purchase
display	byte	%8.0g		= 1 if displayed at time of purchase

summarize

Variable	Obs	Mean	Std. Dev.	Min	Max
id	5466	911.5	526.0141	1	1822
choice	5466	.3333333	.4714476	0	1
price	5466	1.185134	.3059794	.16	2.99
feature	5466	.5087816	.4999686	0	1
display	5466	.3635199	.4810567	0	1

For conditional logit the data must be in a stacked format. There are 3 choices, and thus there must be 3 lines of data for each individual, indicated by the variable id. List the data for the first 3 individuals

list in 1/9

	id	choice	price	feature	display
1.	1	0	1.79	0	0
2.	1	0	1.79	0	0
3.	1	1	1.79	0	0
4.	2	0	1.79	0	0
5.	2	0	1.79	0	0
6.	2	1	.89	1	1
7.	3	0	1.41	0	0
8.	3	0	.84	0	1
9.	3	1	.89	1	0

The lines of data correspond to alternatives 1, 2 and 3, with choice being 1 for the alternative chosen and 0 otherwise. The variable price similarly contains the prices for alternatives 1, 2 and 3 in order, and so on.

It is usually important to include alternative specific constants, like indicator variables, for each brand. These indicator variables serve to capture the effects of market share. Using the automatic observation number variable _n, we can generate a variable that lists the alternatives 1, 2 and 3.

```
sort id, stable
by id:gen alt = _n
```

Note again that this process works because the data are ordered consistently with an observation for Pepsi, then 7-Up and then Coke. List some of the observations to see what we have done.

list in 1/3

	id	choice	price	feature	display	alt
1.	1	0	1.79	0	0	1
2.	1	0	1.79	0	0	2
3.	1	1	1.79	0	0	3

Now, summarize the data by alternative

bysort alt:summarize choice price feature display

-> alt = 1

Variable	Obs	Mean	Std. Dev.	Min	Max
choice	1822	.3457739	.4757505	0	1
price	1822	1.227453	.2902694	.68	1.79
feature	1822	.5148189	.4999176	0	1
display	1822	.3117453	.4633336	0	1

-> alt = 2

Variable	Obs	Mean	Std. Dev.	Min	Max
choice	1822	.3743139	.4840781	0	1
price	1822	1.11764	.3242961	.16	2.99
feature	1822	.5159166	.4998838	0	1
display	1822	.4429199	.4968675	0	1

-> alt = 3

Variable	Obs	Mean	Std. Dev.	Min	Max
choice	1822	.2799122	.4490791	0	1
price	1822	1.210307	.2908002	.68	1.79
feature	1822	.4956092	.500118	0	1
display	1822	.3358946	.4724319	0	1

In the data we have, alternative 2 (7-Up) has slightly lower average price and uses displays more frequently than alternative 1 (Pepsi) and alternative 3 (Coke).

16.4.1 Estimation using asclogit

The command **asclogit** stands for alternative-specific conditional logit. First, we will make an enhancement that, while not strictly necessary, is very convenient when interpreting the results. We will create specific value labels, so that alt will no longer be 1, 2 and 3, but will be represented by the brand names. The first statement below creates the labels, and the second applies them to the variable alt.

```
label define brandlabel 1 "Pepsi"  2  "SevenUp" 3 "Coke"
label values alt brandlabel
```

The command syntax for `asclogit` is found using `help asclogit`.

```
help asclogit                                            dialog:  asclogit
                                                       also see:  asclogit postestimation

Title

     [R] asclogit — Alternative-specific conditional logit (McFadden's choice) model

Syntax

          asclogit depvar [indepvars] [if] [in] [weight], case(varname) alternatives(varname)
                [options]

      options                          description

      Model
      * case(varname)                  use varname to identify cases
      * alternatives(varname)          use varname to identify the alternatives available for each case
```

A dialog box is obtained using `db asclogit` or by following the menu path

Statistics > Categorical outcomes > Alternative-specific conditional logit

For the coke choice model we use

asclogit choice price, case(id) alternatives(alt) basealternative(Coke)

In this command **case** identifies the individual. The command **alternatives** is required. It indicates the choices that are available to each individual. The command **asclogit** will automatically create the alternative specific variables that we called **pepsi** and **sevenup** and add them to the model. The specification of the base alternative, using **basealternative(Coke)**, is not strictly required, but it is usually better to choose the base group rather than follow the internal assignment rules in the software. The results are:

```
Alternative-specific conditional logit        Number of obs    =         5466
Case variable: id                             Number of cases  =         1822

Alternative variable: alt                     Alts per case: min =           3
                                                             avg =         3.0
                                                             max =           3

                                              Wald chi2(1)     =       278.28
Log likelihood = -1824.5621                   Prob > chi2      =       0.0000
```

choice	Coef.	Std. Err.	z	P>|z|	[95% Conf. Interval]	
alt						
price	-2.296368	.1376575	-16.68	0.000	-2.566172	-2.026565
Pepsi						
_cons	.2831663	.062381	4.54	0.000	.1609019	.4054307
SevenUp						
_cons	.103833	.0624705	1.66	0.096	-.0186069	.226273
Coke	(base alternative)					

The **asclogit** command has post-estimation commands. First, there is a nice summary of the choices made in the sample data.

```
estat alternatives
```

```
Alternatives summary for alt
```

| | Alternative | | Cases | Frequency | Percent |
index	value	label	present	selected	selected
1	1	Pepsi	1822	630	34.58
2	2	SevenUp	1822	682	37.43
3	3	Coke	1822	510	27.99

More importantly, there is a post-estimation command that will not only compute the predicted probabilities of each alternative but also the marginal effects. The default command will carry out the calculations at the means of the alternatives of the explanatory variable price.

```
estat mfx
```

Better yet, we can compute the predicted probabilities and marginal effects at specific values of price for each alternative.

```
estat mfx, at(Coke:price=1.10 Pepsi:price=1 SevenUp:price=1.25)
```

```
Pr(choice = Pepsi|1 selected) =  .4831931
```

variable	dp/dx	std. Err.	z	P>|z|	[95% C.I.	]	X
price							
Pepsi	-.573443	.035023	-16.37	0.000	-.642088	-.504799	1
SevenUp	.252391	.014163	17.82	0.000	.224632	.28015	1.25
Coke	.321052	.025424	12.63	0.000	.271221	.370883	1.1

```
Pr(choice = SevenUp|1 selected) = .22746378
```

variable	dp/dx	std. Err.	z	P>|z|	[95% C.I.	]	X
price							
Pepsi	.252391	.014163	17.82	0.000	.224632	.28015	1
SevenUp	-.403527	.018607	-21.69	0.000	-.439996	-.367058	1.25
Coke	.151136	.008372	18.05	0.000	.134727	.167545	1.1

```
Pr(choice = Coke|1 selected) = .28934312
```

variable	dp/dx	std. Err.	z	P>|z|	[95% C.I.	]	X
price							
Pepsi	.321052	.025424	12.63	0.000	.271221	.370883	1
SevenUp	.151136	.008372	18.05	0.000	.134727	.167545	1.25
Coke	-.472188	.029761	-15.87	0.000	-.530519	-.413857	1.1

16.5 ORDERED CHOICE MODELS

The choice options in multinomial and conditional logit models have no natural ordering or arrangement. However, in some cases choices are ordered in a specific way. Examples include:

- Results of opinion surveys in which responses can be strongly disagree, disagree, neutral, agree or strongly agree.
- Assignment of grades or work performance ratings. Students receive grades A, B, C, D, F which are ordered on the basis of a teacher's evaluation of their performance. Employees are often given evaluations on scales such as Outstanding, Very Good, Good, Fair and Poor which are similar in spirit.
- Standard and Poor's rates bonds as AAA, AA, A, BBB and so on, as a judgment about the credit worthiness of the company or country issuing a bond, and how risky the investment might be.

When modeling these types of outcomes numerical values are assigned to the outcomes, but the numerical values are ordinal, and reflect only the ranking of the outcomes. In the first example, we might assign a dependent variable y the values

$$
y = \begin{cases}
1 & \text{strongly disagree} \\
2 & \text{disagree} \\
3 & \text{neutral} \\
4 & \text{agree} \\
5 & \text{strongly agree}
\end{cases}
$$

In *POE4* the problem of choosing what type of college to attend after graduating from high school is used as an illustration. We might rank the possibilities as

$$
y = \begin{cases}
3 & \text{4-year college (the full college experience)} \\
2 & \text{2-year college (a partial college experience)} \\
1 & \text{no college}
\end{cases}
$$

The choices we observe are based on a comparison of "sentiment" towards higher education, y_i^*, which is taken simply to be function of *GRADES* in the text example,

$$
y_i^* = \beta GRADES_i + e_i
$$

to certain thresholds. Because there are $M = 3$ alternatives there are $M-1 = 2$ thresholds μ_1 and μ_2, with $\mu_1 < \mu_2$. The index model does not contain an intercept because it would be exactly collinear with the threshold variables. If sentiment towards higher education is in the lowest category, then $y_i^* \leq \mu_1$ and the alternative "no college" is chosen, if $\mu_1 < y_i^* \leq \mu_2$ then the alternative "2-year college" is chosen, and if sentiment towards higher education is in the highest category, then $y_i^* \leq \mu_1$ and "4-year college" is chosen. That is,

$$y = \begin{cases} 3 \text{ (4-year college)} & \text{if} \quad y_i^* > \mu_2 \\ 2 \text{ (2-year college)} & \text{if} \quad \mu_1 < y_i^* \leq \mu_2 \\ 1 \text{ (no college)} & \text{if} \quad y_i^* \leq \mu_1 \end{cases}$$

The ordinal probit model assumes that the errors e_i are standard normal. The example uses the data file *nels_small.dta*. Open the data file.

```
use nels_small, clear
```

Obtain the detailed summary statistics for the variable *GRADES*.

```
summarize grades, detail
```

```
. summarize grades, detail

                 average grade on 13 point scale with 1 = highest
```

	Percentiles	Smallest		
1%	2.02	1.74		
5%	2.635	1.85		
10%	3.375	1.96	Obs	1000
25%	4.905	2	Sum of Wgt.	1000
50%	6.64		Mean	6.53039
		Largest	Std. Dev.	2.265855
75%	8.24	11.46		
90%	9.525	11.53	Variance	5.134097
95%	10.105	11.77	Skewness	-.0909654
99%	11.13	12.33	Kurtosis	2.243896

Tabulate the choices made by sample members.

```
tab psechoice
```

no college = 1, 2 = 2-year college, 3 = 4-year college	Freq.	Percent	Cum.
1	222	22.20	22.20
2	251	25.10	47.30
3	527	52.70	100.00
Total	1,000	100.00	

The ordered probit syntax is just like the usual regression model. To use a dialog box for specifying the model follow **Statistics > Ordinal outcomes > Orde red probit regression** or enter **db oprobit**.

```
oprobit psechoice grades
```

This is a maximum likelihood estimation problem. The Stata results show that it takes only 3 iterations until the numerical algorithm converges.

```
Iteration 0:   log likelihood = -1018.6575
Iteration 1:   log likelihood = -876.21962
Iteration 2:   log likelihood = -875.82172
Iteration 3:   log likelihood = -875.82172
```

```
Ordered probit regression              Number of obs   =      1000
                                       LR chi2(1)      =    285.67
                                       Prob > chi2     =    0.0000
Log likelihood = -875.82172            Pseudo R2       =    0.1402
```

psechoice	Coef.	Std. Err.	z	P>|z|	[95% Conf. Interval]
grades	-.3066252	.0191735	-15.99	0.000	-.3442045 -.2690459
/cut1	-2.9456	.1468283			-3.233378 -2.657822
/cut2	-2.089993	.1357681			-2.356094 -1.823893

The estimated coefficient of grades is −0.3066 and it is very significant. The "**/cut**" parameters are the estimated thresholds μ_1 and μ_2.

The marginal effects for this model are calculated differently for each outcome.

$$\frac{\partial P[y=1]}{\partial GRADES} = -\phi(\mu_1 - \beta GRADES) \times \beta$$

$$\frac{\partial P[y=2]}{\partial GRADES} = \left[\phi(\mu_1 - \beta GRADES) - \phi(\mu_2 - \beta GRADES)\right] \times \beta$$

$$\frac{\partial P[y=3]}{\partial GRADES} = \phi(\mu_2 - \beta GRADES) \times \beta$$

The margins command in Stata will compute these marginal effects. The additional option that is required indicates for which rank outcome the marginal effect is calculated. If we choose the median grades the marginal effect on the probability of attending a 4-year college is

```
margins, dydx(grades) at(grades=6.64) predict(outcome(3))
```

```
Conditional marginal effects           Number of obs   =      1000
Model VCE    : OIM

Expression   : Pr(psechoice==3), predict(outcome(3))
dy/dx w.r.t. : grades
at           : grades          =        6.64
```

	dy/dx	Delta-method Std. Err.	z	P>|z|	[95% Conf. Interval]
grades	-.1221475	.0076332	-16.00	0.000	-.1371084 -.1071867

If we choose the 5th percentile value, the marginal effect is

```
margins, dydx(grades) at(grades=2.635) predict(outcome(3))
```

```
Conditional marginal effects                    Number of obs    =        1000
Model VCE    : OIM

Expression   : Pr(psechoice==3), predict(outcome(3))
dy/dx w.r.t. : grades
at           : grades          =          2.635
```

	dy/dx	Delta-method Std. Err.	z	P>|z|	[95% Conf. Interval]	
grades	-.0537788	.0035887	-14.99	0.000	-.0608126	-.046745

16.6 MODELS FOR COUNT DATA

When the dependent variable in a regression model is a count of the number of occurrences of an event, the outcome variable is $y = 0, 1, 2, 3, \ldots$ These numbers are actual counts, and thus different from the ordinal numbers of the previous section. While we are again interested in explaining and predicting probabilities, such as the probability that an individual will take two or more trips to the doctor during a year, the probability distribution we use as a foundation is the Poisson, not the normal or the logistic. If Y is a Poisson random variable, then its probability function is

$$f(y) = P(Y = y) = \frac{e^{-\lambda}\lambda^y}{y!}, \quad y = 0, 1, 2, \ldots$$

The factorial (!) term $y! = y \times (y-1) \times (y-2) \times \cdots \times 1$. This probability function has one parameter, λ, which is the mean (and variance) of Y. That is, $E(Y) = \text{var}(Y) = \lambda$. In a regression model we try to explain the behavior of $E(Y)$ as a function of some explanatory variables. We do the same here, keeping the value of $E(Y) \geq 0$ by defining

$$E(Y) = \lambda = \exp(\beta_1 + \beta_2 x)$$

As in other modeling situations we would like to use the estimated model to predict outcomes, determine the marginal effect of a change in an explanatory variable on the mean of the dependent variable, and test the significance of coefficients.

Prediction of the conditional mean of y is straightforward. Given the maximum likelihood estimates $\tilde{\beta}_1$ and $\tilde{\beta}_2$ and given a value of the explanatory variable x_0, then

$$\widehat{E(y_0)} = \tilde{\lambda}_0 = \exp(\tilde{\beta}_1 + \tilde{\beta}_2 x_0)$$

This value is an estimate of the expected number of occurrences observed, if x takes the value x_0. The probability of a particular number of occurrences can be estimated by inserting the estimated conditional mean into the probability function, as

$$\widehat{\Pr(Y=y)} = \frac{\exp\left(-\tilde{\lambda}_0\right)\tilde{\lambda}_0^y}{y!}, \quad y = 0,1,2,\dots$$

The marginal effect of a change in a continuous variable x in the Poisson regression model is not simply given by the parameter, because the conditional mean model is a nonlinear function of the parameters. Using our specification that the conditional mean is given by $E(y_i) = \lambda_i = \exp(\beta_1 + \beta_2 x_i)$, and using rules for derivatives of exponential functions, we obtain the marginal effect

$$\frac{\partial E(y_i)}{\partial x_i} = \lambda_i \beta_2$$

This choice defines the Poisson regression model for count data.

    The example in *Principles of Econometrics, 4th Edition* concerns the number of medals won by a country at the Olympic games in 1988. We will estimate a Poisson regression explaining the number of medals won (*MEDALTOT*) as a function of the logarithms of population and gross domestic product (measure in real 1995 dollars). The data file is *olympics.dta*. Open the data file.

```
use olympics, clear
```

Keep the data for the year 1988.

```
keep if year==88
```

Keep only the variables of interest.

```
keep medaltot pop gdp
```

The Poisson model we will initially estimate has the conditional mean function

$$E(MEDALTOT) = \lambda = \exp\big(\beta_1 + \beta_2 \ln(POP) + \beta_3 \ln(GDP)\big)$$

Create the logarithmic variables.

```
generate lpop = ln(pop)
generate lgdp = ln(gdp)
```

Estimate the Poisson model and store the results. The syntax is just like the usual regression model.

```
poisson medaltot lpop lgdp
```

The estimation results are:

```
Iteration 0:   log likelihood = -722.76694
Iteration 1:   log likelihood = -722.33675
Iteration 2:   log likelihood = -722.33649
Iteration 3:   log likelihood = -722.33649
```

```
Poisson regression                          Number of obs   =         151
                                            LR chi2(2)      =     1728.04
                                            Prob > chi2     =      0.0000
Log likelihood = -722.33649                 Pseudo R2       =      0.5447
```

medaltot	Coef.	Std. Err.	z	P>|z|	[95% Conf. Interval]	
lpop	.1800376	.0322801	5.58	0.000	.1167697	.2433055
lgdp	.5766033	.0247217	23.32	0.000	.5281497	.625057
_cons	-15.88746	.5118048	-31.04	0.000	-16.89058	-14.88434

To reach the **poisson** dialog box enter the command **db poisson**, or on the Stata menu bar select **Statistics > Count outcomes > Poisson regression**

Use the **margins** command to compute the marginal effects at the median values

margins, dydx(*) at((median) lpop lgdp)

```
Conditional marginal effects                Number of obs   =         151
Model VCE      : OIM

Expression     : Predicted number of events, predict()
dy/dx w.r.t.   : lpop lgdp
at             : lpop           =     15.73425 (median)
                 lgdp           =     22.81883 (median)
```

	dy/dx	Delta-method Std. Err.	z	P>|z|	[95% Conf. Interval]	
lpop	.1995122	.0389282	5.13	0.000	.1232143	.2758101
lgdp	.6389744	.0402253	15.88	0.000	.5601343	.7178145

Using margins we can compute the predicted number of events when explanatory variables are at their medians.

margins, predict(n) at((median) lpop lgdp)

```
Adjusted predictions                        Number of obs   =         151
Model VCE      : OIM

Expression     : Predicted number of events, predict(n)
at             : lpop           =     15.73425 (median)
                 lgdp           =     22.81883 (median)
```

	Margin	Delta-method Std. Err.	z	P>|z|	[95% Conf. Interval]	
_cons	1.10817	.0903926	12.26	0.000	.9310035	1.285336

16.7 CENSORED DATA MODELS

An example that illustrates the situation is based on Thomas Mroz's (1987) study of married women's labor force participation and wages. The data are in the file *mroz.dta* and consist of 753 observations on married women. Of these women 325 did not work outside the home, and thus had no hours worked and no reported wages. The histogram of hours worked is shown in Figure 16.3 of *Principles of Econometrics, 4th Edition*. The histogram shows the large fraction of women who did not enter the labor force. This is an example of censored data, meaning that a substantial fraction of the observations on the dependent variable take a limit value, which is zero in the case of market hours worked by married women.

16.7.1 Simulated data example

In *Principles of Econometrics, 4th Edition*, Section 16.7.2 the underlying ideas are presented first using a Monte Carlo experiment and simulated data in the file *tobit.dta*. Using simulation is an excellent way to learn econometrics. It requires us to understand how the data are obtained under a particular set of assumptions. The observed sample is obtained within the framework of an index or latent variable model, similar to the one discussed in Section 16.5 of this manual on the ordered probit model. Let the latent variable be

$$y_i^* = \beta_1 + \beta_2 x_i + e_i = -9 + x_i + e_i$$

In this example we have given the parameters the specific values $\beta_1 = -9$ and $\beta_2 = 1$. The error term is assumed to have a normal distribution, $e_i \sim N(0, \sigma^2 = 16)$. The observable outcome y_i takes the value zero if $y_i^* \leq 0$, but $y_i = y_i^*$ if $y_i^* > 0$. That is,

$$y_i = \begin{cases} 0 & \text{if } y_i^* \leq 0 \\ y_i^* & \text{if } y_i^* > 0 \end{cases}$$

Open *tobit.dta*.

```
use tobit, clear
describe
```

First, examine the data summary statistics for all the data.

```
Summarize
```

Variable	Obs	Mean	Std. Dev.	Min	Max
y	200	2.951102	3.906139	0	14.9416
x	200	9.88019	5.659853	.148959	19.824

Now summarize the data for positive y values

```
summarize if y>0
```

Variable	Obs	Mean	Std. Dev.	Min	Max
y	100	5.902204	3.616079	.106413	14.9416
x	100	14.15509	3.481772	2.00901	19.824

The simulated data has 100 observations with positive *y* values. Estimate the least squares regression of *y* on *x*.

```
reg y x
```

Source	SS	df	MS		
Model	1697.72783	1	1697.72783	Number of obs =	200
Residual	1338.59888	198	6.76060042	F(1, 198) =	251.12
				Prob > F =	0.0000
				R-squared =	0.5591
				Adj R-squared =	0.5569
Total	3036.32671	199	15.2579232	Root MSE =	2.6001

y	Coef.	Std. Err.	t	P>|t|	[95% Conf. Interval]	
x	.5160625	.0325657	15.85	0.000	.4518423	.5802827
_cons	-2.147694	.3705802	-5.80	0.000	-2.878485	-1.416903

Note that the estimates are far from the true values.

Now estimate the regression using only observations for which *y* > 0.

```
reg y x if y>0
```

Source	SS	df	MS		
Model	489.720033	1	489.720033	Number of obs =	100
Residual	804.80632	98	8.21230938	F(1, 98) =	59.63
				Prob > F =	0.0000
				R-squared =	0.3783
				Adj R-squared =	0.3720
Total	1294.52635	99	13.0760238	Root MSE =	2.8657

y	Coef.	Std. Err.	t	P>|t|	[95% Conf. Interval]	
x	.6387869	.0827208	7.72	0.000	.4746302	.8029437
_cons	-3.139881	1.205478	-2.60	0.011	-5.532112	-.7476489

Again the estimates are far from the true values.

The syntax for tobit estimation is like a usual regression, except for the requirement that we specify whether the data are censored from below (lower limit, **ll**) or above (upper limit, **ul**). Enter **help tobit** for the complete syntax. The simulated data has a lower limit, so the estimation command is

```
tobit y x, ll
```

which yields the results:

```
Tobit regression                          Number of obs    =         200
                                          LR chi2(1)       =      205.08
                                          Prob > chi2      =      0.0000
Log likelihood = -301.87794               Pseudo R2        =      0.2535
```

y	Coef.	Std. Err.	t	P>|t|	[95% Conf. Interval]	
x	1.048705	.0789849	13.28	0.000	.8929506	1.20446
_cons	-10.2773	1.096991	-9.37	0.000	-12.44052	-8.114084
/sigma	3.575591	.2610292			3.060853	4.090329

```
   Obs. summary:          100  left-censored observations at y<=0
                          100       uncensored observations
                            0 right-censored observations
```

Note that these maximum likelihood estimates are much close to the true values. The coefficient **/sigma** is the estimate of σ, which in the Monte Carlo experiment was set to be 4.

The tobit dialog box is accessed by entering the command **db tobit**, or following the menu path

> **Statistics > Linear models and related > Censored regression > Tobit regression**

16.7.2 Mroz data example

If we wish to estimate a model explaining the market hours worked by a married woman, what explanatory variables would we include? Factors that would tend to pull a woman into the labor force are her education and her prior labor market experience. Factors that may reduce her incentive to work are her age, the presence of young children in the home. Thus we might propose the regression model

$$HOURS = \beta_1 + \beta_2 EDUC + \beta_3 EXPER + \beta_4 AGE + \beta_4 KIDSL6 + e$$

where the observed variable *HOURS* is either a positive number of hours worked, or zero, for women who did not enter the labor force. *KIDSL6* is the number of children less than 6 years old in the household.

Open *mroz.dta* and describe the regression variables.

```
use mroz, clear
describe lfp hours educ exper age kids16
```

variable name	storage type	display format	value label	variable label
lfp	byte	%8.0g		dummy variable = 1 if woman worked in 1975, else 0
hours	int	%8.0g		wife's hours of work in 1975
educ	byte	%8.0g		wife's educational attainment, in years
exper	byte	%8.0g		Actual years of wife's previous labor market experience
age	byte	%8.0g		wife's age
kids16	byte	%8.0g		Number of children less than 6 years old in household

Examine the data by computing summary statistics for the key variables.

```
summarize lfp hours educ exper age kids16
```

Variable	Obs	Mean	Std. Dev.	Min	Max
lfp	753	.5683931	.4956295	0	1
hours	753	740.5764	871.3142	0	4950
educ	753	12.28685	2.280246	5	17
exper	753	10.63081	8.06913	0	45
age	753	42.53785	8.072574	30	60
kids16	753	.2377158	.523959	0	3

To illustrate the censored nature of the data, construct a histogram for the variable hours.

```
histogram hours, frequency title(Hours worked by married women)
```

A large proportion of married women in the sample have 0 hours of labor market work. Obtain the summary statistics for those with positive hours worked.

```
summarize hours educ exper age kids16 if (hours>0)
```

Variable	Obs	Mean	Std. Dev.	Min	Max
hours	428	1302.93	776.2744	12	4950
educ	428	12.65888	2.285376	5	17
exper	428	13.03738	8.055923	0	38
age	428	41.97196	7.721084	30	60
kids16	428	.1401869	.3919231	0	2

Compare these to the summary statistics for those who are not in the labor force.

```
summarize educ exper age kids16 if (hours==0)
```

Variable	Obs	Mean	Std. Dev.	Min	Max
hours	325	0	0	0	0
educ	325	11.79692	2.181995	5	17
exper	325	7.461538	6.918567	0	45
age	325	43.28308	8.467796	30	60
kids16	325	.3661538	.6368995	0	3

The nonworking women have slightly lower education and experience, are slightly older and have more small children.

Carry out a least squares regression of the model for hours worked using all the sample observations, and then again using only women with positive hours worked.

regress hours educ exper age kids16

Source	SS	df	MS
Model	146771295	4	36692823.7
Residual	424138429	748	567029.985
Total	570909724	752	759188.463

```
Number of obs =     753
F( 4,   748) =   64.71
Prob > F      =  0.0000
R-squared     =  0.2571
Adj R-squared =  0.2531
Root MSE      =  753.01
```

hours	Coef.	Std. Err.	t	P>|t|	[95% Conf. Interval]	
educ	27.08568	12.23989	2.21	0.027	3.057054	51.1143
exper	48.03981	3.641804	13.19	0.000	40.89044	55.18919
age	-31.30782	3.96099	-7.90	0.000	-39.0838	-23.53184
kids16	-447.8547	58.41252	-7.67	0.000	-562.5267	-333.1827
_cons	1335.306	235.6487	5.67	0.000	872.6945	1797.918

regress hours educ exper age kids16 if (hours>0)

Source	SS	df	MS
Model	32193987.4	4	8048496.86
Residual	225117032	423	532191.566
Total	257311020	427	602601.92

```
Number of obs =     428
F( 4,   423) =   15.12
Prob > F      =  0.0000
R-squared     =  0.1251
Adj R-squared =  0.1168
Root MSE      =  729.51
```

hours	Coef.	Std. Err.	t	P>|t|	[95% Conf. Interval]	
educ	-16.46211	15.58083	-1.06	0.291	-47.0876	14.16339
exper	33.93637	5.009185	6.77	0.000	24.09038	43.78237
age	-17.10821	5.457674	-3.13	0.002	-27.83575	-6.380677
kids16	-305.309	96.44904	-3.17	0.002	-494.8881	-115.7299
_cons	1829.746	292.5356	6.25	0.000	1254.741	2404.75

Compare the coefficient estimates of **educ** and **kids16**.

Now obtain the **tobit** estimates.

tobit hours educ exper age kids16, ll

```
Tobit regression                                    Number of obs   =      753
                                                    LR chi2(4)      =   255.50
                                                    Prob > chi2     =   0.0000
Log likelihood = -3827.1433                         Pseudo R2       =   0.0323
```

hours	Coef.	Std. Err.	t	P>|t|	[95% Conf. Interval]	
educ	73.29099	20.47458	3.58	0.000	33.09659	113.4854
exper	80.53527	6.287805	12.81	0.000	68.19145	92.87909
age	-60.7678	6.88819	-8.82	0.000	-74.29025	-47.24534
kids16	-918.9181	111.6606	-8.23	0.000	-1138.123	-699.713
_cons	1349.876	386.2989	3.49	0.001	591.5188	2108.234
/sigma	1133.697	42.06234			1051.123	1216.271

```
Obs. summary:        325  left-censored observations at hours<=0
                     428     uncensored observations
                       0 right-censored observations
```

As previously argued the least squares estimates are unreliable because the least squares estimator is both biased and inconsistent. The Tobit estimates have the anticipated signs and are all statistically significant at the 0.01 level.

To compute and interpret marginal effects we must specify exactly what we want. Two regression functions of interest are $E(HOURS)$, the expectation of the observed hours, and $E(HOURS \mid HOURS > 0)$, the expected hours worked conditional on the woman being in the labor force. For the observed hours, the marginal effect of education, for example is

$$\frac{\partial E(HOURS)}{\partial EDUC} = \Phi\left(\beta_1 + \beta_2 EDUC + \beta_3 EXPER + \beta_4 AGE + \beta_4 KIDSL6\right) \times \beta_2$$

This is the coefficient of $EDUC$ multiplied by a scale factor, $\Phi(\bullet)$. To compute the scale factor required for calculation of the marginal effects we must choose values of the explanatory variables. We choose the sample means for $EDUC$ (12.29), $EXPER$ (10.63), AGE (42.5) and assume one small child at home (rather than the mean value of 0.24). The Stata commands to compute the scale factor after a tobit estimation are

```
scalar xb = _b[_cons]+_b[educ]*12.29+_b[exper]*10.63
        +_b[age]*42.5+_b[kids16]*1
scalar cdf = normal( xb/_b[/sigma])
display "x*beta = " xb
display "Tobit scale Factor: cdf evaluated at zi = " cdf
display "Marginal effect of education = " _b[educ]*cdf
```

```
. display "x*beta = " xb
x*beta = -394.837
```

```
. display "Tobit scale Factor: cdf evaluated at zi = " cdf
Tobit scale Factor: cdf evaluated at zi = .36381726
```

```
. display "Marginal effect of education = " _b[educ]*cdf
Marginal effect of education = 26.664527
```

Thus the marginal effect on observed hours of work of another year of education is

$$\frac{\partial E(HOURS)}{\partial EDUC} = \tilde{\beta}_2 \tilde{\Phi} = 73.29 \times .3638 = 26.66$$

That is, we estimate that another year of education will increase a wife's hours of work by about 26.7 hours, conditional upon the assumed values of the explanatory variables. This marginal effect can be computed using the **margins** command:

```
quietly tobit hours  educ exper age kids16, 11
margins, dydx(educ) at(educ=12.29 exper=10.63 age=42.5 kids16=1)
        predict(ystar(0,.))
```

```
Conditional marginal effects                    Number of obs   =        753
Model VCE    : OIM

Expression   : E(hours*|hours>0), predict(ystar(0,.))
dy/dx w.r.t. : educ
at           : educ          =        12.29
               exper         =        10.63
               age           =         42.5
               kids16        =            1
```

	dy/dx	Delta-method Std. Err.	z	P>|z|	[95% Conf. Interval]
educ	26.66453	7.563667	3.53	0.000	11.84001	41.48904

The marginal effect above is the effect of education on the observed value of y (*HOURS*). The marginal effect can be decomposed into two factors, and is called the "McDonald-Moffit" decomposition,

$$\frac{\partial E(y \mid x)}{\partial x} = \text{Prob}(y>0)\frac{\partial E(y \mid x, y>0)}{\partial x} + E(y \mid x, y>0)\frac{\partial \text{Prob}(y>0)}{\partial x}$$

The first factor accounts for the marginal effect of a change in x for the portion of the population whose y-data is observed already. The second factor accounts for changes in the proportion of the population who switch from the y-unobserved category to the y-observed category when x changes.

The marginal effect on those whose *HOURS* are already positive is

$$\frac{\partial E(y \mid x, y>0)}{\partial x}$$

This marginal effect is computed using

```
margins, dydx(educ) at(educ=12.29 exper=10.63 age=42.5 kids16=1)
        predict(e(0,.))
```

```
Conditional marginal effects                    Number of obs    =       753
Model VCE     : OIM

Expression    : E(hours|hours>0), predict(e(0,.))
dy/dx w.r.t.  : educ
at            : educ           =         12.29
                exper          =         10.63
                age            =          42.5
                kids16         =             1
```

	dy/dx	Delta-method Std. Err.	z	P>|z|	[95% Conf. Interval]	
educ	21.574	5.999972	3.60	0.000	9.814276	33.33373

16.8 SELECTION BIAS

The Heckit model is composed of two equations. The first, is the selection equation that determines whether the variable of interest is observed. The sample consists of N observations, however the variable of interest is observed only for $n < N$ of these. The selection equation is expressed in terms of a latent variable z_i^* which depends on one or more explanatory variables w_i, and is given by

$$z_i^* = \gamma_1 + \gamma_2 w_i + u_i \quad i = 1, \ldots, N$$

For simplicity we will include only one explanatory variable in the selection equation. The latent variable is not observed, but we do observe the binary variable

$$z_i = \begin{cases} 1 & z_i^* > 0 \\ 0 & \text{otherwise} \end{cases}$$

The second equation is the linear model of interest. It is

$$y_i = \beta_1 + \beta_2 x_i + e_i \quad i = 1, \ldots, n \quad N > n$$

A selectivity problem arises when y_i is observed only when $z_i = 1$, and if the errors of the two equations are correlated. In such a situation the usual least squares estimators of β_1 and β_2 are biased and inconsistent.

Consistent estimators are based on the conditional regression function

$$E\left[y_i \mid z_i^* > 0\right] = \beta_1 + \beta_2 x_i + \beta_\lambda \lambda_i \quad i = 1, \ldots, n$$

where the additional variable λ_i is "Inverse Mills Ratio." It is equal to

$$\lambda_i = \frac{\phi(\gamma_1 + \gamma_2 w_i)}{\Phi(\gamma_1 + \gamma_2 w_i)}$$

where, as usual, $\phi(\cdot)$ denotes the standard normal probability density function, and $\Phi(\cdot)$ denotes the cumulative distribution function for a standard normal random variable. While the value of λ_i is not known, the parameters γ_1 and γ_2 can be estimated using a probit model, based on the observed binary outcome z_i. Then the estimated IMR,

$$\tilde{\lambda}_i = \frac{\phi(\tilde{\gamma}_1 + \tilde{\gamma}_2 w_i)}{\Phi(\tilde{\gamma}_1 + \tilde{\gamma}_2 w_i)}$$

is inserted into the regression equation as an extra explanatory variable, yielding the estimating equation

$$y_i = \beta_1 + \beta_2 x_i + \beta_\lambda \tilde{\lambda}_i + v_i \quad i = 1,\ldots,n$$

Least squares estimation of this equation yields consistent estimators of β_1 and β_2. A word of caution, however, as the least squares estimator is inefficient relative to the maximum likelihood estimator, and the usual standard errors and t-statistics produced after estimation by least squares of the augmented equation are incorrect. Proper estimation of standard errors requires the use of specialized software for the "Heckit" model.

As an example we will reconsider the analysis of wages earned by married women using the Mroz (1987) data. In the sample of 753 married women, 428 have market employment and nonzero earnings.

Open *mroz.dta*.

```
use mroz, clear
```

Generate ln(*WAGE*).

```
generate lwage = ln(wage)
```

Estimate a simple wage equation, explaining ln(*WAGE*) as a function of the woman's education, *EDUC*, and years of market work experience (*EXPER*), using the 428 women who have positive wages.

```
regress lwage educ exper if (hours>0)
```

Source	SS	df	MS
Model	33.132458	2	16.566229
Residual	190.194984	425	.447517609
Total	223.327442	427	.523015086

```
Number of obs =      428
F( 2,    425) =    37.02
Prob > F      =   0.0000
R-squared     =   0.1484
Adj R-squared =   0.1444
Root MSE      =   .66897
```

lwage	Coef.	Std. Err.	t	P>|t|	[95% Conf. Interval]	
educ	.1094888	.0141672	7.73	0.000	.0816423	.1373353
exper	.0156736	.0040191	3.90	0.000	.0077738	.0235733
_cons	-.4001744	.1903682	-2.10	0.036	-.7743548	-.0259939

The estimated return to education is about 11%, and the estimated coefficients of both education and experience are statistically significant.

The Heckit procedure starts by estimating a probit model of labor force participation. As explanatory variables we use the woman's age, her years of education, an indicator variable for whether she has children and the marginal tax rate that she would pay upon earnings if employed. Generate a new variable kids which is a dummy variable indicating the presence of any kids in the household.

```
generate kids = (kidsl6+kids618>0)
```

The estimated probit model is

```
probit lfp age educ kids mtr
```

Probit regression

```
Number of obs  =      753
LR chi2(4)     =    41.45
Prob > chi2    =   0.0000
Pseudo R2      =   0.0403
```

Log likelihood = -494.14614

lfp	Coef.	Std. Err.	z	P>|z|	[95% Conf. Interval]	
age	-.0206155	.0070447	-2.93	0.003	-.0344229	-.0068082
educ	.0837753	.023205	3.61	0.000	.0382943	.1292563
kids	-.3138848	.1237108	-2.54	0.011	-.5563535	-.0714162
mtr	-1.393853	.6165751	-2.26	0.024	-2.602318	-.1853878
_cons	1.192296	.7205439	1.65	0.098	-.2199443	2.604536

As expected the effects of age, the presence of children, and the prospects of higher taxes significantly reduce the probability that a woman will join the labor force, while education increases it. Using the estimated coefficients, compute the Inverse Mills Ratio for the 428 women with market wages.

$$\tilde{\lambda} = IMR = \frac{\phi(1.1923 - 0.0206\,AGE + 0.0838\,EDUC - 0.3139\,KIDS - 1.3939\,MTR)}{\Phi(1.1923 - 0.0206\,AGE + 0.0838\,EDUC - 0.3139\,KIDS - 1.3939\,MTR)}$$

This is accomplished in Stata by using the **predict** post-estimation command, and then generating a new variable for the inverse Mills ratio. The function **normalden** is the standard normal *pdf* and the function **normal** is the standard normal *cdf*.

```
predict w, xb
generate imr = normalden(w)/normal(w)
```

This then is included in the wage equation, and least squares estimation applied.

```
regress lwage educ exper imr
```

Source	SS	df	MS
Model	36.2307253	3	12.0769084
Residual	187.096716	424	.441265841
Total	223.327442	427	.523015086

```
Number of obs =      428
F(  3,    424) =    27.37
Prob > F       =   0.0000
R-squared      =   0.1622
Adj R-squared  =   0.1563
Root MSE       =   .66428
```

lwage	Coef.	Std. Err.	t	P>|t|	[95% Conf. Interval]	
educ	.0584579	.0238495	2.45	0.015	.01158	.1053358
exper	.0163202	.0039984	4.08	0.000	.0084612	.0241793
imr	-.8664386	.3269855	-2.65	0.008	-1.509153	-.2237242
_cons	.8105417	.4944723	1.64	0.102	-.1613804	1.782464

Two results are of note. First the estimated coefficient of the Inverse Mills ratio is statistically significant, implying that there is a selection bias present in the least squares results. Secondly, the estimated return to education has fallen from approximately 11% to approximately 6%. The usual standard errors do not account for the fact that the Inverse Mills ratio is itself an estimated value. The correct standard errors which do account for the first stage probit estimation are obtained using Stata's **heckman** command.

```
heckman lwage educ exper, select(lfp=age educ kids mtr) twostep
```

The command has two parts: the first is the equation of interest, second the selection equation. The labor force participation variable **lfp** = 0 when **hours** = 0, and **lfp** = 1 when **hours** > 0. The option **twostep** replicates the steps we have shown, and produces correct standard errors.

The **heckman** dialog box is located by entering **help heckman**. Note that there are separate dialogs for the two-step and maximum likelihood estimator.

```
help heckman                                   dialogs:  heckman_ml  heckman_2step
                                                   svy:  heckman_ml
                                               also see:  heckman postestimation

Title

    [R] heckman — Heckman selection model
```

Alternatively, for the two-step estimator, follow the menu path

Statistics > Sample-selection models > Heckman selection model (two-step)

```
. heckman lwage educ exper, select(lfp=age educ kids mtr) twostep
```

```
Heckman selection model -- two-step estimates        Number of obs    =      753
(regression model with sample selection)             Censored obs     =      325
                                                     Uncensored obs   =      428

                                                     Wald chi2(2)     =    19.53
                                                     Prob > chi2      =   0.0001
```

	Coef.	Std. Err.	z	P>|z|	[95% Conf.	Interval]
lwage						
educ	.0584579	.0296354	1.97	0.049	.0003737	.1165422
exper	.0163202	.0042022	3.88	0.000	.0080842	.0245563
_cons	.8105418	.6107985	1.33	0.185	-.3866012	2.007685
lfp						
age	-.0206155	.0070447	-2.93	0.003	-.0344229	-.0068082
educ	.0837753	.023205	3.61	0.000	.0382943	.1292563
kids	-.3138848	.1237108	-2.54	0.011	-.5563535	-.0714162
mtr	-1.393853	.6165751	-2.26	0.024	-2.602318	-.1853878
_cons	1.192296	.7205439	1.65	0.098	-.2199443	2.604536
mills						
lambda	-.8664387	.3992843	-2.17	0.030	-1.649022	-.0838559
rho	-0.92910					
sigma	.93255927					
lambda	-.86643869	.3992843				

As you can see the adjusted t-statistics are slightly smaller, indicating that the adjusted standard errors are somewhat larger than the usual ones from the least squares regression.

In most instances it is preferable to estimate the full model, both the selection equation and the equation of interest, jointly by maximum likelihood. While the nature of this procedure is beyond the scope of this book, it is available in Stata. Then menu path is

Statistics > Sample-selection models > Heckman selection model (ML)

The maximum likelihood estimated wage equation is

```
heckman lwage educ exper, select(age educ kids mtr)
```

The results are:

```
. heckman lwage educ exper, select(lfp=age educ kids mtr)

Iteration 0:    log likelihood = -922.95945
Iteration 1:    log likelihood = -914.27456
Iteration 2:    log likelihood = -913.56337
Iteration 3:    log likelihood = -913.56101
Iteration 4:    log likelihood = -913.56101

Heckman selection model                   Number of obs    =        753
(regression model with sample selection)  Censored obs     =        325
                                          Uncensored obs   =        428

                                          Wald chi2(2)     =      22.50
Log likelihood =  -913.561                Prob > chi2      =     0.0000
```

	Coef.	Std. Err.	z	P>|z|	[95% Conf.	Interval]
lwage						
educ	.0658159	.0166346	3.96	0.000	.0332126	.0984192
exper	.0117675	.0040935	2.87	0.004	.0037444	.0197906
_cons	.6685864	.2350055	2.84	0.004	.2079841	1.129189
lfp						
age	-.0132621	.005939	-2.23	0.026	-.0249022	-.0016219
educ	.0639306	.0217446	2.94	0.003	.0213119	.1065492
kids	-.1525918	.0995874	-1.53	0.125	-.3477796	.042596
mtr	-2.291885	.5375647	-4.26	0.000	-3.345493	-1.238278
_cons	1.595958	.6237306	2.56	0.011	.3734682	2.818447
/athrho	-1.219374	.1181811	-10.32	0.000	-1.451005	-.9877435
/lnsigma	-.1631751	.0500129	-3.26	0.001	-.2611986	-.0651515
rho	-.8394695	.0348978			-.8958914	-.7563985
sigma	.8494425	.0424831			.770128	.9369255
lambda	-.713081	.0605756			-.831807	-.594355

```
LR test of indep. eqns. (rho = 0):   chi2(1) =      28.64    Prob > chi2 = 0.0000
```

Note that with this procedure we can apply likelihood ratio principles to test whether the errors in the equation of interest and selection equation are correlated. This is the LR test at the bottom of the results.

KEY TERMS

asclogit	latent variable	**normal**
baseoutcome	likelihood ratio test	**normalden**
binary choice models	**lincom**	**oprobit**
censored data	**logit**	ordered probit
censored regression	LR test	**poisson**
conditional logit	**lrtest**	Poisson regression
db	marginal effects	**predict**
delta method	**margins**	**probit**
estat alternatives	**matrix**	selection bias
estat classification	maximum likelihood estimation	selection equation
estat mfx	**mlogit**	**tabstat**
heckit	**modulo**	**tobit**
heckman	Monte Carlo experiment	tobit scale factor
histogram	multinomial logit	Wald test
inverse Mills ratio	**nlcom**	

CHAPTER 16 DO-FILE [CHAP16.DO]

```
* file chap16.do for Using Stata for Principles of Econometrics, 4e

cd c:\data\poe4stata

* Stata Do-file
* copyright C 2011 by Lee C. Adkins and R. Carter Hill
* used for "Using Stata for Principles of Econometrics, 4e"
* by Lee C. Adkins and R. Carter Hill (2011)
* John Wiley and Sons, Inc.

* setup
version 11.1
capture log close
set more off

********** Probit

* open new log
log using chap16_probit, replace text

* examine data
use transport, clear
describe
summarize

* probit estimation
probit auto dtime

* predicted probabililties
predict phat

* beta1 + beta2*2
lincom _b[_cons]+_b[dtime]*2

* standard normal density
```

```
nlcom (normalden(_b[_cons]+_b[dtime]*2))

* marginal effect when dtime=2
nlcom (normalden(_b[_cons]+_b[dtime]*2)*_b[dtime] )

* calulations at mean -.122381
lincom _b[_cons]+_b[dtime]*(-.122381)
nlcom (normalden(_b[_cons]+_b[dtime]*(-.122381)))
nlcom (normalden(_b[_cons]+_b[dtime]*(-.122381))*_b[dtime] )

* direct calculation of predicted probability at dtime=3
nlcom (normal(_b[_cons]+_b[dtime]*3) )

* marginal effect evaluated at each observation
gen ame = normalden(_b[_cons]+_b[dtime]*dtime)*_b[dtime]

* average marginal effect
tabstat ame, stat(n mean sd min max)

* marginal effects at means
margins, dydx(dtime) atmeans

* average marginal effects
margins, dydx(dtime)

* 0.975 percentile of t(19)-distribution
scalar t975 = invttail(19,.025)
di "0.975 critical value 19 df " t975

* 95% interval estimate of AME
scalar lbame =    .0484069   - t975*.003416
scalar ubame =    .0484069   + t975*.003416
di "95% interval estimate AME"
di "lbame = " lbame " ubame = " ubame

* ME at dtime = 2
margins, dydx(dtime) at(dtime=2)

* 95% interval estimate of AME at dtime = 2
scalar lb =  .1036899 - t975*.0326394
scalar ub =  .1036899 + t975*.0326394
di "95% interval estimate marginal effect dtime=2"
di "lb = " lb " ub= " ub

* ME at dtime=3
margins, dydx(dtime) at(dtime=3)

* predicted probability at dtime = 2
margins, predict(pr) at(dtime=2)

* predicted probability at dtime = 3
margins, predict(pr) at(dtime=3)

* 95% interval estimate of predicted probability at dtime = 3
scalar lbp =    .7982919 - t975*.1425387
scalar ubp =    .7982919 + t975*.1425387
di "95% interval estimate predicted probability dtime=3"
di "lb = " lbp " ub= " ubp

* Average predicted probability
margins, predict(pr)

* Average of predicted probability
```

```
summarize phat

*-------------------------------------------
* The Delta-method standard errors
*-------------------------------------------

********** Appendix 16A

* probit
probit auto dtime
ereturn list

matrix list e(V)

* ME at dtime=2
margins, dydx(dtime) at(dtime=2)

* dg-dbeta1
nlcom (-normalden(_b[_cons]+_b[dtime]*2)*(_b[_cons]+_b[dtime]*2)*_b[dtime])

* dg-dbeta2
nlcom (normalden(_b[_cons]+_b[dtime]*2)*(1-(_b[_cons]+_b[dtime]*2)*_b[dtime]*2))

* average marginal effects
margins, dydx(dtime)

* dg2-dbeta1
gen dg21 = -normalden(_b[_cons]+_b[dtime]*dtime)* ///
        (_b[_cons]+_b[dtime]*dtime)*_b[dtime]
gen dg22 = normalden(_b[_cons]+_b[dtime]*dtime)* ///
        (1-(_b[_cons]+_b[dtime]*dtime)*_b[dtime]*dtime)
summarize dg21 dg22

log close

********** A Marketing example

* open new log
log using chap16_coke, replace text
use coke, clear

* examine data
describe
summarize

* linear probability model
regress coke pratio disp_coke disp_pepsi, vce(robust)
estimates store lpm
predict phat

* predict probability when pratio = 1.1
margins, predict(xb) at(pratio=1.1 disp_coke=0 disp_pepsi=0)

* predict outcomes using linear probability model
generate p1 = (phat >=.5)
tabulate p1 coke,row

* probit
probit coke pratio disp_coke disp_pepsi
estimates store probit

* predicted outcomes summary
estat classification
```

```
* average marginal effect of change in price ratio
margins, dydx(pratio)

* average marginal effect when pratio=1.1 and displays are not present
margins, dydx(pratio) at(pratio=1.1 disp_coke=0 disp_pepsi=0)

* average predicted probability when pratio=1.1 and displays are not present
margins, predict(pr) at(pratio=1.1 disp_coke=0 disp_pepsi=0)

* t-test
lincom disp_coke + disp_pepsi

* chi-square tests
test disp_coke + disp_pepsi=0
test disp_coke disp_pepsi

* likelihood ratio test of model significance
scalar lnlu = e(ll)
scalar lnlr = e(ll_0)
scalar lr_test = 2*(lnlu-lnlr)
di "lnlu    = " lnlu
di " lnlr   = " lnlr
di " lr_test = " lr_test

* likelihood ratio test of displays equal but opposite effect
gen disp = disp_pepsi-disp_coke
probit coke pratio disp
estimates store probitr

* automatic test
lrtest probit probitr

* direct calculation
scalar lnlr = e(ll)
scalar lr_test = 2*(lnlu-lnlr)
di "lnlu    = " lnlu
di " lnlr   = " lnlr
di " lr_test = " lr_test

* likelihood ratio of significance of displays
probit coke pratio
estimates store probitr

* automatic test
lrtest probit probitr

* direct calculation
scalar lnlr = e(ll)
scalar lr_test = 2*(lnlu-lnlr)
di "lnlu    = " lnlu
di " lnlr   = " lnlr
di " lr_test = " lr_test

* logit
logit coke pratio disp_coke disp_pepsi
estimates store logit

* predicted outcomes summary
estat classification

* average marginal effects for logit
margins, dydx(pratio)
```

```
margins, dydx(pratio) at(pratio=1.1 disp_coke=0 disp_pepsi=0)
margins, predict(pr) at(pratio=1.1 disp_coke=0 disp_pepsi=0)

* tables comparing models
esttab lpm probit logit , se(%12.4f) b(%12.5f) star(* 0.10 ** 0.05 *** 0.01) ///
      scalars(ll_0 ll chi2)gaps mtitles("LPM" "probit" "logit") ///
        title("Coke-Pepsi Choice Models")

* out of sample forecasting
regress coke pratio disp_coke disp_pepsi in 1/1000
predict phat2
generate p2 = (phat2 >=.5)
tabulate p2 coke in 1001/1140,row

probit coke pratio disp_coke disp_pepsi in 1/1000
estat classification in 1001/1140

logit coke pratio disp_coke disp_pepsi in 1/1000
estat classification in 1001/1140

log close

********** Chapter 16.3 Multinomial logit

log using chap16_mlogit, replace text

use nels_small, clear

* summarize data
describe
summarize grades, detail
tab psechoice

* estimate model
mlogit psechoice grades, baseoutcome(1)

* compute predictions and summarize
predict ProbNo ProbCC ProbColl
summarize ProbNo ProbCC ProbColl

* predicted probabilities
margins, predict(outcome(1)) at(grades=6.64)
margins, predict(outcome(2)) at(grades=6.64)
margins, predict(outcome(3)) at(grades=6.64)
margins, predict(outcome(1)) at(grades=2.635)
margins, predict(outcome(2)) at(grades=2.635)
margins, predict(outcome(3)) at(grades=2.635)

* marginal effects
margins, dydx(grades) at(grades=6.64)
margins, dydx(grades)
margins, dydx(grades) at(grades=2.635)
margins, dydx(grades) predict(outcome(2)) at(grades=6.64)
margins, dydx(grades) predict(outcome(2)) at(grades=2.635)
margins, dydx(grades) predict(outcome(3)) at(grades=6.64)
margins, dydx(grades) predict(outcome(3)) at(grades=2.635)

log close

********* Conditional logit

log using chap16_clogit, replace text
use cola, clear
```

```
* examine data
describe
summarize
list in 1/9

* create alternatives variable
sort id, stable
by id:gen alt = _n

* view some observations
list in 1/3

* summarize by alternative
bysort alt:summarize choice price feature display

* label values
label define brandlabel 1 "Pepsi"  2  "SevenUp" 3 "Coke"
label values alt brandlabel

* estimate model
asclogit choice price, case(id) alternatives(alt) basealternative(Coke)

* post-estimation
estat alternatives
estat mfx
estat mfx, at(Coke:price=1.10 Pepsi:price=1 SevenUp:price=1.25)

log close

********** Ordered probit

log using chap16_oprobit, replace text
use nels_small, clear

* summarize data
summarize grades, detail
tab psechoice

* estimate model
oprobit psechoice grades

* marginal effects
margins, dydx(grades) at(grades=6.64)  predict(outcome(3))
margins, dydx(grades) at(grades=2.635) predict(outcome(3))
log close

********** Poisson Regression
log using chap16_poisson, replace
use olympics, clear

* keep 1988 results
keep if year==88
keep medaltot pop gdp
describe

* log variables
gen lpop = ln(pop)
gen lgdp = ln(gdp)

* estimate poisson model
poisson medaltot lpop lgdp
```

```
* marginal effects at median of log variable
margins, dydx(*) at((median) lpop lgdp)

* predicted number of medals at medians
margins, predict(n) at((median) lpop lgdp)

log close

********** Tobit
log using chap16_tobit, replace text

* using simulated data

use tobit, clear

* examine data
describe
summarize
summarize if y>0

* regression
reg y x
reg y x if y>0

* tobit
tobit y x, ll

* tobit using Mroz data

use mroz, clear

* examine data
describe lfp hours  educ exper age kids16
summarize lfp hours  educ exper age kids16
histogram hours, frequency title(Hours worked by married women)

summarize hours  educ exper age kids16 if (hours>0)
summarize hours  educ exper age kids16 if (hours==0)

* regression
regress hours  educ exper age kids16
regress hours  educ exper age kids16 if (hours>0)

* tobit
tobit hours  educ exper age kids16, ll

* tobit scale factor
scalar xb = _b[_cons]+_b[educ]*12.29+_b[exper]*10.63+_b[age]*42.5+_b[kids16]*1
scalar cdf = normal( xb/_b[/sigma])
display "x*beta = " xb
display "Tobit scale Factor: cdf evaluated at zi = " cdf
display "Marginal effect of education = " _b[educ]*cdf

quietly tobit hours  educ exper age kids16, ll

* marginal effect on E(y|x)
margins, dydx(educ) at(educ=12.29 exper=10.63 age=42.5 kids16=1) predict(ystar(0,.))

* marginal effect on E(y|x,y>0)
margins, dydx(educ) at(educ=12.29 exper=10.63 age=42.5 kids16=1) predict(e(0,.))


********** Heckit
```

```
use mroz, clear

generate lwage = ln(wage)

* ols
regress lwage educ exper if (hours>0)

* probit
generate kids = (kidsl6+kids618>0)
probit lfp age educ kids mtr
predict w, xb

* Inverse Mills Ratio
generate imr = normalden(w)/normal(w)

* Heckit two-step
regress lwage educ exper imr

* Heckit two-step automatic
heckman lwage educ exper, select(lfp=age educ kids mtr) twostep

* Heckit maximum likelihood
heckman lwage educ exper, select(lfp=age educ kids mtr)

log close
```

APPENDIX A

Mathematical Tools

CHAPTER OUTLINE

A.1 STATA MATH AND LOGICAL OPERATORS

The basic arithmetic, logical and relational operators are

```
                                               Relational
        Arithmetic            Logical      (numeric and string)
--------------------     ------------------  --------------------
   +   addition            &   and                >   greater than
   -   subtraction         |   or                 <   less than
   *   multiplication      !   not                >=  > or equal
   /   division            ~   not                <=  < or equal
   ^   power                                      ==  equal
   -   negation                                   != not equal

A double equal sign (==) is used for equality testing.

    The order of evaluation (from first to last) of all operators is !, ^,
 - (negation), /, *, - (subtraction), +, != (or \=), >, <, <=, >=, ==, &,
 and |.
```

Enter **help operators** in the **Command** window.

A.2 MATH FUNCTIONS

Stata offers many math functions. Enter **help math functions**. Some common ones, as listed in Stata help, are:

abs(x)
   Description: returns the absolute value of x.

ceil(x)
   Description: returns the unique integer n such that n - 1 < x < n.
                 Also see floor(x), int(x), and round(x).

exp(x)
   Description: returns the exponential function of e^x. This function
                 is the inverse of ln(x).

floor(x)
   Description: returns the unique integer n such that n <= x < n + 1.
                 Also see ceil(x), int(x), and round(x).

int(x)
   Description: returns the integer obtained by truncating x toward 0;

ln(x)
   Domain: 1e-323 to 8e+307
   Range: -744 to 709
   Description: returns the natural logarithm of x. This function is
                 the inverse of exp(x).

log(x)
   Description: returns the natural logarithm of x, which is a
                 synonym for ln(x).

max(x1,x2,...,xn)
   Description: returns the maximum value of non-missing x1, x2, ..., xn.

min(x1,x2,...,xn)
   Description: returns the minimum value of non-missing x1, x2, ..., xn.

mod(x,y)
   Description: returns the modulus of x with respect to y.
                 mod(x,y) = x - y*int(x/y)

round(x,y) or round(x)
   Description: returns x rounded in units of y or x rounded to the
                 nearest integer if the argument y is omitted.

```
sqrt(x)
   Description:  returns the square root of x.

sum(x)
   Description:  returns the running sum of x treating missing values as
                 zero.


trunc(x) is a synonym for int(x).
```

A.3 EXTENSIONS TO GENERATE

There are some extensions to generate called **egen** functions. Enter **help egen**. The functions work only with **egen**. The syntax is

egen [type] newvar = fcn(arguments) [if] [in] [, options]

```
Some useful ones are:

    count(exp)                                    (allows by varlist:)
        creates a constant (within varlist) containing the number of
        nonmissing observations of exp.  Also see rownonmiss() and
        rowmiss().

    kurt(varname)                                 (allows by varlist:)
        returns the kurtosis (within varlist) varname.

    max(exp)                                      (allows by varlist:)
        creates a constant (within varlist) containing the maximum value
        of exp.

    mean(exp)                                     (allows by varlist:)
        creates a constant (within varlist) containing the mean of exp.

    median(exp)                                   (allows by varlist:)
        creates a constant (within varlist) containing the median of exp.
        Also see pctile().

    min(exp)                                      (allows by varlist:)
        creates a constant (within varlist) containing the minimum value
        of exp.

    pctile(exp) [, p(#)]                          (allows by varlist:)
        creates a constant (within varlist) containing the #th percentile
        of exp.  If p(#) is not specified, 50 is assumed, meaning medians.
        Also see median().
```

```
sd(exp)                                              (allows by varlist:)
    creates a constant (within varlist) containing the standard
    deviation of exp.  Also see mean().

skew(varname)                                        (allows by varlist:)
    returns the skewness (within varlist) of varname.

std(exp) [, mean(#) std(#)]
    may not be combined with by.  It creates the standardized values
    of exp.  The options specify the desired mean and standard
    deviation. The default is mean(0) and std(1), producing a variable
    with mean 0, standard deviation 1.

total(exp)                                           (allows by varlist:)
    creates a constant (within varlist) containing the sum of exp.
    Also see mean().
```

A.4 THE CALCULATOR

Stata includes a handy calculator that we use many times in this manual. It is called display. Enter **help display**. For example, as a hand calculator:

```
display 2 + 2
```

and you can include dialog within quotes,

```
display "two plus two = " 2 + 2
```

Will display in the Results window

```
two plus two = 4
```

A.5 SCIENTIFIC NOTATION

Stata automatically uses scientific notation for very large numbers. For example

```
di 1000000*100000000
```

```
1.000e+14
```

The outcome 1.000e+14 is 1.000 times 1014.

A.6 NUMERICAL DERIVATIVES AND INTEGRALS

In *Principles of Econometrics, 4th Edition*, Appendix A.3, some rules for derivatives are given. Stata has a function that will carry out derivatives numerically. See Exercise A.8 in POE4 for an illustration of how it is done. The derivative of a function at a point is the slope of the tangent at that point. If $f(x)$ is a function, and $\varepsilon > 0$ is a small numerical value, then derivative at x_i is approximately

$$\frac{dy}{dx} \approx \frac{f(x_i + \varepsilon) - f(x_i - \varepsilon)}{2\varepsilon}$$

How to choose ε is a problem, and there are many variations, all of which are outside the scope of this book. You might check http://en.wikipedia.org/wiki/Numerical_differentiation for an introduction and suggested references.

The Stata command for numerical derivatives is **dydx**. See **help dydx** for the basic syntax.

```
dydx yvar xvar [if] [in] , generate(newvar) [dydx_options]
```

To illustrate we use the function $y = x^2 - 8x + 16$ from page 643 of *POE4*. Clear memory and use **range** to generate a sequence of **x** values, $x = 0, 1, ..., 8$. The syntax of **range** is

```
range varname #first #last [#obs]
```

```
clear
range x 0 8 9             //                    create x
```

Generate the values of *y* and label with the function description, then plot the **twoway** graph.

```
gen y = x^2 - 8*x + 16          //generate function
label variable y "x^2-8*x+16"   //label
twoway connected y x            //graph
```

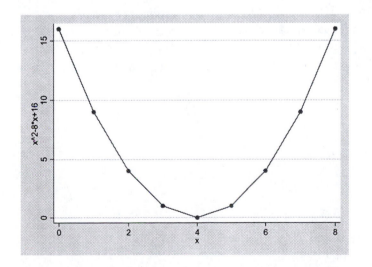

The derivative of this function is created using **dydx**, generating a new variable called **dy** with the derivative values at each point.

```
dydx y x, gen(dy)                  /              /derivative
```

An elasticity at a point (x, y) is the function slope at that point times x/y. Use the **round** function to round the function to two decimal places.

```
gen elas=round(dy*x/y,.01)          /        /elasticity
```

The true derivative of the function is $dy/dx = 2x - 8$. Create this variable and list the values created so far.

```
gen dytrue = 2*x - 8                        //true derivative
list
```

	x	y	dy	elas	dytrue
1.	0	16	-8	0	-8
2.	1	9	-6	-.67	-6
3.	2	4	-4	-2	-4
4.	3	1	-2	-6	-2
5.	4	0	0	.	0
6.	5	1	2	10	2
7.	6	4	4	6	4
8.	7	9	6	4.67	6
9.	8	16	8	4	8

For a function of several variables a partial derivative is the derivative holding all else constant. For example, consider the function $y_2 = 3x^2 + 2x + 3z + 14$. To calculate the partial derivative we fix z at a specific value, say $z = 2$, and then compute the derivative of the resulting function of a single variable.

```
scalar z0 = 2             //            specific value
gen y2 = 3*x^2+2*x+3*z0+14            //new function at z0
dydx y2 x, gen(dy2)                   //partial derivative
gen dy2true = 6*x + 2                 //true partial at z0
list x dy2 dy2true
```

	x	dy2	dy2true
1.	0	2	2
2.	1	8	8
3.	2	14	14
4.	3	20	20
5.	4	26	26
6.	5	32	32
7.	6	38	38
8.	7	44	44
9.	8	50	50

Numerical intergrals are a computing challenge, because we must find the area under a curve between certain limits. An introduction to the concepts can be found at http://en.wikipedia.org/wiki/Numerical_integration. The Stata function for numerical integration is **integ**. Using help integ we find the syntax

```
integ yvar xvar [if] [in] [, integ_options]
```

To illustrate we use the simple function $y = 2x$ discussed in *POE4*, Appendix A.4.1. Clear memory and create 101 x and y values between 0 and 1.

```
clear
range x 0 1 101            //create x
gen y = 2*x               //generate y=f(x)
```

Create a new variable containing integral values from $x = 0$ up to each point, and list some.

```
integ y x, gen(iy)        //integral
list in 41/51        /    /list integral values
```

	x	y	iy
41.	.4	.8	.16
42.	.41	.82	.1681
43.	.42	.84	.1764
44.	.43	.86	.1849
45.	.44	.88	.1936
46.	.45	.9	.2025
47.	.46	.92	.2116
48.	.47	.94	.2209
49.	.48	.96	.2304
50.	.49	.98	.2401
51.	.5	1	.25

KEY TERMS

arithmetic operators	**generate**	**range**
derivative	**integ**	relational operators
display	integral	scientific notation
dydx	logical operators	**twoway**
egen	math functions	

APPENDIX A DO-FILE [APPX A.DO]

```
* file appx_a.do for Using Stata for Principles of Econometrics, 4e

cd c:\data\poe4stata

* Stata do-file
* copyright C 2011 by Lee C. Adkins and R. Carter Hill
* used for "Using Stata for Principles of Econometrics, 4e"
* by Lee C. Adkins and R. Carter Hill (2011)
* John Wiley and Sons, Inc.

* setup
version 11.1
capture log close
set more off

* open log file
log using appx_a, replace text
clear

********** numerical derivatives

range x 0 8 9              //cr            eate x
gen y = x^2 - 8*x + 16         //ge        nerate function
label variable y "x^2-8*x+16"          //label
twoway connected y x       //gr        aph
dydx y x, gen(dy)          //de        rivative
gen elas=round(dy*x/y,.01)      //el      asticity
gen dytrue = 2*x - 8           //true derivative
list

* partial derivative

scalar z0 = 2              //sp         ecific value
gen y2 = 3*x^2+2*x+3*z0+14      //new function at z0
dydx y2 x, gen(dy2)            //partial derivative
gen dy2true = 6*x + 2          //true partial at z0
list x dy2 dy2true

********** numerical integrals
clear
range x 0 1 101            //cr            eate x
gen y = 2*x            //ge        nerate y=f(x)
integ y x, gen(iy)            //in        tegral
list in 41/51         //li        st integral values
log close
```

APPENDIX B

Probability Concepts

B.1 STATA PROBABILILTY FUNCTIONS

Stata includes many built in functions for probability density functions (*pdf*s) and cumulative distribution functions (*cdf*s). Type **help functions** and then select density functions

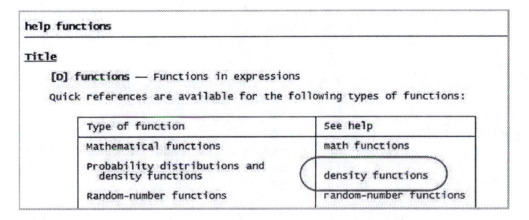

Among those we will use are:

```
binomial(n,k,p)
   Description:  returns the probability of observing (k) or fewer
                 successes in (n) trials when the probability of a
                 success on one trial is p.

chi2(n,x)
   Description:  returns the cumulative chi-squared distribution with n
                 degrees of freedom.

chi2tail(n,x)
   Description:  returns the reverse cumulative (upper-tail)
                 chi-squared distribution with n degrees of freedom.
                 chi2tail(n,x) = 1 - chi2(n,x)

F(n1,n2,f)
   Description:  returns the cumulative F distribution with n1 numerator
                 and n2 denominator degrees of freedom.

Fden(n1,n2,f)
   Description:  returns the probability density function for the F
                 distribution with n1 numerator and n2 denominator
                 degrees of freedom.

Ftail(n1,n2,f)
   Description:  returns the reverse cumulative (upper-tail) F
                 distribution with n1 numerator and n2 denominator
                 degrees of freedom.  Ftail(n1,n2,f) = 1 - F(n1,n2,f)

invchi2(n,p)
   Description:  returns the inverse of chi2():  if chi2(n,x) = p, then
                 invchi2(n,p) = x.

invchi2tail(n,p)
   Description:  returns the inverse of chi2tail(): if chi2tail(n,x) = p,
                 then invchi2tail(n,p) = x.

invF(n1,n2,p)
   Description:  returns the inverse cumulative F distribution: if
                 F(n1,n2,f) = p, then invF(n1,n2,p) = f.

invFtail(n1,n2,p)
   Description:  returns the inverse reverse cumulative (upper-tail,)
                 F distribution: if Ftail(n1,n2,f) = p, then
                 invFtail(n1,n2,p) = f.
```

```
invnormal(p)
    Description:  returns the inverse cumulative standard normal
                    distribution: if normal(z) = p, then
                    invnormal(p) = z.

invttail(n,p)
    Description:  returns the inverse reverse cumulative (upper-tail),
                    Student's t distribution: if ttail(n,t) = p,
                    then invttail(n,p) = t.

normal(z)
    Description:  returns the cumulative standard normal distribution.

normalden(z)
    Description:  returns the standard normal density.

normalden(x,m,s)
    Description:  returns the normal density with mean m and standard
                    deviation s.
                    normalden(x,0,1) = normalden(x)
                    normalden(x,m,s) = normalden((x-m)/s)/s

tden(n,t)
    Description:  returns the probability density function of Student's t
                    distribution.

ttail(n,t)
    Description:  returns the reverse cumulative (upper-tail, survival)
                    Student's t distribution; it returns the
                    probability T > t.
```

B.2 BINOMIAL DISTRIBUTION

A binomial random variable X is the number of successes in n independent trials of identical experiments with probability of success p. Given the number of trials n and the probability of success p, binomial probabilities are given by

$$P(X = x) = f(x) = \binom{n}{x} p^x (1 - p)^{n-x}$$

where

$$\binom{n}{x} = \frac{n!}{x!(n-x)!}$$

is the "number of combinations of n items taken x at a time," and $n!$ is "n factorial," which is given by $n! = n((n-1)(n-2)\cdots(2)(1)$. Suppose that the $n = 13$ games the LSU Tigers play are all independent and in each game they have the probability $p = 0.7$ of winning. What is the probability of them winning at least 8 games during the season? The answer is

$$P(X \geq 8) = \sum_{x=8}^{13} f(x) = 1 - P(X \leq 7) = 1 - F(7)$$

Using the Stata function **binomial** we can compute the probability of 7 or fewer wins to be 0.165 using.

```
scalar prob1 = binomial(13,7,.7)
di "probability <= binomial(13,7,0.7) is " prob1

probability <= binomial(13,7,0.7) is .16539748
```

The probability of more than 7 wins is then 0.8346 using

```
scalar prob2 = 1 - binomial(13,7,.7)
di "probability > binomial(13,7,0.7) is " prob2

probability > binomial(13,7,0.7) is .83460252
```

B.3 NORMAL DISTRIBUTION

B.3.1 Normal density plots

First, let us plot the normal density function using a **twoway function** which plots $y = f(x)$. It makes no difference if x and y are existing variables. The Stata function **normalden** returns the value of the standard normal density $\phi(x)$ for a given x. To plot the density over $[-5, 5]$ use

```
twoway function y = normalden(x), range(-5 5)      /      //
       title("Standard normal density")                  ///
       saving(normal_pdf.emf, replace)
```

The saving option will save the graph to disk as an "enhanced metafile." If the extension ***.emf** is omitted then the graph is saved as a Stata graph (***.gph**). The ***.emf** format is useful when graphs are inserted into Microsoft Word documents as pictures, which is how we are doing it. The plot appears on the following page. We have saved the graph so that we can access it later. It will appear in your default directory, which for the authors is **c:\data\poe4stata**. We will not include this option in future graphs in this Appendix, but it is often a good idea.

The plot of any normal density can be obtained by modifying the command only slightly. Enter **help normalden** to find a **normalden(x,s)** for a normal density with mean 0 and standard deviation **s**, and **normalden(x,m,s)** for a normal density with mean **m** and standard deviation **s**. In this graph we illustrate the use of different line patterns (**lpattern**). The options are:

```
blank              dot              longdash_shortdash  tight_dot
dash               longdash         shortdash           vshortdash
dash_3dot          longdash_3dot    shortdash_dot
dash_dot           longdash_dot     shortdash_dot_dot
dash_dot_dot       longdash_dot_dot solid
```

To recall these at any time enter into the command line **graph query linepatternstyle**. The line width is controlled with **lwidth**. The options are listed with **graph query linewidthstyle**:

```
medium     medthin    thick    vthick    vvthick    vvvthick
medthick   none       thin     vthin     vvthin     vvvthin
```

We will have a different **legend** for the 3 curves. For help with legends enter **help legend_option**. We have used the graph separator notion **||** rather than **()** because it clearly demarks the end of one function and the beginning of another

```
twoway function y = normalden(x), range(-5 5)                       ///
       || function y = normalden(x,0.8),                            ///
          r           ange(-5 5) lpattern(dash)             /     //
       || function y = normalden(x,1,0.8),                          ///
          r           ange(-5 5) lpattern(dash_dot)         /     //
       ||, title("Normal Densities")                        /     //
             legend(label(1 "N(0,1)") label(2 "N(0,0.8^2)")        ///
       l        abel(3 "N(1,0.8^2)"))
```

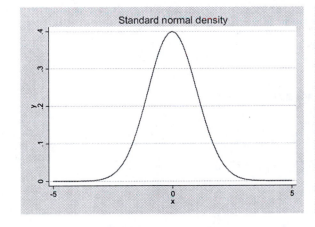

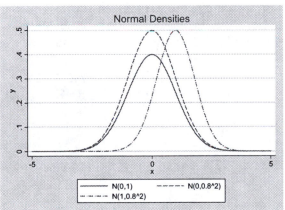

B.3.2 Normal probability calculation

Now calculate some normal probabilities. The *cdf* for the standardized normal variable Z is so widely used that it is given its own special symbol, $\Phi(z) = P(Z \leq z)$. It is used in probability calculations as

$$P[a \leq X \leq b] = P\left[\frac{a-\mu}{\sigma} \leq Z \leq \frac{b-\mu}{\sigma}\right] = \Phi\left(\frac{b-\mu}{\sigma}\right) - \Phi\left(\frac{a-\mu}{\sigma}\right)$$

The Stata function **normal** computes the function $\Phi(z) = P(Z \le z)$. To compute the left tail probability $P[Z \le 1.33] = \Phi(1.33)$ use

```
scalar n_tail = normal(1.33)
di "lower tail probability N(0,1) < 1.33 is " n_tail
```

The result is

```
lower tail probability N(0,1) < 1.33 is .90824086
```

For example, if $X \sim N(3,9)$, then

$$P[4 \le X \le 6] = P[0.33 \le Z \le 1] = \Phi(1) - \Phi(0.33) = 0.8413 - 0.6293 = 0.2120$$

The commands are

```
scalar prob = normal((6-3)/3) - normal((4-3)/3)
di "probability 3<=N(3,9)<=6 is " prob
```

The result is

```
probability 3<=N(3,9)<=6 is .21078609
```

To compute percentiles of the standard normal distribution which are used as critical values for tests or in the calculation of interval estimates, use **invnormal**. For example, for the 95th percentile of the standard normal distribution use

```
scalar n_95 = invnormal(.95)
di "95th percentile of standard normal = " n_95
```

Producing

```
95th percentile of standard normal = 1.6448536
```

B.4 STUDENT'S *t*-DISTRIBUTION

B.4.1 Plot of standard normal and *t*(3)

The *t*-density function can be similarly plotted. The *t*-distribution shape is determined by a single parameter called the degrees of freedom. To plot the *t*-density for 3 degrees of freedom use the **tden** function to generate the density values, and plot them as above. In fact we can overlay this plot against the standard normal to illustrate the differences

```
twoway function y = normalden(x), range(-5 5)                    ///
        || function y = tden(3,x), range(-5 5) lpattern(dash)    ///
        ||, title("standard normal and t(3)")                    ///
              legend(label(1 "N(0,1)") label(2 "t(3)"))
```

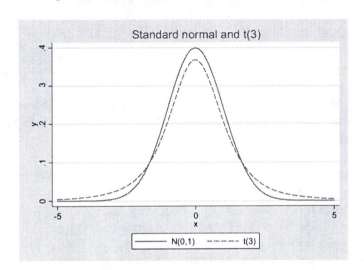

B.4.2 *t*-distribution probabilities

Calculating *t*-distribution probabilities is accomplished using the Stata function **ttail**. This function returns the probability in the **upper tail** of the *t* distribution. For example, to compute the probabilities that a *t*(3) random variable will be greater than 1.33, and then less than 1.33, use

```
scalar t_tail = ttail(3,1.33)
di "upper tail probability t(3) > 1.33 = " t_tail
di "lower tail probability t(3) < 1.33 = " 1 - ttail(3,1.33)
```

These commands produce

```
upper tail probability t(3) > 1.33 = .13779644
lower tail probability t(3) < 1.33 = .86220356
```

Percentiles for the *t*-distribution use the Stata function **invttail**. To compute the 95th, and 5th, percentiles for the *t*(3) distribution use

```
scalar t3_95 = invttail(3,.05)
di "95th percentile of t(3) = " t3_95
di "5th percentile of t(3) = " invttail(3,.95)
```

Producing the results

```
upper tail probability t(3) > 1.33 = .13779644
lower tail probability t(3) < 1.33 = .86220356
```

B.4.3 Graphing tail probabilities

For students, illustrating tail probabilities is a useful skill. Find the 95th percentile of the $t(38)$ distribution.

```
di "95th percentile of t(38) = " invttail(38,.05)
```

The 95th percentile then is

```
95th percentile of t(38) = 1.6859545
```

For the plot we first generate a graph of the tail area, to the right of 1.686, and **recast** the graph to an **area** plot. Second we add the t-density function, a title and locate some text along the horizontal axis. The place(s) option places the text to the "south".

```
twoway function y=tden(38,x), range(1.686 5)              ///
     c      olor(ltblue) recast(area)           /      //
    || function y=tden(38,x), range(-5 5)                ///
     l      egend(off) plotregion(margin(zero))          ///
    ||, ytitle("f(t)") xtitle("t")              /        //
    te      xt(0 1.686 "1.686", place(s))       //       /
    t       itle("Right-tail rejection region")
```

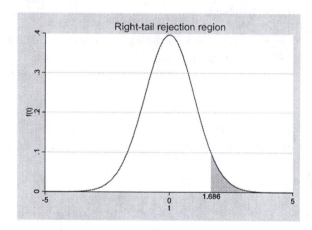

For a two-tail p-value, with the probability that a value from the $t(38)$ distribution will be greater than 1.9216 or less than -1.9216 use

```
twoway function y=tden(38,x), range(1.9216 5)            ///
         color(ltblue) recast(area)             /        //
    || function y=tden(38,x), range(-5 -1.9216)          ///
         color(ltblue) recast(area)             /        //
    || function y=tden(38,x), range(-5 5)                ///
    ||, legend(off) plotregion(margin(zero))             ///
         ytitle("f(t)") xtitle("t")             /        //
         text(0 -1.921578 "-1.9216", place(s))           ///
         text(0 1.9216 "1.9216", place(s))      /        //
         title("Pr|t(38)|>1.9216")
```

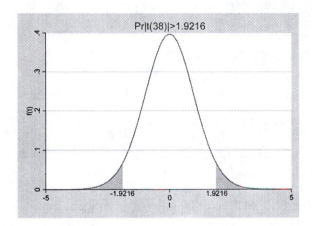

B.5 *F*-DISTRIBUTION

B.5.1 Plotting the *F*-density

The *F*-distribution is said to have *m1* numerator degrees of freedom and *m2* denominator degrees of freedom. The values of *m1* and *m2* determine the shape of the distribution. This random values is takes only positive values, so to plot it create a new variable that goes from near 0 to near 6. As an example we plot the $F(8, 20)$ density using the **twoway function** with Fden()

```
twoway function y = Fden(8,20,x), range(0 6)              ///
        l      egend(off) plotregion(margin(zero))        ///
        y      title("F-density") xtitle("x")        /      //
        ti     tle("F(8,20) density")
```

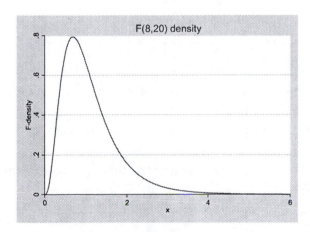

B.5.2 *F*-distribution probability calculation

Probability calculations use the functions Ftail(), which returns upper-tail probabilities, and F(), which the cumulative distribution function. For example, to compute the probability that a random value from the $F(8,20)$ distribution will be greater than 3.0, which is 0.02203345, using either approach

```
scalar f_tail = Ftail(8,20,3.0)
di "upper tail probability F(8,20) > 3.0 = " f_tail
di "upper tail probability F(8,20) > 3.0 = " 1-F(8,20,3.0)
```

```
. di "upper tail probability F(8,20) > 3.0 = " f_tail
upper tail probability F(8,20) > 3.0 = .02203345

. di "upper tail probability F(8,20) > 3.0 = " 1-F(8,20,3.0)
upper tail probability F(8,20) > 3.0 = .02203345
```

The 95th percentile of the $F(8,20)$ density function is calculated using **invFtail()**. This function works with the **upper** tail, so the 95th percentile leaves 5 percent of the probability in the upper tail.

```
scalar f_95 = invFtail(8,20,.05)
di "95th percentile of F(8,20) = " f_95
```

```
95th percentile of F(8,20) = 2.4470637
```

B.6 CHI-SQUARE DISTRIBUTION

B.6.1 Plotting the chi-square density

The chi-square density function is not included as a simple function in Stata. We will take this opportunity to use some of the function is Stata to program this density from a formula. The chi-square density function is

$$f(x) = \frac{1}{2^{m/2}\Gamma(m/2)} x^{0.5m-1} e^{-0.5x} \quad \text{for } x > 0$$

This formula can be found in statistics books, or web. One reference is http://en.wikipedia.org/wiki/Chi-square_distribution. In this expression m is the degrees of freedom parameter that controls the shape of the density function. The term $\Gamma(\cdot)$ represents the gamma function from mathematics. You may have not encountered it before, but it is generalization of the factorial (!) function. Stata has a function **lngamma** that computes the natural logarithm of this function.

```
lngamma(x)
    Description:  returns the natural log of the gamma function of x. For
    integer values of x > 0, this is ln((x-1)!).
```

Clear memory, and set the number of observations to 101. Generate some x values, from near 0 to about 20. Specify a scalar **df** to be 7, for the degrees of freedom.

```
clear
set obs 101
gen xc = _n/5
scalar df = 7
```

Generate a new variable that is the value of the chi-square density function

```
gen chi2_pdf =(1/(2^(df/2)))*(1/exp(lngamma(df/2)))* ///
     xc      ^(df/2 - 1)*exp(-xc/2)
```

Plot the density function using no markers, tick marks from 0 to 21 in increments of 2.

```
twoway (connected chi2_pdf x, msymbol(none)), ///
       xlabel(0(2)21) title(Chi-square density with 7 df)
```

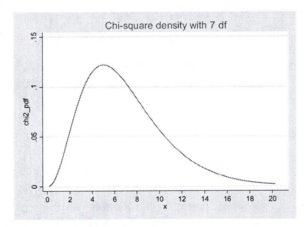

B.6.2 Chi-square probability calculations

Cumulative probabilities use the chi-square cdf function `chi2()`. Compute the probability that a chi-square with 7 degrees of freedom takes a value greater than 15

```
scalar chi2_tail = 1 - chi2(df,15)
di "upper tail probability chi2(7) > 15 is " chi2_tail
```

Yielding

```
upper tail probability chi2(7) > 15 is .0359994
```

Chi-square percentiles can be obtained using `invchi2()` or the upper tail version `invchi2tail()`. To compute the 95th percentile for the chi-square distribution with 7 degrees of freedom use

```
scalar chi2_95 = invchi2tail(df,.05)
di "95th percentile of chi2(7) = " chi2_95
```

Producing

```
95th percentile of chi2(7) = 14.06714
```

B.7 RANDOM NUMBERS

The generation of random numbers is serious business and best left to professionals. The normal users, such as your authors, do not generate random values from first principles when required. Always use the random number generators in Stata. These are

```
runiform()
   Description:  returns uniform random variates.

rbeta(a, b)
   Description:  returns beta(a,b) random variates

rbinomial(n, p)
   Description:  returns binomial(n,p) random variates, where n is the
                 number of trials and p is the success probability.

rchi2(df)
   Description:  returns chi-squared, with df degrees of freedom, random
                 variates.

rgamma(a, b)
   Description:  returns gamma(a,b) random variates, where a is the
                 gamma shape parameter and b is the scale parameter.

rhypergeometric(N, K, n)
   Description:  returns hypergeometric random variates.

rnbinomial(n, p)
   Description:  returns negative binomial random variates.

rnormal()
   Description:  returns standard normal (Gaussian) random variates

rnormal(m)
   Description:  returns normal(m,1) (Gaussian) random variates

rnormal(m, s)
   Description:  returns normal(m,s) (Gaussian) random variates

rpoisson(m)
   Description:  returns Poisson(m) random variates, where m is the
                 distribution mean.
```

```
rt(df)
    Description:   returns Student's t random variates, where df is the
                   degrees of freedom.
```

Nevertheless we believe that should you use random numbers it is important to have a general idea of how they are created. We consider the simplest case of using the "inversion method."

B.7.1 Using inversion method

Suppose you wish to obtain a random number from a specific probability distribution, with *pdf* $f(y)$ and *cdf* $F(y)$.

The Inversion Method: Step by Step

1. Obtain a uniform random number u_1 in the $(0,1)$ interval.

2. Let $u_1 = F(y_1)$

3. Solve the equation in step 2 for y_1.

4. The value y_1 is a random number from the *pdf* $f(y)$.

The inversion method can be used to draw random numbers from any distribution that permits you to carry out step 3. The solution is often denoted $y_1 = F^{-1}(u_1)$, where F^{-1} is called the **inverse cumulative distribution function**.

Suppose the target distribution, from which we want a random number, is $f(y) = 2y, 0 < y < 1$. The *cdf* of Y is $P(Y \le y) = F(y) = y^2, 0 < y < 1$. Set a uniform random number $u_1 = F(y_1) = y_1^2$ and solve to obtain $y_1 = F^{-1}(u_1) = (u_1)^{1/2}$. The value y_1 is a random value, or a **random draw**, from the probability distribution $f(y) = 2y, 0 < y < 1$.

To illustrate in Stata let us create 1000 values **y1** from the triangular density. We use the uniform random number generator **runiform()** with a specific seed value to create the uniform random variable **u1**.

```
clear
set obs 1000
set seed 12345
gen u1 = runiform()
label variable u1 "uniform random values"

histogram u1, bin(10) percent
gen y1 = sqrt(u1)
histogram y1, bin(10) percent
```

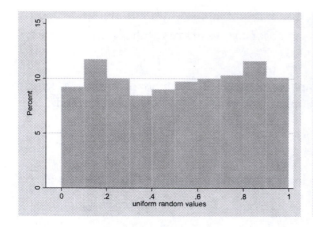

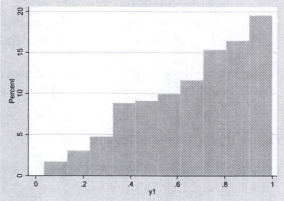

As a second example let us consider a slightly more exotic distribution. The **extreme value distribution** is the foundation of logit choice models that are discussed in *Principles of Econometrics, 4th Edition*, Chapter 16. It has probability density function

$$f(v) = \exp(-v) \cdot \exp(-\exp(-v))$$

The extreme value *cdf* is $F(v) = \exp(-\exp(-v))$. Despite its complicated looking form, we can obtain values from this distribution using $v = F^{-1}(u) = -\ln(-\ln(u))$. To plot this density and create 10,000 random numbers and a histogram using

```
clear
set obs 10000
set seed 12345
gen u1 = runiform()
gen v1=-3+(_n-1)*13/10000
gen fev1 = exp(-v1)*exp(-exp(-v1))
twoway line fev1 v1, ytitle("Extreme value density")
gen ev1 = -log(-log(u1))
histogram ev1, bin(40) percent kdensity kdenopts(gaussian)
```

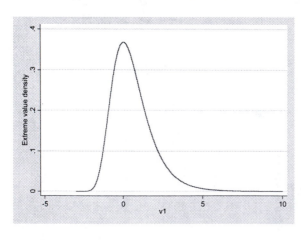

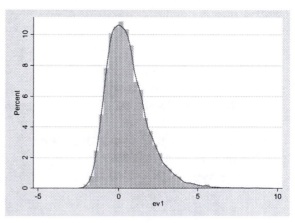

B.7.2 Creating uniform random numbers

A standard method for creating a uniform random number is the **linear congruential generator**[1]. Consider the recursive relationship

$$X_n = (aX_{n-1} + c) \bmod m$$

where a, c and m are constants that we choose. It means, X_n takes the value equal to the remainder obtained by dividing $aX_{n-1} + c$ by m. It is recursive relationship because the nth value depends on the $n-1^{st}$. That means we must choose a starting value X_0, which is called the random number **seed**. Everyone using the same seed, and values a, c and m, will generate the same string of numbers. The value m determines the maximum period of the recursively generated values. The uniform random values falling in the interval $(0,1)$ are obtained as $U_n = X_n/m$. To illustrate we choose $X_0 = 1234567$, $a = 1664525$, $b = 1013904223$, and $m = 2^{32}$, and create 10,000 values of two uniform random numbers **u1** and **u2**.

```
clear
set obs 10001
gen double u1 = 1234567
gen double u2 = 987654321
scalar a = 1664525
scalar c = 1013904223
scalar m = 2^32
replace u1 = (a*u1[_n-1]+c) - m*ceil((a*u1[_n-1]+c)/m) + m if _n >1
replace u1 = u1/m

replace u2 = (a*u2[_n-1]+c) - m*ceil((a*u2[_n-1]+c)/m) + m if _n >1
replace u2 = u2/m

label variable u1 "uniform random number using seed = 1234567"
label variable u2 "uniform random number using seed = 987654321"

list u1 in 1/4
drop if _n==1
histogram u1, bin(20) percent
summarize u1

histogram u2, bin(20) percent
summarize u2
```

The summary statistics and histogram for **u2** are

---

[1] A description and link to sources is http://en.wikipedia.org/wiki/Linear_congruential_generator

```
. summarize u2
```

Variable	Obs	Mean	Std. Dev.	Min	Max
u2	10000	.5009009	.2877264	1.26e-06	.9998045

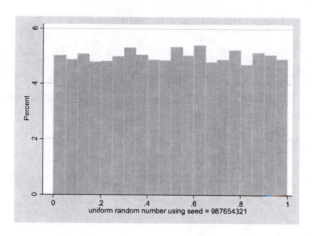

KEY TERMS

binomial distribution	inversion method	random number generator
chi2	**invFtail**	random numbers
chi-square distribution	**invnormal**	**rarea**
degrees of freedom	**invttail**	**runiform()**
density functions	**legend**	**seed**
extreme value distribution	**lngamma**	**set seed**
F distribution	**lpattern**	t distribution
Fden	**lwidth**	**tden**
Ftail	modulus	**title**
gamma function	**msymbol**	**ttail**
histogram	**normal**	**Twoway function**
invchi2	normal distribution	**xlabel**
invchi2tail	**normalden**	

APPENDIX B DO-FILE [APPX_B.DO]

```
* file appx_b.do for Using Stata for Principles of Econometrics, 4e

cd c:\data\poe4stata

* Stata Do-file
* copyright C 2011 by Lee C. Adkins and R. Carter Hill
* used for "Using Stata for Principles of Econometrics, 4e"
* by Lee C. Adkins and R. Carter Hill (2011)
* John Wiley and Sons, Inc.

* setup
```

```
version 11.1
capture log close

* open log file
log using appx_b, replace text
clear

* binomial probabilities
scalar prob1 = binomial(13,7,0.7)
di "probability <= binomial(13,7,0.7) is " prob1

scalar prob2 = 1 - binomial(13,7,0.7)
di "probability > binomial(13,7,0.7) is " prob2

* plot standard normal density
twoway function y = normalden(x), range(-5 5)                    ///
        title("Standard normal density")                        ///
          saving(normal_pdf.emf, replace)

* plot several normal densities
twoway function y = normalden(x), range(-5 5)                    ///
        || function y = normalden(x,0.8),            ///
          rang            e(-5 5) lpattern(dash)          ///
        || function y = normalden(x,1,0.8),          ///
          rang            e(-5 5) lpattern(dash_dot)          ///
      ||, title("Normal Densities")            ///
            legend(label(1 "N(0,1)") label(2 "N(0,0.8^2)")         ///
          labe        l(3 "N(1,0.8^2)"))

* compute normal probabilities
scalar n_tail = normal(1.33)
di "lower tail probability N(0,1) < 1.33 is " n_tail

scalar prob = normal((6-3)/3) - normal((4-3)/3)
di "probability 3<=N(3,9)<=6 is " prob

* compute normal percentiles
scalar n_95 = invnormal(.95)
di "95th percentile of standard normal = " n_95

* plot t(3)
twoway function y = normalden(x), range(-5 5)                    ///
        || function y = tden(3,x), range(-5 5) lpattern(dash)   ///
      ||, title("Standard normal and t(3)")                     ///
            legend(label(1 "N(0,1)") label(2 "t(3)"))

* t probabilities
scalar t_tail = ttail(3,1.33)
di "upper tail probability t(3) > 1.33 = " t_tail
di "lower tail probability t(3) < 1.33 = " 1 - ttail(3,1.33)

* t critical values
scalar t3_95 = invttail(3,0.05)
di "95th percentile of t(3) = " t3_95
di "5th percentile of t(3) = " invttail(3,0.95)

* t(38) shaded tail graphs
di "95th percentile of t(38) = " invttail(38,0.05)

* one-tail rejection region
twoway function y=tden(38,x), range(1.686 5)                    ///
        colo            r(ltblue) recast(area)          ///
      || function y=tden(38,x), range(-5 5)                     ///
```

```
        lege            nd(off) plotregion(margin(zero))                ///
    ||, ytitle("f(t)") xtitle("t")                          ///
        text         (0 1.686 "1.686", place(s))                ///
        titl         e("Right-tail rejection region")

* two-tail p-value
twoway function y=tden(38,x), range(1.9216 5)                           ///
        colo              r(ltblue) recast(area)                ///
    || function y=tden(38,x), range(-5 -1.9216)                        ///
        colo              r(ltblue) recast(area)                ///
    || function y=tden(38,x), range(-5 5)                              ///
    ||, legend(off) plotregion(margin(zero))                           ///
        ytit         le("f(t)") xtitle("t")                    ///
        text         (0 -1.921578 "-1.9216", place(s))              ///
        text         (0 1.9216 "1.9216", place(s))             ///
        titl         e("Pr|t(38)|>1.9216")

* Plot F-density
twoway function y = Fden(8,20,x), range(0 6)                            ///
        lege            nd(off) plotregion(margin(zero))               ///
        ytit         le("F-density") xtitle("x")               ///
        titl         e("F(8,20) density")

* F probabilities
scalar f_tail = Ftail(8,20,3.0)
di "upper tail probability F(8,20) > 3.0 = " f_tail
di "upper tail probability F(8,20) > 3.0 = " 1-F(8,20,3.0)

* F critical values
scalar f_95 = invFtail(8,20,.05)
di "95th percentile of F(8,20) = " f_95

* Chi square density
clear
set obs 101
gen x = _n/5
scalar df = 7
gen chi2_pdf = (1/(2^(df/2)))*(1/exp(lngamma(df/2)))*               ///
        x^(d                  f/2 - 1)*exp(-x/2)

twoway line chi2_pdf x, xlabel(0(2)21)                              ///
            title("Chi-square density with 7 df")

* chi-square probabilities
scalar chi2_tail = 1 - chi2(df,15)
di "upper tail probability chi2(7) > 15 is " chi2_tail

* chi-square critical values
scalar chi2_95 = invchi2tail(df,.05)
di "95th percentile of chi2(7) = " chi2_95

********** Appendix B.4

* generating triangular distribution
clear
set obs 1000
set seed 12345
gen u1 = runiform()
set seed 1010101
label variable u1 "uniform random values"
histogram u1, bin(10) percent
gen y1 = sqrt(u1)
histogram y1, bin(10) percent
```

```
* generating extreme value distribution
clear
set obs 10000
set seed 12345
gen u1 = runiform()
gen v1=-3+(_n-1)*13/10000
gen fev1 = exp(-v1)*exp(-exp(-v1))

twoway line fev1 v1, ytitle("Extreme value density")

* random values
gen ev1 = -log(-log(u1))
histogram ev1, bin(40) percent kdensity kdenopts(gaussian)

* generating uniform random values
clear
set obs 10001
gen double u1 = 1234567
gen double u2 = 987654321
scalar a = 1664525
scalar c = 1013904223
scalar m = 2^32
replace u1 = (a*u1[_n-1]+c) - m*ceil((a*u1[_n-1]+c)/m) + m if _n >1
replace u1 = u1/m

replace u2 = (a*u2[_n-1]+c) - m*ceil((a*u2[_n-1]+c)/m) + m if _n >1
replace u2 = u2/m

label variable u1 "uniform random number using seed = 1234567"
label variable u2 "uniform random number using seed = 987654321"

list u1 in 1/4
drop if _n==1
histogram u1, bin(20) percent
summarize u1

histogram u2, bin(20) percent
summarize u2

log close
```

APPENDIX **C**

Review of Statistical Inference

CHAPTER OUTLINE

C.1 EXAMINING THE HIP DATA

Begin a Stata session with the usual commands, and open a log file. An example that is used throughout the Appendix is the "Hip data," a sample of hip widths of 50 randomly selected U.S. adults. Open the data file *hip.dta*.

```
use hip, clear
describe
```

variable name	type	format	label	variable label
y	double	%10.0g		hip width, inches

C.1.1 Constructing a histogram

When first obtaining data it is useful to examine it graphically and numerically. A histogram showing the percent of values falling in various intervals is obtained using

```
histogram y, percent saving(hip_hist,replace)
```

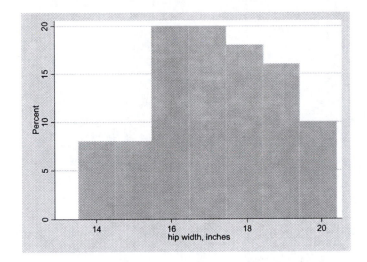

A handy feature of the Stata menu system is that you can enhance a command without knowing the exact syntax required. On the menu select **Graphics > Histogram**.

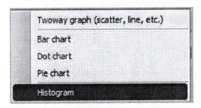

Fill in the dialog box with selections and press OK.

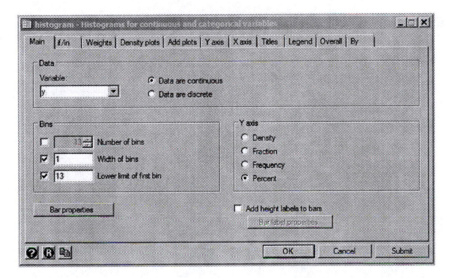

The result is

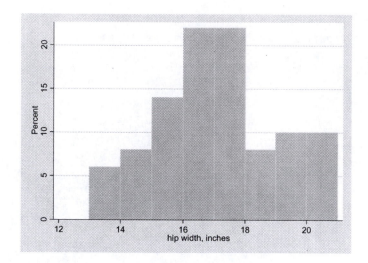

The Stata **Review** and **Results** windows indicate that the line command for this figure is

```
histogram y, width(1) start(13) percent
```

C.1.2 Obtaining summary statistics

Detailed numerical summary statistics are obtained using

```
summarize y, detail
```

Enter into the command window **help summarize**. The Viewer box shows the command syntax and options. Further note the descriptions of items computed and what values are kept for "post-estimation" usage.

```
summarize saves the following in r():

    Scalars
      r(N)            number of observations
      r(mean)         mean
      r(skewness)     skewness (detail only)
      r(min)          minimum
      r(max)          maximum
      r(sum_w)        sum of the weights
      r(p1)           1st percentile (detail only)
      r(p5)           5th percentile (detail only)
etc.

      r(p99)          99th percentile (detail only)
      r(var)          variance
      r(kurtosis)     kurtosis (detail only)
      r(sum)          sum of variable
      r(sd)           standard deviation
```

. summarize y, detail

```
                          hip width, inches
              Percentiles       Smallest
      1%         13.53           13.53
      5%         13.9            13.71
     10%         14.835          13.9        Obs                    50
     25%         15.94           14.21       Sum of Wgt.            50

     50%         17.085                      Mean              17.1582
                                 Largest     Std. Dev.         1.807013
     75%         18.55           20.23
     90%         19.7            20.23        Variance          3.265297
     95%         20.23           20.33        Skewness          -.013825
     99%         20.4            20.4         Kurtosis          2.331534
```

The saved values can be used in further statements in a Stata session, until they are overwritten by a subsequent Stata command. You must "use them or lose them" in pretty short order.

C.1.3 Estimating the population mean

There are several automatic Stata commands to carry out the basic data analysis. To estimate the population mean, and also create an interval estimate the command is **mean varname**. Using this command for the hip data we have:

mean y

```
Mean estimation                          Number of obs     =       50

                  Mean    Std. Err.    [95% Conf. Interval]
        y       17.1582   .2555503     16.64465    17.67175
```

In this output the **Mean** is

$$\bar{y} = \sum y_i / N$$

The unbiased estimator of the population variance σ^2 is

$$\hat{\sigma}^2 = \frac{\sum(y_i - \bar{y})^2}{N-1}$$

You may remember this estimator from a prior statistics course as the "sample variance." Using the sample variance we can estimate the variance of the estimator $\bar{Y}$ as

$$\widehat{\text{var}(\bar{Y})} = \hat{\sigma}^2 / N$$

The square root of the estimated variance is called the standard error of $\bar{Y}$, called by Stata **Std. Err.**, and is also known as the standard error of the mean and the standard error of the estimate,

$$se\left(\bar{Y}\right) = \sqrt{\widehat{var\left(\bar{Y}\right)}} = \hat{\sigma} / \sqrt{N}$$

The 100(1−α)% interval estimator is

$$\bar{Y} \pm t_c \frac{\hat{\sigma}}{\sqrt{N}} \text{ or } \bar{Y} \pm t_c se\left(\bar{Y}\right)$$

where t_c is the (1−α/2)-percentile of the *t*-distribution with $N-1$ degrees of freedom.

C.2 USING SIMULATED DATA VALUES

Using simulated data is an important tool for learning econometrics. There are a variety of ways to simulate data in Stata. The first command we will explore is **drawnorm**. This command will cause Stata to generate normally distributed random variables with given means, standard deviations and correlations. Enter **help drawnorm** for the syntax and options. For a dialog box, enter the command **db drawnorm**, or select the path

Data > Create or change data > Other var iable-creation commands > Dr aw sample fro m normal distribution

The command defaults are to generate observations from uncorrelated normal random variables with zero means and variances (standard deviations) 1. These options can be changed in the dialog box. To create correlated normal variables we can specify the correlations between variables. It is customary to specify an array or matrix, a table, containing the correlations. If we call the correlations matrix *C*, it will be arranged as

$$C = \begin{bmatrix} corr\left(x,x\right) & corr\left(x,y\right) \\ corr\left(y,x\right) & corr\left(y,y\right) \end{bmatrix}$$

The correlation between a variable and itself is 1.0. If the correlation between *x* and *y* is to be 0.5, then

$$C = \begin{bmatrix} 1 & .5 \\ .5 & 1 \end{bmatrix}$$

This matrix or array is symmetric, because the correlation between *x* and *y* is the same as the correlation between *y* and *x*. The Stata command to create this matrix, after clearing memory, is

```
clear
matrix C = (1, .5 \ .5, 1)
```

Within the parentheses rows are separated by "\" and row elements are separated by commas ",". Fill in the **drawnorm** dialog box as

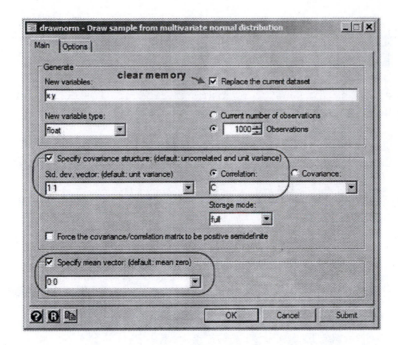

Click the **Option** tab. There you will find an option for setting the random number generator seed. Random numbers are created by a complex algorithm that must have a starting value. See Appendix B of this manual for an explanation of random number generators. This starting value is called the **seed**. If **seed** is selected, then each time you issue a command, or series of commands, the stream of random numbers created will be the same. This can be useful if you are debugging a Do-file, or command sequence, and want to see if the results showing up are the same each time. If a seed is not specified, then Stata will pick one for you.

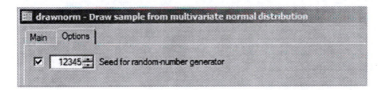

The Stata command implied by the dialog box, which will create these 1000 pairs of random numbers, is

```
drawnorm x y, n(1000) means(0 0) corr(C) sds(1 1) cstorage(full)
     seed(12345)
```

In this case we want the random numbers to have zero means and variance 1 so the options **means()** and **sds()** can be omitted. The simplified command would be

```
drawnorm x y, n(1000) corr(C) seed(12345)
```

Obtain the summary statistics and note that their means are near 0 and standard deviations are near 1.

```
summarize x y
```

Variable	Obs	Mean	Std. Dev.	Min	Max
x	1000	-.0445718	.9996242	-2.949586	2.776384
y	1000	-.0074078	.9974661	-3.595466	3.582233

Another useful command for summary statistics is **tabstat**. To see the full syntax for this command enter **help tabstat**. For a dialog box enter **db tabstat**. Pointing and clicking will take you there too. On the Stata menu select

Statistics > Summaries, tables, and tests > Tables > Table of summary statistics (tabstat)

In the dialog box choose the statistics you desire. The drop down list under each statistic to display is quite complete.

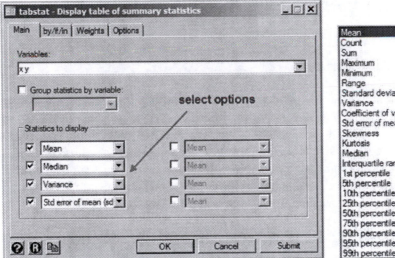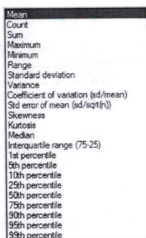

The equivalent Stata command is

```
tabstat x y, statistics( mean median var semean ) columns(variables)
```

The columns option is not required, so that the command can be reduced to

```
tabstat x y, statistics( mean median var semean )
```

stats	x	y
mean	-.0445718	-.0074078
p50	-.0193433	-.0278578
variance	.9992486	.9949387
se(mean)	.0316109	.0315426

We can find the correlation between x and y using the **correlate** command, which can be abbreviated

```
corr x y
```

```
. corr x y
(obs=1000)
```

	x	y
x	1.0000	
y	0.4690	1.0000

The sample correlation is very close to the "true" value we specified. For a scatter diagram enter

```
twoway scatter y x, saving(xynorm ,replace)
```

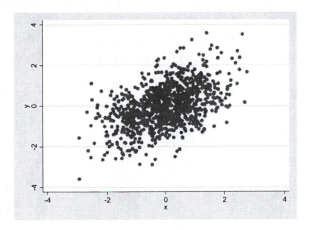

Because there are no overlays the above command can be simplified to `scatter y x`.

C.3 THE CENTRAL LIMIT THEOREM

The powerful central limit theorem is very frequently applied in econometrics. The theorem says: If $Y_1,...,Y_N$ are independent and identically distributed random variables with mean μ and variance σ^2, and $\bar{Y} = \sum Y_i / N$, then $Z_N = (\bar{Y} - \mu)/(\sigma/\sqrt{N})$ has a probability distribution that converges to the standard normal $N(0,1)$ as $N \to \infty$.

To illustrate this powerful result we will use simulated data. Clear memory, set the number of observations to 1000 and set the seed.

```
clear
set obs 1000
set seed 12345
```

Let the continuous random variable Y have a triangular distribution, with probability density function

$$f(y) = \begin{cases} 2y & 0 < y < 1 \\ 0 & \text{otherwise} \end{cases}$$

Draw a sketch of the *pdf* to understand its name. The expected value of Y is $\mu = E(Y) = 2/3$ and its variance is $\sigma^2 = \text{var}(Y) = 1/18$. The Central Limit Theorem says that if $Y_1, \ldots, Y_N$ are independent and identically distributed with density $f(y)$ then

$$Z_N = \frac{\overline{Y} - 2/3}{\sqrt{\dfrac{1/18}{N}}}$$

has a probability distribution that approaches the standard normal distribution as N approaches infinity. To generate random numbers from a triangular density we will use a result Appendix B of this manual. If U is a uniform random number between 0 and 1, then $Y = \sqrt{U}$ has a triangular distribution. Uniform random numbers are obtained using the Stata function `runiform()`.

```
gen y1 = sqrt(runiform())
```

A histogram shows the shape of the distribution

```
histogram y1, saving(triangle_hist ,replace)
```

The distribution is not bell shaped, is it?

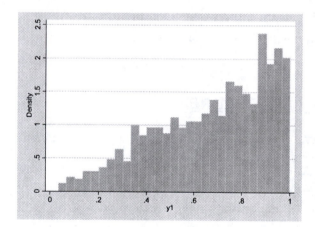

Now create another 11 such variables using a **forvalues** loop. This looping device will repeat a series commands over consecutive values of the indexing variable. The rules for such a loop, quoting from Stata help documenation are:
Braces must be specified with **forvalues**, and (1) the open brace must appear on the same line as forvalues; (2) nothing may follow the open brace except, of course, comments; the first command to be executed must appear on a new line; and (3) the close brace must appear on a line by itself.

Using **rep** as the indexing variable we can create **y2-y12**. In the second line we specify a **generate** command with the variable being **y`rep'**. Each pass through the loop **rep** is replaced by the values 2 through 12.

```
forvalues rep=2/12 {
```

```
    gen y`rep' = sqrt(runiform())
    }
```

We will find the sample means of the first 3, first 7 and all 12 of these triangular variables. The central limit theorem says we should standardize the variables as

$$Z_N = \frac{\bar{Y} - 2/3}{\sqrt{\dfrac{1/18}{N}}}$$

Using a **foreach** loop, which is similar to the **forvalues** loop, except it loops over a list of items, we can efficiently complete several tasks. First, use **egen** to create the means **ybar3**, **ybar7** and **ybar12** of a row of variables **y1-yn**. Then, **generate** the variable Z_N defined above. The **histogram** command includes **normal** so that a normal curve will be fitted to the histogram. Then summarize will show us details. Recall that for a normal variable **Skewness** is 0 and **Kurtosis** is 3.

```
    foreach n in 3 7 12 {
        egen ybar`n' = rowmean(y1-y`n')
        gen z`n' = (ybar`n' - 2/3)/(sqrt((1/18)/`n'))
        histogram z`n', normal saving(ybar`n'_hist , replace)
        summarize z`n', detail
    }
```

Examining the histogram of **z12**, with a normal density function fitted over it, we find

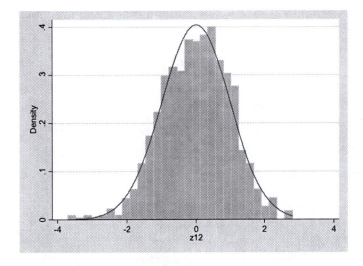

We have averaged together 12 very non-normal random variables and the result has a very symmetric bell shaped distribution.

z12

	Percentiles	Smallest		
1%	-2.549243	-3.697989		
5%	-1.586884	-3.636459		
10%	-1.245175	-3.251922	Obs	1000
25%	-.6835418	-3.213517	Sum of Wgt.	1000
50%	.0323963		Mean	.0038828
		Largest	Std. Dev.	.9859598
75%	.7039524	2.736392		
90%	1.207615	2.747086	Variance	.9721167
95%	1.540365	2.767131	Skewness	-.2156755
99%	2.214441	2.815349	Kurtosis	3.188245

For a standard normal random variable we should find a mean near zero and a standard deviation (and variance) near one. Also, the **Skewness** should be zero and the **Kurtosis** should be 3. Our values are very close to this. The result is even more impressive because the central limit really talks about averaging together a very large number of variables, and we have just used 12.

C.4 INTERVAL ESTIMATION

Let Y be a normally distributed random variable, $Y \sim N(\mu, \sigma^2)$. Assume that we have a random sample of size N from this population, $Y_1, Y_2, \ldots, Y_N$. The estimator of the population mean is $\bar{Y} = \sum_{i=1}^{N} Y_i / N$. Because we have assumed that Y is normally distributed it is also true that $\bar{Y} \sim N(\mu, \sigma^2/N)$. The standardized random variable

$$t = \frac{\bar{Y} - \mu}{\hat{\sigma}/\sqrt{N}} \sim t_{(N-1)}$$

has a t-distribution with $(N-1)$ degrees of freedom. The notation $t_{(N-1)}$ denotes a t-distribution with $N-1$ "degrees of freedom." Let the critical value t_c be the $100(1-\alpha/2)$-percentile value $t_{(1-\alpha/2, N-1)}$. This critical value has the property that $P\left[t_{(N-1)} \leq t_{(1-\alpha/2, N-1)}\right] = 1 - \alpha/2$. If t_c is a critical value from the t-distribution then,

$$P\left[-t_c \leq \frac{\bar{Y} - \mu}{\hat{\sigma}/\sqrt{N}} \leq t_c\right] = 1 - \alpha$$

Rearranging we obtain

$$P\left[\bar{Y} - t_c \frac{\hat{\sigma}}{\sqrt{N}} \leq \mu \leq \bar{Y} + t_c \frac{\hat{\sigma}}{\sqrt{N}}\right] = 1 - \alpha$$

The $100(1-\alpha)\%$ interval estimator for μ is

$$\bar{Y} \pm t_c \frac{\hat{\sigma}}{\sqrt{N}} \text{ or } \bar{Y} \pm t_c \text{se}(\bar{Y})$$

This interval estimator has center and width that vary from sample to sample.

C.4.1 Using simulated data

Clear memory, set the number of sample observations to 30, and set the seed value.

```
clear
set obs 30
set seed 12345
```

Draw 10 independent standard normal $N(0,1)$ random variables.

```
drawnorm x1-x10
```

We modify these to have mean 10 and variance 10, using the properties of the normal distribution. If $X_i \sim N(0,1)$ then $Y_i = a + bX_i \sim N(a, b^2)$. Using a **forvalues** loop we create 10 such variables.

```
forvalues n=1/10 {
        gen y`n' = 10 + sqrt(10)*x`n'
        }
```

To obtain 95% confidence interval estimates we can use the Stata command **ci**. Enter **help ci** in the Command window to see the syntax. To locate the dialog box, type **db ci**. To use the menu select

Statistics > Summaries, tables, and tests > Summary and descriptive statistics > Confidence intervals

Fill in the **ci** dialog box

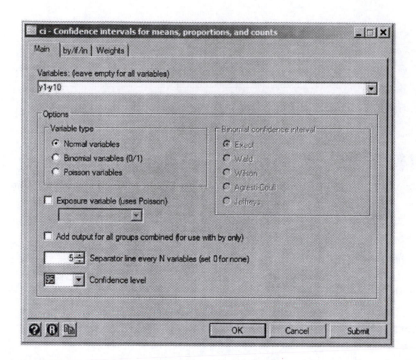

The Stata command is

```
ci y1-y10
```

Variable	Obs	Mean	Std. Err.	[95% Conf.	Interval]
y1	30	10.00381	.5808083	8.81592	11.19169
y2	30	10.93521	.3674302	10.18373	11.68668
y3	30	10.25851	.5594697	9.114271	11.40276
y4	30	8.458479	.5744584	7.28358	9.633378
y5	30	10.11062	.5154498	9.056411	11.16484
y6	30	10.09176	.611673	8.840744	11.34277
y7	30	9.085932	.5962659	7.866432	10.30543
y8	30	9.523076	.4450133	8.612922	10.43323
y9	30	10.96144	.6188641	9.695716	12.22715
y10	30	9.547122	.5854969	8.349646	10.7446

The result shows the sample mean, the standard error and the 95% interval estimates. In this case interval 4 does not contain the true value of the population mean, which is 10. This is the outcome of sampling variation. If this interval estimation procedure is used many times 95% of the intervals obtained using this method will contain the true mean. Any one interval may or may not contain the true population mean.

C.4.2 Using the hip data

Automatic commands are wonderful, but the ability to click does not demonstrate or necessarily promote understanding. Clear memory, and open *hip.dta*.

```
use hip, clear
```

Use the automatic command **ci** to obtain an interval estimate for mean population hip width.

```
ci y
```

Variable	Obs	Mean	Std. Err.	[95% Conf. Interval]
y	50	17.1582	.2555503	16.64465 17.67175

To demonstrate the details of this calculation, obtain detailed summary statistics. We have already seen these, so we can use the option **quietly** to suppress the output.

```
quietly summarize y, detail
return list
```

Stata saves these quantities in an array called **r()**. You can view these values by entering **return list** in the Command window. Some of these scalar values are:

```
       r(N)  =  50
   r(sum_w)  =  50
    r(mean)  =  17.1582
     r(Var)  =  3.265296693877551
      r(sd)  =  1.80701319692955
r(skewness)  =  -.0138249736168214
```

We can use these values, and the formulas in *POE4*, to construct a 95% interval estimate.

```
scalar ybar = r(mean)
scalar nobs = r(N)
scalar df = nobs - 1
scalar tc975 = invttail(df,.025)
scalar sighat = r(sd)
scalar se = sighat/sqrt(nobs)
scalar lb = ybar - tc975*se
scalar ub = ybar + tc975*se
```

Display the results

```
di "lb of 95% confidence interval = " lb
di "ub of 95% confidence interval = " ub
```

The results are

```
lb of 95% confidence interval = 16.644653
ub of 95% confidence interval = 17.671747
```

C.5 TESTING THE MEAN OF A NORMAL POPULATION

Consider the null hypothesis $H_0 : \mu = c$. If the sample data come from a normal population with mean μ and variance σ^2, then

$$t = \frac{\bar{Y} - \mu}{\hat{\sigma}/\sqrt{N}} \sim t_{(N-1)}$$

If the null hypothesis $H_0 : \mu = c$ is true, then

$$t = \frac{\bar{Y} - c}{\hat{\sigma}/\sqrt{N}} \sim t_{(N-1)}$$

The rejection regions are summarized as

- If the alternative hypothesis $H_1 : \mu > c$ is true, then the value of the t-statistic tends to become larger than usual for the t-distribution. Let the critical value t_c be the $100(1-\alpha)$-percentile $t_{(1-\alpha, N-1)}$ from a t-distribution with $N-1$ degrees of freedom. Then $P(t \le t_c) = 1 - \alpha$, where α is the level of significance of the test. If the t-statistic is greater than or equal to t_c then we reject $H_0 : \mu = c$ and accept the alternative $H_1 : \mu > c$.
- If the alternative hypothesis $H_1 : \mu < c$ is true, then the value of the t-statistic tends to become smaller than usual for the t-distribution. The critical value $-t_c$ is the 100α-percentile $t_{(\alpha, N-1)}$ from a t-distribution with $N-1$ degrees of freedom such that $P(t \le -t_c) = \alpha$, where α is the level of significance of the test. If $t \le -t_c$, then we reject $H_0 : \mu = c$ and accept the alternative hypothesis $H_1 : \mu < c$.
- If the alternative hypothesis $H_1 : \mu \ne c$ is true, then values of the test statistic may be unusually "large" or unusually "small." The rejection region consists of the two "tails" of the t-distribution, and this is called a two-tail test. The critical value is the $100(1 - \alpha/2)$-percentile from a t-distribution with $N-1$ degrees of freedom, $t_c = t_{(1-\alpha/2, N-1)}$, so that $P[t \ge t_c] = P[t \le -t_c] = \alpha / 2$. If the value of the test statistic t falls in the rejection region, either tail of the $t_{(N-1)}$-distribution, then we reject the null hypothesis $H_0 : \mu = c$ and accept the alternative hypothesis $H_1 : \mu \ne c$.

C.5.1 Right-tail test

To illustrate a right tail test, test the null hypothesis $H_0 : \mu = 16.5$. The alternative hypothesis is $H_1 : \mu > 16.5$. Obtain the detailed estimates and carry out the calculation.

```
use hip, clear
quietly summarize y, detail
scalar ybar = r(mean)
scalar nobs = r(N)
scalar df = nobs - 1
scalar sighat = r(sd)
scalar se = sighat/sqrt(nobs)
```

```
scalar t1 = (ybar - 16.5)/se
scalar tc95 = invttail(df,.05)
scalar p1 = ttail(df,t1)
di "right tail test"
di "tstat = " t1
di "tc95  = " tc95
di "pval  = " p1
```

Producing the output

```
right tail test
tstat = 2.5756186
tc95  = 1.6765509
pval  = .00653694
```

There is an automatic command for testing the mean of a normal population called **ttest**. Find the syntax by typing **help ttest**. To open the dialog box, type **db ttest**. This yields

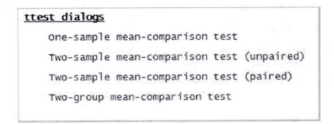

There are several tests depending on the problem. We are using a One-sample mean-comparison test. Open this dialog box, and fill it in as

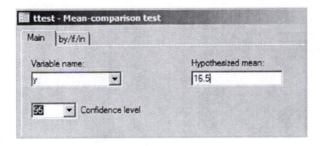

The required Stata command is (using == rather than =)

```
ttest y==16.5
```

```
One-sample t test
```

Variable	Obs	Mean	Std. Err.	Std. Dev.	[95% Conf. Interval]	
y	50	17.1582	.2555503	1.807013	16.64465	17.67175

```
    mean = mean(y)                                              t =    2.5756
Ho: mean = 16.5                             degrees of freedom =        49

    Ha: mean < 16.5           Ha: mean != 16.5             Ha: mean > 16.5
  Pr(T < t) = 0.9935        Pr(|T| > |t|) = 0.0131        Pr(T > t) = 0.0065
```

Lots of output is produced, including the *t*-statistic value 2.5756. For a right tail test the *p*-value is the area under the *t*-distribution with $N-1 = 49$ degrees of freedom. That value is shown to be 0.0065.

C.5.2 Two-tail test

To illustrate a two tail test consider the null hypothesis is $H_0 : \mu = 17$. The alternative hypothesis is $H_1 : \mu \neq 17$.

```
        quietly summarize y, detail
        scalar t2 = (ybar - 17)/se
        scalar p2 = 2*ttail(df,abs(t2))
        di "two tail test"
        di "tstat = " t2
        di "tc975  = " tc975
        di "pval   = " p2
```

The result is

```
        two tail test
        tstat = .61905631
        tc975  = 2.0095752
        pval   = .53874692
```

The automatic test is

```
        ttest y==17
```

```
One-sample t test
```

Variable	Obs	Mean	Std. Err.	Std. Dev.	[95% Conf. Interval]	
y	50	17.1582	.2555503	1.807013	16.64465	17.67175

```
    mean = mean(y)                                              t =    0.6191
Ho: mean = 17                               degrees of freedom =        49

    Ha: mean < 17             Ha: mean != 17               Ha: mean > 17
  Pr(T < t) = 0.7306        Pr(|T| > |t|) = 0.5387        Pr(T > t) = 0.2694
```

The test statistic value is 0.6191 and the two tail *p*-value is 0.5387. In the Stata output "!=" means "not equal to," or "≠".

C.6 TESTING THE VARIANCE OF A NORMAL POPULATION

Let Y be a normally distributed random variable, $Y \sim N(\mu, \sigma^2)$. Assume that we have a random sample of size N from this population, $Y_1, Y_2, \ldots, Y_N$. The estimator of the population mean is $\bar{Y} = \sum Y_i / N$ and the unbiased estimator of the population variance is $\hat{\sigma}^2 = \sum (Y_i - \bar{Y})^2 / (N-1)$. To test the null hypothesis $H_0 : \sigma^2 = \sigma_0^2$ we use the test statistic

$$V = \frac{(N-1)\hat{\sigma}^2}{\sigma_0^2} \sim \chi^2_{(N-1)}$$

If the null hypothesis is true then the test statistic has the indicated chi-square distribution with $(N-1)$ degrees of freedom. If the alternative hypothesis is $H_1 : \sigma^2 > \sigma_0^2$ then we carry out a one-tail test. If we choose the level of significance $\alpha = .05$, then the null hypothesis is rejected if $V \geq \chi^2_{(.95, N-1)}$, where $\chi^2_{(.95, N-1)}$ is the 95th-percentile of the chi-square distribution with $(N-1)$ degrees of freedom.

To illustrate consider the null hypothesis that the variance of the hip population data equals 4. The Stata automatic test is **sdtest**. It specifies the null hypothesis in terms of the standard deviation, rather than the variance. Thus the null hypothesis is $H_0 : \sigma = 2$.

The test command, assuming the hip data are in memory, is

```
sdtest y == 2
```

One-sample test of variance

Variable	Obs	Mean	Std. Err.	Std. Dev.	[95% Conf. Interval]
y	50	17.1582	.2555503	1.807013	16.64465 17.67175

```
     sd = sd(y)                                  c = chi2 =  39.9999
Ho:  sd = 2                        degrees of freedom =       49

     Ha: sd < 2                Ha: sd != 2                Ha: sd > 2
  Pr(C < c) = 0.1832    2*Pr(C < c) = 0.3664       Pr(C > c) = 0.8168
```

The test statistic value is 39.9999 and the right tail p-value is 0.8168. To see the details, specify a scalar equal to the hypothesized variance.

```
quietly summarize y, detail
scalar s0 = 4
scalar sighat2 = r(Var)
scalar df = r(N)-1
scalar v = df*sighat2/s0
scalar chi2_95 = invchi2(df,.95)
scalar chi2_05 = invchi2(df,.05)
scalar p = 2*chi2(df,v)
di "Chi square test stat = " v
di "5th percentile chisquare(49) = " chi2_05
di "95th percentile chisquare(49) = " chi2_95
```

```
di "2 times p value = " p
```

The output is

```
Chi square test stat = 39.999884
5th percentile chisquare(49) = 33.930306
95th percentile chisquare(49) = 66.338649
2 times p value = .36643876
```

C.7 TESTING THE EQUALITY OF TWO NORMAL POPULATION MEANS

Let two normal populations be denoted $N(\mu_1, \sigma_1^2)$ and $N(\mu_2, \sigma_2^2)$. In order to estimate and test the difference between means, $\mu_1 - \mu_2$, we must have random samples of data from each of the two populations. We draw a sample of size N_1 from the first population, and a sample of size N_2 from the second population. Using the first sample we obtain the sample mean $\bar{Y}_1$ and sample variance $\hat{\sigma}_1^2$; from the second sample we obtain $\bar{Y}_2$ and $\hat{\sigma}_2^2$. How the null hypothesis $H_0 : \mu_1 - \mu_2 = c$ is tested depends on whether the two population variances are equal or not.

C.7.1 Population variances are equal

If the population variances are equal, so that $\sigma_1^2 = \sigma_2^2 = \sigma_p^2$, then we use information in both samples to estimate the common value σ_p^2. This "pooled variance estimator" is

$$\hat{\sigma}_p^2 = \frac{(N_1 - 1)\hat{\sigma}_1^2 + (N_2 - 1)\hat{\sigma}_2^2}{N_1 + N_2 - 2}$$

If the null hypothesis $H_0 : \mu_1 - \mu_2 = c$ is true, then

$$t = \frac{(\bar{Y}_1 - \bar{Y}_2) - c}{\sqrt{\hat{\sigma}_p^2 \left(\dfrac{1}{N_1} + \dfrac{1}{N_2} \right)}} \sim t_{(N_1 + N_2 - 2)}$$

As usual we can construct a one-sided alternative, such as $H_1 : \mu_1 - \mu_2 > c$, or the two-sided alternative $H_1 : \mu_1 - \mu_2 \neq c$.

C.7.2 Population variances are unequal

If the population variances are not equal, then we cannot use the pooled variance estimate. Instead we use

$$t^* = \frac{\left(\bar{Y}_1 - \bar{Y}_2\right) - c}{\sqrt{\dfrac{\hat{\sigma}_1^2}{N_1} + \dfrac{\hat{\sigma}_2^2}{N_2}}}$$

The exact distribution of this test statistic is neither normal nor the usual t-distribution. The distribution of t^* can be approximated by a t-distribution with degrees of freedom

$$df = \frac{\left(\hat{\sigma}_1^2/N_1 + \hat{\sigma}_2^2/N_2\right)^2}{\left(\dfrac{\left(\hat{\sigma}_1^2/N_1\right)^2}{N_1 - 1} + \dfrac{\left(\hat{\sigma}_2^2/N_2\right)^2}{N_2 - 1}\right)}$$

This is called Satterthwaite's formula.

To illustrate the test for populations with equal variances, draw two samples from normal populations with means 1 and 2, using **drawnorm**.

```
clear
drawnorm x1 x2, n(50) means(1 2) seed(12345)
```

Calculate the summary statistics.

```
summarize
```

Variable	Obs	Mean	Std. Dev.	Min	Max
x1	50	1.124799	.9030621	-.8845057	3.381427
x2	50	1.945904	.9256588	-.003253	4.517602

Using this information you could compute the test statistic given in POE4. The automatic test uses the command **ttest** with an option.

```
ttest x1 == x2, unpaired
```

Unpaired means that the observations are not matched to each other in any way. The results are shown below. The difference between the two sample means is -0.82 and the t-statistic value is -4.4897 with 98 degrees of freedom. The two tail p-value is 0.0000 leading us to correctly reject the equality of the two population means.

```
Two-sample t test with equal variances
```

Variable	Obs	Mean	Std. Err.	Std. Dev.	[95% Conf. Interval]	
x1	50	1.124799	.1277123	.9030621	.8681512	1.381446
x2	50	1.945904	.1309079	.9256588	1.682835	2.208973
combined	100	1.535351	.0998996	.9989957	1.337129	1.733574
diff		-.8211052	.1828861		-1.184037	-.4581738

```
    diff = mean(x1) - mean(x2)                              t =  -4.4897
Ho: diff = 0                             degrees of freedom =        98

      Ha: diff < 0                 Ha: diff != 0                   Ha: diff > 0
  Pr(T < t) = 0.0000        Pr(|T| > |t|) = 0.0000           Pr(T > t) = 1.0000
```

To illustrate the test when we do not assume variances are equal, generate two normal variables that have $N(1,1)$ and $N(2,4)$ distributions.

drawnorm x3 x4, n(50) means(1 2) sds(1 2) seed(12345)

The command **ttest** now has the option **unequal**.

ttest x3 == x4, unpaired unequal

```
Two-sample t test with unequal variances
```

Variable	Obs	Mean	Std. Err.	Std. Dev.	[95% Conf. Interval]	
x3	50	1.124799	.1277123	.9030621	.8681512	1.381446
x4	50	1.891808	.2618158	1.851318	1.365669	2.417946
combined	100	1.508303	.1499527	1.499527	1.210764	1.805842
diff		-.7670091	.2913039		-1.347843	-.1861754

```
    diff = mean(x3) - mean(x4)                                        t =  -2.6330
Ho: diff = 0                   Satterthwaite's degrees of freedom =    71.069

      Ha: diff < 0                 Ha: diff != 0                   Ha: diff > 0
  Pr(T < t) = 0.0052        Pr(|T| > |t|) = 0.0104           Pr(T > t) = 0.9948
```

The degrees of freedom are calculated to be 71.069, and again the two tail test rejects the null hypothesis that the population means are equal.

C.8 TESTING THE EQUALITY OF TWO NORMAL POPULATION VARIANCES

Given two normal populations, denoted $N(\mu_1, \sigma_1^2)$ and $N(\mu_2, \sigma_2^2)$, we can test the null hypothesis $H_0 : \sigma_1^2 / \sigma_2^2 = 1$. If the null hypothesis is true, then the population variances are equal. The test statistic is derived from the results that $(N_1 - 1)\hat{\sigma}_1^2 / \sigma_1^2 \sim \chi_{(N_1 - 1)}^2$ and $(N_2 - 1)\hat{\sigma}_2^2 / \sigma_2^2 \sim \chi_{(N_2 - 1)}^2$. The ratio

$$F = \frac{\dfrac{(N_1-1)\hat{\sigma}_1^2/\sigma_1^2}{(N_1-1)}}{\dfrac{(N_2-1)\hat{\sigma}_2^2/\sigma_2^2}{(N_2-1)}} = \frac{\hat{\sigma}_1^2/\sigma_1^2}{\hat{\sigma}_2^2/\sigma_2^2} \sim F_{(N_1-1,N_2-1)}$$

If the null hypothesis $H_0 : \sigma_1^2/\sigma_2^2 = 1$ is true then the test statistic is $F = \hat{\sigma}_1^2/\hat{\sigma}_2^2$, which has an F-distribution with (N_1-1) numerator and (N_2-1) denominator degrees of freedom. If the alternative hypothesis is $H_1 : \sigma_1^2/\sigma_2^2 \neq 1$, then we carry out a two-tail test. If we choose level of significance $\alpha = .05$, then we reject the null hypothesis if $F \geq F_{(.975,N_1-1,N_2-1)}$ or if $F \leq F_{(.025,N_1-1,N_2-1)}$ where $F_{(\alpha,N_1-1,N_2-1)}$ denotes the 100α-percentile of the F-distribution with the specified degrees of freedom. If the alternative is one-sided, $H_1 : \sigma_1^2/\sigma_2^2 > 1$ then we reject the null hypothesis if $F \geq F_{(.95,N_1-1,N_2-1)}$.

Using the simulated variables **x3** and **x4**, the test is carried out using the automatic command **sdtest**.

```
     sdtest x3 == x4
```

Variance ratio test

Variable	Obs	Mean	Std. Err.	Std. Dev.	[95% Conf. Interval]	
x3	50	1.124799	.1277123	.9030621	.8681512	1.381446
x4	50	1.891808	.2618158	1.851318	1.365669	2.417946
combined	100	1.508303	.1499527	1.499527	1.210764	1.805842

```
    ratio = sd(x3) / sd(x4)                              f =    0.2379
Ho: ratio = 1                          degrees of freedom =    49, 49

    Ha: ratio < 1              Ha: ratio != 1                Ha: ratio > 1
  Pr(F < f) = 0.0000      2*Pr(F < f) = 0.0000          Pr(F > f) = 1.0000
```

C.9 TESTING NORMALITY

The normal distribution is symmetric, and has a bell-shape with a peakedness and tail-thickness leading to a kurtosis of 3. Thus we can certainly test for departures from normality by checking the skewness and kurtosis from a sample of data. If skewness is not close to zero, and if kurtosis is not close to 3, then we would reject the normality of the population. In *Principles of Econometrics, 4th Edition*, Appendix C.4.2 we developed sample measures of skewness and kurtosis

$$\widetilde{skewness} = S = \frac{\tilde{\mu}_3}{\tilde{\sigma}^3}$$

$$\widetilde{kurtosis} = K = \frac{\tilde{\mu}_4}{\tilde{\sigma}^4}$$

The Jarque-Bera test statistic allows a joint test of these two characteristics,

$$JB = \frac{N}{6}\left(S^2 + \frac{(K-3)^2}{4}\right)$$

If the true distribution is symmetric and has kurtosis 3, which includes the normal distribution, then the JB test statistic has a chi-square distribution with 2 degrees of freedom if the sample size is sufficiently large. If $\alpha = .05$ then the critical value of the $\chi^2_{(2)}$ distribution is 5.99. We reject the null hypothesis and conclude that the data are non-normal if $JB \geq 5.99$. If we reject the null hypothesis then we know the data have non-normal characteristics, but we do not know what distribution the population might have.

Clear memory and open *hip.dta*.

```
use hip, clear
```

Stata offers number of automatic tests. The nature of the tests is beyond the scope of this book. They do offer one test that is similar to, but not exactly the same, as the Jarque-Bera test. It is implemented using

```
sktest y
```

Skewness/Kurtosis tests for Normality

Variable	Obs	Pr(Skewness)	Pr(Kurtosis)	adj chi2(2)	joint Prob>chi2
y	50	0.9645	0.2898	1.17	0.5569

The Jarque-Bera test follows, using the **skewness** and **kurtosis** values generated by **summarize**.

```
quietly summarize y, detail
scalar nobs = r(N)
scalar s = r(skewness)
scalar k = r(kurtosis)
scalar jb = (nobs/6)*(s^2 + ((k-3)^2)/4)
scalar chi2_95 = invchi2(2,.95)
scalar pval = 1 - chi2(2,jb)
di "jb test statistic " jb
di "95th percentile chi2(2) " chi2_95
di "pvalue " pval
```

With output

```
jb test statistic = .93252312
95th percentile chi2(2) = 5.9914645
pvalue = .62734317
```

C.10 MAXIMUM LIKELIHOOD ESTIMATION

Stata offers powerful general command for maximizing likelihood functions. We have used maximum likelihood estimation many times already. For example, binary and multinomial choice models, such as probit, logit, and conditional logit are estimated using maximum likelihood. However it is possible to do maximum likelihood estimation "from scratch" using a likelihood function for a particular problem in which you are interested. Stata's ml command will maximize a user supplied log-likelihood function. Enter **help ml**. These commands are beyond the scope of *POE4*. Advanced users may wish to consider *Maximum Likelihood Estimation with Stata, 4th Edition*, by Gould, Pitblado and Poi, Stata Press, 2010, which is available on www.stata.com. A few simple examples, based on examples from William Greene (2008) Econometrics Analysis, 6th Edition, can be found at http://www.principlesofeconometrics.com/poe4/usingstata.htm.

C.11 KERNEL DENSITY ESTIMATOR

Figure C.19 in *POE4* shows histograms for two data sets. The data used are in the file *kernel.dta*. Let us generate similar, but not identical data. First, clear memory and set the number of observations to 500.

```
clear
set obs 500
```

Specify means and standard deviations for two normal random variables, and draw random values using **drawnorm**.

```
matrix m = (7,9,5)
matrix sd = (1.5,.5,1)
drawnorm x y1 y2, means(m) sds(sd) seed(1234567)
```

Examine these variables

```
summarize
```

Variable	Obs	Mean	Std. Dev.	Min	Max
x	500	6.939916	1.549873	2.666413	11.98759
y1	500	9.00128	.5260826	7.367773	10.70334
y2	500	4.992534	1.070694	2.044742	7.962709

```
correlate
```

	x	y1	y2
x	1.0000		
y1	0.0004	1.0000	
y2	-0.0763	-0.0185	1.0000

Create a mixture variable from **y1** and **y2**, where each observation has a random probability of being included.

```
set seed 987654321
gen u = uniform()
gen p = (u > .5)
gen y = p*y1+(1-p)*y2
```

Now create Figure C.19, which is shown on the following page.

```
histogram x, freq width(.25) xlabel(2(1)12) start(2) ///
        title("X~N(7,1.5^2)") saving(n1, replace)
histogram y, freq width(.25) xlabel(2(1)12) start(2) ///
        title("Y mixture of N(9,0.5^2) & N(5,1)") saving(mix1,replace)
graph combine "n1" "mix1", cols(2) ysize(4) xsize(6) ///
        title("Figure C.19 Histograms of X and Y") saving(figc19,replace)
```

Figure C.20 in *POE4* shows the histograms with superimposed normal densities. These curves are obtained using the formula

$$\widehat{f(x)} = \frac{1}{\hat{\sigma}\sqrt{2\pi}} \exp\left(-\frac{1}{2}\left(\frac{x-\hat{\mu}}{\hat{\sigma}}\right)^2\right)$$

True means and standard deviations are replaced by estimates. These figures, shown on the next page, are obtained by simply adding the **normal** option to the **histogram**. We have tinkered with settings for the histogram so that they will match text figure.

```
histogram x, freq width(.25) xlabel(2(1)12) start(2) ///
        normal title("X~N(7,1.5^2)") saving(n2, replace)
histogram y, freq width(.25) xlabel(2(1)12)  start(2) ///
        normal title("Y mixture of N(9,0.5^2) & N(5,1)")      ///
        saving(mix2,replace)
graph combine "n2" "mix2", cols(2) ysize(4) xsize(6) ///
        title("Figure C.20 Normal Parametric Densities") ///
        saving(figc20,replace)
```

Figure C.21 shows histograms for *Y* with different bin widths. These figures are shown on the page following the next.

```
histogram y, width(1) freq xlabel(2(1)12) start(2) ///
        title("bin width=1") saving(y1,replace)

histogram y, width(.1) freq xlabel(2(1)12) start(2) ///
        title("bin width=0.1") saving(y2,replace)

graph combine "y1" "y2", cols(2) ysize(4) xsize(6) ///
        title("Figure C.21 Different Bin Widths") ///
```

```
saving(figc21,replace)
```

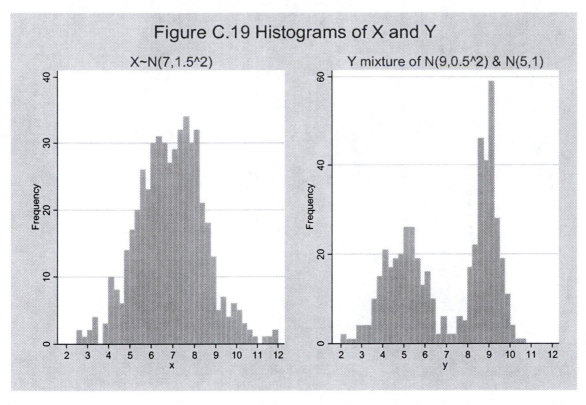

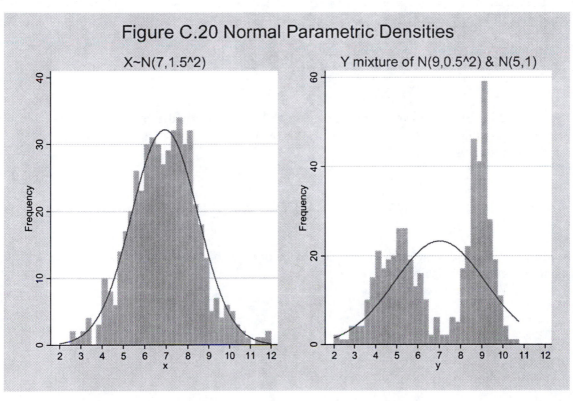

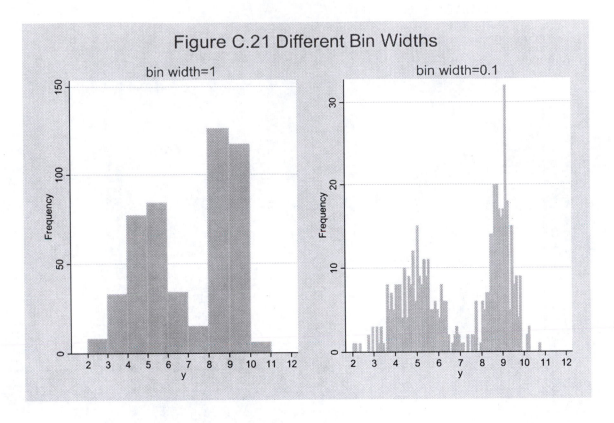

Figure C.21 Different Bin Widths

In Figure C.22 of *POE4* we show the use of so called "kernel densities" superimposed upon the histograms. A kernel density is

$$\widehat{f(x)} = \frac{1}{nh} \sum_{i=1}^{n} K\left(\frac{x_i - x}{h}\right)$$

where K is a kernel, h is a smoothing parameter called the **bandwidth** and x are values over the domain of possible values. There are many kernel functions; one of them is Gaussian and is described as follows:

$$K\left(\frac{x_i - x}{h}\right) = \frac{1}{\sqrt{2\pi}} \exp\left(-\frac{1}{2}\left(\frac{x_i - x}{h}\right)^2\right)$$

To see more about this in Stata enter **help histogram**. Scroll down in the Viewer box a bit to find information on Density plots.

    Density plots

normal specifies that the histogram be overlaid with an appropriately scaled normal density. The normal will have the same mean and standard deviation as the data.

normopts(*line_options***)** specifies details about the rendition of the normal curve, such as the color and style of line used. See [G] **graph twoway line**.

kdensity specifies that the histogram be overlaid with an appropriately scaled kernel density estimate of the density. By default, the estimate will be produced using the Epanechnikov kernel with an "optimal" half-width. This default corresponds to the default of **kdensity**; see [R] **kdensity**. How the estimate is produced can be controlled using the **kdenopts()** option described below.

kdenopts(*kdensity_options***)** specifies details about how the kernel density estimate is to be produced along with details about the rendition of the resulting curve, such as the color and style of line used. The kernel density estimate is described in [G] **graph twoway kdensity**. As an example, if you wanted to produce kernel density estimates by using the Gaussian kernel with optimal half-width, you would specify **kdenopts(gauss)** and if you also wanted a half-width of 5, you would specify **kdenopts(gauss width(5))**.

The Stata code for Figure C.22 is below. Note that we request a Gaussian kernel density in the options.

```
histogram y, width(.25) freq xlabel(2(1)12)  start(2) ///
     kdensity kdenopts(gauss width(1.5)) title("bandwidth=1.5") ///
     saving(b1,replace)

histogram y, width(.25) freq xlabel(2(1)12)  start(2) ///
     kdensity kdenopts(gauss width(1)) title("bandwidth=1") ///
     saving(b2,replace)

histogram y, width(.25) freq xlabel(2(1)12)  start(2) ///
     kdensity kdenopts(gauss width(.4)) title("bandwidth=0.4") ///
     saving(b3,replace)

histogram y, width(.25) freq xlabel(2(1)12)  start(2) ///
     kdensity kdenopts(gauss width(.1)) title("bandwidth=0.1") ///
     saving(b4,replace)

graph combine "b1" "b2" "b3" "b4", cols(2) ysize(4) xsize(6) ///
     title("Figure C.22 Nonparametric Densities") ///
     saving(figc22,replace)
```

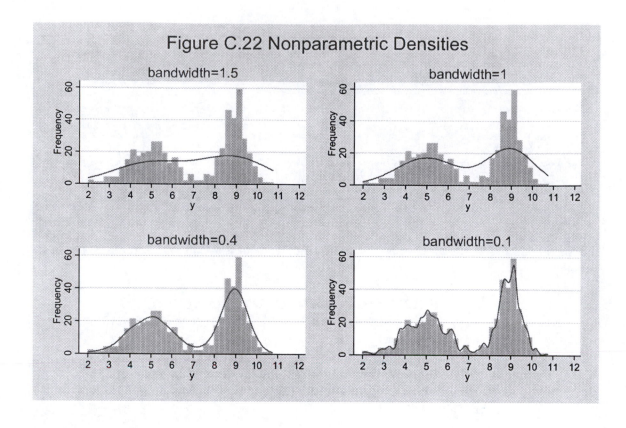

Figure C.22 Nonparametric Densities

KEY TERMS

bandwidth	**kdensity**	skewness
central limit theorem	kernel density	**sktest**
ci	kurtosis	standard error
confidence intervals	**mean**	**summarize**
correlation matrix	mean test	**summarize,detail**
drawnorm	normality test	**tabstat**
Gaussian kernel	post estimation	test of two means
histogram	**return list**	**ttest**
hypothesis tests	**sdtest**	**runiform()**
interval estimation	**set obs**	variance test
Jarque-Bera test	**set seed**	
kdenopts	simulated data	

APPENDIX C DO-FILE [APPX C.DO]

```
* file appx_c.do for Using Stata for Principles of Econometrics, 4e

cd c:\data\poe4stata

* Stata do-file
* copyright C 2011 by Lee C. Adkins and R. Carter Hill
```

```
* used for "Using Stata for Principles of Econometrics, 4e"
* by Lee C. Adkins and R. Carter Hill (2011)
* John Wiley and Sons, Inc.

* setup
version 11.1
capture log close
set more off

********* examine hip data
log using appx_c, replace text

use hip, clear
describe
histogram y, percent saving(hip_hist,replace)

* histogram using pull down menu
histogram y, width(1) start(13) percent

* summary statistics
summarize y, detail

* estimate mean
mean y

* generate several normal variables
clear
matrix C = (1, .5 \ .5, 1)
drawnorm x y, n(1000) corr(C) seed(12345)
summarize x y
tabstat x y, statistics (mean median variance semean)
corr x y
twoway scatter y x, saving(xynorm ,replace)

********* central limit theorem
clear
set obs 1000
set seed 12345

* generate triangular distributed value
gen y1 = sqrt(runiform())
histogram y1, saving(triangle_hist ,replace)

* 11 more
forvalues rep=2/12 {
    gen y`rep' = sqrt(runiform())
    }

* standardize several and plot
foreach n in 3 7 12 {
    egen ybar`n' = rowmean(y1-y`n')
    gen z`n' = (ybar`n' - 2/3)/(sqrt((1/18)/`n'))
    histogram z`n', normal saving(ybar`n'_hist , replace)
    graph export ybar`n'_hist.emf, replace
    summarize z`n', detail
    }

* interval estimates
* simulated data
clear
set obs 30
set seed 12345
drawnorm x1-x10
```

```
* transform
forvalues n=1/10 {
      gen y`n' = 10 + sqrt(10)*x`n'
      }

* compute interval estimates
ci y1-y10

* hip data
use hip, clear

* automatic interval estimate
ci y

* details of interval estimate
quietly summarize y, detail
return list
scalar ybar = r(mean)
scalar nobs = r(N)
scalar df = nobs - 1
scalar tc975 = invttail(df,.025)
scalar sighat = r(sd)
scalar se = sighat/sqrt(nobs)
scalar lb = ybar - tc975*se
scalar ub = ybar + tc975*se

di "lb of 95% confidence interval = " lb
di "ub of 95% confidence interval = " ub

********* hypothesis testing

* right tail test mu = 16.5

* details
use hip, clear
quietly summarize y, detail
scalar ybar = r(mean)
scalar nobs = r(N)
scalar df = nobs - 1
scalar sighat = r(sd)
scalar se = sighat/sqrt(nobs)
scalar t1 = (ybar - 16.5)/se
scalar tc95 = invttail(df,.05)
scalar p1 = ttail(df,t1)
di "right tail test"
di "tstat = " t1
di "tc95  = " tc95
di "pval  = " p1

* automatic version
ttest y==16.5

* two tail test mu = 17

* details
quietly summarize y, detail
scalar t2 = (ybar - 17)/se
scalar p2 = 2*ttail(df,abs(t2))
di "two tail test"
di "tstat = " t2
di "tc975  = " tc975
di "pval  = " p2
```

```
* automatic version
ttest y==17

********* Testing the variance

* automatic test
sdtest y == 2

* details
quietly summarize y, detail
scalar s0 = 4
scalar sighat2 = r(Var)
scalar df = r(N)-1
scalar v = df*sighat2/s0
scalar chi2_95 = invchi2(df,.95)
scalar chi2_05 = invchi2(df,.05)
scalar p = 2*chi2(df,v)
di "Chi square test stat = " v
di "5th percentile chisquare(49) = " chi2_05
di "95th percentile chisquare(49) = " chi2_95
di "2 times p value = " p

********* testing equality of population means
clear
drawnorm x1 x2, n(50) means(1 2) seed(12345)
summarize

* assuming variances are equal
ttest x1 == x2, unpaired

* assuming variances unequal
drawnorm x3 x4, n(50) means(1 2) sds(1 2) seed(12345)
ttest x3 == x4, unpaired unequal

* testing population variances
sdtest x3 == x4

* test normality
use hip, clear

********* Jarque_Bera test
* automatic test
sktest y

* details
quietly summarize y, detail
scalar nobs = r(N)
scalar s = r(skewness)
scalar k = r(kurtosis)
scalar jb = (nobs/6)*(s^2 + ((k-3)^2)/4)
scalar chi2_95 = invchi2(2,.95)
scalar pval = 1 - chi2(2,jb)
di "jb test statistic = " jb
di "95th percentile chi2(2) = " chi2_95
di "pvalue = " pval


********* kernel density estimation
clear
set obs 500

* specify means and standard deviations
```

```
matrix m = (7,9,5)
matrix sd = (1.5,.5,1)

* draw normal random values
drawnorm x y1 y2, means(m) sds(sd) seed(1234567)

* examine
summarize
correlate

* create mixture
set seed 987654321
gen u = uniform()
gen p = (u > .5)
gen y = p*y1+(1-p)*y2

* Figure C.19
histogram x, freq width(.25) xlabel(2(1)12) start(2)              ///
       title("X~N(7,1.5^2)") saving(n1, replace)
histogram y, freq width(.25) xlabel(2(1)12) start(2)              ///
       title("Y mixture of N(9,0.5^2) & N(5,1)") saving(mix1,replace)
graph combine "n1" "mix1", cols(2) ysize(4) xsize(6)             ///
       title("Figure C.19 Histograms of X and Y") saving(figc19,replace)

* Figure C.20
histogram x, freq width(.25) xlabel(2(1)12) start(2)              ///
       normal title("X~N(7,1.5^2)") saving(n2, replace)
histogram y, freq width(.25) xlabel(2(1)12)  start(2)            ///
       normal title("Y mixture of N(9,0.5^2) & N(5,1)")          ///
       saving(mix2,replace)
graph combine "n2" "mix2", cols(2) ysize(4) xsize(6)             ///
       title("Figure C.20 Normal Parametric Densities")         ///
       saving(figc20,replace)

* Figure C.21
histogram y, width(1) freq xlabel(2(1)12) start(2)              ///
       title("bin width=1") saving(y1,replace)

histogram y, width(.1) freq xlabel(2(1)12) start(2)            ///
       title("bin width=0.1") saving(y2,replace)

graph combine "y1" "y2", cols(2) ysize(4) xsize(6)             ///
       title("Figure C.21 Different Bin Widths")               ///
       saving(figc21,replace)

* Figure C.22
histogram y, width(.25) freq xlabel(2(1)12)  start(2)           ///
       kdensity kdenopts(gauss width(1.5)) title("bandwidth=1.5") ///
       saving(b1,replace)

histogram y, width(.25) freq xlabel(2(1)12)  start(2)           ///
       kdensity kdenopts(gauss width(1)) title("bandwidth=1")   ///
       saving(b2,replace)

histogram y, width(.25) freq xlabel(2(1)12)  start(2)           ///
       kdensity kdenopts(gauss width(.4)) title("bandwidth=0.4") ///
       saving(b3,replace)

histogram y, width(.25) freq xlabel(2(1)12)  start(2)           ///
       kdensity kdenopts(gauss width(.1)) title("bandwidth=0.1") ///
       saving(b4,replace)

graph combine "b1" "b2" "b3" "b4", cols(2) ysize(4) xsize(6)    ///
```

```
        title("Figure C.22 Nonparametric Densities")                    ///
        saving(figc22,replace)
log close
```

<u>INDEX</u>